McDougal Littell
Science

INTEGRATED COURSE

1

Space Science

Waves, Sound, and Light

Matter and Energy

Ecology

Earth's Surface

INTEGRATED COURSE 1

Acknowledgments: Excerpts and adaptations from *National Science Education Standards* by the National Academy of Sciences. Copyright © 1996 by the National Academy of Sciences. Reprinted with permission from the National Academies Press, Washington, D.C.

Excerpts and adaptations from *Benchmarks for Science Literacy: Project 2061.* Copyright © 1993 by the American Association for the Advancement of Science. Reprinted with permission.

ISBN: 0-618-42299-4   4 5 6 7 8 VJM 08 07 06 05

Internet Web Site: http://www.mcdougallittell.com

Science Consultants

Chief Science Consultant

James Trefil, Ph.D. is the Clarence J. Robinson Professor of Physics at George Mason University. He is the author or co-author of more than 25 books, including *Science Matters* and *The Nature of Science*. Dr. Trefil is a member of the American Association for the Advancement of Science's Committee on the Public Understanding of Science and Technology. He is also a fellow of the World Economic Forum and a frequent contributor to *Smithsonian* magazine.

Rita Ann Calvo, Ph.D. is Senior Lecturer in Molecular Biology and Genetics at Cornell University, where for 12 years she also directed the Cornell Institute for Biology Teachers. Dr. Calvo is the 1999 recipient of the College and University Teaching Award from the National Association of Biology Teachers.

Kenneth Cutler, M.S. is the Education Coordinator for the Julius L. Chambers Biomedical Biotechnology Research Institute at North Carolina Central University. A former middle school and high school science teacher, he received a 1999 Presidential Award for Excellence in Science Teaching.

Instructional Design Consultants

Douglas Carnine, Ph.D. is Professor of Education and Director of the National Center for Improving the Tools of Educators at the University of Oregon. He is the author of seven books and over 100 other scholarly publications, primarily in the areas of instructional design and effective instructional strategies and tools for diverse learners. Dr. Carnine also serves as a member of the National Institute for Literacy Advisory Board.

Linda Carnine, Ph.D. consults with school districts on curriculum development and effective instruction for students struggling academically. A former teacher and school administrator, Dr. Carnine also co-authored a popular remedial reading program.

Donald Steely, Ph.D. serves as principal investigator at the Oregon Center for Applied Science (ORCAS) on federal grants for science and language arts programs. His background also includes teaching and authoring of print and multimedia programs in science, mathematics, history, and spelling.

Sam Miller, Ph.D. is a middle school science teacher and the Teacher Development Liaison for the Eugene, Oregon, Public Schools. He is the author of curricula for teaching science, mathematics, computer skills, and language arts.

Vicky Vachon, Ph.D. consults with school districts throughout the United States and Canada on improving overall academic achievement with a focus on literacy. She is also co-author of a widely used program for remedial readers.

Content Reviewers

John Beaver, Ph.D.
Ecology
Professor, Director of Science Education Center
College of Education and Human Services
Western Illinois University
Macomb, IL

Donald J. DeCoste, Ph.D.
Matter and Energy, Chemical Interactions
Chemistry Instructor
University of Illinois
Urbana-Champaign, IL

Dorothy Ann Fallows, Ph.D., MSc
Diversity of Living Things, Microbiology
Partners in Health
Boston, MA

Michael Foote, Ph.D.
The Changing Earth, Life Over Time
Associate Professor
Department of the Geophysical Sciences
The University of Chicago
Chicago, IL

Lucy Fortson, Ph.D.
Space Science
Director of Astronomy
Adler Planetarium and Astronomy Museum
Chicago, IL

Elizabeth Godrick, Ph.D.
Human Biology
Professor, CAS Biology
Boston University
Boston, MA

Isabelle Sacramento Grilo, M.S.
The Changing Earth
Lecturer, Department of the Geological Sciences
San Diego State University
San Diego, CA

David Harbster, MSc
Diversity of Living Things
Professor of Biology
Paradise Valley Community College
Phoenix, AZ

Richard D. Norris, Ph.D.
Earth's Waters
Professor of Paleobiology
Scripps Institution of Oceanography
University of California, San Diego
La Jolla, CA

Donald B. Peck, M.S.
Motion and Forces; Waves, Sound, and Light;
Electricity and Magnetism
Director of the Center for Science Education (retired)
Fairleigh Dickinson University
Madison, NJ

Javier Penalosa, Ph.D.
Diversity of Living Things, Plants
Associate Professor, Biology Department
Buffalo State College
Buffalo, NY

Raymond T. Pierrehumbert, Ph.D.
Earth's Atmosphere
Professor in Geophysical Sciences (Atmospheric Science)
The University of Chicago
Chicago, IL

Brian J. Skinner, Ph.D.
Earth's Surface
Eugene Higgins Professor of Geology and Geophysics
Yale University
New Haven, CT

Nancy E. Spaulding, M.S.
Earth's Surface, The Changing Earth, Earth's Waters
Earth Science Teacher (retired)
Elmira Free Academy
Elmira, NY

Steven S. Zumdahl, Ph.D.
Matter and Energy, Chemical Interactions
Professor Emeritus of Chemistry
University of Illinois
Urbana-Champaign, IL

Susan L. Zumdahl, M.S.
Matter and Energy, Chemical Interactions
Chemistry Education Specialist
University of Illinois
Urbana-Champaign, IL

Safety Consultant

Juliana Texley, Ph.D.
Former K–12 Science Teacher and School Superintendent
Boca Raton, FL

English Language Advisor

Judy Lewis, M.A.
Director, State and Federal Programs for reading proficiency
and high risk populations
Rancho Cordova, CA

iv

Teacher Panel Members

Carol Arbour
Tallmadge Middle School,
Tallmadge, OH

Patty Belcher
Goodrich Middle School,
Akron, OH

Gwen Broestl
Luis Munoz Marin Middle School,
Cleveland, OH

Al Brofman
Tehipite Middle School,
Fresno, CA

John Cockrell
Clinton Middle School,
Columbus, OH

Jenifer Cox
Sylvan Middle School,
Citrus Heights, CA

Linda Culpepper
Martin Middle School,
Charlotte, NC

Kathleen Ann DeMatteo
Margate Middle School,
Margate, FL

Melvin Figueroa
New River Middle School,
Ft. Lauderdale, FL

Doretha Grier
Kannapolis Middle School,
Kannapolis, NC

Robert Hood
Alexander Hamilton Middle School,
Cleveland, OH

Scott Hudson
Covedale Elementary School,
Cincinnati, OH

Loretta Langdon
Princeton Middle School,
Princeton, NC

Carlyn Little
Glades Middle School,
Miami, FL

Ann Marie Lynn
Amelia Earhart Middle School,
Riverside, CA

James Minogue
Lowe's Grove Middle School,
Durham, NC

Joann Myers
Buchanan Middle School,
Tampa, FL

Barbara Newell
Charles Evans Hughes Middle School,
Long Beach, CA

Anita Parker
Kannapolis Middle School,
Kannapolis, NC

Greg Pirolo
Golden Valley Middle School,
San Bernardino, CA

Laura Pottmyer
Apex Middle School,
Apex, NC

Lynn Prichard
Booker T. Washington Middle Magnet
School, Tampa, FL

Jacque Quick
Walter Williams High School,
Burlington, NC

Robert Glenn Reynolds
Hillman Middle School,
Youngstown, OH

Stacy Rinehart
Lufkin Road Middle School,
Apex, NC

Theresa Short
Abbott Middle School,
Fayetteville, NC

Rita Slivka
Alexander Hamilton Middle School,
Cleveland, OH

Marie Sofsak
B F Stanton Middle School,
Alliance, OH

Nancy Stubbs
Sweetwater Union Unified School District,
Chula Vista, CA

Sharon Stull
Quail Hollow Middle School,
Charlotte, NC

Donna Taylor
Okeeheelee Middle School,
West Palm Beach, FL

Sandi Thompson
Harding Middle School,
Lakewood, OH

Lori Walker
Audubon Middle School & Magnet Center,
Los Angeles, CA

Teacher Lab Evaluators

Andrew Boy
W.E.B. DuBois Academy,
Cincinnati, OH

Jill Brimm-Byrne
Albany Park Academy,
Chicago, IL

Gwen Broestl
Luis Munoz Marin Middle School,
Cleveland, OH

Al Brofman
Tehipite Middle School,
Fresno, CA

Michael A. Burstein
The Rashi School,
Newton, MA

Trudi Coutts
Madison Middle School,
Naperville, IL

Jenifer Cox
Sylvan Middle School,
Citrus Heights, CA

Larry Cwik
Madison Middle School,
Naperville, IL

Jennifer Donatelli
Kennedy Junior High School,
Lisle, IL

Melissa Dupree
Lakeside Middle School,
Evans, GA

Carl Fechko
Luis Munoz Marin Middle School,
Cleveland, OH

Paige Fullhart
Highland Middle School,
Libertyville, IL

Sue Hood
Glen Crest Middle School,
Glen Ellyn, IL

William Luzader
Plymouth Community Intermediate School,
Plymouth, MA

Ann Min
Beardsley Middle School,
Crystal Lake, IL

Aileen Mueller
Kennedy Junior High School,
Lisle, IL

Nancy Nega
Churchville Middle School,
Elmhurst, IL

Oscar Newman
Sumner Math and Science Academy,
Chicago, IL

Lynn Prichard
Booker T. Washington Middle Magnet
School, Tampa, FL

Jacque Quick
Walter Williams High School,
Burlington, NC

Stacy Rinehart
Lufkin Road Middle School,
Apex, NC

Seth Robey
Gwendolyn Brooks Middle School,
Oak Park, IL

Kevin Steele
Grissom Middle School,
Tinley Park, IL

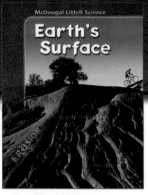

McDougal Littell Science

Earth's Surface

(eEdition

UNIT A
Earth's Surface

Unit Features

1 Views of Earth Today   A6

2 Minerals   A40

Why can gold be separated from other minerals and rocks in a river? page A40

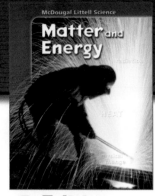

eEdition

UNIT B
Matter and Energy

Unit Features

1 Introduction to Matter   B6

the BIG idea

Everything that has mass and takes up space is matter.

2 Properties of Matter   B38

the BIG idea

Matter has properties that can be changed by physical and chemical processes.

What properties could help you identify this sculpture as sugar? page B38

*What different forms of
energy are shown in this
photograph? page B68*

Visual Highlights

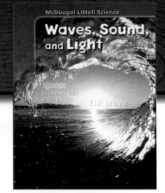

eEdition

UNIT C
Waves, Sound, and Light

Unit Features

1 Waves

the BIG idea

Waves transfer energy and interact in predictable ways.

2 Sound

the BIG idea

Sound waves transfer energy through vibrations.

How is this guitar player producing sound? page C34

How does this phone stay connected? page C70

Visual Highlights

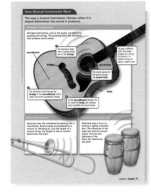

UNIT D
Ecology

eEdition

Unit Features

the BIG idea

Matter and energy together support life within an environment.

How many living and nonliving things can you identify in this photograph? page D6

How do living things interact? page D42

Visual Highlights

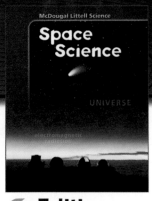

eEdition

UNIT E
Space Science

Unit Features

1 Exploring Space E6

the BIG idea

People develop and use technology to explore and study space.

2 Earth, Moon, and Sun E40

the BIG idea

Earth and the Moon move in predictable ways as they orbit the Sun.

What would you see if you looked at the Moon with a telescope? page E40

This image shows Jupiter with one of its large moons. How big are these objects compared with Earth? page E76

Visual Highlights

Features

Math in Science

Think Science

Connecting Sciences

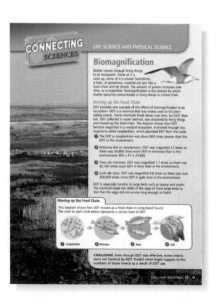

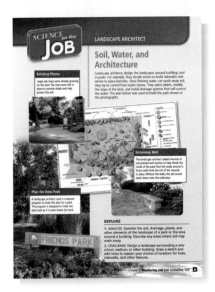

Science on the Job

Extreme Science

Frontiers in Science

Timelines in Science

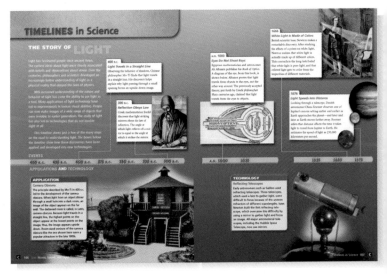

Internet Resources @ ClassZone.com

Simulations

Visualizations

Career Centers

Resource Centers

EARTH'S SURFACE
Resources for the following topics may be found at ClassZone.com: *Satellite Mapping, Map Projections, GIS, Precious Metals, Minerals, Gemstones, Meteorites and Impacts, Igneous Rocks, Sedimentary Rocks, Metamorphic Rocks, Earth System Research, Weathering, Soil, Mudflows, Rivers and Erosion, Glaciers.*

MATTER AND ENERGY
Resources for the following topics may be found at ClassZone.com: *Scale Views of Matter, Volume, Scanning Tunneling Microscope Images, Mixtures, Chemical Properties of Matter, Melting Points and Boiling Points, Separating Materials from Mixtures, Kinetic Energy and Potential Energy, Electric Cars, Alternative Energy Sources, Temperature and Heat Research, Temperature and Temperature Scales, Thermal Energy.*

WAVES, SOUND, AND LIGHT
Resources for the following topics may be found at ClassZone.com: *Waves, Wave Speed, Supersonic Aircraft, Sound Safety, Musical Instruments, the Electromagnetic Spectrum, Visible Light, Light Research, Optics, Microscopes and Telescopes, Lasers.*

ECOLOGY
Resources for the following topics may be found at ClassZone.com: *Prairie Ecosystems, Ecosystems, Cycles in Nature, Land and Aquatic Biomes, Symbiotic Relationships, Succession, Conservation Efforts, The Environment, Urban Expansion, Natural Resources, Ecosystem Recovery.*

SPACE SCIENCE
Resources for the following topics may be found at ClassZone.com: *Telescopes, Space Exploration, Seasons, Tides, Advances in Astronomy, Impact Craters, Moons of Giant Planets, Life Cycles of Stars, Galaxies, Galaxy Collisions.*

Math Tutorials

NSTA SciLinks

Codes for use with the NSTA SciLinks site may be found on every chapter opener.

Content Review

There is a content review for every chapter at ClassZone.com

Test Practice

There is a standardized test practice for every chapter at ClassZone.com

Explore the Big Idea

Chapter Opening Inquiry

Each chapter opens with hands-on explorations that introduce the chapter's Big Idea.

Chapter Investigations

Full-Period Labs

The Chapter Investigations are in-depth labs that let you form and test a hypothesis, build a model, or sometimes design your own investigation.

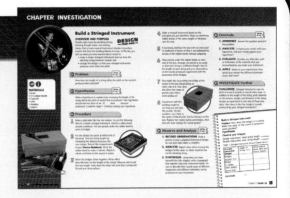

Explore

Introductory Inquiry Activities

Most sections begin with a simple activity that lets you
explore the Key Concept before you read the section.

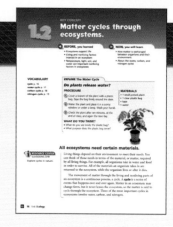

Investigate

Skill Labs

Each Investigate activity gives you a chance to practice a specific science skill related to the content that you're studying.

Standards and Benchmarks

Each unit addresses some of the learning goals described in the *National Science Education Standards* (NSES) and the Project 2061 *Benchmarks for Science Literacy.* The following National Science Education Standards are also addressed in the book introduction, unit and chapter features, and lab investigations in all the units: A.9 Understandings About Scientific Inquiry, E.6 Understandings About Science and Technology, F.5 Science and Technology in Society, G.1 Science as a Human Endeavor, G.2 Nature of Science, G.3 History of Science.

National Science Education Standards

Content Standards

UNIT A Earth's Surface

A.9.d | Technology is used to gather more detailed and accurate data to help scientists in their investigations.

D.1.a | Earth consists of an inner and outer core, a mantle, and a crust.

D.1.c | Landforms are shaped by weathering and erosion.

D.1.d | In the rock cycle, old rocks at Earth's surface weather and become sediments. The sediments are buried, then compressed and heated to form new rock.

D.1.e | Soil consists of weathered rocks, organic plant and animal matter, and bacteria.

D.1.k | Living organisms have produced some types of rocks and have contributed to the weathering of rocks.

E.6.c | Technology allows scientists to observe or measure phenomena that would otherwise be beyond scientists' reach.

UNIT B Matter and Energy

B.1.a | A substance has characteristic properties, such as density, a boiling point, and solubility.
A mixture of substances often can be separated into the original substances using these properties.

B.1.c | There are more than 100 known elements that combine to produce compounds.

B.3.a | Energy is a property of substances and is often associated with heat, light, electricity, mechanical motion, and sound
Energy is transferred in many ways.

B.3.b | Heat flows from warmer objects to cooler ones, until both reach the same temperature.

UNIT C Waves, Sound, and Light

B.3.a | Energy is often associated with sound, light, mechanical motion. Energy is transferred in many ways.

B.3.c | Light interacts with matter by transmission, absorption, or scattering.
To see an object, light from that object must enter the eye.

B.3.f | Energy from the Sun is transferred to Earth in the form of visible light, infrared light, or ultraviolet light.

UNIT D Ecology

C.4.a | A population consists of all individuals of a species that occur together at a given place and time. An ecosystem includes both living and nonliving things.

C.4.b | Different populations have different roles in an ecosystem. Food webs show the relationship between producers and consumers.

C.4.c | Most energy in ecosystems enters as sunlight, gets transferred by producers into chemical energy through photosynthesis, and passes from organism to organism as food.

C.4.d | Factors can limit population growth.

D.1.f | Water circulates through Earth's crust, oceans, and atmosphere.

D.3.d | The Sun is the major source of energy affecting plant growth, winds, ocean currents, the water cycle, and seasonal variations.

E.6.e | All designs have limits, including availability, safety, and environmental impact.

F.2.a | Human overpopulation can cause increased use of resources, decline in resources, and decline in other populations.

F.2.b | Causes of pollution and resource loss vary from place to place.

UNIT E Space Science

A.9.d | Technology allows scientists to be more accurate and to use data.

B.3.a | Energy is associated with heat, light, electricity, motion, sound, nuclei, and the nature of a chemical.

B.3.f | Energy from the Sun has a range of wavelengths, including visible light, infrared radiation, and ultraviolet radiation.

D.3.a | The Sun is the central and largest body in a system of nine planets and their moons and objects such as asteroids and comets.

D.3.b | The regular and predictable motions of objects in the solar system explain such phenomena as the day, the year, phases of the Moon, and eclipses.

D.3.d | Seasons result from varying amounts of the Sun's energy hitting the surface due to the tilt of Earth's axis and the length of the day.

F.5.c | Technology influences society through its products and processes.

G.2.a | Scientists use observations, experiments, and models to test their explanations.

Process and Skill Standards

A.1 | Identify questions that can be answered through scientific methods.

A.2 | Design and conduct a scientific investigation.

A.3 | Use appropriate tools and techniques to gather and analyze data.

A.4 | Use evidence to describe, predict, explain, and model.

A.5 | Think critically to find relationships between results and interpretations.

A.6 | Give alternative explanations and predictions.

A.7 | Communicate procedures and explanations.

A.8 | Use mathematics in scientific inquiry.

E.1 | Identify a problem to be solved.

E.2 | Design a solution or product.

E.3 | Implement the proposed solution.

E.4 | Evaluate the solution or design.

Project 2061 Benchmarks

Content Benchmarks

UNIT A Earth's Surface

1.C.6	Computers speed up and extend scientists' ability to collect, store, compile, analyze, and prepare data.
4.B.2	Earth is a rocky planet surrounded by a thin blanket of air, with water covering nearly three-quarters of its surface.
4.B.10	The ability to recover valuable minerals is just as important as how abundant or rare they are in nature. As minerals are used up, obtaining them becomes more difficult.
4.C.2	Earth's surface is shaped in part by the motion of wind and water over a long time.
4.C.3	In the rock cycle, sediments are buried and cemented together by dissolved minerals to form solid rock again.
4.C.4	Rocks bear evidence of the minerals, temperatures, and forces that formed them in the rock cycle.
4.C.6	Soil composition, texture, fertility, and resistance to erosion are influenced by plant roots and debris and by organisms living in the soil.
9.C.3	The spherical Earth is distorted when projected onto a flat map.
9.C.5	It takes two numbers to locate a point on a map.
11.A.2	Thinking about things as systems means looking at how each part relates to the others.

UNIT B Matter and Energy

4.D.1	All matter is made up of atoms.
4.D.2	Equal volumes of different substances usually have different weights.
4.D.3	Atoms and molecules are always in motion.
4.E.1	Energy cannot be created or destroyed, but it can be changed from one form to another.
4.E.2	Most of what goes on in the universe involves energy transformations.
4.E.3	Heat can be transferred through materials by the collisions of atoms or across space by radiation.
4.E.4	Energy appears in different forms, including heat, mechanical, chemical, and gravitational.
8.B.1	The choice of materials for a job depends on their properties.
8.C.1	Energy can change from one form to another. In the process, some energy is always converted to heat. Some systems transform energy with less loss of heat than others.

UNIT C Waves, Sound, and Light

4.F.1	Light from the sun is made up of a mixture of many different colors of light, even though the light looks almost white.
4.F.2	Something can be "seen" when light waves emitted or reflected by it enter the eye—just as something can be "heard" when sound waves from it enter the ear.
4.F.4	Vibrations in materials set up wavelike disturbances that spread away from the source. Sound and earthquake waves are examples. These and other waves move at different speeds through different materials.
4.F.5	Human eyes respond to only a narrow range of wavelengths of electromagnetic radiation—visible light. Differences of wavelength within that range are perceived as differences in color.

UNIT D Ecology

3.C.6	Rarely are technology issues simple.
4.B.8	Water is, necessary for life, limited, and becoming depleted and polluted.
4.C.7	Human activities affect the environment.
5.A.5	All organisms are part of two connected food webs.
5.D.1	Species with similar needs may compete.
5.D.2	Populations may interact in diverse ways.
5.E.2	Matter is transferred between living things and the environment.
5.E.3	Energy can change form in living things.
6.E.5	The health of individuals requires keeping soil, air, and water safe.
11.A.2	Studying a system involves studying interactions among its parts.

UNIT E Space Science

4.A.2	Light takes time to travel, so distant objects seen from Earth appear as they were long ago. It takes light a few minutes to reach Earth from the Sun, the closest star, and several billion years to reach Earth from very distant galaxies.
4.A.3	Nine planets that vary in size, composition, and surface features orbit the Sun in nearly circular orbits. Some planets have rings and a variety of moons. Some planets and moons show signs of geological activity.
4.A.4	Chunks of rock that orbit the Sun sometimes impact Earth's atmosphere and sometimes reach Earth's surface. Other
4.A.4 cont'd.	chunks of rock and ice produce long, illuminated tails when they pass close to the Sun.
4.B.5	Phases of the Moon occur because the Moon's orbit changes the amount of the sunlit part of the Moon that can be seen from Earth.
4.G.2	The Sun's gravitational pull holds Earth in its orbit, just as Earth's gravitational pull holds the Moon in orbit.
11.B.1	Models are often used to think about processes that cannot be observed directly, changed deliberately, or examined safely.

Process and Skill Benchmarks

1.A.3	Some knowledge in science is very old and yet is still used today.
1.B.1	Design an investigation in which you collect evidence, reason logically, and use imagination to devise hypotheses.
3.A.2	Technology is essential to access outer space and remote locations; to collect, use, and share data; and to communicate.
3.B.1	Design requires taking constraints into account.
9.B.3	Use graphs to show the relationship between two variables.
9.C.4	Use graphs to show patterns and make predictions.
11.A.2	Think about things as systems by looking for the ways each part relates to others.
11.B.1	Use models to think about processes.
11.C.4	Use equations to summarize observed changes.
11.D.2	With complex systems, use summaries, averages, ranges, and examples.
12.B.1	Find what percentage one number is of another.
12.B.2	Use and compare numbers in equivalent forms such as decimals and percents.
12.B.7	Determine, use, and convert units.
12.C.1	Compare amounts proportionally.
12.C.3	Use and read measurement instruments.
12.D.1	Use tables and graphs to organize information and identify relationships.
12.E.3	Be skeptical of biased samples.
12.E.4	Recognize more than one way to interpret a given set of findings.
12.E.5	Criticize faulty reasoning.

Introducing Science

Scientists are curious. Since ancient times, they have been asking and answering questions about the world around them. Scientists are also very suspicious of the answers they get. They carefully collect evidence and test their answers many times before accepting an idea as correct.

In this book you will see how scientific knowledge keeps growing and changing as scientists ask new questions and rethink what was known before. The following sections will help get you started.

What Is Science?

Science is the systematic study of all of nature, from particles too small to see to the human body to the entire universe. However, no individual scientist can study all of nature. Therefore science is divided into many different fields. For example, some scientists are biologists, others are geologists, and still others are chemists or astronomers.

All the different scientific fields can be grouped into three broad categories: life science, earth science, and physical science.

- Life science focuses on the study of living things; it includes the fields of cell biology, botany, ecology, zoology, and human biology.
- Earth science focuses on the study of our planet and its place in the universe; it includes the fields of geology, oceanography, meteorology, and astronomy.
- Physical science focuses on the study of what things are made of and how they change; it includes the fields of chemistry and physics.

Integrated Science Course 1

Integrated Science pulls together units from the different categories of science to give you a broad picture of how scientists study nature. For example, scientists from the three broad categories might all study a river, but from different points of view. You will learn in Unit A that a geologist might study how the river formed and how it has changed the land through which it flows. In Unit B, you will see how a chemist might study the river's water and the different substances dissolved in it. In Unit D, you will learn how an ecologist might study the river as an ecosystem—all the living and nonliving things that interact in the river.

Even though science has many different fields, all scientists have similar ways of thinking and approaching their work. For example, scientists use instruments as well as their minds to look for patterns in nature. Scientists also try to find explanations for the patterns they discover. As you study each unit, you will in part focus on the patterns that scientists have found within that particular specialized branch. At the same time, as you move from one unit to another, you will be blending knowledge from the different branches of science together to form a more general understanding of our universe.

Unifying Principles

As you learn, it helps to have a big picture of science as a framework for new information. McDougal Littell Science has identified unifying principles from each of the three broad categories of science: life science, earth science, and physical science. These unifying principles are described on the following pages. However, keep in mind that the broad categories of science do not have fixed borders. Earth science shades into life science, which shades into physical science, which shades back into earth science.

> ## the BIG idea
>
> Each chapter begins with a big idea. Keep in mind that each big idea relates to one or more of the unifying principles.

What Is Life Science?

Life science is the study of the great variety of living things that have lived or now live on Earth. Life science includes the study of the characteristics and needs that all living things have in common. It is also a study of changes—both daily changes and those that take place over millions of years. Probably most important, in studying life science you will explore the many ways that all living things—including you—depend on Earth and its resources.

A moose, like any other living thing, interacts with its environment. Eating is one obvious but important interaction. Food provides energy as well as most of the materials a moose needs to survive.

UNIFYING PRINCIPLES of Life Science

All living things share common characteristics.

Despite the variety of living things on Earth, there are certain characteristics common to all. The basic unit of life is the **cell.** Any living thing, whether it has one cell or many, is described as an **organism.** All organisms are characterized by

- organization—the way that an organism's body is arranged
- growth—the way that an organism grows and develops over its lifetime
- reproduction—the way that an organism produces offspring like itself
- response—the ways an organism interacts with its surroundings

All living things share common needs.

All living things have three basic needs: energy, materials, and living space. Energy enables an organism to carry out all the activities of life. The body of an organism needs water and other materials. Water is important because most of the chemical reactions in a cell take place in water. Organisms also require other materials. Plants, for example, need carbon dioxide to make energy-rich sugars, and most living things need oxygen. Living space is the environment in which an organism gets the energy and materials it needs.

Living things meet their needs through interactions with the environment.

The **environment** is everything that surrounds a living thing. This includes other organisms as well as nonliving factors, such as rainfall, sunlight, and soil. Any exchange of energy or materials between the living and nonliving parts of the environment is an **interaction.** Plants interact with the environment by capturing energy from the Sun and changing that energy into chemical energy that is stored in sugar. Animals can interact with plants by eating the plants and getting energy from the sugars that the plants have made.

The types and numbers of living things change over time.

A **species** is a group of living things so closely related that they can produce offspring together that can also reproduce. Scientists have named about 1.4 million different species. The great variety of species on Earth today is called **biodiversity.** Different species have different characteristics, or **adaptations,** that allow the members of that species to get their needs met in a particular environment. Over the millions of years that life has existed on Earth, new species have come into being and others have disappeared. The disappearance of a species is called **extinction.** Fossils of now extinct organisms is one way that scientists have of seeing how living things have changed over time.

What Is Earth Science?

Earth science is the study of Earth's interior, its rocks and soil, its oceans, its atmosphere, and outer space. For many years, scientists studied each of these topics separately. They learned many important things. More recently, however, scientists have looked more and more at the connections among the different parts of Earth—its oceans, atmosphere, living things, and rocks and soil. Scientists have also been learning more about other planets in our solar system, as well as stars and galaxies far away. Through these studies they have learned much about Earth and its place in the universe.

The universe is everything that exists, and everything in the universe is governed by the same physical laws. The same laws govern the stars shown in this picture and the page on which the picture is printed.

UNIFYING PRINCIPLES of Earth Science

Heat energy inside Earth and radiation from the Sun provide energy for Earth's processes.

Energy is the ability to cause change. All of Earth's processes need energy to occur. Earth's interior is very hot. This heat energy moves up to Earth's surface, where it provides the energy to build mountains, cause earthquakes, and make volcanoes erupt. Earth also receives energy from the Sun as **radiation**—energy that travels across distances in the form of certain types of waves. Energy from the Sun causes winds to blow, ocean currents to flow, and water to move from the ground to the atmosphere and back again.

Physical forces, such as gravity, affect the movement of all matter on Earth and throughout the universe.

What do the stars in a galaxy, the planet Earth, and your body have in common? For one thing, they are all made of matter. **Matter** is anything that has mass and takes up space. Rocks are matter. You are matter. Even the air around you is matter. Everything in the universe is also affected by the same physical forces. A **force** is a push or a pull. Forces affect how matter moves everywhere in the universe.

Matter and energy move among Earth's rocks and soil, atmosphere, waters, and living things.

Think of Earth as a huge system, or an organized group of parts that work together. Within this system, matter and energy move among the different parts. The four major parts of Earth's system are the

- **atmosphere,** which includes all the air surrounding the solid planet
- **geosphere,** which includes all of Earth's rocks and minerals, as well as Earth's interior
- **hydrosphere,** which includes oceans, rivers, lakes, and every drop of water on or under Earth's surface
- **biosphere,** which includes all the living things on Earth

Earth has changed over time and continues to change.

Events are always changing Earth's surface. Some events, such as the building or wearing away of mountains, occur over millions of years. Others, such as earthquakes, occur within seconds. A change can affect a small area or even the entire planet.

What Is Physical Science?

Physical science is the study of what things are made of and how they change. It combines the study of both physics and chemistry. Physics is the study of matter, energy, and forces, and it includes such topics as motion, light, and electricity and magnetism. Chemistry is the study of the structure and properties of matter. It focuses especially on how substances change into different substances.

Like the tiles that make up this picture, the particles that make up all substances combine to make structures that we can see. Unlike these tiles, the individual particles themselves are too small to see.

UNIFYING PRINCIPLES of Physical Science

Matter is made of particles too small to see.

The tiny particles that make up all matter are called **atoms.** Just how tiny are atoms? They are far too small to see even through a powerful microscope. In fact, an atom is about a million times smaller than the period at the end of this sentence. There are more than 100 basic kinds of matter called **elements.** The atoms of any element are all alike but different from the atoms of any other element. Everything around you is made of atoms and combinations of atoms.

Matter changes form and moves from place to place.

You see objects moving and changing all around you. All changes in matter are the result of atoms moving and combining in different ways. Regardless of how much matter may change, however, under ordinary conditions it is never created or destroyed. Matter that seems to disappear merely changes into another form of matter.

Energy changes from one form to another, but it cannot be created or destroyed.

All the changes you see around you depend on energy. Energy, in fact, means the ability to cause change. Using energy means changing energy. But energy is never created or destroyed, no matter how often it changes form. This fact is known as the **law of conservation of energy.** The energy you may think you've lost when a match has burned out has only been changed into other forms of energy that are less useful to you.

Physical forces affect the movement of all matter on Earth and throughout the universe.

A **force** is a push or a pull. Every time you push or pull an object, you are applying a force to that object, whether or not the object moves. There are several forces—several pushes or pulls—acting on you right now. All these forces are necessary for you to do the things you do, even sitting and reading. **Gravity** keeps you on the ground. Gravity also keeps the Moon moving around Earth, and Earth moving around the Sun. **Friction** is the force that opposes motion. The friction between the bottoms of your shoes and the floor makes it possible for you to walk without slipping. Too much friction between a heavy box and the floor makes it hard to push the box across the floor.

The Nature of Science

You may think of science as a body of knowledge or a collection of facts. More important, however, science is an active process that involves certain ways of looking at the world.

Scientific Habits of Mind

Scientists are curious. They ask questions. A scientist who finds an unusual rock by the side of a river would ask questions such as, "Did this rock form in this area?" or "Did this rock form elsewhere and get moved here?" Questions like these make a scientist want to investigate.

Scientists are observant. They look closely at the world around them. A scientist who studies rocks can learn a lot about a rock just by picking it up, looking at its color, and feeling how heavy it is.

Scientists are creative. They draw on what they know to form possible explanations for a pattern, an event, or an interesting phenomenon that they have observed. Then scientists put together a plan for testing their ideas.

Scientists are skeptical. Scientists don't accept an explanation or answer unless it is based on evidence and logical reasoning. They continually question their own conclusions as well as the conclusions suggested by other scientists. Scientists only trust evidence that can be confirmed by other people or other methods.

Scientists use seismographs to observe and measure vibrations that move through the ground.

This scientist is collecting a sample of melted rock from a hot lava flow in Hawaii.

Science Processes at Work

You can think of science as a continuous cycle of asking and seeking answers to questions about the world. Although there are many processes that scientists use, all scientists typically do the following:

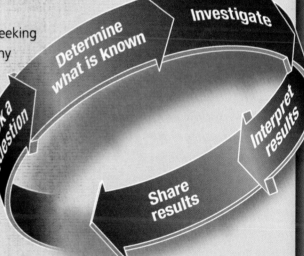

- Observe and ask a question
- Determine what is known
- Investigate
- Interpret results
- Share results

Observe and Ask a Question

It may surprise you that asking questions is an important skill. A scientific investigation may start when a scientist asks a question. Perhaps scientists observe an event or a process that they don't understand, or perhaps answering one question leads to another.

Determine What Is Known

When beginning an inquiry, scientists find out what is already known about a question. They study results from other scientific investigations, read journals, and talk with other scientists. The scientist who is trying to figure out where an unusual rock came from will study maps that show what types of rocks are already known to be in the area where the rock was found.

Investigate

Investigating is the process of collecting evidence. Two important ways of doing this are experimenting and observing.

An **experiment** is an organized procedure to study something under controlled conditions. For example, the scientist who found the rock by the river might notice that it is lighter in color where it is chipped. The scientist might design an experiment to determine why the rock is a different color on the inside. The scientist could break off a small piece of the inside of the rock and heat it up to see if it becomes the same color as the outside. The scientist would need to use a piece of the same rock that is being studied. A different rock might react differently to heat.

A scientist may use photography to study fast events, such as multiple flashes of lightning.

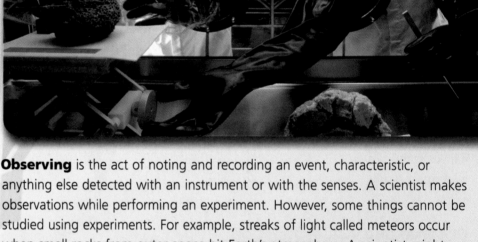

Rocks, such as this one from the Moon, can be subjected to different conditions in a laboratory.

Observing is the act of noting and recording an event, characteristic, or anything else detected with an instrument or with the senses. A scientist makes observations while performing an experiment. However, some things cannot be studied using experiments. For example, streaks of light called meteors occur when small rocks from outer space hit Earth's atmosphere. A scientist might study meteors by taking pictures of the sky at a time when meteors are likely to occur.

Forming hypotheses and making predictions are two other skills involved in scientific investigations. A **hypothesis** is a tentative explanation for an observation or a scientific problem that can be tested by further investigation. For example, the scientist might make the following hypothesis about the rock from the beach:

The rock is a meteorite, which is a rock that fell to the ground from outer space. The outside of the rock changed color because it was heated up from passing through Earth's atmosphere.

A **prediction** is an expectation of what will be observed or what will happen. To test the hypothesis that the rock's outside is black because it is a meteorite, the scientist might predict that a close examination of the rock will show that it has many characteristics in common with rocks that are already known to be meteorites.

Interpret Results

As scientists investigate, they analyze their evidence, or data, and begin to draw conclusions. **Analyzing data** involves looking at the evidence gathered through observations or experiments and trying to identify any patterns that might exist in the data. Scientists often need to make additional observations or perform more experiments before they are sure of their conclusions. Many times scientists make new predictions or revise their hypotheses.

Scientists use computers to gather and interpret data.

Scientists make images such as this computer drawing of a landscape to help share their results with others.

Share Results

An important part of scientific investigation is sharing results of experiments. Scientists read and publish in journals and attend conferences to communicate with other scientists around the world. Sharing data and procedures gives scientists a way to test each others' results. They also share results with the public through newspapers, television, and other media.

The Nature of Technology

When you think of technology, you may think of cars, computers, and cell phones. Imagine having no refrigerator or radio. It's difficult to think of a world without the products of what we call technology. Technology, however, is more than just devices that make our daily activities easier. Technology is the process of using scientific knowledge to design solutions to real-world problems.

Science and Technology

Science and technology go hand in hand. Each depends upon the other. Even a device as simple as a thermometer is designed using knowledge of the ways different materials respond to changes in temperature. In turn, thermometers have allowed scientists to learn more about the world. Greater knowledge of how materials respond to changes in temperature helped engineers to build items such as refrigerators. They have also built thermometers that could be read automatically by computers. New technologies lead to new scientific knowledge and new scientific knowledge leads to even better technologies.

The Process of Technological Design

The process of technological design involves many choices. What, for example, should be done to protect the residents of an area prone to severe storms such as tornadoes and hurricanes? Build stronger homes that can withstand the winds? Try to develop a way to detect the storms long before they occur? Or learn more about hurricanes in order to find new ways to protect people from the dangers? The steps people take to solve the problem depend a great deal on what they already know about the problem as well as what can reasonably be done. As you learn about the steps in the process of technological design, think about the different choices that could be made at each step.

Identify a Need

To study hurricanes, scientists needed to know what happens inside the most dangerous parts of the storm. However, it was not safe for scientists to go near the centers of hurricanes because the winds were too strong and changed direction too fast. Scientists needed a way to measure conditions deep inside the storm without putting themselves in danger.

Design and Develop

One approach was to design a robotic probe to take the measurements. The probe and instruments needed to be strong enough to withstand the fast winds near the center of a hurricane. The scientists also needed a way to send the probe into the storm and to get the data from the instruments quickly.

Scientists designed a device called a dropsonde, which could be dropped from an airplane flying over the hurricane. A dropsonde takes measurements from deep inside the storm and radios data back to the scientists.

Test and Improve

Even good technology can usually be improved. When scientists first used dropsondes, they learned about hurricanes. They also learned what things about the dropsondes worked well and what did not. For example, the scientists wanted better ways to keep track of where the probe moved. Newer dropsondes make use of the Global Positioning System, which is a way of pinpointing any position on Earth by using satellite signals.

Using McDougal Littell Science

Reading Text and Visuals

This book is organized to help you learn. Use these boxed pointers as a path to help you learn and remember the **Big Ideas** and **Key Concepts**.

Take notes.

Use the strategies on the **Getting Ready to Learn** page.

Read the Big Idea.

As you read **Key Concepts** for the chapter, relate them to **the Big Idea**.

CHAPTER

2 Min

the **BIG** idea

Minerals are basic building blocks of Earth.

Key Concepts

SECTION 2.1 Minerals are all around us.
Learn about the characteristics all minerals share.

SECTION 2.2 A mineral is identified by its properties.
Learn how to identify minerals by observing and testing their properties.

SECTION 2.3 Minerals are valuable resources.
Learn how minerals form, how they are mined, and how they are used.

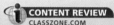

Internet Preview

CLASSZONE.COM
Chapter 2 online resources: Content Review, Visualization, three Resource Centers, Math Tutorial, Test Practice

---

CHAPTER 2

Getting Ready to Learn

CONCEPT REVIEW

- Earth has four main layers: crust, mantle, outer core, and inner core.
- Matter exists in the forms of gas, liquid, and solid.
- People use maps to show many different features of Earth.

VOCABULARY REVIEW

atom *See Glossary.*
geosphere p. 12

CONTENT REVIEW
CLASSZONE.COM
Review concepts and vocabulary.

TAKING NOTES

SCIENCE NOTEBOOK

SUPPORTING MAIN IDEAS

Make a chart to show each main idea and the information that supports it. Copy each blue heading. Below each heading, add supporting information, such as reasons, explanations, and examples.

VOCABULARY STRATEGY

Place each vocabulary term at the center of a description wheel. On the spokes write some words explaining it.

See the Note-Taking Handbook on pages R45–R51.

Minerals have four characteristics.

- Minerals form naturally.
- All minerals are solids.
- Each mineral is always made of the same element or elements.
- All minerals have crystal structures.

atoms joined in a repeating 3-D pattern

CRYSTAL

formed by all minerals

KEY CONCEPT

2.1 Minerals are all around us.

◀ **BEFORE,** you learned

• Earth is made of layers
• Earth's outermost rocky layer is the crust

▶ **NOW,** you will learn

• What the characteristics of minerals are
• How minerals are classified into groups
• Which mineral group is most common

VOCABULARY

mineral p. 43
element p. 45
crystal p. 46

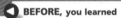

EXPLORE Minerals

What are some characteristics of a mineral?

PROCEDURE

① Sprinkle some table salt on a sheet of colored paper. Look at a few grains of the salt through a magnifying glass. Then rub a few grains between your fingers.

② In your notebook, describe all the qualities of the salt that you observe.

③ Examine the rock salt in the same way and describe its qualities in your notebook. How do the two differ?

MATERIALS

• colored paper
• table salt
• rock salt
• magnifying glass

WHAT DO YOU THINK?

Salt is a mineral. From your observations of salt, what do you think are some characteristics of minerals?

Minerals have four characteristics.

You use minerals all the time. Every time you turn on a microwave oven or a TV, you depend on minerals. The copper in the wires that carry electricity to the device is a mineral. Table salt, or halite (HAYL-YT), is another mineral that you use in your everyday life.

Minerals have four characteristics. A **mineral** is a substance that

• forms in nature
• is a solid
• has a definite chemical makeup
• has a crystal structure

VOCABULARY
Add a description wheel for *mineral* in your notebook.

Chapter 2: **Minerals** 43 **A**

Reading Text and Visuals

Study the visuals.

- Read the title.
- Read all labels and captions.
- Figure out what the picture is showing. Notice colors, arrows, and lines.

Minerals in Rocks

Most rocks are made up of minerals.

Quartz

Feldspar

Mica

granite

This piece of granite contains the minerals quartz, feldspar, and mica.

Answer the questions.

Check Your Reading questions will help you remember what you read.

READING TiP
Proportions show relationships between amounts. For example, a quartz crystal always has two oxygen atoms for every silicon atom.

Read one paragraph at a time.

Look for a topic sentence that explains the main idea of the paragraph. Figure out how the details relate to that idea. One paragraph might have several important ideas; you may have to reread to understand.

READING TiP
Molten rock refers to rock that has become so hot that it has melted.

You might think that minerals and rocks are the same things. But a mineral must have the four characteristics listed on page 43. A rock has only two of these characteristics—it is a solid and it forms naturally. A rock usually contains two or more types of minerals.

Two samples of the same type of rock may vary greatly in the amounts of different minerals they contain. Minerals, however, are always made up of the same materials in the same proportions. A ruby is a mineral. Therefore, a ruby found in India has the same makeup as a ruby found in Australia.

CHECK YOUR READING How are minerals different from rocks?

Formed in Nature

Minerals are formed by natural processes. Every type of mineral can form in nature by processes that do not involve living organisms. As you will read, a few minerals can also be produced by organisms as part of their shells or bones.

Minerals form in many ways. The mineral halite, which is used as table salt, forms when water evaporates in a hot, shallow part of the ocean, leaving behind the salt it contained. Many types of minerals, including the ones in granite, develop when molten rock cools. Talc, a mineral that can be used to make baby powder, forms deep in Earth as high pressure and temperature cause changes in solid rock.

Doing Labs

To understand science, you have to see it in action. Doing labs helps you understand how things really work.

① Read the entire lab first.

② Follow the procedure.

③ Record the data.

CHAPTER INVESTIGATION

Mineral Identification

OVERVIEW AND PURPOSE In this activity, you will observe and perform tests on minerals. Then you will compare your observations to a mineral identification key.

▶ Procedure

1. Make a data table like the one shown in the notebook on the next page.

2. You will examine and identify five minerals. Get a numbered mineral sample from the mineral set. Record the number of your sample in your table.

3. First, observe the sample. Note the color and the luster of the sample. Write your observations in your table. In the row labeled "Luster," write *metallic* if the mineral appears shiny like metal. Write *nonmetallic* if the sample does not look like metal. For example, it may look glassy, pearly, or dull.

step 3

4. Observe the sample through the hand lens. Look to see any signs of how the crystals in the mineral broke. If it appears that the crystals have broken along straight lines, put a check in the row labeled "Cleavage." If it appears that the sample has fractured, put a check in the appropriate row of your table.

step 4

5. CAUTION: Keep the streak plate on your desktop or table while you are doing the streak test. A broken streak plate can cause serious cuts. Rub the mineral sample on the streak plate. If the sample does not leave a mark, the mineral is harder than the streak plate. Write *no* in the row labeled "Streak." If the sample does leave a mark on the streak plate, write the color of the streak in that row.

step 5

MATERIALS
- numbered mineral samples
- hand lens
- streak plate
- copper penny
- steel file
- magnet
- dilute hydrochloric acid
- eyedropper
- Mohs scale
- Mineral Identification Key

A 58 Unit: Earth's Surface

6. Test each sample for its hardness on the Mohs scale. Try to scratch the sample with each of these items in order: a fingernail, a copper penny, and a steel file. In the Mohs scale, find the hardness number of the object that first scratches the sample. Write in the table that the mineral's hardness value is between that of the hardest item that did not scratch the sample and that of the item that did scratch it.

7. Test the sample with the magnet. If the magnet is attracted to the sample, put a check in the row labeled "Magnetic."

step 7

8. Repeat steps 2 through 7 for each of the other numbered samples.

▶ Observe and Analyze *Write It Up*

1. **INTERPRET DATA** Use the Mineral Identification Key and the information in your data table to identify your samples. Write the names of the minerals in your table.

2. **COLLECT DATA CAUTION: Before doing the acid test, put on your safety glasses, protective gloves, and lab apron. Acids can cause burns.** If you identified one of the samples as a carbonate mineral, such as calcite, you can check your identification with the acid test. Use the eyedropper to put a few drops of dilute hydrochloric acid on the mineral. If the acid bubbles, the sample is a carbonate.

▶ Conclude *Write It Up*

1. **COMPARE AND CONTRAST** How are the minerals calcite and halite alike? Which property can you use to test whether a sample is calcite or halite?

2. **INTERPRET** Look at the data in your table. Name any minerals that you could identify on the basis of a single property.

3. **APPLY** Examine a piece of granite rock. On the basis of your examination of granite and your observations of the samples, try to determine what the light-colored, translucent mineral in the granite is and what the flaky, darker mineral is.

▶ INVESTIGATE Further

Specific gravity is another property used to identify minerals. The specific gravity of a mineral is determined by comparing the mineral's density with the density of water.

Find the specific gravity of an unknown mineral chosen from your teacher's samples. Attach your mineral with a string to a spring scale. Record its mass and label this value M1. Then suspend the mineral in a beaker of water. Record the measurement of the mineral's mass in water. Label this value M2. To determine the mineral's specific gravity, use the following equation:

$$\frac{M1}{M1 - M2} = \text{specific gravity}$$

Do all the other steps to identify the sample. Does the specific gravity you measured match the one listed for that mineral in the identification key?

Mineral Identification

Table 1 Mineral Properties

Property	Sample Number				
	1	2	3	4	5
Color					
Luster					
Cleavage					
Fracture					
Streak					
Hardness					
Magnetic					
Acid test					
Name of mineral					

Chapter 2: Minerals 59 A

④ Analyze your results.

⑤ Write your lab report.

Using Technology

The Internet is a great source of information about up-to-date science. The ClassZone Website and SciLinks have exciting sites for you to explore. Video clips and simulations can make science come alive.

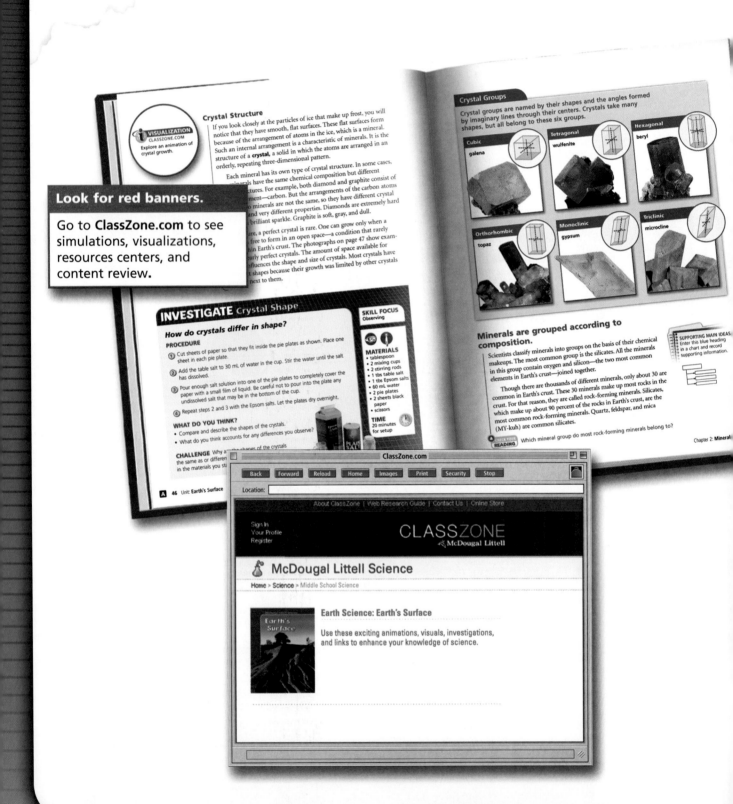

Look for red banners.

Go to **ClassZone.com** to see simulations, visualizations, resources centers, and content review.

FRONTIERS in Science

SCIENTIFIC AMERICAN FRONTIERS

REMOTE SENSING

...nology high above Earth's surface is giving scientists ...ole new look at our planet. This image is of Jasper ...r near Palo Alto, California.

SCIENTIFIC AMERICAN FRONTIERS

View the video segment "All That Glitters" to learn how explorers use remote sensing and... methods to find valuable materials.

A 2 ... Earth's Surface

Watch the videos.

See science at work in the **Scientific American Frontiers video.**

Look up SciLinks.

Go to **scilinks.org** to explore the topic.

NSTA
scilinks.org
SCI LINKS

The Sun Code: MDL060

Earth's Surface

biosphere

sedimentary
rock

EROSION

geosphere

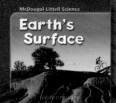

Earth's Surface
Contents Overview

Unit Features

1 Views of Earth Today   6

(the **BIG** idea)

Modern technology has changed the
way we view and map Earth.

2 Minerals   40

(the **BIG** idea)

Minerals are basic building
blocks of Earth.

3 Rocks   72

(the **BIG** idea)

Rocks change into other rocks
over time.

4 Weathering and Soil Formation   112

(the **BIG** idea)

Natural forces break rocks apart
and form soil, which supports life.

5 Erosion and Deposition   142

(the **BIG** idea)

Water, wind, and ice shape
Earth's surface.

REMOTE SENSING

Technology high above Earth's surface is giving scientists a whole new look at our planet. This image is of Jasper Ridge, near Palo Alto, California.

SCIENTIFIC AMERICAN FRONTIERS

View the video segment "All That Glitters" to learn how explorers use remote sensing and other methods to find valuable materials.

This research jet aircraft carries instruments to study Earth's land surface, ocean, and atmosphere. It flies at high altitudes, allowing it to collect data and images over large areas during a single flight.

Mapping Earth

You're probably familiar with images of gold prospectors in the Old West. Maybe you've seen them in old movies or read about them in history books. Prospectors wandered through the mountains, looking for signs of ores or gemstones, going here and there in response to rumors or stories, pitching camp in remote canyons on a hunch. People still prospect for minerals today, but they're more likely to fly in airplanes than to ride mules. And stories of fabled mines are just stories and fables. Today's prospectors rely on scientific evidence from remote sensing.

Remote sensing—the use of instruments to gather data from a distance—has two great advantages. The first is that sensors mounted in satellites and airplanes can collect vast amounts of detailed information over large areas. The second is that the sensors can easily collect information about the same area again and again.

For example, scientists use remote sensing to make better and more detailed maps of Earth and to track changes over time. Thanks to remote sensing, scientists now know that Mount Everest, the highest point on Earth, is actually getting higher by about 1 centimeter (0.4 in.) per year. Remote sensors on satellites are also mapping global ocean temperatures and showing how they change over the course of a year.

Uncut diamond

Detecting Minerals from Above

One of the many uses of remote sensing is to find new sources of valuable minerals, such as diamonds. To detect minerals from airplanes or satellites, remote sensors make use of the energy in sunlight. Sunlight reaches Earth as radiation, which travels in the form of waves. All objects absorb some types of radiation and reflect others. The particular wavelengths absorbed or reflected depend upon the materials that make up the objects. Each kind of material has a unique "fingerprint" of the wavelengths it absorbs and the wavelengths it reflects.

When sunlight strikes Earth's surface, some of it is reflected back into the sky. Some of the radiation is absorbed by rocks and other objects and then emitted, or given off, in a different form. Remote sensors in airplanes and satellites collect the reflected and emitted radiation and analyze it to determine which types of rocks and minerals lie on the surface. The remote sensing

Sun

Energy from the Sun reflects at different wavelengths from materials at Earth's surface. Instruments on the jet analyze the reflected energy and map the surface.

systems collect so much data that computer processing and analysis are difficult and expensive. Still, the data are usually clear enough to show the types of minerals located in the regions scanned. However, minerals that are buried cannot be detected by remote sensing from aircraft or satellites. The sensors receive only energy from or near the surface.

SCIENTIFIC AMERICAN FRONTIERS

View the "All that Glitters" segment of your *Scientific American Frontiers* video to see how finding certain common minerals can indicate the presence of a valuable mineral like diamond.

IN THIS SCENE FROM THE VIDEO ⊙ a mineral prospector searches for diamonds in a cylinder of rock drilled from beneath Earth's surface.

SEARCHING FOR DIAMONDS People used to think that North America did not have many diamonds. However, northern Canada is geologically similar to the world's major diamond-producing areas: southern Africa, Russia, and Australia. A few diamond prospectors kept searching, using remote sensing and other techniques. The prospectors looked for more common minerals that form under the same conditions as diamonds. They made maps showing where these minerals were most plentiful and used the maps to search for diamond-rich rock. Once the prospectors realized that the glaciers of the last ice age had moved the minerals, they looked for and found diamonds farther northward. Canada is now a big producer of diamonds.

Remote sensing can show the presence of minerals that occur with diamonds, but people must still use older methods to collect samples for further analysis.

Prospecting for Diamonds

One of the major regions of mineral exploration in which remote sensing is used is in the Northwest Territories of Canada, where the first diamond mine began operating in 1998. The Canada Centre for Remote Sensing has helped develop sensing equipment that can fit easily onto light airplanes and computer equipment to analyze results quickly. The sensing equipment is used to detect certain types of minerals that are often found along with diamonds.

Using remote sensing to locate minerals associated with diamonds or valuable ores is only a beginning. The data cannot show how far the minerals or ores extend underground. Prospectors must still explore the area and take samples. However, remote sensing gives mineral prospectors an excellent idea of where to start looking.

UNANSWERED Questions

As scientists use remote sensing to study Earth's land surface, ocean, and atmosphere, they work to answer new questions.

- Can remote sensing be used to locate sources of iron, platinum, or gold in areas that are difficult to explore on foot?

- How do changes in water temperature at the ocean surface affect long-range weather patterns and the health of ocean organisms?

- How do different types of clouds affect the amount of sunlight reaching Earth's surface and the average temperature of the surface?

UNIT PROJECTS

As you study this unit, work alone or with a group on one of the projects listed below.

Hiker's Guide Video

Like prospectors, wilderness hikers must be able to read maps that show the shape of the land. Prepare a video to teach hikers how to choose hiking and camping areas by reading maps.

- Obtain a topographic map of a wilderness area in a national or state park.

- Write a script outlining what you will teach and how you will videotape it.

- Present your video and display the maps you used.

Diamond Mine Model

Diamonds can be carried toward Earth's surface by kimberlite pipes. Show how diamonds are mined from kimberlite.

- Build a model of a diamond-mine tunnel that passes through kimberlite.

- Present your model to your class. Explain the relationship between kimberlite and diamonds.

Glacier Photo Essay

Make a photo essay showing how glaciers reshape Earth's surface as they move and melt.

- Find images of areas that are or have been affected by glaciers. Write captions for them.

- Present the images as a photo essay on a poster or in a portfolio.

CAREER CENTER
CLASSZONE.COM

Learn more about careers in mineralogy.

Views of Earth Today

the BIG idea

Modern technology has changed the way we view and map Earth.

Key Concepts

SECTION

1.1 Technology is used to explore the Earth system.
Learn how technology has changed people's view of Earth.

SECTION

1.2 Maps and globes are models of Earth.
Learn how to locate any place on Earth and how Earth's sphere is portrayed on flat maps.

SECTION

1.3 Topographic maps show the shape of the land.
Learn about representing the features of Earth's surface on flat maps.

SECTION

1.4 Technology is used to map Earth.
Learn how satellites and computers are used to provide more detailed maps of Earth.

Internet Preview

CLASSZONE.COM

Chapter 1 online resources: Content Review, Simulation, Visualization, three Resource Centers, Math Tutorial, and Test Practice

What do all these views show about Earth?

Swirling clouds over North and South America: NASA Terra satellite data

Warm and cool ocean-surface temperatures: NASA satellite image

Chlorophyll levels (green) on land and sea: SeaStar spacecraft image

Earth's rocky surface without the oceans: NASA satellite data

EXPLORE (the BIG idea)

Earth's Changing Surface

Go outside and find evidence of how wind, water, or living things change the surface of Earth. You might look in alleyways, parks, wooded areas, or backyards. For example, you might find a path worn through a grassy area near a parking lot.

Observe and Think What changes do you observe? What do you think caused the changes?

Using Modern Maps

Find a map of a city, a bus or rail system, or a state. Study the names, colors, and symbols on the map and any features of interest.

Observe and Think Which direction on the map is north? What do the symbols mean? How do you measure the distance from one point to another?

Internet Activity: Mapping

Go to **ClassZone.com** to learn more about mapping Earth from space. Find out about a NASA mission to develop the most accurate map of Earth ever made.

Observe and Think Why do you think scientists need different maps produced from satellite data?

NSTA
scilinks.org
SCiLINKS

Earth's Spheres **Code: MDL013**

Getting Ready to Learn

◀ CONCEPT REVIEW

- Earth, like all planets, is shaped roughly like a sphere.
- Earth supports a complex web of life.
- The planet consists of many parts that interact with one another.

◀ VOCABULARY REVIEW

See Glossary for definitions.

energy

matter

planet

satellite

 CONTENT REVIEW
CLASSZONE.COM
Review concepts and vocabulary.

▶ TAKING NOTES

MAIN IDEA AND DETAIL NOTES

Make a two-column chart. Write the main ideas, such as those in the blue headings, in the column on the left. Write details about each of those main ideas in the column on the right.

VOCABULARY STRATEGY

Draw a **word triangle** diagram for each new vocabulary term. On the bottom line write and define the term. Above that, write a sentence that uses the term correctly. At the top, draw a picture to show what the term looks like.

See the Note-Taking Handbook on pages R45–R51.

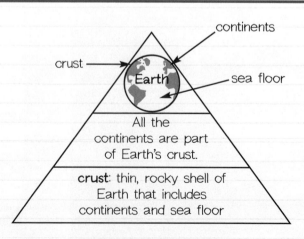

SCIENCE NOTEBOOK

MAIN IDEAS	DETAIL NOTES
1. The Earth system has four main parts.	1. Atmosphere = mixture of gases surrounding Earth 1. Hydrosphere = all waters on Earth

continents

crust → Earth

sea floor

All the continents are part of Earth's crust.

crust: thin, rocky shell of Earth that includes continents and sea floor

Technology is used to explore the Earth system.

 BEFORE, you learned

- Earth has a spherical shape and supports a complex web of life
- Earth's environment is a system with many parts

NOW, you will learn

- About the Earth system and its four major parts
- How technology is used to explore the Earth system
- How the parts of the Earth system shape the surface

VOCABULARY

system p. 9
atmosphere p. 10
hydrosphere p. 10
biosphere p. 11
geosphere p. 12

VOCABULARY
Remember to draw a word triangle in your notebook for each vocabulary term.

THINK ABOUT

How do these parts work together?

Look closely at this terrarium. Notice that the bowl and its cover form a boundary between the terrarium and the outside world. What might happen to the entire terrarium if any part were taken away? What might happen if you placed the terrarium in a dark closet?

The Earth system has four major parts.

A terrarium is a simple example of a **system** —an organized group of parts that work together to form a whole. To understand a system, you need to see how all its parts work together. This principle is true for a small terrarium, and it is true for planet Earth.

Both a terrarium and Earth are closed systems. They are closed because matter, such as soil or water, cannot enter or leave. However, energy can flow into or out of the system. Just as light and heat pass through the glass of the terrarium, sunlight and heat enter and leave the Earth system through the atmosphere.

Within the Earth system are four connected parts: the atmosphere (Earth's air), the hydrosphere (Earth's waters), the biosphere (Earth's living things), and the geosphere (Earth's interior and its rocks and soils). Each of these parts is an open system because both matter and energy move into and out of it. The four open systems work together to form one large, closed system called Earth.

Atmosphere

READING TiP

The names of the Earth system's four parts contain Greek prefixes. *Atmo-* refers to vapor or gas. *Hydro-* refers to water. *Bio-* refers to life, and *geo-* refers to earth.

The **atmosphere** (AT-muh-SFEER) is the mixture of gases and particles that surrounds and protects the surface of Earth. The most abundant gases are nitrogen (about 78%) and oxygen (nearly 21%). The atmosphere also contains carbon dioxide, water vapor, and a few other gases.

Before the 1800s, all studies of the atmosphere had to be done from the ground. Today, scientists launch weather balloons, fly specially equipped planes, and view the atmosphere in satellite images. The data they collect show that the atmosphere interacts with the other parts of the Earth system to form complex weather patterns that circulate around Earth. The more scientists learn about these patterns, the more accurately they can predict local weather.

Hydrosphere

The **hydrosphere** (HY-druh-SFEER) is made up of all the water on Earth in oceans, lakes, glaciers, rivers, and streams and underground. Water covers nearly three-quarters of Earth's surface. Only about 3 percent of the hydrosphere is fresh water. Nearly 70 percent of Earth's fresh water is frozen in glaciers and polar ice caps.

Parts of the Earth System

Atmosphere

Over 400 cones make this weather balloon more stable as it gathers data about the atmosphere.

Hydrosphere

Scientists need special diving equipment to study Earth's oceans.

In the past 50 years, scientists have used deep-sea vehicles, special buoys, satellite images, and diving suits, such as the one shown on page 10, to study the world's oceans. They have discovered that the oceans contain several layers of cold and warm water. As these layers circulate, they form cold and warm ocean currents. The currents interact with wind patterns in the atmosphere and affect Earth's weather.

 CHECK YOUR READING How does the hydrosphere affect the atmosphere?

Biosphere

The **biosphere** (BY-uh-SFEER) includes all life on Earth, in the air, on the land, and in the waters. The biosphere can be studied with a variety of technologies. For example, satellite photos are used to track yearly changes in Earth's plant and animal life. As the photograph below shows, special equipment allows scientists to study complex environments, such as rain forests, without damaging them.

Scientists have learned a lot about how the biosphere interacts with the other parts of the Earth system. For example, large forests act as Earth's "lungs," absorbing carbon dioxide and releasing oxygen into the atmosphere. When dead trees decay, they return nutrients to the soil.

 CHECK YOUR READING Name one way the biosphere and the atmosphere interact.

MAIN IDEA AND DETAILS
As you read this section, use this strategy to take notes.

Biosphere

These platforms, built in the treetops, are used to observe forest plants and animals.

Geosphere

In mines dug deep underground, scientists can explore Earth's minerals and rocks.

Geosphere

The **geosphere** (JEE-uh-SFEER) includes all the features on Earth's surface—the continents, islands, and sea floor—and everything below the surface. As the diagram illustrates, the geosphere is made up of several layers: crust, mantle, and outer and inner core.

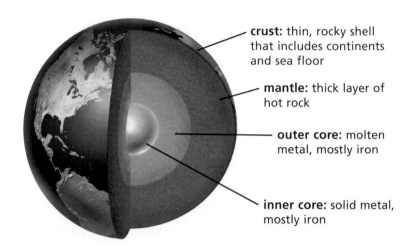

crust: thin, rocky shell that includes continents and sea floor

mantle: thick layer of hot rock

outer core: molten metal, mostly iron

inner core: solid metal, mostly iron

People have studied the surface of the geosphere for centuries. Not until the 1900s, however, were people able to study Earth from space or to explore deep within the planet. Today, scientists use satellite images, sound waves, and computer modeling to develop accurate pictures of features on and below Earth's surface. These images show that Earth constantly changes. Some changes are sudden—a volcano explodes, releasing harmful gases and dust into the air. Other changes, such as the birth of new islands, happen over millions of years.

Earth's continents have many unique landforms such as these rock towers in Cathedral Valley, Utah.

CHECK YOUR READING Give an example of matter moving from the geosphere to the atmosphere.

INVESTIGATE Geosphere's Layers

How can you model the geosphere's layers?

PROCEDURE

1. To model the layers of the geosphere, you will be using a quarter of an apple that your teacher has cut. Note: NEVER eat food in the science classroom.

2. Hold the apple slice and observe it carefully. Compare it with the diagram of the geosphere's layers on page 12.

3. Draw a diagram of the apple and label it with the names of the layers of the geosphere.

WHAT DO YOU THINK?

- What are the four parts of the apple slice?
- What major layer of the geosphere does each part of the apple resemble?

CHALLENGE What other object do you think would make a good model of the geosphere's layers? What model could you build or make yourself?

SKILL FOCUS
Modeling

MATERIALS
apple slice

TIME
15 minutes

All four parts of the Earth system shape the planet's surface.

Earth's surface is worn away, built up, and reshaped every day by the atmosphere, the hydrosphere, the biosphere, and the geosphere. Here are some of the ways they affect the surface.

Atmosphere and Hydrosphere Not even the hardest stone can withstand wind and water. Over millions of years, rain, wind, and flowing water carve huge formations such as the Grand Canyon in Arizona or the rock towers of Utah, shown on page 12.

Geosphere Landmasses pushing together have set off earthquakes and formed volcanoes and mountain ranges around the world.

Biosphere Plants, animals, and human beings have also changed Earth's surface. For instance, earthworms help make soils more fertile. And throughout human history, people have dammed rivers and cleared forests for farmland.

You are part of this process, too. Every time you walk or ride a bike across open land, you are changing Earth's surface. Your feet or the bike's tires dig into the dirt, wearing away plants and exposing soil to sunlight, wind, and water. If you take the same route every day, over time you will wear a path in the land.

READING TIP

Landmass is a compound word made up of the words *land* and *mass*. Landmass means "a large area of land."

Mudslide in California

Atmosphere and Hydrosphere Heavy winter rains soak the ground until it cannot absorb any more water.

Biosphere People who build on fragile hillsides remove plants whose roots help hold the soil in place.

Geosphere With nothing to hold the water-soaked ground, it slides downhill, leaving a deep trench.

The photograph above shows a good example of how the four parts can suddenly change Earth's surface. A mudslide like this one can happen in a matter of minutes. Sometimes the side of a mountain may collapse, becoming a river of mud that can bury an entire town.

The four parts of the Earth system continue to shape the surface with every passing year. Scientists will continue to record these changes to update maps and other images of the planet's complex system.

CHECK YOUR READING Find three examples on pages 13 and 14 that show how the parts of the Earth system shape the planet's surface.

1.1 Review

KEY CONCEPTS

1. Define *system*. Compare an open and a closed system.

2. Name the four parts of the Earth system. List one fact about each part that scientists learned through modern technology.

3. Give two examples of how the Earth system's four parts can interact with each other.

CRITICAL THINKING

4. **Apply** One day you see that plants are dying in the class terrarium. What part might be missing from its system?

5. **Infer** You visit a state park and see a thin rock wall with a hole, like a window, worn through it. Which of the four parts of the Earth system might have made the hole? Explain.

◑ CHALLENGE

6. **Predict** Imagine that a meteorite 200 meters wide strikes Earth, landing in a wooded area. Describe one way that this event would affect the biosphere or the geosphere. **Hint:** A meteorite is traveling several thousand kilometers per hour when it strikes the ground.

1.2 Maps and globes are models of Earth.

◀ BEFORE, you learned

- The Earth system has four main parts: atmosphere, hydrosphere, biosphere, and geosphere
- Technology is used to study and map the Earth system
- The Earth system's parts interact to shape Earth's surface

▶ NOW, you will learn

- What information maps can provide about natural and human-made features
- How to find exact locations on Earth
- Why all maps distort Earth's surface

VOCABULARY

relief map p. 16
map scale p. 17
map legend p. 17
equator p. 18
latitude p. 18
prime meridian p. 19
longitude p. 19
projection p. 20

EXPLORE Mapping

What makes a good map?

PROCEDURE

MATERIALS
- paper
- pencil or pen

1. Draw a map to guide someone from your school to your home or to a point of interest, such as a park, statue, or store, near your school.

2. Trade maps with a classmate. Is his or her map easy to understand? Why or why not?

3. Use feedback from your partner to revise your own map.

WHAT DO YOU THINK?
What visual clues make a map easy to understand and use?

Maps show natural and human-made features.

Have you ever drawn a map to help someone get to your home? If so, your map is actually a rough model of your neighborhood, showing important streets and landmarks. Any map you use is a flat model of Earth's surface, showing Earth's features as seen from above.

On the other hand, a globe represents Earth as if you were looking at it from outer space. A globe is a sphere that shows the relative sizes and shapes of Earth's land features and waters.

In this section you will learn how maps and globes provide different types of information about Earth's surface. They can show everything from city streets to land features to the entire world.

 CHECK YOUR READING How are maps and globes alike? How are they different?

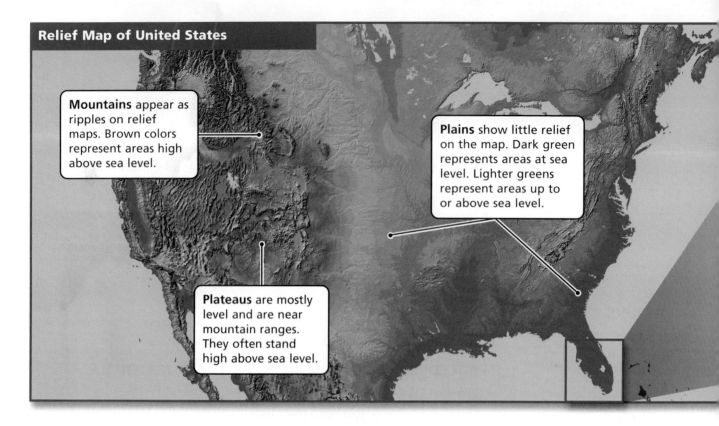

Relief Map of United States

Mountains appear as ripples on relief maps. Brown colors represent areas high above sea level.

Plains show little relief on the map. Dark green represents areas at sea level. Lighter greens represent areas up to or above sea level.

Plateaus are mostly level and are near mountain ranges. They often stand high above sea level.

Land Features on Maps

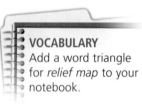

VOCABULARY
Add a word triangle for *relief map* to your notebook.

When scientists or travelers want to know what the landscape of an area actually looks like, they will often use a relief map. A **relief map,** such as the one above, shows how high or low each feature is on Earth. A mapmaker uses photographs or satellite images to build a three-dimensional view of Earth's surface. A relief map shows three main types of land features: mountains, plains, and plateaus.

Mountains stand higher than the land around them. A mountain's base may cover several square kilometers. A group of mountains is called a mountain range. Mountain ranges connected in a long chain form a mountain belt. The Rocky Mountains in the United States are part of a huge mountain belt that includes the Canadian Rockies and the Andes Mountains in South America.

Plateaus have fairly level surfaces but stand high above sea level. Plateaus are often found near large mountain ranges. In the United States, the Colorado Plateau is about 3350 meters (11,000 ft) above sea level. This plateau includes parts of Arizona, Colorado, New Mexico, and Utah.

Plains are gently rolling or flat features. The United States has two types of plains—coastal plains near the eastern and southeastern shores, and interior plains in the center of the nation. The interior Great Plains cover the middle third of the United States.

CHECK YOUR READING How is a plateau different from either a mountain or a plain?

Southern Florida

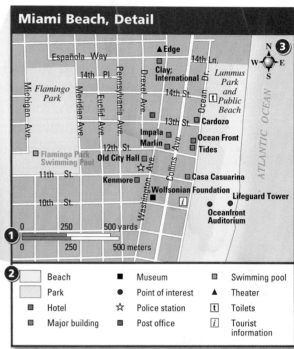

Miami Beach, Detail

Scale and Symbols on Maps

The maps most people use are road and city maps like the ones above. These maps provide information about human-made features as well as some natural features. To use these maps, you need to know how to read a map scale and a map legend, or key.

① A **map scale** relates distances on a map to actual distances on Earth's surface. Notice that on the map of southern Florida above, the scale is in kilometers and miles. On the Miami Beach map, the scale is in meters and yards. The smaller the area a map shows, the more detail it includes.

The scale can be expressed as a ratio, a bar, or equivalent units of distance. For example, a ratio of 1:25,000 means that 1 centimeter on the map represents 25,000 centimeters (0.25 kilometer) on Earth.

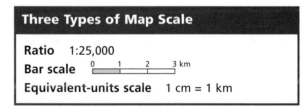

Three Types of Map Scale

Ratio	1:25,000
Bar scale	0 1 2 3 km
Equivalent-units scale	1 cm = 1 km

② A **map legend,** also called a key, is a chart that explains the meaning of each symbol used on a map. Symbols can stand for highways, parks, and other features. The legend on the Miami Beach map shows major points of interest for tourists.

③ A map usually includes a compass rose to show which directions are north, south, east, and west. In general, north on a map points to the top of the page.

READING TiP

As used here, *legend* does not refer to a story. It is based on the Latin word *legenda,* which means "to be read."

CHECK YOUR READING What information do map scales and map legends provide?

VISUALIZATION
CLASSZONE.COM

Explore how latitude and longitude help you find locations on Earth's surface.

Latitude and longitude show locations on Earth.

Suppose you were lucky enough to find dinosaur bones in the desert. Would you know how to find that exact spot again? You would if you knew the longitude and latitude of the place. Latitude and longitude lines form an imaginary grid over the entire surface of Earth. This grid provides everyone with the same tools for navigation. Using latitude and longitude, you can locate any place on the planet.

Latitude

READING TiP

Hemi- is a Greek prefix meaning "half."

Latitude is based on an imaginary line that circles Earth halfway between the north and south poles. This line is called the **equator,** and it divides Earth into northern and southern hemispheres. A hemisphere is one half of a sphere.

Latitude is a distance in degrees north or south of the equator, which is 0°. A degree is 1/360 of the distance around a full circle. If you start at one point on the equator and travel all the way around the world back to that point, you have traveled 360 degrees.

The illustration below shows that latitude lines are parallel to the equator and are evenly spaced between the equator and the poles. Also, latitude lines are always labeled north or south of the equator to

Latitude and Longitude

The **equator** divides Earth into northern and southern hemispheres.

30° N
NORTHERN HEMISPHERE
Equator
SOUTHERN HEMISPHERE
30° S

The **prime meridian** divides Earth into eastern and western hemispheres.

30° W   30° E
WESTERN HEMISPHERE   EASTERN HEMISPHERE
Prime Meridian

60° N
● Paris, France
30° N   ● Cairo, Egypt
60° W   60° E
30° W   30° E
0°
30° S
60° S

Latitude is a distance in degrees north or south of the equator.

Longitude is a distance in degrees east or west of the prime meridian.

You can find a location by noting where latitude and longitude lines cross.

READING VISUALS What are the approximate latitudes and longitudes of Cairo, Egypt, and Paris, France?

show whether a location is in the northern or southern hemisphere. For instance, the North Pole is 90° north, or 90°N, while the South Pole is 90° south, or 90°S. Latitude, however, is only half of what you need to locate any spot on Earth. You also need to know its longitude.

Longitude

Longitude is based on an imaginary line that stretches from the North Pole through Greenwich, England, to the South Pole. This line is called the **prime meridian.** Any place up to 180° west of the prime meridian is in the Western Hemisphere. Any place up to 180° east of the prime meridian is in the Eastern Hemisphere.

Longitude is a distance in degrees east or west of the prime meridian, which is 0°. Beginning at the prime meridian, longitude lines are numbered 0° to 180° west and 0° to 180° east.

Longitude lines are labeled east or west to indicate whether a location is in the eastern or western hemisphere. For example, the longitude of Washington, D.C., is about 78° west, or 78°W. The city of Hamburg, Germany, is about 10° east, or 10°E. If you understand latitude and longitude, you can find any spot on Earth's surface.

READING TiP
There is an easy way to remember the difference between latitude and longitude. Think of longitude lines as the "long" lines that go from pole to pole.

CHECK YOUR READING Why do all cities in the United States have a north latitude and a west longitude?

Global Positioning System

The Global Positioning System (GPS) is a network of satellites that are used to find the latitude, longitude, and elevation, or height above sea level, of any site. Twenty-four GPS satellites circle Earth and send signals that are picked up by receivers on the surface. At least three satellites need to be above the horizon for GPS to work. A computer inside a receiver uses the satellite signals to calculate the user's exact location—latitude, longitude, and elevation. GPS is an accurate, easy method for finding location.

GPS devices are used by many people, including pilots, sailors, hikers, and map makers. Some cars now have GPS receivers and digital road maps stored in their computers. A driver types in an address, and the car's computer finds the best way to get there.

CHECK YOUR READING Explain how GPS can help someone find their exact location.

Never be lost again. This hiker turns on his GPS unit to find out his current latitude and longitude. He then locates these data on his map to pinpoint his exact location.

Map projections distort the view of Earth's surface.

The most accurate way to show Earth's surface is on a globe. A globe, however, cannot show much detail, and it is awkward to carry. People use flat maps for their detail and convenience. A **projection** is a way of representing Earth's curved surface on a flat map. Mapmakers use different types of projections, all of which distort, or misrepresent, Earth's surface in different ways.

Cylindrical Projection

The Mercator projection shows Earth as if the map were a large cylinder wrapped around the planet. The outlines of the landmasses and seas are then drawn onto the map. As shown in the diagram on page 21, the cylinder is unrolled to form a flat map. Latitude and longitude appear as straight lines, forming a grid of rectangles.

The Mercator projection is useful for navigating at sea or in the air. It shows the entire world, except for regions near the poles, on one map. Sailors and pilots can draw a straight line from one point to

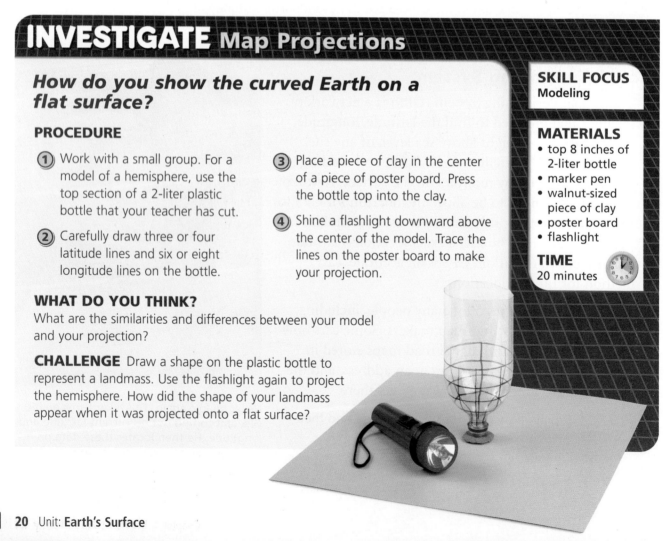

INVESTIGATE Map Projections

How do you show the curved Earth on a flat surface?

PROCEDURE

1. Work with a small group. For a model of a hemisphere, use the top section of a 2-liter plastic bottle that your teacher has cut.

2. Carefully draw three or four latitude lines and six or eight longitude lines on the bottle.

3. Place a piece of clay in the center of a piece of poster board. Press the bottle top into the clay.

4. Shine a flashlight downward above the center of the model. Trace the lines on the poster board to make your projection.

WHAT DO YOU THINK?
What are the similarities and differences between your model and your projection?

CHALLENGE Draw a shape on the plastic bottle to represent a landmass. Use the flashlight again to project the hemisphere. How did the shape of your landmass appear when it was projected onto a flat surface?

SKILL FOCUS
Modeling

MATERIALS
- top 8 inches of 2-liter bottle
- marker pen
- walnut-sized piece of clay
- poster board
- flashlight

TIME
20 minutes

another to plot a course. The problem with Mercator maps is that areas far away from the equator appear much larger than they really are. On the map below, Greenland looks bigger than South America. In reality, South America is about eight times larger than Greenland.

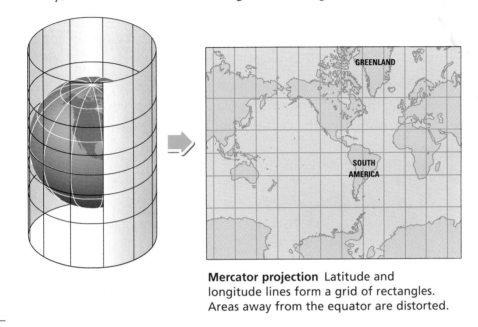

Mercator projection Latitude and longitude lines form a grid of rectangles. Areas away from the equator are distorted.

Conic Projections

Conic projections are based on the shape of a cone. The diagram below shows how a cone of paper might be wrapped around the globe. The paper touches the surface only at the middle latitudes, halfway between the equator and the North Pole.

When the cone is flattened out, the latitude lines are curved slightly. The curved lines represent the curved surface of Earth. This allows the map to show the true sizes and shapes of some landmasses.

Conic projections are most useful for mapping large areas in the middle latitudes, such as the United States. However, landmasses near the equator or near the north or south pole will be distorted.

CHECK YOUR READING What are the main uses of Mercator and conic projections?

Conic projection Latitude lines are slightly curved. Only mid-latitude areas are the correct size and shape.

Planar Projections

RESOURCE CENTER
CLASSZONE.COM

Find out more about
map projections and
how they are used.

Planar projections were developed to help people find the shortest distance between two points. They are drawn as if a circle of paper were laid on a point on Earth's surface. As you look at the diagram below, notice how the shape of the sphere is transferred to the flat map. When a planar map represents the polar region, the longitude lines meet at the center like the spokes of a wheel.

A planar map is good for plotting ocean or air voyages and for showing the north and south polar regions. However, landmasses farther away from the center point are greatly distorted.

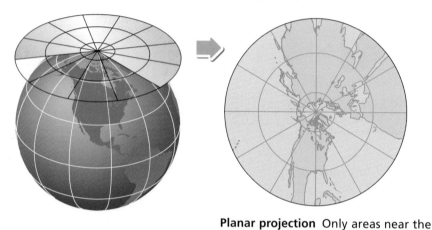

Planar projection Only areas near the center point are the correct size and shape.

The Mercator, conic, and planar projections are all attempts to solve the problem of representing a curved surface on a flat map. Each projection can show certain areas of the world accurately but distorts other areas.

CHECK YOUR READING What areas does the planar projection show accurately?

1.2 Review

KEY CONCEPTS

1. What natural and human-made features can maps show? Give two examples of each.

2. Explain how latitude and longitude can help you locate any place on Earth.

3. Why do all flat maps distort Earth's surface?

CRITICAL THINKING

4. **Provide Examples** Imagine that your family is on a long car trip. What symbols on a road map would you pay the most attention to? Explain.

5. **Apply** Use a world map to find the approximate latitudes and longitudes of Moscow, Russia; Tokyo, Japan; Denver, Colorado; and La Paz, Bolivia.

○ CHALLENGE

6. **Apply** Working with a partner or with a small group, select the shortest airline route from Chicago to London, using a globe and a Mercator map. **Hint:** Notice that as you go farther north on the globe, the longitude lines become closer together.

MATH TUTORIAL
CLASSZONE.COM
Click on Math Tutorial for more help with solving proportions.

How Far Is It?

A science class is visiting Chicago and is using the map on the left to walk to the lakefront museums. Remember, a map scale shows how distances on the map compare to actual distances on the ground.

Buckingham Fountain

Example

In this case, the map scale indicates that 1 centimeter on the map represents 300 meters on the ground. The map scale shows this as equivalent units. By using these units to write a proportion, you can use cross products to determine actual distances.

What distance does 3 cm on the map represent? Set up the problem like this:

$$\frac{1 \text{ cm}}{300 \text{ m}} = \frac{3 \text{ cm}}{x}$$

(1) $1 \text{ cm} \cdot x = 3 \text{ cm} \cdot 300 \text{ m}$

(2) $x = 3 \cdot 300 \text{ m}$

(3) $x = 900 \text{ m}$

ANSWER 3 centimeters on the map represents 900 meters on the ground.

Use cross products and a metric ruler to answer the following questions.

1. The science class divides into two groups. Each group starts at Buckingham Fountain. How far, in meters, will one group walk to get to the Adler Planetarium if they follow the red dotted line?

2. How far, in meters, will the other group walk to get to the end of Navy Pier if they follow the blue dotted line?

3. The group that walked to Adler decides to take a boat to join the other group at Navy Pier. How far, in meters, is their boat ride along the red dotted line?

CHALLENGE What is the total distance, in kilometers, that the two groups traveled? Set up the problem as a proportion. **Hint:** There are 1000 meters in a kilometer.

Map labels:
AVE · LAKE SHORE DR · SUPERIOR ST · MICHIGAN · NAVY PIER · Chicago River · RANDOLPH ST · DR · Art Institute of Chicago · DR · Chicago Harbor · Buckingham Fountain · CONGRESS PKWY · LAKE SHORE DR · MICHIGAN AVE · COLUMBUS · LAKE · Lake Michigan · Shedd Aquarium · Adler Planetarium · ROOSEVELT RD · Field Museum of Natural History · Northerly Island · LAKE SHORE DR · LAKEFRONT TRAIL · AVE · 18TH ST · N W E S · RMAK RD · MC CORMICK PLACE · MICHIGAN

0 150 300 meters
1 cm = 300 m

Topographic maps show the shape of the land.

◀ **BEFORE,** you learned

- Different maps provide information about natural and human-made features
- Latitude and longitude are used to find places on Earth
- All flat maps distort Earth's surface

▶ **NOW,** you will learn

- How contour lines show elevation, slope, and relief
- What rules contour lines follow
- What common symbols are used on topographic maps

VOCABULARY

topography p. 24
contour line p. 25
elevation p. 25
slope p. 25
relief p. 25
contour interval p. 26

EXPLORE Topographic Maps

How can you map your knuckles?

PROCEDURE

1. Hold your fist closed, knuckles up, as shown in the photo.

2. Draw circles around the first knuckle. Make sure the circles are the same distance from each other.

3. Flatten out your hand. Observe what happens. Write down your observations.

WHAT DO YOU THINK?

- How does the height of your knuckles change when you clench your fist, then flatten out your hand?
- What do you think the circles represent?

MATERIAL
washable colored pen

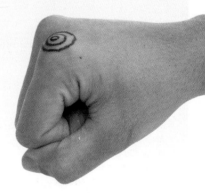

VOCABULARY

Add a word triangle for *topography* to your notebook.

Topographic maps use contour lines to show features.

Imagine you are on vacation with your family in a national park. You have a simple trail map that shows you where to hike. But the map does not tell you anything about what the land looks like. Will you have to cross any rivers or valleys? How far uphill or downhill will you have to hike?

To answer these questions, you need to know something about the topography of the area. **Topography** is the shape, or features, of the land. These features can be natural—such as mountains, plateaus, and plains—or human-made—such as dams and roads. To show the topography of an area, mapmakers draw a topographic map.

A topographic map is a flat map that uses lines to show Earth's surface features. Distance and elevation can be given in feet or meters. Take a look at the topographic map of Mount Hood on this page. The wiggly lines on the map are called **contour lines,** and they show an area's elevation, slope, and relief.

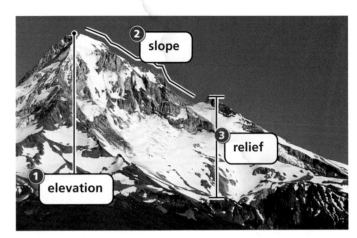

1 The **elevation** of a place is how high above sea level it is. An area can range from a few meters to several thousand meters above sea level. The numbers on the contour lines show the elevations of different points in the Mount Hood area.

2 The **slope** of a landform or area is how steep it is. The more gradual the slope, the farther apart the contour lines on the map. The steeper the slope, the closer together the contour lines.

3 The **relief** of an area is the difference between its high and low points. For example, subtracting the lowest elevation on the map from the highest gives you a measure of the area's relief.

CHECK YOUR READING What is the difference between elevation and slope?

Mount Hood Topographic Map

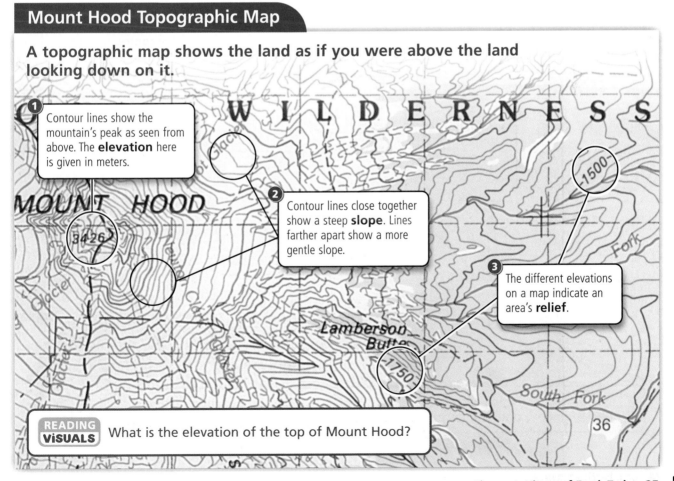

A topographic map shows the land as if you were above the land looking down on it.

1 Contour lines show the mountain's peak as seen from above. The **elevation** here is given in meters.

2 Contour lines close together show a steep **slope**. Lines farther apart show a more gentle slope.

3 The different elevations on a map indicate an area's **relief**.

WILDERNESS

MOUNT HOOD
3426

1500

Fork

Lamberson Butte

1750

South Fork

36

READING VISUALS What is the elevation of the top of Mount Hood?

Contour lines follow certain rules.

MAIN IDEA AND DETAILS
Use your main idea and details chart to take notes on the rules for reading a topographic map.

Contour lines on topographic maps can help you visualize landforms. Think of the following statements as rules for reading such maps:

- **Lines never cross.** Contour lines never cross, because each line represents an exact elevation.

- **Circles show highest and lowest points.** Contour lines form closed circles around mountaintops, hilltops, and the centers of depressions, which are sunken areas in the ground. Sometimes, the elevation of a mountain or hill is written in meters or feet in the middle of the circle.

- **Contour interval is always the same on a map.** The **contour interval** is the difference in elevation from one contour line to the next. For example, the contour interval on the map below is 10 feet. This means that the change in elevation between contour lines is always 10 feet. The contour interval can differ from map to map, but it is always the same on a particular map.

Ely, Minnesota, Topographic Map

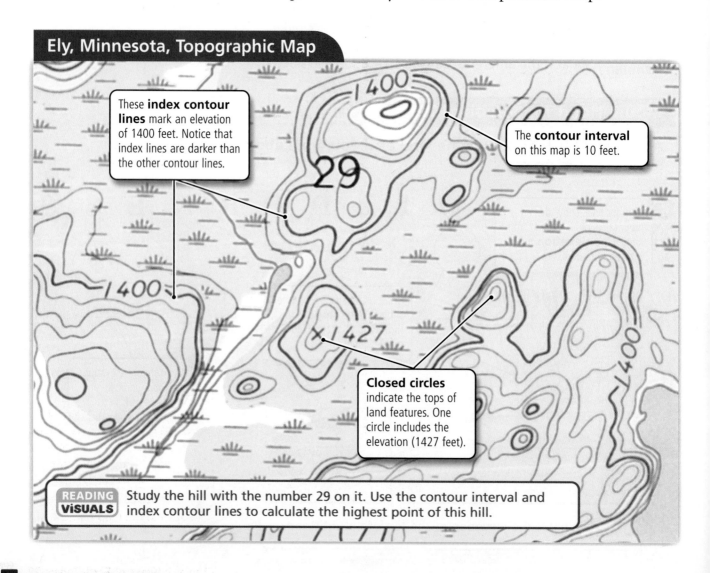

These **index contour lines** mark an elevation of 1400 feet. Notice that index lines are darker than the other contour lines.

The **contour interval** on this map is 10 feet.

Closed circles indicate the tops of land features. One circle includes the elevation (1427 feet).

READING VISUALS Study the hill with the number 29 on it. Use the contour interval and index contour lines to calculate the highest point of this hill.

- **Index contour lines mark elevations.** The darker contour lines on a map are called index contour lines. Numbers that indicate elevations are often written on these lines. To calculate higher or lower elevations, simply count the number of lines above or below an index line. Then multiply that number by the contour interval. For instance, on the Ely map, one index line marks 1400 feet. To find the elevation of a point three lines up from this index line, you would multiply 10 feet (the contour interval) by 3. Add the result, 30, to 1400. The point's elevation is 1430 feet.

SIMULATION
CLASSZONE.COM

Discover the relationship between topographic maps and surface features.

 CHECK YOUR READING What information do index contour lines provide?

Besides contour lines, topographic maps also contain symbols for natural and human-made features. Below are some common map symbols that the United States Geological Survey (USGS) uses on its topographic maps.

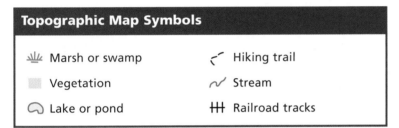

Topographic Map Symbols

⚶ Marsh or swamp	⌒ Hiking trail
▢ Vegetation	⌁ Stream
⌒ Lake or pond	╫ Railroad tracks

The USGS provides topographic maps for nearly every part of the United States. These maps cover urban, rural, and wilderness areas. Hikers and campers are not the only ones who use topographic maps. Engineers, archaeologists, forest rangers, biologists, and others rely on them as well.

 **Review**

KEY CONCEPTS

1. How do contour lines show elevation, slope, and relief?

2. Why do contour lines never cross on a topographic map?

3. How would you show the top of a hill, an area of vegetation, or a hiking trail on a topographic map?

CRITICAL THINKING

4. **Apply** For an area with gently sloping hills and little relief, would you draw contour lines close together or far apart? Explain why.

5. **Compare and Contrast** How would a road map and a topographic map of the same area differ? What information would each provide?

⬤ CHALLENGE

6. **Synthesize** Work with a group to make a topographic map of the area around your school. First decide how big an area you will include. Then choose a contour interval, a map scale, and symbols for buildings, sports fields, and other features. Let other students test the map's accuracy.

CHAPTER INVESTIGATION

Bright
Lake
1391

1400

1400

Investigate Topographic Maps

OVERVIEW AND PURPOSE Topographic maps show the shape of the land. In this lab you will use what you have learned about how Earth's three-dimensional surface is represented on maps to

- make a terrain model out of clay
- produce a topographic map of the model

▶ Procedure

1 Build a simple landscape about 6–8 cm high from modeling clay. Include a variety of land features. Make sure your model is no taller than the sides of the container.

2 Place your model into the container. Stand a ruler upright inside the container and tape it in place.

3 Lay the clear plastic sheet over the container and tape it on one side like a hinge. Carefully trace the outline of your clay model.

4 Add 2 cm of colored water to the container.

step 3

5 Insert spaghetti sticks into the model all around the waterline. Place the sticks about 3 cm apart. Make sure the sticks are vertical and are no taller than the sides of the container.

6 Lower the plastic sheet back over the container. Looking straight down on the container, make a dot on the sheet wherever you see a spaghetti stick. Connect the dots to trace the contour line accurately onto your map.

7 Continue adding water, 2 cm at a time. Each time you add water, insert the sticks into the model at the waterline and repeat step 6. Continue until the model landscape is underwater. Carefully drain the water when finished.

MATERIALS

- half-gallon cardboard juice container
- scissors
- modeling clay
- clear plastic sheet (transparency or sheet protector)
- cellophane tape
- ruler
- water
- food coloring
- box of spaghetti
- erasable marker pen

step 5

Observe and Analyze

Write It Up

1. Compare your topographic map with the three-dimensional model. Remember that contour lines connect points of equal elevation. What do widely spaced or tightly spaced contour lines mean? What does a closed circle mean?

2. Make a permanent record of your map to keep in your **Science Notebook** by carefully tracing the contour lines onto a sheet of white paper. To make reading the map easier, use a different color for an index contour line.

3. What is the contour interval of your model landscape? For example, each 2 centimeters might represent 20 meters in an actual landscape. Record the elevation of the index contour line on your map.

Conclude

Write It Up

1. **INFER** How would you determine the elevation of a point located halfway between two contour lines?

2. **EVALUATE** Describe any errors that you may have made in your procedure or any places where errors might have occurred.

3. **APPLY** Explain how you would use a topographic map if you were planning a hiking trip or a cross-country bike race.

INVESTIGATE Further

CHALLENGE Choose one feature on a topographic map—such as the map on page 26—to translate into a cross-sectional diagram.

1. Lay a piece of ruled paper across the center of the topographical feature.

2. Mark each of the contour lines on the ruled paper and label each mark with the elevation.

3. Mark the same elevations on the side of the paper, as shown in the example.

4. Use a ruler to draw a straight line down from each mark to the matching elevation on the side of the paper.

5. Connect the points to draw a profile of the landform.

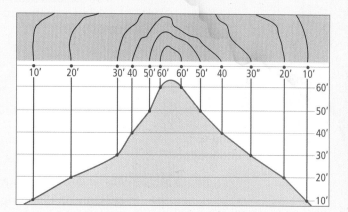

INVESTIGATE TOPOGRAPHIC MAPS

Observe and Analyze

Figure 1. Topographic Map of Model

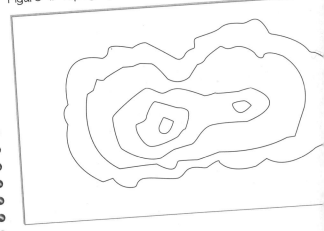

Conclude

Technology is used to map Earth.

BEFORE, you learned

- Contour lines are used on topographic maps to show elevation, slope, and relief
- Contour lines follow certain rules
- Map symbols show many natural and human-made features

NOW, you will learn

- How remote-sensing images can provide detailed and accurate information about Earth
- How geographic data can be displayed in layers to build maps

VOCABULARY

remote sensing p. 30
sensor p. 31
false-color image p. 32
geographic information systems p. 33

THINK ABOUT

What can you see in this image?

Satellites can record all types of information about Earth's surface. This image shows a section of Washington, D.C. The satellite that collected the data is 680 kilometers (420 mi) above Earth. What familiar items can you see in the picture? How might images like this be useful to scientists, mapmakers, and engineers?

Remote sensing provides detailed images of Earth.

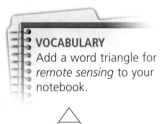

VOCABULARY
Add a word triangle for *remote sensing* to your notebook.

If you have ever looked at an object through a pair of binoculars, you have used remote sensing. **Remote sensing** is the use of scientific equipment to gather information about something from a distance. Remote-sensing technology can be as simple as a camera mounted on an airplane or as complex as a satellite orbiting Earth.

To get an idea of how important remote sensing is, imagine you are a mapmaker in the 1840s. You have been asked to draw a map of a state, but you have no cameras, no photographs from airplanes, and no satellites to help you. To get a good view of the land, you have to climb to the highest points and carefully draw every hill, valley, river, and landform below you. It will take you months to map the state.

Today, that same map would take far less time to make. Modern mapmakers use remote-sensing images from airplanes and satellites to develop highly detailed and accurate maps of Earth's surface.

Airplane cameras use film to record data, but satellites use sensors to build images of Earth. A **sensor** is a mechanical or electrical device that receives and responds to a signal, such as light. Satellite sensors detect far more than your eyes can see. They collect information about the different types of energy coming from Earth's surface. The satellites then send that information to computers on Earth.

The computers turn the information into images, as shown in the illustration below. Satellite data can be used to build an image of the entire planet, a single continent, or a detail of your area. For example, the image on the right shows a closeup of the Jefferson Memorial in Washington, D.C.

This satellite image includes the Jefferson Memorial, walkways, and roads. See if you can find the memorial in the image on page 30.

⬭ CHECK YOUR READING   Explain how remote sensing is used to gather information about Earth.

Satellite Imaging

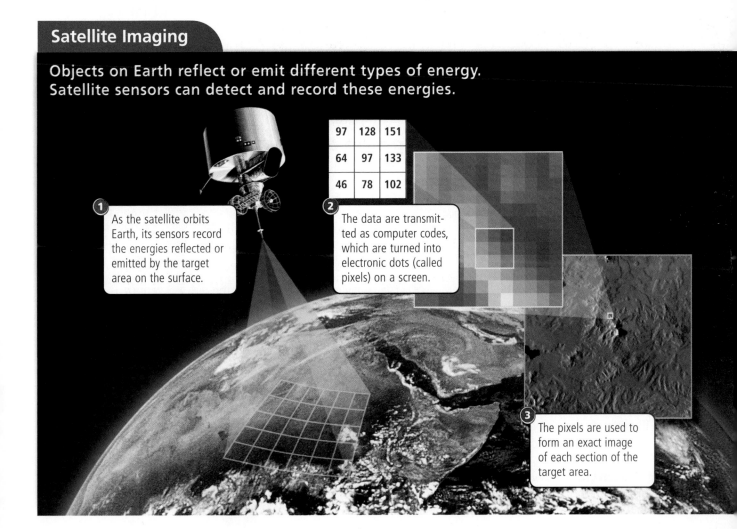

Objects on Earth reflect or emit different types of energy. Satellite sensors can detect and record these energies.

97	128	151
64	97	133
46	78	102

1 As the satellite orbits Earth, its sensors record the energies reflected or emitted by the target area on the surface.

2 The data are transmitted as computer codes, which are turned into electronic dots (called pixels) on a screen.

3 The pixels are used to form an exact image of each section of the target area.

One of the ways scientists study changes is by using false-color images. In one type of **false-color image,** Earth's natural colors are replaced with artificial ones to highlight special features. For example, fire officials used false-color images like the ones below to track the spread of a dangerous wildfire in southern Oregon.

OREGON

July 21, 2002

Small fires break out.

In this false-color image, vegetation is bright green, burned areas are red, fire is bright pink, and smoke is blue.

August 14, 2002

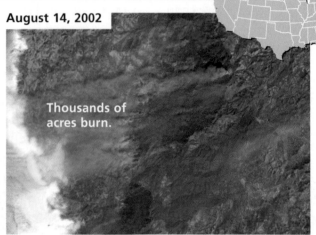

Thousands of acres burn.

Three weeks later, as this false-color image clearly shows, the fires had spread over a large area.

INVESTIGATE Satellite Imaging

How do satellites send images to Earth?

PROCEDURE

①　Work with a partner. One of you will be the "sensor," and the other will be the "receiving station."

②　The sensor draws the initials of a famous person on a piece of graph paper. The receiving station does NOT see the drawing.

③　The sensor sends the picture to the receiving station. For blank squares, the sensor says "Zero." For filled-in squares, the sensor says "One." Be sure to start at the top row and read left to right, telling the receiving station when a new row begins.

④　The receiving station transfers the code to the graph paper. At the end, the receiver has three tries to guess whose initials were sent.

SKILL FOCUS
Modeling

MATERIALS
- graph paper
- pen or pencil
- *for Challenge:* colored pens or pencils

TIME
25 minutes

WHAT DO YOU THINK?

- What would happen if you accidentally skipped or repeated a row?
- If you increased or decreased the number and size of the squares, how would this affect the picture?

CHALLENGE Use a variety of colors to send other initials or an image. Your code must tell the receiver which color to use for each square.

Geographic information systems display data in layers.

RESOURCE CENTER
CLASSZONE.COM

Find out more about how GIS is used.

Any good city map will show you what is on the surface—buildings, streets, parks, and other features. But suppose you need to know about tunnels under the city. Or maybe you want to know where the most students live. An ordinary map, even one based on remote-sensing images, will not tell you what you want to know.

Instead, you would turn to geographic information systems. **Geographic information systems** (GIS) are computer systems that can store and arrange geographic data and display the data in many different types of maps. Scientists, city planners, and engineers all use GIS maps to help them make decisions. For example, suppose your city wants to build a new airport. It must be away from populated areas and near major highways. The illustration below shows how city officials might use GIS to pick the best site.

Geographic Information Systems

GIS can be used to produce maps that help people make decisions.

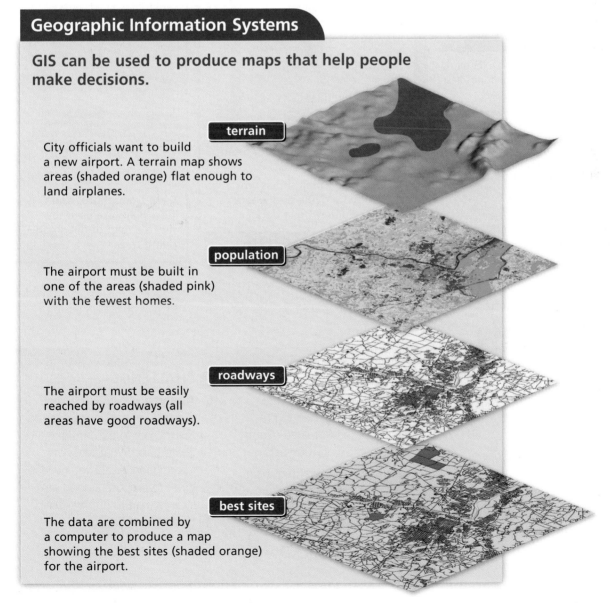

City officials want to build a new airport. A terrain map shows areas (shaded orange) flat enough to land airplanes.

terrain

The airport must be built in one of the areas (shaded pink) with the fewest homes.

population

The airport must be easily reached by roadways (all areas have good roadways).

roadways

The data are combined by a computer to produce a map showing the best sites (shaded orange) for the airport.

best sites

Any geographic information can be entered into GIS and converted into a map. These systems are especially useful in displaying information about changes in the environment.

For example, near Long Valley in California, the volcano known as Mammoth Mountain began giving off carbon dioxide, or CO_2. As the gas rose through the soil, it began killing the roots of trees nearby. Scientists measured the flow of CO_2 around Horseshoe Lake and other areas. They used computer software to build the maps shown below.

⚠ **CHECK YOUR READING** Summarize the ways GIS maps can be helpful to engineers, city planners, and scientists.

Mammoth Mountain

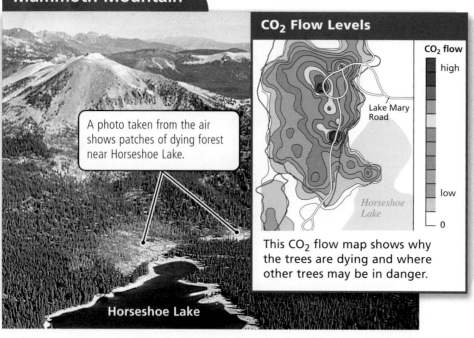

A photo taken from the air shows patches of dying forest near Horseshoe Lake.

Horseshoe Lake

CO_2 Flow Levels

CO_2 flow
high
low
0

Lake Mary Road

Horseshoe Lake

This CO_2 flow map shows why the trees are dying and where other trees may be in danger.

Area Map

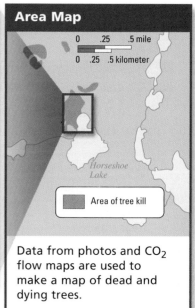

0   .25   .5 mile
0   .25   .5 kilometer

Horseshoe Lake

Area of tree kill

Data from photos and CO_2 flow maps are used to make a map of dead and dying trees.

1.4 Review

KEY CONCEPTS

1. How are satellites used to make images of Earth from outer space?

2. What are some of the types of information obtained by remote sensing?

3. Explain in your own words what a GIS map is.

CRITICAL THINKING

4. **Infer** Explain how satellite images might be used to predict what a natural area might look like in 50 or 100 years.

5. **Evaluate** If you wanted to compare a region before and during a flood, how could false-color images help you?

⚠ CHALLENGE

6. **Analyze** Work with a small group. Suppose you wanted to ask the city to build a skateboard park. What types of information would you need in order to propose a good site? Draw a map to display each type of information.

Trains and Bus Lines

▤ Train lines
— Bus lines

Streets and Freeways

▭ Freeway
— Streets

Restaurants and Shopping

▤▤▤ Shops and restaurants

Which Site Is Best for an Olympic Stadium?

Imagine you live in a city that has been chosen to host the Summer Olympics. The only question is where to build the Olympic stadium—in the center of town, in the suburbs, or on the site of an old baseball park. The city government has developed maps to help them decide which is the best site. The planners know that thousands of people will come to see the games. Therefore, they reason, the stadium should be (1) easy to reach by car, (2) close to mass-transit stops, and (3) near restaurants and shops.

▶ Analyzing Map Data

As you study the maps, keep these requirements in mind.

1. Which site(s) is/are easiest to reach by car?
2. Which site(s) is/are closest to bus and train lines?
3. Which site(s) is/are close to shopping areas?

▶ Interpreting Data

In your **Science Notebook,** create a chart like the one below to help you interpret the data displayed on the maps. As you fill in the chart, think about which site offers the greatest benefits to all the people who will attend the Olympic Games.

	Site Ⓐ		Site Ⓑ		Site Ⓒ	
	Yes	No	Yes	No	Yes	No
Near mass transit						
Near highways and roads						
Near shopping areas						

As a group Choose the best site based on your interpretation of the data. Discuss your choice with other groups to see if they agree.

CHALLENGE Once the site is chosen, the planners will start building the stadium. What types of information about the site will they need? Sketch maps displaying the information. **Hint:** The stadium will need electricity, water, and delivery of supplies.

the **BIG** idea

Modern technology has changed the way we view and map Earth.

CONTENT REVIEW
CLASSZONE.COM

◀ KEY CONCEPTS SUMMARY

1.1 Technology is used to explore the Earth system.

The atmosphere, hydrosphere, biosphere, and geosphere work together to form one large system called Earth.

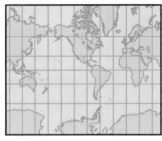

VOCABULARY
system p. 9
atmosphere p. 10
hydrosphere p. 10
biosphere p. 11
geosphere p. 12

1.2 Maps and globes are models of Earth.

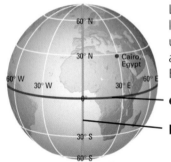

60° N
30° N
• Cairo, Egypt
60° W
30° W
0°
30° E
60° E
30° S
60° S

Latitude and longitude are used to locate any point on Earth.

— **equator**

— **prime meridian**

All map projections distort Earth's surface.

VOCABULARY
relief map p. 16
map scale p. 17
map legend p. 17
equator p. 18
latitude p. 18
prime meridian p. 19
longitude p. 19
projection p. 20

1.3 Topographic maps show the shape of the land.

Contour lines show elevation, slope, and relief.

×1427

1400

Contour lines never cross.

Closed circles represent hilltops.

Contour lines show steepness of slope.

Index contour lines show elevation.

VOCABULARY
topography p. 24
contour line p. 25
elevation p. 25
slope p. 25
relief p. 25
contour interval p. 26

1.4 Technology is used to map Earth.

Remote-sensing technology gathers accurate data about Earth.

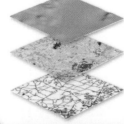

Geographic information systems are computer programs used to merge layers of information.

VOCABULARY
remote sensing p. 30
sensor p. 31
false-color image p. 32
geographic information systems p. 33

Reviewing Vocabulary

Copy and complete the chart below, using vocabulary terms from this chapter.

Term	Use	Appearance
map legend	to explain map symbols	chart of symbols
1. latitude	to show distance from the equator	
2. longitude		lines going from pole to pole
3.	to show land features	rippled and smooth areas
4. map scale	to represent distances	
5. equator		line at 0° latitude
6. prime meridian	to separate east and west hemispheres	
7.	to show height above sea level	line showing elevation
8. false-color image	to highlight information	

Reviewing Key Concepts

Multiple Choice *Choose the letter of the best answer.*

9. Which Greek prefix is matched with its correct meaning?
   a. *hydro* = life
   b. *atmo* = gas
   c. *bio* = earth
   d. *geo* = water

10. What portion of Earth is covered by water?
   a. one-quarter
   b. one-half
   c. three-quarters
   d. nine-tenths

11. The continents and ocean basins are part of Earth's
   a. crust
   b. mantle
   c. outer core
   d. inner core

12. Which Earth system includes humans?
   a. atmosphere
   b. biosphere
   c. hydrosphere
   d. geosphere

13. One way the atmosphere shapes Earth's surface is by
   a. winds
   b. floods
   c. earthquakes
   d. tunnels

14. How are the major parts of the Earth system related to each other?
   a. They rarely can be studied together.
   b. They often are in conflict.
   c. They usually work independently.
   d. They continually affect each other.

15. A flat map shows Earth's curved surface by means of
   a. elevation
   b. topography
   c. relief
   d. projection

16. People use latitude and longitude lines mostly to identify
   a. map scales
   b. country names
   c. exact locations
   d. distances

17. The most accurate way to show Earth's surface is a
   a. globe
   b. conic projection
   c. cylindrical projection
   d. planar projection

18. One example of remote sensing is the use of
   a. contour lines
   b. projections
   c. GIS
   d. binoculars

Short Answer *Write a few sentences to answer each question.*

19. How does the Global Positioning System work? In your answer use each of the following terms. Underline each term in your answer.

24 satellites	computer	longitude
receiver	latitude	elevation

20. How do Mercator maps distort the view of Earth's surface?

21. How do people use sensors in making maps?

Thinking Critically

Use the topographic map below to answer the next seven questions.

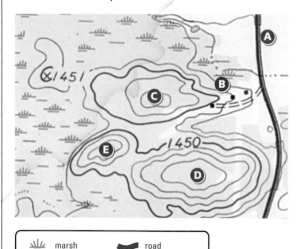

Symbol	Feature	Symbol	Feature
marsh		road	
buildings		unpaved road	

22. APPLY Imagine you are hiking through this area. Which hill—*C, D,* or *E*—has the steepest slope? How do you know?

23. ANALYZE What is the topography of the land through which the curved road *A* goes?

24. IDENTIFY CAUSE The squares at *B* represent buildings. Why do you think the buildings were placed here instead of somewhere else in the area?

25. APPLY The contour interval is 10 meters. What is the elevation of the highest point on the map?

26. SYNTHESIZE Sketch the two hills *D* and *E.* What would they look like to someone on the ground?

27. INFER Suppose someone wanted to build a road through the terrain on the far left side of the map. What are the advantages and disadvantages of such a route?

28. EVALUATE Do you think this area would be a good place to ride mountain bikes? Why or why not?

CHART INFORMATION *On a separate sheet of paper, write a word to fill each blank in the chart.*

Feature	Shown on Topographic Maps?	Belongs to Which Major System?
rivers	*yes*	*hydrosphere*
29. slope		
30. winds		
31. plants		
32. lakes		
33. relief		

the BIG idea

34. APPLY Look again at the photographs on pages 6–7. Now that you have finished the chapter, reread the question on the main photograph. What would you change in or add to your answer?

35. SYNTHESIZE Describe some of the types of information that new technology has provided about Earth.

36. DRAW CONCLUSIONS What type of technology do you think has done the most to change the way people view and map Earth? Explain your conclusion.

UNIT PROJECTS

If you are doing a unit project, make a folder for your project. Include in your folder a list of the resources you will need, the date on which the project is due, and a schedule to track your progress. Begin gathering data.

Analyzing a Diagram

This diagram shows the four major parts of the Earth system. Use it to answer the questions below.

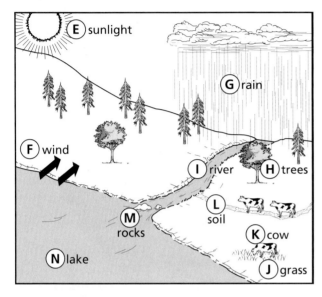

1. Where is the main source of energy for the Earth system?

a. E   c. G
b. F   d. L

2. Where is the biosphere shaping the geosphere?

a. E   c. L
b. F   d. M

3. Where is matter moving from one part of the hydrosphere to another?

a. I to N   c. J to H
b. G to H   d. N to M

4. Which items belong to the geosphere?

a. F and G   c. I and N
b. H and J   d. M and L

5. Which process is occurring at M where water is running over the rocks?

a. The geosphere is shaping the atmosphere.
b. The atmosphere is shaping the biosphere.
c. The hydrosphere is shaping the geosphere.
d. The biosphere is shaping the geosphere.

6. Where is matter moving from the atmosphere to the biosphere?

a. E and F   c. G and H
b. F and M   d. I and G

7. At K, the cow is eating grass. What kind of movement in the Earth system does this represent?

a. from the atmosphere to the hydrosphere
b. from the hydrosphere to the biosphere
c. between two parts of the geosphere
d. between two parts of the biosphere

8. Which is an example of how the hydrosphere is supported by the geosphere?

a. I, because the river receives the rain
b. H, because the trees are rooted in the ground
c. M, because the river drains into the lake
d. N, because the lake is contained by a basin

Extended Response

Answer the two questions below in detail. Include some of the terms shown in the word box. In your answers, underline each term you use.

geosphere	surface	system
atmosphere	hydrosphere	biosphere

9. Rain falls and soaks into the soil. Plants and animals use some of the water. More of the water drains into a river, then enters the ocean. Describe this process as movements among the major parts of the Earth system.

10. Describe an example of how people can shape the surface of the geosphere.

2 Minerals

the BIG idea

Minerals are basic building blocks of Earth.

Key Concepts

SECTION

2.1 Minerals are all around us.
Learn about the characteristics all minerals share.

SECTION

2.2 A mineral is identified by its properties.
Learn how to identify minerals by observing and testing their properties.

SECTION

2.3 Minerals are valuable resources.
Learn how minerals form, how they are mined, and how they are used.

Internet Preview

CLASSZONE.COM

Chapter 2 online resources: Content Review, Visualization, three Resource Centers, Math Tutorial, Test Practice

Why can gold be separated from other minerals and rocks in a river?

How Do You Turn Water into a Mineral?

Freeze some water into ice cubes. Then compare water, an ice cube, and a penny. Liquid water is not a mineral, but ice is. The surface of the penny is made of the mineral copper.

Observe and Think
How are the water, ice cube, and penny similar? How are they different? What do you think one of the properties of a mineral is?

What Makes Up Rocks?

Find three different rocks near your home or school. Examine them closely with a magnifying glass.

Observe and Think
Describe the rocks. How many materials can you see in each rock? How do you think they got there?

Internet Activity: Minerals

Go to **ClassZone.com** to find out more about minerals that are also precious metals.

Observe and Think
In addition to jewelry, how many different uses can you find for gold?

NSTA
scilinks.org
*SCI*LINKS
Identifying Minerals **Code: MDL014**

Getting Ready to Learn

◀ CONCEPT REVIEW

- Earth has four main layers: crust, mantle, outer core, and inner core.
- Matter exists in the forms of gas, liquid, and solid.
- People use maps to show many different features of Earth.

◀ VOCABULARY REVIEW

atom *See Glossary.*

geosphere p. 12

CONTENT REVIEW
CLASSZONE.COM
Review concepts and vocabulary.

▶ TAKING NOTES

SUPPORTING MAIN IDEAS

Make a chart to show each main idea and the information that supports it. Copy each blue heading. Below each heading, add supporting information, such as reasons, explanations, and examples.

VOCABULARY STRATEGY

Place each vocabulary term at the center of a **description wheel**. On the spokes write some words explaining it.

See the Note-Taking Handbook on pages R45–R51.

SCIENCE NOTEBOOK

Minerals have four characteristics.

→ Minerals form naturally.

→ All minerals are solids.

→ Each mineral is always made of the same element or elements.

→ All minerals have crystal structures.

formed by all minerals

atoms joined in a repeating 3-D pattern

CRYSTAL

Minerals are all around us.

 BEFORE, you learned

- Earth is made of layers
- Earth's outermost rocky layer is the crust

 NOW, you will learn

- What the characteristics of minerals are
- How minerals are classified into groups
- Which mineral group is most common

VOCABULARY

mineral p. 43
element p. 45
crystal p. 46

EXPLORE Minerals

What are some characteristics of a mineral?

PROCEDURE

1. Sprinkle some table salt on a sheet of colored paper. Look at a few grains of the salt through a magnifying glass. Then rub a few grains between your fingers.

2. In your notebook, describe all the qualities of the salt that you observe.

3. Examine the rock salt in the same way and describe its qualities in your notebook. How do the two differ?

WHAT DO YOU THINK?
Salt is a mineral. From your observations of salt, what do you think are some characteristics of minerals?

MATERIALS
- colored paper
- table salt
- rock salt
- magnifying glass

Minerals have four characteristics.

You use minerals all the time. Every time you turn on a microwave oven or a TV, you depend on minerals. The copper in the wires that carry electricity to the device is a mineral. Table salt, or halite (HAYL-YT), is another mineral that you use in your everyday life.

Minerals have four characteristics. A **mineral** is a substance that

- forms in nature
- is a solid
- has a definite chemical makeup
- has a crystal structure

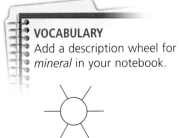
VOCABULARY
Add a description wheel for *mineral* in your notebook.

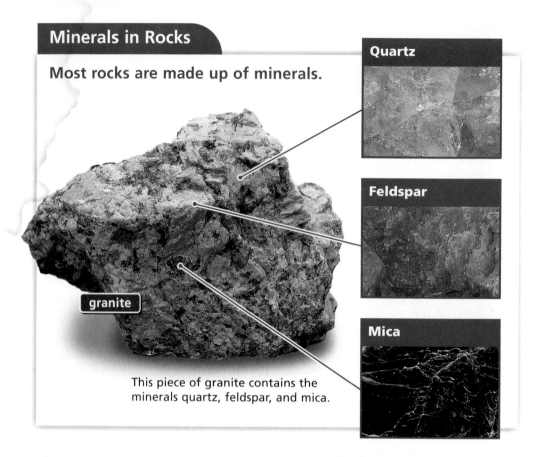

Minerals in Rocks

Most rocks are made up of minerals.

Quartz

Feldspar

Mica

granite

This piece of granite contains the minerals quartz, feldspar, and mica.

You might think that minerals and rocks are the same things. But a mineral must have the four characteristics listed on page 43. A rock has only two of these characteristics—it is a solid and it forms naturally. A rock usually contains two or more types of minerals.

Two samples of the same type of rock may vary greatly in the amounts of different minerals they contain. Minerals, however, are always made up of the same materials in the same proportions. A ruby is a mineral. Therefore, a ruby found in India has the same makeup as a ruby found in Australia.

READING TiP

Proportions show relationships between amounts. For example, a quartz crystal always has two oxygen atoms for every silicon atom.

CHECK YOUR READING How are minerals different from rocks?

Formed in Nature

Minerals are formed by natural processes. Every type of mineral can form in nature by processes that do not involve living organisms. As you will read, a few minerals can also be produced by organisms as part of their shells or bones.

Minerals form in many ways. The mineral halite, which is used as table salt, forms when water evaporates in a hot, shallow part of the ocean, leaving behind the salt it contained. Many types of minerals, including the ones in granite, develop when molten rock cools. Talc, a mineral that can be used to make baby powder, forms deep in Earth as high pressure and temperature cause changes in solid rock.

READING TiP

Molten rock refers to rock that has become so hot that it has melted.

Solid

A mineral is a solid—that is, it has a definite volume and a rigid shape. Volume refers to the amount of space an object takes up. For example, a golf ball has a smaller volume than a baseball, and a baseball has a smaller volume than a basketball.

A substance that is a liquid or a gas is not a mineral. However, in some cases its solid form is a mineral. For instance, liquid water is not a mineral, but ice is.

Definite Chemical Makeup

Each mineral has a definite chemical makeup: it consists of a specific combination of atoms of certain elements. An **element** is a substance that contains only one type of atom. In turn, an atom is the smallest particle an element can be divided into.

Everything you can see or touch is made up of atoms. Some substances, including the minerals gold and copper, consist of just one element. All the atoms in gold or copper are of the same type. However, most substances contain atoms of more than one element. Most minerals are compounds, substances consisting of several elements in specific proportions. Halite, for example, has one atom of sodium for every atom of chlorine.

The types of atoms that make up a mineral are part of what makes the mineral unique. The way in which the atoms are bonded, or joined together, is also important. As you will read, many properties of minerals are related to how strong or weak the bonds are.

READING **TiP**

You may remember *compound* from compound words—words formed by joining together smaller words: *note + book = notebook*. Likewise, a chemical compound has two or more elements joined together.

Atoms in Minerals

Atoms in Copper

The mineral copper is made up only of copper atoms.

copper

copper

halite

The mineral halite is made up of equal numbers of sodium and chlorine atoms.

Atoms in Halite

chlorine

sodium

READING **VISUALS** How do the diagrams show that copper consists of only one element and halite is a compound?

Crystal Structure

VISUALIZATION
CLASSZONE.COM

Explore an animation of crystal growth.

If you look closely at the particles of ice that make up frost, you will notice that they have smooth, flat surfaces. These flat surfaces form because of the arrangement of atoms in the ice, which is a mineral. Such an internal arrangement is a characteristic of minerals. It is the structure of a **crystal,** a solid in which the atoms are arranged in an orderly, repeating three-dimensional pattern.

Each mineral has its own type of crystal structure. In some cases, two minerals have the same chemical composition but different crystal structures. For example, both diamond and graphite consist of just one element—carbon. But the arrangements of the carbon atoms in these two minerals are not the same, so they have different crystal structures and very different properties. Diamonds are extremely hard and have a brilliant sparkle. Graphite is soft, gray, and dull.

In nature, a perfect crystal is rare. One can grow only when a mineral is free to form in an open space—a condition that rarely exists within Earth's crust. The photographs on page 47 show examples of nearly perfect crystals. The amount of space available for growth influences the shape and size of crystals. Most crystals have imperfect shapes because their growth was limited by other crystals forming next to them.

INVESTIGATE Crystal Shape

How do crystals differ in shape?
PROCEDURE

1. Cut sheets of paper so that they fit inside the pie plates as shown. Place one sheet in each pie plate.

2. Add the table salt to 30 mL of water in the cup. Stir the water until the salt has dissolved.

3. Pour enough salt solution into one of the pie plates to completely cover the paper with a small film of liquid. Be careful not to pour into the plate any undissolved salt that may be in the bottom of the cup.

4. Repeat steps 2 and 3 with the Epsom salts. Let the plates dry overnight.

WHAT DO YOU THINK?
- Compare and describe the shapes of the crystals.
- What do you think accounts for any differences you observe?

CHALLENGE Why are the shapes of the crystals the same as or different from the shapes in the materials you started with?

SKILL FOCUS
Observing

MATERIALS
- tablespoon
- 2 mixing cups
- 2 stirring rods
- 1 tbs table salt
- 1 tbs Epsom salts
- 60 mL water
- 2 pie plates
- 2 sheets black paper
- scissors

TIME
20 minutes for setup

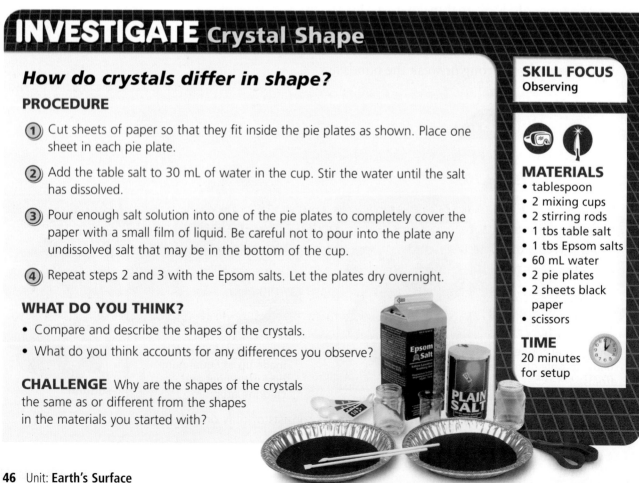

Crystal Groups

Crystal groups are named by their shapes and the angles formed by imaginary lines through their centers. Crystals take many shapes, but all belong to these six groups.

Cubic — galena

Tetragonal — wulfenite

Hexagonal — beryl

Orthorhombic — topaz

Monoclinic — gypsum

Triclinic — microcline

Minerals are grouped according to composition.

Scientists classify minerals into groups on the basis of their chemical makeups. The most common group is the silicates. All the minerals in this group contain oxygen and silicon—the two most common elements in Earth's crust—joined together.

Though there are thousands of different minerals, only about 30 are common in Earth's crust. These 30 minerals make up most rocks in the crust. For that reason, they are called rock-forming minerals. Silicates, which make up about 90 percent of the rocks in Earth's crust, are the most common rock-forming minerals. Quartz, feldspar, and mica (MY-kuh) are common silicates.

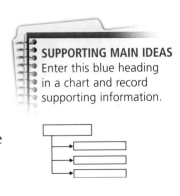

SUPPORTING MAIN IDEAS
Enter this blue heading in a chart and record supporting information.

CHECK YOUR READING Which mineral group do most rock-forming minerals belong to?

The sand on many beaches consists mainly of quartz, an important silicate mineral.

Common Elements of Earth's Crust

Oxygen 46.6%
Silicon 27.7%
Calcium 3.6%
Iron 5.0%
Aluminum 8.1%
Other 9.0%

Source: Brian Mason, *Principles of Geochemistry*

READING VISUALS How much of Earth's crust is made up of oxygen and silicon?

RESOURCE CENTER
CLASSZONE.COM

Find information on minerals.

The second most common group of rock-forming minerals is the carbonates. All the minerals in this group contain carbon and oxygen joined together. Calcite (KAL-SYT), which is common in seashells, is a carbonate mineral.

There are many other mineral groups. All are important, even though their minerals may not be as common as rock-forming minerals. For instance, the mineral group known as oxides contains the minerals from which most metals, such as tin and copper, are refined. An oxide consists of an element, usually a metal, joined to oxygen. This group includes hematite (HEE-muh-TYT), a source of iron.

CHECK YOUR READING Why is the oxide mineral group important?

2.1 Review

KEY CONCEPTS

1. What are the four characteristics of a mineral?

2. On what basis do scientists classify minerals?

3. What is the most common group of minerals? What percentage of the crust do they make up?

CRITICAL THINKING

4. **Classify** Can oil and natural gas be classified as minerals? Why or why not?

5. **Apply** When a piece of quartz is heated to a very high temperature, it melts into a liquid. Is it still a mineral? Why or why not?

▲ CHALLENGE

6. **Interpret** You can see perfect crystals lining the inside of certain rocks when they are broken open. How do you think the crystals were able to form?

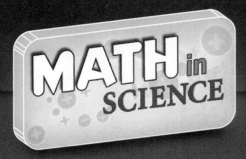

MATH TUTORIAL

CLASSZONE.COM

Click on Math Tutorial for more help with percents and fractions.

Minerals in Rocks

Like most rocks, granite is a mixture of several minerals. Each mineral makes up a certain proportion, or fraction, of the granite. You can compare mineral amounts by expressing each mineral's fraction as a percentage.

Granite

Example

To change a fraction to a percentage, you must find an equivalent fraction with 100 as the denominator. Suppose, for example, you want to change the fraction $\frac{1}{5}$ to a percentage. First, divide 100 by the denominator 5, which gives you 20. Then, multiply both the numerator and denominator by 20 to find the percentage.

$$\frac{1}{5} \cdot \frac{20}{20} = \frac{20}{100} \text{ or } 20\% \qquad \frac{1}{5} \text{ is } 20\%$$

The table below shows the fraction of each mineral in a granite sample.

Minerals in Granite Sample

Mineral	Fraction of Granite Sample	Percentage of Granite
Quartz	$\frac{1}{4}$	?
Feldspar	$\frac{13}{20}$	?
Mica	$\frac{3}{50}$	?
Dark minerals	$\frac{1}{25}$	?

Answer the following questions.

1. On your paper, copy the table and fill in the percentage of each mineral in the granite sample above.

2. Which minerals make up the greatest and smallest percentages of the granite?

3. In another granite sample, feldspar makes up $\frac{3}{5}$ and mica makes up $\frac{2}{25}$. What is the percentage of each mineral in the rock?

CHALLENGE The mineral hornblende is often one of the dark minerals in granite. If hornblende makes up $\frac{1}{32}$ of a granite sample, what percentage of the rock is hornblende?

2.2 A mineral is identified by its properties.

◀ BEFORE, you learned

- All minerals have four characteristics
- Most minerals in Earth's crust are silicates

▶ NOW, you will learn

- Which mineral properties are most important in identification
- How minerals are identified by their properties

VOCABULARY

streak p. 51
luster p. 52
cleavage p. 53
fracture p. 53
density p. 54
hardness p. 55

THINK ABOUT

What can you tell by looking at a mineral?

The photographs at the right show five pieces of the mineral fluorite (FLUR-YT). As you can see, the pieces are very different in color and size. Fluorite occurs in many colors, even in colorless forms. Its crystals can be well formed or poorly formed. Also, the sides of the crystals may be smooth or rough.

If you came across fluorite while hiking, would you know what it was by just looking at it? Probably not. Read on to find out how you could identify it.

A mineral's appearance helps identify it.

READING **TiP**

The word *characteristic* is used for a feature that is typical of a person or thing. It can be used as a noun or an adjective.

To identify a mineral, you need to observe its properties—characteristic features that identify it. You might begin by looking at the mineral's color. However, many minerals occur in more than one color, so you would need to examine other properties as well. You might also notice how the mineral reflects light, which determines how shiny or dull it is. Most minerals reflect light in characteristic ways. In this section you will read about how the properties of a mineral—including its appearance—are used to identify it.

○ **CHECK YOUR READING** Why do you need to look at properties other than color to identify a mineral?

Color and Streak

Some minerals can be almost any color, but most minerals have a more limited color range. For example, a particular mineral may almost always be brown to black.

Three main factors cause minerals to vary in color. First, a mineral may get its color from tiny amounts of an element that is not part of its normal chemical makeup. For example, a sample of pure quartz is clear and colorless, but tiny amounts of iron can give quartz a violet color. This violet variety of quartz is called amethyst. Second, a mineral's color can change when it is at or near Earth's surface and is in contact with the atmosphere or water. Third, mineral crystals can have defects in their crystal structures that change their color.

Some minerals have a different color when they are ground into a fine powder than when they are left whole. A mineral's **streak** is the color of the powder left behind when the mineral is scraped across a surface. Geologists use a tile of unglazed porcelain, called a streak plate, as a tool to identify minerals by their streaks. Streak is a better clue to a mineral's identity than surface color is. Look at the photographs of hematite below. Even though the mineral samples are different colors, both leave a reddish brown streak when scraped across a streak plate. All samples of the same mineral have the same streak.

READING TiP
A geologist is a scientist who studies Earth.

CHECK YOUR READING What is the difference between color and streak?

Streak

These samples are of the mineral hematite. They are different colors, but they have the same streak.

This hematite looks dull because it has tiny crystals that reflect light in all directions.

This hematite looks shiny because it has larger crystals.

READING VISUALS What is a clue that both samples are of the same mineral?

Luster

READING TiP

Luster comes from the Latin *lūstrāre*, "to make bright." But luster isn't always bright or shiny. Some minerals have lusters that are waxlike or dull.

A mineral's **luster** is the way in which light reflects from its surface. The two major types of luster are metallic and nonmetallic. The mineral pyrite has a metallic luster. It looks as if it were made of metal. A mineral with a nonmetallic luster can be shiny, but it does not appear to be made of metal. An example of a nonmetallic luster is the glassy luster of garnet. Compare the lusters of pyrite and garnet in the photographs below.

Pyrite has a metallic luster.

Garnet crystals in this rock have a nonmetallic luster.

Like a mineral's color, its luster may vary from sample to sample. If a mineral has been exposed to the atmosphere or to water, its surface luster can become dull. However, if the mineral is broken to reveal a fresh surface, its characteristic luster can be seen.

The way a mineral breaks helps identify it.

SUPPORTING MAIN IDEAS
Enter this blue heading in a chart and record supporting information.

If you hit a piece of calcite with a hammer, the calcite will break into tilted blocks. You can peel off layers of mica because it splits into thin, flat sheets. Each kind of mineral always breaks in the same way, and this property can help identify a mineral. In fact, the way a mineral breaks is a better clue to its identity than are its color and luster.

Cleavage

Cleavage is a tendency to break along flat surfaces.

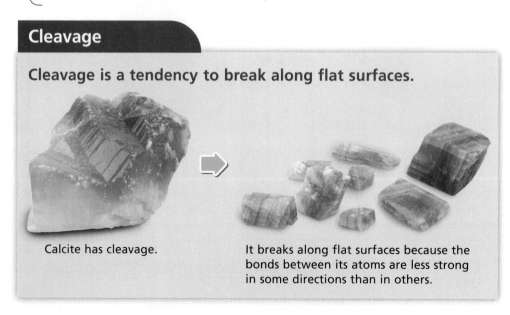

Calcite has cleavage.

It breaks along flat surfaces because the bonds between its atoms are less strong in some directions than in others.

Cleavage

Cleavage is the tendency of a mineral to break along flat surfaces. The way in which a mineral breaks depends on how its atoms are bonded, or joined together. In a mineral that displays cleavage, the bonds of the crystal structure are weaker in the directions in which the mineral breaks.

When geologists describe the cleavage of a mineral, they consider both the directions in which the mineral breaks and the smoothness of the broken surfaces. Mica has cleavage in one direction and breaks into sheets. The photographs on page 52 show that calcite has cleavage in three directions and breaks into tilted blocks. Because the broken surfaces of both mica and calcite are smooth, these minerals are said to have perfect cleavage.

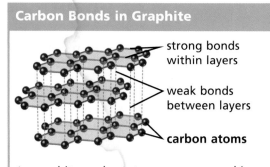

Carbon Bonds in Graphite

strong bonds within layers

weak bonds between layers

carbon atoms

In graphite, carbon atoms are arranged in layers. Graphite has cleavage because the weak bonds between the layers break easily.

Fracture

Fracture is the tendency of a mineral to break into irregular pieces. Some minerals such as quartz break into pieces with curved surfaces, as shown below. Other minerals may break differently—perhaps into splinters or into rough or jagged pieces.

In a mineral that displays fracture, the bonds that join the atoms are fairly equal in strength in all directions. The mineral does not break along flat surfaces because there are no particular directions of weakness in its crystal structure.

VOCABULARY
Add a description wheel for *fracture* in your notebook.

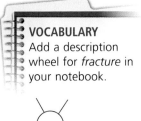

CHECK YOUR READING How does the strength of the bonds between atoms determine whether a mineral displays cleavage or fracture?

Fracture

Fracture is a tendency to break into irregular pieces.

Quartz does not have cleavage. It breaks by fracturing.

It breaks along irregular surfaces because the bonds between its atoms are about the same strength in every direction.

A mineral's density and hardness help identify it.

A tennis ball is not as heavy or as hard as a baseball. You would be able to tell the two apart even with your eyes closed by how heavy and hard they feel. You can identify minerals in a similar way.

Density

Even though a baseball and a tennis ball are about the same size, the baseball has more mass and so is more dense. A substance's **density** is the amount of mass in a given volume of the substance. For example, 1 cubic centimeter of the mineral pyrite has a mass of 5.1 grams, so pyrite's density is 5.1 grams per cubic centimeter.

Density is very helpful in identifying minerals. For example, gold and pyrite look very similar. Pyrite is often called fool's gold. However, you can tell the two minerals apart by comparing their densities. Gold is much denser than pyrite. The mass of a piece of gold is almost four times the mass of a piece of pyrite of the same size. A small amount of a very dense mineral, such as gold, can have more mass and be heavier than a larger amount of a less dense mineral, such as pyrite. A mineral's density is determined by the kinds of atoms that make up

Comparing Densities

Differences in density can be used to tell minerals apart.

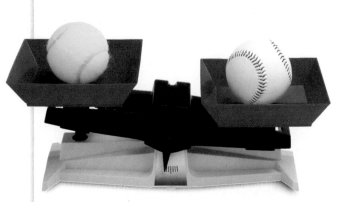

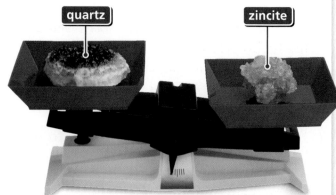

The baseball on the right has more mass, and so is denser, than a tennis ball that is about the same size.

The zincite sample on the right is about twice as dense as the quartz sample.

READING VISUALS Estimate the size a piece of quartz would have to be to balance the zincite sample.

the mineral, as well as how closely the atoms are joined together. An experienced geologist can estimate the density of a mineral by lifting it. But to get an exact measurement, geologists use special scales.

 CHECK YOUR READING Why does a piece of gold weigh much more than a piece of pyrite that is the same size?

Hardness

One way to tell a tennis ball from a baseball without looking at them is to compare their densities. Another way is to test which one is harder. Hardness is another dependable clue to a mineral's identity.

A mineral's **hardness** is its resistance to being scratched. Like a mineral's cleavage, a mineral's hardness is determined by its crystal structure and the strength of the bonds between its atoms. Harder minerals have stronger bonds.

A scale known as the Mohs scale is often used to describe a mineral's hardness. This scale is based on the fact that a harder mineral will scratch a softer one. As you can see in the chart at the right, ten minerals are numbered in the scale, from softest to hardest. Talc is the softest mineral and has a value of 1. Diamond, the hardest of all minerals, has a value of 10.

A mineral can be scratched only by other minerals that have the same hardness or are harder. To determine the hardness of an unknown mineral, you test whether it scratches or is scratched by the minerals in the scale. For example, if you can scratch an unknown mineral with apatite but not with fluorite, the mineral's hardness is between 4 and 5 in the Mohs scale.

In place of minerals, you can use your fingernail, a copper penny, and a steel file to test an unknown mineral. To avoid damage to the minerals, you can test whether the mineral scratches these items. When using a penny to test hardness, make sure its date is 1982 or earlier. Only older pennies are made mainly of copper, which has a hardness of about 3.

Mohs Scale

1 Talc

2 Gypsum — gypsum

Your fingernail has a hardness of about 2.5, so it can scratch gypsum.

3 Calcite

4 Fluorite

5 Apatite — apatite

A steel file has a hardness of about 6.5. You can scratch apatite with it.

6 Feldspar

7 Quartz

8 Topaz

Diamond is the hardest mineral. Only a diamond can scratch another diamond.

9 Corundum

10 Diamond — diamond

How hard are some common minerals?

PROCEDURE

1. Try to scratch each mineral with your fingernail, the penny, and the steel file. Record the results in a chart.

2. Assign a hardness range to each mineral.

3. In the last column of your chart, rank the minerals from hardest to softest.

WHAT DO YOU THINK?

- Use your results to assign a hardness range in the Mohs scale to each sample.
- If two minerals have the same hardness range according to your tests, how could you tell which is harder?

CHALLENGE If you had a mineral that could not be scratched by the steel file, what else might you test it with to estimate its hardness?

MATERIALS
- samples of 5 minerals
- copper penny (1982 or earlier)
- steel file

TIME
20 minutes

Some minerals have special properties.

The photographs on page 57 show how geologists test some minerals. Such tests help them identify minerals that have unusual properties.

Minerals in the carbonate group, such as calcite, react with acid. Chalk is a familiar item that is made up of carbonate minerals. The test consists of putting a drop of a weak solution of hydrochloric acid on a mineral sample. If the acid reacts with the mineral, carbon dioxide gas will form and bubble out of the acid. The bubbles show that the mineral is a carbonate.

Some minerals have a property known as fluorescence (flu-REHS-uhns). Fluorescent minerals glow when they are exposed to ultraviolet (UHL-truh-VY-uh-liht) light. The word *fluorescence* comes from the name of the mineral fluorite, which has this property. Other minerals that display fluorescence include calcite and willemite. Although fluorescence is an interesting and sometimes dramatic property, it has limited value in mineral identification. Different samples of the same mineral may or may not display fluorescence, and they may glow in different colors.

 CHECK YOUR READING To identify calcite, why would it be more useful to test with dilute hydrochloric acid than to check for fluorescence?

Special Properties

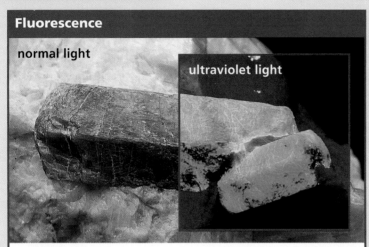

Fluorescence

normal light

ultraviolet light

These minerals look ordinary in normal light but display red and green fluorescence under ultraviolet light.

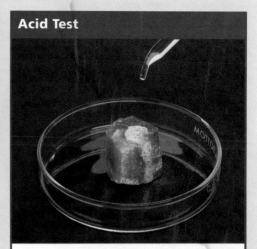

Acid Test

Acid in contact with carbonate minerals, such as calcite, forms bubbles.

A few minerals respond to magnets. A magnet is pulled toward these minerals. The mineral magnetite strongly attracts magnets, and some other minerals weakly attract magnets. To test a mineral, hold a magnet loosely and bring it close to the mineral. You will be able to notice if there is even a small pull of the magnet toward the mineral. Magnets are commonly used in laboratories and industries to separate magnetic minerals from other minerals.

Some rare minerals have a property known as radioactivity. They contain unstable elements that change into other elements over time. As this happens, they release energy. Geologists can measure this energy and use it to identify minerals that contain unstable elements.

2.2 Review

KEY CONCEPTS

1. Why is color not a reliable clue to the identity of a mineral?

2. What is the difference between cleavage and fracture?

3. Describe what would happen if you rubbed a mineral with a Mohs hardness value of 7 against a mineral with a value of 5.

CRITICAL THINKING

4. **Analyze** Which mineral-identification tests would be easy for a person to perform at home? Which would be difficult?

5. **Draw Conclusions** Diamond and graphite contain only carbon atoms. How can you tell which mineral's atoms are bonded more closely?

⚠ CHALLENGE

6. **Apply** The mineral topaz has perfect cleavage in one direction. It also displays fracture. Explain why a mineral such as topaz can display both cleavage and fracture.

CHAPTER INVESTIGATION

Mineral Identification

OVERVIEW AND PURPOSE In this activity, you will observe and perform tests on minerals. Then you will compare your observations to a mineral identification key.

▶ Procedure

1. Make a data table like the one shown in the notebook on the next page.

2. You will examine and identify five minerals. Get a numbered mineral sample from the mineral set. Record the number of your sample in your table.

step 3

3. First, observe the sample. Note the color and the luster of the sample. Write your observations in your table. In the row labeled "Luster," write *metallic* if the mineral appears shiny like metal. Write *nonmetallic* if the sample does not look like metal. For example, it may look glassy, pearly, or dull.

4. Observe the sample through the hand lens. Look to see any signs of how the crystals in the mineral broke. If it appears that the crystals have broken along straight lines, put a check in the row labeled "Cleavage." If it appears that the sample has fractured, put a check in the appropriate row of your table.

step 4

5. **CAUTION: Keep the streak plate on your desktop or table while you are doing the streak test. A broken streak plate can cause serious cuts.** Rub the mineral sample on the streak plate. If the sample does not leave a mark, the mineral is harder than the streak plate. Write *no* in the row labeled "Streak." If the sample does leave a mark on the streak plate, write the color of the streak in that row.

step 5

MATERIALS

- numbered mineral samples
- hand lens
- streak plate
- copper penny
- steel file
- magnet
- dilute hydrochloric acid
- eyedropper
- Mohs scale
- Mineral Identification Key

DILUTE HCl

6 Test each sample for its hardness on the Mohs scale. Try to scratch the sample with each of these items in order: a fingernail, a copper penny, and a steel file. In the Mohs scale, find the hardness number of the object that first scratches the sample. Write in the table that the mineral's hardness value is between that of the hardest item that did not scratch the sample and that of the item that did scratch it.

7 Test the sample with the magnet. If the magnet is attracted to the sample, put a check in the row labeled "Magnetic."

step 7

8 Repeat steps 2 through 7 for each of the other numbered samples.

Observe and Analyze
Write It Up

1. **INTERPRET DATA** Use the Mineral Identification Key and the information in your data table to identify your samples. Write the names of the minerals in your table.

2. **COLLECT DATA CAUTION: Before doing the acid test, put on your safety glasses, protective gloves, and lab apron. Acids can cause burns.** If you identified one of the samples as a carbonate mineral, such as calcite, you can check your identification with the acid test. Use the eyedropper to put a few drops of dilute hydrochloric acid on the mineral. If the acid bubbles, the sample is a carbonate.

Conclude
Write It Up

1. **COMPARE AND CONTRAST** How are the minerals calcite and halite alike? Which property can you use to test whether a sample is calcite or halite?

2. **INTERPRET** Look at the data in your table. Name any minerals that you could identify on the basis of a single property.

3. **APPLY** Examine a piece of granite rock. On the basis of your examination of granite and your observations of the samples, try to determine what the light-colored, translucent mineral in the granite is and what the flaky, darker mineral is.

▶ INVESTIGATE Further

Specific gravity is another property used to identify minerals. The specific gravity of a mineral is determined by comparing the mineral's density with the density of water.

Find the specific gravity of an unknown mineral chosen from your teacher's samples. Attach your mineral with a string to a spring scale. Record its mass and label this value M1. Then suspend the mineral in a beaker of water. Record the measurement of the mineral's mass in water. Label this value M2. To determine the mineral's specific gravity, use the following equation:

$$\frac{M1}{M1 - M2} = \text{specific gravity}$$

Do all the other steps to identify the sample. Does the specific gravity you measured match the one listed for that mineral in the identification key?

Mineral Identification
Table 1. Mineral Properties

Property	Sample Number				
	1	2	3	4	5
Color					
Luster					
Cleavage					
Fracture					
Streak					
Hardness					
Magnetic					
Acid test					
Name of mineral					

2.3 Minerals are valuable resources.

◀ BEFORE, you learned	▶ NOW, you will learn
• Minerals are classified according to their compositions and crystal structures • A mineral can be identified by its properties	• How minerals are used in industry and art • How minerals form • How minerals are mined

VOCABULARY

magma p. 62
lava p. 62
ore p. 64

EXPLORE Minerals at Your Fingertips

What is an everyday use of minerals?

PROCEDURE

① Observe the core of a wooden pencil. Even though it is called lead, it is made of a mixture of minerals—clay and graphite. A No. 4 pencil has more clay in its lead.

② Use each pencil to draw something, noticing how each marks the page.

WHAT DO YOU THINK?

• How is using a pencil similar to a streak test?
• When would a No. 4 pencil be more useful than a No. 2 pencil?

MATERIALS

• No. 2 wooden pencil
• No. 4 wooden pencil
• paper

Minerals have many uses in industry.

Minerals are necessary to our modern way of life. Mineral deposits are sources of

- metals for cars and airplanes
- quartz and feldspar for glass
- fluorite and calcite for toothpaste
- silver compounds for photographic film
- mica and talc for paint

These examples illustrate just a few of the many ways we depend on minerals.

 CHECK YOUR READING Give three examples of the use of minerals in familiar products.

Minerals have many uses in the arts.

No matter what month you were born in, there is a mineral associated with it—your birthstone. The tradition of birthstones is hundreds of years old. It is one example of the value that people place on the particularly beautiful minerals known as gemstones. In fact, the ancient Egyptians used gems in necklaces and other jewelry at least 4000 years ago.

When gemstones are found, they are usually rough and irregularly shaped. Before a gemstone is used in jewelry, a gem cutter grinds it into the desired shape and polishes it. This process increases the gemstone's beauty and sparkle. The material used to shape and polish a gemstone must be at least as hard as the gemstone itself. Metals, such as gold and silver, also are used in jewelry making and other decorative arts. Both gold and silver are usually combined with copper to increase their hardness.

○ **CHECK YOUR READING** How are minerals prepared for use in jewelry? What other questions do you have about how minerals are used?

ⓘ **RESOURCE CENTER**
CLASSZONE.COM
Learn more about gemstones.

READING TIP
Corundum and diamond are the two hardest minerals in the Mohs scale. They are often used to grind and polish gemstones.

Uses of Minerals

Common Uses of Minerals	
Mineral	**Products**
Quartz (source of silicon)	Optics, glass, abrasives, gems
Hematite (source of iron)	Machines, nails, cooking utensils
Gibbsite (source of aluminum)	Soda cans, shopping carts
Dolomite (source of magnesium)	Insulators, medicines
Chromite (source of chromium)	Automobile parts, stainless steel
Galena (source of lead)	Batteries, fiber optics, weights
Kaolinite (found in clay)	Ceramics, paper, cosmetics
Beryl (source of beryllium)	Aircraft frames, gems (green form is emerald)

Technology

A clear quartz crystal was sliced to make this computer chip. Minerals such as copper, silver, and gold are commonly used in electronics.

Industry

Diamonds are used as abrasives, as in this drill tip. Minerals are also used in such products as insulators and water filters.

Arts

Cinnabar is ground up to make the pigment known as vermilion. Other minerals are also used as pigments in dyes and paints. Gemstones are used in jewelry, as are platinum and gold.

Minerals form in several ways.

Minerals form within Earth or on Earth's surface by natural processes. Minerals develop when atoms of one or more elements join together and crystals begin to grow. Recall that each type of mineral has its own chemical makeup. Therefore, what types of minerals form in an area depends in part on which elements are present there. Temperature and pressure also affect which minerals form.

Water evaporates. Water usually has many substances dissolved in it. Minerals can form when the water evaporates. For example, when salt water evaporates, the atoms that make up halite, which is used as table salt, join to form crystals. Other minerals form from evaporation too, depending on the substances dissolved in the water. The mineral gypsum often forms as water evaporates.

Hot water cools. As hot water within Earth's crust moves through rocks, it can dissolve minerals. When the water cools, the dissolved minerals separate from the water and become solid again. In some cases, minerals are moved from one place to another. Gold can dissolve in hot water that moves through the crust. As the water cools and the gold becomes solid again, it can fill cracks in rocks. In other cases, the minerals that form are different from the ones that dissolved. Lead from the mineral galena can later become part of the mineral wulfenite as atoms join together into new minerals.

Molten rock cools. Many minerals grow from magma. **Magma**—molten rock inside Earth—contains all the types of atoms that are found in minerals. As magma cools, the atoms join together to form different minerals. Minerals also form as lava cools. **Lava** is molten rock that has reached Earth's surface. Quartz is one of the many minerals that crystallize from magma and lava.

Heat and pressure cause changes. Heat and pressure within Earth cause new minerals to form as bonds between atoms break and join again. The mineral garnet can grow and replace the minerals chlorite and quartz as their atoms combine in new ways. The element carbon is present in some rocks. At high temperatures carbon forms the mineral graphite, which is used in pencils.

Organisms produce minerals. A few minerals are produced by living things. For example, ocean animals such as oysters and clams produce calcite and other carbonate minerals to form their shells. Even you produce minerals. Your body produces one of the main minerals in your bones and teeth—apatite.

 CHECK YOUR READING How is the formation of minerals as molten rock cools similar to the formation of minerals as water evaporates?

Mineral Formation

Minerals form at Earth's surface and within Earth.

Water evaporates.

As water evaporates along a shoreline, it leaves behind substances that were dissolved in it. Here, gypsum is forming.

Hot water cools.

Gold dissolved in hot water can fill cracks in rocks as the water cools.

Molten rock cools.

Minerals such as quartz grow as molten rock cools.

Heat and pressure cause changes.

Graphite forms inside Earth when carbon is subjected to great heat.

READING VISUALS Each of the four processes shown involves heat. What is the heat source for rapid evaporation of water at Earth's surface?

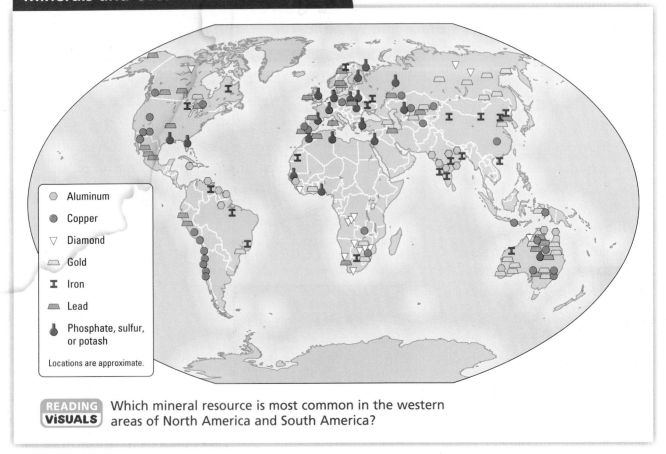

Aluminum
Copper
Diamond
Gold
Iron
Lead
Phosphate, sulfur, or potash

Locations are approximate.

Which mineral resource is most common in the western areas of North America and South America?

Many minerals are mined.

Before minerals can be used to make products, they must be removed from the ground. Some minerals are found near Earth's surface, while others lie deep underground. Some minerals are found at a wide range of depths, from the surface to deep within Earth.

Most minerals are combined with other minerals in rocks. For any mineral to be worth mining, there must be a fairly large amount of the mineral present in a rock. Rocks that contain enough of a mineral to be mined for a profit are called **ores.**

READING TiP

To make a profit, mine owners must be able to sell ores for more than it cost them to dig the ores out.

Surface Mining

Minerals at or near Earth's surface are recovered by surface mining. Some minerals, such as gold, are very dense. These minerals can build up in riverbeds as less dense minerals are carried away by the water. In a method called panning, a miner uses a pan to wash away unwanted minerals that are less dense. The gold and other dense minerals stay in the bottom of the pan and can then be further separated. In bigger riverbed mining operations, miners use machines to dig out and separate the valuable minerals.

Another method of surface mining is strip mining. Miners strip away plants, soil, and unwanted rocks from Earth's surface. Then they use special machines to dig out an ore.

Like strip mining, open-pit mining involves removing the surface layer of soil. Miners then use explosives to break up the underlying rock and recover the ore. As they dig a deep hole, or pit, to mine the ore, they build roads up the sides of the pit. Trucks carry the ore to the surface. Ores of copper and of iron are obtained by open-pit mining.

If an Olympic-sized swimming pool were filled with rock from this mine, it might contain enough copper to make a solid "beach ball" 146 cm (60 in.) in diameter.

 CHECK YOUR READING How are strip mining and open-pit mining similar? How are they different?

INVESTIGATE Mining

What are the benefits and costs of mining ores?

SKILL FOCUS
Drawing
conclusions

PROCEDURE

1. Put the birdseed into a pan. Add the beads to the birdseed and mix well.

2. Search through the seeds and separate out the beads and sunflower seeds, placing each kind in a different pile. Take no more than 3 minutes.

3. Assign a value to each of the beads and seeds: red bead, $5; green bead, $4; blue bead, $3; sunflower seed, $2. Count up the value of your beads and seeds. For every yellow bead, subtract $100, which represents the cost of restoring the land after mining.

WHAT DO YOU THINK?

- How does the difficulty of finding the red beads relate to the difficulty of finding the most valuable ores?
- How does the total value of the blue beads and the sunflower seeds compare to the total value of the red and green beads? What can you conclude about deciding which materials to mine?

CHALLENGE The sunflower seeds and the red, green, and blue beads could represent minerals that contain copper, gold, iron, and silver. Which bead or seed is most likely to represent each mineral? Explain your choices.

MATERIALS
- 1 pound wild-birdseed mix with sunflower seeds
- shallow pan
- 2 small red beads
- 4 small green beads
- 8 small blue beads
- 3 medium yellow beads

TIME
25 minutes

Deep Mining

Deep-mining methods are needed when an ore lies far below Earth's surface. These methods are used to obtain many minerals. Miners dig an opening to reach a deep ore. When the ore is inside a mountain or hill, miners can cut a level passage to reach the mineral they want. Miners dig a vertical passage to reach an ore that lies underground in a flat area or under a mountain.

From the main passage, miners blast, drill, cut, or dig the ore. If the passage is horizontal, they keep digging farther and farther into the hill or mountain. If it is vertical, they remove the ore in layers.

These gold miners are working underground near Carlin, Nevada. The world's deepest gold mine is in South Africa and extends almost 3 km (2 mi) underground.

2.3 Review

KEY CONCEPTS

1. Give two examples of the use of minerals in industry and two examples of the use of minerals in the arts.

2. What are the five ways in which minerals form?

3. What is required for rocks to be considered ores?

CRITICAL THINKING

4. **Infer** Would an ore at Earth's surface or an ore deep underground be more expensive to mine? Explain.

5. **Apply** The mineral quartz has been used as a gemstone for thousands of years. What minerals could jewelry makers use to grind and polish quartz?

⬤ CHALLENGE

6. **Analyze** Both strip mining and open-pit mining are types of surface mining. When might miners choose to use open-pit mining rather than strip mining to obtain an ore?

Geometry for Gems

If you found a gemstone in nature, it would probably look dull and rough. You might want to take it to a gem cutter, who would use a grinding wheel to shape and polish your rough stone into a beautiful gem. You would also discover that a lot of the rough gemstone is ground away into powder.

Gem cutters use geometry to help them choose the best final shapes of gems. Geometry also helps them to shape gems with many small, flat surfaces at specific angles. These surfaces are called facets, and they make the gems sparkle.

Starred Gems

Some gems—such as certain rubies, sapphires, and forms of quartz—show a six-pointed star when cut in a rounded shape instead of facets. These gems contain tiny flaws aligned at 120-degree angles. When light hits the flaws, it scatters in a star-shaped pattern. The star ruby shown here is a good example of these beautiful gems.

Deeply Colored Gems

Some gems are shaped to show off their rich colors rather than their sparkle. These gems have fewer and larger facets. Also, many brightly colored gems contain lighter and darker areas of color. The gems are shaped so that the richest color is toward the bottom. Light entering one of these gems strikes the bottom and reflects the rich color to the viewer's eye.

Sparkling Gems

How much a gem sparkles depends on the geometric angles at which it is cut. If the overall angle of the bottom part of a gem is too shallow **(A)** or too steep **(C)**, light will go through the gem.

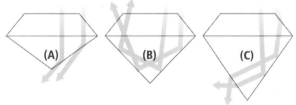

However, if the angles are correct **(B),** light will bounce around inside the gem as it is reflected to the viewer's eye. The more facets a gem has, the more the light will bounce, and the more the gem will sparkle.

EXPLORE

1. **COMPARE** Table salt, which is the mineral halite, sparkles as light is reflected from its crystal faces. Snow, which is the mineral ice, also sparkles in sunlight. How are the crystal faces of salt and snow similar to facets? How are they different?

2. **CHALLENGE** When would it be best for a gem cutter to split an irregularly shaped crystal into two or more smaller stones before grinding them into finished gems? Remember, one larger stone is usually more valuable than two smaller ones.

the BIG idea

Minerals are basic building blocks of Earth.

CONTENT REVIEW
CLASSZONE.COM

◀ KEY CONCEPTS SUMMARY

2.1 **Minerals are all around us.**

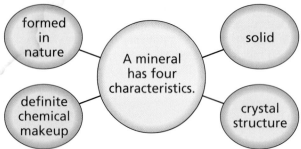

formed in nature

A mineral has four characteristics.

solid

definite chemical makeup

crystal structure

VOCABULARY
mineral p. 43
element p. 45
crystal p. 46

2.2 **A mineral is identified by its properties.**

Mineral Properties	wulfenite
color	orange
streak	white
luster	nonmetallic
cleavage	yes
density	6.9
hardness	3

VOCABULARY
streak p. 51
luster p. 52
cleavage p. 53
fracture p. 53
density p. 54
hardness p. 55

2.3 **Minerals are valuable resources.**

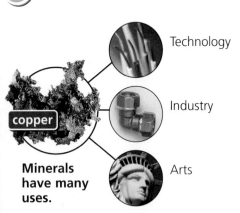

Technology

Industry

copper

Minerals have many uses.

Arts

Mineral Formation

Water evaporates.

Organisms form shells or bones.

Hot water cools.

Molten rock cools.

Heat and pressure cause changes.

VOCABULARY
magma p. 62
lava p. 62
ore p. 64

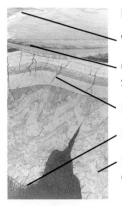

Reviewing Vocabulary

On a separate sheet of paper, write a sentence describing the relationship between the two vocabulary terms.

1. mineral, crystal

2. cleavage, fracture

3. magma, lava

4. element, density

5. mineral, ore

6. element, magma

Reviewing Key Concepts

Multiple Choice *Choose the letter of the best answer.*

7. A mineral is a substance that forms
   a. from rocks   c. from one element
   b. in nature   d. in liquid

8. A crystal structure is characteristic of
   a. an element   c. magma
   b. a rock   d. a mineral

9. A mineral is made up of one or more
   a. ores   c. compounds
   b. rocks   d. elements

10. How is it possible for two different minerals to have the same chemical composition?
    a. They have different crystal structures.
    b. One is formed only by organisms.
    c. Only one is a rock-forming mineral.
    d. They have different appearances.

11. Most minerals in Earth's crust belong to the silicate mineral group because this group contains the
    a. rarest elements on Earth
    b. most common elements on Earth
    c. most valuable metals on Earth
    d. largest crystals on Earth

12. Which of the following is the least reliable clue to a mineral's identity?
    a. color   c. hardness
    b. density   d. luster

13. Many properties of a mineral are related to the
    a. number of elements of which it is made
    b. other types of minerals present as it formed
    c. strength of bonds between its atoms
    d. speed at which it formed

14. What types of minerals form in an area depends in part on
    a. which elements are present
    b. the types of rock present
    c. the density of rocks present
    d. whether crystals can form

15. Open-pit mining is used to obtain ores that lie
    a. under flat land
    b. deep in Earth's crust
    c. near the surface of Earth
    d. in riverbeds

16. Gemstones are used in
    a. building materials
    b. paper products
    c. automobile parts
    d. jewelry making

Short Answer *Write a short answer for each question.*

17. Why aren't all solids minerals? Include the term *crystal structure* in your answer.

18. Why is a mineral's streak more useful in identifying it than its color?

19. If you drop dilute hydrochloric acid on the mineral aragonite, it bubbles. What mineral group do you think aragonite belongs to? Why?

20. Describe how the strength of the bonds between atoms in a mineral determines whether the mineral displays cleavage or fracture.

Thinking Critically

Properties such as hardness and density are used to identify minerals. Use the information from the chart to answer the next five questions.

Mineral	Hardness	Density (g/cm^3)
platinum	4.5	19.0
aragonite	4	3
topaz	8	3.5
quartz	7	2.7
arsenic	3.5	5.7

21. COMPARE Platinum can combine with arsenic to form the mineral sperrylite. How do you think the density of sperrylite compares with the densities of platinum and arsenic?

22. APPLY Gems made of topaz are much more valuable than those made of quartz, even though the two minerals can look similar. Describe two methods you could use to identify quartz.

23. APPLY Would a miner be more likely to use the method of panning to find platinum or to find topaz? Why?

24. INFER Aragonite forms very attractive crystals, yet this common mineral is rarely used in jewelry. Why do you think this is?

25. DEDUCE About how many times heavier than a piece of quartz would you expect a piece of platinum of the same size to be? Show your work.

26. HYPOTHESIZE *Halite* is the mineral name for table salt. Thick layers of halite are mined near Detroit, Michigan. At one time, an ocean covered the area. Write a hypothesis that explains how the halite formed there.

27. PREDICT The mineral chromite is the main ore of the metal chromium. What might happen after all the chromite on Earth is mined?

28. PREDICT The mineral apatite is a compound in your bones and teeth. Apatite contains the elements phosphorus and calcium. How might your bones be affected if you do not have enough of these elements in your diet?

29. DRAW CONCLUSIONS You live on the surface of Earth's crust. The average density of the crust is about 2.8 grams per cubic centimeter. Most metal ores have densities greater than 5 grams per cubic centimeter. How common do you think metal ores are in the crust? Why?

the BIG idea

30. ANALYZE Minerals are basic components of planets such as Earth and Mars. Other planets in our solar system, such as Jupiter and Saturn, are called gas giants because they are composed mainly of the gases hydrogen and helium. They do not have solid surfaces. Do you think that minerals are basic components of gas giants? Why or why not?

Mars

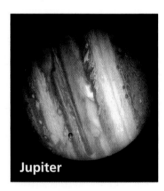

Jupiter

31. INFER Minerals make up much of Earth. People use minerals as sources of many materials, such as metals. Some metals are used to make machine parts or build houses. How would your life be different if minerals that contain metals were rare in Earth's crust?

UNIT PROJECTS

If you need to do an experiment for your unit project, gather the materials. Be sure to allow enough time to observe results before the project is due.

Analyzing a Table

This table shows characteristics of four minerals. Use it to answer the questions below.

Sample	Cleavage or Fracture	Density (g/cm³)	Hardness (in Mohs scale)	Magnetic
E	cleavage	3.7	8.5	no
F	fracture	5.2	5.5	yes
G	fracture	2.7	7.0	no
H	cleavage	2.7	3.0	no

1. Which sample is most dense?

 a. E **c.** G

 b. F **d.** H

2. Which sample is hardest?

 a. E **c.** G

 b. F **d.** H

3. What will happen if G is rubbed against each of the other samples?

 a. It will scratch only E.

 b. It will scratch only F.

 c. It will scratch only H.

 d. It will scratch F and H.

4. Which statement accurately describes how one of the samples will affect a magnet?

 a. E will attract the magnet.

 b. F will attract the magnet.

 c. G will be pushed away from the magnet.

 d. H will be pushed away from the magnet.

5. Which sample or samples have a crystal structure?

 a. E, F, G, and H **c.** E and H

 b. only F **d.** F and G

6. Which samples are likely to break along flat surfaces?

 a. E and G **c.** G and H

 b. F and G **d.** E and H

7. An unidentified mineral sample has a density of 2.9 grams per cubic centimeter and a hardness of 6.7. Which mineral is it most like?

 a. E **c.** G

 b. F **d.** H

8. Which is true about one-cubic-centimeter pieces of these samples?

 a. Each would have the same weight.

 b. E would be heaviest.

 c. F would be heaviest.

 d. H would be heaviest.

Extended Response

Answer the two questions below in detail. Include some of the terms shown in the word box. In your answers underline each term you use.

chemical makeup	element	compound
crystal structure	Mohs scale	hardness

9. Describe the characteristics of minerals that make them different from rocks.

10. Describe the type of mineral that would work best on the tip of a drill designed to make holes in hard materials.

Rocks

the BIG idea

Rocks change into other rocks over time.

How long will these rocks remain as they are?

Key Concepts

Internet Preview

CLASSZONE.COM

Chapter 3 online resources: Content Review, Simulation, Visualization, four Resource Centers, Math Tutorial, Test Practice

EXPLORE (the BIG idea)

How Can Rocks Disappear?

Chalk is made of carbonate minerals, as is a type of rock called limestone. Put a piece of chalk in a cup. Pour vinegar over the chalk.

Observe and Think Describe what happens to the chalk. How do you think this change could happen to limestone in nature? **Hint:** Think about the amount of time it might take.

What Causes Rocks to Change?

Make two balls out of modeling clay and freeze them. Take the clay balls out of the freezer and put them on paper. Cover one ball with plastic wrap and stack books on top of it.

Observe and Think Observe how the clay balls change over time. How might rocks respond to changes in temperature, pressure, or both?

Internet Activity: Rocks

Go to **ClassZone.com** to explore how rocks form and change.

Observe and Think Give three examples of the ways in which rocks are continually changing.

NSTA
scilinks.org

SCiLINKS

The Rock Cycle **Code: MDL015**

Getting Ready to Learn

◀ CONCEPT REVIEW

- Every mineral has a specific chemical composition.
- A mineral's atoms are arranged in a crystal structure.
- Minerals form under a variety of conditions.

◀ VOCABULARY REVIEW

mineral p. 43

crystal p. 46

magma p. 62

lava p. 62

 CONTENT REVIEW
CLASSZONE.COM
Review concepts and vocabulary.

▶ TAKING NOTES

MAIN IDEA WEB

Write each new blue heading in the center box. In the boxes around it, take notes about important terms and details that relate to the main idea.

VOCABULARY STRATEGY

Draw a **magnet word** diagram for each new vocabulary term. Around the "magnet" write words and ideas related to the term.

See the Note-Taking Handbook on pages R45–R51.

SCIENCE NOTEBOOK

Rocks are not the same as minerals.

Different types of rocks contain different minerals.

Most rocks are made of minerals.

A rock may be made up of only one mineral.

A few kinds of rocks contain no minerals at all.

Solid

ROCK

Formed naturally

Usually made up of minerals

KEY CONCEPT

The rock cycle shows how rocks change.

◀ **BEFORE, you learned**

- Minerals are basic components of Earth
- Minerals form in many different ways

▶ **NOW, you will learn**

- What the three types of rocks are
- How one type of rock can change into another
- How common each rock type is in Earth's crust

VOCABULARY

rock p. 75
rock cycle p. 78
igneous rock p. 78
sedimentary rock p. 78
metamorphic rock p. 78

EXPLORE Rocks and Minerals

How do rocks differ from minerals?

PROCEDURE

① Closely examine the rock and mineral samples. What do you notice about the forms, shapes, colors, and textures of the rock and the mineral?

② In your notebook, make lists of the characteristics of the rock and of the mineral.

MATERIALS
- mineral sample
- rock sample
- magnifying glass

WHAT DO YOU THINK?

- What are the similarities and differences between the rock and the mineral?
- What additional observations or tests might help you determine other differences between rocks and minerals?

Most rocks are made of minerals.

If you have ever put together a jigsaw puzzle, you know that each piece is an important part of the final picture. Just as the pieces combine to form the picture, minerals combine to form most rocks. Another way to consider the relationship between minerals and rocks is to compare rocks to words. Just as letters combine to make up words, minerals combine to make up rocks. A **rock** is a naturally formed solid that is usually made up of one or more types of minerals.

The structure of rocks is different from that of minerals. A mineral is always made of the same elements in the same proportions. All minerals have an orderly crystal structure. In contrast, the proportion of different minerals in a particular kind of rock may vary. In addition, the minerals in a rock can be all jumbled together.

A few types of rocks are made up of one kind of mineral, and a few contain no minerals at all. Limestone, for example, can be composed entirely of the mineral calcite. Obsidian (ahb-SIHD-ee-uhn) is a rock that contains no minerals. It consists of natural glass, which is not a mineral because it does not have a crystal structure. Coal is another rock that is not composed of minerals. It is made up of the remains of ancient plants that have been buried and pressed into rock.

Gabbro, like most rocks, is made up of several types of minerals.

Obsidian is an unusual rock because it contains no minerals.

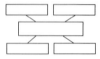

MAIN IDEA WEB
As you read, write each blue heading in a central box and record important details in boxes around it.

These huge cliffs on the coast of the Hawaiian island of Kauai show only a tiny part of the rock that makes up Earth.

Our world is built of rocks.

Earth is built almost entirely of rock. When you look at Earth's surface, you can see soil, plants, rivers, and oceans. These surface features, however, form only a very thin covering on the planet. Between this thin layer and Earth's metallic core, Earth is made of solid and molten rock.

Because rocks are so common, it is not surprising that people use them for many different purposes, including

- the building of houses and skyscrapers
- the sources of metals, such as iron, aluminum, and copper
- the carving of statues and other works of art
- as a base for pavement for roads and highways

People value rocks because rocks last a long time and because some are beautiful. Ancient rock structures and carvings give us a link to our distant past. Many famous monuments and sculptures are made from rocks. Granite blocks form part of the Great Wall of China. Limestone blocks make up the Great Pyramid in Egypt. The faces of four U.S. presidents are carved in the granite of Mount Rushmore.

This sculptor in Indonesia, like artists throughout the world, shapes rocks into lasting works of art.

CHECK YOUR READING Why do people use rocks for many different purposes?

People study rocks to learn how areas have changed through time. For example, rocks show that North America, as well as most of the rest of the world, has been buried under thick layers of ice many times. You could learn about the types of rocks in your area by collecting and identifying them. You could also examine a map that shows types of rocks and where they are located. This type of map is called a geologic map. The map may be of a large area, such as your state, or a smaller area, such as your county.

INVESTIGATE Classification of Rocks

How can rocks be classified?

Geologists classify rocks by their physical characteristics. Design your own system for classifying rocks, as a scientist might.

PROCEDURE

1. Examine the rock samples. Look at their physical characteristics.
2. Make a list of the differences in the physical characteristics of the rocks.
3. Use your list to decide which characteristics are most important in classifying the rocks into different types. Make a chart in which these characteristics are listed and used to classify the rocks into types.

WHAT DO YOU THINK?

- Which physical characteristic is most helpful in classifying the rocks?
- Which physical characteristic is least helpful in classifying the rocks?

CHALLENGE Is it possible to classify rocks only by the characteristics you can see?

SKILL FOCUS
Classifying

MATERIALS
6 rock samples

TIME
20 minutes

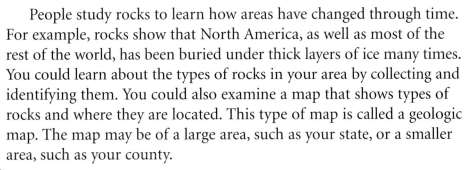

Rocks change as they move through the rock cycle.

When you want to describe a person you can depend on, you may say that he or she is "like a rock." That's the way people think of rocks—as solid and unchanging. Nevertheless, rocks do change. But the changes usually occur over a huge span of time—thousands to millions of years. The **rock cycle** is the set of natural processes that form, change, break down, and re-form rocks.

A cycle is made up of repeating events that happen one after another. This does not mean that rocks move through the rock cycle in a particular order. As the illustration shows on page 79, a rock at any point in the cycle can change in two or three different ways. Like all cycles, the rock cycle has no beginning or ending but goes on continually.

VOCABULARY
Add a magnet word diagram for *rock cycle* to your notebook. Then add diagrams for the names of the rock types.

Rock Types

The three types of rocks are classified by how they form.

- **Igneous rock** (IHG-nee-uhs) forms when molten rock cools and becomes solid. Igneous rock can form within Earth, or it can form on Earth's surface. Igneous rocks that originally formed at great depths can reach Earth's surface over time. Deep rocks may be raised closer to the surface when mountains are pushed up. At the same time, other processes can wear away the rocks that cover the deeper rocks.

- Most **sedimentary rock** (SEHD-uh-MEHN-tuh-ree) forms when pieces of older rocks, plants, and other loose material get pressed or cemented together. Loose material is carried by water or wind and then settles out, forming layers. The lower layers of material can get pressed into rock by the weight of the upper layers. Also, new minerals can grow in the spaces within the material, cementing it together. Some sedimentary rocks form in other ways, as when water evaporates, leaving behind minerals that were dissolved in it.

- **Metamorphic rock** (MEHT-uh-MAWR-fihk) forms when heat or pressure causes older rocks to change into new types of rocks. For example, a rock can get buried deeper in the crust, where pressure and temperature are much greater. The new conditions cause the structure of the rock to change and new minerals to grow in place of the original minerals. The rock becomes a metamorphic rock. Like igneous rocks, metamorphic rocks can be raised to Earth's surface over time.

READING TiP

When material dissolves in water, it breaks into many tiny parts. When the water evaporates, the parts join together and the material becomes solid again.

CHECK YOUR READING What are the three rock types? What questions do you have about how rocks move through the rock cycle?

The Rock Cycle

In the rock cycle, natural processes change each type of rock into other types. Rocks can take many paths through the rock cycle and change into other types in any order.

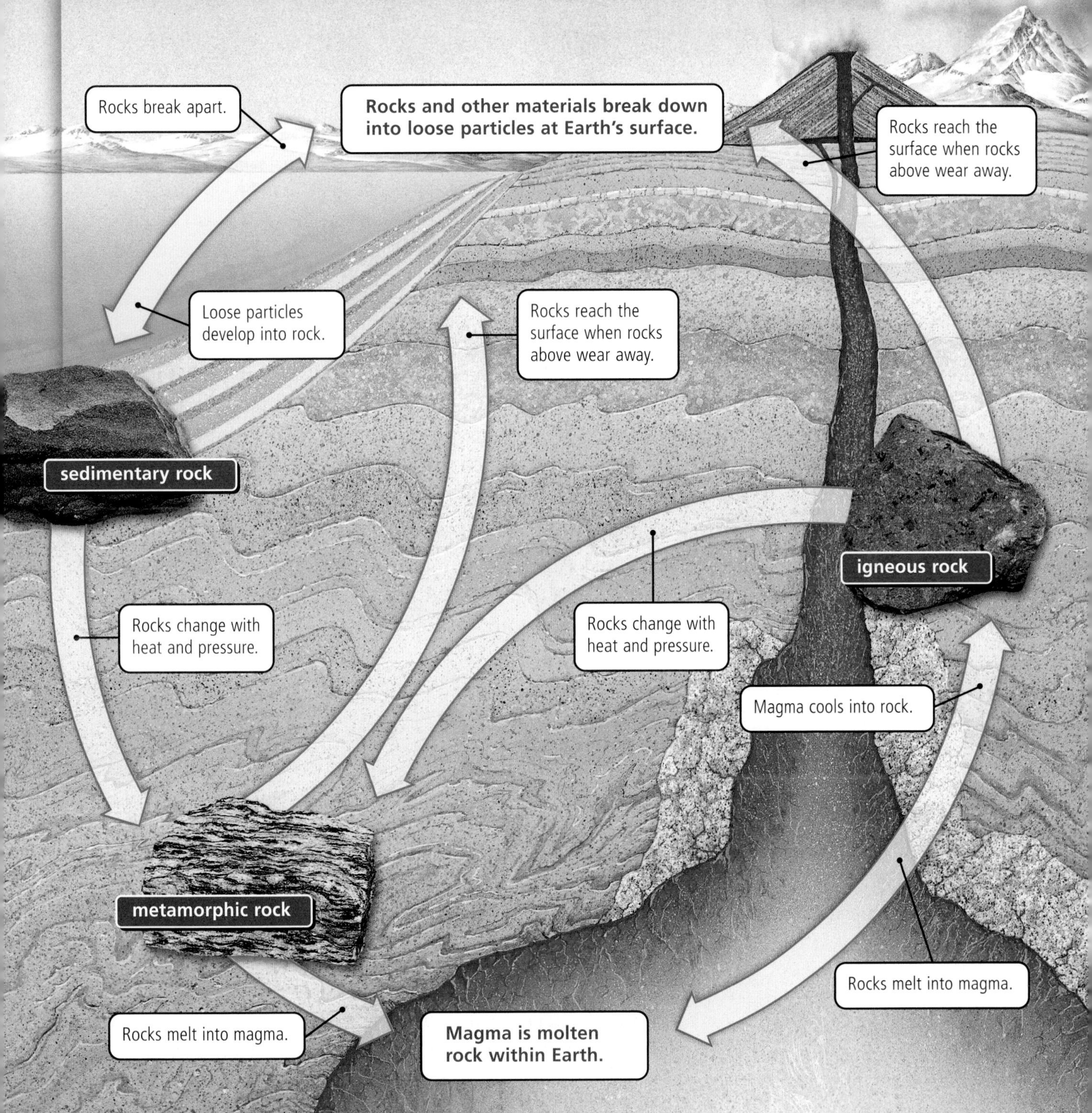

Rocks break apart.

Rocks and other materials break down into loose particles at Earth's surface.

Rocks reach the surface when rocks above wear away.

Loose particles develop into rock.

Rocks reach the surface when rocks above wear away.

sedimentary rock

igneous rock

Rocks change with heat and pressure.

Rocks change with heat and pressure.

Magma cools into rock.

metamorphic rock

Rocks melt into magma.

Rocks melt into magma.

Magma is molten rock within Earth.

READING VISUALS What are three different ways an igneous rock can change as it moves to another stage of the rock cycle?

Rocks in the Crust

Even though sedimentary rock is common at Earth's surface, as a whole the crust consists mainly of igneous and metamorphic rock.

Surface of Crust

Igneous and metamorphic rock 25%

Sedimentary rock 75%

Entire Crust

Sedimentary rock 5%

Igneous and metamorphic rock 95%

Rocks in the Crust

Igneous, sedimentary, and metamorphic rocks are all found in Earth's crust. But these rock types are not evenly distributed. Most of Earth's crust—95 percent of it—consists of igneous rock and metamorphic rock. Sedimentary rock, which forms a thin covering on Earth's surface, makes up only 5 percent of the crust.

The distribution of rock types is a reflection of the rock cycle. Sedimentary rocks are most common at the surface because they are formed by processes that occur at the surface. Most igneous rocks and metamorphic rocks are formed by processes that occur deeper within Earth.

 CHECK YOUR READING Would you expect to find sedimentary rock deep in Earth's crust? Why or why not?

3.1 Review

KEY CONCEPTS

1. How are rocks and minerals different?

2. What are the three types of rock?

3. Which rock types are most common within Earth's crust? Which type is most common at Earth's surface?

CRITICAL THINKING

4. **Analyze** Why is the set of natural processes by which rocks change into other types of rocks called a cycle?

5. **Infer** Which type of rock would you expect to be common on the floor of a large, deep lake? Why?

CHALLENGE

6. **Synthesize** Draw a diagram showing how an igneous rock could change into a metamorphic rock and how the metamorphic rock could change into a sedimentary rock.

Rocks from Space

Earth makes its own rocks. But some rocks come from space and land on Earth's surface. About 30,000 rocks with masses greater than 100 grams (3.5 oz) fall to Earth's surface every year. That's a rate of more than 80 rocks per day!

- A rock from space that reaches Earth's surface after passing through its atmosphere is called a meteorite.

- Most meteorites go unnoticed when they strike Earth. Either they fall in areas where there are few people, or they fall into the ocean.

- The largest rock from space ever found on Earth is called the Hoba meteorite. It weighs 60 tons! It landed in what is now Namibia, Africa, about 80,000 years ago.

This rock is a piece of the meteorite that formed Barringer Crater.

A meteorite impact formed Barringer Crater, which is located in the Arizona desert.

Meteorite Hunters Search Ice

Meteorite hunters search the icy wastes of Antarctica for these rocks. Do more meteorites fall there? No. But they are easy to see against the ice. The cold also helps preserve them in their original condition. In addition, the movements of the ice gather meteorites together in certain locations.

Meteorites Blast Earth

Large meteorites are very rare. This is fortunate, because they hit with great power. About 50,000 years ago, a meteorite that was about 45 meters (150 ft) in diameter slammed into what is now Arizona and blasted a crater 1.2 kilometers (0.75 mi) wide. Craters from ancient impacts may be hard to recognize because the land has been reshaped by geological processes. Evidence can still be found, though. The energy of an impact is so high that some minerals, such as quartz, are permanently altered.

EXPLORE

1. **PREDICT** Oceans cover about 71 percent of Earth's surface. Calculate how many meteorites with masses greater than 100 grams are likely to fall into the ocean each year. How many are likely to fall on land?

2. **CHALLENGE** Use information from the Resource Center to describe how a meteorite impact could have helped cause the dinosaurs to become extinct.

RESOURCE CENTER
CLASSZONE.COM
Learn more about meteorites and meteorite impacts.

A streak of light marks the path of a rock from space through Earth's atmosphere. The rock probably burned up completely before it could land.

3.2 Igneous rocks form from molten rock.

 BEFORE, you learned

- Earth's interior is very hot
- Most minerals in Earth's crust are silicates

NOW, you will learn

- Why igneous rocks formed at Earth's surface are different from those formed within Earth
- Why silica content is important in classifying igneous rocks
- Why igneous rocks can make long-lasting landforms

VOCABULARY

intrusive igneous rock p. 83

extrusive igneous rock p. 83

THINK ABOUT

Why do two rocks made of the same minerals look very different?

Look at a sample of granite and a sample of rhyolite (RY-uh-LYT). These two igneous rocks contain the same minerals, so their chemical compositions are very similar. Yet granite and rhyolite look very different. What do you think might cause this difference?

granite

rhyolite

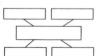

MAIN IDEA WEB
Remember to make a web for each main idea.

Magma and lava form different types of igneous rocks.

Igneous rocks form from molten rock, but where does molten rock come from? The temperature inside Earth increases with depth. That is, the farther down you go, the hotter it gets. Deep within Earth, temperatures are hot enough—750°C to 1250°C (about 1400°F to 2300°F)—to melt rock. This molten rock is called magma. Molten rock that reaches Earth's surface is called lava.

An igneous rock is classified on the basis of its mineral composition and the size of its mineral crystals. A rock formed from magma can have the same composition as a rock formed from lava. The rocks, though, will have different names, because the sizes of their crystals will be very different. You will read why later in this section.

People's decisions about how to use igneous rocks are based in part on the rocks' crystal sizes. For example, rocks with large mineral crystals are often used as building stones because they are attractive.

Origin of Igneous Rocks

Depending on where they form, igneous rocks are classified as intrusive (ihn-TROO-sihv) or extrusive (ihk-STROO-sihv). An **intrusive igneous rock** is one that forms when magma cools within Earth. An **extrusive igneous rock** is one that forms when lava cools on Earth's surface.

Granite is a common intrusive rock in continents. If magma with the same composition reaches the surface, it forms extrusive rocks such as rhyolite and pumice (PUHM-ihs). Basalt (buh-SAWLT) is an extrusive igneous rock that forms the ocean floor. Gabbro is an intrusive rock that has the same composition as basalt.

CHECK YOUR READING How are gabbro and basalt similar? How are they different?

You can see extrusive igneous rocks at Earth's surface. But intrusive igneous rocks form within Earth. How do they reach the surface? Forces inside Earth can push rocks up, as when mountains form. Also, water and wind break apart and carry away surface rocks. Then deeper rocks are uncovered at the surface.

VOCABULARY
Add magnet word diagrams for *intrusive igneous rock* and *extrusive igneous rock* to your notebook.

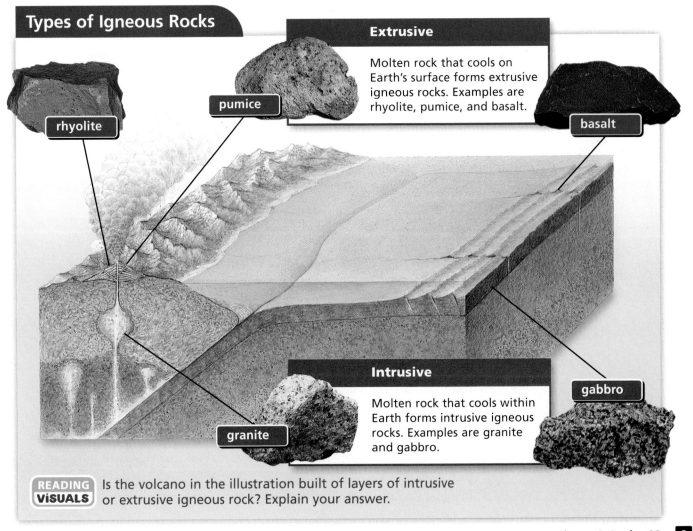

Types of Igneous Rocks

Extrusive
Molten rock that cools on Earth's surface forms extrusive igneous rocks. Examples are rhyolite, pumice, and basalt.

rhyolite

pumice

basalt

Intrusive
Molten rock that cools within Earth forms intrusive igneous rocks. Examples are granite and gabbro.

granite

gabbro

READING VISUALS Is the volcano in the illustration built of layers of intrusive or extrusive igneous rock? Explain your answer.

Textures of Igneous Rocks

The texture of an igneous rock—that is, the size of its mineral crystals—depends on how quickly magma or lava cooled to form it. In an icemaker, crystals form as water freezes into ice. In a similar way, mineral crystals form as molten rock freezes into solid rock.

The magma that forms intrusive igneous rocks stays below the surface of Earth. Large crystals can form in intrusive rocks because

- the interior of Earth is very hot
- the high temperatures allow magma to cool slowly
- slow cooling allows time for large mineral crystals to form

The lava that forms extrusive igneous rocks reaches Earth's surface. Very small crystals form in extrusive rocks because

- the surface of Earth is cooler than Earth's interior
- the lower temperatures cause the lava to cool quickly
- there is no time for large mineral crystals to form

Some igneous rocks contain crystals of very different sizes. These rocks formed from magma that started cooling within Earth and then erupted onto the surface. The large crystals grew as the magma cooled slowly. The small crystals grew as the lava cooled quickly.

CHECK YOUR READING How does an igneous rock that has both large and small mineral crystals form?

Crystal Size and Cooling Time

The more slowly molten rock cools within Earth, the larger the igneous rocks' mineral crystals will be.

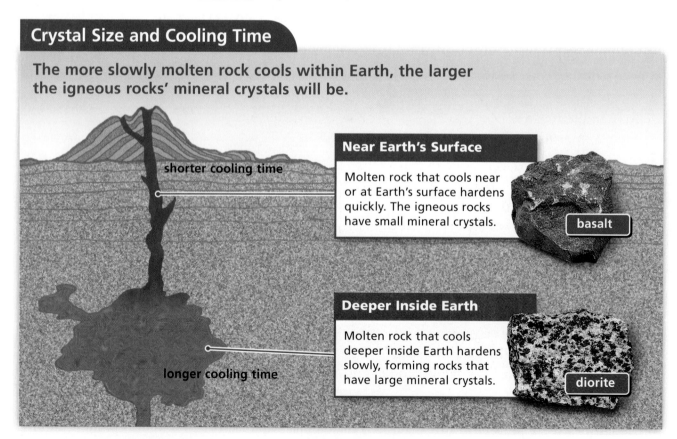

shorter cooling time

Near Earth's Surface

Molten rock that cools near or at Earth's surface hardens quickly. The igneous rocks have small mineral crystals.

basalt

Deeper Inside Earth

Molten rock that cools deeper inside Earth hardens slowly, forming rocks that have large mineral crystals.

diorite

longer cooling time

INVESTIGATE Crystal Size

How does cooling time affect crystal size?

PROCEDURE

1. Look at the Mineral Crystal Diagrams datasheet.

2. Describe your observations of the crystals in each of the igneous-rock diagrams A–C on the lines provided.

3. Describe what is shown in each of graphs 1–3 on the lines provided.

4. Match each igneous-rock diagram with its corresponding graph.

5. On the back of the paper, explain why you matched each crystal diagram with a particular graph.

WHAT DO YOU THINK?

- Which diagram shows an intrusive igneous rock, such as gabbro?
- Where do you think the rock shown in diagram B formed? Explain your answer.

CHALLENGE Write a hypothesis to explain why the rock shown in diagram C might be found at a shallow depth in Earth's crust.

SKILL FOCUS
Analyzing

MATERIALS
Mineral Crystal
Diagrams datasheet

TIME
20 Minutes

Composition of Igneous Rocks

Texture is not enough to identify an igneous rock. Think about substances that have similar textures, such as sugar and salt. A spoonful of sugar and a spoonful of salt both consist of small white grains. However, sugar and salt are different materials—that is, they have different compositions. Likewise, different igneous rocks might have similar textures. To identify them, you must also consider their compositions.

Most igneous rocks are mainly made up of silicate minerals, which you read about in the last chapter. The silicate mineral group is the most common group in Earth's crust. Silicate minerals contain varying amounts of silica, a compound of silicon and oxygen. After identifying the texture of an igneous rock, geologists classify the rock on the basis of how rich it is in silica.

Special equipment must be used to determine a rock's exact composition, but you can estimate the level of silica in an igneous rock by looking at its color. Igneous rocks with high levels of silica, such as granite and rhyolite, are typically light in color. Those with low levels of silica, such as gabbro and basalt, are dark in color.

CHECK YOUR READING Would you expect a light gray igneous rock to be rich or poor in silica? Why?

Igneous rocks make long-lasting landforms.

In northwestern New Mexico, a great peak rises out of a flat, barren desert. The Navajo call the peak Tsé Bit'a'í (tseh biht-ah-ih), meaning "rock with wings." In English, it's called Ship Rock, because it looks something like a sailing ship. Ship Rock is an example of the kinds of landforms that are made of igneous rocks. A landform is a natural feature on Earth's land surface.

Intrusive Rock Formations

Ship Rock actually formed about one kilometer below the surface of Earth 30 million years ago. It is all that remains of magma that once fed a volcano. The magma cooled slowly and formed intrusive igneous rock.

As magma pushes up toward Earth's surface, it makes channels and other formations underground. Formations of intrusive igneous rock can be harder and more lasting than other types of rock. Notice in the illustration below how igneous rock has been left at the surface as other, weaker types of rock have been worn away.

Intrusive Rock Formation

Wind and water wear away surrounding, weaker rock to reveal intrusive rock formations, such as Ship Rock.

Ancient Land Surface

Magma that remains below the surface will later become intrusive igneous rock.

Present-Day Land Surface

Surface rock has worn away to reveal some of the intrusive rock.

READING VISUALS Where in the bottom illustration is more intrusive rock likely to be uncovered next?

Extrusive Rock Formations

When magma makes its way to Earth's surface through a volcano or crack, the lava may erupt in different ways. Some lava can build huge plateaus when it erupts from long cracks in Earth's surface. Lava that is low in silica, such as basalt lava, flows easily and spreads out in thin sheets over great distances. The Columbia Plateau in Oregon and Washington is made of basalt. When lava that is low in silica erupts at a single point, it can build up a huge volcano with gently sloping sides. The Hawaiian Islands are a chain of volcanoes that are built of basalt lava. The volcanoes started erupting on the sea floor and over a very long time grew tall enough to rise above the surface of the ocean as islands.

READING **TiP**

Notice what properties of basalt lava allow it to build large plateaus.

Lava that contains a greater amount of silica does not flow easily. Silica-rich lava tends to build cone-shaped volcanoes with steep sides. Volcanoes fed by silica-rich magma tend to erupt explosively. Because the magma is thick and sticky, pressure can build up in volcanoes until they explode. An example is Mount St. Helens in the state of Washington. Its 1980 eruption reduced the volcano's height by 400 meters (about 1300 ft). Lava flows are adding new extrusive igneous rock. At the current rate it will take more than 200 years for the volcano to reach its pre-1980 height.

Basalt lava can flow long distances. Here it is spreading over a road in Hawaii.

 CHECK YOUR READING — Why does silica-rich lava tend to build steep volcanoes instead of spreading out?

3.2 Review

KEY CONCEPTS

1. What is the main difference between intrusive and extrusive igneous rocks?

2. What are the two major properties used to classify igneous rocks?

3. Why can intrusive igneous rocks be left behind when surrounding rocks are worn away?

CRITICAL THINKING

4. **Draw Conclusions** If granite within Earth melts and then erupts at the surface, what type of extrusive rock is likely to form?

5. **Analyze** Would you expect extrusive rocks produced by an explosive volcano to be light or dark in color? Why?

CHALLENGE

6. **Synthesize** Why are the names *intrusive* and *extrusive* appropriate for the two types of igneous rocks?

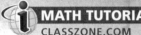

MATH TUTORIAL
CLASSZONE.COM

Click on Math Tutorial for more help with estimating areas.

Resurfacing Earth

Lava flows from volcanoes are common on the island of Hawaii. The map below shows lava flows from the Kilauea volcano. The flow shown in blue destroyed more than 180 homes and covered the region in a layer of lava up to 25 meters thick.

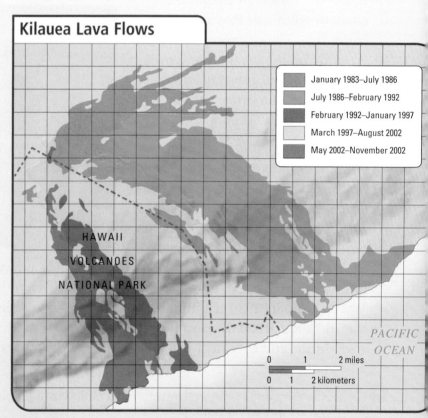

Kilauea Lava Flows

- January 1983–July 1986
- July 1986–February 1992
- February 1992–January 1997
- March 1997–August 2002
- May 2002–November 2002

HAWAII

VOLCANOES

NATIONAL PARK

PACIFIC OCEAN

0   1   2 miles

0   1   2 kilometers

Use the map to answer the following questions.

1. How many squares does the lava flow shown in yellow cover? First, count the complete grid squares covered by the lava flow shown in yellow. Next, think of partially covered grid squares as fractions, and add them together to get whole squares. Finally, add the number of these squares to the number of complete squares.

2. What is the area of the flow in square kilometers?

3. Use the same method to estimate the areas of the flows shown in purple and blue.

CHALLENGE To estimate the area covered by all the lava flows shown on the map, would it be better to estimate the area of each flow separately and then add the results together? Or would it be better to estimate the total area of the flows in one step? Explain your reasoning.

3.3 Sedimentary rocks form from earlier rocks.

◀ **BEFORE, you learned**

- Most rocks are made of minerals
- Some ocean organisms build their shells from minerals
- Dissolved minerals re-form as water evaporates

▶ **NOW, you will learn**

- What kinds of materials make up sedimentary rocks
- What the processes that form sedimentary rocks are
- How sedimentary rocks record past conditions

VOCABULARY

sediment p. 89

EXPLORE Particle Layers

What happens as rock particles settle in water?

PROCEDURE

1. Pour 2 cups of water into the jar.

2. Add the gravel and sand to the water.

3. Shake the jar for a few seconds and then set it down on a counter. Observe and record what happens to the materials in the water.

WHAT DO YOU THINK?

- What determines how the materials settle to the bottom of the jar?

- In a lake, how would a mixture of different-sized rock particles settle to the bottom?

MATERIALS

- jar
- measuring cup
- water
- 1/3 cup gravel
- 1/3 cup sand

Some rocks form from rock particles.

If the sand grains on a beach become naturally cemented together, they form a sedimentary rock called sandstone. Most sedimentary rock forms as sandstone does—from loose material that gets pressed together or cemented into rock. Sedimentary rock forms in other ways, too.

Sedimentary rock takes its name from the word *sediment*, which means "something that settles." **Sediments** are materials that settle out of water or air. In addition to loose pieces of rocks and minerals, pieces of plant and animal remains can also make up sediments. Sedimentary rocks develop from layers of sediments that build up on land or underwater.

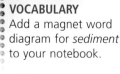

VOCABULARY
Add a magnet word diagram for *sediment* to your notebook.

⬤ **CHECK YOUR READING** What types of material can make up sediments?

Forming and Transporting Rock Particles

A sandy ocean beach, a gravel bar in a river, and a muddy lake bottom all consist mainly of rock particles. These particles were broken away from rocks by the action of water or wind or a combination of both. Such particles may vary in size from boulders to sand to tiny bits of clay.

Just as water washes mud off your hands as it runs over them, rainwater washes away rock particles as it flows downhill. The water carries these rock particles to streams and rivers, which eventually empty into lakes or oceans. Strong winds also pick up sand and rock dust and carry them to distant places.

As winds or water currents slow down, rock particles settle on the land or at the bottom of rivers, lakes, and oceans. The sediments form layers as larger particles settle first, followed by smaller ones.

RESOURCE CENTER
CLASSZONE.COM
Find information on sedimentary rocks.

Forming Loose Sediments into Rocks

If you have ever watched workers building a road, you know that they first put down layers of gravel and other materials. Then they press the layers together, using a huge roller. In a similar way, layers of sediments

Sorting Sediments by Size

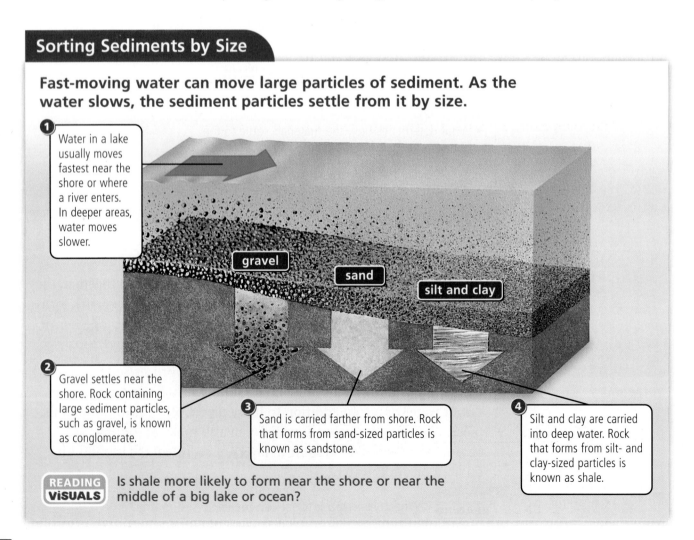

Fast-moving water can move large particles of sediment. As the water slows, the sediment particles settle from it by size.

1 Water in a lake usually moves fastest near the shore or where a river enters. In deeper areas, water moves slower.

gravel

sand

silt and clay

2 Gravel settles near the shore. Rock containing large sediment particles, such as gravel, is known as conglomerate.

3 Sand is carried farther from shore. Rock that forms from sand-sized particles is known as sandstone.

4 Silt and clay are carried into deep water. Rock that forms from silt- and clay-sized particles is known as shale.

READING VISUALS Is shale more likely to form near the shore or near the middle of a big lake or ocean?

composed of rock particles may get pressed together to form rock. One layer gets buried by another, and then another. The overlying layers apply pressure to, or press down on, the sediments underneath.

Small particles of sediment, such as silt and clay, may be formed into rock by pressure alone. In other sedimentary rocks the particles are held together by minerals that have crystallized between them, acting as cement. Over a long time, these processes transform loose sediments into sedimentary rocks.

 CHECK YOUR READING What are two processes that can change sediments into rocks?

Some rocks form from plants or shells.

Processes similar to the ones that produce sedimentary rocks from rock particles also produce rocks from shells or plant remains. These remains are fossils. A fossil is the remains or trace of an organism from long ago.

MAIN IDEA WEB
Add a web to your notebook for each main idea.

Coal

If you look at a piece of coal through a magnifying glass, you may be able to make out the shapes of bits of wood or leaves. That is because coal is made up of remains of plants—dead wood, bark, leaves, stems, and roots. Coal is an unusual sedimentary rock because it forms from plants instead of earlier rocks.

The coal people use today started forming millions of years ago in swamps. As plants died, their remains fell upon the remains of earlier plants. Then layers of other sediments buried the layers of plant remains. The weight of the sediments above pressed the plant material into coal.

The dark layer in these rocks is coal.

Here, you can see fossils of ancient plants preserved in coal.

Limestone

Limestone is made up of carbonate minerals, such as calcite. The shells and skeletons of ocean organisms are formed of these minerals. When the organisms die, the shells and skeletons settle on the ocean floor as layers of sediment. Over time, the layers become buried, pressed together, and cemented to form limestone. The photographs below show how loose shells can become limestone.

These shells were made by ocean organisms.

1. The shells get cemented together into limestone as some of their minerals dissolve and re-form.

2. Individual shells become harder to see as minerals in the limestone continue to dissolve and re-form.

3. Over time, what was once loose sediment becomes limestone with no recognizable shells.

READING TiP

Notice that limestone made up of cemented shells and the limestone in coral reefs were both formed by ocean organisms.

The famous white cliffs of Dover, England, consist of a type of limestone called chalk. The limestone began to form millions of years ago, when the land was under the ocean. The rock developed from shells of tiny organisms that float in the ocean. Most limestone comes from shells and skeletons of ocean organisms. The materials the organisms use to build their shells and skeletons are present in ocean water because they were dissolved from earlier rocks. Like almost all sedimentary rock, limestone forms from material that came from older rocks.

Coral reefs also consist of limestone that comes from organisms. However, in the case of reefs, the limestone is produced directly as coral organisms build their skeletons one on top of another. In the formation of coral, the rock does not go through a loose-sediment stage.

The skeletons of these tiny coral organisms eventually make huge coral reefs.

Some rocks form when dissolved minerals re-form from water.

If you have grown crystals in a container, you know that some substances can dissolve in water and then re-form as the water evaporates. The same process happens in nature. Some sedimentary rocks are made up of minerals that crystallized as water dried up.

The water in oceans, lakes, rivers, and streams contains minerals that came from rocks. Some of these minerals are in solid form. As rainwater washes over rocks, it picks up pieces of minerals and rock particles and carries them into streams and rivers, where many of them settle to the bottom. However, some of the minerals dissolve in the water and are carried along with it.

Water often flows through cracks in rock that is near Earth's surface. As water moves through limestone, some of the rock dissolves. A large open space, or cave, can be left in the rock. As the water flows and drips through the cave, some of it evaporates. The new limestone that forms can take many odd and beautiful shapes.

Sometimes minerals crystallize along the edges of lakes and oceans where the climate is dry and a lot of water evaporates quickly. Over time, the minerals build up and form layers of sedimentary rock. Rock salt and gypsum form in this way. Under the city of Detroit, for example, is a large bed of rock salt that developed when part of an ancient ocean dried up.

Water is shaping this limestone cavern. Water dissolves and transports minerals, then leaves the minerals behind as it evaporates.

 CHECK YOUR READING How are the origins of rock salt and some limestone similar?

These limestone towers in Mono Lake, California, formed underwater. They are now above the surface because the lake level has dropped.

INVESTIGATE Rock Layers

How do sedimentary rocks form in layers?

PROCEDURE

1. Prepare the plaster of Paris by mixing it with the water.

2. Mix 2 tablespoons of the gravel with 2 tablespoons of the plaster of Paris and pour the mixture into the paper cup.

3. Mix the sand with 2 tablespoons of the plaster of Paris and the food coloring. Add the mixture to the paper cup, on top of the gravel mixture.

4. Mix the rest of the gravel with the rest of the plaster of Paris. Add the mixture to the paper cup, on top of the sand mixture.

5. After the mixtures harden for about 5 minutes, tear apart the paper cup and observe the layers.

MATERIALS
- 1 paper cup
- 3 mixing cups
- 6 tbs plaster of Paris
- 3 tbs water
- 4 tbs gravel
- 2 tbs sand
- 3 drops food coloring

TIME
20 minutes

WHAT DO YOU THINK?

- How is the procedure you used to make your model similar to the way sedimentary rock forms?

- Describe how similar layers of real rock could form.

CHALLENGE How would you create a model to show the formation of fossil-rich limestone?

Sedimentary rocks show the action of wind and water.

READING TiP

Notice that sedimentary rocks are laid down in layers. As conditions in an area change, so do the characteristics of the layers.

Sedimentary rocks are laid down in layers, with the oldest layers on the bottom. A geologist studying layers of sedimentary rocks can tell something about what conditions were like in the past. For instance, fossils of fish or shells in a layer of rock show that the area was covered by a lake or an ocean long ago.

Fossils are not the only way to tell something about what past conditions were like. The sediments themselves contain a great deal of information. For example, a layer of sedimentary rock may contain sediment particles of different sizes. The largest particles are at the very bottom of the layer. Particles higher in the layer become increasingly smaller. A layer like this shows that the water carrying the sediment was slowing down. The largest particles dropped out when the water was moving quickly. Then smaller and smaller particles dropped out

Crossbeds	Ripples	Mud Cracks
	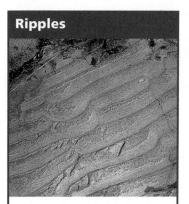	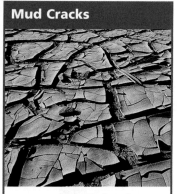
The tilted layers in these sandstone rocks are called crossbeds. The layers were once moving sand dunes.	The surface of this sandstone preserves ancient sand ripples.	As wet silt and clay dry out, cracks develop on the surface of the sediment.

as the water slowed. This type of layer is often created by a flood, when a large amount of water is at first moving quickly.

Sedimentary rocks can give information about the directions in which long-ago wind or water currents were traveling when sediments settled from them. Sand can be laid down in tilted layers on the slopes of sand dunes or sandbars. Sand can also form ripples as water or wind moves over its surface. If the sand has been buried and cemented into sandstone, a geologist can examine it and tell the direction in which the water or wind was moving.

Some rocks made of clay or silt have cracks that developed when the mud from which they formed dried out. Mud cracks show that the rocks formed in areas where wet periods were followed by dry periods.

 CHECK YOUR READING What could a geologist learn by finding rocks that have ripples or mud cracks?

 **3.3 Review**

KEY CONCEPTS

1. What types of material can make up sediments?

2. Describe the three processes by which sedimentary rocks form.

3. Describe how a sedimentary rock can show how fast water was flowing when its sediments were laid down.

CRITICAL THINKING

4. **Infer** Why is coal called a fossil fuel?

5. **Analyze** How could the speed of flowing water change to lay down alternating layers of sand and mud?

△ CHALLENGE

6. **Synthesize** How is it possible for a single sedimentary rock to contain rock particles, animal shells, and minerals that crystallized from water?

Metamorphic rocks form as existing rocks change.

◀ **BEFORE,** you learned	▶ **NOW,** you will learn
• Igneous rocks form as molten rock cools • Sedimentary rocks form from earlier rocks	• How a rock can change into another type of rock • How new minerals can grow in existing rocks

VOCABULARY

metamorphism p. 96
recrystallization p. 97
foliation p. 100

THINK ABOUT

How does a rock change into another kind of rock?

Examine a sample of shale and a sample of schist (shihst). Shale, a sedimentary rock, can change into schist. Think about how this change could occur without the shale's melting or breaking apart. Make a prediction about what process changes shale into schist.

shale

schist

Heat and pressure change rocks.

When you cook popcorn, you use heat to increase the pressure within small, hard kernels until they explode into a fluffy snack. Cooking popcorn is just one example of the many ways in which heat and pressure can change the form of things—even things like rocks.

The process in which an existing rock is changed by heat or pressure—or both—is called **metamorphism** (MEHT-uh-MAWR-FIHZ-uhm). The original sedimentary or igneous rock is called the parent rock. The resulting rock is a metamorphic rock. Even a metamorphic rock can be a parent rock for another type of metamorphic rock.

Many of the metamorphic rocks people use were once sedimentary rocks. Limestone is the parent rock of marble, which is used by builders and artists. Shale can be the parent rock of schist, which can be a source of the gemstone garnet. Some schists are a source of the mineral graphite, which is used in pencils.

READING TiP

Rocks change into other rocks by the process of metamorphism. A similar word, *metamorphosis,* refers to what happens when a caterpillar changes into a butterfly.

 Give an example of a way people use metamorphic rocks.

During metamorphism, rocks undergo many changes. One type of change occurs when pressure causes a rock's minerals to flatten out in one direction. Other changes can occur in a rock's minerals, but the rock remains solid. Rocks do not melt when they undergo metamorphism. If the temperature gets high enough to melt the rock, the end result is an igneous rock, not a metamorphic rock.

Heat and pressure can break the bonds that join atoms in minerals. Then the atoms can join together differently as new bonds form. This process is called **recrystallization.** It has two main results. First, individual mineral crystals can grow larger as more atoms join their crystal structures. Second, atoms can combine in different ways, and new minerals can form in place of older ones. For example, shale is a sedimentary rock that is formed from silt and clay. During recrystallization, garnet can form from these materials.

How Rocks Change

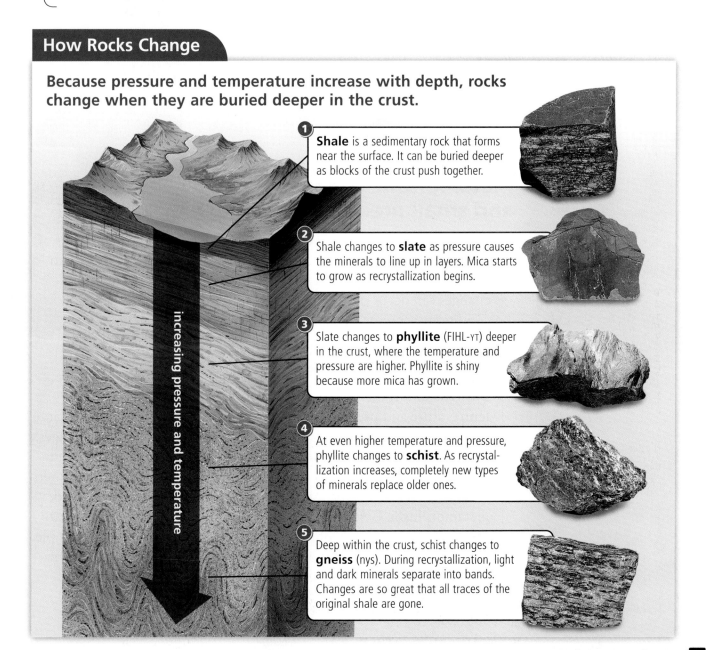

Because pressure and temperature increase with depth, rocks change when they are buried deeper in the crust.

increasing pressure and temperature

1. **Shale** is a sedimentary rock that forms near the surface. It can be buried deeper as blocks of the crust push together.

2. Shale changes to **slate** as pressure causes the minerals to line up in layers. Mica starts to grow as recrystallization begins.

3. Slate changes to **phyllite** (FIHL-YT) deeper in the crust, where the temperature and pressure are higher. Phyllite is shiny because more mica has grown.

4. At even higher temperature and pressure, phyllite changes to **schist**. As recrystallization increases, completely new types of minerals replace older ones.

5. Deep within the crust, schist changes to **gneiss** (nys). During recrystallization, light and dark minerals separate into bands. Changes are so great that all traces of the original shale are gone.

INVESTIGATE Metamorphic Changes

How can pressure and temperature change a solid?

PROCEDURE

① Use a vegetable peeler to make a handful of wax shavings of three different colors. Mix the shavings.

② Use your hands to warm the shavings, and then squeeze them into a wafer.

WHAT DO YOU THINK?

- Describe what happened to the wax shavings.
- How do the changes you observed resemble metamorphic changes in rocks?

CHALLENGE What changes that occur in metamorphic rocks were you unable to model in this experiment?

SKILL FOCUS
Modeling

MATERIALS
- 3 candles of different colors
- vegetable peeler

TIME
10 minutes

Metamorphic changes occur over large and small areas.

The types of metamorphic changes that occur depend on the types of parent rocks and the conditions of temperature and pressure. When both high temperature and high pressure are present, metamorphic changes can occur over very large areas. When only one of these conditions is present, changes tend to occur over smaller areas.

Change over Large Areas

Most metamorphic changes occur over large areas in which both temperature and pressure are high. An example is a region where large blocks of rock are pressing together and pushing up mountain ranges. This process can affect an area hundreds of kilometers wide and tens of kilometers deep. In such an area, rocks are buried, pressed together, bent, and heated. The pressure and heat cause the rocks to undergo metamorphism. Generally, the deeper below the surface the rocks are, the greater the metamorphic changes that occur in them. For example, a sedimentary rock may change to slate near the surface but become gneiss deep inside a mountain.

CHECK YOUR READING Where can metamorphic changes occur over large areas?

Change over Small Areas

Some metamorphic changes occur over small areas. For example, magma can push into rocks underground, or surface rock can be covered by a lava flow. The magma or lava heats the rock it is in contact with, causing recrystallization. These changes are mainly due to high temperature, not pressure. The rocks get roasted but not squeezed. The thickness of rock changed by the heat can range from less than one meter to several hundred meters, depending on the amount and temperature of the molten rock.

Small areas of metamorphic rock can also be formed by high pressure alone. At or near Earth's surface, rocks move and grind past one another during earthquakes. Rocks that grind together in this way can be subjected to high pressures that cause metamorphic changes.

RESOURCE CENTER
CLASSZONE.COM

Find information on metamorphic rocks.

Metamorphic Changes

Changes can occur over hundreds of kilometers or over just a few centimeters.

Changes over Large Areas

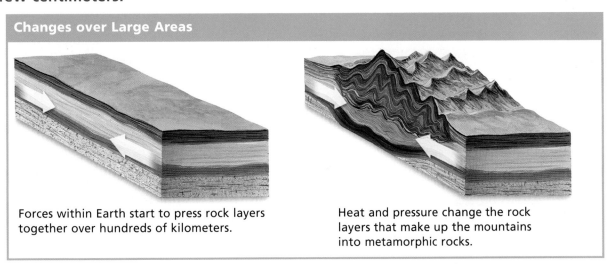

Forces within Earth start to press rock layers together over hundreds of kilometers.

Heat and pressure change the rock layers that make up the mountains into metamorphic rocks.

Changes over Small Areas

Magma can push into rock layers and cause changes over areas ranging from a few centimeters to tens of meters.

The magma is hot enough to bake the surrounding rocks into metamorphic rocks.

READING VISUALS Compare how heat and pressure cause changes over the large and small areas shown above.

Most metamorphic rocks develop bands of minerals.

VOCABULARY
Add a magnet word diagram for *foliation* to your notebook.

Some buildings have floors covered with tiles of the metamorphic rock slate. This rock is especially useful for tiles because it displays foliation, a common property of metamorphic rocks. **Foliation** is an arrangement of minerals in flat or wavy parallel bands. Slate can be split into thin sheets along the boundaries between its flat bands of minerals.

You may be familiar with the word *foliage.* Both *foliage* and *foliation* come from the Latin word *folium,* meaning "leaf." Foliated rocks either split easily into leaflike sheets or have bands of minerals that are lined up and easy to see.

Foliated Rocks

Foliation develops when rocks are under pressure. Foliation is common in rocks produced by metamorphic changes that affect large areas. However, as you will see, a metamorphic rock that consists almost entirely of one type of mineral does not show foliation.

Foliation in Metamorphic Rocks

Metamorphic rocks that contain several minerals develop foliation under pressure.

phyllite

Phyllite is a foliated metamorphic rock that contains several types of minerals.

marble

Marble is a nonfoliated metamorphic rock that consists almost entirely of only one mineral.

Foliated

Using a microscope, you can see that the minerals are lined up in bands.

Nonfoliated

The mineral crystals in this rock are not lined up.

READING VISUALS Compare the pictures of the minerals in the foliated rock and the nonfoliated rock. What is different about their arrangements?

Foliation develops when minerals flatten out or line up in bands. At low levels of metamorphism, the bands are extremely thin, as in slate. With higher pressure and temperature, the mineral mica can grow and make the rock look shiny, as is common in phyllite and schist. At even higher levels of metamorphism, the minerals in the rock tend to separate into light and dark bands, like those in gneiss.

 CHECK YOUR READING How do rocks change as foliation develops?

Nonfoliated Rocks

Metamorphic rocks that do not show foliation are called nonfoliated rocks. One reason a metamorphic rock may not display foliation is that it is made up mainly of one type of mineral, so that different minerals cannot separate and line up in layers. One common nonfoliated metamorphic rock is marble, which develops from limestone. Marble is used as a decorative stone. It is good for carving and sculpting. Because marble is nonfoliated, it does not split into layers as an artist is working with it. Another example of a nonfoliated rock is quartzite. It forms from sandstone that is made up almost entirely of pieces of quartz.

Another reason that a metamorphic rock may lack foliation is that it has not been subjected to high pressure. Hornfels is a metamorphic rock that can form when a rock is subjected to high temperatures. Hornfels, which often forms when magma or lava touches other rock, is nonfoliated.

 CHECK YOUR READING What are two reasons a metamorphic rock might not show foliation?

3.4 Review

KEY CONCEPTS

1. What conditions can cause a sedimentary or igneous rock to change into a metamorphic rock?

2. How do new minerals grow within existing rocks?

3. Why do bands of minerals develop in most metamorphic rocks?

CRITICAL THINKING

4. **Draw Conclusions** Would gneiss be more likely to form at shallow depths or at great depths where mountains are being pushed up? Why?

5. **Infer** Would you expect to find foliated or nonfoliated metamorphic rocks next to a lava flow? Why?

CHALLENGE

6. **Synthesize** What features of sedimentary rocks are unlikely to be found in metamorphic rocks? What features of metamorphic rocks do not occur in sedimentary rocks?

CHAPTER INVESTIGATION

Rock Classification

OVERVIEW AND PURPOSE In this activity you will examine rock samples and refer to a rock classification key. You will classify each sample as igneous, sedimentary, or metamorphic.

▶ Procedure

1. Make a data table like the one shown on the **Science Notebook** page.

2. Get a numbered rock sample. Record its number in your data table.

3. Observe the sample as a whole. Then closely examine it with the hand lens. Record in your table all visible properties of the sample. For example, include properties such as mineral or sediment size, layering, or banding.

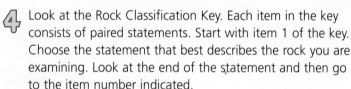

step 3

4. Look at the Rock Classification Key. Each item in the key consists of paired statements. Start with item 1 of the key. Choose the statement that best describes the rock you are examining. Look at the end of the statement and then go to the item number indicated.

MATERIALS
- magnifying glass
- 6–8 rock samples
- Rock Classification Key

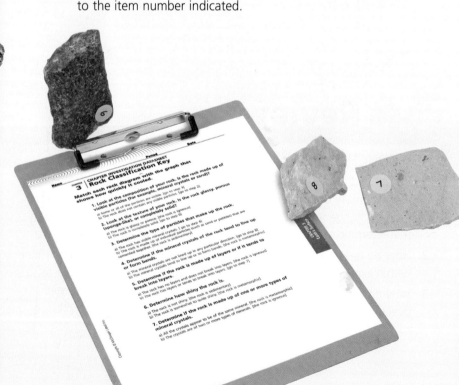

5 Examine the rock sample again and choose the statement that best describes the rock.

6 Continue to work through the key until your choices lead you to a classification that fits your rock. Repeat steps 2–5 for each of the numbered samples.

▶ Observe and Analyze   Write It Up

1. **INTERPRET** Referring to the Rock Classification Key and the observations you recorded, write the type of each rock in your data table.

2. **IDENTIFY LIMITS** What problems, if any, did you experience in applying the key? Which samples did not seem to fit easily into a category? How could you improve the key?

▶ Conclude   Write It Up

1. **COMPARE AND CONTRAST** How are igneous and metamorphic rocks similar? How can you tell them apart?

2. **ANALYZE** Examine a sample of sedimentary rock in which visible particles are cemented together. In addition to sight, what other sense could help you classify this sample?

3. **APPLY** What have you learned from this investigation that would help you make a classification key that someone else could follow? How might you make a key to classify the recordings in a music collection? Write two pairs of numbered statements that would start the classification process.

▶ INVESTIGATE Further

CHALLENGE Make a rock classification key to distinguish between rocks from Earth and rocks from the Moon. Here are some facts to consider. The surface of the Moon was once covered by a thick layer of magma. The Moon has no running water and almost no atmosphere. Minerals on Earth often contain tiny amounts of water. Minerals on the Moon almost never contain any water. The Moon does not have processes that can cause a rock to change into another type of rock.

An astronaut photographed this rock on the Moon. The rock sits in a valley that formed 4 billion years ago. The rock may not have changed or moved since that time.

Rock Classification
Observe and Analyze
Table 1. Rock Sample Properties

Sample Number	Description of Visible Properties	Rock Type

Conclude

3

the BIG idea

Rocks change into other rocks over time.

CONTENT REVIEW
CLASSZONE.COM

◀ KEY CONCEPTS SUMMARY

3.1 **The rock cycle shows how rocks change.**

Processes at Earth's surface and heat within Earth cause rocks to change into other types of rocks.

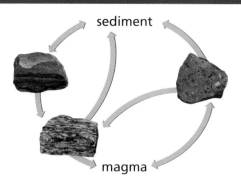
sediment

magma

VOCABULARY
rock p. 75
rock cycle p. 78
igneous rock p. 78
sedimentary rock p. 78
metamorphic rock p. 78

3.2 **Igneous rocks form from molten rock.**

As molten rock cools, minerals crystallize and form igneous rocks.

igneous

Extrusive igneous rocks cool quickly at Earth's surface.

Intrusive igneous rocks cool slowly within Earth.

VOCABULARY
intrusive igneous rock p. 83
extrusive igneous rock p. 83

3.3 **Sedimentary rocks form from earlier rocks.**

Layers of sedimentary rocks form as
• sediments are pressed or cemented together
• dissolved minerals re-form as water evaporates

sedimentary

Larger particles of sediment settle faster.

VOCABULARY
sediment p. 89

3.4 **Metamorphic rocks form as existing rocks change.**

Metamorphic rocks form as the structures of the parent rocks change and as their minerals recrystallize.

metamorphic

shale

heat and pressure

schist

VOCABULARY
metamorphism p. 96
recrystallization p. 97
foliation p. 100

Reviewing Vocabulary

Copy and complete the chart below. There may be more than one correct response.

Rock Type	Forms From	Example
		Identifying characteristic
intrusive igneous rock	magma	**1.**
		large mineral crystals
extrusive igneous rock	**2.**	basalt
		3.
sedimentary rock	**4.**	conglomerate
		contains large pieces of earlier rocks
sedimentary rock	ancient plant remains	**5.**
		may contain plant fossils
sedimentary rock	**6.**	limestone
		7.
foliated metamorphic rock	parent rock that has several types of minerals	**8.**
		minerals are lined up
nonfoliated metamorphic rock	**9.**	**10.**
		11.

Reviewing Key Concepts

Multiple Choice *Choose the letter of the best answer.*

12. The three groups of rock are sedimentary, metamorphic, and
  a. limestone
  b. granite
  c. igneous
  d. coal

13. The rock cycle shows how rocks continually
  a. increase in size
  b. increase in number
  c. become more complex
  d. change over time

14. Which kind of rock forms when molten rock cools?
  a. metamorphic
  b. sedimentary
  c. igneous
  d. extrusive

15. An existing rock can change into another type of rock when it is subjected to great
  a. pressure
  b. winds
  c. flooding
  d. foliation

16. Which kind of rock forms by recrystallization?
  a. intrusive igneous
  b. extrusive igneous
  c. sedimentary
  d. metamorphic

17. Geologists classify an igneous rock on the basis of its crystal size and the amount of _____ its minerals contain.
  a. carbon
  b. silica
  c. sediment
  d. foliation

18. Pieces of rock can settle from water and get cemented into
  a. metamorphic rock
  b. sedimentary rock
  c. igneous rock
  d. extrusive rock

19. Rock salt is an example of a sedimentary rock that develops from dissolved minerals as
  a. water evaporates
  b. magma cools
  c. sediments break down
  d. sand settles in water

Short Answer *Write a short answer to each question.*

20. What is the difference between a rock and a mineral?

21. Compare the distribution of rock types at Earth's surface to their distribution in the entire crust. How are any differences related to processes occurring in the rock cycle?

22. How is the texture of an igneous rock related to the rate at which it cooled?

Thinking Critically

Use the photograph below to answer the next four questions.

23. INFER What are the dark markings on the rock?

24. OBSERVE Which of the three groups of rocks does this rock belong to? How do you know?

25. SUMMARIZE Describe the process by which this rock most likely formed.

26. PREDICT If this rock were subjected to metamorphism, how might it change?

27. APPLY Copy and complete the concept map below.

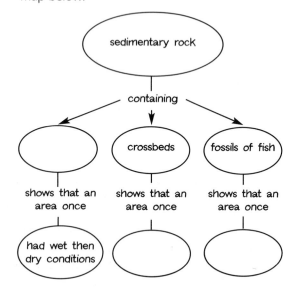

PREDICT Which of the three rock types—igneous, sedimentary, or metamorphic—would you be most likely to find in each area?

Area	Rock Type
28. the bottom of a large lake	
29. older rock surrounding an igneous intrusion	
30. a lava flow from a volcano	
31. a part of the surface that was once deep within a mountain range	
32. the sides of a cave	

the **BIG** idea

33. ANALYZE Look again at the photograph on pages 72–73. Using your knowledge of the rock cycle, draw a diagram showing how sedimentary rocks can form cliffs at Earth's surface. Then add to the diagram by showing how the rocks are likely to change over time.

34. CONNECT Describe how material in a rock near the top of a mountain can later be used by an ocean organism in forming its shell.

UNIT PROJECTS

Check your schedule for your unit project. How are you doing? Be sure that you've placed data or notes from your research in your project folder.

Analyzing a Diagram

*This diagram shows a simple version of the rock cycle.
Use it to answer the questions below.*

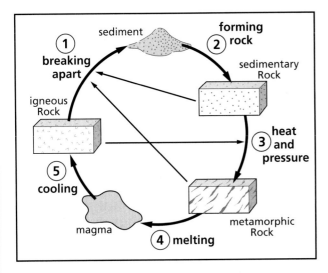

1. Where are loose materials developing into rock?

a. 1   c. 4

b. 2   d. 5

2. Where are sand and other small particles forming from rock?

a. 1   c. 4

b. 2   d. 5

3. Where is magma developing into rock?

a. 1   c. 4

b. 3   d. 5

4. Where is molten rock forming?

a. 1   c. 4

b. 3   d. 5

5. Where are heat and pressure changing solid rock into another type of rock without melting it?

a. 1   c. 4

b. 3   d. 5

6. According to the diagram, what can happen to sedimentary rock?

a. It can become sediment or magma.

b. It can become igneous rock or magma.

c. It can become sediment or metamorphic rock.

d. It can become sediment, metamorphic rock, or magma.

7. How could you change the diagram to show that igneous rock can become magma again?

a. Add an arrow from igneous rock to metamorphic rock.

b. Add an arrow from heat and pressure to igneous rock.

c. Add an arrow from igneous rock to melting.

d. Add an arrow from melting to igneous rock.

8. What must happen to rock that formed inside Earth before it can become sediment?

a. It must reach the surface as rock above it wears away.

b. It must become magma and erupt from a volcano.

c. Heat and pressure must change it into sediment.

d. It must become sedimentary rock while inside Earth.

Extended Response

Answer the two questions below in detail. Include some of the terms shown in the word box. In your answers underline each term you use.

| pressed together   buried   mineral crystals |
| cooling time |

9. Most sedimentary rock forms from pieces of existing rocks. Explain why coal is an unusual sedimentary rock and how coal forms.

10. Melba is trying to decide whether an igneous rock formed deep inside Earth or at the surface. What should she look for? Why?

TIMELINES in Science

HISTORY OF THE EARTH SYSTEM

Systems of air, water, rocks, and living organisms have developed on Earth during the planet's 4.6 billion years of history. More and more scientists have become curious about how these parts of Earth work together. Today, scientists think of these individual systems as part of one large Earth system.

The timeline shows a few events in the history of the Earth system. Scientists have developed special tools and procedures to study this history. The boxes below the timeline show how technology has led to new knowledge about the Earth system and how that knowledge has been applied.

4.6 BYA

Earth Forms in New Solar System
The Sun and nine planets, one of which is Earth, form out of a cloud of gas and dust. Earth forms and grows larger as particles collide with it. While Earth is still young, a slightly smaller object smashes into it and sends huge amounts of material flying into space. Some of this material forms a new object—the Moon.

EVENTS

5 BYA
Billion Years Ago

APPLICATIONS AND TECHNOLOGY

TECHNOLOGY

Measuring Age of Solar System
In 1956, Clair C. Patterson published his estimate that the solar system was 4.55 billion years old. Previously, scientists had learned how to use radioactive elements present in rocks to measure their ages. Patterson used this technology to determine the ages of meteorites that were formed along with the solar system and later fell to Earth. Since 1956, scientists have studied more samples and used new technologies. These studies have generally confirmed Patterson's estimate.

This iron meteorite fell in Siberia in 1947. Data from such meteorites are clues to how and when the solar system formed.

4.4 BYA

Earth Gains Atmosphere, Ocean

Earth's atmosphere forms as volcanoes release gases, including water vapor. Though some gases escape into space, Earth's gravity holds most of them close to the planet. The atmosphere contains no free oxygen. As Earth starts to cool, the water vapor becomes water droplets and falls as rain. Oceans begin to form.

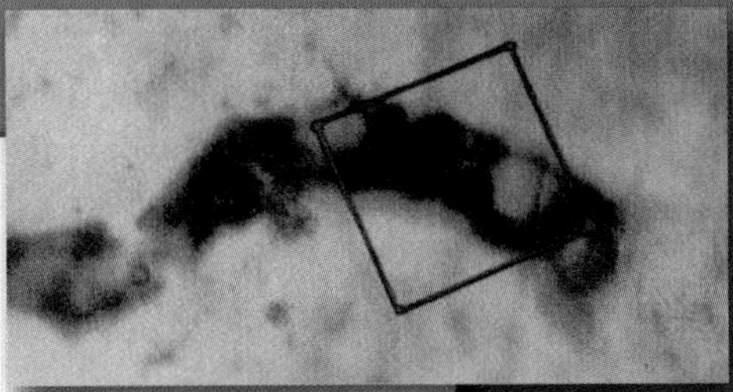

3.5 BYA

Organisms Affect Earth System

Tiny organisms use energy from sunlight to make their food, giving off oxygen as a waste product. The oxygen combines with other gases and with minerals. It may be another billion years before free oxygen starts to build up in the atmosphere.

1.8 BYA

First Supercontinent Forms

All of Earth's continents come together to form one huge supercontinent. The continents and ocean basins are still moving and changing.
This supercontinent will break apart in the future. New supercontinents will form and break apart as time goes on.

4 BYA   **3 BYA**   **2 BYA**   **1 BYA**

APPLICATION

Measuring Ozone Levels

In 1924, scientists developed the first instrument to measure ozone, the Dobson spectrophotometer. Ozone is a molecule that consists of three oxygen atoms. In the 1970s, scientists realized that levels of ozone in the upper atmosphere were falling. Countries have taken action to preserve the ozone layer, which protects organisms—including humans—from dangerous ultraviolet radiation. Today, computers process ozone data as they are collected and make them quickly available to researchers around the world.

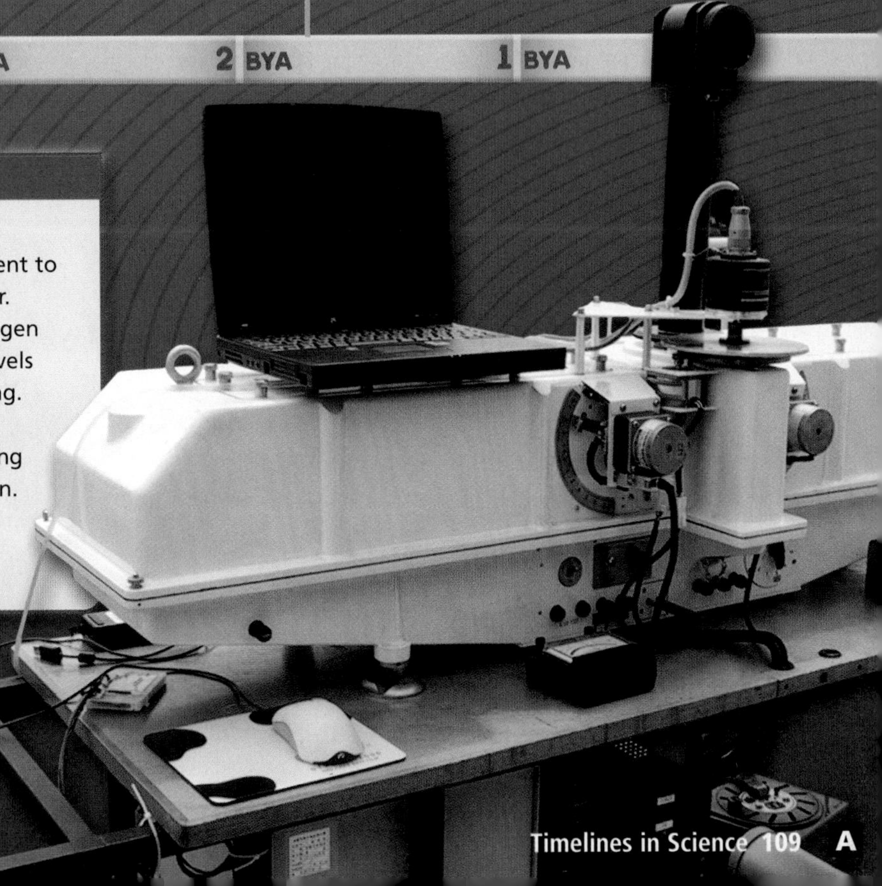

A Dobson spectrophotometer measures the total amount of ozone in the atmosphere above it.

600 MYA
New Animals Appear

The first multi-celled animals appear in the ocean. Some types of these animals are fastened to the sea floor and get food from particles in water flowing past them. Worms are the most complex type of animals to appear so far.

480 MYA
Plants Appear on Land

The earliest plants appear. These plants, perhaps similar to mosses, join the lichens that already live on land. Through photosynthesis, plants and lichens decrease the amount of carbon dioxide in the air and increase the amount of oxygen. These changes may lead to the eventual development of large, complex animals.

200 MYA
Atlantic Ocean Forms

Earth's continents, which have been combined into the supercontinent Pangaea, start to separate. As what are now the continents of North America and Africa spread apart, the Atlantic Ocean forms.

| 800 MYA | 600 MYA | 400 MYA | 200 MYA |

Million Years Ago

TECHNOLOGY

Ocean-Floor Core Samples

In the 1960s, scientists began drilling holes into the sea floor to collect long cores, or columns, of sediment and rock. The cores give clues about Earth's climate, geology, and forms of life for millions of years.

The research ship *JOIDES Resolution* has a drilling rig built into it. Equipment attached to the rig is lowered to the sea floor to collect core samples.

12,000 years ago
Earth Emerges from Ice—Again
Earth's temperature warms slightly. Kilometers-thick ice sheets that formed during the latest of Earth's many ice ages start to melt. Forests and grasslands expand. Sea level rises about 100 meters (330 ft), and the ocean floods the edges of the continents.

1972
New View of Earth
Harrison "Jack" Schmitt, an astronaut traveling 24,000 kilometers (15,000 mi) above Earth, takes a photograph. It is the first to show Earth fully lit by the Sun, and the image is sometimes called the Blue Marble. It helps people see the planet as one system.

RESOURCE CENTER
CLASSZONE.COM

Learn more about the Earth system.

100 MYA   Today

APPLICATION

International Space Station
The International Space Station has laboratories in which scientists study Earth, the solar system, and the universe. Also, scientists are doing research to better understand the effects of very low gravity on people. This work is part of an effort to develop the life-support systems needed for people to remain in space a long time. Eventually it might aid in the further exploration of space by humans.

INTO THE FUTURE

In almost every area of life, from music to food to sports, the world has become more connected. Science is no exception. In the past century, scientists have begun to monitor the ozone layer. They have realized that the processes that cause continents to change positions also cause earthquakes and volcanic eruptions to occur.

Changes in technology are likely to help scientists increase their understanding of the Earth system. For example, instruments on artificial satellites measure changes in clouds, ocean life, and land temperatures. These types of data help scientists understand how changes in one part of Earth affect other parts.

ACTIVITIES

Taking a Core Sample
Add layers of damp sand of different colors to a paper cup. Switch cups with a partner. Press a clear straw through the sand, put your finger over the top of the straw, and pull the straw out. Determine the order in which your partner added the sand layers. How would you know if there was a layer of sand that did not go across the entire cup?

Writing About Science
Imagine you are living in micro-gravity like the astronauts on the International Space Station. Write a detailed description of two hours of your day.

CHAPTER 4

Weathering and Soil Formation

the **BIG** idea

Natural forces break rocks apart and form soil, which supports life.

How is rock related to soil?

Key Concepts

SECTION
4.1 Mechanical and chemical forces break down rocks.
Learn about the natural forces that break down rocks.

SECTION
4.2 Weathering and organic processes form soil.
Learn about the formation and properties of soil.

SECTION
4.3 Human activities affect soil.
Learn how land use affects soil and how soil can be protected and conserved.

Internet Preview

CLASSZONE.COM

Chapter 4 online resources: Content Review, two Visualizations, two Resource Centers, Math Tutorial, Test Practice

EXPLORE (the BIG idea)

Ice Power

Fill a plastic container to the top with water and seal the lid tightly. Place it in the freezer overnight. Check on your container the next morning.

Observe and Think
What happened to the container? Why?

Getting the Dirt on Soil

Remove the top and bottom of a tin can. Be careful of sharp edges. Measure and mark 2 cm from one end of the can. Insert the can 2 cm into the ground, up to the mark. Fill the can with water and time how long it takes for the can to drain. Repeat the procedure in a different location.

Observe and Think
What do you think affects how long it takes for soil to absorb water?

Internet Activity:
Soil Formation

Go to **ClassZone.com** to watch how soil forms. Learn how materials break down and contribute to soil buildup over time.

Observe and Think
What do rocks and soil have in common? What do organic matter and soil have in common?

NSTA
scilinks.org
SCiLINKS

Soil Conservation Code: MDL016

Getting Ready to Learn

CONCEPT REVIEW

- The atmosphere, hydrosphere, biosphere, and geosphere interact to shape Earth's surface.
- Natural processes form, change, break down, and re-form rocks.

VOCABULARY REVIEW

cleavage p. 53

fracture p. 53

rock p. 75

rock cycle p. 78

sediment p. 89

CONTENT REVIEW
CLASSZONE.COM
Review concepts and vocabulary.

TAKING NOTES

COMBINATION NOTES

To take notes about a new concept, first make an informal outline of the information. Then make a sketch of the concept and label it so that you can study it later.

CHOOSE YOUR OWN STRATEGY

Take notes about new vocabulary terms, using one or more of the strategies from earlier chapters—**magnet word, word triangle,** or **description wheel.** Feel free to mix and match the strategies, or use an entirely different vocabulary strategy.

See the Note-Taking Handbook on pages R45–R51.

SCIENCE NOTEBOOK

NOTES

Causes of Mechanical Weathering
- Ice
- Pressure Release
- Plant Roots
- Moving Water

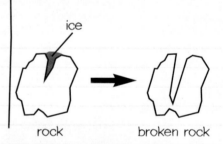

rock   broken rock

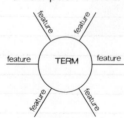

Description Wheel

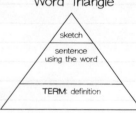

Word Triangle

Magnet Word

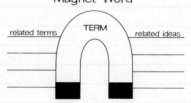

KEY CONCEPT

Mechanical and chemical forces break down rocks.

◀ **BEFORE, you learned**

- Minerals make up most rocks
- Different minerals have different properties
- Rocks are broken down to form sediments

▶ **NOW, you will learn**

- How mechanical weathering breaks down rocks
- How chemical weathering changes rocks
- What factors affect the rate at which weathering occurs

VOCABULARY

weathering p. 115
mechanical weathering
 p. 116
exfoliation p. 116
abrasion p. 116
chemical weathering
 p. 118

EXPLORE Mechanical Weathering

What causes rocks to break down?

PROCEDURE

① Place a handful of rocks on a piece of dark-colored construction paper. Observe the rocks and take notes on their appearance.

② Place the rocks in a coffee can. Put the lid on the can and shake the can forcefully for 2 minutes, holding the lid tightly shut.

③ Pour the rocks onto the construction paper. Observe them and take notes on any changes in their appearance.

WHAT DO YOU THINK?

- What happened to the rocks and why?
- What forces in nature might affect rocks in similar ways?

MATERIALS

- coffee can with lid
- rocks
- dark-colored construction paper

Weathering breaks rocks into smaller pieces.

Think about the tiniest rock you have ever found. How did it get so small? It didn't start out that way! Over time, natural forces break rocks into smaller and smaller pieces. If you have ever seen a concrete sidewalk or driveway that has been cracked by tree roots, you have seen this process. The same thing can happen to rocks.

Weathering is the process by which natural forces break down rocks. In this section you will read about two kinds of weathering. One kind occurs when a rock is physically broken apart—like the cracked sidewalk. Another kind occurs when a chemical reaction changes the makeup of a rock.

VOCABULARY
Remember to add *weathering* to your notebook, using the vocabulary strategy of your choice.

Chapter 4: **Weathering and Soil Formation** 115 **A**

Mechanical weathering produces physical changes in rocks.

RESOURCE CENTER
CLASSZONE.COM

Learn more about weathering.

If you smash a walnut with a hammer, you will break it into a lot of small pieces, but you will not change what it is. Even though the pieces of the walnut are no longer connected together, they are still composed of the same materials. **Mechanical weathering**—the breaking up of rocks by physical forces—works in much the same way. In this natural process, physical forces split rocks apart but do not change their composition—what they are made of. Ice wedging, pressure release, plant root growth, and abrasion can all cause mechanical weathering.

READING TIP

The word *expand* means "to increase in size or volume."

1 Ice Wedging When water freezes, it expands. When water freezes in the cracks and pores of rocks, the force of its expansion is strong enough to split the rocks apart. This process, which is called ice wedging, can break up huge boulders. Ice wedging is common in places where temperatures rise above and fall below the freezing point for water, which is 0°C (32°F).

2 Pressure Release Rock deep within Earth is under great pressure from surrounding rocks. Over time, Earth's forces can push the rock up to the surface, or the overlying rocks and sediment can wear away. In either case, the pressure inside the rock is still high, but the pressure on the surface of the rock is released. This release of pressure causes the rock to expand. As the rock expands, cracks form in it, leading to exfoliation. **Exfoliation** (ehks-FOH-lee-AY-shuhn) is a process in which layers or sheets of rock gradually break off. This process is sometimes called onion-skin weathering, because the rock surface breaks off in thin layers similar to the layers of an onion.

3 Plant Root Growth Trees, bushes, and other plants may take root in cracks in rocks. As the roots of these plants grow, they wedge open the cracks. The rock—even if it is large—can be split completely apart.

4 Abrasion Water can wear down rocks on riverbeds and along shorelines by abrasion. **Abrasion** (uh-BRAY-zhuhn) is the process of wearing down by friction, the rubbing of one object or surface against another. The force of moving water alone can wear away particles of rock. Water also causes rocks to tumble downstream. The tumbling rocks wear down as they grind against the riverbed and against each other. Ocean waves beating against a rocky shore also wear down rocks by abrasion.

 CHECK YOUR READING How does moving water weather rocks?

Mechanical Weathering

Ice wedging, pressure release, plant root growth, and abrasion can all break apart rocks.

① Ice Wedging

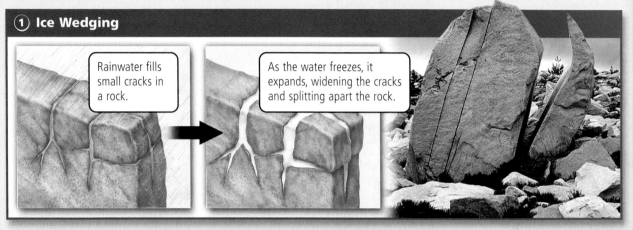

Rainwater fills small cracks in a rock.

As the water freezes, it expands, widening the cracks and splitting apart the rock.

② Pressure Release

Earth's forces can push rock that formed deep underground up to the surface.

The release of pressure causes the rock to expand and crack.

③ Plant Root Growth

When plants grow in cracks in a rock, their roots can widen the cracks and force the rock apart.

④ Abrasion

Flowing water can move rocks, causing them to rub together and wear down into rounded shapes.

READING VISUALS What evidence of mechanical weathering can you see in each photograph above?

Chemical weathering changes the mineral composition of rocks.

VISUALIZATION
CLASSZONE.COM

Watch chemical weathering in action.

If you have seen an old rusty nail, you have witnessed the result of a chemical reaction and a chemical change. The steel in the nail contains iron. Oxygen in air and water react with the iron to form rust.

Minerals in rocks also undergo chemical changes when they react with water and air. **Chemical weathering** is the breakdown of rocks by chemical reactions that change the rocks' makeup, or composition. When minerals in rocks come into contact with air and water, some dissolve and others react and are changed into different minerals.

Dissolving

Water is the main cause of chemical weathering. Some minerals completely dissolve in ordinary water. The mineral halite, which is the same compound as table salt, dissolves in ordinary water. Many more minerals dissolve in water that is slightly acidic—like lemonade. In the atmosphere, small amounts of carbon dioxide dissolve in rainwater. The water and carbon dioxide react to form a weak acid. After falling to Earth, the rainwater moves through the soil, picking up additional

INVESTIGATE Chemical Weathering

What is necessary for rust to form?

PROCEDURE

1. Place a piece of steel wool in a cup filled to the top with water. Place a second piece of steel wool in a cup with a small amount of water. The water should touch but not cover the steel wool. Place a third piece in a cup with no water.

2. Allow the three cups to sit overnight. Observe the appearance of the steel wool in each container the next day.

WHAT DO YOU THINK?

• What happened to the steel wool in each cup?

• Judging by the appearance of the pieces of steel wool, what do you think is necessary for rusting to occur?

CHALLENGE Tear the steel wool that rusted most apart and compare the appearances of the inside and the outside. Why might the inside and the outside look different?

SKILL FOCUS
Identifying variables

MATERIALS
• steel wool
• 3 cups
• water

TIME
15 minutes

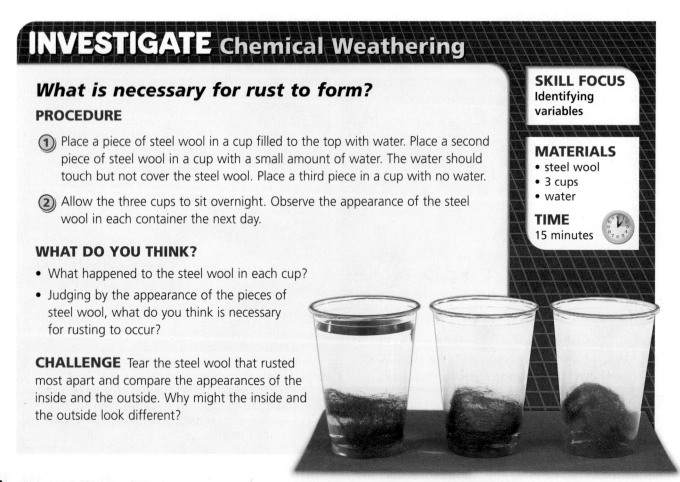

About 100 Years Ago

Today

READING VISUALS **INFER** This ancient stone monument was moved from a desert in Egypt to New York City in 1881. How and why has it changed?

carbon dioxide from decaying plants. The slightly acidic water breaks down minerals in rocks. In the process, the rocks may also break apart into smaller pieces.

Air pollution can make rainwater even more acidic than it is naturally. Power plants and automobiles produce gases such as sulfur dioxide and nitric oxide, which react with water vapor in the atmosphere to form acid rain. Acid rain causes rocks to weather much faster than they would naturally. The photographs above show how acid rain can damage a granite column in just a hundred years.

Rusting

The oxygen in the air is also involved in chemical weathering. Many common minerals contain iron. When these minerals dissolve in water, oxygen in the air and the water combines with the iron to produce iron oxides, or rust. The iron oxides form a coating that colors the weathered rocks like those you see in the photograph of Oak Creek Canyon in Arizona.

The rocks in Oak Creek Canyon are reddish because iron in the rocks reacted with water and air to produce iron oxides.

CHECK YOUR READING How is air involved in chemical weathering?

Weathering occurs at different rates.

COMBINATION NOTES
Record in your notes three factors that affect the rate at which rock weathers.

Most weathering occurs over long periods of time—hundreds, thousands, or even millions of years. It can take hundreds or thousands of years for a very hard rock to wear down only a few millimeters—a few times the thickness of your fingernail. But the rate of weathering is not the same for all rocks. Factors such as surface area, rock composition, and location influence the rate of weathering.

Surface Area The more of a rock's surface that is exposed to air and water, the faster the rock will break down. A greater surface area allows chemical weathering to affect more of a rock.

① Over time, mechanical weathering breaks a rock into smaller pieces.

② As a result, more of the rock's surface is exposed to chemical weathering.

Rock Composition Different kinds of rock break down at different rates. Granite, for example, breaks down much more slowly than limestone. Both of these rocks are often used for tombstones and statues.

Climate Water is needed for chemical weathering to occur, and heat speeds up chemical weathering. As a result, chemical weathering occurs faster in hot, wet regions than it does in cold, dry regions. However, mechanical weathering caused by freezing and thawing occurs more in cold regions than in hot regions.

 Review

KEY CONCEPTS

1. What is weathering?
2. What are four causes of mechanical weathering?
3. How do water and air help cause chemical weathering?
4. Describe three factors that affect the rate at which weathering occurs.

CRITICAL THINKING

5. **Infer** How does mechanical weathering affect the rate of chemical weathering?
6. **Predict** Would weathering affect a marble sculpture inside a museum? Explain your answer.

⚫ CHALLENGE

7. **Infer** The word *weather* is most commonly used to refer to the state of the atmosphere at a certain time. Why do you think the same word is used to refer to the breakdown of rocks?

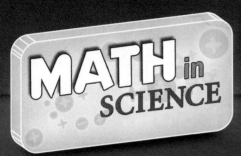

MATH in SCIENCE

MATH TUTORIAL

Click on Math Tutorial for more help with finding the surface areas of rectangular prisms.

Weathering has broken apart these rocks in the Isles of Scilly, England.

Rock Weathering

How quickly a rock weathers depends, in part, on its surface area. The greater the surface area, the more quickly the rock weathers. Do you think a rock will weather more quickly if you break it in half? You can find out by using a rectangular prism to represent the rock.

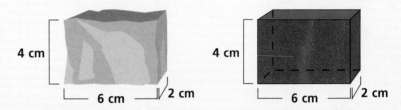

Example

To find the surface area of the prism, add the areas of its faces.

(1) Find the area of each face.

Area of top (or bottom) face: 6 cm × 2 cm = 12 cm^2
Area of front (or back) face: 6 cm × 4 cm = 24 cm^2
Area of right (or left) face: 4 cm × 2 cm = 8 cm^2

(2) Add the areas of all six faces to find the surface area.

Surface area = 12 cm^2 + 12 cm^2 + 24 cm^2 + 24 cm^2
+ 8 cm^2 + 8 cm^2
= 88 cm^2

ANSWER The surface area of the prism is 88 cm^2.

For the rock broken in half, you can use two smaller rectangular prisms to represent the two halves.

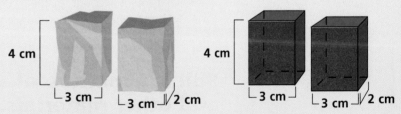

Answer the following questions.

1. What is the surface area of each of the smaller rectangular prisms?

2. How does the total surface area of the two smaller prisms compare with the surface area of the larger prism?

3. Will the rock weather more quickly in one piece or broken in half?

CHALLENGE If the two smaller prisms both broke in half, what would be the total surface area of the resulting four prisms?

KEY CONCEPT

4.2 Weathering and organic processes form soil.

 BEFORE, you learned

- Weathering processes break down rocks
- Climate influences the rate of weathering

 NOW, you will learn

- What soil consists of
- How climate and landforms affect a soil's characteristics
- How the activities of organisms affect a soil's characteristics
- How the properties of soil differ

VOCABULARY

humus p. 123
soil horizon p. 124
soil profile p. 124

EXPLORE Soil Composition

What makes soils different?

PROCEDURE

① Spread some potting soil on a piece of white paper. Spread another type of soil on another piece of white paper.

② Examine the two soil samples with a hand lens. Use the tweezers to look for small pieces of rock or sand, humus, and clay. Humus is brown or black, and clay is lighter in color. Record your observations.

WHAT DO YOU THINK?

- How do the two soil samples differ? How are they alike?
- What might account for the differences between the two soils?

MATERIALS

- potting soil
- local soil sample
- white paper (2 pieces)
- hand lens
- tweezers

Soil is a mixture of weathered rock particles and other materials.

Soil may not be the first thing you think of when you wake up in the morning, but it is a very important part of your everyday life. You have spent your whole life eating food grown in soil, standing on soil, and living in buildings built on soil. Soil is under your feet right now—or at least there used to be soil there before the building you are in was constructed. In this section you will learn more about the world of soil beneath your feet.

 Why is soil important?

Soil Composition

Soil is a mixture of four materials: weathered rock particles, organic matter, water, and air. Weathered rock particles are the main ingredient of soil. Soils differ, depending on what types of rock the rock particles came from—for example, granite or limestone.

Water and air each make up about 20 to 30 percent of a soil's volume. Organic matter makes up about 5 percent. The word *organic* (awr-GAN-ihk) means "coming from living organisms." Organic matter in soil comes from the remains and waste products of plants, animals, and other living organisms. For example, leaves that fall to a forest floor decay and become part of the soil. The decayed organic matter in soil is called **humus** (HYOO-muhs).

All soils are not the same. Different soils are made up of different ingredients and different amounts of each ingredient. In the photographs below, the black soil contains much more decayed plant material than the red soil. The black soil also contains more water. The kind of soil that forms in an area depends on a number of factors, including

- the kind of rock in the area
- the area's climate, or overall weather pattern over time
- the landforms in the area, such as mountains and valleys
- the plant cover in the area
- the animals and other organisms in the area
- time

The composition of a soil determines what you can grow in it, what you can build on it, and what happens to the rainwater that falls on it.

VOCABULARY
A description wheel would be a good choice for taking notes about the term *humus*.

READING VISUALS **COMPARE AND CONTRAST** These two soils look different because they contain different ingredients. How would you describe their differences?

Soil Horizons

This soil profile in Hagerstown, Maryland, shows distinct A, B, and C horizons.

If you dig a deep hole in the ground, you might notice that the deeper soil looks different. As you dig down, you will find larger rock particles that are less weathered. There is also less organic matter in deeper soil.

Soil develops in a series of horizontal layers called soil horizons. A **soil horizon** is a layer of soil with properties that differ from those of the layer above or below it. Geologists label the main horizons A, B, and C. In some places there may also be a layer of dead leaves and other organic matter at the surface of the ground.

- **The A horizon** is the upper layer of soil and is commonly called topsoil. It contains the most organic matter of the three horizons. Because of the humus the A horizon contains, it is often dark in color.

- **The B horizon** lies just below the A horizon. It has little organic matter and is usually brownish or reddish in color. It contains clay and minerals that have washed down from the A horizon.

- **The C horizon** is the deepest layer of soil. It consists of the largest and least-weathered rock particles. Its color is typically light yellowish brown.

The soil horizons in a specific location make up what geologists call a **soil profile.** Different locations can have very different soil profiles. The A horizon, for example, may be very thick in some places and very thin in others. In some areas, one or more horizons may even be missing from the profile. For example, a soil that has had only a short time to develop might be missing the B horizon.

 CHECK YOUR READING What are soil horizons?

Climate and landforms affect soil.

COMBINATION NOTES
Record in your notes four categories of soil that form in different climate regions.

Different kinds of soils form in different climates. The soil that forms in a hot, wet climate is different from the soil of a cold, dry climate. Climate also influences the characteristics and thickness of the soil that develops from weathered rock. Tropical, desert, temperate, and arctic soils are four types of soil that form in different climate regions.

The shape of the land also affects the development of soil. For example, mountain soils may be very different from the soils in nearby valleys. The cold climate on a mountain results in slow soil formation, and the top layer of soil continually washes down off the slopes. As a result, mountain slopes have soils with thin A horizons that cannot support large plants. The soil that washes down the slopes builds up in the surrounding valleys, so the valleys may have soils with thick A horizons that can support many plants.

World Soil Types

Different types of soils form in different climates.

Tropical Soils

Tropical soils form in warm, rainy regions. Heavy rains wash away minerals, leaving only a thin surface layer of humus. Tropical soils are not suitable for growing most crops.

Desert Soils

Desert soils form in dry regions. These soils are shallow and contain little organic matter. Because of the low rainfall, chemical weathering and soil formation occur very slowly in desert regions.

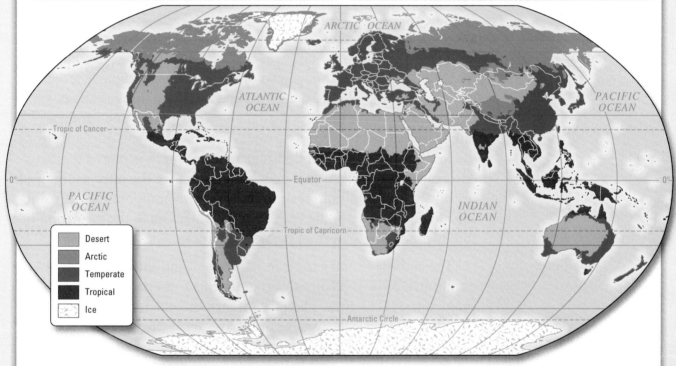

ARCTIC OCEAN

ATLANTIC OCEAN

PACIFIC OCEAN

Tropic of Cancer

0°

PACIFIC OCEAN

Equator

INDIAN OCEAN

Tropic of Capricorn

0°

Antarctic Circle

Legend:
- Desert
- Arctic
- Temperate
- Tropical
- Ice

Temperate Soils

Temperate soils form in regions with moderate rainfall and temperatures. Some temperate soils are dark-colored, rich in organic matter and minerals, and good for growing crops.

Arctic Soils

Arctic soils form in cold, dry regions where chemical weathering is slow. They typically do not have well-developed horizons. Arctic soils contain a lot of rock fragments.

The activities of organisms affect soil.

COMBINATION NOTES
Record in your notes three types of organisms that affect soil characteristics.

READING TiP
A decomposer is an organism that decomposes, or breaks down, dead plants and animals.

Under the ground beneath your feet is a whole world of life forms that are going about their daily activities. The living organisms in a soil have a huge impact on the soil's characteristics. In fact, without them, the soil would not be able to support the wide variety of plants that people depend on to live. The organisms that affect the characteristics of soils include plants, microorganisms (MY-kroh-AWR-guh-NIHZ-uhmz), and animals.

Plants, such as trees and grasses, provide most of the organic matter that gets broken down to form humus. Trees add to the organic matter in soil as they lose their branches and leaves. Trees and other plants also contribute to humus when they die and decompose, or break down.

 CHECK YOUR READING How are plants and humus related?

Microorganisms include decomposers such as bacteria and fungi (FUHN-jy). The prefix *micro-* means "very small." Microorganisms are so small that they can be seen only with a microscope. A spoonful of soil may contain more than a million microorganisms! These microorganisms decompose dead plants and animals and produce nutrients that plants need to grow. Plants absorb these nutrients from the soil through their roots. Nitrogen, for example, is one of the nutrients plants need to grow. Microorganisms change the nitrogen in dead organic matter—and nitrogen in the air—into compounds that plants can absorb and use. Some bacteria also contribute to the formation of soil by producing acids that break down rocks.

The cycling of nutrients through the soil and through plants is a continual process. Plants absorb nutrients from the soil and use those nutrients to grow. Then they return the nutrients to the soil when they die or lose branches and leaves. New plants then absorb the nutrients from the soil and start the cycle over again.

Animals such as earthworms, ants, termites, mice, gophers, moles, and prairie dogs all make their homes in the soil. All of these animals loosen and mix the soil as they tunnel through it. They create spaces in the soil, thereby adding to its air content and improving its ability to absorb and drain water. Burrowing animals also bring partly weathered rock particles to the surface of the ground, where they become exposed to more weathering. Just like plants, animals return nutrients to the soil when their bodies decompose after death.

 CHECK YOUR READING How do animals affect soil? Name at least three ways.

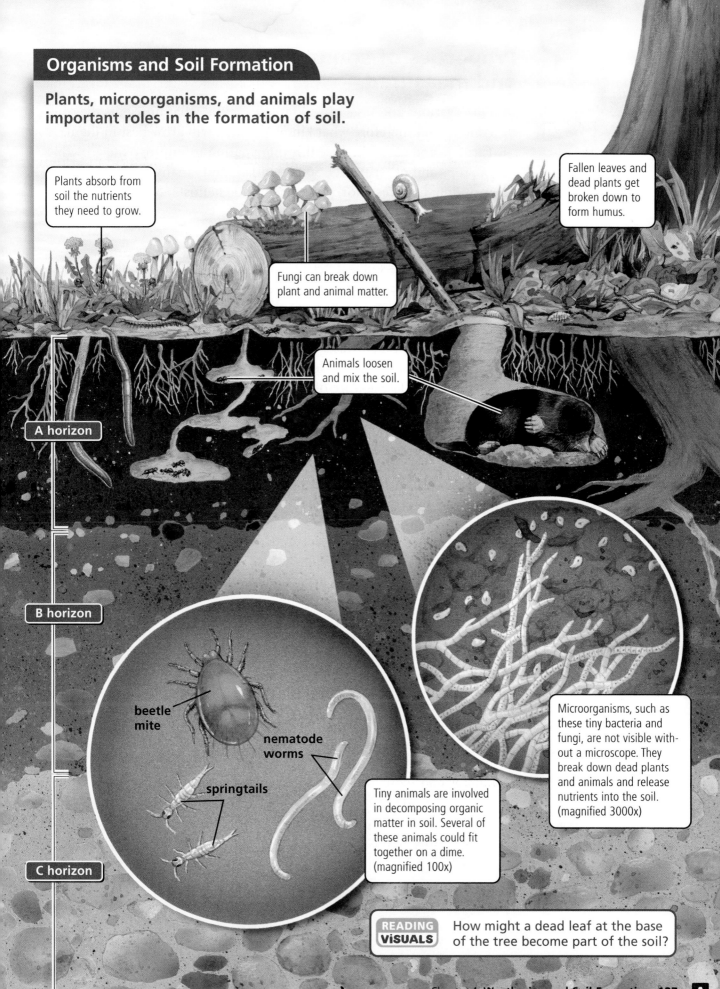

Organisms and Soil Formation

Plants, microorganisms, and animals play important roles in the formation of soil.

Plants absorb from soil the nutrients they need to grow.

Fungi can break down plant and animal matter.

Fallen leaves and dead plants get broken down to form humus.

Animals loosen and mix the soil.

A horizon

B horizon

C horizon

beetle mite

nematode worms

springtails

Tiny animals are involved in decomposing organic matter in soil. Several of these animals could fit together on a dime. (magnified 100x)

Microorganisms, such as these tiny bacteria and fungi, are not visible without a microscope. They break down dead plants and animals and release nutrients into the soil. (magnified 3000x)

READING VISUALS How might a dead leaf at the base of the tree become part of the soil?

Properties of soil can be observed and measured.

Observations and tests of soil samples reveal what nutrients the soils contain and therefore what kinds of plants will grow best in them. Farmers and gardeners use this information to improve the growth of crops and other plants. Soil scientists study many soil properties, including texture, color, pore space, and chemistry.

Texture

The texture of a soil is determined by the size of the weathered rock particles it contains. Soil scientists classify the rock particles in soils into three categories, on the basis of size: sand, silt, and clay. Sand particles are the largest and can be seen without a microscope. Silt particles are smaller than sand particles—too small to be seen without a microscope. Clay particles are the smallest. Most soils contain a mixture of sand, silt, and clay. The texture of a soil influences how easily air and water move through the soil.

Soil Texture

The texture of a soil is determined by the amounts of sand, silt, and clay it contains.

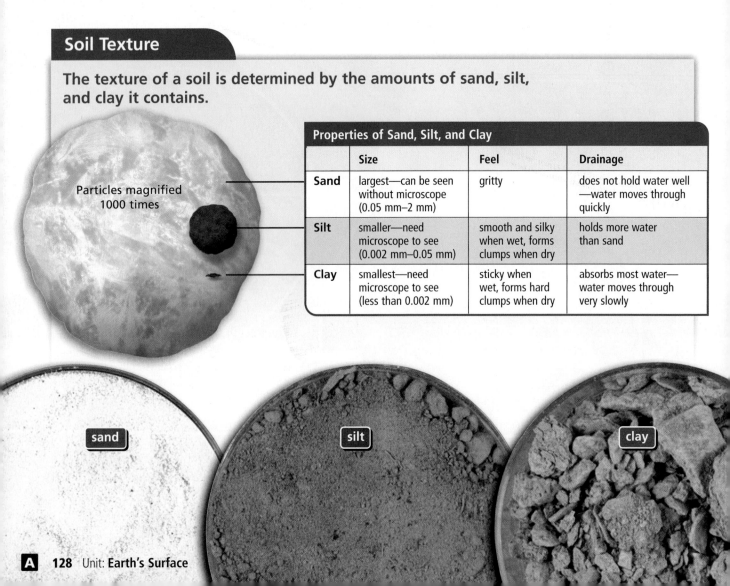

Particles magnified 1000 times

Properties of Sand, Silt, and Clay

	Size	Feel	Drainage
Sand	largest—can be seen without microscope (0.05 mm–2 mm)	gritty	does not hold water well—water moves through quickly
Silt	smaller—need microscope to see (0.002 mm–0.05 mm)	smooth and silky when wet, forms clumps when dry	holds more water than sand
Clay	smallest—need microscope to see (less than 0.002 mm)	sticky when wet, forms hard clumps when dry	absorbs most water—water moves through very slowly

sand

silt

clay

Color

The color of a soil is a clue to its other properties. Soil colors include red, brown, yellow, green, black, and even white. Most soil colors come from iron compounds and humus. Iron gives soil a reddish color. Soils with a high humus content are usually black or brown. Besides indicating the content of a soil, color may also be a clue to how well water moves through the soil—that is, how well the soil drains. Bright-colored soils, for instance, drain well.

RESOURCE CENTER
CLASSZONE.COM

Investigate soil.

Pore Space

Pore space refers to the spaces between soil particles. Water and air move through the pore spaces in a soil. Plant roots need both water and air to grow. Soils range from about 25 to 60 percent pore space. An ideal soil for growing plants has 50 percent of its volume as pore space, with half of the pore space occupied by air and half by water.

This gardener is adding lime to the soil to make it less acidic.

Chemistry

Plants absorb the nutrients they need from the water in soil. These nutrients may come from the minerals or the organic matter in the soil. To be available to plant roots, the nutrients must be dissolved in water. How well nutrients dissolve in the water in soil depends on the water's pH, which is a measure of acidity. Farmers may apply lime to make soil less acidic. To make soil more acidic, an acid may be applied.

 CHECK YOUR READING How does soil acidity affect whether the nutrients in soil are available to plants?

4.2 Review

KEY CONCEPTS

1. What are the main ingredients of soil?
2. How do climate and landforms affect soils' characteristics?
3. How do the activities of organisms affect the characteristics of soil?
4. Describe four properties of soil.

CRITICAL THINKING

5. **Compare and Contrast** How would a soil containing a lot of sand differ from a soil with a lot of clay?
6. **Infer** Which would you expect to be more fertile, the soil on hilly land or the soil on a plain? Why?

CHALLENGE

7. **Synthesize** What kinds of roots might you expect to find on plants that grow in arctic soils? Why?

CHAPTER INVESTIGATION

MATERIALS
- dried soil sample
- 250 mL graduated cylinder
- 1 qt jar, with lid
- water
- 2 L plastic bottle
- scissors
- window screening
- rubber band
- pH test strips
- clock with second hand
- *for Challenge:* Texture Flow Chart

Testing Soil

OVERVIEW AND PURPOSE Soil is necessary for life. Whether a soil is suitable for farming or construction, and whether it absorbs water when it rains, depends on the particular properties of that soil. In this investigation you will
- test a soil sample to measure several soil properties
- identify the properties of your soil sample

▶ Procedure

PORE-SPACE TEST

1. Measure 200 mL of the dried soil sample in a graduated cylinder. Pour it into the jar.

2. Rinse the graduated cylinder, then fill it with 200 mL of water. Slowly pour the water into the jar until the soil is so soaked that any additional water would pool on top.

3. Record the amount of water remaining in the graduated cylinder. Then determine by subtraction the amount you added to the soil sample. Make a soil properties chart in your **Science Notebook** and record this number in it.

4. Discard the wet soil according to your teacher's instructions, and rinse the jar.

pH TEST AND DRAINAGE TEST

5. Cut off the top of a plastic bottle and use a rubber band to attach a piece of window screening over its mouth. Place the bottle top, mouth down, into the jar.

6. Use the graduated cylinder to measure 200 mL of soil, and pour the soil into the inverted bottle top.

7. Rinse the graduated cylinder, and fill it with 100 mL of water. Test the water's pH, using a pH test strip. Record the result in the "before" space in your soil properties chart.

8. Pour the water into the soil. Measure the amount of time it takes for the first drips to fall into the jar. Record the result in your soil properties chart.

top of plastic bottle

jar

step 5

window screening

9 Once the water stops dripping, remove the bottle top. Use a new pH strip to measure the pH of the water in the jar. Record this measurement in the "after" space in your soil properties chart and note any differences in the appearance of the water before and after its filtering through the soil.

10 Discard the wet soil according to your teacher's instructions, and rinse the jar.

PARTICLE-TYPE TEST

11 Add water to the jar until it is two-thirds full. Pour in soil until the water level rises to the top of the jar, then replace the lid. Shake the jar, and set it to rest undisturbed on a countertop overnight.

12 The next day, observe the different soil layers. The sample should have separated into sand (on the bottom), silt (in the middle), and clay (on the top). Measure the height of each layer, as well as the overall height of the three layers. Record your measurements in your soil properties chart.

13 Use the following formula to calculate the percentage of each kind of particle in the sample:

$$\frac{\text{height of layer}}{\text{total height of all layers}} \times 100$$

Record your results and all calculations in your soil properties chart.

▶ Observe and Analyze *Write It Up*

1. RECORD Complete your soil properties chart.

2. IDENTIFY How did steps 1–3 test your soil sample's pore space?

3. IDENTIFY How did steps 5–9 test your soil sample's drainage rate?

▶ Conclude *Write It Up*

1. EVALUATE In step 3 you measured the amount of space between the soil particles in your sample. In step 8 you measured how quickly water passed through your sample. Are these two properties related? Explain your answer.

2. EVALUATE Would packing down or loosening up your soil sample change any of the properties you tested? Explain your answer.

3. INTERPRET What happened to the pH of the water that passed through the soil? Why do you think that happened?

4. ANALYZE Look at the percentages of sand, silt, and clay in your sample. How do the percentages help to explain the properties you observed and measured?

▶ INVESTIGATE Further

CHALLENGE Soil texture depends on the size of the weathered rock particles the soil contains. Use the Texture Flow Chart to determine the texture of your soil sample.

Testing Soil

Observe and Analyze

Table 1. Soil Properties Chart

Property	Result	Notes and Calculations
Pore space	_ mL water added	
pH	before: pH = _ after: pH = _	
Drainage	_ seconds	
Particle type	height of sand = _ cm height of silt = _ cm height of clay = _ cm total height = _ cm	

Conclude

4.3 Human activities affect soil.

 BEFORE, you learned

- Soils consist mainly of weathered rock and organic matter
- Soils vary, depending on climate
- Organisms affect the characteristics of soil
- Soil properties can be measured

 NOW, you will learn

- Why soil is a necessary resource
- How people's use of land affects soil
- How people can conserve soil

VOCABULARY

desertification p. 133

THINK ABOUT

How does land use affect soil?

Look outside for evidence of ways that people have affected the soil. Make a list of all the things that you can see or think of. Use your list to make a two-column table with the headings "Activity" and "Effects."

Soil is a necessary resource.

Soil helps sustain life on Earth—including your life. You already know that soil supports the growth of plants, which in turn supply food for animals. Therefore, soil provides you with nearly all the food you eat. But that's not all. Many other items you use, such as cotton clothing and medicines, come from plants. Lumber in your home comes from trees. Even the oxygen you breathe comes from plants.

Besides supporting the growth of plants, soil plays other life-sustaining roles. Soil helps purify, or clean, water as it drains through the ground and into rivers, lakes, and oceans. Decomposers in soil also help recycle nutrients by breaking down the remains of plants and animals, releasing nutrients that living plants use to grow. In addition, soil provides a home for a variety of living things, from tiny one-celled organisms to small mammals.

 CHECK YOUR READING Why is soil a necessary resource?

Land-use practices can harm soil.

The way people use land can affect the levels of nutrients and pollution in soil. Any activity that exposes soil to wind and rain can lead to soil loss. Farming, construction and development, and mining are among the main activities that impact soil resources.

Farming

Farming is very important to society because almost all of the world's food is grown on farms. Over the 10,000 years humans have been farming, people have continually improved their farming methods. However, farming has some harmful effects and can lead to soil loss.

COMBINATION NOTES
Remember to take notes about how farming affects soil.

Farmers often add nutrients to soil in the form of organic or artificial fertilizers to make their crops grow better. However, some fertilizers can make it difficult for microorganisms in the soil to produce nutrients naturally. Fertilizers also add to water pollution when rainwater draining from fields carries the excess nutrients to rivers, lakes, and oceans.

Over time, many farming practices lead to the loss of soil. All over the world, farmers clear trees and other plants and plow up the soil to plant crops. Without its natural plant cover, the soil is more exposed to rain and wind and is therefore more likely to get washed or blown away. American farmers lose about five metric tons of soil for each metric ton of grain they produce. In many other parts of the world, the losses are even higher.

Another problem is overgrazing. Overgrazing occurs when farm animals eat large amounts of the land cover. Overgrazing destroys natural vegetation and causes the soil to wash or blow away more easily. In many dry regions of the world, overgrazing and the clearing of land for farming have led to desertification. **Desertification** (dih-ZUR-tuh-fih-KAY-shuhn) is the expansion of desert conditions in areas where the natural plant cover has been destroyed.

Exposed soil can be blown away by wind or washed away by rain.

Construction and Development

To make roads, houses, shopping malls, and other buildings, people need to dig up the soil. Some of the soil at construction sites washes or blows away because its protective plant cover has been removed. The soil that is washed or blown away ends up in nearby low-lying areas, in rivers and streams, or in downstream lakes or reservoirs. This soil can cause problems by making rivers and lakes muddy and harming the organisms that live in them. The buildup of soil on riverbeds raises the level of the rivers and may cause flooding. The soil can also fill up lakes and reservoirs.

The top of this hill in San Bernardino County, California, was cleared for a housing development. A house will be built on each flat plot of land.

Mining

Some methods of mining cause soil loss. For example, the digging of strip mines and open-pit mines involves the removal of plants and soil from the surface of the ground.

By exposing rocks and minerals to the air and to rainwater, these forms of mining speed up the rate of chemical weathering. In mining operations that expose sulfide minerals, the increased chemical weathering causes a type of pollution known as acid drainage. Abandoned mines can fill with rainwater. Sulfide minerals react with the air and the water to produce sulfuric acid. Then the acid water drains from the mines, polluting the soil in surrounding areas.

CHECK YOUR READING   How do some methods of mining affect the soil?

To make this open-pit mine in Cananea, Mexico, plants and soil were removed from the surface of the ground.

Soil can be protected and conserved.

Soil conservation is very important, because soil can be difficult or impossible to replace once it has been lost. Soil takes a very long time to form. A soil with well-developed horizons may take hundreds of thousands of years to form! Most soil conservation methods are designed to hold soil in place and keep it fertile. Below are descriptions of a few of the many soil conservation methods that are used by farmers around the world.

Crop rotation is the practice of planting different crops on the same field in different years or growing seasons. Grain crops, such as wheat, use up a lot of the nitrogen—a necessary plant nutrient—in the soil. The roots of bean crops, such as soybeans, contain bacteria that restore nitrogen to the soil. By rotating these crops, farmers can help maintain soil fertility.

Conservation tillage includes several methods of reducing the number of times fields are tilled, or plowed, in a year. The less soil is disturbed by plowing, the less likely it is to be washed or blown away. In one method of conservation tillage, fields are not plowed at all. The remains of harvested crops are simply left on the fields to cover and protect the soil. New seeds are planted in narrow bands of soil.

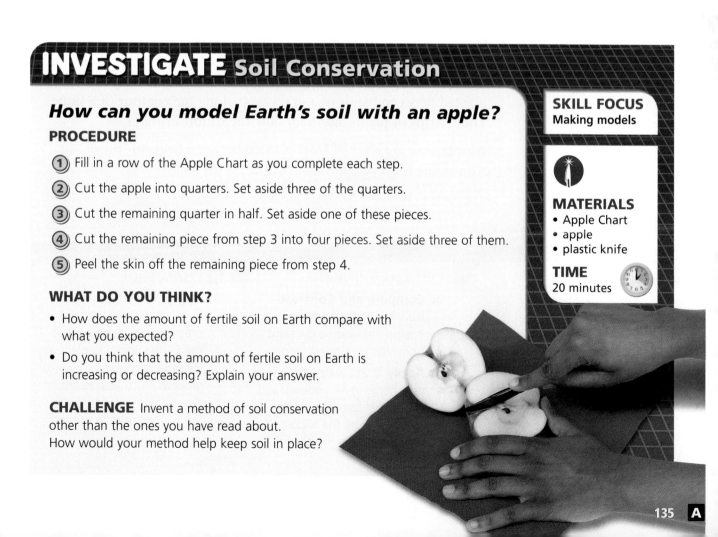

INVESTIGATE Soil Conservation

How can you model Earth's soil with an apple?

PROCEDURE

1. Fill in a row of the Apple Chart as you complete each step.
2. Cut the apple into quarters. Set aside three of the quarters.
3. Cut the remaining quarter in half. Set aside one of these pieces.
4. Cut the remaining piece from step 3 into four pieces. Set aside three of them.
5. Peel the skin off the remaining piece from step 4.

WHAT DO YOU THINK?

- How does the amount of fertile soil on Earth compare with what you expected?
- Do you think that the amount of fertile soil on Earth is increasing or decreasing? Explain your answer.

CHALLENGE Invent a method of soil conservation other than the ones you have read about. How would your method help keep soil in place?

SKILL FOCUS
Making models

MATERIALS
- Apple Chart
- apple
- plastic knife

TIME
20 minutes

Terracing

Contour Plowing

READING VISUALS **COMPARE** Both terracing and contour plowing are soil conservation methods used on sloping land. How does each method help conserve soil?

Terraces are flat, steplike areas built on a hillside to hold rainwater and prevent it from running downhill. Crops are planted on the flat tops of the terraces.

Contour plowing is the practice of plowing along the curves, or contours, of a slope. Contour plowing helps channel rainwater so that it does not run straight downhill, carrying away soil with it. A soil conservation method called strip-cropping is often combined with contour plowing. Strips of grasses, shrubs, or other plants are planted between bands of a grain crop along the contour of a slope. These strips of plants also help slow the runoff of water.

Windbreaks are rows of trees planted between fields to "break," or reduce, the force of winds that can carry off soil.

4.3 Review

KEY CONCEPTS

1. Why is soil a necessary resource?

2. How do land-use practices in farming, construction and development, and mining affect soil?

3. Describe at least three methods of soil conservation.

CRITICAL THINKING

4. **Compare and Contrast** How might the problem of soil loss on flat land be different from that on sloping land?

5. **Apply** If you were building a new home in an undeveloped area, what steps would you take to reduce the impact of construction on the soil?

⬤ CHALLENGE

6. **Apply** You have advised an inexperienced farmer to practice strip-cropping, but the farmer wants to plant all the land in wheat in order to grow as much as possible. What argument would you use to convince the farmer?

Soil, Water, and Architecture

Landscape architects design the landscapes around buildings and in parks. For example, they decide where to build sidewalks and where to place benches. Since flowing water can wash away soil, they try to control how water moves. They select plants, modify the slope of the land, and install drainage systems that will control the water. The plan below was used to build the park shown in the photographs.

Existing Plants

Large oak trees were already growing on the land. The trees were left in place to provide shade and help protect the soil.

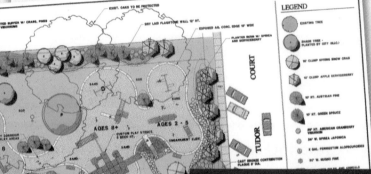

Retaining Wall

The landscape architect added mounds of soil planted with bushes to help divide the inside of the park from the roads around it. Stone walls hold the soil of the mounds in place. Without the walls, the soil would wash down onto the walkways.

Plan for New Park

A landscape architect used a computer program to draw this plan for a park. The program is designed to make the plan look as if it were drawn by hand.

EXPLORE

1. ANALYZE Examine the soil, drainage, plants, and other elements of the landscape of a park or the area around a building. Describe any areas where soil may wash away.

2. CHALLENGE Design a landscape surrounding a new school, stadium, or other building. Draw a sketch and add notes to explain your choices of locations for trees, sidewalks, and other features.

the **BIG** idea

Natural forces break rocks apart and form soil, which supports life.

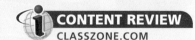
CONTENT REVIEW
CLASSZONE.COM

◀ KEY CONCEPTS SUMMARY

4.1 Mechanical and chemical forces break down rocks.

Over time, **mechanical weathering** breaks a rock into smaller pieces.

Chemical weathering affects exposed rock surfaces.

VOCABULARY
weathering p. 115
mechanical weathering p. 116
exfoliation p. 116
abrasion p. 116
chemical weathering p. 118

4.2 Weathering and organic processes form soil.

Soil has measurable properties, such as color, texture, pore space, and chemistry.

Soil is a mixture of weathered rock, organic matter, water, and air.

Plants, microorganisms, and animals affect soil characteristics.

VOCABULARY
humus p. 123
soil horizon p. 124
soil profile p. 124

4.3 Human activities affect soil.

Soil is essential to life and takes a long time to form. It is difficult or impossible to replace soil that has been lost.

Soil Loss

Farming, construction and development, and mining are three human activities that affect soil.

Soil Conservation

Soil conservation practices help keep soil from blowing or washing away.

VOCABULARY
desertification p. 133

Reviewing Vocabulary

Copy the three-column chart below. Complete the chart for each term. The first one has been done for you.

Term	Definition	Example
EXAMPLE chemical weathering	the breakdown of rocks by chemical reactions that change the rocks' mineral composition	Iron reacts with air and water to form iron oxides or rust.
1. mechanical weathering		
2. abrasion		
3. exfoliation		
4. desertification		

Reviewing Key Concepts

Multiple Choice *Choose the letter of the best answer.*

5. The force of expanding water in the cracks and pores of a rock is an example of
   a. chemical weathering
   b. mechanical weathering
   c. oxidation
   d. desertification

6. The breakdown of a rock by acidic water is an example of
   a. chemical weathering
   b. mechanical weathering
   c. oxidation
   d. desertification

7. Soil is a mixture of what four materials?
   a. granite, limestone, nitrogen, and air
   b. plant roots, iron oxides, water, and air
   c. rock particles, plant roots, humus, and nitrogen
   d. rock particles, humus, water, and air

8. What is the main component of soil?
   a. humus
   b. water
   c. air
   d. rock particles

9. What is humus?
   a. the decomposed rock particles in soil
   b. the decomposed organic matter in soil
   c. the material that makes up the B horizon
   d. the material that makes up the C horizon

10. Three factors that affect the rate of weathering are
   a. microorganisms, plants, and animals
   b. weather, landforms, and rainfall
   c. surface area, rock composition, and climate
   d. texture, color, and pore space

11. Microorganisms affect the quality of soil by
   a. decomposing organic matter
   b. creating tunnels
   c. absorbing water
   d. increasing mechanical weathering

12. The movement of air and water through a soil is influenced most by the soil's
   a. color and chemistry
   b. texture and pore space
   c. pH and nitrogen content
   d. microorganisms

13. Contour plowing, strip-cropping, and terracing are conservation methods designed to reduce the
   a. runoff of water
   b. activity of microorganisms
   c. acidity of soil
   d. pore space of soil

Short Answer *Write a few sentences to answer each question.*

14. How do farming, construction and development, and mining affect soil?

15. How do ice wedging, pressure release, plant root growth, and abrasion cause mechanical weathering?

16. How do air and water cause chemical weathering?

Use the photograph to answer the next three questions.

17. APPLY Make a sketch of the soil profile above, labeling the A, B, and C horizons.

18. OBSERVE What does the color of the top layer indicate about this soil?

19. APPLY Which part of the profile is most affected by chemical and mechanical weathering? Why?

20. APPLY Suppose that you own gently sloping farmland. Describe the methods that you would use to hold the soil in place and maintain its fertility.

21. SYNTHESIZE Describe the composition, color, texture, and amount of pore space of a soil that would be good for growing crops.

22. COMPARE AND CONTRAST How does mechanical weathering differ from chemical weathering? How are the two processes similar?

23. PREDICT What effect will the continued growth of the world's population likely have on soil resources?

24. ANALYZE Soil loss is a problem all over the world. Where might lost soil end up?

25. ANALYZE Can lost soil be replaced? Explain.

26. ANALYZE Copy the concept map below and fill it in with the following terms and phrases.

acidic water	chemical weathering
damaged statue	exfoliation
mechanical weathering	moving water
oxygen and water	pressure release
rounded rocks	rust

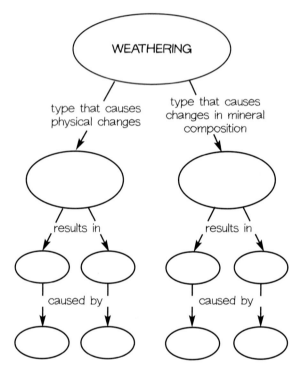

27. ANALYZE Add to the concept map to show the three factors that affect the rate of weathering.

the BIG idea

28. MODEL Draw a diagram that shows an example of a natural force breaking rocks apart to form soil that supports life.

29. SYNTHESIZE A cycle is a series of events or actions that repeats regularly. Describe a cycle that involves soil and living things.

UNIT PROJECTS

If you need to create graphs or other visuals for your project, be sure you have grid paper, poster board, markers, or other supplies.

Analyzing a Table

The table indicates some of the characteristics of four soil samples. Use the table to answer the questions below.

Sample	Color	Ability to Hold Water	Percentage of Pore Space	Percentage of Humus
1	black	average	50%	9%
2	yellowish brown	low	70%	3%
3	reddish brown	average	60%	3%
4	very red	average to low	65%	2%

1. Soils that contain a lot of sand do not hold water very well. Which sample probably contains the most sand?

a. 1   **c.** 3
b. 2   **d.** 4

2. Iron gives soil a reddish color. Which sample probably contains the most iron?

a. 1   **c.** 3
b. 2   **d.** 4

3. Crops grow best in soils with about half of their volume consisting of pore space. Which soil has an ideal amount of pore space for growing crops?

a. 1   **c.** 3
b. 2   **d.** 4

4. What soil color might indicate a high level of organic matter?

a. black   **c.** red-brown
b. yellow   **d.** red

5. Imagine you have an additional soil sample. The sample is dark brown, has an average ability to hold water, and has 55% pore space. What percentage of humus would this soil most likely contain?

a. 1%   **c.** 3%
b. 2%   **d.** 8%

Extended Response

Answer the two questions below in detail. Include some of the terms shown in the word box. In your answers, underline each term you use.

abrasion	moving water
chemical weathering	plant roots
ice	rusting
mechanical weathering	

6. Jolene is comparing a rock from a riverbed and a rock from deep underground. One is very smooth. The other has very sharp edges. Explain which rock was probably found in each location.

7. In a museum, Hank sees two iron knives that were made in the early 1800s. One has spent 200 years on the top of a fortress wall. The other one has been stored in the museum for 200 years. Why might the two knives look different?

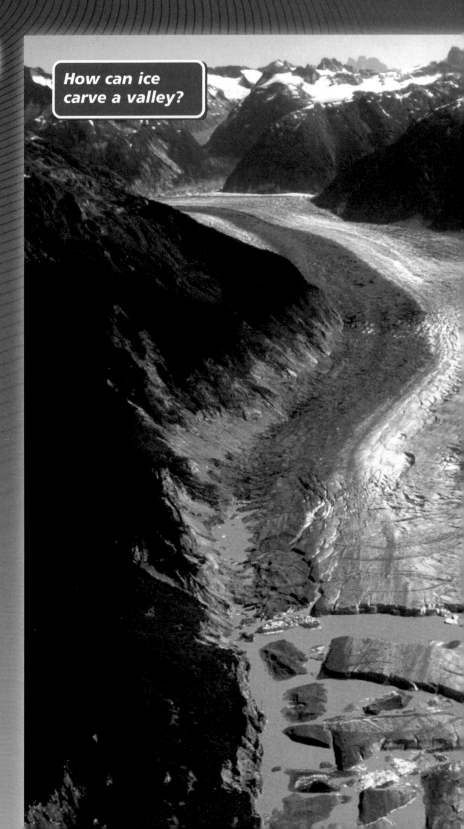

CHAPTER

Erosion and Deposition

the **BIG** idea

Water, wind, and ice shape Earth's surface.

How can ice carve a valley?

Key Concepts

SECTION
5.1 **Forces wear down and build up Earth's surface.**
Learn how natural forces shape and change the land.

SECTION
5.2 **Moving water shapes land.**
Learn about the effects of water moving over land and underground.

SECTION
5.3 **Waves and wind shape land.**
Discover how waves and wind affect land.

SECTION
5.4 **Glaciers carve land and move sediments.**
Learn about the effect of ice moving over land.

Internet Preview

CLASSZONE.COM

Chapter 5 online resources: Content Review, two Visualizations, three Resource Centers, Math Tutorial, Test Practice

EXPLORE (the BIG idea)

Where Has Water Been?

Think about what water does when it falls and flows on the ground. Go outside your school or home and look at the ground and pavement carefully. Look in dry places for evidence of where water has been.

Observe and Think What evidence did you find? How does it show that water was in a place that is now dry?

How Do Waves Shape Land?

Pile a mixture of sand and gravel on one side of a pie tin to make a "beach." Slowly add water away from the beach until the tin is about one-third full. Use your hand to make waves in the tin and observe what happens.

Observe and Think What happened to the beach? How did the waves affect the sand and gravel?

Internet Activity: Wind Erosion

Go to **ClassZone.com** to learn about one type of wind erosion. See how wind can form an arch in rock.

Observe and Think How long do you think it would take for wind to form an arch?

NSTA
scilinks.org
SC*LINKS*

Wind Erosion **Code: MDL017**

Getting Ready to Learn

◀ CONCEPT REVIEW

- Weathering breaks down rocks.
- Water and ice are agents of weathering.
- Soil contains weathered rock and organic material.

◀ VOCABULARY REVIEW

sediment p. 89
weathering p. 115
abrasion p. 116

CONTENT REVIEW
CLASSZONE.COM
Review concepts and vocabulary.

▶ TAKING NOTES

CHOOSE YOUR OWN STRATEGY

Take notes using one or more of the strategies from earlier chapters— **main idea and detail notes, supporting main ideas, main idea web,** or **combination notes.** Feel free to mix and match the strategies, or use an entirely different note-taking strategy.

VOCABULARY STRATEGY

Write each new vocabulary term in the center of a **four square** diagram. Write notes in the squares around each term. Include a definition, some characteristics, and some examples of the term. If possible, write some things that are not examples of the term.

See the Note-Taking Handbook on pages R45–R51.

SCIENCE NOTEBOOK

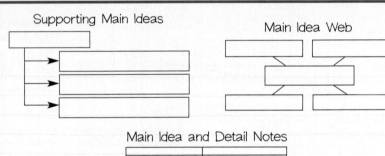

Supporting Main Ideas

Main Idea Web

Main Idea and Detail Notes

Definition	Characteristics
process in which weathered particles are picked up and moved	gravity is important part; wind and ice are agents

EROSION

Examples	Nonexamples
mass wasting, mudflow, slump, creep	longshore current, humus

5.1 Forces wear down and build up Earth's surface.

 BEFORE, you learned

- Weathering breaks rocks apart
- Weathering forms soil

 NOW, you will learn

- How erosion moves and deposits rock and soil
- How gravity causes movement of large amounts of rock and soil

VOCABULARY

erosion p. 145
deposition p. 145
mass wasting p. 147

THINK ABOUT

How did natural forces shape this landform?

This valley in Iceland was formed by the action of water. How long might it have taken to form? Where did the material that once filled the valley go?

Natural forces move and deposit sediments.

The valley in the photograph was formed by the movement of water. The water flowed over the land and carried away weathered rock and soil, shaping a valley where the water flows. In this section you will learn about the processes that shape landscapes.

The process in which weathered particles are picked up and moved from one place to another is called **erosion** (ih-ROH-zhuhn). Erosion has a constant impact on Earth's surface. Over millions of years, it wears down mountains by removing byproducts of weathering and depositing them elsewhere. The part of the erosion process in which sediment is placed in a new location, or deposited, is called **deposition** (DEHP-uh-ZIHSH-uhn).

The force of gravity is an important part of erosion and deposition. Gravity causes water to move downward, carrying and depositing sediment as it flows. Gravity can pull huge masses of ice slowly down mountain valleys. And gravity causes dust carried by the wind to fall to Earth.

 VOCABULARY
Use four square diagrams to take notes about the terms *erosion* and *deposition*.

Erosion of weathered rock by the movement of water, wind, and ice occurs in three major ways:

- **Water** Rainwater and water from melting snow flow down sloping land, carrying rock and soil particles. The water makes its way to a river, which then carries the sediment along. The sediment gets deposited on the river's bottom, banks, or floodplain, or near its mouth. Waves in oceans and lakes also carry sediment and deposit it to form beaches and other features.

- **Wind** Strong winds lift tiny particles of dust and carry them long distances. When the wind dies down, the particles drop to the ground. Wind can also push larger particles of sand along the ground.

- **Ice** As ice moves slowly downhill, it transports rock and soil particles that are embedded in it.

CHECK YOUR READING What are the three major ways in which erosion moves sediment?

INVESTIGATE Erosion

How does the effect of rainwater on sloping land differ from its effect on flat land?

DESIGN — YOUR OWN — EXPERIMENT

Streams are one of the main agents of erosion on Earth. Design an experiment to show the effect that rainwater has on sloping land.

PROCEDURE

1. Figure out how to use the soil, water, and trays to test the effects of rainwater on sloping land and on flat land.

2. Write up your procedure.

3. Carry out your experiment.

WHAT DO YOU THINK?

- What were the results of your experiment? Did it work? Why or why not?

- What were the variables in your experiment?

- What does your experiment demonstrate about erosion and running water?

CHALLENGE How would you design an experiment to demonstrate the relationship between floods and erosion?

SKILL FOCUS
Designing experiments

MATERIALS
- soil
- 2 large trays
- pitcher of water

TIME
25 minutes

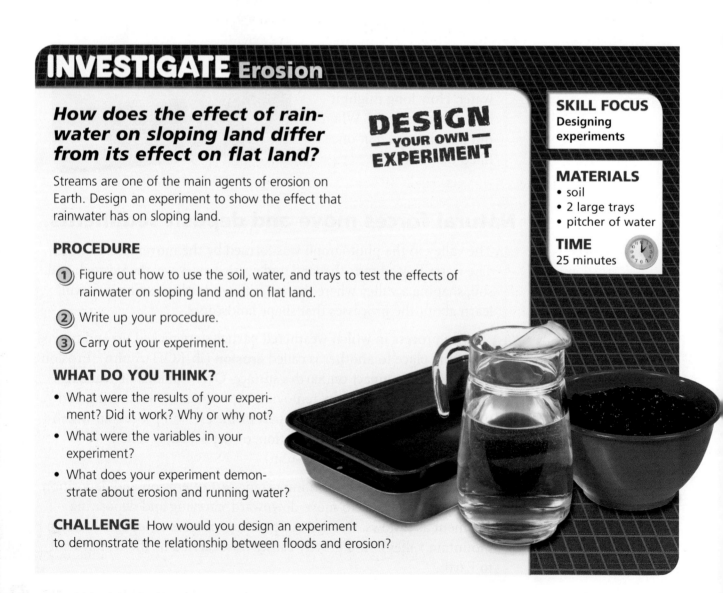

Gravity can move large amounts of rock and soil.

Along the California coast many homes are built atop beautiful cliffs, backed by mountains and looking out to the sea. These homes may seem like great places to live. They are, however, in a risky location.

The California coast region and other mountainous areas have many landslides. A landslide is one type of **mass wasting**—the downhill movements of masses of rock and soil.

In mass wasting, gravity pulls material downward. A triggering event, such as heavy rain or an earthquake, might loosen the rock and soil. As the material becomes looser, it gives way to the pull of gravity and moves downward.

Mass wasting can occur suddenly or gradually. It can involve tons of rock sliding down a steep mountain slope or moving little by little down a gentle hillside. One way to classify an occurrence of mass wasting is by the type of material that is moved and the speed of the movement. A sudden, fast movement of rock and soil is called a landslide. Movements of rock are described as slides or falls. Movement of mud or soil is described as a mudflow.

VOCABULARY
Be sure to make a four square diagram for *mass wasting* in your notebook.

Mass Wasting of Rock

Mass wasting of rock includes rockfalls and rockslides:

- In a rockfall, individual blocks of rock drop suddenly and fall freely down a cliff or steep mountainside. Weathering can break a block of rock from a cliff or mountainside. The expansion of water that freezes in a crack, for example, can loosen a block of rock.

- In a rockslide, a large mass of rock slides as a unit down a slope. A rockslide can reach a speed of a hundred kilometers per hour. Rockslides can be triggered by earthquakes.

Mass wasting of rock often takes place in high mountains. In some places, rocks can fall or slide onto roads. You might also see evidence of rockfalls and rockslides at the base of steep cliffs, where piles of rock slope outward.

Rockslides, such as this one in California, can drop huge amounts of rock onto highways.

Mudflows in 1999 in Venezuela happened very quickly and took as many as 30,000 lives.

RESOURCE CENTER
CLASSZONE.COM

Learn more about mudflows.

In this example of slump, at Mesa Verde National Park in Colorado, a huge mass of rock and soil moved downward.

Mudflow

Sometimes a mountain slope collapses. Then a mixture of rock, soil, and plants—called debris (duh-BREE)—falls or slides down. Like mass wasting of rock, mass movements of debris are common in high mountains with steep slopes.

A major type of mass wasting of debris is a mudflow. A mudflow consists of debris with a large amount of water. Mudflows often happen in mountain canyons and valleys after heavy rains. The soil becomes so heavy with water that the slope can no longer hold it in place. The mixture of soil, water, and debris flows downward, picking up sediment as it rushes down. When it reaches a valley, it spreads in a thin sheet over the land.

Mudflows also occur on active volcanoes. In 1985, a huge mudflow destroyed the town of Armero, Colombia, and killed more than 20,000 people. When a volcano erupted there, the heat caused ice and snow near the top of the volcano to melt, releasing a large amount of water that mixed with ash from the volcano. The mixture of ash and water rushed down the volcano and picked up debris. It formed gigantic mudflows that poured into all the surrounding valleys.

Mount St. Helens, a volcanic mountain in the state of Washington, is a place where large mudflows have occurred. During an eruption in 1980, some mudflows from the volcano traveled more than 90 kilometers (56 mi) from the mountain.

CHECK YOUR READING What causes a mudflow to occur?

Slumps and Creep

Slumps and creep are two other main types of mass wasting on hilly land. These forms of mass wasting can be much less dramatic than rockslides or mudflows. But they are the types of mass movement that you are most likely to see evidence of.

A slump is a slide of loose debris that moves as a single unit. Slumps can occur along roads and highways where construction has made slopes unstable. They can cover sections of highway with debris. Like other types of mass movement, slumps can be triggered by heavy rain.

The slowest form of mass movement of soil or debris is creep. The soil or debris moves at a rate of about 1 to 10 millimeters a year—a rate too slow to actually be seen. But evidence of creep can be seen on hillsides that have old fences or telephone poles. The fences or poles may lean downward, or some may be out of line. They have been moved by the creeping soil. The soil closer to the surface moves faster than the soil farther down, which causes the fences or poles to lean.

Even the slight slope of this land in Alberta, Canada, caused these posts to tilt because of creep.

Originally, the fence posts stand vertically in the ground.

Over many years, the soil holding the posts slowly shifts downhill, and the posts lean.

Creep can affect buildings as well. The weight of a heavy mass of soil moving slowly downhill can be great enough to crack a building's walls. Creep affects all hillsides covered with soil, but its rate varies. The wetter the soil, the faster it will creep downhill.

5.1 Review

KEY CONCEPTS

1. How does erosion change landscapes?

2. Describe why weathering is important in erosion.

3. How can gravity move large amounts of rock and soil?

CRITICAL THINKING

4. **Compare and Contrast** What is the main difference between erosion and mass wasting?

5. **Infer** What force and what cause can contribute to both erosion and mass wasting?

◐ CHALLENGE

6. **Rank** Which of the four locations would be the best and worst places to build a house? Rank the four locations and explain your reasoning.

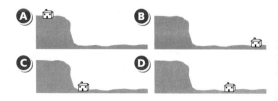

5.2 Moving water shapes land.

▶ **NOW, you will learn**

◀ **BEFORE, you learned**

- Erosion is the movement of rock and soil
- Gravity causes mass movements of rock and soil

NOW, you will learn

- How moving water shapes Earth's surface
- How water moving under-ground forms caves and other features

VOCABULARY

drainage basin p. 151
divide p. 151
floodplain p. 152
alluvial fan p. 153
delta p. 153
sinkhole p. 155

EXPLORE Divides

How do divides work?

PROCEDURE

① Fold the sheet of paper in thirds and tape it as shown to make a "ridge."

② Drop the paper clips one at a time directly on top of the ridge from a height of about 30 cm. Observe what happens and record your observations.

WHAT DO YOU THINK?

How might the paper clips be similar to water falling on a ridge?

MATERIALS

- sheet of paper
- tape
- paper clips

Streams shape Earth's surface.

If you look at a river or stream, you may be able to notice something about the land around it. The land is higher than the river. If a river is running through a steep valley, you can easily see that the river is the low point. But even in very flat places, the land is sloping down to the river, which is itself running downhill in a low path through the land.

Running water is the major force shaping the landscape over most of Earth. From the broad, flat land around the lower Mississippi River to the steep mountain valleys of the Himalayas, water running downhill changes the land. Running water shapes a variety of landforms by moving sediment in the processes of erosion and deposition. In this section, you will learn how water flows on land in systems of streams and rivers and how water shapes and changes landscapes. You also will learn that water can even carve out new features underground.

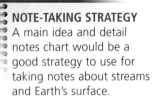

NOTE-TAKING STRATEGY
A main idea and detail notes chart would be a good strategy to use for taking notes about streams and Earth's surface.

Drainage Basins and Divides

When water falls or ice melts on a slope, some of the water soaks into the ground and some of it flows down the slope in thin sheets. But within a short distance this water becomes part of a channel that forms a stream. A stream is any body of water—large or small—that flows down a slope along a channel.

Streams flow into one another to form complex drainage systems, with small streams flowing into larger ones. The area of land in which water drains into a stream system is called a **drainage basin.** In most drainage basins, the water eventually drains into a lake or an ocean. For example, in the Mississippi River drainage basin, water flows into the Mississippi, and then drains into the Gulf of Mexico, which is part of the ocean.

Drainage basins are separated by ridges called divides, which are like continuous lines of high land. A **divide** is a ridge from which water drains to one side or the other. Divides can run along high mountains. On flatter ground, a divide can simply be the the highest line of land and can be hard to see.

Divides are the borders of drainage basins. A basin can be just a few kilometers wide or can drain water from a large portion of a continent. The Continental Divide runs from Alaska to Mexico. Most water that falls west of the Continental Divide ends up draining into the Pacific Ocean. Most water that falls east of it drains into the Gulf of Mexico and Atlantic Ocean.

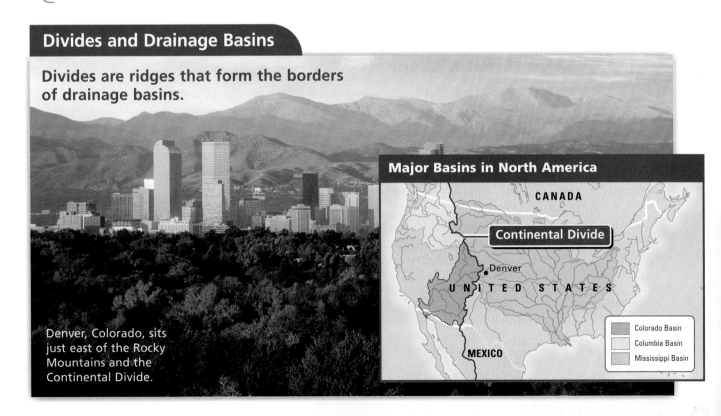

Divides and Drainage Basins

Divides are ridges that form the borders of drainage basins.

Denver, Colorado, sits just east of the Rocky Mountains and the Continental Divide.

Major Basins in North America

CANADA

Continental Divide

Denver

UNITED STATES

MEXICO

Colorado Basin
Columbia Basin
Mississippi Basin

Downtown Davenport, Iowa, sits in the floodplain of the Mississippi River and was covered with water when the river flooded in 1993.

Valleys and Floodplains

As streams flow and carry sediment from the surface of the land, they form valleys. In high mountains, streams often cut V-shaped valleys that are narrow and steep walled. In lower areas, streams may form broad valleys that include floodplains. A **floodplain** is an area of land on either side of a stream that is underwater when the stream floods. The floodplain of a large river may be many kilometers wide.

When a stream floods, it deposits much of the sediment that it carries onto its floodplain. This sediment can make the floodplain very fertile—or able to support a lot of plant growth. In the United States, the floodplains of the Mississippi River are some of the best places for growing crops.

RESOURCE CENTER
CLASSZONE.COM

Find out more about rivers and erosion.

CHECK YOUR READING Why is fertile land often found on flat land around rivers?

Stream Channels

As a stream flows through a valley, its channel may run straight in some parts and curve around in other parts. Curves and bends that form a twisting, looping pattern in a stream channel are called meanders (mee-AN-duhrz). The moving water erodes the outside banks and deposits sediment along the inside banks. Over many years, meanders shift position.

During a flood, the stream may cut a new channel that bypasses a meander. The cut-off meander forms a crescent-shaped lake, which is called an oxbow lake. This term comes from the name of a U-shaped piece of wood that fits under the neck of an ox and is attached to its yoke.

The meanders of this river and oxbow lakes formed as the river deposited sediment and changed course.

Alluvial Fans and Deltas

Besides shaping valleys and forming oxbow lakes, streams also create landforms called alluvial fans and deltas. Both of these landforms are formed by the deposition of sediment.

An **alluvial fan** (uh-LOO-vee-uhl) is a fan-shaped deposit of sediment at the base of a mountain. It forms where a stream leaves a steep valley and enters a flatter plain. The stream slows down and spreads out on the flatter ground. As it slows down, it can carry less sediment. The slower-moving water drops some of its sediment, leaving it at the base of the slope.

A **delta** is an area of land formed by the buildup of sediment at the end, or mouth, of a river. When a river enters the ocean, the river's water slows down, and the river drops much of its sediment. This sediment gradually builds up to form a plain. Like alluvial fans, deltas tend to be fan-shaped. Over a very long time, a river may build up its delta far out into the sea. A large river, such as the Mississippi, can build up a huge delta. Like many other large rivers on Earth, the Mississippi has been building up its delta out into the sea for many thousands of years.

This alluvial fan was formed by a stream flowing into the Jago River in Alaska.

From Divide to Delta

On their path to the ocean, streams and rivers slow down and flatten out.

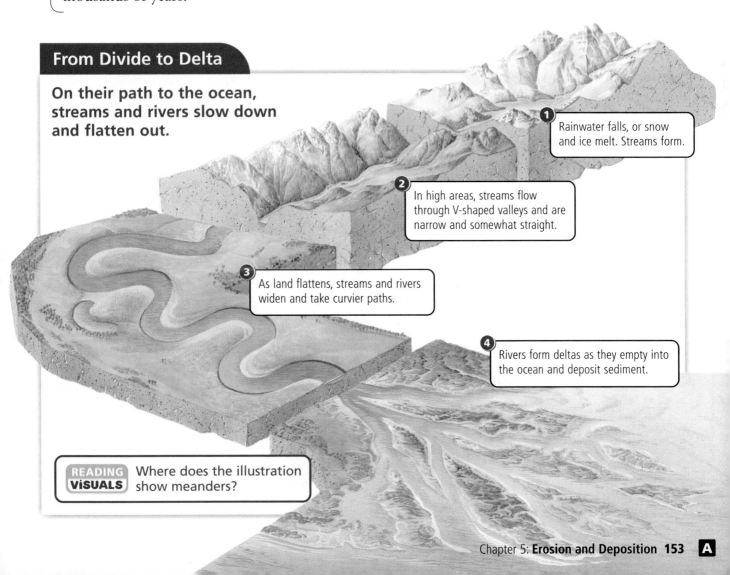

1 Rainwater falls, or snow and ice melt. Streams form.

2 In high areas, streams flow through V-shaped valleys and are narrow and somewhat straight.

3 As land flattens, streams and rivers widen and take curvier paths.

4 Rivers form deltas as they empty into the ocean and deposit sediment.

READING VISUALS Where does the illustration show meanders?

Water moving underground forms caverns.

Not all rainwater runs off the land and flows into surface streams. Some of it evaporates, some is absorbed by plants, and some soaks into the ground and becomes groundwater. At a certain depth below the surface, the spaces in soil and rock become completely filled with water. The top of this water-filled region is called the water table. The water below the water table is called groundwater.

The water table is at different distances below the surface in different places. Its level also can change over time in the same location, depending on changes in rainfall. Below the water table, groundwater flows slowly through underground beds of rock and soil, where it causes erosion to take place.

You have read that chemicals in water and air can break down rock. As you read in Chapter 4, rainwater is slightly acidic. This acidic water can dissolve certain rocks, such as limestone. In some areas, where the underground rock consists of limestone, the groundwater can dissolve some of the limestone and carry it away. Over time, this

VISUALIZATION
CLASSZONE.COM

Observe the process of cave formation.

Cavern Formation

Caves form as water underground dissolves limestone, leaving open spaces.

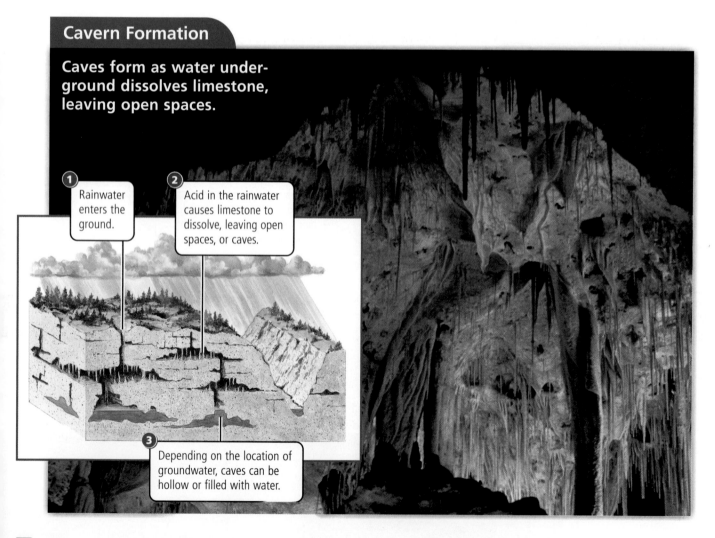

① Rainwater enters the ground.

② Acid in the rainwater causes limestone to dissolve, leaving open spaces, or caves.

③ Depending on the location of groundwater, caves can be hollow or filled with water.

This sinkhole took down a large part of a parking lot in Atlanta, Georgia.

process produces open spaces, or caves. Large caves are called caverns. If the water table drops, a cavern may fill with air.

Some caverns have huge networks of rooms and passageways. Mammoth Cave in Kentucky, for example, is part of a cavern system that has more than 560 kilometers (about 350 mi) of explored passageways. Within the cavern are lakes and streams.

A surface feature that often occurs in areas with caverns is a sinkhole. A **sinkhole** is a basin that forms when the roof of a cave becomes so thin that it suddenly falls in. Sometimes it falls in because water that supported the roof has drained away. Landscapes with many sinkholes can be found in southern Indiana, south central Kentucky, and central Tennessee. In Florida, the collapse of shallow underground caverns has produced large sinkholes that have destroyed whole city blocks.

 Why do caverns form in areas with limestone?

KEY CONCEPTS

1. What is the difference between a drainage basin and a divide?

2. How do streams change as they flow from mountains down to plains?

3. How do caverns form?

CRITICAL THINKING

4. **Sequence** Draw a cartoon with three panels showing how a sinkhole forms.

5. **Compare and Contrast** Make a Venn diagram to compare and contrast alluvial fans and deltas.

△ CHALLENGE

6. **Apply** During a flood, a river drops the largest pieces of its sediment on the floodplain close to its normal channel. Explain why. (**Hint:** Think about the speed of the water.)

CHAPTER INVESTIGATION

Creating Stream Features

OVERVIEW AND PURPOSE A view from the sky reveals that a large river twists and bends in its channel. But as quiet as it might appear, the river constantly digs and dumps Earth materials along its way. This erosion and deposition causes twists and curves called meanders, and forms a delta at the river's mouth. In this investigation you will

- create a "river" in a stream table to observe the creation of meanders and deltas
- identify the processes of erosion and deposition

▶ Problem

Write It Up

How does moving water create meanders and deltas?

▶ Procedure

1 Arrange the stream table on a counter so that it drains into a sink or bucket. If possible, place a sieve beneath the outlet hose to keep sand out of the drain. You can attach the inlet hose to a faucet if you have a proper adapter. Or you can gently pour water in with a pitcher or use a recirculating pump and a bucket.

2 Place wood blocks beneath the inlet end of the stream table so that the table tilts toward the outlet at about a 20 degree angle. Fill the upper two-thirds of the stream table nearly to the top with sand. Pack the sand a bit, and level the surface with the edge of a ruler. The empty bottom third of the stream table represents the lake or bay into which the river flows.

3 Using the end of the ruler, dig a gently curving trench halfway through the thickness of the sand from its upper to its lower end.

MATERIALS

- stream table, with hose attachment or recirculating pump
- sieve (optional)
- wood blocks
- sand
- ruler
- water
- sink with drain
- pitcher (optional)
- bucket (optional)

4. Direct a gentle flow of tap water into the upper end of the trench. Increase the flow slightly when the water begins to move through the trench. You may have to try this several times before you find the proper rate of flow to soak the sand and fill the stream channel. Avoid adding so much water that it pools at the top before moving into the channel. You can also change the stream table's tilt.

5. Once you are successful in creating a river, observe its shape and any movement of the sand. Continue until the top part of the sand is completely washed away and your river falls apart. Scrape the sand back into place with the ruler and repeat the procedure until you thoroughly understand the stream and sand movements.

▶ Observe and Analyze
Write It Up

1. **RECORD** Diagram your stream-table setup, and make a series of drawings showing changes in your river over time. Be sure to label the river's features, as well as areas of erosion and deposition. Be sure to diagram the behavior of the sand at the river's mouth.

2. **RECORD** Write a record of the development of your river from start to finish. Include details such as the degree of tilt you used, your method of introducing water into the stream table, and features you observed forming.

▶ Conclude
Write It Up

1. **EVALUATE** How do you explain the buildup of sand at the mouth of your river? Use the words *speed, erosion,* and *deposition* in your answer. Did the slope of the stream change over time?

2. **INTERPRET** Where in your stream table did you observe erosion occurring? Deposition? What features did each process form?

3. **INFER** What might have occurred if you had increased the amount or speed of the water flowing into your river?

4. **IDENTIFY LIMITS** In what ways was your setup a simplified version of what would actually occur on Earth? Describe the ways in which an actual stream would be more complex.

5. **APPLY** Drawing on what you observed in this investigation, make two statements that relate the age of a stream to (1) the extent of its meanders and (2) to the size of its delta or alluvial fan.

▶ INVESTIGATE Further

CHALLENGE Revise this activity to test a problem statement about a specific stream feature. You could choose to vary the stream's slope, speed, or volume to test the changes' effects on meanders and deltas, for example. Or you could vary the sediment size and observe the movements of each size. Write a hypothesis and design an experimental procedure. Identify the independent and dependent variables.

Creating stream features
Observe and Analyze
1. Before adding water

2. After one minute

5.3 Waves and wind shape land.

◀ **BEFORE, you learned**

- Stream systems shape Earth's surface
- Groundwater creates caverns and sinkholes

▶ **NOW, you will learn**

- How waves and currents shape shorelines
- How wind shapes land

VOCABULARY

longshore drift p. 159
longshore current p. 159
sandbar p. 160
barrier island p. 160
dune p. 161
loess p. 162

THINK ABOUT

How did these pillars of rock form?

The rock formations in this photograph stand along the shoreline near the small town of Port Campbell, Australia. What natural force created these isolated stone pillars? What evidence of this force can you see in the photograph?

Waves and currents shape shorelines.

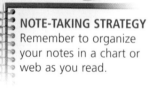

NOTE-TAKING STRATEGY
Remember to organize your notes in a chart or web as you read.

The stone pillars, or sea stacks, in the photograph above are a major tourist attraction in Port Campbell National Park. They were formed by the movement of water. The constant action of waves breaking against the cliffs slowly wore them away, leaving behind pillarlike formations. Waves continue to wear down the pillars and cliffs at the rate of about two centimeters (one inch) a year. In the years to come, the waves will likely wear away the stone pillars completely.

The force of waves, powered by wind, can wear away rock and move thousands of tons of sand on beaches. The force of wind itself can change the look of the land. Moving air can pick up sand particles and move them around to build up dunes. Wind can also carry huge amounts of fine sediment thousands of kilometers.

In this section, you'll read more about how waves and wind shape shorelines and a variety of other landforms.

Shorelines

Some shorelines, like the one near Port Campbell, Australia, are made up of steep, rock cliffs. As waves crash against the rock, they wear away the bottom of the cliffs. Eventually, parts of the cliffs above break away and fall into the water, where they are worn down and carried away by the water.

While high, rocky coasts get worn away, low coastlines often get built up. As you read earlier, when a stream flows into an ocean or a lake, it deposits its sediment near its mouth. This sediment mixes with the sediment formed by waves beating against the coast. Waves and currents move this sediment along the shore, building up beaches. Two terms are used to describe the movement of sediment and water along a shore: *longshore drift* and *longshore current.*

- **Longshore drift** is the zigzag movement of sand along a beach. Waves formed by wind blowing across the water far from shore may hit a shoreline at an angle. These angled waves carry sand up onto the shore, and then gravity pulls the water and sand directly back into the water. The sand gradually moves down the beach. The illustration below shows longshore drift.

- A **longshore current** is movement of water along a shore as waves strike the shore at an angle. The direction of the longshore current can change from day to day as the direction of the waves striking the shore changes.

Longshore drift moves large amounts of sand along beaches. It can cause a beach to shrink at one location and grow at another.

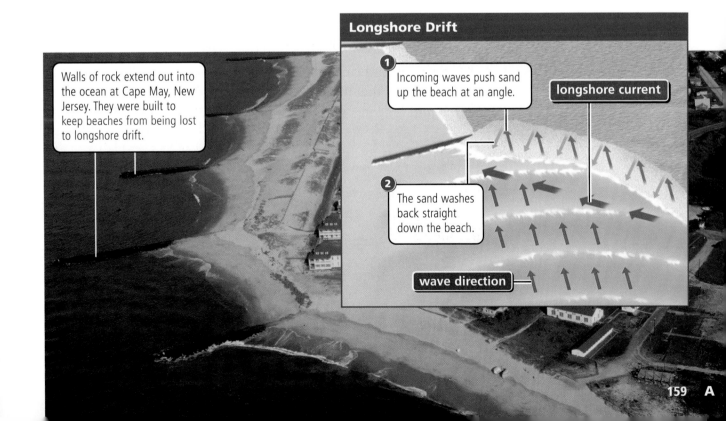

Walls of rock extend out into the ocean at Cape May, New Jersey. They were built to keep beaches from being lost to longshore drift.

Longshore Drift

1 Incoming waves push sand up the beach at an angle.

longshore current

2 The sand washes back straight down the beach.

wave direction

INVESTIGATE Longshore Drift

How does sand move along a beach?

PROCEDURE

1. Prop up a book as shown.

2. Hold a coin with your finger against the bottom right corner of the book.

3. Gently flick the coin up the slope of the book at an angle. The coin should slide back down the book and fall off the bottom. If necessary, readjust the angle of the book and the strength with which you are flicking the coin.

4. Repeat step 3 several times. Observe the path the coin takes. Record your observations. Include a diagram that shows the general path the coin takes as it slides up and down the book.

WHAT DO YOU THINK?

- What path did the coin take on its way up? On its way down?
- In this model of longshore drift, what represents the beach, what represents the sand, and what represents a wave?

CHALLENGE In this model, in which direction will the longshore current move? How could you change the model to change the direction of the current?

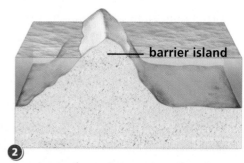

Sandbars and Barrier Islands

As they transport sand, ocean waves and currents shape a variety of coastal landforms. Longshore currents, for example, often deposit sand along shorelines. The sand builds up to form sandbars. A **sandbar** is a ridge of sand built up by the action of waves and currents. A sandbar that has built up above the water's surface and is joined to the land at one end is called a spit. The tip of Cape Cod, Massachusetts, is a spit.

Strong longshore currents that mostly move in one direction may produce sandbars that build up over time into barrier islands. A **barrier island** is a long, narrow island that develops parallel to a coast.

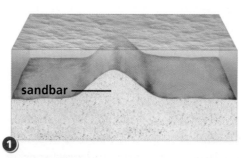

sandbar

barrier island

① Waves and currents move and build up sand deposits to form a sandbar under the water surface.

② As more sand is deposited, the sandbar rises above the surface to become a barrier island.

This lighthouse on a barrier island in North Carolina had to be moved because of beach erosion. The photograph shows the lighthouse before it was moved.

A barrier island gets its name from the fact that it forms a barrier between the ocean waves and the shore of the mainland. As a barrier island builds up, grasses, bushes, and trees begin to grow on it.

Barrier islands are common along gently sloping coasts around the world. They occur along the coasts of New Jersey and North Carolina and along the coastline of the Gulf of Mexico. Padre Island in Texas is a barrier island about 180 kilometers (110 mi) in length.

Barrier islands constantly change shape. Hurricanes or other storms can speed up the change. During large storms, waves can surge across the land, carrying away huge amounts of sediment and depositing it elsewhere. Houses on beaches can be destroyed in storms.

 CHECK YOUR READING How and where do barrier islands form?

Wind shapes land.

At Indiana Dunes National Lakeshore, not far from the skyscrapers of Chicago, you can tumble or slide down huge sand dunes. First-time visitors to the Indiana dunes find it hard to believe that sand formations like these can be found so far from a desert or an ocean. What created this long stretch of dune land along the southern shore of Lake Michigan? The answer: wind. A **dune** is a mound of sand built up by wind.

Like water, wind has the power to transport and deposit sediment. Although wind is a less powerful force of erosion than moving water, it can still shape landforms, especially in dry regions and in areas that have few or no plants to hold soil in place. Wind can build up dunes, deposit layers of dust, or make a land surface as hard as pavement.

wind

sand-particle movement

dune movement

Wind makes sand particles build up and tumble down, causing a dune to migrate, or move.

These hills of sand are at the Great Sand Dunes National Monument in Colorado.

Dune Formation

Even a light breeze can carry dust. A moderate wind can roll and slide grains of sand along a beach or desert, creating ripples. Only a strong wind, however, can actually pick up and carry sand particles. When the wind dies down or hits something—such as a cliff or a hill—it drops the sand. Over time, the deposits of sand build up to create dunes.

Some dunes start out as ripples that grow larger. Others form as wind-carried sand settles around a rock, log, or other obstacle. In climates with enough rainfall, plants begin to grow on dunes a short distance from beaches.

Dunes form only where there are strong winds and a constant supply of loose sand. They can be found on the inland side of beaches of oceans and large lakes, on the sandy floodplains of large rivers, and in sandy deserts.

Dunes can form in a variety of sizes and shapes. They can reach heights of up to 300 meters (about 1000 ft). Some dunes are curved; others are long, straight ridges; still others are mound-shaped hills. A dune usually has a gentle slope on the side that faces the wind and a steeper slope on the side sheltered from the wind.

Loess

Besides forming dunes, wind also changes the soil over large regions of Earth by depositing dust. A strong windstorm can move millions of tons of dust. As the wind dies down, the dust drops to the ground. Deposits of fine wind-blown sediment are called **loess** (LOH-uhs).

In some regions, deposits of loess have built up over thousands and even millions of years. Loess is a valuable resource because it forms good soil for growing crops.

This loess deposit in Iowa built up over many thousands of years.

Loess covers about 10 percent of the land surface of Earth. China has especially large deposits of loess, covering hundreds of thousands of square kilometers. Some of the deposits are more than 300 meters (about 1000 ft) thick. Such thick deposits take a long time to develop. Some of the loess deposits in China are 2 million years old. Winds blowing over the deserts and dry regions of central Asia carried the dust that formed these deposits.

Parts of east central Europe and the Mississippi Valley in the United States also contain significant loess deposits. In the central United States, loess deposits are between 8 and 30 meters (25 and 100 ft) thick.

Desert Pavement

Not only does wind shape land surfaces by depositing dust; it also shapes land surfaces by removing dust. When wind blows away all the smallest particles from a mixture of sand, silt, and gravel, it leaves behind just a layer of stones and gravel. This stony surface is called desert pavement because it looks like a cobblestone pavement. The coarse gravel and rocks are too large to be picked up by wind.

 CHECK YOUR READING How are both loess and desert pavement formed by wind?

Desert pavement is made up of particles too large to be picked up by wind.

5.3 Review

KEY CONCEPTS

1. What kinds of landforms do longshore drift and longshore currents produce?

2. How do dunes form?

3. How does loess form, and why is it important?

CRITICAL THINKING

4. **Identify Cause and Effect** Is longshore drift the cause or effect of a longshore current? Explain.

5. **Predict** What effect would a barrier island have on the shoreline of the mainland?

⬤ CHALLENGE

6. **Hypothesize** The south and east shores of Lake Michigan have large areas of sand dunes, but the north and west shores do not. Write a hypothesis that explains why. You might want to use a map and draw the shape of Lake Michigan to explain.

Life on Dunes

The leaves of American beach grass contain silica, the main component of sand. The leaves are therefore very tough. Why is this important on a dune?

Sand dunes are a difficult environment for most organisms. For example, few plants can gather enough nutrition from sand to grow quickly. However, any plant that grows slowly is likely to be buried by the shifting sand. Plants and animals that thrive on dunes generally have unusual traits that help them survive in dune conditions.

American Beach Grass

Among the first plants to grow on new coastal dunes is American beach grass. It grows faster as sand begins to bury it, and it can grow up to 1 meter (more than 3 ft) per year. Its large root system—reaching down as much as 3 meters (about 10 ft)—helps it gather food and water. The roots also help hold sand in place. As the grass's roots make the dunes stable, other plants can begin to grow there.

Sand Food

One of the most unusual plants in desert dunes is called sand food. It is one of the few plants that cannot convert sunlight into energy it can use. Instead, its long underground stem grabs onto the root of another plant and sucks food from it. Most of the plant is the stem. Sand food plants may be more than 2 meters (almost 7 ft) long.

In spring, sand food produces a small head of purple flowers that barely comes out of the ground. How does growing mostly underground help sand food survive?

Fowler's Toad

Fowler's toad is one of the animals that can live in coastal dunes. During the day, sunlight can make the top layer of the sand very hot and dry. These toads dig down into the sand, where they are safe, cool, and moist. They are most active at night.

Fowler's toads have a brownish or greenish color that makes them hard to see against a sandy background. How would this help protect them from animals that want to eat them?

EXPLORE

1. **GENERALIZE** Dune plants often have long roots. Propose an explanation for this.

2. **CHALLENGE** Use library or Internet resources to learn about another plant or animal that lives on dunes. Describe how it has adapted to the conditions in which it lives.

KEY CONCEPT

5.4 Glaciers carve land and move sediments.

BEFORE, you learned	**NOW,** you will learn
• Running water shapes landscapes • Wind changes landforms	• How moving ice erodes land • How moving ice deposits sediment and changes landforms

VOCABULARY

glacier p. 165
till p. 168
moraine p. 168
kettle lake p. 169

EXPLORE Glaciers

How do glaciers affect land?

PROCEDURE

1. Flatten the clay on top of a paper towel.

2. Drag the ice cube across the clay as shown. Record your observations.

3. Leave the ice cube to melt on top of the clay.

WHAT DO YOU THINK?

• What happened when you dragged the ice cube across the clay?

• What happened to the sand and gravel in the ice cube as it melted?

MATERIALS
• modeling clay
• paper towel
• ice cube containing sand and gravel

VOCABULARY
Remember to add a four square diagram for *glacier* to your notebook.

Glaciers are moving bodies of ice.

You might not think of ice as something that moves. But think about what happens to an ice cube on a table. The cube begins to melt, makes a small puddle, and may slide a little. The water under the cube makes the table surface slippery, which allows the ice cube to slide.

A similar process happens on a much larger scale with glaciers. A **glacier** is a large mass of ice that moves over land. A glacier forms in a cold region when more snow falls than melts each year. As the snow builds up, its weight presses the snow on the bottom into ice. On a mountain, the weight of a heavy mass of ice causes it to flow downward, usually slowly. On flatter land, the ice spreads out as a sheet. As glaciers form, move, and melt away, they shape landscapes.

Chapter 5: **Erosion and Deposition** 165 **A**

Extent of Glaciers

Glaciers can exist only in places where it is cold enough for water to stay frozen year round. Glaciers are found in mountain ranges all over the world and in land regions near the north and south poles.

Today, glaciers cover about 10 percent of Earth's land surface. However, the amount of land surface covered by glaciers has varied greatly over Earth's history. Glaciers have expanded during long cold periods called ice ages and have disappeared during long warm periods. About 30,000 years ago—during the last major ice age—glaciers extended across the northern parts of North America and Eurasia. They covered nearly 30 percent of the present land surface of Earth.

There are two major types of glaciers: alpine glaciers and continental glaciers.

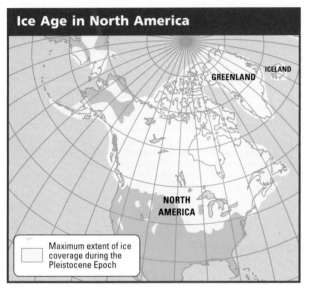

Ice Age in North America

ICELAND

GREENLAND

NORTH AMERICA

Maximum extent of ice coverage during the Pleistocene Epoch

RESOURCE CENTER
CLASSZONE.COM

Learn more about the movement and effects of glaciers.

Alpine Glaciers

Alpine glaciers, also called valley glaciers, form in mountains and flow down through valleys. As these glaciers move, they cause erosion, breaking up rock and carrying and pushing away the resulting sediment. Over time, an alpine glacier can change a V-shaped mountain valley into a U-shaped valley with a wider, flatter bottom.

Some glaciers extend all the way down into the lower land at the bases of mountains. At an alpine glacier's lower end, where temperatures are warmer, melting can occur. The melting glacier drops sediment, and streams flowing from the glacier carry some of the sediment away. If an alpine glacier flows into the ocean, big blocks may break off and become icebergs.

Continental Glaciers

Continental glaciers, also called ice sheets, are much larger than alpine glaciers. They can cover entire continents, including all but the highest mountain peaks. An ice sheet covered most of Canada and the northern United States during the last ice age. This ice sheet melted and shrank about 10,000 years ago.

Today, ice sheets cover most of Greenland and Antarctica. Each of these glaciers is shaped like a wide dome over the land. The ice on Antarctica is as much as 4500 meters (15,000 ft) thick.

CHECK YOUR READING What are the two major types of glaciers and where do they form?

Types of Glaciers and Movement

A glacier is a large mass of ice that moves over land.

Alpine Glaciers

A glacier, such as this one in Alaska, changes the landscape as it moves down a mountain valley.

Continental Glaciers

Huge sheets of ice cover the continent of Antarctica and other land regions.

Glacier Movement

Gravity causes the ice in a glacier to move downhill. Two different processes cause glaciers to move: flowing and sliding.

Flowing The ice near the surface of a glacier is brittle, and cracks often form in it. However, deep inside a glacier, ice does not break as easily because it is under great pressure from the weight of the ice above it. Instead of breaking, ice inside a glacier flows like toothpaste being squeezed in its tube.

As a glacier moves, it breaks up rock and pushes and carries sediment.

Sliding The weight of a glacier and heat from Earth cause ice at the bottom of a glacier to melt. A layer of water forms under the glacier. The glacier slides along on this layer of water just as an ice cube might slide on a countertop.

READING VISUALS In the illustration, why are cracks shown near the surface of the glacier and not at the bottom?

A moving glacier left visible abrasion lines on this rock.

Glaciers deposit large amounts of sediment.

As glaciers have melted and retreated, they have shaped the landscapes of many places on Earth. As a glacier moves or expands, it transports a vast amount of sediment—a mix of boulders, small rocks, sand, and clay. It acts like a plow, pushing rock and soil and plucking out big blocks of rock. As a glacier moves over rock, it scratches and scrapes the rock in a process called abrasion. Abrasion leaves visible grooves on rock surfaces.

Moraines

When glaciers expand and advance and then melt and retreat, they affect both the land underneath them and the land around them. A glacier pushes huge amounts of sediment to its sides and front. When the glacier retreats, the deposits of sediment remain as visible evidence that ice once moved through. The sediment left directly on the ground surface by a retreating glacier is called **till**.

A deposit of till left behind by a retreating glacier is called a **moraine** (muh-RAYN). The ridges of till deposited at the sides of a glacier are called lateral moraines. The till that marks the farthest advance of a glacier forms a deposit called an end moraine. Moraines formed by continental glaciers, such as those in North America during the ice age, can be huge—many kilometers long.

The blanket of till that a glacier deposits along its bottom is called a ground moraine. Rock deposits from glaciers can often be identified as till because the till rocks are different, in type or age, from the rock that was present before the glacier formed.

A glacier scooped out this valley in California and left behind lateral moraines.

⬤ CHECK YOUR READING Draw a sketch of a glacier and label where lateral, end, and ground moraines would form.

Lateral moraines

Lakes

Besides ridges, hills, and blankets of till, melting glaciers also leave behind depressions of various sizes that can become lakes. Landscapes shaped by glaciers are often dotted with small kettle lakes as well as larger lakes. A **kettle lake** is a bowl-shaped depression that was formed by a block of ice from a glacier and then became filled with water.

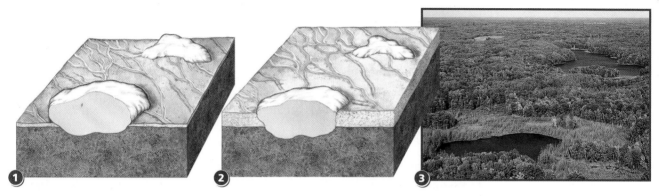

① As a glacier moves away, it leaves huge blocks of ice.

② Over time, sediment builds up around the ice.

③ The ice melts, leaving behind bowls that become kettle lakes. These lakes are in Wisconsin.

The last ice sheet in North America formed many kettle lakes in some regions. Kettle lakes are common in Michigan, Wisconsin, and Minnesota.

INVESTIGATE Kettle Lake Formation

How do kettle lakes form?

DESIGN — YOUR OWN —

Kettle lakes form when sediment builds up around blocks of ice left behind by a retreating glacier. Use what you know about kettle lake formation to design a model of the process.

PROCEDURE

① Use the tray, the ice cubes, and the other materials to model how sediment builds up around ice blocks.

② Write a description of the process you used to make your model.

WHAT DO YOU THINK?

- Describe how your model worked. What did you do first? What happened next?
- Did your model accurately represent the formation of kettle lakes? Did it work? Why or why not?
- What were the limitations of your model? Are there any aspects of kettle lake formation that are not represented? If so, what are they?

SKILL FOCUS
Designing models

MATERIALS
- shallow tray
- ice cubes
- modeling clay
- sand
- gravel
- water

TIME
30 minutes

Great Lakes Formation

① 14,000 Years Ago

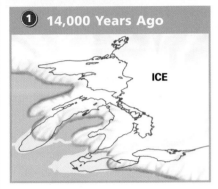

The ice sheet covering a land of river valleys began to retreat.

② 7000 Years Ago

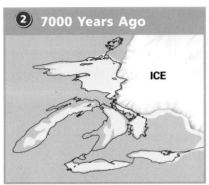

Water filled the bowls carved out by the ice.

③ Today

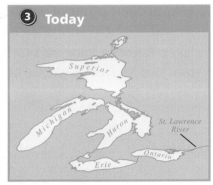

The Great Lakes contain 20 percent of the world's fresh lake water.

Many large lakes are the result of ice ages. In some places, lakes formed after glaciers in valleys melted and left behind moraines that dammed the valleys. Many of these lakes are long and narrow, like the Finger Lakes in New York, which are named for their slender shape.

The Great Lakes were formed thousands of years ago as an ice sheet moved over the land and then melted. A million years ago, the region of the Great Lakes had many river valleys. The ice sheet gouged out large depressions in the land and left piles of rock and debris that blocked water from draining out. In some areas, where the deepest Great Lakes are now, the enormous weight of the glacier actually caused the land to sink as much as one kilometer.

The ice sheet started to melt about 14,000 years ago. By about 7000 years ago, it had melted past what would become Lake Erie and Lake Ontario, the lakes farthest to the east.

CHECK YOUR READING What are two ways the ice sheet formed the Great Lakes?

5.4 Review

KEY CONCEPTS

1. Describe the two processes that cause glaciers to move.
2. What are the two major types of glaciers, and where are they found?
3. Describe the land features left behind by glaciers that have melted and shrunk.

CRITICAL THINKING

4. **Compare and Contrast** Identify two ways in which the erosion effects of glaciers differ from those of rivers.
5. **Predict** How would glaciers be affected by changes in climate, such as global warming and global cooling?

◯ CHALLENGE

6. **Infer** Regions near the equator are generally the warmest on Earth. However, in one small area of Africa, there are glaciers close to the equator. Form a hypothesis to explain why these glaciers exist.

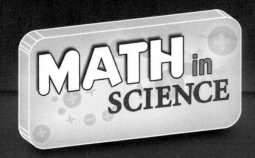

MATH in SCIENCE

 MATH TUTORIAL

Click on Math Tutorial for more help with making line graphs.

Snow Line Elevation and Latitude

Glaciers form above the snow line, the lowest elevation at which there is permanent snow in the summer. The snow line elevation depends on temperature and precipitation. In the hot tropics the snow line is high in the mountains, while at the poles it is near sea level. The table shows the snow line elevations at different locations on Earth. The latitude of each location indicates how far the location is from the equator; the latitude of the equator is 0 degrees, and the latitude of the North Pole is 90 degrees.

Location	Latitude (degrees north)	Snow Line Elevation (meters)
North Pole	90	0
Juneau, Alaska	58	1050
Glacier National Park	49	2600
Sierra Nevada	37	3725
Himalayas (East Nepal)	28	5103
Ecuador	0	4788

Follow the steps below to make a line graph of the data.

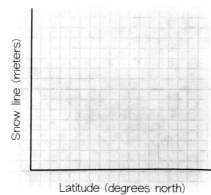

(1) On a sheet of graph paper, draw and label axes. Put latitude on the horizontal axis and snow line elevation on the vertical axis.

(2) Choose and mark a scale for each axis.

(3) Graph each point.

(4) Draw line segments to connect the points.

Use your graph to answer the following questions.

1. Mount Kenya is very close to the equator. Estimate the snow line elevation on Mount Kenya.

2. Mount Rainier is at 47 degrees north latitude and is 4389 meters tall. Can there be glaciers on Mount Rainier? If so, estimate the elevation above which the glaciers form.

3. Mount Washington in New Hampshire is at 45 degrees north latitude and is 1917 meters tall. Can there be glaciers on Mount Washington? If so, estimate their lowest elevation.

CHALLENGE Temperatures are hotter at the equator than at 28 degrees north latitude. Why is the snow line lower at the equator in Ecuador? (**Hint:** The answer involves precipitation.)

CONTENT REVIEW
CLASSZONE.COM

the **BIG** idea

Water, wind, and ice shape Earth's surface.

◀ **KEY CONCEPTS SUMMARY**

5.1 Forces wear down and build up Earth's surface.

Water, wind, and ice move sediment in the process called **erosion**. The placement of sediment in a new location is **deposition**, part of the erosion process.

VOCABULARY
erosion p. 145
deposition p. 145
mass wasting p. 147

5.2 Moving water shapes land.

Water drains from land in **drainage basins,** which are separated by **divides.** As water flows over land and underground, it moves sediment and changes land features.

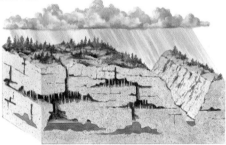

VOCABULARY
drainage basin p. 151
divide p. 151
floodplain p. 152
alluvial fan p. 153
delta p. 153
sinkhole p. 155

5.3 Waves and wind shape land.

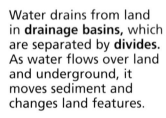

The action of water moves sand and builds up new landforms, such as sandbars and barrier islands. Wind forms dunes.

VOCABULARY
longshore drift p. 159
longshore current
  p. 159
sandbar p. 160
barrier island p. 160
dune p. 161
loess p. 162

5.4 Glaciers carve land and move sediments.

Glaciers are large bodies of ice that change landscapes as they move.

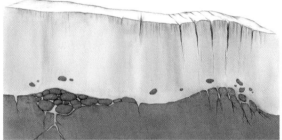

VOCABULARY
glacier p. 165
till p. 168
moraine p. 168
kettle lake p. 169

Reviewing Vocabulary

Copy and complete the chart below. Explain how each landscape feature is formed.

Feature	How It Forms
EXAMPLE delta	A river deposits sediment as it enters the ocean.
1. alluvial fan	
2. sinkhole	
3. sandbar	
4. barrier island	
5. dune	
6. loess	
7. moraine	
8. kettle lake	

Reviewing Key Concepts

Multiple Choice *Choose the letter of the best answer.*

9. The first stage in the erosion process is
   a. deposition
   b. mass wasting
   c. drainage
   d. weathering

10. The main natural force responsible for mass movements of rocks and debris is
    a. rainwater   c. gravity
    b. wind   d. fire

11. A sinkhole is formed by the collapse of
    a. an alluvial fan
    b. a cavern
    c. a moraine
    d. a kettle lake

12. Rivers transport sediment to
    a. drainage basins
    b. oceans and lakes
    c. the water table
    d. moraines

13. Drainage basins are separated by a
    a. moraine   c. tributary
    b. divide   d. barrier island

14. In high mountains, a valley carved by a stream has the shape of a
    a. U   c. plate
    b. crescent   d. V

15. An oxbow lake is formed by the cutting off of a
    a. meander   c. sinkhole
    b. drainage basin   d. glacier

16. Sandbars, spits, and barrier islands can all be built up by
    a. glaciers   c. wind
    b. ocean waves   d. mass wasting

17. A dune is a sand mound built up primarily by
    a. gravity   c. glaciers
    b. running water   d. wind

18. Strong winds can transport large quantities of
    a. gravel   c. dry sand
    b. wet sand   d. clay

19. A mountain valley carved by a glacier has the shape of a
    a. U   c. bowl
    b. crescent   d. V

Short Answer *Answer each of the following questions in a sentence or two.*

20. How is deposition part of the erosion process?

21. How can rainwater in the Rocky Mountains end up in the ocean?

22. What is the effect of a longshore current on a beach?

23. Why is a mass movement of mud called a flow?

24. What visual evidence is a sign of creep?

25. What is the connection between icebergs and glaciers?

Thinking Critically

This photograph shows two glaciers joining to form one (A). Make a sketch of the glaciers to answer the next three questions.

26. **APPLY** Place an arrow to show in which direction the main glacier (A) is moving.

27. **ANALYZE** Mark the places where you think till would be found.

28. **APPLY** Mark the location of a lateral moraine.

29. **ANALYZE** Why does the main glacier not have an end moraine?

30. **COMPARE AND CONTRAST** Compare the main glacier valley in the photograph with the valley at the far right (B). How are the valleys different? Explain why they might be different.

31. **APPLY** In exploring an area of land, what clues would you look for to determine whether glaciers were once there?

32. **COMPARE AND CONTRAST** How is a deposit of till from a glacier similar to a river delta? How is it different?

33. **EVALUATE** If you were growing crops on a field near a slow-moving, curvy river, what would an advantage of the field's location be? What might be a disadvantage?

34. **COMPARE AND CONTRAST** How are mudflows and mass wasting of rock similar? How are they different? Include references to speed and types of material in your answer.

35. **INFER** If the wind usually blows from west to east over a large area of land, and the wind usually slows down over the eastern half of the area, where would you be likely to find loess in the area? Explain your answer.

36. **APPLY** If you were considering a location for a house and were concerned about creep, what two factors about the land would you consider?

37. **SYNTHESIZE** Describe how the processes of erosion and deposition are involved in the formation of kettle lakes.

the **BIG** idea

38. **SYNTHESIZE** Describe how snow falling onto the Continental Divide in the Rocky Mountains can be part of the process of erosion and deposition. Include the words *divide, glacier, stream,* and *ocean* in your answer.

39. **PROVIDE EXAMPLES** Choose three examples of erosion processes—one each from Sections 5.2, 5.3, and 5.4. Explain how gravity is involved in each of these processes.

UNIT PROJECTS

Evaluate all the data, results, and information in your project folder. Prepare to present your project. Be ready to answer questions posed by your classmates about your results.

Analyzing a Diagram

Use the diagram to answer the questions below.

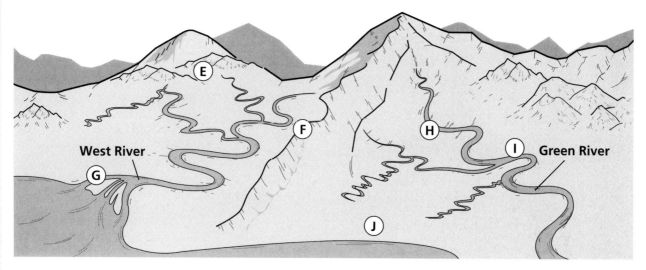

1. Where would a glacier be most likely to form?

  a. E   **c.** G

  b. F   **d.** H

2. Where is a divide?

  a. E   **c.** H

  b. F   **d.** I

3. Where is a delta?

  a. E   **c.** G

  b. F   **d.** J

4. Which process could move sediment from point E to point G?

  a. weathering   **c.** deposition

  b. erosion   **d.** drifting

5. Which word best describes the building up of sediment at point G?

  a. weathering   **c.** deposition

  b. erosion   **d.** drifting

6. Why might the water in the Green River move faster at point H than at point I?

  a. The river at point H is warmer.

  b. The river at point H is smaller.

  c. The slope at point H is steeper.

  d. More rain falls at point H.

Extended Response

Answer the two questions below in detail. Include some of the terms shown in the word box. In your answers, underline each term you use.

ocean waves	currents	barrier island
grass	glaciers	kettle lakes

7. Each year, Clark and his family visit the ocean. Clark notices that a sandbar near the coast is slightly larger each year. Predict what will happen if this trend continues.

8. Annika often goes fishing at one of several small, round lakes that are within 20 miles of her house in Minnesota. How might these lakes have formed?

UNIT B

Matter and Energy

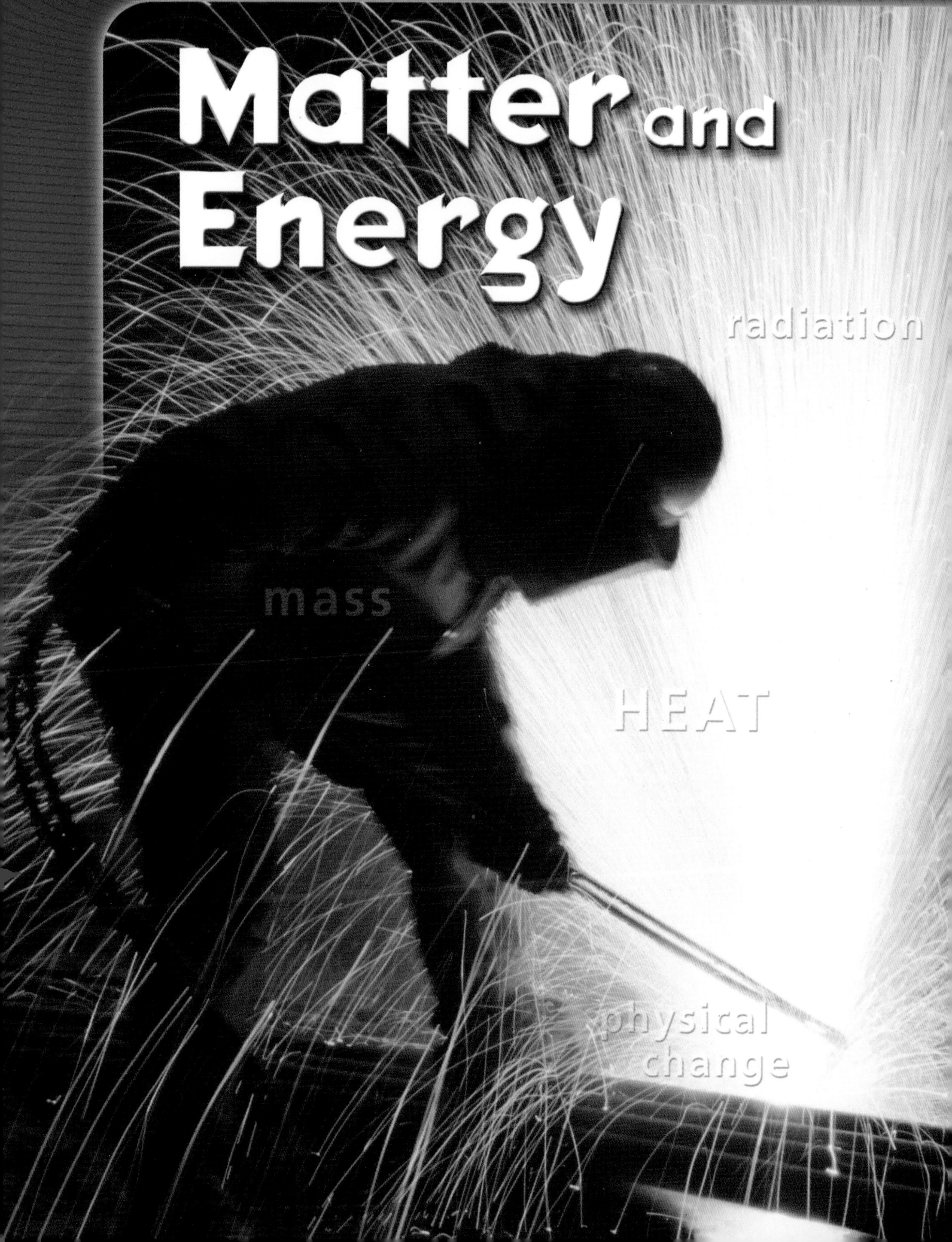
radiation
mass
HEAT
physical change

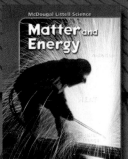

Matter and Energy
Contents Overview

B

Unit Features

1 Introduction to Matter   6

(the **BIG** idea)

Everything that has mass and takes up space is matter.

2 Properties of Matter   38

(the **BIG** idea)

Matter has properties that can be changed by physical and chemical processes.

3 Energy   68

(the **BIG** idea)

Energy has different forms, but it is always conserved.

4 Temperature and Heat   100

(the **BIG** idea)

Heat is a flow of energy due to temperature differences.

FUELS of the FUTURE

Where does this spacecraft get its fuel?

SCIENTIFIC AMERICAN FRONTIERS

View the "Sunrayce" segment of your *Scientific American Frontiers* video to learn about a cross-country race in which cars use solar power instead of gasoline.

Deep Space 1 was an experimental design. Its successful mission prepared the way to the development of more ion-propelled spacecraft.

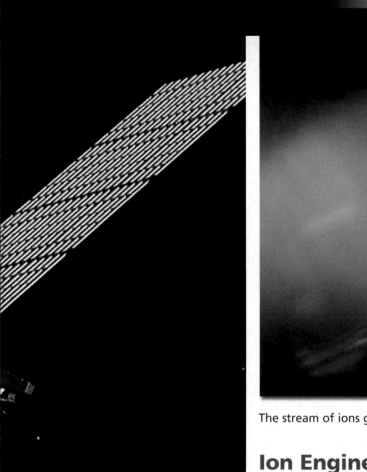

The stream of ions glows blue as it is shot out of an ion-propulsion engine.

Ion Engines for Long Voyages

Rocket engines must provide huge amounts of energy to move spacecraft away from Earth and keep them in orbit. The fuel required can weigh more than the spacecraft themselves. That is why scientists and engineers are always looking for more efficient ways to give spacecraft and other vehicles the energy to move.

One method of powering spacecraft uses electrically charged particles called ions. The atoms of a gas—usually xenon—are first made into ions. An electric field is then used to pull these ions out of the engine at a very high speed—faster than 100,000 kilometers per hour (62,000 mi/h). This stream of rapidly moving ions works like the gases coming out of a jet engine on a plane—propelling the spacecraft in the direction opposite to the ion stream.

An advantage of ion propulsion is that its fuel is much lighter than the chemical fuel used in rockets. Ion propulsion does not provide enough thrust to be used for a rocket launch, but it can be used to move a spacecraft through long distances in outer space. This method of propulsion provides a small force to the spacecraft; however, over time the spacecraft can reach great speeds.

The space probe *Deep Space 1* was the first to use an ion engine to travel between planets. The engine generated enough speed for the probe to follow and photograph comet Borrelly in 2001.

Solar sails will reflect sunlight to move a spacecraft through space.

Running on Sunlight

Solar energy is used for travel in outer space, where there is plenty of sunlight and very little friction to slow down a spacecraft. However, once a spacecraft travels far away from the Sun—as far as the outer planets Jupiter and Saturn—the amount of energy reaching it is far less than the energy it was getting near Earth. The sunlight can be helpful only if solar cells on the vehicle can collect enough of it. One solution is to reflect sunlight. Scientists are developing solar sails, which will act like enormous mirrors. The pressure of reflected sunlight on the sails can be used to move a large ship through space—even far from the Sun.

Beaming Energy from Earth

Another way to power a spacecraft is to send energy to it all the way from Earth. This idea is called beamed energy propulsion. A beam delivers energy to solar sails on the spacecraft. The energy can be in the form of microwaves—the same energy that heats food in a microwave oven or delivers calls on a cell phone. Or it can be in the form of laser light, a very concentrated beam of visible light. This method has already been used successfully to power very small vehicles, 10 centimeters (4 in.) long. Experiments are under way with larger spacecraft.

Combined Technologies

Some recent space flights have combined common and experimental technologies. For example, the *Cassini* space probe has two regular rocket engines for propulsion. Other energy comes from three generators powered by radioactive decay. This combination of engines allowed *Cassini* to be the largest and most complicated spacecraft ever launched. Its goal is to explore Saturn.

SCIENTIFIC AMERICAN FRONTIERS

View the "Sunrayce" segment of your *Scientific American Frontiers* video to see what is involved in solar-car racing.

IN THIS SCENE FROM THE VIDEO ▸ Students from California State University, Los Angeles, work on their solar car.

CATCHING THE SUN'S RAYS Since 1990 teams of college students have built and raced solar-powered cars. The races are held every two years to promote awareness of solar energy and to inspire young people to work in science and engineering.

Solar cells on the cars' bodies convert sunlight into electricity. The goal is to make lightweight cars that convert sunlight efficiently. Today's solar cars can reach speeds of up to 75 miles per hour, but the average racing speed is 25 miles per hour. On cloudy or rainy days, the teams conserve power by traveling more slowly—or risk running down their batteries.

In 2003 the American Solar Challenge took place on historic Route 66 from Chicago to Claremont, California. At 3700 kilometers (2300 mi), the ten-day event was the longest solar-car race in the world.

Alternative Fuels on Earth

Scientists and inventors have long been looking for practical alternative fuels to power vehicles on Earth as well as in outer space. Most vehicle engines on Earth use gasoline or other fossil fuels. These fuels are based on resources, such as petroleum, that are found in underground deposits. Those deposits will not be replaced for millions of years. Solar energy, by contrast, is endlessly renewable, so it seems to be a good alternative to nonrenewable fossil fuels.

Solar-powered cars rely on solar cells, which convert the energy of sunlight directly into electrical energy that can be stored in batteries. One outstanding solar car was built by Dutch students and entered in the 2001 World Solar Challenge.

The students' car, called the *Nuna,* used several technologies that had been developed for space travel. Its body was reinforced with Kevlar, a space-age material that is also used in satellites, space suits, and bulletproof vests. During the race, the *Nuna* covered 3010 kilometers of desert in Australia, breaking solar-car speed records, and won the race.

Does the development of solar cars like the *Nuna* mean that most people will be driving solar cars soon? Unfortunately, such cars run only when the Sun is shining unless they rely on batteries—and it takes hundreds of pounds of batteries to store the amount of energy in a gallon of gasoline. As with spacecraft, the goal is to design a vehicle in which the fuel doesn't outweigh the vehicle itself.

UNANSWERED Questions

Even as scientists and inventors solve problems in solar technology, new questions arise.

- Can solar technology be made affordable?
- Is solar technology practical for large-scale public transportation?
- Are there any hidden costs to the use of alternative fuels?

UNIT PROJECTS

As you study this unit, work alone or with a group on one of these projects.

Build a Solar Oven

Design and build a solar oven that can boil a quarter cup of water.

- Plan and sketch a design for a solar oven that can reach 100°C.
- Collect materials and assemble your oven. Then conduct trials and improve your design.

Multimedia Presentation

Create an informative program on solar race cars and the way they work.

- Collect information about solar race cars. Research how they are powered.
- Examine why solar cars have specific shapes. Learn how the solar panels and batteries work together.
- Give a multimedia presentation describing what you learned.

Design an Experiment

Design an experiment that compares how well two of the following alternative energy sources move an object: solar energy, wind power, biomass (fuel from plant material), waste-material fuel, hydrogen fuel cells, heat exchangers.

- Research the energy sources, and pick two types to compare.
- List materials for your experiment. Create a data table and write up your procedure.
- Describe your experiment for the class.

CAREER CENTER
CLASSZONE.COM

Learn more about careers in electrical engineering.

CHAPTER

Introduction to Matter

the **BIG** idea

Everything that has mass and takes up space is matter.

What matter can you identify in this photograph?

Key Concepts

SECTION

1.1 **Matter has mass and volume.**
Learn what mass and volume are and how to measure them.

SECTION

1.2 **Matter is made of atoms.**
Learn about the movement of atoms and molecules.

SECTION

1.3 **Matter combines to form different substances.**
Learn how atoms form compounds and mixtures.

SECTION

1.4 **Matter exists in different physical states.**
Learn how different states of matter behave.

Internet Preview

CLASSZONE.COM

Chapter 1 online resources: Content Review, two Simulations, four Resource Centers, Math Tutorial, Test Practice

EXPLORE (the BIG idea)

What Has Changed?

Blow up a balloon. Observe it. Let the air out of the balloon slowly. Observe it again.

Observe and Think Did the amount of material that makes up the balloon change? Did the amount of air inside the balloon change? How did the amount of air inside the balloon affect the size of the balloon?

Where Does the Sugar Go?

Stir some sugar into a glass of water. Observe what happens.

Observe and Think What happened to the sugar as you stirred? Do you think you would be able to separate the sugar from the water? If so, how?

Internet Activity: Scale

Go to **ClassZone.com** to explore the smallest units of matter. Start with a faraway view of an object. Then try closer and closer views until you see that object at the atomic level.

Observe and Think Are all objects seen at faraway views made up of the same parts at an atomic level? Explain your answer.

NSTA
scilinks.org
SCiLINKS

Solids, Liquids, and Gases **Code: MDL061**

Getting Ready to Learn

◀ CONCEPT REVIEW

- Matter is made of particles too small to see.
- Energy and matter change from one form to another.
- Energy cannot be created or destroyed.

◀ VOCABULARY REVIEW

See Glossary for definitions.

particle

substance

 CONTENT REVIEW
CLASSZONE.COM
Review concepts and vocabulary.

▶ TAKING NOTES

MAIN IDEA AND DETAIL NOTES

Make a two-column chart. Write the main ideas, such as those in the blue headings, in the column on the left. Write details about each of those main ideas in the column on the right.

VOCABULARY STRATEGY

Write each new vocabulary term in the center of a **four square** diagram. Write notes in the squares around each term. Include a definition, some characteristics, and some examples of the term. If possible, write some things that are not examples of the term.

See the Note-Taking Handbook on pages R45–R51.

SCIENCE NOTEBOOK

MAIN IDEAS	DETAIL NOTES
1. All objects are made of matter.	1. All objects and living organisms are matter.
	1. Light and sound are not matter.
2. Mass is a measure of the amount of matter.	2. A balance can be used to compare masses.
	2. Standard unit of mass is kilogram (kg).

Definition	Characteristics
the downward pull on an object due to gravity	• standard unit is newton (N) • is measured by using a scale

WEIGHT

Examples	Nonexamples
On Earth, a 1 kg object has a weight of 9.8 N.	not the same as mass, which is a measure of how much matter an object contains

Matter has mass and volume.

◀ **BEFORE, you learned**

- Scientists study the world by asking questions and collecting data
- Scientists use tools such as microscopes, thermometers, and computers

▶ **NOW, you will learn**

- What matter is
- How to measure the mass of matter
- How to measure the volume of matter

VOCABULARY

matter p. 9
mass p. 10
weight p. 11
volume p. 11

EXPLORE Similar Objects

How can two similar objects differ?

PROCEDURE

① Look at the two balls but do not pick them up. Compare their sizes and shapes. Record your observations.

② Pick up each ball. Compare the way the balls feel in your hands. Record your observations.

WHAT DO YOU THINK?
How would your observations be different if the larger ball were made of foam?

MATERIALS
2 balls of different sizes

VOCABULARY
Make four square diagrams for *matter* and for *mass* in your notebook to help you understand their relationship.

All objects are made of matter.

Suppose your class takes a field trip to a museum. During the course of the day you see mammoth bones, sparkling crystals, hot-air balloons, and an astronaut's space suit. All of these things are matter.

Matter is what makes up all of the objects and living organisms in the universe. As you will see, **matter** is anything that has mass and takes up space. Your body is matter. The air that you breathe and the water that you drink are also matter. Matter makes up the materials around you. Matter is made of particles called atoms, which are too small to see. You will learn more about atoms in the next section.

Not everything is matter. Light and sound, for example, are not matter. Light does not take up space or have mass in the same way that a table does. Although air is made of atoms, a sound traveling through air is not.

CHECK YOUR READING What is matter? How can you tell if something is matter?

Mass is a measure of the amount of matter.

MAIN IDEA AND DETAILS
As you read, write the blue headings on the left side of a two-column chart. Add details in the other column.

Different objects contain different amounts of matter. **Mass** is a measure of how much matter an object contains. A metal teaspoon, for example, contains more matter than a plastic teaspoon. Therefore, a metal teaspoon has a greater mass than a plastic teaspoon. An elephant has more mass than a mouse.

CHECK YOUR READING How are matter and mass related?

Measuring Mass

When you measure mass, you compare the mass of the object with a standard amount, or unit, of mass. The standard unit of mass is the kilogram (kg). A large grapefruit has a mass of about one-half kilogram. Smaller masses are often measured in grams (g). There are 1000 grams in a kilogram. A penny has a mass of between two and three grams.

How can you compare the masses of two objects? One way is to use a pan balance, as shown below. If two objects balance each other on a pan balance, then they contain the same amount of matter. If a basketball balances a metal block, for example, then the basketball and the block have the same mass. Beam balances work in a similar way, but instead of comparing the masses of two objects, you compare the mass of an object with a standard mass on the beam.

A bowling ball and a basketball are about the same size, but a bowling ball has more mass.

Measuring Weight

When you hold an object such as a backpack full of books, you feel it pulling down on your hands. This is because Earth's gravity pulls the backpack toward the ground. Gravity is the force that pulls two masses toward each other. In this example, the two masses are Earth and the backpack. **Weight** is the downward pull on an object due to gravity. If the pull of the backpack is strong, you would say that the backpack weighs a lot.

Weight is measured by using a scale, such as a spring scale like the one shown on the right, that tells how hard an object is pushing or pulling on it. The standard scientific unit for weight is the newton (N). A common unit for weight is the pound (lb).

Gravity is pulling down on both the girl and the backpack. The heavier the backpack is, the stronger the pull of gravity is on it.

Mass and weight are closely related, but they are not the same. Mass describes the amount of matter an object has, and weight describes how strongly gravity is pulling on that matter. On Earth, a one-kilogram object has a weight of 9.8 newtons (2.2 lb). When a person says that one kilogram is equal to 2.2 pounds, he or she is really saying that one kilogram has a weight of 2.2 pounds on Earth. On the Moon, however, gravity is one-sixth as strong as it is on Earth. On the Moon, the one-kilogram object would have a weight of 1.6 newtons (0.36 lb). The amount of matter in the object, or its mass, is the same on Earth as it is on the Moon, but the pull of gravity is different.

SIMULATION
CLASSZONE.COM

Compare weights on different planets.

CHECK YOUR READING What is the difference between mass and weight?

Volume is a measure of the space matter occupies.

Matter takes up space. A bricklayer stacks bricks on top of each other to build a wall. No two bricks can occupy the same place because the matter in each brick takes up space.

The amount of space that matter in an object occupies is called the object's **volume.** The bowling ball and the basketball shown on page 10 take up approximately the same amount of space. Therefore, the two balls have about the same volume. Although the basketball is hollow, it is not empty. Air fills up the space inside the basketball. Air and other gases take up space and have volume.

Determining Volume by Formula

RESOURCE CENTER
CLASSZONE.COM

Find out more about volume.

There are different ways to find the volume of an object. For objects that have well-defined shapes, such as a brick or a ball, you can take a few measurements of the object and calculate the volume by substituting these values into a formula.

A rectangular box, for example, has a length, a width, and a height that can be measured. To find the volume of the box, multiply the three values.

$$\text{Volume} = \text{length} \cdot \text{width} \cdot \text{height}$$
$$V = lwh$$

If you measure the length, the width, and the height of the box in centimeters (cm), the volume has a unit of centimeters times centimeters times centimeters, or centimeters cubed (cm^3). If the measurements are meters, the unit of volume is meters cubed (m^3). All measurements must be in the same unit to calculate volume.

Other regular solids, such as spheres and cylinders, also have formulas for calculating volumes. All formulas for volume require multiplying three dimensions. Units for volume are often expressed in terms of a length unit cubed, that is, a length to the third power.

Calculating Volume

▶ Sample Problem

What is the volume of a pizza box that is 8 cm high, 38 cm wide, and 38 cm long?

What do you know?	length = 38 cm, width = 38 cm, height = 8 cm
What do you want to find out?	Volume
Write the formula:	$V = lwh$
Substitute into the formula:	$V = 38 \text{ cm} \cdot 38 \text{ cm} \cdot 8 \text{ cm}$
Calculate and simplify:	$11{,}552 \text{ cm} \cdot \text{cm} \cdot \text{cm} = 11{,}552 \text{ cm}^3$
Check that your units agree:	Unit is cm^3. Unit of volume is cm^3. Units agree.
Answer:	$11{,}552 \text{ cm}^3$

▶ Practice the Math

1. A bar of gold is 10 cm long, 5 cm wide, and 7 cm high. What is its volume?
2. What is the volume of a large block of wood that is 1 m long, 0.5 m high, and 50 cm wide?

Measuring Volume by Displacement

Although a box has a regular shape, a rock does not. There is no simple formula for calculating the volume of something with an irregular shape. Instead, you can make use of the fact that two objects cannot be in the same place at the same time. This method of measuring is called displacement.

1 Add water to a graduated cylinder. Note the volume of the water by reading the water level on the cylinder.

2 Submerge the irregular object in the water. Because the object and the water cannot share the same space, the water is displaced, or moved upward. Note the new volume of the water with the object in it.

3 Subtract the volume of the water before you added the object from the volume of the water and the object together. The result is the volume of the object. The object displaces a volume of water equal to the volume of the object.

You measure the volume of a liquid by measuring how much space it takes up in a container. The volume of a liquid usually is measured in liters (L) or milliliters (mL). One liter is equal to 1000 milliliters. Milliliters and cubic centimeters are equivalent. This can be written as $1\ mL = 1\ cm^3$. If you had a box with a volume of one cubic centimeter and you filled it with water, you would have one milliliter of water.

In the first photograph, the graduated cylinder contains 50 mL of water. Placing a rock in the cylinder causes the water level to rise from 50 mL to 55 mL. The difference is 5 mL; therefore, the volume of the rock is $5\ cm^3$.

Measure the volume of water without the rock.

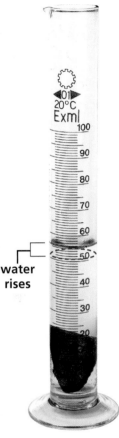

water rises

Measure the volume of water with the rock in it.

1.1 Review

KEY CONCEPTS

1. Give three examples of matter.

2. What do weight and mass measure?

3. How can you measure the volume of an object that has an irregular shape?

CRITICAL THINKING

4. **Calculate** What is the volume of a box that is 12 cm long, 6 cm wide, and 4 cm high?

5. **Synthesize** What is the relationship between the units of measurement for the volume of a liquid and of a solid object?

⬥ CHALLENGE

6. **Infer** Why might a small increase in the dimensions of an object cause a large change in its volume?

CHAPTER INVESTIGATION

Mass and Volume

OVERVIEW AND PURPOSE In order for scientists around the world to communicate with one another about calculations in their research, they use a common system of measurement called the metric system. Scientists use the same tools and methods for the measurement of length, mass, and volume. In this investigation you will

- use a ruler, a graduated cylinder, and a balance to measure the mass and the volume of different objects
- determine which method is best for measuring the volume of the objects

▶ Procedure

1 Make a data table like the one shown on the sample notebook page.

2 Measure the mass of each object: rock, pennies, sponge, and tissue box. Record each mass.

step 2

3 For each object, conduct three trials for mass. Average the trials to find a final mass measurement.

4 Decide how you will find the volume of each object.

For rectangular objects, you will use the following formula:

Volume = length · width · height

For irregular objects, you will use the displacement method and the following formula:

Volume of object = volume of water with object – volume of water without object

MATERIALS
- small rock
- 5 pennies
- rectangular sponge
- tissue box
- beam balance
- large graduated cylinder
- water
- ruler

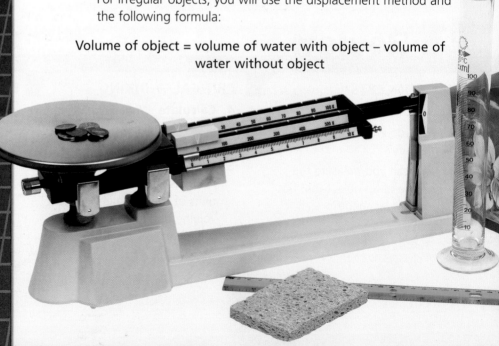

5. For each object, you will conduct three trials for measuring volume. Average the trials to find a final volume measurement.

6. For rectangular objects, use metric units for measuring the length, width, and height. Record the measurements in your data table.

step 6

7. For irregular objects, fill the graduated cylinder about half full with water. Record the exact volume of water in the cylinder. **Note:** The surface of the liquid will be curved in the graduated cylinder. Read the volume of the liquid at the bottom of the curve called the meniscus.

step 7

8. Carefully place the object you are measuring into the cylinder. The object must be completely under the water. Record the exact volume of water in the cylinder containing the object by reading the meniscus.

▶ Observe and Analyze
Write It Up

1. **RECORD OBSERVATIONS** Make sure you have filled out your data table completely.

2. **INTERPRET** For each object, explain why you chose a particular method for measuring the volume.

▶ Conclude
Write It Up

1. **IDENTIFY LIMITS** Which sources of error might have affected your measurements?

2. **APPLY** Doctors need to know the mass of a patient before deciding how much of a medication to prescribe. Why is it important to measure each patient's mass before prescribing medicine?

3. **APPLY** Scientists in the United States work closely with scientists in other countries to develop new technology. What are the advantages of having a single system of measurement?

▶ INVESTIGATE Further

CHALLENGE Measuring cups and spoons used in cooking often include both customary and metric units. Convert the measurements in a favorite recipe into metric units. Convert the amounts of solid ingredients to grams, and liquid ingredients to milliliters or liters. If possible, use the new measurements to follow the recipe and prepare the food. Were your conversions accurate?

Mass and Volume
Observe and Analyze
Table 1. Masses of Various Objects

Object	Mass (g)			Average
	Trial 1	Trial 2	Trial 3	
rock				
5 pennies				
sponge				
tissue box				

Table 2. Volumes of Various Objects

Object	Method Used	Volume (cm³ or mL)			
		Trial 1	Trial 2	Trial 3	Average
rock					
5 pennies					
sponge					
tissue box					

Matter is made of atoms.

 BEFORE, you learned

- Matter has mass
- Matter has volume

 NOW, you will learn

- About the smallest particles of matter
- How atoms combine into molecules
- How atoms and molecules move

VOCABULARY

atom p. 16
molecule p. 18

THINK ABOUT

How small is an atom?

All matter is made up of very tiny particles called atoms. It is hard to imagine exactly how small these particles are. Suppose that each of the particles making up the pin shown in the photograph on the right were actually the size of the round head on the pin. How large would the pin be in that case? If you could stick such a pin in the ground, it would cover about 90 square miles—about one-seventh the area of London, England. It would also be about 80 miles high—almost 15 times the height of Mount Everest.

Atoms are extremely small.

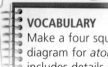

VOCABULARY
Make a four square diagram for *atom* that includes details that will help you remember the term.

How small can things get? If you break a stone wall into smaller and smaller pieces, you would have a pile of smaller stones. If you could break the smaller stones into the smallest pieces possible, you would have a pile of atoms. An **atom** is the smallest basic unit of matter.

The idea that all matter is made of extremely tiny particles dates back to the fifth century B.C., when Greek philosophers proposed the first atomic theory of matter. All matter, they said, was made of only a few different types of tiny particles called atoms. The different arrangements of atoms explained the differences among the substances that make up the world. Although the modern view of the atom is different from the ancient view, the idea of atoms as basic building blocks has been confirmed. Today scientists have identified more than 100 different types of atoms.

 CHECK YOUR READING What are atoms? How are they like building blocks?

Atoms

It is hard to imagine that visible matter is composed of particles too tiny to see. Although you cannot see an individual atom, you are constantly seeing large collections of them. You are a collection of atoms. So are your textbook, a desk, and all the other matter around you. Matter is not something that contains atoms; matter is atoms. A desk, for example, is a collection of atoms and the empty space between those atoms. Without the atoms, there would be no desk—just empty space.

Atoms are so small that they cannot be seen even with very strong optical microscopes. Try to imagine the size of an atom by considering that a single teaspoonful of water contains approximately 500,000,000,000,000,000,000,000 atoms. Although atoms are extremely small, they do have a mass. The mass of a single teaspoonful of water is about 5 grams. This mass is equal to the mass of all the atoms that the water is made of added together.

READING TiP

The word *atom* comes from the Greek word *atomos,* meaning "indivisible," or "cannot be divided."

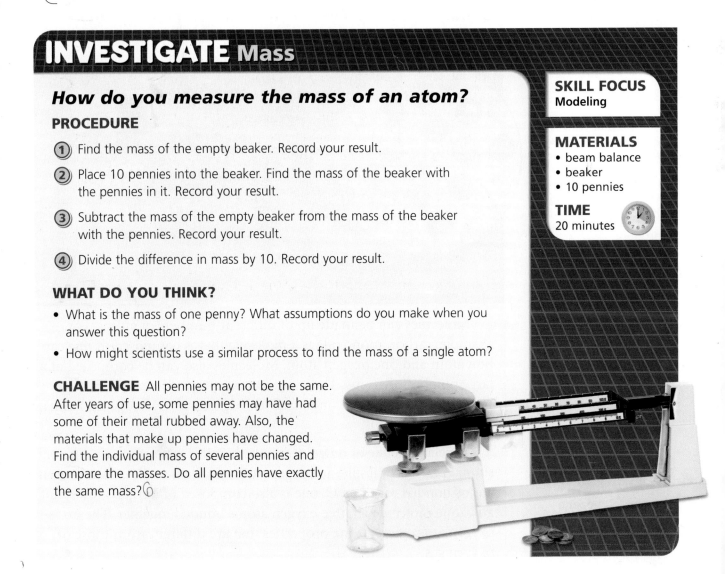

INVESTIGATE Mass

How do you measure the mass of an atom?

PROCEDURE

1. Find the mass of the empty beaker. Record your result.

2. Place 10 pennies into the beaker. Find the mass of the beaker with the pennies in it. Record your result.

3. Subtract the mass of the empty beaker from the mass of the beaker with the pennies. Record your result.

4. Divide the difference in mass by 10. Record your result.

WHAT DO YOU THINK?

- What is the mass of one penny? What assumptions do you make when you answer this question?

- How might scientists use a similar process to find the mass of a single atom?

CHALLENGE All pennies may not be the same. After years of use, some pennies may have had some of their metal rubbed away. Also, the materials that make up pennies have changed. Find the individual mass of several pennies and compare the masses. Do all pennies have exactly the same mass?

SKILL FOCUS
Modeling

MATERIALS
- beam balance
- beaker
- 10 pennies

TIME
20 minutes

Molecules

When two or more atoms bond together, or combine, they make a particle called a **molecule.** A molecule can be made of atoms that are different or atoms that are alike. A molecule of water, for example, is a combination of different atoms—two hydrogen atoms and one oxygen atom (also written as H_2O). Hydrogen gas molecules are made of the same atom—two hydrogen atoms bonded together.

A molecule is the smallest amount of a substance made of combined atoms that is considered to be that substance. Think about what would happen if you tried to divide water to find its smallest part. Ultimately you would reach a single molecule of water. What would you have if you divided this molecule into its individual atoms of hydrogen and oxygen? If you break up a water molecule, it is no longer water. Instead, you would have hydrogen and oxygen, two different substances.

READING TiP

Not all atoms and molecules have color. In this book atoms and molecules are given colors to make them easier to identify.

CHECK YOUR READING How is a molecule related to an atom?

The droplets of water in this spider web are made of water molecules. Each molecule contains two hydrogen atoms (shown in white) and one oxygen atom (shown in red).

hydrogen

oxygen

water

oxygen   **ozone**

Molecules can be made up of different numbers of atoms. For example, carbon monoxide is a molecule that is composed of one carbon atom and one oxygen atom. Molecules also can be composed of a large number of atoms. The most common type of vitamin E molecule, for example, contains 29 carbon atoms, 50 hydrogen atoms, and 2 oxygen atoms.

Molecules made of different numbers of the same atom are different substances. For example, an oxygen gas molecule is made of two oxygen atoms bonded together. Ozone is also composed of oxygen atoms, but an ozone molecule is three oxygen atoms bonded together. The extra oxygen atom gives ozone properties that are different from those of oxygen gas.

This photograph shows the interior of Grand Central Terminal in New York City. Light from the window reflects off dust particles that are being moved by the motion of the molecules in air.

Atoms and molecules are always in motion.

If you have ever looked at a bright beam of sunlight, you may have seen dust particles floating in the air. If you were to watch carefully, you might notice that the dust does not fall toward the floor but instead seems to dart about in all different directions. Molecules in air are constantly moving and hitting the dust particles. Because the molecules are moving in many directions, they collide with the dust particles from different directions. This action causes the darting motion of the dust that you observe.

Atoms and molecules are always in motion. Sometimes this motion is easy to observe, such as when you see evidence of molecules in air bouncing dust particles around. Water molecules move too. When you place a drop of food coloring into water, the motion of the water molecules eventually causes the food coloring to spread throughout the water.

The motion of individual atoms and molecules is hard to observe in solid objects, such as a table. The atoms and molecules in a table cannot move about freely like the ones in water and air. However, the atoms and molecules in a table are constantly moving—by shaking back and forth, or by twisting—even if they stay in the same place.

1.2 Review

KEY CONCEPTS

1. What are atoms?

2. What is the smallest particle of a substance that is still considered to be that substance?

3. Why do dust particles in the air appear to be moving in different directions?

CRITICAL THINKING

4. **Apply** How does tea flavor spread from a tea bag throughout a cup of hot water?

5. **Infer** If a water molecule (H_2O) has two hydrogen atoms and one oxygen atom, how would you describe the make-up of a carbon dioxide molecule (CO_2)?

⚪ CHALLENGE

6. **Synthesize** Assume that a water balloon has the same number of water molecules as a helium balloon has helium atoms. If the mass of the water is 4.5 times greater than the mass of the helium, how does the mass of a water molecule compare with the mass of a helium atom?

EXTREME SCIENCE

Particles Too Small to See

Atoms are so small that you cannot see them through an ordinary microscope. In fact, millions of them could fit in the period at the end of this sentence. Scientists can make images of atoms, however, using an instrument called a scanning tunneling microscope (STM).

Bumps on a Surface

The needle of the scanning tunneling microscope has a very sharp tip that is only one atom wide. The tip is brought close to the surface of the material being observed, and an electric current is applied to the tip. The microscope measures the interaction between the electrically charged needle tip and the nearest atom on the surface of the material. An image of the surface is created by moving the needle just above the surface. The image appears as a series of bumps that shows where the atoms are located. The result is similar to a contour map.

Moving Atoms

Scientists also can use the tip of the STM needle to move atoms on a surface. The large image at left is an STM image of a structure made by pushing individual atoms into place on a very smooth metal surface. This structure was designed as a corral to trap individual atoms inside.

Scientists can manipulate individual atoms to build structures, such as this one made of iron atoms.

Tiny Pieces of Matter

- Images of atoms did not exist until 1970.

- Atoms are so small that a single raindrop contains more than 500 billion trillion atoms.

- If each atom were the size of a pea, your fingerprint would be larger than Alaska.

- In the space between stars, matter is so spread out that a volume of one liter contains only about 1000 atoms.

needle
material
tip of needle
atoms of material

An STM maps the position of atoms using a needle with a tip that is one atom wide.

EXPLORE

1. **INFER** Why must the tip of a scanning tunneling microscope be only one atom wide to make an image of atoms on a surface?

2. **CHALLENGE** Find out more about images of atoms on the Internet. How are STM images used in research to design better materials?

RESOURCE CENTER
CLASSZONE.COM
Find more images from scanning tunneling microscopes.

1.3 Matter combines to form different substances.

 BEFORE, you learned

- Matter is made of tiny particles called atoms
- Atoms combine to form molecules

 NOW, you will learn

- How pure matter and mixed matter are different
- How atoms and elements are related
- How atoms form compounds

VOCABULARY

element p. 22
compound p. 23
mixture p. 23

EXPLORE Mixed Substances

What happens when substances are mixed?

PROCEDURE

(1) Observe and describe a teaspoon of cornstarch and a teaspoon of water.

(2) Mix the two substances together in the cup. Observe and describe the result.

WHAT DO YOU THINK?

- After you mixed the substances, could you still see each substance?
- How was the new substance different from the original substances?

MATERIALS

- cornstarch
- water
- small cup
- spoon

Matter can be pure or mixed.

MAIN IDEA AND DETAILS
Continue to organize your notes in a two-column chart as you read.

Matter can be pure, or it can be two or more substances mixed together. Most of the substances you see around you are mixed, although you can't always tell that by looking at them. For example, the air you breathe is a combination of several substances. Wood, paper, steel, and lemonade are all mixed substances.

You might think that the water that you drink from a bottle or from the tap is a pure substance. However, drinking water has minerals dissolved in it and chemicals added to it that you cannot see. Often the difference between pure and mixed substances is apparent only on the atomic or molecular level.

A pure substance has only one type of component. For example, pure water contains only water molecules. Pure silver contains only silver atoms. Coins and jewelry that look like silver are often made of silver in combination with other metals.

If you could look at the atoms in a bar of pure gold, you would find only gold atoms. If you looked at the atoms in a container of pure water, you would find water molecules, which are a combination of hydrogen and oxygen atoms. Does the presence of two types of atoms mean that water is not really a pure substance after all?

A substance is considered pure if it contains only a single type of atom, such as gold, or a single combination of atoms that are bonded together, such as a water molecule. Because the hydrogen and oxygen atoms are bonded together as molecules, water that has nothing else in it is considered a pure substance.

Elements

One type of pure substance is an element. An **element** is a substance that contains only a single type of atom. The number of atoms is not important as long as all the atoms are of the same type. You cannot separate an element into other substances.

You are probably familiar with many elements, such as silver, oxygen, hydrogen, helium, and aluminum. There are as many elements as there are types of atoms—more than 100. You can see the orderly arrangement of atoms in the element gold, on the left below.

△ CHECK YOUR READING   Why is an element considered to be a pure substance?

Element: Gold

The atoms in gold are all the same type of atom. Therefore, gold is an element.

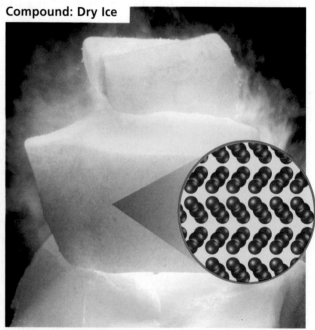

Compound: Dry Ice

Dry ice is frozen carbon dioxide, a compound. Each molecule is made of one carbon atom and two oxygen atoms.

Compounds

A **compound** is a substance that consists of two or more different types of atoms bonded together. A large variety of substances can be made by combining different types of atoms to make different compounds. Some types of compounds are made of molecules, such as water and carbon dioxide, shown on page 22. Other compounds are made of atoms that are bonded together in a different way. Table salt is an example.

A compound can have very different properties from the individual elements that make up that compound. Pure table salt is a common compound that is a combination of sodium and chlorine. Although table salt is safe to eat, the individual elements that go into making it—sodium and chlorine—are poisonous.

 CHECK YOUR READING What is the relationship between atoms and a compound?

Mixtures

Most of the matter around you is a mixture of different substances. Seawater, for instance, contains water, salt, and other minerals mixed together. Your blood is a mixture of blood cells and plasma. Plasma is also a mixture, made up of water, sugar, fat, protein, salts, and minerals.

A **mixture** is a combination of different substances that remain the same individual substances and can be separated by physical means. For example, if you mix apples, oranges, and bananas to make a fruit salad, you do not change the different fruits into a new kind of fruit. Mixtures do not always contain the same amount of the various substances. For example, depending on how the salad is made, the amount of each type of fruit it contains will vary.

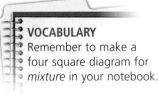

VOCABULARY
Remember to make a four square diagram for *mixture* in your notebook.

APPLY In what ways can a city population be considered a mixture?

INVESTIGATE Mixtures

How well do oil and water mix?

PROCEDURE

① Add a few drops of food coloring to the water in the beaker. Swirl the water around in the beaker until the water is evenly colored throughout.

② Pour the colored water from the beaker into the jar until the jar is about one-fourth full.

③ Add the same amount of vegetable oil to the jar. Screw the lid tightly on the jar.

④ Carefully shake the jar several times with your hand over the cover, and then set it on the table. Observe and record what happens to the liquids in the jar.

⑤ Turn the jar upside down and hold it that way. Observe what happens to the liquids and record your observations.

WHAT DO YOU THINK?

• Does water mix with food coloring? What evidence supports your answer?

• Do water and oil mix? What evidence supports your answer?

• What happened when you turned the jar upside down?

• Based on your observations, what can you infer about the ability of different liquids to mix?

CHALLENGE To clean greasy dishes, you add soap to the dishwater. Try adding soap to your mixture. What does the soap do?

SKILL FOCUS
Inferring

MATERIALS
• food coloring
• beaker of water
• jar with lid
• vegetable oil
for Challenge:
• dish soap

TIME
20 minutes

Comparing Mixtures and Compounds

RESOURCE CENTER
CLASSZONE.COM

Find out more about mixtures.

Although mixtures and compounds may seem similar, they are very different. Consider how mixtures and compounds compare with each other.

• The substances in mixtures remain the same substances. Compounds are new substances formed by atoms that bond together.

• Mixtures can be separated by physical means. Compounds can be separated only by breaking the bonds between atoms.

• The proportions of different substances in a mixture can vary throughout the mixture or from mixture to mixture. The proportions of different substances in a compound are fixed because the type and number of atoms that make up a basic unit of the compound are always the same.

CHECK YOUR READING How is a mixture different from a compound?

Parts of mixtures can be the same or different throughout.

It is obvious that something is a mixture when you can see the different substances in it. For example, if you scoop up a handful of soil, you might see that it contains dirt, small rocks, leaves, and even insects. You can separate the soil into its different parts.

Exactly what you see depends on what part of the soil you scoop up. One handful of soil might have more pebbles or insects in it than another handful would. There are many mixtures, such as soil, that have different properties in different areas of the mixture. Such a mixture is called a hetero-geneous (HEHT-uhr-uh-JEE-nee-uhs) mixture.

In some types of mixtures, however, you cannot see the individual substances. For example, if you mix sugar into a cup of water and stir it well, the sugar seems to disappear. You can tell that the sugar is still there because the water tastes sweet, but you cannot see the sugar or easily separate it out again.

When substances are evenly spread throughout a mixture, you cannot tell one part of the mixture from another part. For instance, one drop of sugar water will be almost exactly like any other drop. Such a mixture is called a homogeneous (HOH-muh-JEE-nee-uhs) mixture. Homogenized milk is processed so that it becomes a homogeneous mixture of water and milk fat. Milk that has not been homogenized will separate—most of the milk fat will float to the top as cream while leaving the rest of the milk low in fat.

> **READING TiP**
> The prefix *hetero* means "different," and the prefix *homo* means "same." The Greek root *genos* means "kind."

 **Review**

KEY CONCEPTS

1. What is the difference between pure and mixed matter?
2. How are atoms and elements related?
3. How are compounds different from mixtures?

CRITICAL THINKING

4. **Infer** What can you infer about the size of sugar particles that are dissolved in a mixture of sugar and water?
5. **Infer** Why is it easier to remove the ice cubes from cold lemonade than it is to remove the sugar?

⚊ CHALLENGE

6. **Apply** A unit of sulfuric acid is a molecule of 2 atoms of hydrogen, 1 atom of sulfur, and 4 atoms of oxygen. How many of each type of atom are there in 2 molecules of sulfuric acid?

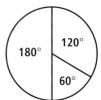

MATH TUTORIAL
CLASSZONE.COM
Click on Math Tutorial for more help with circle graphs.

A Mixture of Spices

Two different mixtures of spices may contain the exact same ingredients but have very different flavors. For example, a mixture of cumin, nutmeg, and ginger powder can be made using more cumin than ginger, or it can be made using more ginger than cumin.

One way to show how much of each substance a mixture contains is to use a circle graph. A circle graph is a visual way to show how a quantity is divided into different parts. A circle graph represents quantities as parts of a whole.

Example

Make a circle graph to represent a spice mixture that is 1/2 cumin, 1/3 nutmeg, and 1/6 ginger.

(1) To find the angle measure for each sector of the circle graph, multiply each fraction in your mixture by 360°.

Cumin: $\frac{1}{2} \cdot 360° = 180°$

Nutmeg: $\frac{1}{3} \cdot 360° = 120°$

Ginger: $\frac{1}{6} \cdot 360° = 60°$

(2) Use a compass to draw a circle. Use a protractor to draw the angle for each sector.

(3) Label each sector and give your graph a title.

ANSWER
Spice Mixture

Answer the following questions.

1. Draw a circle graph representing a spice mixture that is 1/2 ginger, 1/4 cumin, and 1/4 crushed red pepper.

2. A jeweler creates a ring that is 3/4 gold, 3/16 silver, and 1/16 copper. Draw a circle graph representing the mixture of metals in the ring.

3. Draw a circle graph representing a mixture that is 1/5 sand, 2/5 water, and 2/5 salt.

CHALLENGE Dry air is a mixture of about 78 percent nitrogen, 21 percent oxygen, and 1 percent other elements. Create a circle graph representing the elements found in air.

Matter exists in different physical states.

 BEFORE, you learned

- Matter has mass
- Matter is made of atoms
- Atoms and molecules in matter are always moving

 **NOW, you will learn**

- About the different states of matter
- How the different states of matter behave

VOCABULARY

states of matter p. 27
solid p. 28
liquid p. 28
gas p. 28

EXPLORE Solids and Liquids

How do solids and liquids compare?

PROCEDURE

① Observe the water, ice, and marble. Pick them up and feel them. Can you change their shape? their volume?

② Record your observations. Compare and contrast each object with the other two.

WHAT DO YOU THINK?

- How are the ice and the water in the cup similar? How are they different?
- How are the ice and the marble similar? How are they different?

MATERIALS
- water in a cup
- ice cube
- marble
- pie tin

Particle arrangement and motion determine the state of matter.

When you put water in a freezer, the water freezes into a solid (ice). When you place an ice cube on a warm plate, the ice melts into liquid water again. If you leave the plate in the sun, the water becomes water vapor. Ice, water, and water vapor are made of exactly the same type of molecule—a molecule of two hydrogen atoms and one oxygen atom. What, then, makes them different?

Ice, water, and water vapor are different states of water. **States of matter** are the different forms in which matter can exist. The three familiar states are solid, liquid, and gas. When a substance changes from one state to another, the molecules in the substance do not change. However, the arrangement of the molecules does change, giving each state of matter its own characteristics.

Solid, liquid, and gas are common states of matter.

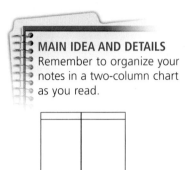

MAIN IDEA AND DETAILS
Remember to organize your notes in a two-column chart as you read.

A substance can exist as a solid, a liquid, or a gas. The state of a substance depends on the space between its particles and on the way in which the particles move. The illustration on page 29 shows how particles are arranged in the three different states.

1 A **solid** is a substance that has a fixed volume and a fixed shape. In a solid, the particles are close together and usually form a regular pattern. Particles in a solid can vibrate but are fixed in one place. Because each particle is attached to several others, individual particles cannot move from one location to another, and the solid is rigid.

2 A **liquid** has a fixed volume but does not have a fixed shape. Liquids take on the shape of the container they are in. The particles in a liquid are attracted to one another and are close together. However, particles in a liquid are not fixed in place and can move from one place to another.

3 A **gas** has no fixed volume or shape. A gas can take on both the shape and the volume of a container. Gas particles are not close to one another and can move easily in any direction. There is much more space between gas particles than there is between particles in a liquid or a solid. The space between gas particles can increase or decrease with changes in temperature and pressure.

 CHECK YOUR READING   Describe two differences between a solid and a gas.

The particles in a solid are usually closer together than the particles in a liquid. For example, the particles in solid steel are closer together than the particles in molten—or melted—steel. However, water is an important exception. The molecules that make up ice actually have more space between them than the molecules in liquid water do.

The fact that the molecules in ice are farther apart than the molecules in liquid water has important consequences for life on Earth. Because there is more space between its molecules, ice floats on liquid water. By contrast, a piece of solid steel would not float in molten steel but would sink to the bottom.

Because ice floats, it remains on the surface of rivers and lakes when they freeze. The ice layer helps insulate the water and slow down the freezing process. Animals living in rivers and lakes can survive in the liquid water layer below the ice layer.

States of Matter

Matter can exist in different states. The state of matter depends on the arrangement and motion of the particles.

① Solid

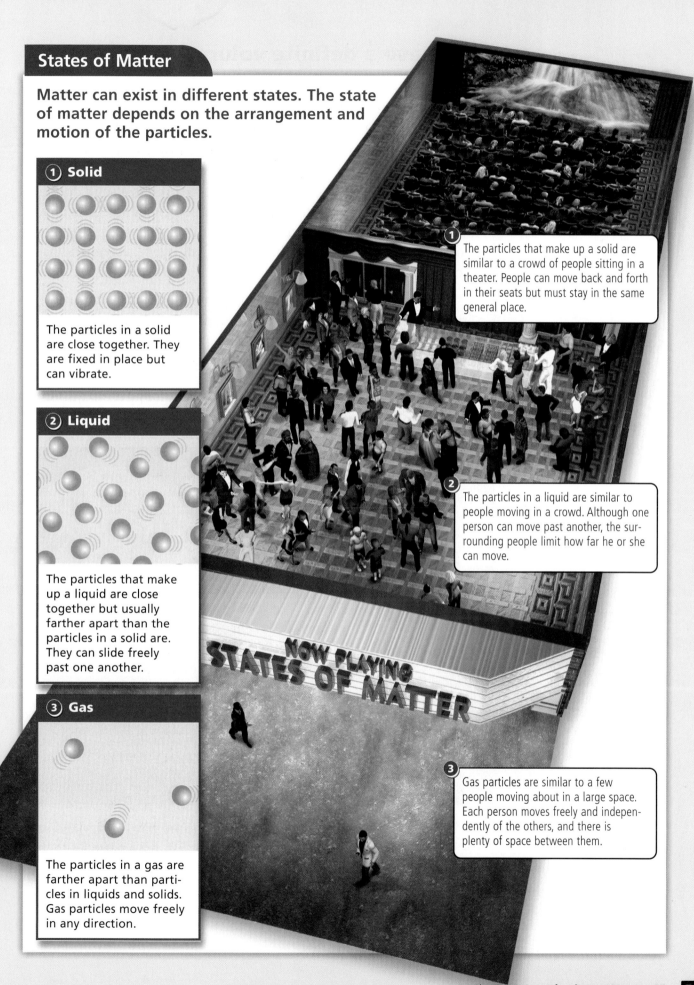

The particles in a solid are close together. They are fixed in place but can vibrate.

① The particles that make up a solid are similar to a crowd of people sitting in a theater. People can move back and forth in their seats but must stay in the same general place.

② Liquid

The particles that make up a liquid are close together but usually farther apart than the particles in a solid are. They can slide freely past one another.

② The particles in a liquid are similar to people moving in a crowd. Although one person can move past another, the surrounding people limit how far he or she can move.

③ Gas

The particles in a gas are farther apart than particles in liquids and solids. Gas particles move freely in any direction.

③ Gas particles are similar to a few people moving about in a large space. Each person moves freely and independently of the others, and there is plenty of space between them.

NOW PLAYING
STATES OF MATTER

Solids have a definite volume and shape.

▼ REMINDER

Volume is the amount of space that an object occupies.

A piece of ice, a block of wood, and a ceramic cup are solids. They have shapes that do not change and volumes that can be measured. Any matter that is a solid has a definite shape and a definite volume.

The molecules in a solid are in fixed positions and are close together. Although the molecules can still vibrate, they cannot move from one part of the solid to another part. As a result, a solid does not easily change its shape or its volume. If you force the molecules apart, you can change the shape and the volume of a solid by breaking it into pieces. However, each of those pieces will still be a solid and have its own particular shape and volume.

The particles in some solids, such as ice or table salt, occur in a very regular pattern. The pattern of the water molecules in ice, for example, can be seen when you look at a snowflake like the one shown below. The water molecules in a snowflake are arranged in hexagonal shapes that are layered on top of one another. Because the molecular pattern has six sides, snowflakes form with six sides or six points. Salt also has a regular structure, although it takes a different shape.

The particles in many solids, such as the water molecules in this snowflake, have a regular pattern.

Not all solids have regular shapes in the same way that ice and salt do, however. Some solids, such as plastic or glass, have particles that are not arranged in a regular pattern.

CHECK YOUR READING   What two characteristics are needed for a substance to be a solid?

Liquids have a definite volume but no definite shape.

Water, milk, and oil are liquids. A liquid has a definite volume but does not have a definite shape. The volume of a certain amount of oil can be measured, but the shape that the oil takes depends on what container it is in. If the oil is in a tall, thin container, it has a tall, thin shape. If it is in a short, wide container, it has a short, wide shape. Liquids take the shape of their containers.

The molecules in a liquid are close together, but they are not tightly attached to one another as the molecules in a solid are. Instead, molecules in liquids can move independently. As a result, liquids can flow. Instead of having a rigid form, the molecules in a liquid move and fill the bottom of the container they are in.

MAIN IDEA AND DETAILS
As you read, organize the headings and details in a two-column chart.

 CHECK YOUR READING How is a liquid different from a solid?

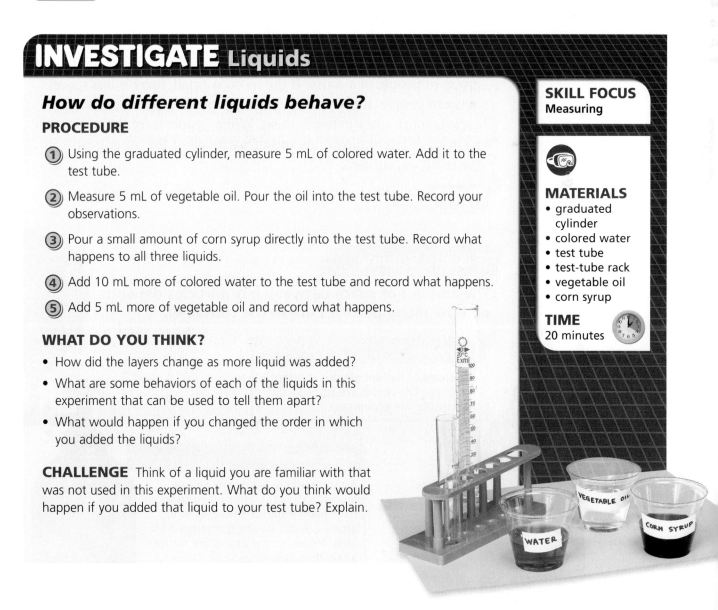

INVESTIGATE Liquids

How do different liquids behave?

PROCEDURE

1. Using the graduated cylinder, measure 5 mL of colored water. Add it to the test tube.

2. Measure 5 mL of vegetable oil. Pour the oil into the test tube. Record your observations.

3. Pour a small amount of corn syrup directly into the test tube. Record what happens to all three liquids.

4. Add 10 mL more of colored water to the test tube and record what happens.

5. Add 5 mL more of vegetable oil and record what happens.

WHAT DO YOU THINK?

- How did the layers change as more liquid was added?
- What are some behaviors of each of the liquids in this experiment that can be used to tell them apart?
- What would happen if you changed the order in which you added the liquids?

CHALLENGE Think of a liquid you are familiar with that was not used in this experiment. What do you think would happen if you added that liquid to your test tube? Explain.

SKILL FOCUS
Measuring

MATERIALS
- graduated cylinder
- colored water
- test tube
- test-tube rack
- vegetable oil
- corn syrup

TIME
20 minutes

Gases have no definite volume or shape.

VOCABULARY
Add a four square diagram to your notebook for *gas.*

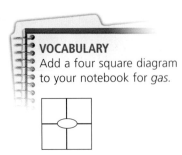

The air that you breathe, the helium in a balloon, and the neon inside the tube in a neon light are gases. A gas is a substance with no definite volume and no definite shape. Solids and liquids have volumes that do not change easily. If you have a container filled with one liter of a liquid that you pour into a two-liter container, the liquid will occupy only half of the new container. A gas, on the other hand, has a volume that changes to match the volume of its container.

Gas Composition

The molecules in a gas are very far apart compared with the molecules in a solid or a liquid. The amount of space between the molecules in a gas can change easily. If a rigid container—one that cannot change its shape—has a certain amount of air and more air is pumped in, the volume of the gas does not change. However, there is less space between the molecules than there was before. If the container is opened, the molecules spread out and mix with the air in the atmosphere.

As you saw, gas molecules in a container can be compared to a group of people in a room. If the room is small, there is less space between people. If the room is large, people can spread out so that there is more space between them. When people leave the room, they go in all different directions and mix with all of the other people in the surrounding area.

 CHECK YOUR READING Contrast the molecules in a gas with those of a liquid and a solid.

Gas and Volume

The amount of space between gas particles depends on how many particles are in the container.

Before Use

The atoms of helium gas are constantly in motion. The atoms are spread throughout the entire tank.

After Use

Although there are fewer helium atoms in the tank after many balloons have been inflated, the remaining atoms are still spread throughout the tank. However, the atoms are farther apart than before.

Gas Behavior

Because gas molecules are always in motion, they are continually hitting one another and the sides of any container they may be in. As the molecules bounce off one another and the surfaces of the container, they apply a pressure against the container. You can feel the effects of gas pressure if you pump air into a bicycle tire. The more air you put into the tire, the harder it feels because more gas molecules are pressing the tire outward.

The speed at which gas molecules move depends on the temperature of the gas. Gas molecules move faster at higher temperatures than at lower temperatures. The volume, pressure, and temperature of a gas are related to one another, and changing one can change the others.

SIMULATION
CLASSZONE.COM
Explore the behavior of a gas.

Pressure ▲ Volume ▼ Temp. ■	Pressure ▲ Volume ■ Temp. ▲	Pressure ■ Volume ▲ Temp. ▲

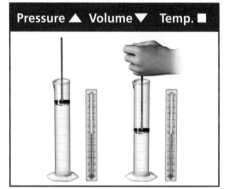

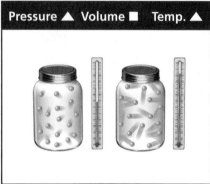

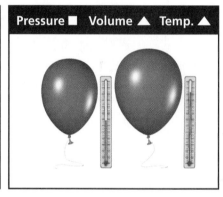

If the temperature of a gas stays the same, increasing the pressure of the gas decreases its volume.

If the volume of a gas stays the same, increasing the temperature of the gas also increases the pressure.

If the pressure of a gas stays the same, increasing the temperature of the gas also increases the volume.

In nature, volume, pressure, and temperature may all be changing at the same time. By studying how gas behaves when one property is kept constant, scientists can predict how gas will behave when all three properties change.

1.4 Review

KEY CONCEPTS

1. What are the characteristics of the three familiar states of matter?

2. How can you change the shape and volume of a liquid?

3. How does gas behave inside a closed container?

CRITICAL THINKING

4. **Infer** What happens to a liquid that is not in a container?

5. **Synthesize** What is the relationship between the temperature and the volume of a gas?

⬥ CHALLENGE

6. **Synthesize** Can an oxygen canister ever be half empty? Explain.

Chapter Review

the BIG idea

Everything that has mass and takes up space is matter.

CONTENT REVIEW
CLASSZONE.COM

◀ KEY CONCEPTS SUMMARY

1.1 Matter has mass and volume.

Mass is a measure of how much matter an object contains.

Volume is the measure of the amount of space matter occupies.

VOCABULARY
matter p. 9
mass p. 10
weight p. 11
volume p. 11

1.2 Matter is made of atoms.

An atom is the smallest basic unit of matter. Two or more atoms bonded together form a molecule. Atoms and molecules are always in motion.

VOCABULARY
atom p. 16
molecule p. 18

1.3 Matter combines to form different substances.

Matter can be pure, such as an element (gold), or a compound (water).

Matter can be a mixture. Mixtures contain two or more pure substances.

VOCABULARY
element p. 22
compound p. 23
mixture p. 23

1.4 Matter exists in different physical states.

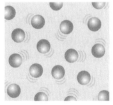 

Solids have a fixed volume and a fixed shape.

Liquids have a fixed volume but no fixed shape.

Gases have no fixed volume and no fixed shape.

VOCABULARY
states of matter p. 27
solid p. 28
liquid p. 28
gas p. 28

Reviewing Vocabulary

Copy and complete the chart below. If the right column is blank, give a brief description or definition. If the left column is blank, give the correct term.

Term	Description
1.	the downward pull of gravity on an object
2. liquid	
3.	the smallest basic unit of matter
4. solid	
5.	state of matter with no fixed volume and no fixed shape
6.	a combination of different substances that remain individual substances
7. matter	
8.	a measure of how much matter an object contains
9. element	
10.	a particle made of two or more atoms bonded together
11. compound	

Reviewing Key Concepts

Multiple Choice *Choose the letter of the best answer.*

12. The standard unit for measuring mass is the
   a. kilogram
   b. gram per cubic centimeter
   c. milliliter
   d. milliliter per cubic centimeter

13. A unit for measuring the volume of a liquid is the
   a. kilogram
   b. gram per cubic centimeter
   c. milliliter
   d. milliliter per cubic centimeter

14. The weight of an object is measured by using a scale that
   a. compares the mass of the object with a standard unit of mass
   b. shows the amount of space the object occupies
   c. indicates how much water is displaced by the object
   d. tells how hard the object is pushing or pulling on it

15. To find the volume of a rectangular box,
   a. divide the length by the height
   b. multiply the length, width, and height
   c. subtract the mass from the weight
   d. multiply one atom's mass by the total

16. Compounds can be separated only by
   a. breaking the atoms into smaller pieces
   b. breaking the bonds between the atoms
   c. using a magnet to attract certain atoms
   d. evaporating the liquid that contains the atoms

17. Whether a substance is a solid, a liquid, or a gas depends on how close its atoms are to one another and
   a. the volume of each atom
   b. how much matter the atoms have
   c. how free the atoms are to move
   d. the size of the container

18. A liquid has
   a. a fixed volume and a fixed shape
   b. no fixed volume and a fixed shape
   c. a fixed volume and no fixed shape
   d. no fixed volume and no fixed shape

Short Answer *Answer each of the following questions in a sentence or two.*

19. Describe the movement of particles in a solid, a liquid, and a gas.

20. In bright sunlight, dust particles in the air appear to dart about. What causes this effect?

21. Why is the volume of a rectangular object measured in cubic units?

22. Describe how the molecules in the air behave when you pump air into a bicycle tire.

Thinking Critically

23. CLASSIFY Write the headings *Matter* and *Not Matter* on your paper. Place each of these terms in the correct category: wood, water, metal, air, light, sound.

24. INFER If you could break up a carbon dioxide molecule, would you still have carbon dioxide? Explain your answer.

25. MODEL In what ways is sand in a bowl like a liquid? In what ways is it different?

26. INFER If you cut a hole in a basketball, what happens to the gas inside?

27. COMPARE AND CONTRAST Create a Venn diagram that shows how mixtures and compounds are alike and different.

28. ANALYZE If you place a solid rubber ball into a box, why doesn't the ball change its shape to fit the container?

29. CALCULATE What is the volume of an aquarium that is 120 cm long, 60 cm wide, and 100 cm high?

30. CALCULATE A truck whose bed is 2.5 m long, 1.5 m wide, and 1 m high is delivering sand for a sand-sculpture competition. How many trips must the truck make to deliver 7 cubic meters of sand?

Use the information in the photograph below to answer the next three questions.

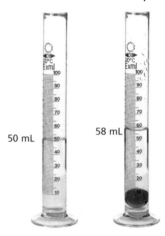

50 mL   58 mL

31. INFER One way to find the volume of a marble is by displacement. To determine a marble's volume, add 50 mL of water to a graduated cylinder and place the marble in the cylinder. Why does the water level change when you put the marble in the cylinder?

32. CALCULATE What is the volume of the marble?

33. PREDICT If you carefully removed the marble and let all of the water on it drain back into the cylinder, what would the volume of the water be? Explain.

the **BIG** idea

34. SYNTHESIZE Look back at the photograph on pages 6–7. Describe the picture in terms of states of matter.

35. WRITE Make a list of all the matter in a two-meter radius around you. Classify each as a solid, liquid, or gas.

UNIT PROJECTS

If you are doing a unit project, make a folder for your project. Include in your folder a list of the resources you will need, the date on which the project is due, and a schedule to track your progress. Begin gathering data.

Interpreting Graphs

The graph below shows the changing volume of a gas as it was slowly heated, with the pressure held constant.

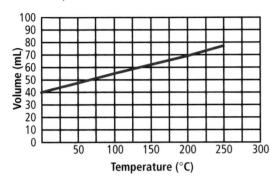

Use the graph to answer the questions.

1. As the temperature of the gas rises, what happens to its volume?

   a. It increases.

   b. It stays the same.

   c. It decreases.

   d. It changes without pattern.

2. What is the volume of the gas at 250°C as compared with the volume at 0°C?

   a. about three times greater

   b. about double

   c. about one-half

   d. about the same

3. What happens to a gas as it is cooled below 0°C?

   a. The volume would increase.

   b. The volume would continue to decrease.

   c. The volume would remain at 40 mL.

   d. A gas cannot be cooled below 0°C.

4. If you raised the temperature of this gas to 300°C, what would be its approximate volume?

   a. 70 mL   **c.** 80 mL

   b. 75 mL   **d.** 85 mL

5. If the volume of the gas at 0°C was 80 mL instead of 40 mL, what would you expect the volume to be at 200°C?

   a. 35 mL   **c.** 80 mL

   b. 70 mL   **d.** 140 mL

Extended Response

Answer the two questions below in detail. Include some of the terms from the word box. Underline each term you use in your answer.

gravity	mass	molecule
states of matter	weight	

6. An astronaut's helmet, measured on a balance, has the same number of kilograms on both Earth and the Moon. On a spring scale, though, it registers more newtons on Earth than on the Moon. Why?

7. Explain how water changes as it moves from a solid to a liquid and then to a gas.

2 Properties of Matter

the BIG idea

Matter has properties that can be changed by physical and chemical processes.

Key Concepts

SECTION
2.1 Matter has observable properties.
Learn how to recognize physical and chemical properties.

SECTION
2.2 Changes of state are physical changes.
Learn how energy is related to changes of state.

SECTION
2.3 Properties are used to identify substances.
Learn how the properties of substances can be used to identify them and to separate mixtures.

Internet Preview

CLASSZONE.COM

Chapter 2 online resources:
Content Review, Simulation,
three Resource Centers,
Math Tutorial, Test Practice

What properties could help you identify this sculpture as sugar?

EXPLORE (the BIG idea)

Float or Sink

Form a piece of clay into a solid ball or cube. Place it in a bowl of water. Notice if it floats or sinks. Then mold the clay into a boatlike shape. Notice if this new object floats or sinks.

Observe and Think
What did you change about the clay? What didn't you change? What would happen if you filled the boat with water?

Hot Chocolate

Place two candy-coated chocolates on a paper towel. Place two more in your hand and close your hand. Wait three minutes. Break open the candies and examine the chocolate.

Observe and Think What happened to the chocolate in your hand? on the towel? What do you think accounts for any differences you see?

Internet Activity: Physical and Chemical Changes

Go to **ClassZone.com** to see how materials can go through physical and chemical changes.

Observe and Think
Think about each change. What can you infer about the difference between a physical change and a chemical change?

NSTA
scilinks.org
SCiLINKS

Physical Properties of Matter **Code: MDL062**

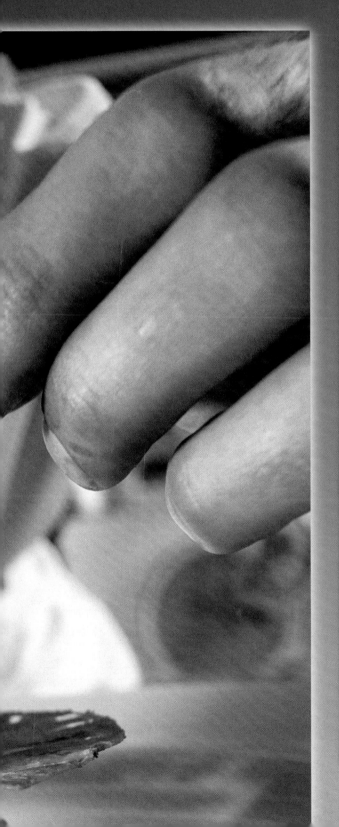

Getting Ready to Learn

◀ CONCEPT REVIEW

- Everything is made of matter.
- Matter has mass and volume.
- Atoms combine to form molecules.

◀ VOCABULARY REVIEW

mass p. 10

volume p. 11

molecule p. 18

states of matter p. 27

 CONTENT REVIEW
CLASSZONE.COM
Review concepts and vocabulary.

▶ TAKING NOTES

MAIN IDEA WEB

Write each new blue heading in a box. Then write notes in boxes around the center box that give important terms and details about that heading.

VOCABULARY STRATEGY

Think about a vocabulary term as a **magnet word** diagram. Write related terms and ideas in boxes around it.

See the Note-Taking Handbook on pages R45–R51.

SCIENCE NOTEBOOK

color, shape, size, texture, volume, mass

melting point, boiling point

Physical properties describe a substance.

density: a measure of the amount of matter in a given volume

CHEMICAL CHANGE

burning

rusting

tarnishing

change in temperature

change in color

formation of bubbles

KEY CONCEPT

Matter has observable properties.

◀ **BEFORE,** you learned

- Matter has mass and volume
- Matter is made of atoms
- Matter exists in different states

▶ **NOW,** you will learn

- About physical and chemical properties
- About physical changes
- About chemical changes

VOCABULARY

physical property p. 41
density p. 43
physical change p. 44
chemical property p. 46
chemical change p. 46

EXPLORE Physical Properties

How can a substance be changed?

PROCEDURE

① Observe the clay. Note its physical characteristics, such as color, shape, texture, and size.

② Change the shape of the clay. Note which characteristics changed and which ones stayed the same.

MATERIAL
rectangular piece of clay

WHAT DO YOU THINK?
- How did reshaping the clay change its physical characteristics?
- How were the mass and the volume of the clay affected?

Physical properties describe a substance.

What words would you use to describe a table? a chair? the sandwich you ate for lunch? You would probably say something about the shape, color, and size of each item. Next you might consider whether it is hard or soft, smooth or rough to the touch. Normally, when describing an object, you identify the characteristics of the object that you can observe without changing the identity of the object.

The characteristics of a substance that can be observed without changing the identity of the substance are called **physical properties.** In science, observation can include measuring and handling a substance. All of your senses can be used to detect physical properties. Color, shape, size, texture, volume, and mass are a few of the physical properties you probably have encountered.

VOCABULARY
Make a magnet word diagram in your notebook for *physical property.*

⬤ **CHECK YOUR READING** Describe some of the physical properties of your desk.

Physical Properties

How do you know which characteristics are physical properties? Just ask yourself whether observing the property involves changing the substance to a different substance. For example, you can stretch a rubber band. Does stretching the rubber band change what it is made of? No. The rubber band is still a rubber band before and after it is stretched. It may look a little different, but it is still a rubber band.

Mass and volume are two physical properties. Measuring these properties does not change the identity of a substance. For example, a lump of clay might have a mass of 200 grams (g) and a volume of 100 cubic centimeters (cm^3). If you were to break the clay in half, you would have two 100 g pieces of clay, each with a volume of 50 cm^3. You can bend and shape the clay too. Even if you were to mold a realistic model of a car out of the clay, it still would be a piece of clay. Although you have changed some of the properties of the object, such as its shape and volume, you have not changed the fact that the substance you are observing is clay.

REMINDER

Because all formulas for volume involve the multiplication of three measurements, volume has a unit that is cubed (such as cm^3).

CHECK YOUR READING Which physical properties listed above are found by taking measurements? Which are not?

Physical Properties

Physical properties of clay—such as volume, mass, color, texture, and shape—can be observed without changing the fact that the substance is clay.

Block of Clay

Shaped Clay

READING VISUALS COMPARE AND CONTRAST Which physical properties do the two pieces of clay have in common? Which are different?

Density

The relationship between the mass and the volume of a substance is another important physical property. For any substance, the amount of mass in a unit of volume is constant. For different substances, the amount of mass in a unit of volume may differ. This relationship explains why you can easily lift a shoebox full of feathers but not one filled with pennies, even though both are the same size. A volume of pennies contains more mass than an equal volume of feathers. The relationship between mass and volume is called density.

Density is a measure of the amount of matter present in a given volume of a substance. Density is normally expressed in units of grams per cubic centimeter (g/cm^3). In other words, density is the mass in grams divided by the volume in cubic centimeters.

$$\text{Density} = \frac{\text{mass}}{\text{Volume}} \qquad D = \frac{m}{V}$$

How would you find the density of 200 g of clay with a volume of $100\ cm^3$? You calculate that the clay has a density of 200 g divided by $100\ cm^3$, or $2\ g/cm^3$. If you divide the clay in half and find the density of one piece of clay, it will be $100\ g/50\ cm^3$, or $2\ g/cm^3$—the same as the original piece. Notice that density is a property of a substance that remains the same no matter how much of the substance you have.

READING TiP

The density of solids is usually measured in grams per cubic centimeter (g/cm^3). The density of liquids is usually measured in grams per milliliter (g/mL). Recall that $1\ mL = 1\ cm^3$.

Calculating Density

▶ Sample Problem

A glass marble has a volume of 5 cm³ and a mass of 13 g. What is the density of glass?

What do you know? Volume = 5 cm³, mass = 13 g

What do you want to find out? Density

Write the formula: $D = \frac{m}{V}$.

Substitute into the formula: $D = \frac{13\ g}{5\ cm^3}$

Calculate and simplify: $D = 2.6\ g/cm^3$

Check that your units agree: Unit is g/cm^3.
Unit of density is g/cm^3. Units agree.

Answer: $D = 2.6\ g/cm^3$

▶ Practice the Math

1. A lead sinker has a mass of 227 g and a volume of 20 cm³. What is the density of lead?

2. A glass of milk has a volume of 100 mL. If the milk has a mass of 103 g, what is the density of milk?

Physical Changes

You have read that a physical property is any property that can be observed without changing the identity of the substance. What then would be a physical change? A **physical change** is a change in any physical property of a substance, not in the substance itself. Breaking a piece of clay in half is a physical change because it changes only the size and shape of the clay. Stretching a rubber band is a physical change because the size of the rubber band changes. The color of the rubber band sometimes can change as well when it is stretched. However, the material that the rubber band is made of does not change. The rubber band is still rubber.

What happens when water changes from a liquid into water vapor or ice? Is this a physical change? Remember to ask yourself what has changed about the material. Ice is a solid and water is a liquid, but both are the same substance—both are composed of H_2O molecules. As you will read in more detail in the next section, a change in a substance's state of matter is a physical change.

 CHECK YOUR READING How is a physical change related to a substance's physical properties?

A substance can go through many different physical changes and still remain the same substance. Consider, for example, the changes that happen to the wool that ultimately becomes a sweater.

1 Wool is sheared from the sheep. The wool is then cleaned and placed into a machine that separates the wool fibers from one another. Shearing and separating the fibers are physical changes that change the shape, volume, and texture of the wool.

2 The wool fibers are spun into yarn. Again, the shape and volume of the wool change. The fibers are twisted so that they are packed more closely together and are intertwined with one another.

3 The yarn is dyed. The dye changes the color of the wool, but it does not change the wool into another substance. This type of color change is a physical change.

4 Knitting the yarn into a sweater also does not change the wool into another substance. A wool sweater is still wool, even though it no longer resembles the wool on a sheep.

It can be difficult to determine if a specific change is a physical change or not. Some changes, such as a change in color, also can occur when new substances are formed during the change. When deciding whether a change is a physical change or not, ask yourself whether you have the same substance you started with. If the substance is the same, then the changes it underwent were all physical changes.

Physical Changes

The process of turning wool into a sweater requires that the wool undergo physical changes. Changes in shape, volume, texture, and color occur as raw wool is turned into a colorful sweater.

1 Shearing

Preparing the wool produces physical changes. The wool is removed from the sheep and then cleaned before the wool fibers are separated.

2 Spinning

Further physical changes occur as a machine twists the wool fibers into a long, thin rope of yarn.

3 Dyeing

Dyeing produces color changes but does not change the basic substance of the wool.

4 The final product, a wool sweater, is still wool.

READING VISUALS How does the yarn in the sweater differ from the wool on the sheep?

Chemical properties describe how substances form new substances.

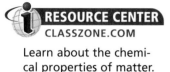

RESOURCE CENTER
CLASSZONE.COM

Learn about the chemical properties of matter.

If you wanted to keep a campfire burning, would you add a piece of wood or a piece of iron? You would add wood, of course, because you know that wood burns but iron does not. Is the ability to burn a physical property of the wood? The ability to burn seems to be quite different from physical properties such as color, density, and shape. More important, after the wood burns, all that is left is a pile of ashes and some new substances in the air. The wood has obviously changed into something else. The ability to burn, therefore, must describe another kind of property that substances have—not a physical property but a chemical property.

Chemical Properties and Changes

Chemical properties describe how substances can form new substances. Combustibility, for example, describes how well an object can burn. Wood burns well and turns into ashes and other substances. Can you think of a chemical property for the metal iron? Especially when left outdoors in wet weather, iron rusts. The ability to rust is a chemical property of iron. The metal silver does not rust, but eventually a darker substance called tarnish forms on its surface. You may have noticed a layer of tarnish on some silver spoons or jewelry.

INFER The bust of Abraham Lincoln is made of bronze. Why is the nose a different color from the rest of the head?

The chemical properties of copper cause it to become a blue-green color when it is exposed to air. A famous example of tarnished copper is the Statue of Liberty. The chemical properties of bronze are different. Some bronze objects tarnish to a dark brown color, like the bust of Abraham Lincoln in the photograph on the left.

Chemical properties can be identified by the changes they produce. The change of one substance into another substance is called a **chemical change.** A piece of wood burning, an iron fence rusting, and a silver spoon tarnishing are all examples of chemical changes. A chemical change affects the substances involved in the change. During a chemical change, combinations of atoms in the original substances are rearranged to make new substances. For example, when rust forms on iron, the iron atoms combine with oxygen atoms in the air to form a new substance that is made of both iron and oxygen.

A chemical change is also involved when an antacid tablet is dropped into a glass of water. As the tablet dissolves, bubbles of gas appear. The water and the substances in the tablet react to form new substances. One of these substances is carbon dioxide gas, which forms the bubbles that you see.

Not all chemical changes are as destructive as burning, rusting, or tarnishing. Chemical changes are also involved in cooking. When you boil an egg, for example, the substances in the raw egg change into new substances as energy is added to the egg. When you eat the egg, further chemical changes take place as your body digests the egg. The process forms new molecules that your body then can use to function.

CHECK YOUR READING Give three examples of chemical changes.

The only true indication of a chemical change is that a new substance has been formed. Sometimes, however, it is difficult to tell whether new substances have been formed or not. In many cases you have to judge which type of change has occurred only on the basis of your observations of the change and your previous experience. However, some common signs can suggest that a chemical change has occurred. You can use these signs to guide you as you try to classify a change that you are observing.

INVESTIGATE Chemical Changes

What are some signs of a chemical change?

PROCEDURE

1. Measure 80 mL of water and pour it into one of the cups.
2. Add 3 full droppers of iodine solution. Record your observations.
3. Add 1 spoonful of cornstarch to the iodine solution and stir. Record your observations.
4. Measure 50 mL of water and pour it into the second cup.
5. Using a clean eyedropper, add 4 full droppers of the iodine/cornstarch solution to the second cup.
6. Drop a vitamin C tablet into the second cup and stir the liquid with a clean spoon until the tablet is dissolved. Record your observations.

WHAT DO YOU THINK?

- What changes did you observe in the first cup? in the second cup?
- Do you think that chemical changes occurred? Why or why not?
- What are some characteristics of chemical changes?

CHALLENGE Describe some chemical changes that you have seen take place in your home or school.

SKILL FOCUS
Measuring

MATERIALS
- graduated cylinder
- water
- 2 clear plastic cups
- 2 eyedroppers
- iodine solution
- cornstarch
- spoon
- vitamin C tablet

TIME
15 minutes

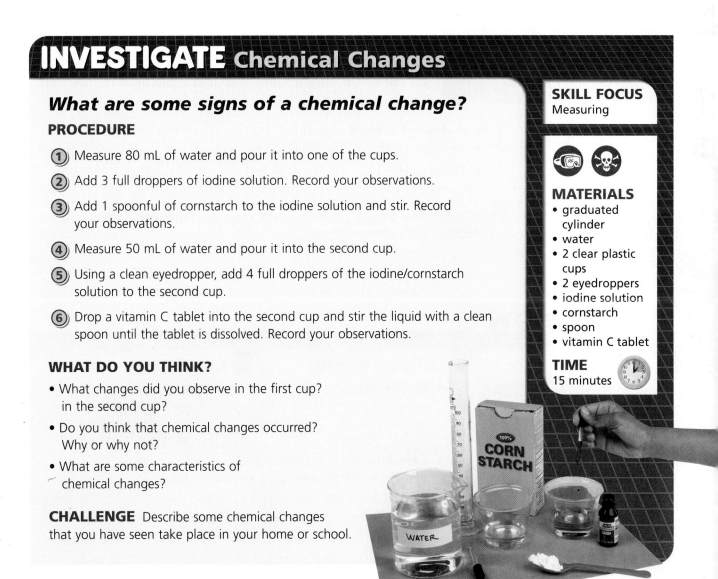

Signs of a Chemical Change

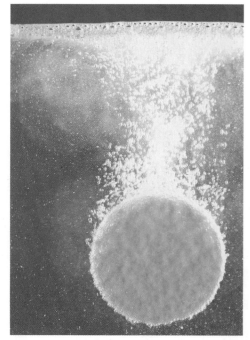

Carbon dioxide bubbles form as substances in the tablet react with water.

You may not be able to see that any new substances have formed during a change. Below are some signs that a chemical change may have occurred. If you observe two or more of these signs during a change, you most likely are observing a chemical change.

Production of an Odor Some chemical changes produce new smells. The chemical change that occurs when an egg is rotting produces the smell of sulfur. If you go outdoors after a thunderstorm, you may detect an unusual odor in the air. The odor is an indication that lightning has caused a chemical change in the air.

Change in Temperature Chemical changes often are accompanied by a change in temperature. You may have noticed that the temperature is higher near logs burning in a campfire.

Change in Color A change in color is often an indication of a chemical change. For example, fruit may change color when it ripens.

Formation of Bubbles When an antacid tablet makes contact with water, it begins to bubble. The formation of gas bubbles is another indicator that a chemical change may have occurred.

Formation of a Solid When two liquids are combined, a solid called a precipitate can form. The shells of animals such as clams and mussels are precipitates. They are the result of a chemical change involving substances in seawater combining with substances from the creatures.

 CHECK YOUR READING Give three signs of chemical changes. Describe one that you have seen recently.

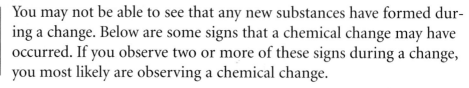

2.1 Review

KEY CONCEPTS

1. What effect does observing a substance's physical properties have on the substance?

2. Describe how a physical property such as mass or texture can change without causing a change in the substance.

3. Explain why burning is a chemical change in wood.

CRITICAL THINKING

4. **Synthesize** Why does the density of a substance remain the same for different amounts of the substance?

5. **Calculate** What is the density of a block of wood with a mass of 120 g and a volume of 200 cm^3?

○ CHALLENGE

6. **Infer** Iron can rust when it is exposed to oxygen. What method could be used to prevent iron from rusting?

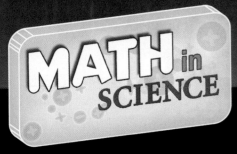

MATH in SCIENCE

MATH TUTORIAL
CLASSZONE.COM

Click on Math Tutorial for more help with solving proportions.

Density of Materials

Two statues are made of the same type of marble. One is larger than the other. However, they both have the same density because they are made of the same material. Recall the formula for density.

$$\text{Density} = \frac{\text{mass}}{\text{Volume}}$$

Because the density is the same, you know that the mass of one statue divided by its volume is the same as the mass of the other statue divided by its volume. You can set this up and solve it as a proportion.

Example

A small marble statue has a mass of 2.5 kg and a volume of 1000 cm³. A large marble statue with the same density has a mass of 10 kg. What is the volume of the large statue?

(1) Write the information as an equation showing the proportion.

$$\frac{\text{mass of small statue}}{\text{volume of small statue}} = \frac{\text{mass of large statue}}{\text{volume of large statue}}$$

(2) Insert the known values into your equation.

$$\frac{2.5 \text{ kg}}{1000 \text{ cm}^3} = \frac{10 \text{ kg}}{\text{volume of large statue}}$$

(3) Compare the numerators: 10 kg is 4 times greater than 2.5 kg.

(4) The denominators of the fractions are related in the same way. Therefore, the volume of the large statue is 4 times the volume of the small one.

volume of large statue = 4 • 1000 cm³ = 4000 cm³

ANSWER The volume of the large statue is 4000 cm³.

Answer the following questions.

1. A lump of gold has a volume of 10 cm³ and a mass of 193 g. Another lump of gold has a mass of 96.5 g. What is the volume of the second lump of gold?

2. A carpenter saws a wooden beam into two pieces. One piece has a mass of 600 g and a volume of 1000 cm³. What is the mass of the second piece if its volume is 250 cm³?

3. A 200 mL bottle is completely filled with cooking oil. The oil has a mass of 180 g. If 150 mL of the oil is poured into a pot, what is the mass of the poured oil?

CHALLENGE You have two spheres made of the same material. One has a diameter that is twice as large as the other. How do their masses compare?

If the marble statue and the marble bust both have the same density, their masses are proportional to their volumes.

KEY CONCEPT

Changes of state are physical changes.

<table>
<tr><td>

◀ **BEFORE,** you learned

- Substances have physical and chemical properties
- Physical changes do not change a substance into a new substance
- Chemical changes result in new substances

</td><td>

▶ **NOW,** you will learn

- How liquids can become solids, and solids can become liquids
- How liquids can become gases, and gases can become liquids
- How energy is related to changes of state

</td></tr>
</table>

VOCABULARY

melting p. 51
melting point p. 51
freezing p. 52
freezing point p. 52
evaporation p. 53
sublimation p. 53
boiling p. 54
boiling point p. 54
condensation p. 55

THINK ABOUT

Where does dew come from?

On a cool morning, droplets of dew cover the grass. Where does this water come from? You might think it had rained recently. However, dew forms even if it has

not rained. Air is made of a mixture of different gases, including water vapor. Some of the water vapor condenses—or becomes a liquid—on the cool grass and forms drops of liquid water.

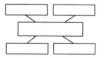

MAIN IDEA WEB
Remember to place each blue heading in a box. Add details around it to form a web.

Matter can change from one state to another.

Matter is commonly found in three states: solid, liquid, and gas. A solid has a fixed volume and a fixed shape. A liquid also has a fixed volume but takes the shape of its container. A gas has neither a fixed volume nor a fixed shape. Matter always exists in one of these states, but it can change from one state to another.

When matter changes from one state to another, the substance itself does not change. Water, ice, and water vapor are all the same basic substance. As water turns into ice or water vapor, the water molecules themselves do not change. What changes are the arrangement of the molecules and the amount of space between them. Changes in state are physical changes because changes in state do not change the basic substance.

 CHECK YOUR READING Why is a change in state a physical change rather than a chemical change?

Solids can become liquids, and liquids can become solids.

If you leave an ice cube on a kitchen counter, it changes to the liquid form of water. Water changes to the solid form of water, ice, when it is placed in a freezer. In a similar way, if a bar of iron is heated to a high enough temperature, it will become liquid iron. As the liquid iron cools, it becomes solid iron again.

Melting

Melting is the process by which a solid becomes a liquid. Different solids melt at different temperatures. The lowest temperature at which a substance begins to melt is called its **melting point.** Although the melting point of ice is 0°C (32°F), iron must be heated to a much higher temperature before it will melt.

Remember that particles are always in motion, even in a solid. Because the particles in a solid are bound together, they do not move from place to place—but they do vibrate. As a solid heats up, its particles gain energy and vibrate faster. If the vibrations are fast enough, the particles break loose and slide past one another. In other words, the solid melts and becomes a liquid.

Some substances have a well-defined melting point. If you are melting ice, for example, you can predict that when the temperature reaches 0°C, the ice will start to melt. Substances with an orderly structure start melting when they reach a specific temperature.

VOCABULARY
Add magnet word diagrams for *melting* and *melting point* to your notebook.

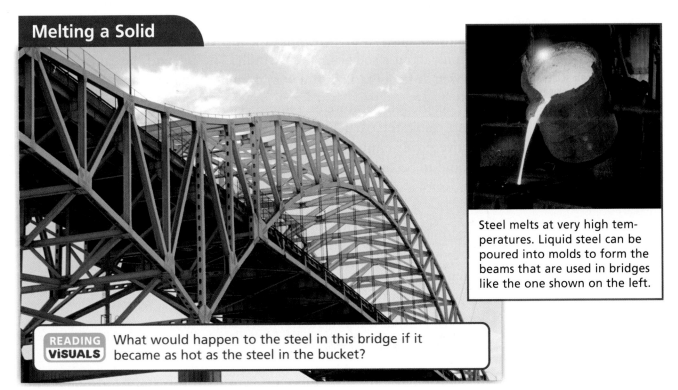

Melting a Solid

Steel melts at very high temperatures. Liquid steel can be poured into molds to form the beams that are used in bridges like the one shown on the left.

READING VISUALS What would happen to the steel in this bridge if it became as hot as the steel in the bucket?

Other substances, such as plastic and chocolate, do not have a well-defined melting point. Chocolate becomes soft when the temperature is high enough, but it still maintains its shape. Eventually, the chocolate becomes a liquid, but there is no specific temperature at which you can say the change happened. Instead, the melting happens gradually over a range of temperatures.

CHECK YOUR READING Describe the movement of molecules in a substance that is at its melting point.

Icicles grow as water drips down them, freezes, and sticks to the ice that is already there. On a warm day, the frozen icicles melt again.

Freezing

Freezing is the process by which a liquid becomes a solid. Although you may think of cold temperatures when you hear the word *freezing*, many substances are solid, or frozen, at room temperature and above. Think about a soda can and a candle. The can and the candle are frozen at temperatures you would find in a classroom.

As the temperature of a liquid is lowered, its particles lose energy. As a result, the particles move more slowly. Eventually, the particles move slowly enough that the attractions among them cause the liquid to become a solid. The temperature at which a specific liquid becomes a solid is called the **freezing point** of the substance.

The freezing point of a substance is the same as that substance's melting point. At this particular temperature, the substance can exist as either a solid or a liquid. At temperatures below the freezing/melting point, the substance is a solid. At temperatures above the freezing/melting point, the substance is a liquid.

CHECK YOUR READING What is the relationship between a substance's melting point and freezing point?

Liquids can become gases, and gases can become liquids.

Suppose you spill water on a picnic table on a warm day. You might notice that the water eventually disappears from the table. What has happened to the water molecules? The liquid water has become water vapor, a gas. The water vapor mixes with the surrounding air. At the same picnic, you might also notice that a cold can of soda has beads of water forming on it. The water vapor in the air has become the liquid water found on the soda can.

Evaporation

Evaporation is a process by which a liquid becomes a gas. It usually occurs at the surface of a liquid. Although all particles in a liquid move, they do not all move at the same speed. Some particles move faster than others. The fastest moving particles at the surface of the liquid can break away from the liquid and escape to become gas particles.

As the temperature increases, the energy in the liquid increases. More particles can escape from the surface of the liquid. As a result, the liquid evaporates more quickly. This is why spilled water will evaporate faster in hot weather than in cold weather.

READING TiP

The root of the word *evaporation* is *vapor,* a Latin word meaning "steam."

CHECK YOUR READING Describe the movement of particles in a liquid as it evaporates.

It is interesting to note that under certain conditions, solids can lose particles through a process similar to evaporation. When a solid changes directly to a gas, the process is called **sublimation.** You may have seen dry ice being used in a cooler to keep foods cold. Dry ice is frozen carbon dioxide that sublimates in normal atmospheric conditions.

Evaporation

During evaporation, fast-moving particles escape from the surface of a liquid and become gas particles.

Boiling

RESOURCE CENTER
CLASSZONE.COM

Explore melting points
and boiling points.

Boiling is another process by which a liquid becomes a gas. Unlike evaporation, boiling produces bubbles. If you heat a pot of water on the stove, you will notice that after a while tiny bubbles begin to form. These bubbles contain dissolved air that is escaping from the liquid. As you continue to heat the water, large bubbles suddenly form and rise to the surface. These bubbles contain energetic water molecules that have escaped from the liquid water to form a gas. This process is boiling.

Boiling can occur only when the liquid reaches a certain temperature, called the **boiling point** of the liquid. Liquids evaporate over a wide range of temperatures. Boiling, however, occurs at a specific temperature for each liquid. Water, for example, has a boiling point of 100°C (212°F) at normal atmospheric pressure.

In the mountains, water boils at a temperature lower than 100°C. For example, in Leadville, Colorado, which has an elevation of 3094 m (10,152 ft) above sea level, water boils at 89°C (192°F). This happens because at high elevations the air pressure is much lower than at sea level. Because less pressure is pushing down on the surface of the water, bubbles can form inside the liquid at a lower temperature. Less energetic water molecules are needed to expand the bubbles under these conditions. The lower boiling point of water means that foods cooked in water, such as pasta, require a longer time to prepare.

Different substances boil at different temperatures. Helium, which is a gas at room temperature, boils at −270°C (−454°F). Aluminum, on the other hand, boils at 2519°C (4566°F). This fact explains why some substances usually are found as gases but others are not.

Boiling

Bubbles of vapor form inside the boiling water.

Tiny droplets of water form on a window as water vapor from the air condenses into liquid water.

Condensation

The process by which a gas changes its state to become a liquid is called **condensation.** You probably have seen an example of condensation when you enjoyed a cold drink on a warm day. The beads of water that formed on the glass or can were water vapor that condensed from the surrounding air.

The cold can or glass cooled the air surrounding it. When you cool a gas, it loses energy. As the particles move more slowly, the attractions among them cause droplets of liquid to form. Condensed water often forms when warm air containing water vapor comes into contact with a cold surface, such as a glass of ice or ground that has cooled during the night.

As with evaporation, condensation can occur over a wide range of temperatures. Like the particles in liquids, the individual particles in a gas are moving at many different speeds. Slowly moving particles near the cool surface condense as they lose energy. The faster moving particles also slow down but continue to move too fast to stick to the other particles in the liquid that is forming. However, if you cool a gas to a temperature below its boiling point, almost all of the gas will condense.

READING TiP

The root of the word *condensation* is *condense,* which comes from a Latin word meaning "to thicken."

2.2 Review

KEY CONCEPTS

1. Describe three ways in which matter can change from one state to another.

2. Compare and contrast the processes of evaporation and condensation.

3. How does adding energy to matter by heating it affect the energy of its particles?

CRITICAL THINKING

4. **Synthesize** Explain how water can exist as both a solid and a liquid at 0°C.

5. **Apply** Explain how a pat of butter at room temperature can be considered to be frozen.

○ CHALLENGE

6. **Infer** You know that water vapor condenses from air when the air temperature is lowered. Should it be possible to condense oxygen from air? What would have to happen?

CHAPTER INVESTIGATION

Freezing Point

OVERVIEW AND PURPOSE Stearic acid is a substance used in making candles. In this experiment you will
- observe melted stearic acid as it changes from a liquid to a solid
- record the freezing point of stearic acid

▶ Problem

What is the freezing point of stearic acid?

▶ Procedure

1. Make a data table like the one shown on the sample notebook page.

2. Use the test-tube tongs to take the test tube of melted stearic acid and place it in the test-tube rack. Keep the test tube in the rack for the entire experiment.

3. Use the wire-loop stirrer and stir the liquid to make sure that it is the same temperature throughout.

4. Place the thermometer into the stearic acid to take a reading. Hold the thermometer so that it does not touch the sides or bottom of the test tube. Wait until the temperature stops rising. Then record the temperature on your data table. Also note whether the stearic acid is a liquid or a solid—or whether both states are present.

5. Take the temperature of the stearic acid every minute, stirring the stearic acid with the stirrer before each reading. To get an accurate reading, place the loop of the stirrer around the thermometer and use an up-and-down motion.

6. Continue taking temperature readings until two minutes after the acid has become totally solid or you are no longer able to stir it.

MATERIALS
- large test tube
- stearic acid
- test-tube tongs
- test-tube rack
- wire-loop stirrer
- thermometer

7 Make a note of the temperature on your data table when the first signs of a solid formation appear.

8 Make a note of the temperature on your data table when the stearic acid is completely solid.

9 Leave the thermometer and stirrer in the test tube and carry it carefully in the test-tube rack to your teacher.

▶ Observe and Analyze   [Write It Up]

1. **RECORD OBSERVATIONS** Make a line graph showing the freezing curve of stearic acid. Label the vertical axis **Temperature** and the horizontal axis **Time.**

2. **RECORD OBSERVATIONS** Label your graph to show when the stearic acid was a liquid, when it was a solid, and when it was present in both states.

3. **ANALYZE** Explain how your graph tells you the freezing point of stearic acid.

▶ Conclude   [Write It Up]

1. **INTERPRET** Answer the question in the problem.

2. **IDENTIFY** How does the freezing point of stearic acid compare with the freezing point of water?

3. **INFER** What happened to the energy of the molecules as the stearic acid changed from a liquid to a solid?

4. **INFER** From your observations, infer the melting point of stearic acid. How is the melting point of stearic acid related to its freezing point?

5. **APPLY** Why do you think stearic acid is used as an ingredient in bar soaps but not in liquid soaps?

▶ INVESTIGATE Further

CHALLENGE What do you think would happen if you mixed in another substance with the stearic acid? How would that affect the freezing point? What experiment would you perform to find the answer?

Freezing Point
Problem What is the freezing point of stearic acid?
Observe and Analyze
Table 1. Freezing Point of Stearic Acid

Time (min)	Temperature (°C)	Liquid	Solid	Both
0.0				
1.0				
2.0				
3.0				
4.0				
5.0				
6.0				
7.0				

KEY CONCEPT

2.3 Properties are used to identify substances.

 BEFORE, you learned

- Matter can change from one state to another
- Changes in state require energy changes

 NOW, you will learn

- How properties can help you identify substances
- How properties of substances can be used to separate substances

---

EXPLORE Identifying Substances

How can properties help you identify a substance?

PROCEDURE

MATERIALS
- substance A
- substance B
- 2 cups
- water

① Place some of substance A into one cup and some of substance B into the other cup. Label the cups.

② Carefully add some water to each cup. Observe and record what happens.

WHAT DO YOU THINK?
- Which result was a physical change? a chemical change? Explain.
- The substances are baking soda and baking powder. Baking powder and water produce carbon dioxide gas. Which substance is baking powder?

Substances have characteristic properties.

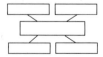

MAIN IDEA WEB
As you read, place each blue heading in a box. Add details around it to form a web.

You often use the properties of a substance to identify it. For example, when you reach into your pocket, you can tell the difference between a ticket stub and a folded piece of tissue because one is stiff and smooth and the other is soft. You can identify nickels, dimes, and quarters without looking at them by feeling their shapes and comparing their sizes. To tell the difference between a nickel and a subway token, however, you might have to use another property, such as color. Texture, shape, and color are physical properties that you use all the time to identify and sort objects.

CHECK YOUR READING How can physical properties be used to identify a substance?

Identifying Unknown Substances

Suppose you have a glass of an unknown liquid that you want to identify. It looks like milk, but you cannot be sure. How could you determine what it is? Of course, you would not taste an unknown substance, but there are many properties other than taste that you could use to identify the substance safely.

To proceed scientifically, you could measure several properties of the unknown liquid and compare them with the properties of known substances. You might observe and measure such properties as color, odor, texture, density, boiling point, and freezing point. A few of these properties might be enough to tell you that your white liquid is glue rather than milk.

To determine the difference among several colorless liquids, scientists would use additional tests. Their tests, however, would rely on the same idea of measuring and comparing the properties of an unknown with something that is already known.

Properties Used for Identifying Substances

You are already familiar with the most common physical properties of matter. Some of these properties, such as mass and volume, depend upon the specific object in question. You cannot use mass to tell one substance from another because two very different objects can have the same mass—a kilogram of feathers has the same mass as a kilogram of peanut butter, for example.

aerogel

Other properties, such as density, can be used to identify substances. They do not vary from one sample of the same substance to another. For example, you could see a difference between a kilogram of liquid soap and a kilogram of honey by measuring their densities.

The physical properties described below can be used to identify a substance.

Aerogel, an extremely lightweight material used in the space program, has such a low density that it can float on soap bubbles.

Density The densities of wood, plastic, and steel are all different. Scientists already have determined the densities of many substances. As a result, you can conveniently compare the density of an unknown substance with the densities of known substances. Finding any matching densities will give you information about the possible identity of the unknown substance. However, it is possible for two different substances to have the same density. In that case, in order to identify the substance positively, you would need additional data.

 Why can't you identify a substance on the basis of density alone?

These fibers act as heat insulators to keep the inside of the sleeping bag warm.

READING TiP

The root of the word *solubility* is the Latin word *solvere,* which means "to loosen."

Iron filings are attracted by the magnet. The wood chips, however, are not.

Heating Properties Substances respond to heating in different ways. Some warm up very quickly, and others take a long while to increase in temperature. This property is important in selecting materials for different uses. Aluminum and iron are good materials for making pots and pans because they conduct heat well. Various materials used in household insulation are poor heat conductors. Therefore, these insulators are used to keep warm air inside a home on a cold day. You can measure the rate at which a substance conducts heat and compare that rate with the heat conduction rates of other substances.

Solubility Solubility is a measure of how much of a substance dissolves in a given volume of a liquid. Sugar and dirt, for instance, have very different solubilities in water. If you put a spoonful of sugar into a cup of water and stir, the sugar dissolves in the water very rapidly. If you put a spoonful of dirt into water and stir, most of the dirt settles to the bottom as soon as you stop stirring.

Electric Properties Some substances conduct electricity better than others. This means that they allow electric charge to move through them easily. Copper wire is used to carry electricity because it is a good conductor. Materials that do not conduct easily, such as rubber and plastics, are used to block the flow of charge. With the proper equipment, scientists can test the electric conductivity of an unknown substance.

Magnetic Properties Some substances are attracted to magnets, but others are not. You can use a magnet to pick up a paper clip but not a plastic button or a wooden match. The elements iron, cobalt, and nickel are magnetic—meaning they respond to magnets— but copper, aluminum, and zinc are not. Steel, which contains iron, is also magnetic.

Mixtures can be separated by using the properties of the substances in them.

Suppose you have a bag of cans that you want to recycle. The recycling center accepts only aluminum cans. You know that some of your cans contain steel. You would probably find it difficult to tell aluminum cans from steel ones just by looking at them. How could you separate the cans? Aluminum and steel may look similar, but they have different magnetic properties. You could use a magnet to test each can. If the magnet sticks to the can, the can contains steel. Recycling centers often use magnets to separate aluminum cans from steel cans.

Some mixtures contain solids mixed with liquids. A filter can be used to separate the solid from the liquid. One example of this is a tea bag. The paper filter allows the liquid water to mix with the tea, because water molecules are small enough to pass through the filter. The large pieces of tea, however, cannot pass through the filter and remain inside the tea bag.

INVESTIGATE Separating Mixtures

How can a mixture of sand, salt, and pepper be separated?

DESIGN
— YOUR OWN —
EXPERIMENT

Scientists often have to isolate a single substance from a mixture. Use your knowledge of the properties of sand, salt, and pepper to design a method for separating each of these substances from the mixture.

PROCEDURE

1. Examine the mixture and the materials provided. Design a procedure for separating the different substances in your mixture. Carefully consider the order in which you will try each step.

2. Write up your procedure. Explain why you chose the steps you did for each substance.

3. Carry out your procedure.

WHAT DO YOU THINK?

- Was your procedure successful? How would you modify your procedure if you were to perform the separation again?

- How does knowing the properties of matter help you separate the substances in mixtures?

MATERIALS
- mixture of sand, salt, and pepper
- 2 index cards
- comb
- felt
- graduated cylinder
- spoon
- water
- coffee filter
- funnel
- small cup
- pie tin

TIME
30 minutes

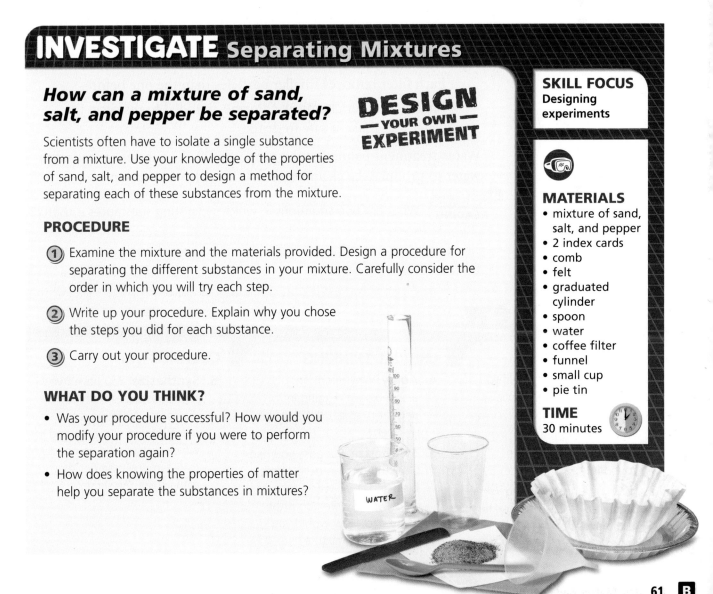

WATER

Some mixtures are more difficult to separate than others. For example, if you stir sugar into water, the sugar dissolves and breaks up into individual molecules that are too tiny to filter out. In this case, you can take advantage of the fact that water is a liquid and will evaporate from an open dish. Sugar, however, does not evaporate. The mixture can be heated to speed the evaporation of the water, leaving the sugar behind.

There are many important reasons for separating substances. One reason is to make a substance safe to consume, such as drinking water. In order to produce drinking water, workers at a water-treatment plant must separate many of the substances that are mixed in with the water.

This water-treatment plant separates harmful substances from the water.

The process in water-treatment plants generally includes these steps:

- First, a chemical is added to the water that causes the larger particles to stick together. They settle to the bottom of the water, where they can be removed.
- Next, the water is run through a series of special molecular filters. Each filter removes smaller particles than the one before.
- Finally, another chemical, chlorine, is added to disinfect the water and make it safe to drink.

Water-treatment plants use the properties of the substances found in water to produce the clean water that flows from your tap.

CHECK YOUR READING What are two situations in which separating substances is useful?

2.3 Review

KEY CONCEPTS

1. How can properties help you distinguish one substance from another?

2. What are two physical properties that can help you identify a substance?

3. How can understanding properties help you separate substances from a mixture?

CRITICAL THINKING

4. **Apply** Why might an archaeologist digging in ancient ruins sift dirt through a screen?

5. **Synthesize** Suppose you had a mixture of iron pellets, pebbles, and small wood spheres, all of which were about the same size. How would you separate this mixture?

○ CHALLENGE

6. **Synthesize** You have two solid substances that look the same. What measurements would you take and which tests would you perform to determine whether they actually are the same?

Separating Minerals

A few minerals, such as rock salt, occur in large deposits that can be mined in a form that is ready to use. Most minerals, however, are combined with other materials, so they need to be separated from the mixtures of which they are a part. Scientists and miners use the differences in physical properties to analyze samples and to separate the materials removed from a mine.

Appearance

Gemstones are prized because of their obvious physical properties, such as color, shininess, and hardness. Particularly valuable minerals, such as diamonds and emeralds, are often located by digging underground and noting the differences between the gemstone and the surrounding dirt and rock.

Density

When gold deposits wash into a streambed, tiny particles of gold mix with the sand. It is hard to separate them by appearance because the pieces are so small. In the 1800s, as prospectors swirled this sand around in a pan, the lighter particles of sand washed away with the water. The denser gold particles collected in the bottom of the pan. Some modern gold mines use the same principle in machines that handle tons of material, washing away the lighter dirt and rock to leave bits of gold.

Magnetism

Machines called magnetic separators divide a mixture into magnetic and nonmagnetic materials. In order to separate iron from other materials, rocks are crushed and carried past a strong magnet. Particles that contain iron are drawn toward the magnet and fall into one bin, while the nonmagnetic materials fall into another bin.

Melting Point

Thousands of years ago, people discovered that when some minerals are placed in a very hot fire, metals—such as copper, tin, and zinc—can be separated from the rock around them. When the ores reach a certain temperature, the metal melts and can be collected as a liquid.

Workers can identify garnets in a mine because their physical properties are different from the physical properties of their surroundings.

EXPLORE

1. **INFER** At a copper ore mine in Chile, one of the world's largest magnets is used to remove pieces of iron from the ore. What can you infer about the copper ore?

2. **CHALLENGE** Electrostatic precipitators are important tools for protecting the environment from pollution. Use the Internet to learn how they are used in power plants and other factories that burn fuels.

RESOURCE CENTER
CLASSZONE.COM

Find out more about separating materials from mixtures.

Chapter Review

the **BIG** idea

Matter has properties that can be changed by physical and chemical processes.

CONTENT REVIEW
CLASSZONE.COM

◀ KEY CONCEPTS SUMMARY

2.1 Matter has observable properties.

- Physical properties can be observed without changing the substance.
- Physical changes can change some physical properties but do not change the substance.

- Chemical properties describe how substances form new substances.
- Chemical changes create new substances.

VOCABULARY
physical property p. 41
density p. 43
physical change p. 44
chemical property p. 46
chemical change p. 46

2.2 Changes of states are physical changes.

Matter is commonly found in three states: solid, liquid, and gas.

◀ freezing
Solid   **Liquid**
melting ▶

◀ condensation
Liquid   **Gas**
evaporation, boiling ▶

VOCABULARY
melting p. 51
melting point p. 51
freezing p. 52
freezing point p. 52
evaporation p. 53
sublimation p. 53
boiling p. 54
boiling point p. 54
condensation p. 55

2.3 Properties are used to identify substances.

Physical properties that can be used to identify substances include:

- density
- heating properties
- solubility
- electric properties
- magnetic properties

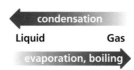 

Mixtures can be separated by using the properties of the substances they contain.

Reviewing Vocabulary

Describe how the terms in the following sets of terms are related.

1. physical property, physical change

2. chemical property, chemical change

3. density, matter

4. melting, melting point, freezing point

5. boiling, boiling point, liquid

6. evaporation, condensation

7. sublimation, solid

Reviewing Key Concepts

Multiple Choice *Choose the letter of the best answer.*

8. Color, shape, size, and texture are
   a. physical properties
   b. chemical properties
   c. physical changes
   d. chemical changes

9. Density describes the relationship between a substance's
   a. matter and mass
   b. mass and volume
   c. volume and area
   d. temperature and mass

10. Dissolving sugar in water is an example of a
    a. physical change
    b. chemical change
    c. change in state
    d. pressure change

11. An electric current can be used to decompose, or break down, water into oxygen gas and hydrogen gas. This is an example of a
    a. physical change
    b. chemical change
    c. change in state
    d. pressure change

12. The formation of rust on iron is a chemical change because
    a. the color and shape have changed
    b. the mass and volume have changed
    c. the substance remains the same
    d. a new substance has been formed

13. The process by which a solid becomes a liquid is called
    a. boiling
    b. freezing
    c. melting
    d. evaporating

14. The process by which a liquid becomes a solid is called
    a. boiling
    b. freezing
    c. melting
    d. evaporating

15. Two processes by which a liquid can become a gas are
    a. evaporation and boiling
    b. melting and freezing
    c. sublimation and condensation
    d. evaporation and condensation

Short Answer *Answer each of the following questions in a sentence or two.*

16. When a sculptor shapes marble to make a statue, is this a physical or a chemical change? Explain your answer.

17. Describe and identify various physical changes that water can undergo.

18. Why does dew often form on grass on a cool morning, even if there has been no rain?

19. Describe the difference between evaporation and boiling in terms of the movement of the liquid's particles in each case.

20. What effect does altitude have on the boiling point of water?

Thinking Critically

21. **ANALYZE** Whole milk is a mixture. When bacteria in the milk digest part of the mixture, changes occur. Lactic acid is produced, and the milk tastes sour. Explain why this process is a chemical change.

22. **INFER** Sharpening a pencil leaves behind pencil shavings. Why is sharpening a pencil a physical change instead of a chemical change?

23. **ANALYZE** Dumping cooked spaghetti and water into a colander separates the two substances because the liquid water can run through the holes in the colander but the solid spaghetti cannot. Explain how this is an example of separating a mixture based on the physical properties of its components.

24. **INFER** The density of water is 1.0 g/mL. Anything with a density less than 1.0 g/mL will float in water. The density of a fresh egg is about 1.2 g/mL. The density of a spoiled egg is about 0.9 g/mL. If you place an egg in water and it floats, what does that tell you about the egg?

Use the photograph below to answer the next three questions.

25. **COMPARE** Which physical properties of the puddle change as the water evaporates? Which physical properties remain the same?

26. **ANALYZE** Can water evaporate from this puddle on a cold day? Explain your answer.

27. **PREDICT** What would happen to any minerals and salts in the water if the water completely evaporated?

Use the chart below to answer the next two questions.

Densities Measured at 20°C

Material	Density (g/cm³)
gold	19.3
lead	11.3
silver	10.5
copper	9.0
iron	7.9

28. **PREDICT** Suppose you measure the mass and the volume of a shiny metal object and find that its density is 10.5 g/mL. Could you make a reasonable guess as to what material the object is made of? What factor or factors might affect your guess?

29. **CALCULATE** A solid nickel bar has a mass of 2.75 kg and a volume of 308.71 cm³. Between which two materials would nickel fall on the chart?

the **BIG** idea

30. **PREDICT** Look again at the photograph on pages 38–39. The chef has melted sugar to make a sculpture. Describe how the sugar has changed in terms of its physical and chemical properties. Predict what will happen to the sculpture over time.

31. **RESEARCH** Think of a question you have about the properties of matter that is still unanswered. For example, there may be a specific type of matter about which you are curious. What information do you need in order to answer your question? How might you find the information?

UNIT PROJECTS

Check your schedule for your unit project. How are you doing? Be sure that you have placed data or notes from your research in your project folder.

Analyzing Experiments

Read the following description of an experiment together with the chart.
Then answer the questions that follow.

Archimedes was a Greek mathematician and scientist who lived in the third century B.C. He figured out that any object placed in a liquid displaced a volume of that liquid equal to its own volume. He used this knowledge to solve a problem.

The king of Syracuse had been given a crown of gold. But he was not sure whether the crown was pure gold. Archimedes solved the king's problem by testing the crown's density.

He immersed the crown in water and measured the volume of water it displaced. Archimedes compared the amount of water displaced by the crown with the amount of water displaced by a bar of pure gold with the same mass. The comparison told him whether the crown was all gold or a mixture of gold and another element.

Element	Density (g/cm^3)
copper	8.96
gold	19.30
iron	7.86
lead	11.34
silver	10.50
tin	7.31

1. Which problem was Archimedes trying to solve?
   a. what the density of gold was
   b. what the crown was made of
   c. what the mass of the crown was
   d. how much water the crown displaced

2. Archimedes used the method that he did because a crown has an irregular shape and the volume of such an object cannot be measured in any other way. Which one of the following objects would also require this method?
   a. a square wooden box
   b. a cylindrical tin can
   c. a small bronze statue
   d. a rectangular piece of glass

3. Suppose Archimedes found that the crown had a mass of 772 grams and displaced 40 milliliters of water. Using the formula $D = m/V$, what would you determine the crown to be made of?
   a. pure gold
   b. half gold and half another element
   c. some other element with gold plating
   d. cannot be determined from the data

4. Using the formula, compare how much water a gold crown would displace if it had a mass of 579 grams.
   a. 10 mL   **c.** 30 mL
   b. 20 mL   **d.** 193 mL

5. If you had crowns made of each element in the chart that were the same mass, which would displace more water than a gold crown of that mass?
   a. all   **c.** tin only
   b. lead only   **d.** none

Extended Response

Answer the two questions below in detail.

6. What is the difference between a physical change and a chemical change? Include examples of each type in your explanation.

7. Why does someone cooking spaghetti at a high elevation need to boil it longer than someone cooking spaghetti at a lower elevation?

CHAPTER 3 Energy

the BIG idea

Energy has different forms, but it is always conserved.

Key Concepts

Internet Preview

CLASSZONE.COM

Chapter 3 online resources: Content Review, Simulation, Visualization, three Resource Centers, Math Tutorial, Test Practice

What different forms of energy are shown in this photograph?

EXPLORE (the BIG idea)

A Penny for Your Energy

Chill an empty glass bottle. Immediately complete the following steps: Rub a drop of cooking oil around the rim of the bottle. Place a coin on the rim so the oil forms a seal between the coin and the bottle. Wrap your hands around the bottle.

Observe and Think What happened to the coin? What do you think caused this to happen?

Hot Dog!

Cover a piece of cardboard with aluminum foil, and bend it into the shape of a U. Poke a wooden skewer through a hot dog, and through each side of the cardboard. Push corks over both ends of the skewer so the cardboard does not flatten out. Place your setup in direct sunlight for 30 minutes.

Observe and Think What happened to the hot dog? Were there any changes you had to make while the hot dog was in sunlight?

Internet Activity: Energy

Go to **ClassZone.com** to investigate the relationship between potential energy and kinetic energy.

Observe and Think How did you change potential energy? How do these changes affect kinetic energy?

NSTA
scilinks.org
SCiLINKS

Forms of Energy **Code: MDL063**

Getting Ready to Learn

CONCEPT REVIEW

- Matter has mass and is made of tiny particles.
- Matter can be changed physically or chemically.
- A change in the state of matter is a physical change.

VOCABULARY REVIEW

matter p. 9

mass p. 10

atom p. 16

physical change p. 44

chemical change p. 46

CONTENT REVIEW
CLASSZONE.COM
Review concepts and vocabulary.

TAKING NOTES

MIND MAP

Write each main idea, or blue heading, in an oval; then write details that relate to each other and to the main idea. Organize the details so that each spoke of the web has notes about one part of the main idea.

VOCABULARY STRATEGY

Write each new vocabulary term in the center of a **frame game** diagram. Decide what information to frame it with. Use examples, descriptions, parts, sentences that use the term in context, or pictures. You can change the frame to fit each term.

See the Note-Taking Handbook on pages R45–R51.

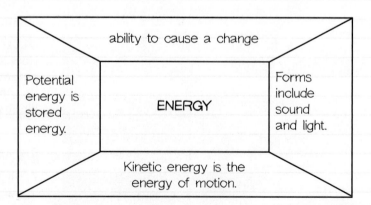

SCIENCE NOTEBOOK

ability to cause a change

different changes from different forms

DIFFERENT FORMS OF ENERGY HAVE DIFFERENT USES.

sunlight — electromagnetic energy

motion — mechanical energy

food — chemical energy

ability to cause a change

Potential energy is stored energy.

ENERGY

Forms include sound and light.

Kinetic energy is the energy of motion.

Energy exists in different forms.

 BEFORE, you learned

- All substances are made of matter
- Matter has both physical and chemical properties
- Matter can exist in different physical states

 NOW, you will learn

- How energy causes change
- About common forms of energy
- About kinetic energy and potential energy

VOCABULARY

energy p. 72
kinetic energy p. 74
potential energy p. 75

EXPLORE Energy

How can you demonstrate energy?

PROCEDURE

1 Fill the bowl halfway with sand. Place the bowl on the floor as shown. Make sure the sand is level.

2 Place a pebble and a rock near the edge of a table above the bowl of sand.

3 Gently push the pebble off the table into the sand. Record your observations.

4 Remove the pebble, and make sure the sand is level. Gently push the rock off the table into the sand. Record your observations.

WHAT DO YOU THINK?

- What happened to the sand when you dropped the pebble? when you dropped the rock?
- How can you explain any differences you observed?

MATERIALS
- large plastic bowl
- sand
- pebble
- rock

Different forms of energy have different uses.

Energy takes many different forms and has many different effects. Just about everything you see happening around you involves energy. Lamps and other appliances in your home operate on electrical energy. Plants use energy from the Sun to grow. You use energy provided by the food you eat to carry out all of your everyday activities—eating, exercising, reading, and even sitting and thinking. In this chapter, you will learn what these and other forms of energy have in common.

Energy

All forms of energy have one important point in common—they cause changes to occur. The flow of electrical energy through a wire causes a cool, dark bulb to get hot and glow. The energy of the wind causes a flag to flutter.

You are a source of energy that makes changes in your environment. For example, when you pick up a tennis racquet or a paintbrush, you change the position of that object. When you hit a tennis ball or smooth paint on a canvas, you cause further changes. Energy is involved in every one of these actions. At its most basic level, **energy** is the ability to cause change.

CHECK YOUR READING Provide your own example of energy and how it causes a change.

The photograph below shows a city street. All of the activities that take place on every street in any city require energy, so there are many changes taking place in the picture. Consider one of the cars. A person's energy is used to turn the key that starts the car. The key's movement starts the car's engine and gasoline begins burning. Gasoline provides the energy for the car to move. The person's hand, the turning key, and the burning gasoline all contain energy that causes change.

VOCABULARY
Remember to use a frame game diagram for *energy* and other vocabulary terms.

The motion of the cars and the glow of the streetlights are changes produced by energy.

Forms of Energy

Scientists classify energy into many forms, each of which causes change in a different way. Some of these forms are described below.

Mechanical Energy The energy that moves objects is mechanical energy. The energy that you use to put a book on a shelf is mechanical energy, as is energy that a person uses to turn a car key.

Sound Energy Sound results from the vibration of particles in a solid, liquid, or gas. People and other animals are able to detect these tiny vibrations with structures in their ears that vibrate due to the sound. So, when you hear a car drive past, you are detecting vibrations in the air produced by sound energy. Sound cannot travel through empty space. If there were no air or other substance between you and the car, you would not hear sounds from the car.

Chemical Energy Energy that is stored in the chemical composition of matter is chemical energy. The amount of chemical energy in a substance depends on the types and arrangement of atoms in the substance. When wood or gasoline burns, chemical energy produces heat. The energy used by the cells in your body comes from chemical energy stored in the foods you eat.

Thermal Energy The total amount of energy from the movement of particles in matter is thermal energy. Recall that matter is made of atoms, and atoms combined in molecules. The atoms and molecules in matter are always moving. The energy of this motion in an object is the object's thermal energy. You will learn more about thermal energy in the next chapter.

Electromagnetic Energy Electromagnetic (ih-LEHK-troh-mag-NEHT-ihk) energy is transmitted through space in the form of electromagnetic waves. Unlike sound, electromagnetic waves can travel through empty space. These waves include visible light, x-rays, and microwaves. X-rays are high energy waves used by doctors and dentists to look at your bones and teeth. Microwaves can be used to cook food or to transmit cellular telephone calls but contain far less energy than x-rays. The Sun releases a large amount of electromagnetic energy, some of which is absorbed by Earth.

Nuclear Energy The center of an atom—its nucleus—is the source of nuclear energy. A large amount of energy in the nucleus holds the nuclear particles together. When a heavy atom's nucleus breaks apart, or when the nuclei (NOO-klee-EYE) of two small atoms join together, energy is released. Nuclear energy released from the fusing of small nuclei to form larger nuclei keeps the Sun burning.

 CHECK YOUR READING How does chemical energy cause a change? What about electromagnetic energy?

APPLY Where in this photograph can you find chemical, sound, and mechanical energy?

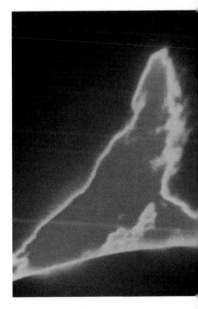

This solar flare releases electromagnetic energy and thermal energy produced by nuclear energy in the Sun.

Kinetic energy and potential energy are the two general types of energy.

RESOURCE CENTER
CLASSZONE.COM

Learn more about kinetic energy and potential energy.

All of the forms of energy can be described in terms of two general types of energy—kinetic energy and potential energy. Anything that is moving, such as a car that is being driven or an atom in the air, has kinetic energy. All matter also has potential energy, or energy that is stored and can be released at a later time.

Kinetic Energy

READING TiP

Kinetic means "related to motion."

The energy of motion is called **kinetic energy.** It depends on both an object's mass and the speed at which the object is moving.

All objects are made of matter, and matter has mass. The more matter an object contains, the greater its mass. If you held a bowling ball in one hand and a soccer ball in the other, you could feel that the bowling ball has more mass than the soccer ball.

- **Kinetic energy increases as mass increases.** If the bowling ball and the soccer ball were moving at the same speed, the bowling ball would have more kinetic energy because of its greater mass.

- **Kinetic energy increases as speed increases.** If two identical bowling balls were rolling along at different speeds, the faster one would have more kinetic energy because of its greater speed. The speed skater in the photographs below has more kinetic energy when he is racing than he does when he is moving slowly.

High Speed

This skater has a large amount of kinetic energy when moving at a high speed.

Low Speed

When the same skater is moving more slowly, he has less kinetic energy.

READING VISUALS **APPLY** How could a skater with less mass than another skater have more kinetic energy?

Potential Energy

Suppose you are holding a soccer ball in your hands. Even if the ball is not moving, it has energy because it has the potential to fall. **Potential energy** is the stored energy that an object has due to its position or chemical composition. The ball's position above the ground gives it potential energy.

The most obvious form of potential energy is potential energy that results from gravity. Gravity is the force that pulls objects toward Earth's surface. The giant boulder on the right has potential energy because of its position above the ground. The mass of the boulder and its height above the ground determine how much potential energy it has due to gravity.

It is easy to know whether an object has kinetic energy because the object is moving. It is not so easy to know how much and what form of potential energy an object has, because objects can have potential energy from several sources. For example, in addition to potential energy from gravity, substances contain potential energy due to their chemical composition—the atoms they contain.

Because the boulder could fall, it has potential energy from gravity.

 CHECK YOUR READING How can you tell kinetic energy and potential energy apart?

INVESTIGATE Potential Energy

How can you change the amount of potential energy?

Use what you know about potential energy to design an experiment that shows how potential energy can be increased or decreased.

DESIGN —YOUR OWN— EXPERIMENT

PROCEDURE

1. Using the materials in the list, design an experiment to investigate the potential energy of the model car. Use the cardboard as a ramp.

2. Write up your hypothesis and your procedure. Remember to include the variables and constants in the experiment.

3. Conduct your experiment and record your results.

WHAT DO YOU THINK?

- What variables did you change? Why?
- How do your results demonstrate a change in potential energy?

SKILL FOCUS
Designing experiments

MATERIALS
- model car
- meter stick
- weights
- balance
- tape
- cardboard
- books

TIME
30 minutes

Another form of potential energy related to an object's position comes from stretching or compressing an object. Think about the spring that is pushed down in a jack-in-the-box. The spring's potential energy increases when the spring is compressed and decreases when it is released. Look at the bow that is being bent in the photograph on the left. When the bowstring is pulled, the bow bends and stores energy. When the string is released, both the string and the bow return to their normal shape. Stored energy is released as the bow and the string straighten out and the arrow is pushed forward.

Pulling the string, which bends the bow, gives the bow potential energy.

When a rock falls or a bow straightens, potential energy is released. In fact, in these examples, the potential energy produced either by gravity or by bending is changed into kinetic energy.

Chemical energy, such as the energy stored in food, is less visible, but it is also a form of potential energy. This form of potential energy depends on chemical composition rather than position. It is the result of the atoms, and the bonds between atoms, that make up the molecules in food. When these molecules are broken apart, and their atoms rearranged through a series of chemical changes, energy is released.

Chemical energy in the fuel of a model rocket engine is potential energy.

The fuel in a model rocket engine also contains chemical energy. Like the molecules that provide energy in your body, the molecules in the fuel store potential energy. When the fuel ignites in the rocket engine, the arrangement of atoms in the chemical fuel changes and its potential energy is released.

 CHECK YOUR READING Why is chemical energy a form of potential energy?

3.1 Review

KEY CONCEPTS

1. List three ways you use energy. How does each example involve a change?

2. What are some changes that can be caused by sound energy? by electromagnetic energy?

3. What two factors determine an object's kinetic energy?

CRITICAL THINKING

4. **Synthesize** How do the different forms of potential energy depend on an object's position or chemical composition?

5. **Infer** What forms of potential energy would be found in an apple on the branch of a tree? Explain.

⬤ CHALLENGE

6. **Synthesize** Describe a stone falling off a tabletop in terms of both kinetic energy and potential energy.

Gasoline or Electric?

Cars use a significant amount of the world's energy. Most cars get their energy from the chemical energy of gasoline, a fossil fuel. Cars can also get their energy from sources other than gasoline. For many years, engineers have been working to design cars that run only on electricity. The goals of developing these new cars include reducing air pollution and decreasing the use of fossil fuels. So why have electric cars not replaced gasoline-powered cars?

▶ Advantages of Electric Cars

- Electric motors are more simple than gasoline engines.
- Electric cars use energy more efficiently than gasoline-powered cars, so they are cheaper to operate.
- Controlling pollution at power plants that produce electricity is easier than controlling pollution from cars.
- Electric motors are quieter than gasoline engines.
- Electric cars do not produce smog, which is a major health concern in large cities.

▶ Disadvantages of Electric Cars

- At this time, electric cars can travel only about 100 miles on a single battery charge.
- It takes several hours to recharge the batteries of an electric car using today's charging systems.
- The batteries of an electric car need to be replaced after being recharged about 600 times.
- An electric car's range is decreased by heating or cooling the inside of the car because, unlike batteries in gasoline-powered cars, its batteries are not recharged during driving.

▶ Finding Solutions

As a Group

What technology would need to be improved for electric cars to replace gasoline-powered cars? What facilities that do not exist today would be needed to serve electric cars?

As a Class

Compare your group's solutions to those of other groups. Use the Internet to research hybrid vehicles. How would these vehicles solve some of the problems that you identified?

RESOURCE CENTER
CLASSZONE.COM

Find out more about electric cars.

3.2 Energy can change forms but is never lost.

◀ BEFORE, you learned	▶ NOW, you will learn
• Energy causes change • Energy has different forms • Kinetic energy and potential energy are the two general types of energy	• How energy can be converted from one form to another • About the law of conservation of energy • How energy conversions may be inefficient

VOCABULARY

law of conservation of energy p. 82
energy efficiency p. 83

THINK ABOUT

How does energy change form?

Potential energy is stored in the chemicals on the head of a match. The flame of a burning match releases that energy as light and heat. Where does the energy to strike the match come from in the first place?

Energy changes forms.

MIND MAP
Use a mind map to take notes about how energy changes forms.

A match may not appear to have any energy by itself, but it does contain potential energy that can be released. The chemical energy stored in a match can be changed into light and heat. Before the chemical energy in the match changes forms, however, other energy conversions must take place.

Plants convert energy from the Sun into chemical energy, which is stored in the form of sugars in their cells. When a person eats food that comes from plants—or from animals that have eaten plants—the person's cells can release this chemical energy. Some of this chemical energy is converted into the kinetic energy that a person uses to rub the match over a rough surface to strike it. The friction between the match and the striking surface produces heat. The heat provides the energy needed to start the chemical changes that produce the flame. From the Sun to the flame, at least five energy conversions have taken place.

 CHECK YOUR READING How is a person's chemical energy changed into another form of energy in the lighting of a match?

Conversions Between Potential Energy and Kinetic Energy

The results of some energy conversions are obvious, such as when electrical energy in a light bulb is changed into light and heat. Other energy conversions are not so obvious. The examples below and on page 80 explore, step by step, some ways in which energy conversions occur in the world around you.

Potential energy can be changed into kinetic energy and back into potential energy. Look at the illustrations and photograph of the ski jumper shown below.

1 At first, the ski jumper is at the top of the hill. This position gives him potential energy (PE) due to gravity.

2 As the ski jumper starts moving downhill, some of his potential energy changes into kinetic energy (KE). Kinetic energy moves him down the slope to the ramp.

3 When the ski jumper takes off from the ramp, some of his kinetic energy is changed back into potential energy as he rises in the air.

When the ski jumper descends to the ground, his potential energy once again changes into kinetic energy. After the ski jumper lands and stops moving, how might he regain the potential energy that he had at the top of the hill? The kinetic energy of a ski lift can move the ski jumper back up the mountain and give him potential energy again.

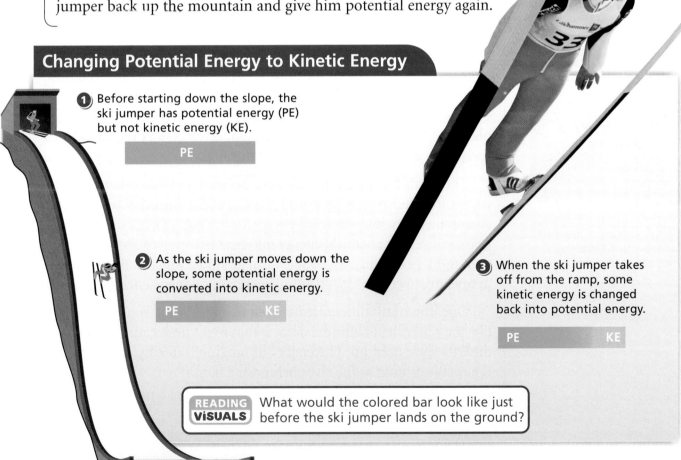

Changing Potential Energy to Kinetic Energy

1 Before starting down the slope, the ski jumper has potential energy (PE) but not kinetic energy (KE).

PE

2 As the ski jumper moves down the slope, some potential energy is converted into kinetic energy.

PE   KE

3 When the ski jumper takes off from the ramp, some kinetic energy is changed back into potential energy.

PE   KE

READING VISUALS What would the colored bar look like just before the ski jumper lands on the ground?

Using Energy Conversions

People have developed ways to convert energy from one form to another for many purposes. Read about the energy conversion process below, and follow that process in the illustrations on page 81 to see how energy in water that is stored behind a dam is changed into electrical energy.

READING TiP

As you read about the process for producing electrical energy, follow the steps on page 81.

1 The water held behind the dam has potential energy because of its position.

2 Some of the water is allowed to flow through a tunnel within the dam. The potential energy in the stored water changes into kinetic energy when the water moves through the tunnel.

3 The kinetic energy of the moving water turns turbines within the dam. The water's kinetic energy becomes kinetic energy in the turbines. The kinetic energy of the turning turbines is converted into electrical energy by electrical generators.

4 Electrical energy is transported away from the dam through wires. The electrical energy is converted into many different forms of energy and is used in many different ways. For example, at a concert or a play, electrical energy is converted into light and heat by lighting systems and into sound energy by sound systems.

As you can see, several energy conversions occur in order to produce a usable form of energy—potential energy becomes kinetic energy, and kinetic energy becomes electrical energy.

Other sources of useful energy begin with electromagnetic energy from the Sun. In fact, almost all of the energy on Earth began as electromagnetic energy from the Sun. This energy can be converted into many other forms of energy. Plants convert the electromagnetic energy of sunlight into chemical energy as they grow. This energy, stored by plants hundreds of millions of years ago, is the energy found in fossil fuels, such as petroleum, coal, and natural gas.

The chemical energy in fossil fuels is converted into other forms of energy for specific uses. In power plants, people burn coal to convert its chemical energy into electrical energy. In homes, people burn natural gas to convert its chemical energy into heat that warms them and cooks their food. In car engines, people burn gasoline, which is made from petroleum, to convert its chemical energy into kinetic energy.

One important difference between fossil fuels and sources of energy like the water held behind a dam, is that fossil fuels cannot be replaced once they are used up. The energy of moving water, by contrast, is renewable as long as the river behind the dam flows.

Hoover Dam produces a large amount of electrical energy for California, Nevada, and Arizona.

 CHECK YOUR READING How can potential energy be changed into a usable form of energy?

Converting Energy

Energy is often converted from one form to another in order to meet everyday needs.

1 Water held behind the dam has **potential energy.**

2 **Potential energy** is converted to **kinetic energy** when the water moves through the tunnel.

3 **Kinetic energy** is used to turn turbines. This **mechanical energy** is converted into **electrical energy** by generators.

4 **Electrical energy** is transmitted through wires, and then converted into many other forms of energy.

Potential Energy to Kinetic Energy

The potential energy of water behind the dam becomes the kinetic energy of moving water.

Kinetic Energy to Electrical Energy

The kinetic energy of turning turbines becomes electrical energy in these generators.

READING VISUALS How many different energy conversions are described in this diagram?

Energy is always conserved.

When you observe energy conversions in your daily life, it may seem that energy constantly disappears. After all, if you give a soccer ball kinetic energy by kicking it along the ground, it will roll for a while but eventually stop. Consider what might have happened to the ball's kinetic energy.

As the ball rolls, it rubs against the ground. Some kinetic energy changes into heat as a result of friction. Some of the ball's energy also changes into sound energy that you can hear as the ball moves. Although the ball loses kinetic energy, the overall amount of energy in the universe does not decrease. The photograph below shows how the soccer ball's kinetic energy decreases.

The soccer ball's kinetic energy decreases as that energy is changed into sound energy and heat.

kinetic energy
converted to heat

kinetic energy
converted to sound

In the soccer ball example, the ball loses energy, but this energy is transferred to other parts of the universe. Energy is conserved. The **law of conservation of energy** states that energy can neither be created nor destroyed. Conservation of energy is called a law because this rule is true in all known cases. Although in many instances it may appear that energy is gained or lost, it is really only changed in form.

READING TIP

Conservation refers to a total that does not change.

CHECK YOUR READING   Explain what is meant by the law of conservation of energy.

Conservation of energy is a balance of energy in the universe. When a soccer ball is kicked, a certain amount of energy is transferred by the kick. The ball gains an equal amount of energy, mostly in the form of kinetic energy. However, the ball's kinetic energy decreases as some of that energy is converted into sound energy and heat from the friction between the ball and the ground.

According to the law of conservation of energy, the amount of energy that a soccer player gives to the ball by kicking it is equal to the energy the ball gains. The energy the ball loses, in turn, is equal to the amount of energy that is transferred to the universe as sound energy and heat as the ball slows down.

Energy conversions may produce unwanted forms of energy.

When energy changes forms, the total amount of energy is conserved. However, the amount of useful energy is almost always less than the total amount of energy. For example, consider the energy used by an electric fan. The amount of electrical energy used is greater than the kinetic energy of the moving fan blades. Because energy is always conserved, some of the electrical energy flowing into the fan's motor is obviously changed into unusable or unwanted forms.

Some electrical energy is converted into unwanted sound energy.

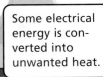

Some electrical energy is converted into kinetic energy of the fan blades.

Some electrical energy is converted into unwanted heat.

The fan converts a significant portion of the electrical energy into the kinetic energy of the fan blades. At the same time, some electrical energy changes into heat in the fan's motor. If the fan shakes, some of the electrical energy is being turned into unwanted kinetic energy. The more efficiently the fan uses electrical energy, though, the more energy will be transformed into kinetic energy that moves the air.

Energy efficiency is a measurement of usable energy after an energy conversion. You may be familiar with energy-efficient household appliances. These appliances convert a greater percentage of energy into the desired form than inefficient ones. The more energy-efficient a fan is, the more electrical energy it turns into kinetic energy in the moving blades. Less electrical energy is needed to operate appliances that are energy efficient.

CHECK YOUR READING   What does it mean when an energy conversion is efficient?

3.2 Review

KEY CONCEPTS

1. Describe an energy conversion you have observed in your own life.

2. Explain the law of conservation of energy in your own words.

3. Give an example of an energy conversion that produces unwanted forms of energy.

CRITICAL THINKING

4. **Synthesize** Suppose you are jumping on a trampoline. Describe the conversions that occur between kinetic energy and potential energy.

5. **Infer** Look at the ski jumper on page 79. Has all of his potential energy likely been changed into kinetic energy at the moment he lands? Explain.

CHALLENGE

6. **Communicate** Draw and label a diagram that shows at least three different energy conversions that might occur when a light bulb is turned on.

CHAPTER INVESTIGATION

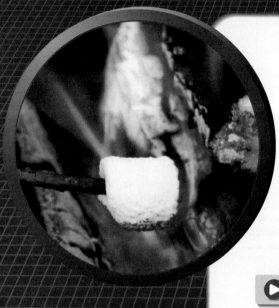

Energy Conversions

OVERVIEW AND PURPOSE All foods contain stored chemical energy, but some foods contain more chemical energy than others. People need this chemical energy for all of their activities. The amount of chemical energy stored in foods like marshmallows can be measured by burning the foods. In this investigation, you will

- construct an apparatus to investigate the amount of energy in samples of food
- calculate the amount of energy released when the foods are burned

▶ Problem
Write It Up

How much energy is stored in different types of food?

▶ Hypothesize
Write It Up

Write a hypothesis to explain which type of food contains a greater amount of chemical energy. Your hypothesis should take the form of an "If . . . , then . . . , because . . ." statement.

▶ Procedure

1 Create a data table similar to the one shown on the sample notebook page.

2 Using the can opener, punch two holes directly opposite each other near the top of the can. Slide the dowel rod through the holes as shown in the photograph to the left.

3 Measure 50 mL of water with a graduated cylinder, and pour the water into the can. Record the mass of the water. (**Hint:** 1 mL of water = 1 gram)

4 Rest the ends of the dowel rod on the ring in the ring stand to hold the can in the air. Carefully place the thermometer in the can. Measure and record the initial temperature (T1) of the water in the can.

5 Make a collar of aluminum foil and tape it around the can as shown. Leave enough room to insert the burner platform and food sample.

MATERIALS
- can opener
- empty aluminum can
- dowel rod
- water
- graduated cylinder
- ring stand with ring
- thermometer
- aluminum pie plate
- aluminum foil
- tape
- large paper clip
- cork
- modeling clay
- crouton
- caramel rice cake
- balance
- wooden matches

6 Construct the burner platform as follows: Open up the paper clip. Push the straightened end into a cork, and push the bottom of the cork into the clay. Push the burner onto the pie plate so it will not move. Put the pie plate under the ring.

step 6

7 Find and record the mass of the crouton. Place the crouton on the flattened end of the burner platform. Adjust the height of the ring so the bottom of the can is about 4 cm above the crouton.

8 Use a match to ignite the crouton. Allow the crouton to burn completely. Measure and record the final temperature (T2) of the water.

9 Empty the water from the can and repeat steps 3–8 with a caramel rice cake. The mass of the rice cake should equal the mass of the crouton.

▶ Observe and Analyze

Write It Up

1. **RECORD OBSERVATIONS** Make sure to record all measurements in the data table.

2. **CALCULATE** Find the energy released from the food samples by following the next two steps.

   Calculate and record the change in temperature.
   change in temperature = T2 − T1

   Calculate and record the energy released in calories. One calorie is the energy needed to raise the temperature of 1 g of water by 1°C.
   energy released = (mass of water · change in temperature · 1 cal/g°C)

3. **GRAPH** Make a bar graph showing the number of calories in each food sample. Which type of food contains a greater amount of chemical energy?

▶ Conclude

Write It Up

1. **INTERPRET** Answer the question posed in the problem.

2. **INFER** Did your results support your hypothesis? Explain.

3. **EVALUATE** What happens to any energy released by the burning food that is not captured by the water? How could you change the setup for a more accurate measurement?

4. **APPLY** Find out how much fat and carbohydrate the different foods contain. Explain the relationship between this information and the number of calories in the foods.

▶ INVESTIGATE Further

CHALLENGE The Calories listed in foods are equal to 1000 calories (1 kilocalorie). Calculate the amount of energy in your food samples in terms of Calories per gram of food (Calories/g). Using a balance, find the mass of any ash that remains after burning the food. Subtract that mass from the original mass of the sample to calculate mass burned. Divide total calories by mass burned, then divide that value by 1000 to find Calories/g. Compare your results to those given on the product labels.

Energy Conversions

Problem How much energy is stored in different types of food?

Hypothesize

Observe and Analyze

Table 1. Energy in Food

	Sample 1	Sample 2
Mass of water (g)		
Initial water temp. (T1) (°C)		
Final water temp. (T2) (°C)		
Mass of food (g)		
Change in temp. (T2 − T1) (°C)		
Energy released (mass·change in temp.·cal/g°C)		

Conclude

3.3 Technology improves the ways people use energy.

◀ BEFORE, you learned

- Energy can change forms
- When energy changes forms, the overall amount of energy remains the same
- Energy conversions usually produce unwanted forms of energy

▶ NOW, you will learn

- How technology can improve energy conversions
- About advantages and disadvantages of different types of energy conversions
- How technology can improve the use of natural resources

VOCABULARY

solar cell p. 88

EXPLORE Solar Cells

Why does a solar calculator need a large solar cell?

PROCEDURE

1. Measure the area of the calculator's solar cell. (**Hint:** area = length • width)

2. Turn the calculator on. Make sure that there is enough light for the calculator to work.

3. Gradually cover the solar cell with the index card. Observe the calculator's display as you cover more of the cell.

4. Measure the uncovered area of the solar cell when the calculator no longer works.

MATERIALS

- solar calculator without backup battery
- ruler
- index card

WHAT DO YOU THINK?

- How much of the solar cell is needed to keep the calculator working?
- Why might a solar calculator have a solar cell that is larger than necessary?

MIND MAP
Use a mind map to take notes about technology that improves energy conversions.

Technology improves energy conversions.

In many common energy conversions, most of the wasted energy is released as heat. One example is the common incandescent light bulb. Amazingly, only about 5 percent of the electrical energy that enters an incandescent light bulb is converted into light. That means that 95 percent of the electrical energy turns into unwanted forms of energy. Most is released as heat and ends up in the form of thermal energy in the surrounding air. To decrease this amount of wasted energy, scientists have investigated several more efficient types of lights.

Efficient Lights

Research to replace light bulbs with a more energy-efficient source of light has resulted in the light-emitting diode, or LED. LEDs have the advantage of converting almost all of the electrical energy they use into light.

The first LEDs were not nearly as bright as typical light bulbs, but over time scientists and engineers have been able to produce brighter LEDs. LEDs have many uses, including television remote controls, computer displays, outdoor signs, giant video boards in stadiums, and traffic signals. LEDs are also used to transmit information through fiber optic cables that connect home audio and visual systems.

 CHECK YOUR READING How are LEDs more efficient than incandescent lights?

LEDs that produce infrared light are used in remote controls.

Efficient Cars

Another common but inefficient energy conversion is the burning of gasoline in cars. A large percentage of gasoline's chemical energy is not converted into the car's kinetic energy. Some of the kinetic energy is then wasted as heat from the car's engine, tires, and brakes. Here, too, efficiency can be improved through advances in technology.

Fuel injectors, common in cars since the 1980s, have improved the efficiency of engines. These devices carefully monitor and control the amount of gasoline that is fed into a car's engine. This precise control of fuel provides a significant increase in the distance a car can travel on a tank of gasoline. More recently, hybrid cars have been developed. These cars use both gasoline and electrical energy from batteries. These cars are very fuel efficient. Even better, some of the kinetic energy lost during braking in hybrid cars is used to generate electrical energy to recharge the car's batteries.

Hybrid cars may look very similar to typical gasoline-powered cars, but their engines are different.

Technology improves the use of energy resources.

Much of the energy used on Earth comes from fossil fuels such as coal, petroleum, and natural gas. However, the supply of fossil fuels is limited. So, scientists and engineers are exploring the use of several alternative energy sources. Today, for example, both solar energy and wind energy are used on a small scale to generate electrical energy.

Solar energy and wind energy have several advantages compared to fossil fuels. Their supply is not limited, and they do not produce the same harmful waste products that fossil fuels do. However, there are also many obstacles that must be overcome before solar energy and wind energy, among other alternative energy sources, are as widely used as fossil fuels.

 CHECK YOUR READING What are the advantages of solar energy and wind energy as compared to fossil fuels?

Solar Energy

VISUALIZATION
CLASSZONE.COM

Observe how solar cells produce electricity.

Solar cells are important in today's solar energy technology. Modern **solar cells** are made of several layers of light-sensitive materials, which convert sunlight directly into electrical energy. Solar cells provide the electrical energy for such things as satellites in orbit around Earth, hand-held calculators, and, as shown below, experimental cars.

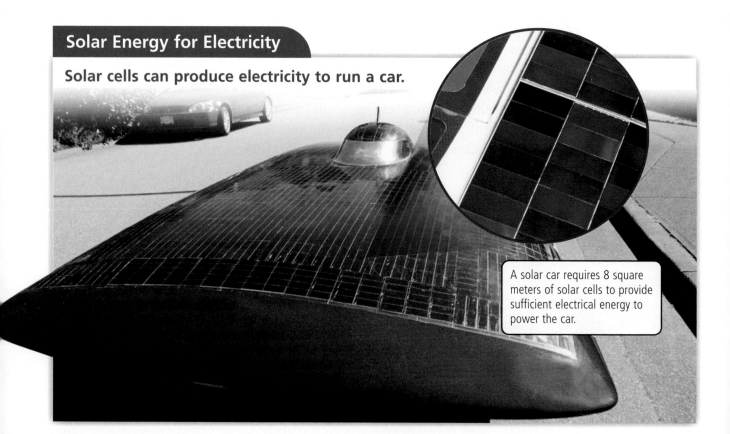

Solar Energy for Electricity

Solar cells can produce electricity to run a car.

A solar car requires 8 square meters of solar cells to provide sufficient electrical energy to power the car.

Solar cells produce electrical energy quietly and cleanly. However, they are not yet commonly used because the materials used to make them are very expensive. What's more, solar cells are not very efficient in producing electrical energy. Large numbers of solar cells produce only a relatively small amount of electrical energy. Typical solar cells convert only about 12 to 15 percent of the sunlight that reaches them into electrical energy. However, solar cells currently being developed could have efficiencies close to 40 percent.

Solar energy can be used in homes to provide heat and electrical energy.

In addition to converting the Sun's light directly into electrical energy, people have used the Sun's radiation for heating. In ancient Rome, glass was used to trap solar energy indoors so that plants could be grown in the winter. Today radiation from the Sun is still used to grow plants in greenhouses and to warm buildings. The photograph above shows a house that uses solar energy in both ways. The solar cells on the roof provide electrical energy, and the large windows help to trap the warmth. In fact, some solar power systems also use that warmth to produce additional electrical energy.

CHECK YOUR READING How can energy from the Sun be used by people?

INVESTIGATE Solar Energy

What improves the collection of solar energy?

PROCEDURE

1. Cover the top of one cup with white plastic, and cover the top of the other cup with black plastic. Secure the plastic with a rubber band.

2. Use the scissors to make a small hole in the center of each cup's plastic lid. Insert a thermometer through each opening.

3. Place the cups in direct sunlight, and record their temperatures every minute for 10 minutes.

WHAT DO YOU THINK?

- Which cup showed a greater temperature change? Why do you think this happened?

- Make a line graph of your results to show the change in temperature in each cup.

CHALLENGE Try the experiment again, using aluminum foil instead of white plastic. How do the results differ with the aluminum foil? Why might this be the case?

SKILL FOCUS
Observing

MATERIALS
- 2 plastic cups
- white plastic
- black plastic
- 2 rubber bands
- scissors
- 2 thermometers
- stopwatch
for Challenge:
- aluminum foil

TIME
20 minutes

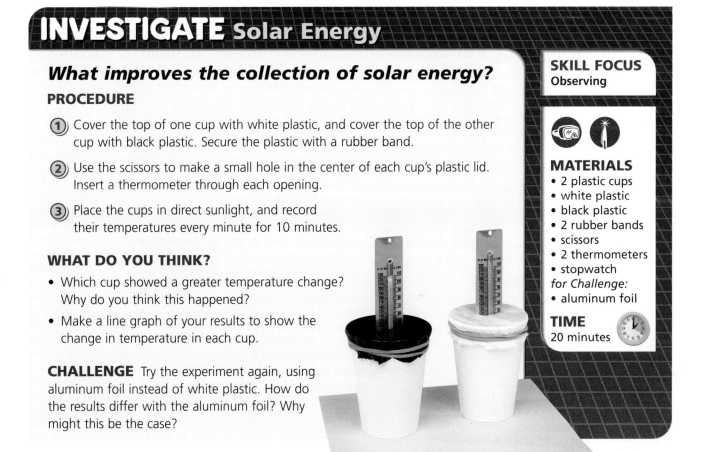

INFER Why might so many windmills be needed at a windfarm?

Wind Energy

RESOURCE CENTER
CLASSZONE.COM

Find out more about alternative energy sources.

For many centuries, people have used the kinetic energy of wind to sail ships, and, by using windmills, to grind grain and pump water. More recently, windmills have been used to generate electrical energy. In the early 1900s, for example, windmills were already being used to produce electrical energy in rural areas of the United States.

Like the technological advances in the use of solar energy, advances in capturing and using wind energy have helped to improve its efficiency and usefulness. One way to better capture the wind's energy has been to build huge windmill farms in areas that receive a consistent amount of wind. Windmill farms are found in several states, including Kansas, California, and New York. Other methods of more efficiently capturing wind energy include the use of specially shaped windmill blades that are made of new, more flexible materials.

 CHECK YOUR READING   How has the use of wind energy changed over time?

3.3 Review

KEY CONCEPTS

1. Provide an example of a common technology that does not efficiently convert energy. Explain.

2. Describe two ways in which hybrid cars are more energy-efficient than gasoline-powered cars.

3. List two advantages and two disadvantages of solar power.

CRITICAL THINKING

4. **Compare and Contrast** How are LEDs similar to incandescent light bulbs? How are they different?

5. **Synthesize** What are two ways in which the Sun's energy can be captured and used? How can both be used in a home?

▲ CHALLENGE

6. **Draw Conclusions** Satellites orbiting Earth use solar cells as their source of electrical energy. Why are solar cells ideal energy sources for satellites?

MATH TUTORIAL
CLASSZONE.COM
Click on Math Tutorial
for more help with rates.

Cool Efficiency

Energy efficiency is important because energy supplies are limited. The energy used by appliances such as air conditioners is measured in British thermal units, or BTUs. One BTU warms one pound of water by 1°F. The cooling ability of an air conditioner is measured by the number of BTUs it can move. Consider the number of BTUs that an air conditioning system must move in an ice rink.

An air conditioner typically has an energy efficiency ratio (EER) rating. The EER measures how efficiently a cooling system operates when the outdoor temperature is 95°F. The EER is the ratio of cooling per hour to the amount of electricity used, which is measured in watts. The higher the EER, the more energy efficient the air conditioner is.

$$EER = \frac{BTUs/hr}{watts\ used}$$

Example

Suppose an air conditioner uses 750 watts of electricity to cool 6000 BTUs per hour at 95°F. Calculate the air conditioner's EER.

(1) Use the formula above to calculate the EER.

$$EER = \frac{BTUs/hr}{watts\ used}$$

(2) Enter the known values into the formula.

$$EER = \frac{6000\ BTUs/hr}{750\ watts\ used}$$

(3) Solve the formula for the unknown value.

$$EER = \frac{6000\ BTUs/hr}{750\ watts\ used} = 8$$

ANSWER EER = 8 BTUs/hr per watt used

Answer the following questions.

1. What is the EER of a cooling system that uses 500 watts of electricity to move 6000 BTUs per hour at 95°F?

2. What is the EER of a cooling system that uses 1500 watts of electricity to move 12,000 BTUs per hour at 95°F?

3. Which air conditioner in the two questions above is more efficient?

CHALLENGE How many BTUs per hour would an air conditioner move at 95°F if it had an EER of 10 and used 1200 watts of electricity?

Indoor ice rinks require cooling systems that can keep ice frozen even when the outdoor temperature is 95°F.

Chapter Review

the BIG idea

Energy has different forms, but it is always conserved.

CONTENT REVIEW
CLASSZONE.COM

KEY CONCEPTS SUMMARY

3.1 Energy exists in different forms.

- Energy is the ability to cause a change.
- Different forms of energy produce changes in different ways.
- Kinetic energy depends on mass and speed.

Potential energy depends on position and chemical composition.

VOCABULARY
energy p. 72
kinetic energy p. 74
potential energy p. 75

3.2 Energy can change forms but is never lost.

- Energy often needs to be transformed in order to produce a useful form of energy.
- The law of conservation of energy states that energy is never created or destroyed.

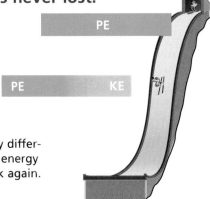

PE

PE   KE

Energy can be transformed in many different ways, including from potential energy (PE) to kinetic energy (KE) and back again.

VOCABULARY
law of conservation of energy p. 82
energy efficiency p. 83

3.3 Technology improves the ways people use energy.

- Different forms of technology are being developed and used to improve the efficiency of energy conversions.
- Solar cells convert sunlight into electrical energy.

New solar cells convert light into electrical energy more efficiently than those in the past.

VOCABULARY
solar cell p. 88

Reviewing Vocabulary

Review vocabulary terms by making a four square diagram for each term as shown in the example below. Include a definition, characteristics, examples from real life, and, if possible, nonexamples of the term.

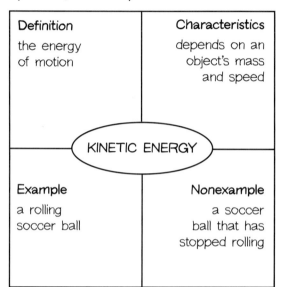

Definition	Characteristics
the energy of motion	depends on an object's mass and speed

KINETIC ENERGY

Example	Nonexample
a rolling soccer ball	a soccer ball that has stopped rolling

1. energy

2. potential energy

3. conservation of energy

4. energy efficiency

Reviewing Key Concepts

Multiple Choice *Choose the letter of the best answer.*

5. All forms of energy are a combination of
   a. mechanical energy and chemical energy
   b. chemical energy and kinetic energy
   c. potential energy and thermal energy
   d. potential energy and kinetic energy

6. Which type of energy is transmitted by vibrations of air?
   a. electromagnetic   c. nuclear
   b. sound   d. chemical

7. When energy is converted from one form to another, what is usually produced?
   a. chemical energy   c. heat
   b. gravity   d. nuclear energy

8. An object's kinetic energy is determined by its
   a. position and composition
   b. speed and position
   c. mass and speed
   d. height and width

9. Which of the following is a conversion from chemical energy to mechanical energy?
   a. a dark light bulb starting to glow
   b. food being heated in an oven
   c. a ball rolling down a hill
   d. a person lifting a weight

10. An energy-efficient electric fan converts a large portion of the electrical energy that enters it into
   a. an unwanted form of energy
   b. kinetic energy of the fan blades
   c. thermal energy in the fan's motor
   d. sound energy in the fan's motor

11. The energy in wind used to generate electricity is
   a. chemical energy
   b. sound energy
   c. potential energy
   d. kinetic energy

12. A skier on a hill has potential energy due to
   a. speed   c. compression
   b. energy efficiency   d. position

Short Answer *Write a short answer to each question.*

13. Explain how the law of conservation of energy might apply to an energy conversion that you observe in your daily life.

14. Describe a situation in which chemical energy is converted into mechanical energy. Explain each step of the energy conversion process.

The illustrations below show an in-line skater on a ramp. Use the illustrations to answer the next five questions.

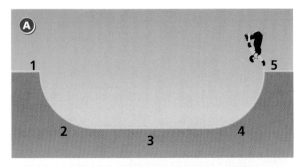

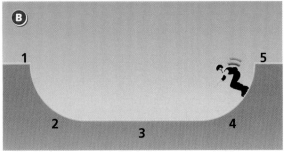

15. **OBSERVE** At what point in the illustrations would the skater have the most potential energy? the most kinetic energy? Explain.

16. **SYNTHESIZE** At what point in illustration B will the skater's kinetic energy begin to be changed back into potential energy? Explain.

17. **INFER** When the skater's kinetic energy is changed back into potential energy, will this amount of potential energy likely be equal to the skater's potential energy in illustration A? Why or why not?

18. **PREDICT** Describe how energy may appear to decrease in the example shown above. What energy conversions that produce unwanted forms of energy are occurring? Explain.

19. **SYNTHESIZE** Draw colored bars that might represent the potential energy and kinetic energy of the skater at each of the five labeled points on illustration A. Explain why you drew the bars the way you did. (**Hint:** See the illustration on p. 79.)

20. **SYNTHESIZE** How are plants and solar cells similar? How are the ways in which they capture sunlight and convert it into other forms of energy different? Explain.

21. **COMPARE** Explain how energy sources such as solar energy and wind energy have similar problems that must be overcome. How have scientists tried to address these problems?

22. **INFER** Suppose that one air conditioner becomes very hot when it is working but another air conditioner does not. Which air conditioner is more energy efficient? How can you tell?

23. **DRAW CONCLUSIONS** Suppose a vacuum cleaner uses 100 units of electrical energy. All of this energy is converted into thermal and sound energy (from the motor), and into the kinetic energy of air being pulled into the vacuum cleaner. If 60 units of electrical energy are converted into thermal energy and sound energy, how much electrical energy is converted into the desired form of energy? How do you know?

24. **COMMUNICATE** Describe a process in which energy changes forms at least twice. Draw and label a diagram that shows these energy conversions.

the BIG idea

25. **APPLY** Look again at the photograph on pages 68 and 69 and consider the opening question. How might your answer have changed after reading the chapter?

26. **COMMUNICATE** How have your ideas about energy and its different forms changed after reading the chapter? Provide an example from your life to describe how you would have thought of energy compared to how you might think about it now.

UNIT PROJECTS

If you need to do an experiment for your unit project, gather the materials. Be sure to allow enough time to observe results before the project is due.

Interpreting Graphs

Study the graph below. Then answer the first five questions.

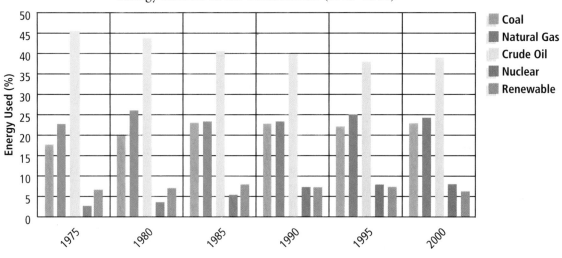

Energy Sources in the United States (1975–2000)

Legend:
- Coal
- Natural Gas
- Crude Oil
- Nuclear
- Renewable

Source: U.S. Energy Information Administration,
Monthly Energy Review (June 2003)

1. In which year did the greatest percentage of energy used in the United States come from crude oil?

a. 1975   **c.** 1995
b. 1980   **d.** 2000

2. What three sources of energy account for about 80 percent of all energy used in each year shown?

a. coal, crude oil, nuclear
b. natural gas, crude oil, renewable
c. coal, natural gas, crude oil
d. crude oil, nuclear, renewable

3. Which sources of energy show a greater percentage in 2000 as compared to 1980?

a. crude oil, renewable   **c.** coal, nuclear
b. natural gas, crude oil   **d.** coal, crude oil

4. The use of which energy source tended to decrease between 1975 and 2000?

a. coal   **c.** crude oil
b. natural gas   **d.** nuclear

5. The use of which source of energy steadily increased between 1975 and 1995?

a. coal   **c.** nuclear
b. crude oil   **d.** renewable

Extended Response

Answer the questions in detail. Include some of the terms from the word box on the right. Underline each term you use in your answers.

chemical energy	potential energy
electrical energy	sound energy
mechanical energy	thermal energy

6. When gasoline is burned in a moving car's engine, which forms of energy are being used? Which forms of energy are produced? Explain.

7. Name two appliances in your home that you believe are inefficient. What about them indicates that they may be inefficient?

TIMELINES in Science

ABOUT TEMPERATURE AND HEAT

Most likely, the first fires early people saw were caused by lightning. Eventually, people realized that fire provided warmth and light, and they learned how to make it themselves. During the Stone Age 25,000 years ago, people used firewood to cook food as well as to warm and light their shelters. Wood was the first fuel.

This timeline shows a few of the many steps on the path toward understanding temperature and heat. Notice how the observations and ideas of previous thinkers sparked new theories by later scientists. The boxes below the timeline show how technology has led to new insights and to applications related to temperature and heat.

445 B.C.

Four Basic Substances Named

Greek philosopher Empedocles says that everything on Earth is made of some combination of four basic substances: earth, air, fire, and water. Different types of matter have different qualities depending on how they combine these substances.

350 B.C.

Aristotle Expands Theory of Matter

Greek philosopher Aristotle names four basic qualities of matter: dryness, wetness, hotness, and coldness. Each of the four basic substances has two of these qualities.

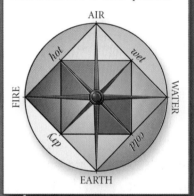

EVENTS

480 B.C.	440 B.C.	400 B.C.	360 B.C.	320 B.C.

APPLICATIONS AND TECHNOLOGY

People have been trying to understand and control heat since early times.

A.D. 1617
Heat Is Motion

English philosopher Francis Bacon uses observation and experimentation to demonstrate that heat is a form of motion. Most people remain unconvinced. They consider heat to be a fluid, which they call caloric.

1762
Calorimetry Founded

Scottish chemist Joseph Black founds the science of calorimetry, which describes the amount of energy as heat a substance can hold. His research in boiling and evaporation is valuable to his friend James Watt, who is making improvements to the steam engine.

1724
Mercury Used for Thermometer

Gabriel Fahrenheit, a German instrument maker, reports that mercury works well for measuring temperature. It expands evenly as temperature rises, and its silvery appearance makes it easy to see inside a glass tube. On Fahrenheit's scale, the boiling point of pure water is 212 degrees and the freezing point is 32 degrees.

1742
New Temperature Scale Used

Swedish astronomer Anders Celsius devises a scale for measuring temperature in which the freezing point of water is 0 degrees. The boiling point of pure water is 100 degrees. He calls this the Centigrade scale, from Latin words meaning "one hundred steps."

A.D. 1600	1640	1680	1720	1760

APPLICATION

Alchemy: The Quest to Create Gold

Alchemists, who hoped to turn less valuable metals into gold, took up the Greeks' theory of the four basic substances. They thought they could convert one substance into another by changing the balance of the four basic substances. Their ideas spread to the Byzantine Empire after A.D. 641, where these concepts were combined with advances in techniques for manipulating heat. Alchemy spread to Western Europe during the 1100s and 1200s.

Alchemists used chemical processes such as heating in furnaces, boiling in pots or cauldrons, distillation, pounding, and grinding. Because it was difficult to control the temperature, and thermometers had not yet been invented, alchemists usually had many different kinds of furnaces. Although alchemy is not considered a true science today, it did contribute methods and processes still used by chemists. It remained popular until around 1700.

1798
Heat and Friction Linked
While observing cannons at a weapons factory, American-born scientist Benjamin Thompson (Count Rumford) notices that friction between the cutting tools and the metal cannon barrels generates large amounts of heat. He concludes that friction is an unending source of heat. This observation helps put an end to the theory that heat is a fluid.

1906
Absolute Zero Identified
German physicist Walther Nernst suggests that absolute zero is the temperature at which the individual particles in an object would be practically motionless. Absolute zero, equivalent to –273°C, is the lowest temperature any object can reach. This limit was identified by British physicist Lord Kelvin in 1848. However, this temperature can never actually be reached by any real object.

1824
Heat Moves from Warmer to Cooler Objects
French physicist Nicolas Sadi Carnot shows that heat is a flow of energy from an object with a higher temperature to an object with a lower temperature. This explains why ice placed in a hot liquid melts and becomes a liquid rather than the liquid becoming ice.

1845
Various Energies Produce Heat
British physicist James Joule shows that mechanical energy can be converted to heat. Using a paddle-wheel device, he shows that the various forms of energy, such as mechanical and thermal, are basically the same and can change from one form to another. Joule also states that a given amount of energy of whatever form always yields that same amount of heat.

1800   **1840**   **1880**   **1920**

TECHNOLOGY
Keeping Heat In or Out
In 1892 Scottish physicist James Dewar invented the vacuum flask—a container in which warm fluids could be kept warm and cool fluids cool. A vacuum between the inner and outer walls of the container reduced conduction, which is the transfer of heat between two objects that are touching each other. Because a vacuum contains no matter, it does not conduct heat. Dewar's flask had silver walls to reflect radiated energy. As long as the flask was sealed, the vacuum was maintained and the temperature of a liquid inside the flask did not change much. A variation on Dewar's flask was produced in the early 1900s under the trade name Thermos. Today we call any vacuum container used for keeping beverages hot or cold a thermos.

This cutaway shows the inside of one of Dewar's experimental flasks.

2003

Wasps Stay Cool

Scientists in Israel have found evidence that some wasps have an internal air-conditioning system. Like a refrigerator, the wasp uses energy to stay cooler than the air around it. The energy may come from several sources, such as the energy generated by an electric current produced when the wasp's shell is exposed to sunlight. This ability to stay cool allows wasps to hunt for food even on very hot days.

RESOURCE CENTER
CLASSZONE.COM

Learn about current temperature and heat research.

1960   2000

APPLICATION

Using Thermal Energy from Ponds

Ponds can be used to store solar energy. The goal is to turn the solar energy into energy people can use. Salt must be added to the ponds, however, so that the water at the bottom is denser than the water at the top. This prevents thermal energy stored on the bottom from moving up to the surface, where it would be lost to the air through evaporation. A net on the surface helps prevent wind from mixing the water layers.

INTO THE FUTURE

As scientists are able to create colder and colder temperatures in the laboratory, they gain new insight into the scientific theories that explain temperature and heat. Advances in our knowledge of temperature and heat will lead to future applications.

- Scientists have developed a car that can run on hydrogen cooled into its liquid state. Before cars that run on this supercooled fuel become common, a system of refueling stations must be established.

- Understanding how some materials, such as silicon, conduct energy as heat may result in medical advances through better scanning and imaging technology.

- At temperatures approaching absolute zero (–273°C), a unique state of matter can be formed that is different from a solid, liquid, or gas. This rare state of matter could possibly be used to help produce extremely small circuits for use in miniature computers or other electronics.

ACTIVITIES

Design a Procedure

Many people claim that it is possible to determine the temperature by listening to the chirping of crickets. Crickets are sensitive to changes in air temperature and chirp more quickly when the temperature rises. To calculate the temperature in degrees Celsius, count the number of chirps in 7 seconds and add 5.

Write a procedure for an experiment that would test this claim. What factors would you consider testing? What range of temperatures would you test?

Writing About Science

Alchemy has fascinated people for centuries. Research its influence on both the technology and procedures of modern chemistry. Write a short report.

Temperature and Heat

the **BIG** idea

Heat is a flow of energy due to temperature differences.

Key Concepts

SECTION
4.1 Temperature depends on particle movement.
Learn how kinetic energy is the basis of temperature.

SECTION
4.2 Energy flows from warmer to cooler objects.
Learn about differences between temperature and heat, and how temperature changes in different substances.

SECTION
4.3 The transfer of energy as heat can be controlled.
Learn how energy is transferred through heat, and how that transfer can be controlled.

Internet Preview

CLASSZONE.COM

Chapter 4 online resources: Content Review, two Simulations, two Resource Centers, Math Tutorial, Test Practice

How does heat from the Sun increase this giraffe's temperature?

Moving Colors

Fill a clear plastic cup halfway with cold water. Fill another cup halfway with hot water. Using an eyedropper, place a drop of food coloring at the very bottom of each cup. Observe.

Observe and Think What happened to the drop of food coloring in cold water? in hot water? Why might this have happened?

Does It Chill?

Place an outdoor thermometer in an empty paper cup, and place the cup in the freezer. Check the thermometer every minute and record the time it takes for the temperature to reach 0°C (32°F). Remove the cup from the freezer. After it returns to room temperature, fill the cup with soil and repeat the experiment.

Observe and Think How long did it take for the temperature to reach 0°C each time? Why might there have been a difference?

Internet Activity: Kinetic Theory

Go to **ClassZone.com** to explore how temperature affects the speed of particles. Examine the effects of particle size as well.

Observe and Think What is the relationship between temperature and kinetic energy? How does particle mass affect temperature?

NSTA
scilinks.org
SC/LINKS

Kinetic Theory **Code: MDL064**

Getting Ready to Learn

◀ CONCEPT REVIEW

- Matter is made of particles too small to see.
- Matter can be solid, liquid, or gas.
- Energy is the ability to cause a change.
- There are different forms of energy.

◀ VOCABULARY REVIEW

matter p. 9
energy p. 72
kinetic energy p. 74

 **CONTENT REVIEW**
CLASSZONE.COM
Review concepts and vocabulary.

▶ TAKING NOTES

CHOOSE YOUR OWN STRATEGY

Take notes using one or more of the strategies from earlier chapters—**main idea and detail notes, main idea web,** or **mind map.** Feel free to mix and match the strategies, or use an entirely different note-taking strategy.

VOCABULARY STRATEGY

Place each vocabulary term at the center of a **description wheel** diagram. Write some words describing it on the spokes.

See the Note-Taking Handbook on pages R45–R51.

SCIENCE NOTEBOOK

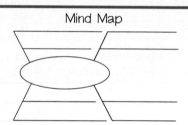

Main Idea and Detail Notes

Mind Map

Main Idea Web

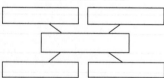

solids, liquids, gases

temperature

KINETIC THEORY OF MATTER

kinetic energy

particle movement

4.1 Temperature depends on particle movement.

◀ **BEFORE, you learned**

- All matter is made of particles
- Kinetic energy is the energy of motion
- Energy can be transferred or changed but is never created or destroyed

▶ **NOW, you will learn**

- How temperature depends on kinetic energy
- How temperature is measured
- How changes in temperature can affect matter

VOCABULARY

kinetic theory of matter p. 104
temperature p. 105
degree p. 106
thermometer p. 107

EXPLORE Temperature

What can cause a change in temperature?

PROCEDURE

1. Work with a partner. Hold the rubber band with both hands. Without stretching it, hold it to the underside of your partner's wrist.

2. Move the rubber band away, then quickly stretch it once and keep it stretched. Hold it to the underside of your partner's wrist.

3. Move the rubber band away and quickly let it return to its normal size. Hold it to the underside of your partner's wrist.

WHAT DO YOU THINK?
- What effect did stretching the rubber band have on the temperature of the rubber band?
- What may have caused this change to occur?

MATERIALS
large rubber band

All matter is made of moving particles.

NOTE-TAKING STRATEGY
You could take notes on the movement of particles in matter by using a main idea web.

You have read that any object in motion has kinetic energy. All the moving objects you see around you—from cars to planes to butterflies—have kinetic energy. Even objects so small that you cannot see them, such as atoms, are in motion and have kinetic energy.

You might think that a large unmoving object, such as a house or a wooden chair, does not have any kinetic energy. However, all matter is made of atoms, and atoms are always in motion, even if the objects themselves do not change their position. The motion of these tiny particles gives the object energy. The chair you are sitting on has some amount of energy. You also have energy, even when you are not moving.

The Kinetic Theory of Matter

REMINDER

Kinetic energy is the energy of motion.

Physical properties and physical changes are the result of how particles of matter behave. The **kinetic theory of matter** states that all of the particles that make up matter are constantly in motion. As a result, all particles in matter have kinetic energy. The kinetic theory of matter helps explain the different states of matter—solid, liquid, and gas.

1 The particles in a solid, such as concrete, are not free to move around very much. They vibrate back and forth in the same position and are held tightly together by forces of attraction.

2 The particles in a liquid, such as water in a pool, move much more freely than particles in a solid. They are constantly sliding around and tumbling over each other as they move.

3 In a gas, such as the air around you or in a bubble in water, particles are far apart and move around at high speeds. Particles might collide with one another, but otherwise they do not interact much.

Particles do not always move at the same speed. Within any group of particles, some are moving faster than others. A fast-moving particle might collide with another particle and lose some of its speed. A slow-moving particle might be struck by a faster one and start moving faster. Particles have a wide range of speeds and often change speeds.

READING TiP

In illustrations of particle movement, more motion lines mean a greater speed.

CHECK YOUR READING What is the kinetic theory of matter?

Matter in Motion

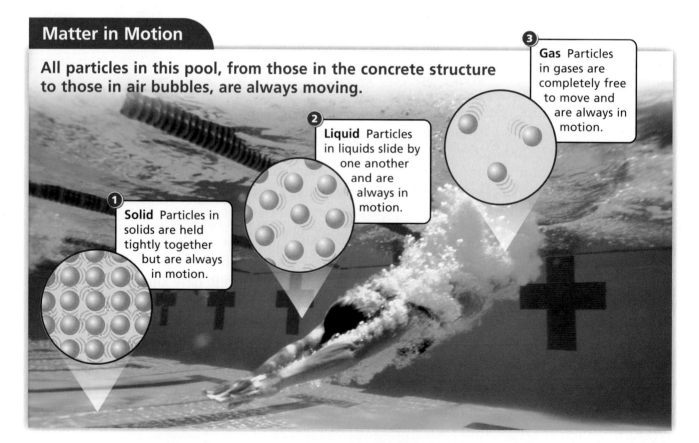

All particles in this pool, from those in the concrete structure to those in air bubbles, are always moving.

1 Solid Particles in solids are held tightly together but are always in motion.

2 Liquid Particles in liquids slide by one another and are always in motion.

3 Gas Particles in gases are completely free to move and are always in motion.

Temperature and Kinetic Energy

Particles of matter moving at different speeds have different kinetic energies because kinetic energy depends on speed. It is not possible to know the kinetic energy of each particle in an object. However, the average kinetic energy of all the particles in an object can be determined.

Temperature is a measure of the average kinetic energy of all the particles in an object. If a liquid, such as hot cocoa, has a high temperature, the particles in the liquid are moving very fast and have a high average kinetic energy. The cocoa feels hot. If a drink, such as a fruit smoothie, has a low temperature, the particles in the liquid are moving more slowly and have a lower average kinetic energy. The smoothie feels cold.

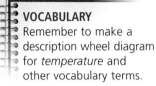

VOCABULARY
Remember to make a description wheel diagram for *temperature* and other vocabulary terms.

hot liquid

cold liquid

You experience the connection between temperature and the kinetic energy of particles every day. For example, to raise the temperature of your hands on a cold day—to warm your hands—you have to add energy, perhaps by putting your hands near a fire or a hot stove. The added energy makes the particles in your hands move faster. If you let a hot bowl sit on a table for a while, the particles in the bowl slow down due to collisions with particles in the air and in the table. The temperature of the bowl decreases, and it becomes cooler.

Temperature is the measurement of the average kinetic energy of particles, not just their speed. Recall that kinetic energy depends on mass as well as speed. Particles in a metal doorknob do not move as fast as particles in air. However, the particles in a doorknob have more mass and they can have the same amount of kinetic energy as particles in air. As a result, the doorknob and the air can have equal temperatures.

 How does temperature change when kinetic energy increases?

Temperature can be measured.

RESOURCE CENTER
CLASSZONE.COM

Find out more about temperature and temperature scales.

You have read that a warmer temperature means a greater average kinetic energy. How is temperature measured and what does that measurement mean? Suppose you hear on the radio that the temperature outside is 30 degrees. Do you need to wear a warm coat to spend the day outside? The answer depends on the temperature scale being used. There are two common temperature scales, both of which measure the average kinetic energy of particles. However, 30 degrees on one scale is quite different from 30 degrees on the other scale.

Temperature Scales

To establish a temperature scale, two known values and the number of units between the values are needed. The freezing and boiling points of pure water are often used as the standard values. These points are always the same under the same conditions and they are easy to reproduce. In the two common scales, temperature is measured in units called **degrees** (°), which are equally spaced units between two points.

The scale used most commonly in the United States for measuring temperature—in uses ranging from cooking directions to weather reports—is the Fahrenheit (FAR-uhn-HYT) scale (°F). It was developed in the early 1700s by Gabriel Fahrenheit. On the Fahrenheit scale, pure water freezes at 32°F and boils at 212°F. Thus, there are 180 degrees—180 equal units—between the freezing point and the boiling point of water.

During a summer day in Death Valley, California, the temperature can reach 49°C (120°F).

The temperature scale most commonly used in the rest of the world, and also used more often in science, is the Celsius (SEHL-see-uhs) scale (°C). This scale was developed in the 1740s by Anders Celsius. On the Celsius scale, pure water freezes at 0°C and boils at 100°C, so there are 100 degrees—100 equal units—between these two temperatures.

Recall the question asked in the first paragraph of this page. If the outside temperature is 30 degrees, do you need to wear a warm coat? If the temperature is 30°F, the answer is yes, because that temperature is colder than the freezing point of water. If the temperature is 30°C, the answer is no—it is a nice warm day (86°F).

 CHECK YOUR READING How are the Fahrenheit and Celsius temperature scales different? How are they similar?

Thermometers

Temperature is measured by using a device called a thermometer. A **thermometer** measures temperature through the regular variation of some physical property of the material inside the thermometer. A mercury or alcohol thermometer, for example, can measure temperature because the liquid inside the thermometer always expands or contracts by a certain amount in response to a change in temperature.

Liquid-filled thermometers measure how much the liquid expands in a narrow tube as the temperature increases. The distances along the tube are marked so that the temperature can be read. At one time, thermometers were filled with liquid mercury because it expands or contracts evenly at both high and low temperatures. This means that mercury expands or contracts by the same amount in response to a given change in temperature. However, mercury is dangerous to handle, so many thermometers today are filled with alcohol instead.

Some thermometers work in a different way—they use a material whose electrical properties change when the temperature changes. These thermometers can be read by computers. Some show the temperature on a display panel and are often used in cars and in homes.

 CHECK YOUR READING How do liquid-filled thermometers work?

INVESTIGATE Temperature Measurements

How does a thermometer work?

PROCEDURE

1. To make your own thermometer, fill the bottle halfway with the alcohol solution. Add a small amount of food coloring and mix thoroughly.

2. Place the straw into the bottle. Use clay to suspend the straw above the bottom of the bottle and to seal the bottle's mouth completely.

3. Pour ice water into the bowl and place the bottle into the ice water. Record your observations, and then empty the bowl.

4. Pour hot water into the bowl and place the bottle into the hot water. Record your observations.

WHAT DO YOU THINK?

- What happened to the level of the alcohol solution in the straw when the bottle was put into the ice water? into the hot water?
- Why do you think these changes happened?

CHALLENGE How could you modify your thermometer so that you could use it to measure a temperature?

SKILL FOCUS
Modeling

MATERIALS
- plastic bottle
- alcohol solution
- food coloring
- clear plastic straw
- clay
- bowl
- ice water
- hot tap water

TIME
30 minutes

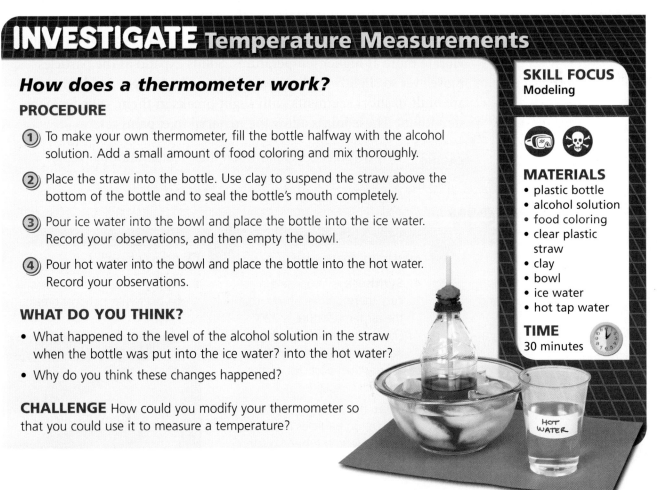

During construction of the Gateway Arch in St. Louis, engineers had to account for thermal expansion.

Thermal Expansion

The property that makes liquid-filled thermometers work is called thermal expansion. Thermal expansion affects many substances, not just alcohol and liquid mercury. All gases, many liquids, and most solids expand when their temperature increases.

Construction engineers often have to take thermal expansion into account because steel and concrete both expand with increasing temperature. An interesting example involves the construction of the Gateway Arch in St. Louis, which is built mostly of steel.

The final piece of the Arch to be put into place was the top segment joining the two legs. The Arch was scheduled to be completed in the middle of the day for its opening ceremony. However, engineers knew that the side of the Arch facing the Sun would get hot and expand due to thermal expansion.

This expansion would narrow the gap between the legs and prevent the last piece from fitting into place. In order to complete the Arch, workers sprayed water on the side facing the Sun. The water helped cool the Arch and decreased the amount of thermal expansion. Once the final segment was in place, engineers made the connection strong enough to withstand the force of the expanding material.

Thermal expansion occurs in solids because the particles of solids vibrate more at higher temperatures. Solids expand as the particles move ever so slightly farther apart. This is why bridges and highways are built in short segments with slight breaks in them, called expansion joints. These joints allow the material to expand safely.

 CHECK YOUR READING — Why do objects expand when their temperatures increase?

4.1 Review

KEY CONCEPTS

1. Describe the relationship between temperature and kinetic energy.
2. Describe the way in which thermometers measure temperature.
3. How can you explain thermal expansion in terms of kinetic energy?

CRITICAL THINKING

4. **Synthesize** Suppose a mercury thermometer shows that the air temperature is 22°C (72°F). Do particles in the air have more average kinetic energy than particles in the mercury? Explain.
5. **Infer** If a puddle of water is frozen, do particles in the ice have kinetic energy? Explain.

CHALLENGE

6. **Apply** Why might a sidewalk be built with periodic breaks in it?

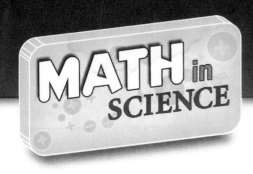

MATH in SCIENCE

MATH TUTORIAL
CLASSZONE.COM

Click on Math Tutorial for more help with temperature conversions.

How Hot Is Hot?

Temperatures on Earth can vary greatly, from extremely hot in some deserts to frigid in polar regions. The meaning of a temperature measurement depends on which temperature scale is being used. A very high temperature on the Fahrenheit scale is equal to a much lower temperature on the Celsius scale. The table shows the formulas used to convert temperatures between the two scales.

Conversion	Formula
Fahrenheit to Celsius	$°C = \frac{5}{9}(°F - 32)$
Celsius to Fahrenheit	$°F = \frac{9}{5}°C + 32$

Example

The boiling point of pure water is 212°F. Convert that temperature to a measurement on the Celsius scale.

(1) Use the correct conversion formula.

$$°C = \frac{5}{9} (°F - 32)$$

(2) Substitute the temperature given for the correct variable in the formula.

$$°C = \frac{5}{9} (212 - 32) = \frac{5}{9} \cdot 180 = 100$$

ANSWER $°C = 100$

Use the information in the table below to answer the questions that follow.

Highest and Lowest Temperatures Recorded on Earth			
Location	Highest Temp. (°F)	Location	Lowest Temp. (°F)
El Azizia, Libya	136	Vostok, Antarctica	−129
Death Valley, California	134	Oimekon, Russia	−90
Tirat Tsvi, Israel	129	Verkhoyansk, Russia	−90
Cloncurry, Australia	128	Northice, Greenland	−87
Seville, Spain	122	Snag, Yukon, Canada	−81

1. What is the highest temperature in °C?

2. What is the temperature difference in °C between the highest and second highest temperatures?

3. What is the difference between the highest and lowest temperatures in °F? in °C?

CHALLENGE The surface of the Sun is approximately 5500°C. What is this temperature in °F?

Temperatures on Earth, ranging from the extremes of frigid polar regions to the hottest deserts, can differ by more than 250°F.

4.2 Energy flows from warmer to cooler objects.

◀ **BEFORE,** you learned

- All matter is made of moving particles
- Temperature is the measurement of average kinetic energy of particles in an object
- Temperature can be measured

▶ **NOW,** you will learn

- How heat is different from temperature
- How heat is measured
- Why some substances change temperature more easily than others

VOCABULARY

heat p. 110
thermal energy p. 111
calorie p. 112
joule p. 112
specific heat p. 113

THINK ABOUT

Why does water warm up so slowly?

If you have ever seen food being fried in oil or butter, you know that the metal frying pan heats up very quickly, as does the oil or butter used to coat the pan's surface.

However, if you put the same amount of water as you put oil in the same pan, the water warms up more slowly. Why does water behave so differently from the metal, oil, or butter?

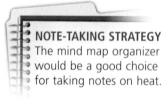

NOTE-TAKING STRATEGY
The mind map organizer would be a good choice for taking notes on heat.

Heat is different from temperature.

Heat and temperature are very closely related. As a result, people often confuse the concepts of heat and temperature. However, they are not the same. Temperature is a measurement of the average kinetic energy of particles in an object. **Heat** is a flow of energy from an object at a higher temperature to an object at a lower temperature.

If you add energy as heat to a pot of water, the water's temperature starts to increase. The added energy increases the average kinetic energy of the water molecules. Once the water starts to boil, however, adding energy no longer changes the temperature of the water. Instead, the heat goes into changing the physical state of the water from liquid to gas rather than increasing the kinetic energy of the water molecules. This fact is one demonstration that heat and temperature are not the same thing.

CHECK YOUR READING What is heat?

Heat and Thermal Energy

RESOURCE CENTER
CLASSZONE.COM

Learn more about
thermal energy.

Suppose you place an ice cube in a bowl on a table. At first, the bowl and the ice cube have different temperatures. However, the ice cube melts, and the water that comes from the ice will eventually have the same temperature as the bowl. This temperature will be lower than the original temperature of the bowl but higher than the original temperature of the ice cube. The water and the bowl end up at the same temperature because the particles in the ice cube and the particles in the bowl continually bump into each other and energy is transferred from the bowl to the ice.

Heat is always the transfer of energy from an object at a higher temperature to an object at a lower temperature. So energy flows from the particles in the warmer bowl to the particles in the cold ice and, later, the cooler water. If energy flowed in the opposite direction— from cooler to warmer—the ice would get colder and the bowl would get hotter, and you know that never happens.

CHECK YOUR READING In which direction does heat always transfer energy?

When energy flows from a warmer object to a cooler object, the thermal energy of both of the objects changes. **Thermal energy** is the total random kinetic energy of particles in an object. Note that temperature and thermal energy are different from each other. Temperature is an average and thermal energy is a total. A glass of water can have the same temperature as Lake Superior, but the lake has far more thermal energy because the lake contains many more water molecules.

Another example of how energy is transferred through heat is shown on the right. Soon after you put ice cubes into a pitcher of lemonade, energy is transferred from the warmer lemonade to the colder ice. The lemonade's thermal energy decreases and the ice's thermal energy increases. Because the particles in the lemonade have transferred some of their energy to the particles in the ice, the average kinetic energy of the particles in the lemonade decreases. As a result, the temperature of the lemonade decreases.

lemonade   heat

ice

Energy is transferred from the warmer lemonade to the cold ice through heat until their temperatures are equal.

CHECK YOUR READING How are heat and thermal energy related to each other?

Measuring Heat

The most common units of heat measurement are the calorie and the joule (jool). One **calorie** is the amount of energy needed to raise the temperature of 1 gram of water by 1°C. The **joule** (J) is the standard scientific unit in which energy is measured. One calorie is equal to 4.18 joules.

You probably think of calories in terms of food. However, in nutrition, one Calorie—written with a capital C—is actually one kilocalorie, or 1000 calories. This means that one Calorie in food contains enough energy to raise the temperature of 1 kilogram of water by 1°C. So, each Calorie in food contains 1000 calories of energy.

How do we know how many Calories are in a food, such as a piece of chocolate cake? The cake is burned inside an instrument called a calorimeter. The amount of energy released from the cake through heat is the number of Calories transferred from the cake to the calorimeter. The energy transferred to the calorimeter is equal to the amount of energy originally in the cake. A thermometer inside the calorimeter measures the increase in temperature from the burning cake, which is used to calculate how much energy is released.

CHECK YOUR READING How is heat measured?

INVESTIGATE Heat Transfer

Which substances change temperature faster?

PROCEDURE

① Using the graduated cylinder and the balance, separately measure 20 g of room-temperature water, 20 g of pennies, and 20 g of aluminum foil. Pour the water into a beaker until it is needed.

② Using the graduated cylinder, pour 50 mL of hot water into each of the cups. Record the water temperature in each cup.

③ Pour the room-temperature water into one cup. Place the pennies in the second cup and the foil in the third. After 5 minutes, record the temperature of the water in each of the cups.

WHAT DO YOU THINK?

• How did the temperature changes in the three cups compare?

• What might account for the differences you observed?

CHALLENGE Why might items such as pots and pans be made of materials like copper, stainless steel, or iron?

SKILL FOCUS
Measuring

MATERIALS
• graduated cylinder
• balance
• room-temperature water
• pennies
• aluminum foil
• hot tap water
• 100 mL beaker
• 3 plastic cups
• thermometer
• stopwatch

TIME
30 minutes

HOT WATER

Some substances change temperature more easily than others.

Have you ever seen an apple pie taken right out of the oven? If you put a piece of pie on a plate to cool, you can touch the pie crust in a few minutes and it will feel only slightly warm. But if you try to take a bite, the hot pie filling will burn your mouth. The pie crust cools much more quickly than the filling, which is mostly water.

Specific Heat

The amount of energy required to raise the temperature of 1 gram of a substance by 1°C is the **specific heat** of that substance. Every substance has its own specific heat value. So, each substance absorbs a different amount of energy in order to show the same increase in temperature.

If you look back at the definition of a calorie, you will see that it is defined in terms of water—one calorie raises the temperature of 1 gram of water by 1°C. So, water has a specific heat of exactly 1.00 calorie per gram per °C. Because one calorie is equal to 4.18 J, it takes 4.18 J to raise the temperature of one gram of water by 1°C. In joules, water's specific heat is 4.18 J per gram per °C. If you look at the specific heat graph shown below, you will see that 4.18 is an unusually large value. For example, one gram of iron has to absorb only 0.45 joules for its temperature to increase by 1°C.

A substance with a high specific heat value, like water, not only has to absorb a large quantity of energy for its temperature to increase, but it also must release a large quantity of energy for its temperature to decrease. This is why the apple pie filling can still be hot while the pie crust is cool. The liquid filling takes longer to cool. The high specific heat of water is also one reason it is used as a coolant in car radiators. The water can absorb a great deal of energy and protect the engine from getting too hot.

⬭ CHECK YOUR
READING How is specific heat related to a change in temperature?

READING **TIP**

Joules per gram per °C is shown as $\frac{J}{g°C}$.

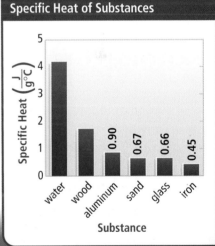

Specific Heat of Substances

Specific Heat $\left(\frac{J}{g°C}\right)$

water	wood	aluminum	sand	glass	iron
	0.90	0.67	0.66	0.45	

Substance

APPLY More energy is needed to warm water than many other substances. What materials in this photograph might be warmer than the water?

Specific Heat and Mass

Recall that thermal energy is the total kinetic energy of all particles in an object. So, thermal energy depends on the object's mass. Suppose you have a cup of water at a temperature of 90°C (194°F) and a bathtub full of water at a temperature of 40°C (104°F). Which mass of water has more thermal energy? There are many more water molecules in the bathtub, so the water in the tub has more thermal energy.

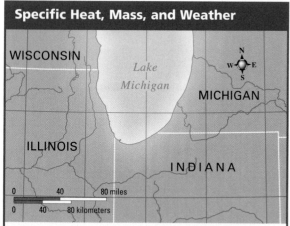

Specific Heat, Mass, and Weather

WISCONSIN

Lake Michigan

MICHIGAN

ILLINOIS

INDIANA

0   40   80 miles
0 40   80 kilometers

The temperature of a large body of water influences the temperature of nearby land. The green shading shows how far this effect extends.

The water in the cup has the same specific heat as the water in the tub. However, the cup of water will cool more quickly than the water in the bathtub. The tub of water has to release more thermal energy to its surroundings, through heat, to show a decrease in temperature because it has so much more mass.

This idea is particularly relevant to very large masses. For example, Lake Michigan holds 4.92 quadrillion liters (1.30 quadrillion gallons) of water. Because of the high specific heat of water and the mass of water in the lake, the temperature of Lake Michigan changes very slowly.

The temperature of the lake affects the temperatures on its shores. During spring and early summer, the lake warms slowly, which helps keep the nearby land cooler. During the winter, the lake cools slowly, which helps keep the nearby land warmer. Temperatures within about 15 miles of the lake can differ by as much as 6°C (about 10°F) from areas farther away from the lake.

As you will read in the next section, the way in which a large body of water can influence temperatures on land depends on how energy is transferred through heat.

CHECK YOUR READING   How does an object's thermal energy depend on its mass?

4.2 Review

KEY CONCEPTS

1. How is temperature related to heat?

2. How do the units that are used to measure heat differ from the units that are used to measure temperature?

3. Describe specific heat in your own words.

CRITICAL THINKING

4. **Compare and Contrast** How are a calorie and a joule similar? How are they different?

5. **Synthesize** Describe the relationships among kinetic energy, temperature, heat, and thermal energy.

○ CHALLENGE

6. **Infer** Suppose you are spending a hot summer day by a pool. Why might the water in the pool cool the air near the pool?

Cooking with Heat

A chef makes many decisions about cooking a meal based on heat and temperature. The appropriate temperature and cooking method must be used. A chef must calculate the cooking time of each part of the meal so that everything is finished at the same time. A chef also needs to understand how heat moves through food. For example, if an oven temperature is too hot, meat can be overcooked on the outside and undercooked on the inside.

Bread vs. Meat

Chefs have to understand how energy as heat is transferred to different foods. For example, the fluffy texture of bread comes from pockets of gas that separate its fibers. The gas is a poor conductor of energy. Therefore, more energy and a longer cooking time are needed to cook bread than to cook an equal amount of meat.

Roasting and Heat

The shape of the food being roasted is just as important as what is being roasted. Heat moves more quickly through food with a thin shape than it will through food with a thicker shape.

What Temperature?

Eggs cook very differently under different temperatures. For example, temperature is important when baking meringue, which is made of egg whites and sugar. A Key lime pie topped with meringue is baked at 400°F to make a meringue that is soft. However, meringue baked at 275°F makes light and crisp dessert shells.

EXPLORE

1. **COMPARE** Using a cookbook, find the oven temperatures for baking biscuits, potatoes, and beef. Could you successfully cook a roast and biscuits in the oven at the same time?

2. **CHALLENGE** Crack open three eggs. Lightly beat one egg in each of three separate bowls. Follow the steps below.

   1. Heat about two cups of water to 75°C in a small pan.
   2. Pour one of the eggs into the water in the pan.
   3. Observe the egg and record your observations.
   4. Repeat steps 1–3 twice, once with boiling water and then with room-temperature water.

   Describe the differences that you observed among the three eggs. What may account for these differences?

The transfer of energy as heat can be controlled.

◀ **BEFORE, you learned**

- Temperature is the average amount of kinetic energy of particles in an object
- Heat is the flow of energy from warmer objects to cooler objects

▶ **NOW, you will learn**

- How energy is transferred through heat
- How materials are used to control the transfer of energy through heat

VOCABULARY

conduction p. 117
conductor p. 117
insulator p. 117
convection p. 118
radiation p. 119

EXPLORE Conduction

How can you observe a flow of energy?

PROCEDURE

1. Fill the large beaker halfway with hot tap water. Fill the small beaker halfway with cold water. Place a thermometer in each beaker. Record the temperature of the water in each beaker.

2. Without removing the water in either beaker, place the small beaker inside the large beaker. Record the temperature in each beaker every 30 seconds for 2 minutes.

MATERIALS
- 500 mL beaker
- hot tap water
- 200 mL beaker
- cold water
- 2 thermometers
- stopwatch

WHAT DO YOU THINK?
- How did the water temperature in each beaker change?
- In which direction did energy flow? How do you know?

NOTE-TAKING STRATEGY
Main idea and detail notes would be a useful strategy for taking notes on how heat transfers energy.

Energy moves as heat in three ways.

Think about what you do to keep warm on a cold day. You may wear several layers of clothing, sit next to a heater, or avoid drafty windows. On a hot day, you may wear light clothing and sit in the shade of a tree. In all of these situations, you are trying to control the transfer of energy between yourself and your surroundings.

Recall that heat is always a transfer of energy from objects at a higher temperature to objects at a lower temperature. How does energy get transferred from a warmer object to a cooler one? There are three different ways in which this transfer of energy can occur—by conduction, convection, and radiation. So, in trying to control heat, it is necessary to control conduction, convection, and radiation.

Conduction

One way in which energy is transferred as heat is through direct contact between objects. **Conduction** is the process that moves energy from one object to another when they are touching physically. If you have ever picked up a bowl of hot soup, you have experienced conduction.

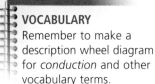

VOCABULARY
Remember to make a description wheel diagram for *conduction* and other vocabulary terms.

Conduction occurs any time that objects at different temperatures come into contact with each other. The average kinetic energy of particles in the warmer object is greater than that of the particles in the cooler object. When particles of the objects collide, some of the kinetic energy of the particles in the warmer object is transferred to the cooler object. As long as the objects are in contact, conduction continues until the temperatures of the objects are equal.

Conduction can also occur within a single object. In this case, energy is transferred from the warmer part of the object to the cooler part of the object by heat. Suppose you put a metal spoon into a cup of hot cocoa. Energy will be conducted from the warm end of the spoon to the cool end until the temperature of the entire spoon is the same.

Some materials transfer the kinetic energy of particles better than others. **Conductors** are materials that transfer energy easily. Often, conductors also have a low specific heat. For example, metals are typically good conductors. You know that when one end of a metal object gets hot, the other end quickly becomes hot as well. Consider pots or pans that have metal handles. A metal handle becomes too hot to touch soon after the pan is placed on a stove that has been turned on.

Other materials, called **insulators,** are poor conductors. Insulators often have high specific heats. Some examples of insulators are wood, paper, and plastic foam. In fact, plastic foam is a good insulator because it contains many small spaces that are filled with air. A plastic foam cup will not easily transfer energy by conduction. As a result, plastic foam is often used to keep cold drinks cold or hot drinks hot. Think about the pan handle mentioned above. Often, the handle is made of a material that is an insulator, such as wood or plastic. Although a wood or plastic handle will get hot when the pan is on a stove, it takes a much longer time for wood or plastic to get hot as compared to a metal handle.

Conduction transfers energy from the cocoa to the mug to the person's hands.

CHECK YOUR READING How are conductors and insulators different?

Convection

Energy can also be transferred through the movement of gases or liquids. **Convection** is the process that transfers energy by the movement of large numbers of particles in the same direction within a liquid or gas. In most substances, as the kinetic energy of particles increases, the particles spread out over a larger area. An increased distance between particles causes a decrease in the density of the substance. Convection occurs when a cooler, denser mass of the gas or liquid replaces a warmer, less dense mass of the gas or liquid by pushing it upward.

Convection is a cycle in nature responsible for most winds and ocean currents. When the temperature of a region of air increases, the particles in the air spread out and the air becomes less dense.

① Cooler, denser air flows in underneath the warmer, less dense air, and pushes the warmer air upward.

② When this air cools, it becomes more dense than the warmer air beneath it.

③ The cooled air sinks and moves under the warmer air.

Convection in liquids is similar. Warm water is less dense than cold water, so the warm water is pushed upward as cooler, denser water moves underneath. When the warm water that has been pushed up cools, its density increases. The cycle continues when this more dense water sinks, pushing warmer water up again.

Recall that a large body of water, such as Lake Michigan, influences the temperature of the land nearby. This effect is due to convection. During the spring and early summer, the lake is cool and warms more slowly than the land. The air above the land gets warmer than the air over the water. The warmer air above the land is less dense than the cooler air above the water. The cooler, denser air moves onshore and pushes the warmer air up. The result is a cooling breeze from the lake.

REMINDER

Density = $\dfrac{\text{mass}}{\text{Volume}}$

READING TiP

As you read about the cycle that occurs during convection, follow the steps in the illustration below.

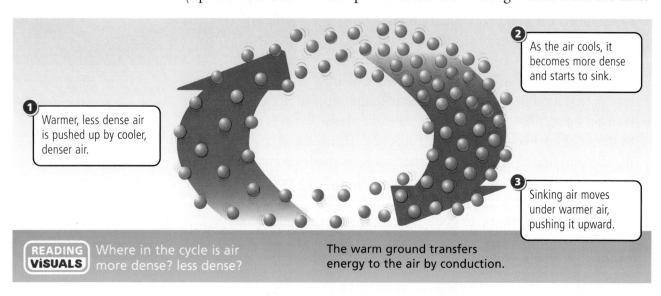

① Warmer, less dense air is pushed up by cooler, denser air.

② As the air cools, it becomes more dense and starts to sink.

③ Sinking air moves under warmer air, pushing it upward.

READING VISUALS Where in the cycle is air more dense? less dense?

The warm ground transfers energy to the air by conduction.

Radiation

Radiation is another way in which energy can be transferred from one place to another. **Radiation** is energy that travels as electromagnetic waves, which include visible light, microwaves, and infrared (IHN-fruh-REHD) light. The Sun is the most significant source of radiation that you experience on a daily basis. However, all objects—even you—emit radiation and release energy to their surroundings.

Consider radiation from the Sun. You can feel radiation as heat when radiation from the Sun warms your skin. The radiation emitted from the Sun strikes the particles in your body and transfers energy. This transfer of energy increases the movement of particles in your skin, which you detect as an increase in temperature. Of course, you are not the only object on Earth that absorbs the Sun's radiation. Everything—from air to concrete sidewalks—absorbs radiation that increases particle motion and produces an increase in temperature.

When radiation is emitted from one object and then is absorbed by another, the result is often a transfer of energy through heat. Like both conduction and convection, radiation can transfer energy from warmer to cooler objects. However, radiation differs from conduction and convection in a very significant way. Radiation can travel through empty space, as it does when it moves from the Sun to Earth. If this were not the case, radiation from the Sun would have no effect on Earth.

When radiation from the Sun is absorbed, energy is transferred through heat.

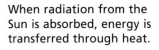

SIMULATION
CLASSZONE.COM

Identify examples of conduction, convection, or radiation.

 CHECK YOUR READING How does radiation transfer energy?

Different materials are used to control the transfer of energy.

Energy is always being transferred between objects at different temperatures. It is often important to slow this movement of energy. For example, if energy were always transferred quickly and efficiently through heat, it would not be possible to keep a building warm during a cold day or to keep cocoa hot in a thermos.

Insulation

Insulators used by people are similar to insulators in nature. Polar bears are so well insulated that they tend to overheat.

The polar bear's hollow guard hair is an effective insulator because air inside the hair does not easily conduct energy.

hollow hair

Vacuum Flask

hot liquid (inside flask)

air (outside flask)

inner reflective layer

outer case

empty space

The empty space between layers in a vacuum flask prevents the conduction of energy through heat.

Polar bears have several layers of insulation. They have a layer of fat up to 11 cm thick, a 2.5–5.0 cm thick layer of fur, and an outer layer of hollow guard hairs.

READING VISUALS How is the polar bear's hollow hair similar to the empty space in a vacuum flask? How is it different?

Insulators are used to control and slow the transfer of energy from warmer objects to cooler objects because they are poor conductors of energy. You can think of an insulator as a material that keeps cold things cold or hot things hot.

Sometimes people say that insulation "keeps out the cold." An insulator actually works by trapping energy. During the winter, you use insulators such as wool to slow the loss of your body heat to cold air. The wool traps air against your body, and because both air and wool are poor conductors, you lose body heat at a slower rate. Fiberglass insulation in the outer walls of a building works in the same way. The fiberglass slows the movement of energy from a building to the outside during cold weather, and it slows the movement of energy into the building during hot weather.

A vacuum flask, or thermos, works in a slightly different way to keep liquids either hot or cold. Between two layers of the flask is an empty space. This space prevents conduction between the inside and outside walls of the flask. Also, the inside of the flask is covered with a shiny material that reflects much of the radiation that strikes it. This prevents radiation from either entering or leaving the flask.

Insulators that people use are often very similar to insulators in nature. Look at the photograph of the polar bear on page 120. Because of the arctic environment in which the polar bear lives, it needs several different types of insulation. The polar bear's fur helps to trap a layer of air against its body to keep warmth inside. Polar bears also have guard hairs that extend beyond the fur. These guard hairs are hollow and contain air. Because air is a poor conductor, the bear's body heat is not easily released into the air.

 How does insulation keep a building warm?

KEY CONCEPTS

1. What are three ways in which energy can be transferred through heat? Provide an example of each.

2. Explain how convection is a cycle in nature.

3. Describe how an insulator can slow a transfer of energy.

CRITICAL THINKING

4. **Compare and Contrast** Describe the similarities and differences among conduction, convection, and radiation.

5. **Synthesize** Do you think solids can undergo convection? Why or why not? Explain.

◯ CHALLENGE

6. **Infer** During the day, wind often blows from a body of water to the land. What do you think would happen at night? Explain.

CHAPTER INVESTIGATION

Insulators

OVERVIEW AND PURPOSE

To keep warm in cold weather, a person needs insulation. A down-filled coat, such as the one worn by the girl in the photograph, is a very effective insulator because it contains a great deal of air. Energy is transferred rapidly through some substances and quite slowly through others. In this investigation, you will

- design and build an insulator for a bottle to maintain the temperature of the water inside
- test an unchanged bottle and your experimental bottle to see which maintains the water's temperature more effectively

▶ Problem

Write It Up

How can a bottle be insulated most effectively?

▶ Procedure

1. Create a data table similar to the one shown on the sample notebook page to record your measurements.

2. Set aside plastic bottles, thermometers, modeling clay, and a graduated cylinder. Decide whether you will test hot or cold water in your bottles.

3. From the other materials available to you, design a way to modify one of the bottles so that it will keep the temperature of the water constant for a longer period of time than the control bottle.

4. Build your modified bottle by using one or more of the insulating materials available.

MATERIALS
- 2 small plastic bottles
- 2 thermometers
- modeling clay
- graduated cylinder
- tap water (hot or cold)
- foam packing peanuts
- plastic wrap
- aluminum foil
- soil
- sand
- rubber bands
- coffee can
- beaker
- stopwatch

5 Fill each bottle with 200 mL of hot or cold water. Make sure that the water in each bottle is the same temperature.

6 Place a thermometer into each bottle. The thermometers should touch only the water, not the bottom or sides of the bottles. Use modeling clay to hold the thermometers in place in the bottles.

7 Record the starting temperature of the water in both bottles. Continue to observe and record the temperature of the water in both bottles every 2 minutes for 30 minutes. Record these temperatures in your data table.

step 6

Observe and Analyze
Write It Up

1. **COMMUNICATE** Draw the setup of your experimental bottle in your notebook. Be sure to label the materials that you used to insulate your experimental bottle.

2. **RECORD OBSERVATIONS** Make sure you record all of your measurements and observations in the data table.

3. **GRAPH** Make a double line graph of the temperature data. Graph temperature versus time. Plot the temperature on the vertical axis, or *y*-axis, and the time on the horizontal axis, or *x*-axis. Use different colors to show the data from the different bottles.

4. **IDENTIFY VARIABLES, CONTROLS, AND CONSTANTS** Which bottle was the control? What was the variable? What were the constants in both setups?

5. **ANALYZE** Obtain the experimental results from two other groups that used a different insulator. Compare your results with the results from the other groups. Which bottle changed temperature most quickly?

Conclude

Write It Up

1. **EVALUATE** Explain why the materials used by different groups might have been more or less effective as insulators. How might you change your design to improve its insulating properties?

2. **IDENTIFY LIMITS** Describe possible sources of error in the procedure or any points at which errors might have occurred. Why is it important to use the same amount of water in both bottles?

3. **APPLY** Energy can be transferred as heat by radiation, conduction, and convection. Which of these processes might be slowed by the insulation around your bottle? Explain.

INVESTIGATE Further

CHALLENGE We depend on our clothing to keep us from losing body heat when we go outside in cold weather. How might you determine the type of clothing that would provide the best insulation? Design an experiment that would test your hypothesis.

Insulators

Problem How can a bottle be insulated most effectively?

Observe and Analyze

Table 1. Water Temperature Measurements

Time (min)	Control Bottle Temperature (°C)	Experimental Bottle Temperature (°C)
0		
2		
4		
6		
8		
10		

Conclude

Chapter Review

the BIG idea

Heat is a flow of energy due to temperature differences.

CONTENT REVIEW
CLASSZONE.COM

KEY CONCEPTS SUMMARY

 4.1 **Temperature depends on particle movement.**
- All particles in matter have kinetic energy.
- Temperature is the measurement of the average kinetic energy of particles in an object.
- Temperature is commonly measured on the Fahrenheit or Celsius scales.

VOCABULARY
kinetic theory of matter p. 104
temperature p. 105
degree p. 106
thermometer p. 107

hot liquid   cold liquid

Particles in a warmer substance have a greater average kinetic energy than particles in a cooler substance.

 4.2 **Energy flows from warmer to cooler objects.**
- Heat is a transfer of energy from an object at a higher temperature to an object at a lower temperature.
- Different materials require different amounts of energy to change temperature.

VOCABULARY
heat p. 110
thermal energy p. 111
calorie p. 112
joule p. 112
specific heat p. 113

Energy is transferred from the warmer lemonade to the cold ice through heat.

heat

ice

 4.3 **The transfer of energy as heat can be controlled.**
- Energy can be transferred by conduction, convection, and radiation.
- Different materials are used to control the transfer of energy.

VOCABULARY
conduction p. 117
conductor p. 117
insulator p. 117
convection p. 118
radiation p. 119

Types of Energy Transfer		
Conduction	**Convection**	**Radiation**
• Energy transferred by direct contact • Energy flows directly from warmer object to cooler object • Can occur within one object • Continues until object temperatures are equal	• Occurs in gases and liquids • Movement of large number of particles in same direction • Occurs due to difference in density • Cycle occurs while temperature differences exist	• Energy transferred by electromagnetic waves such as light, microwaves, and infrared radiation • All objects radiate energy • Can transfer energy through empty space

Reviewing Vocabulary

Make a frame for each of the vocabulary terms listed below. Write the term in the center. Decide what information to frame it with. Use definitions, examples, descriptions, parts, or pictures.

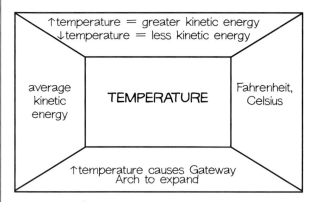

↑temperature = greater kinetic energy
↓temperature = less kinetic energy

average kinetic energy

TEMPERATURE

Fahrenheit, Celsius

↑temperature causes Gateway Arch to expand

1. kinetic theory of matter
2. heat
3. thermal energy
4. conduction
5. convection
6. radiation

In two or three sentences, describe how the terms in the following pairs are related to each other. Underline each term in your answers.

7. calorie, joule

8. conductor, insulator

Reviewing Key Concepts

Multiple Choice *Choose the letter of the best answer.*

9. What is the zero point in the Celsius scale?
   a. the freezing point of pure water
   b. the boiling point of pure water
   c. the freezing point of mercury
   d. the boiling point of alcohol

10. Energy is always transferred through heat from?
   a. an object with a lower specific heat to one with a higher specific heat
   b. a cooler object to a warmer object
   c. an object with a higher specific heat to one with a lower specific heat
   d. a warmer object to a cooler object

11. The average kinetic energy of particles in an object can be measured by its
   a. heat   c. calories
   b. thermal energy d. temperature

12. How is energy transferred by convection?
   a. by direct contact between objects
   b. by electromagnetic waves
   c. by movement of groups of particles in gases or liquids
   d. by movement of groups of particles in solid objects

13. The total kinetic energy of particles in an object is
   a. heat   c. calories
   b. thermal energy d. temperature

14. Water requires more energy than an equal mass of iron for its temperature to increase by a given amount because water has a greater
   a. thermal energy c. temperature
   b. specific heat   d. kinetic energy

15. Energy from the Sun travels to Earth through which process?
   a. temperature   c. radiation
   b. conduction   d. convection

16. An insulator keeps a home warm by
   a. slowing the transfer of cold particles from outside to inside
   b. increasing the specific heat of the air inside
   c. slowing the transfer of energy from inside to outside
   d. increasing the thermal energy of the walls

17. Conduction is the transfer of energy from a warmer object to a cooler object through
   a. a vacuum   c. direct contact
   b. a gas   d. empty space

Short Answer *Write a short answer to each question.*

18. How are kinetic energy and temperature related to each other?

19. What is the difference between heat and temperature?

The illustrations below show particle movement in a substance at two different temperatures. Use the illustrations to answer the next four questions.

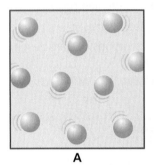 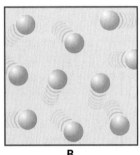

A   B

20. OBSERVE Which illustration represents the substance when it is at a higher temperature? Explain.

21. PREDICT What would happen to the particles in illustration A if the substance were chilled? What would happen if the particles in illustration B were warmed?

22. PREDICT If energy is transferred from one of the substances to the other through heat, in which direction would the energy flow (from A to B, or from B to A)? Why?

23. COMMUNICATE Suppose energy is transferred from one of the substances to the other through heat. Draw a sketch that shows what the particles of both substances would look like when the transfer of energy is complete. Explain.

24. COMPARE AND CONTRAST How are conduction and convection similar? How are they different?

25. DRAW CONCLUSIONS Suppose you are outdoors on a hot day and you move into the shade of a tree. Which form of energy transfer are you avoiding? Which type of energy transfer are you still feeling? Explain.

26. COMMUNICATE Draw a sketch that shows how convection occurs in a liquid. Label the sketch to indicate how the process occurs in a cycle.

Use the illustrations of the two thermometers below to answer the next four questions.

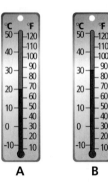

A   B

27. How much of a change in temperature occurred between A and B in the Fahrenheit scale?

28. Suppose the temperatures were measured in 10 g of water. How much energy, in calories, would have been added to cause that increase in temperature? (**Hint:** 1 calorie raises the temperature of 1 g of water by 1°C.)

29. Again, suppose the temperatures shown above were measured in 10 g of water. How much energy, in joules, would have been added? (**Hint:** 1 calorie = 4.18 joules.)

30. Suppose that the temperatures were measured for 10 g of iron. How much energy, in joules, would have been added to cause the increase in temperature? (**Hint:** see graph on p. 113.)

the BIG idea

31. ANALYZE Look back at the photograph and the question on pages 100 and 101. How has your understanding of temperature and heat changed after reading the chapter?

32. COMMUNICATE Explain the kinetic theory of matter in your own words. What, if anything, about the kinetic theory of matter surprised you?

UNIT PROJECTS

Evaluate all the data, results, and information from your project folder. Prepare to present your project.

Interpreting Diagrams

The diagrams below illustrate the process that occurs in sea and land breezes.

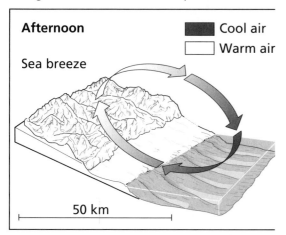

Afternoon
Sea breeze
■ Cool air
□ Warm air
50 km

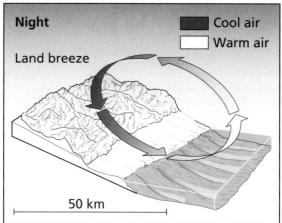

Night
Land breeze
■ Cool air
□ Warm air
50 km

Use the diagrams above to answer the next five questions.

1. What happens during the day?

  a. Cool air from the land flows out to sea.

  b. Warm air from the land flows out to sea close to sea level.

  c. Cool air from the sea flows to the land.

  d. Warm air from the sea flows to the land.

2. What characteristic of large bodies of water explains why the seawater is cooler than the land in the hot afternoon sun?

  a. Water is liquid while the land is solid.

  b. Water has a higher specific heat than land.

  c. Land is a better insulator than water.

  d. Land has a higher specific heat than water.

3. What process causes the warm air to move upward over the land during the day?

  a. convection   **c.** evaporation

  b. condensation   **d.** radiation

4. Warm air is pushed upwards by cooler air during convection because the warm air

  a. is more dense   **c.** is less dense

  b. has more mass   **d.** has less mass

5. About how far over water does this land breeze extend?

  a. 1 kilometer   **c.** 25 kilometers

  b. 10 kilometers   **d.** 50 kilometers

Extended Response

Answer the two questions below in detail. Include some of the terms from the word box on the right. Underline each term that you use in your answer.

| boiling point | heat | specific heat |
| conduction | freezing point | zero point |

6. What are the differences between the Fahrenheit and Celsius temperature scales? Which one is used in science? Why might this be the case?

7. Suppose you place three spoons—one metal, one plastic, and one wood—into a cup filled with hot water. The bowl end of the spoon is inside the cup and the handle is sticking up into the air. On each handle, you place a bead, held to the spoon by a dab of margarine. From which spoon will the bead fall first, and why?

UNIT C

Waves, Sound, and Light

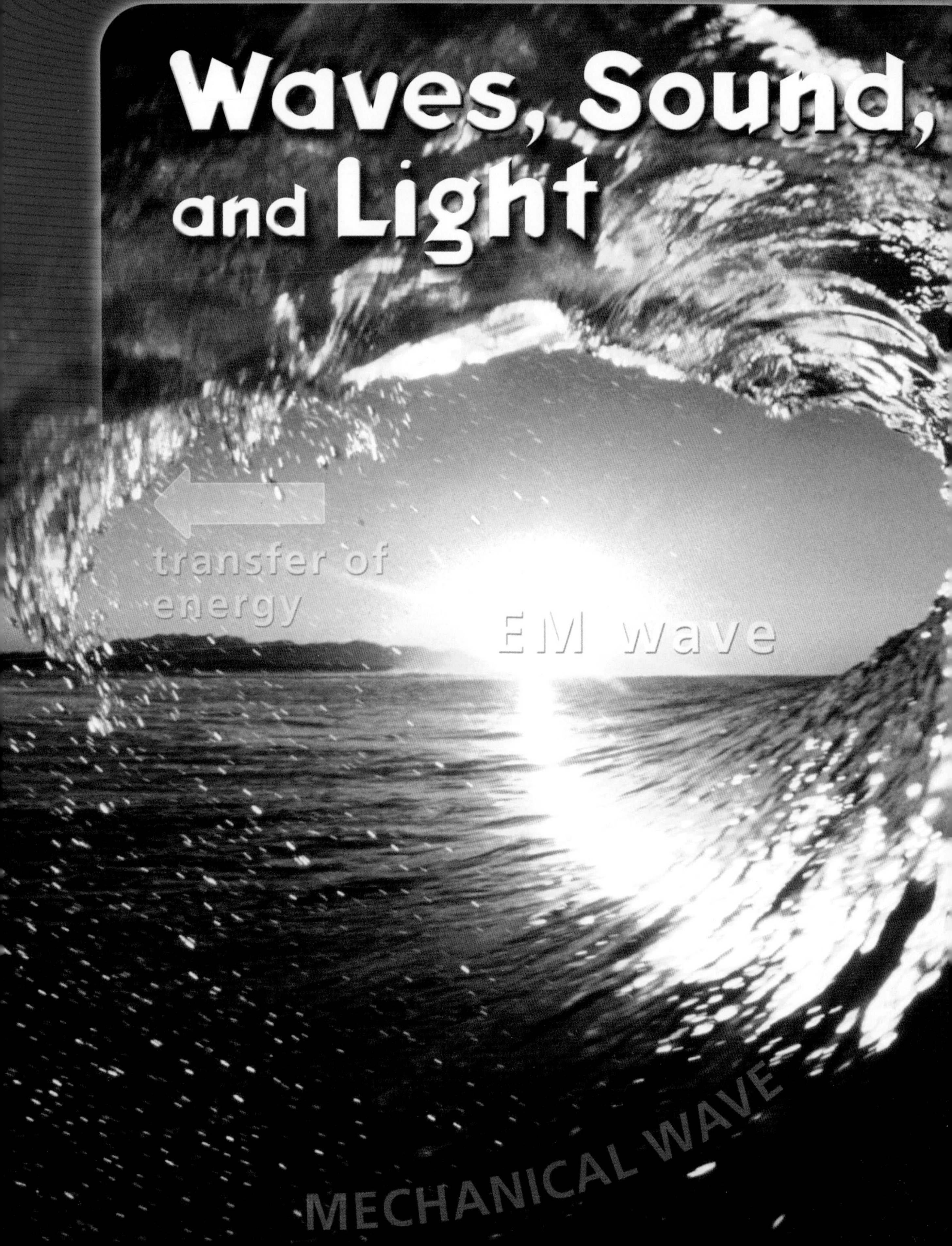
transfer of energy
EM wave
MECHANICAL WAVE

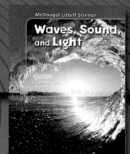

Waves, Sound, and Light
Contents Overview

Unit Features

the BIG idea

Waves transfer energy and
interact in predictable ways.

the BIG idea

Sound waves transfer energy
through vibrations.

the BIG idea

Electromagnetic waves transfer
energy through radiation.

the BIG idea

Optical tools depend on
the wave behavior of light.

SOUND Medicine

How will sound waves be used in the future of medicine?

SCIENTIFIC AMERICAN FRONTIERS

View the video segment "Each Sound Is a Present" to learn how advances in medicine are restoring people's hearing.

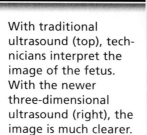

With traditional ultrasound (top), technicians interpret the image of the fetus. With the newer three-dimensional ultrasound (right), the image is much clearer.

Seeing Inside the Body

Have you ever wondered what the inside of your body looks like? Doctors have tried for many years to find ways of seeing what goes on inside a person's body that makes that person sick. Around 100 years ago, scientists found that a kind of wave called x-rays could be used to make images of the bones inside a person. This common method of seeing inside a body, is used mainly to show bones and teeth. However, repeated exposure to x-rays can be damaging to body cells. In the 1960s doctors started using a different kind of wave called ultrasound to make images of the organs inside the body.

Waves are now used in many medical applications. For example, cochlear implants use radio waves to help people hear. Ultrasound now has many new medical applications, from breaking up kidney stones to monitoring the flow of blood in the body.

Sound and Ultrasound

Sound is a type of wave, a vibration in the air. Humans can hear a wide range of different sounds, from very low pitches to very high. Sounds that are higher in pitch than humans can hear are referred to as ultrasound. They are no different from sounds we can hear, except they vibrate much faster than human ears can detect. Many animals can detect ultrasound; for example, dog whistles are in the ultrasound range.

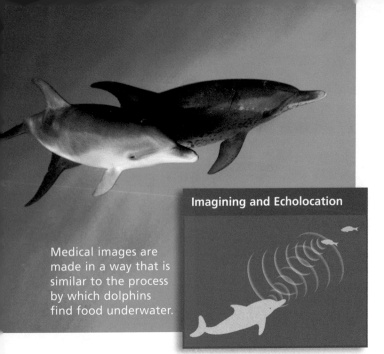

Imagining and Echolocation

Medical images are made in a way that is similar to the process by which dolphins find food underwater.

for the sound to travel to the object and return. Echolocation enables bats to capture flying insects at night and dolphins to catch fish in the ocean depths, where light doesn't penetrate.

Similarly, in ultrasound imaging, a machine sends a beam of ultrasound into a person's body and detects any echoes. The waves reflect whenever they strike a boundary between two objects with different densities. A computer measures the time required for the wave to travel to the boundary and reflect back; this information is used to determine the location and shape of the organ. The computer can then generate a live image of the organ inside the body.

The technology of ultrasound in medicine is based upon a process similar to that used by bats and dolphins to find food, a process called echolocation. The animal emits an ultrasound click or chirp and then listens for an echo. The echo indicates that an object has reflected the sound back to the animal. Over time, these animals have evolved the ability to judge the distance of the object by noting the time required

Ultrasound imaging has been used most often to monitor the development of a fetus inside its mother and to observe the valves of the heart. Blood flow can be color coded with faster flow in one color and slower flow in another color. The colors make it easier to see the location of blockages affecting the rate of flow in the blood vessels. This helps doctors detect blockages and diagnose heart problems.

HEARING IS A GIFT A recent development in technology is about to give seven-year-old Kelley Flynn something she has always wanted —better hearing. Kelley has been almost completely deaf since she was two years old, and now she is losing the little hearing she does have. The development is a device called a cochlear implant. Cochlear implants work inside the ear, stimulating the brain when a sound is detected.

Normally, sound travels as vibrations from the outer ear, through the middle ear to the inner ear, where thousands of tiny cells—called hair cells— register the quality of the sound and send a signal to the brain. In a cochlear implant, tiny electrical sensors, or electrodes, mimic the hair cells by registering the sound and sending a signal to the brain. The signals get to the electrodes through a system including a computer, microphone, and radio transmitter and receiver. Using this system, people with little or no hearing are able to sense sounds.

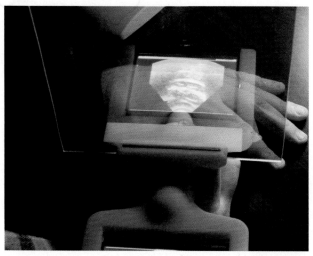

Recent advances in ultrasound technology include the development of portable devices that display images of the body, such as this hand-held device.

Advances in Ultrasound

Waves, including ultrasound, transfer energy. Physical therapists often use this fact when applying ultrasound to sore joints, heating the muscles and ligaments so they can move more freely. If the ultrasound waves are given stronger intensity and sharper focus, they can transfer enough energy to break up kidney stones in the body. The use of focused sound waves is now being tested for its ability to treat other problems, such as foot injuries.

Other recent advances in medical ultrasound include the development of devices that produce clearer images and use equipment that is smaller in size. In the late 1990's portable ultrasound devices were developed that allow the technology to be brought to the patient.

UNANSWERED Questions

As scientists learn more about the use of sound and other types of waves, new questions will arise.

- Will new methods of imaging the body change the way diseases are diagnosed?
- How closely do sounds heard using a cochlear implant resemble sounds heard by the ear?

UNIT PROJECTS

As you study this unit, work alone or with a group on one of these projects.

Magazine Article

Write a magazine article about the medical uses of ultrasound.

- Collect information about medical ultrasound and take notes about applications that interest you.
- If possible, conduct an interview with a medical practitioner who uses ultrasound.
- Read over all your notes and decide what information to include in your article.

Make a Music Video

Make a music video for a song of your choice, and explain how the video uses sound waves and light waves.

- Plan the sound portion of the video, including how the music will be played and amplified.
- For the lighting, use colored cellophane or gels to mix different colors of light. Explain your choices.
- Rehearse the video. Record the video and present it to the class.

Design a Demonstration

Design a hands-on demonstration of echolocation.

- Research the use of echolocation by animals.
- Design a demonstration of echolocation using a tennis ball and an obstacle.
- Present your demonstration to the class.

CAREER CENTER
CLASSZONE.COM

Learn more about careers in audiology.

1 Waves

the BIG idea

Waves transfer energy and interact in predictable ways.

Key Concepts

SECTION
1.1 Waves transfer energy.
Learn about forces and energy in wave motion.

SECTION
1.2 Waves have measurable properties.
Learn how the amplitude, wavelength, and frequency of a wave are measured.

SECTION
1.3 Waves behave in predictable ways.
Learn about reflection, refraction, diffraction, and interference.

Internet Preview

CLASSZONE.COM

Chapter 1 online resources: Content Review, Simulation, Visualization, two Resource Centers, Math Tutorial, Test Practice

What is moving these surfers?

EXPLORE (the BIG idea)

How Can Energy Be Passed Along?

Stand several videos up in a line. Knock over the first video, and notice the motion of the other videos.

Observe and Think Write down your observations. How far did each video move? What traveled from the beginning to the end of the line? Where did the energy to move the last video come from?

How Can You Change a Wave?

Fill a large bowl half-full of water. Dip a pencil into the water and pull it out quickly. Observe the wave that forms. Now try tapping the bowl with the eraser end of your pencil. What will happen if you use more energy to make the waves? Less energy?

Observe and Think What happened to the size of the waves? The speed? Why do you think that is so?

Internet Activity: Waves

Go to **ClassZone.com** to simulate the effect that different degrees of force have on a wave.

Observe and Think What do you think would happen to the wave if you increased the number of times the flapper moved? What other ways could you affect the wave in the pool?

NSTA
scilinks.org
SCiLINKS

Seismic Waves **Code: MDL027**

Getting Ready to Learn

◀ CONCEPT REVIEW

- Forces change the motion of objects in predictable ways.
- Energy can be transferred from one place to another.

◀ VOCABULARY REVIEW

See Glossary for definitions.

force

kinetic energy

potential energy

CONTENT REVIEW
CLASSZONE.COM

Review concepts and vocabulary.

▶ TAKING NOTES

COMBINATION NOTES

To take notes about a new concept, write an explanation of the concept in a table. Then make a sketch of the concept and label it so you can study it later.

VOCABULARY STRATEGY

Write each new vocabulary term in the center of a **four square** diagram. Write notes in the squares around each term. Include a definition, some characteristics, and some examples of the term. If possible, write some things that are not examples of the term.

See the Note-Taking Handbook on pages R45–R51.

SCIENCE NOTEBOOK

Concept	Explanation	Sketch
Forces and waves	Forces move a medium up and down or back and forth. A wave moves forward.	direction of force / direction of wave

Definition	Characteristics
A disturbance that transfers energy from one place to another	Matter moves in place. Energy travels entire distance.

WAVE

Examples	Nonexamples
Water wave Sound wave	Ball rolling Water rushing downstream

KEY CONCEPT

Waves transfer energy.

◀ **BEFORE,** you learned

- Forces can change an object's motion
- Energy can be kinetic or potential

▶ **NOW,** you will learn

- How forces cause waves
- How waves transfer energy
- How waves are classified

VOCABULARY

wave p. 9
medium p. 11
mechanical wave p. 11
transverse wave p. 13
longitudinal wave p. 14

EXPLORE Waves

How will the rope move?

PROCEDURE

① Tie a ribbon in the middle of a rope. Then tie one end of the rope to a chair.

② Holding the loose end of the rope in your hand, stand far enough away from the chair that the rope is fairly straight.

③ Flick the rope by moving your hand up and down quickly. Observe what happens.

MATERIALS
- ribbon
- rope
- chair

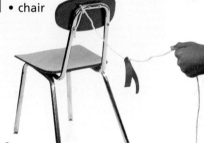

WHAT DO YOU THINK?
- How did the rope move? How did the ribbon move?
- What do you think starts a wave, and what keeps it going?

A wave is a disturbance.

You experience the effects of waves every day. Every sound you hear depends on sound waves. Every sight you see depends on light waves. A tiny wave can travel across the water in a glass, and a huge wave can travel across the ocean. Sound waves, light waves, and water waves seem very different from one another. So what, exactly, is a wave?

> **READING** **TiP**
> To *disturb* means to agitate or unsettle.

A **wave** is a disturbance that transfers energy from one place to another. Waves can transfer energy over distance without moving matter the entire distance. For example, an ocean wave can travel many kilometers without the water itself moving many kilometers. The water moves up and down—a motion known as a disturbance. It is the disturbance that travels in a wave, transferring energy.

 CHECK YOUR READING How does an ocean wave transfer energy across the ocean?

Forces and Waves

READING TiP

As you read each example, think of how it is similar to and different from the other examples.

You know that a force is required to change the motion of an object. Forces can also start a disturbance, sending a wave through a material. The following examples describe how forces cause waves.

Example 1 Rope Wave Think of a rope that is tied to a doorknob. You apply one force to the rope by flicking it upward and an opposite force when you snap it back down. This sends a wave through the rope. Both forces—the one that moves the rope up and the one that moves the rope down—are required to start a wave.

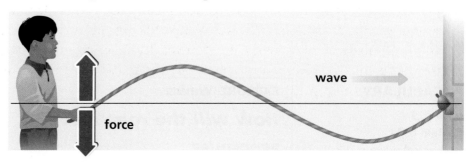

Example 2 Water Wave Forces are also required to start a wave in water. Think of a calm pool of water. What happens if you apply a force to the water by dipping your finger into it? The water rushes back after you remove your finger. The force of your finger and the force of the water rushing back send waves across the pool.

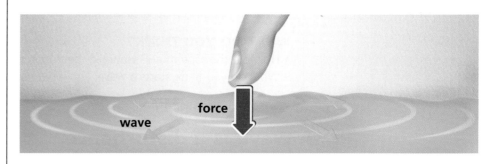

Example 3 Earthquake Wave An earthquake is a sudden release of energy that has built up in rock as a result of the surrounding rock pushing and pulling on it. When these two forces cause the rock to suddenly break away and move, the energy is transferred as a wave through the ground.

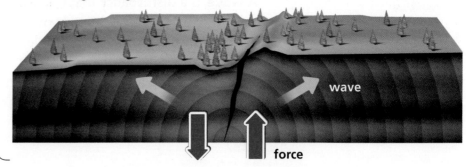

Materials and Waves

A rope tied to a doorknob, water, and the ground all have something in common. They are all materials through which waves move. A **medium** is any substance that a wave moves through. Water is the medium for an ocean wave; the ground is the medium for an earthquake wave; the rope is the medium for the rope wave. In the next chapter, you will learn that sound waves can move through many mediums, including air.

Waves that transfer energy through matter are known as **mechanical waves.** All of the waves you have read about so far, even sound waves, are mechanical waves. Water, the ground, a rope, and the air are all made up of matter. Later, you will learn about waves that can transfer energy through empty space. Light is an example of a wave that transfers energy through empty space.

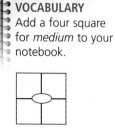

VOCABULARY

Add a four square for *medium* to your notebook.

 CHECK YOUR READING   How are all mechanical waves similar?

Energy and Waves

The waves caused by an earthquake are good examples of energy transfer. The disturbed ground shakes from side to side and up and down as the waves move through it. Such waves can travel kilometers away from their source. The ground does not travel kilometers away from where it began; it is the energy that travels in a wave. In the case of an earthquake, it is kinetic energy, or the energy of motion, that is transferred.

This photograph was taken after a 1995 earthquake in Japan. A seismic wave transferred enough energy through the ground to bend the railroad tracks, leaving them in the shape of a wave.

A Wave Model

When these fans do "the wave" in a stadium, they are modeling the way a disturbance travels through a medium.

Each person only moves up and down.

The wave can move all the way around the stadium.

READING VISUALS In which direction do people move when doing the stadium wave? In which direction does the wave move?

Look at the illustration of people modeling a wave in a stadium. In this model, the crowd of people represents a wave medium. The people moving up and down represent the disturbance. The transfer of the disturbance around the stadium represents a wave. Each person only moves up and down, while the disturbance can move all the way around the stadium.

Ocean waves are another good example of energy transfer. Ocean waves travel to the shore, one after another. Instead of piling up all the ocean water on the shore, however, the waves transfer energy. A big ocean wave transfers enough kinetic energy to knock someone down.

CHECK YOUR READING How does the stadium wave differ from a real ocean wave?

Waves can be classified by how they move.

As you have seen, one way to classify waves is according to the medium through which they travel. Another way to classify waves is by how they move. You have read that some waves transfer an up-and-down or a side-to-side motion. Other waves transfer a forward-and-backward motion.

Transverse Waves

Think again about snapping the rope with your hand. The action of your hand causes a vertical, or up-and-down, disturbance in the rope. However, the wave it sets off is horizontal, or forward. This type of wave is known as a transverse wave. In a **transverse wave,** the direction in which the wave travels is perpendicular, or at right angles, to the direction of the disturbance. *Transverse* means "across" or "crosswise." The wave itself moves crosswise as compared with the vertical motion of the medium.

READING **TiP**

Perpendicular means at a 90° angle.

90°

Transverse Wave

direction of disturbance   direction of wave

Water waves are also transverse. The up-and-down motion of the water is the disturbance. The wave travels in a direction that is perpendicular to the direction of the disturbance. The medium is the water, and energy is transferred outward in all directions from the source.

 CHECK YOUR READING What is a transverse wave? Find two examples in the paragraphs above.

INVESTIGATE Wave Types

How do waves compare?

PROCEDURE

① Place the spring toy on the floor on its side. Stretch out the spring. To start a disturbance in the spring, take one end and move it from side to side. Observe the movement in the spring. Remember that a transverse wave travels at right angles to the disturbance.

② Put the spring toy on the floor in the same position as before. Think about how you could make a different kind of disturbance to produce a different kind of wave. (**Hint:** Suppose you push the spring in the direction of the wave you expect to make.) Observe the movement in the spring.

WHAT DO YOU THINK?

• Compare the waves you made. How are they alike? How are they different?

• What kind of wave did you produce by moving the spring from side to side?

CHALLENGE Can you think of a third way to make a wave travel through a spring?

SKILL FOCUS
Comparing

MATERIALS
spring toy

TIME
10 minutes

Longitudinal Waves

READING TiP

The word *long* can help you remember longitudinal waves. The disturbance moves along the length of the spring.

Another type of wave is a longitudinal wave. In a **longitudinal wave** (LAHN-jih-TOOD-n-uhl), the wave travels in the same direction as the disturbance. A longitudinal wave can be started in a spring by moving it forward and backward. The coils of the spring move forward and bunch up and then move backward and spread out. This forward and backward motion is the disturbance. Longitudinal waves are sometimes called compressional waves because the bunched-up area is known as a compression. How is a longitudinal wave similar to a transverse wave? How is it different?

Longitudinal Wave

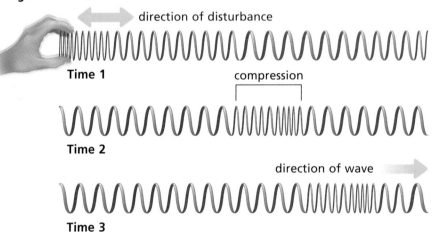

direction of disturbance

Time 1

compression

Time 2

direction of wave

Time 3

RESOURCE CENTER
CLASSZONE.COM

Learn more about waves.

Sound waves are examples of longitudinal waves. Imagine a bell ringing. The clapper inside the bell strikes the side and makes it vibrate, or move back and forth rapidly. The vibrating bell pushes and pulls on nearby air molecules, causing them to move forward and backward. These air molecules, in turn, set more air molecules into motion. A sound wave pushes forward. In sound waves, the vibrations of the air molecules are in the same direction as the movement of the wave.

1.1 Review

KEY CONCEPTS

1. Describe how forces start waves.

2. Explain how a wave can travel through a medium and yet the medium stays in place. Use the term *energy* in your answer.

3. Describe two ways in which waves travel, and give an example of each.

CRITICAL THINKING

4. **Analyze** Does water moving through a hose qualify as a wave? Explain why or why not.

5. **Classify** Suppose you drop a cookie crumb in your milk. At once, you see ripples spreading across the surface of the milk. What type of waves are these? What is the disturbance?

CHALLENGE

6. **Predict** Suppose you had a rope long enough to extend several blocks down the street. If you were to start a wave in the rope, do you think it would continue all the way to the other end of the street? Explain why or why not.

MATH in SCIENCE

MATH TUTORIAL
CLASSZONE.COM

Click on Math Tutorial for more help with finding the mean, median, and mode.

Before going out on the water, boaters can check reports on wave conditions in their area.

Wave Heights

Tracking stations throughout the world's oceans measure and record the height of water waves that pass beneath them. The data recorded by the stations can be summarized as average wave heights over one hour or one day.

How would you summarize the typical wave heights over one week? There are a few different ways in which data can be summarized. Three common ways are finding the mean, median, and mode.

Example

Wave height data for one week are shown below.

| 1.2 m | 1.5 m | 1.4 m | 1.7 m | 2.0 m | 1.4 m | 1.3 m |

(1) Mean To find the mean of the data, divide the sum of the values by the number of values.

$$\text{Mean} = \frac{1.2 + 1.5 + 1.4 + 1.7 + 2.0 + 1.4 + 1.3}{7} = 1.5 \text{ m}$$

ANSWER The mean wave height is 1.5 m.

(2) Median To find the median of the data, write the values in order from least to greatest. The value in the middle is the median.

1.2 m   1.3 m   1.4 m   (1.4 m)   1.5 m   1.7 m   2.0 m

ANSWER The median wave height is 1.4 m.

(3) Mode The mode is the number that occurs most often.

ANSWER The mode for the data is also 1.4 m.

Use the data to answer the following questions.

The data below show wave heights taken from a station off the coast of Florida over two weeks.

| Wk 1 | 1.2 m | 1.1 m | 1.1 m | 1.5 m | 4.7 m | 1.2 m | 1.1 m |
| Wk 2 | 0.7 m | 0.8 m | 0.9 m | 0.8 m | 1.0 m | 1.1 m | 0.8 m |

1. Find the mean, median, and mode of the data for Week 1.

2. Find the mean, median, and mode of the data for Week 2.

CHALLENGE A storm carrying strong winds caused high waves on the fifth day of the data shown above for Week 1. Which of the following was most affected by the high value—the mean, median, or mode?

1.2 Waves have measurable properties.

BEFORE, you learned

- Forces cause waves
- Waves transfer energy
- Waves can be transverse or longitudinal

NOW, you will learn

- How amplitude, wavelength, and frequency are measured
- How to find a wave's speed

VOCABULARY

crest p. 17
trough p. 17
amplitude p. 17
wavelength p. 17
frequency p. 17

THINK ABOUT

How can a wave be measured?

This enormous wave moves the water high above sea level as it comes crashing through. How could you find out how high a water wave actually goes? How could you find out how fast it is traveling? In what other ways do you think a wave can be measured? Read on to find out.

Waves have amplitude, wavelength, and frequency.

The tallest ocean wave ever recorded was measured from the deck of a ship during a storm. An officer on the ship saw a wave reach a height that was level with a point high on the ship, more than 30 meters (100 ft)! Height is a property of all waves—from ripples in a glass of water to gigantic waves at surfing beaches—and it can be measured.

The speed of a water wave is another property that can be measured—by finding the time it takes for one wave peak to travel a set distance. Other properties of a wave that can be measured include the time between waves and the length of a single wave. Scientists use the terms *amplitude*, *wavelength*, and *frequency* to refer to some commonly measured properties of waves.

COMBINATION NOTES
Use combination notes in your notebook to describe how waves can be measured.

 CHECK YOUR READING   What are three properties of a wave that can be measured?

Measuring Wave Properties

A **crest** is the highest point, or peak, of a wave. A **trough** is the lowest point, or valley, of a wave. Suppose you are riding on a boat in rough water. When the boat points upward and rises, it is climbing to the crest of a wave. When it points downward and sinks, the boat is falling to the trough of the wave.

1 **Amplitude** for a transverse wave is the distance between a line through the middle of a wave and a crest or trough. In an ocean wave, amplitude measures how far the wave rises above, or dips below, its original position, or rest position.

Amplitude is an important measurement, because it indicates how much energy a wave is carrying. The bigger the amplitude, the more energy the wave has. Find amplitude on the diagram below.

2 The distance from one wave crest to the very next crest is called the **wavelength.** Wavelength can also be measured from trough to trough. Find wavelength on the diagram below.

3 The number of waves passing a fixed point in a certain amount of time is called the **frequency.** The word *frequent* means "often," so frequency measures how often a wave occurs. Frequency is often measured by counting the number of crests or troughs that pass by a given point in one second. Find frequency on the diagram below.

VOCABULARY
Remember to add a four square to your notebook for each new term on this page.

CHECK YOUR READING How is amplitude related to energy?

Wave Properties

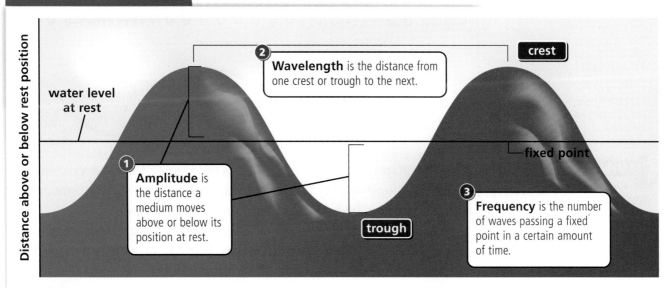

Distance above or below rest position

water level at rest

2 **Wavelength** is the distance from one crest or trough to the next.

crest

fixed point

1 **Amplitude** is the distance a medium moves above or below its position at rest.

trough

3 **Frequency** is the number of waves passing a fixed point in a certain amount of time.

READING VISUALS How many wavelengths are shown in this diagram? How do you know?

How Frequency and Wavelength Are Related

The frequency and wavelength of a wave are related. When frequency increases more wave crests pass a fixed point each second. That means the wavelength shortens. So, as frequency increases, wavelength decreases. The opposite is also true—as frequency decreases, wavelength increases.

Suppose you are making waves in a rope. If you make one wave crest every second, the frequency is one wave per second (1/s). Now suppose you want to increase the frequency to more than one wave per second. You flick the rope up and down faster. The wave crests are now closer together. In other words, their wavelengths have decreased.

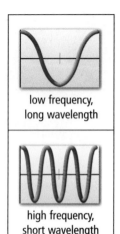

low frequency,
long wavelength

high frequency,
short wavelength

Graphing Wave Properties

The graph of a transverse wave looks much like a wave itself. The illustration on page 19 shows the graph of an ocean wave. The measurements for the graph come from a float, or buoy (BOO-ee), that keeps track of how high or low the water goes. The graph shows the position of the buoy at three different points in time. These points are numbered. Since the graph shows what happens over time, you can see the frequency of the waves.

Unlike transverse waves, longitudinal waves look different from their graphs. The graph of a longitudinal wave in a spring is drawn below. The coils of the spring get closer and then farther apart as the wave moves through them.

REMINDER

Frequency is the number of waves that pass a given point in a certain amount of time.

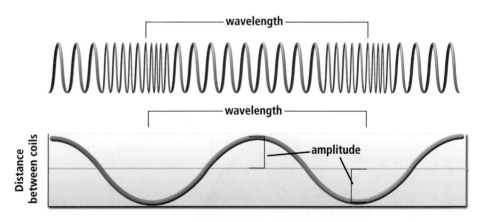

wavelength

wavelength

amplitude

Distance between coils

VISUALIZATION
CLASSZONE.COM
Watch the graph of a wave form.

The shape of the graph resembles the shape of a transverse wave. The wavelength on a longitudinal wave is the distance from one compression to the next. The amplitude of a longitudinal wave measures how compressed the medium gets. Just as in a transverse wave, frequency in a longitudinal wave is the number of waves passing a fixed point in a certain amount of time.

CHECK YOUR READING   How are longitudinal waves measured?

Graphing a Wave

The graph of a transverse wave looks like a wave itself. The graph shows what happens over time.

The buoy moves up and down as the waves pass.

1 **Time: 0 s** The buoy is below the rest position.

2 **Time: 1 s** The buoy is equal with the rest position.

3 **Time: 2 s** The buoy is above the rest position.

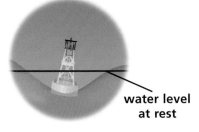

water level at rest

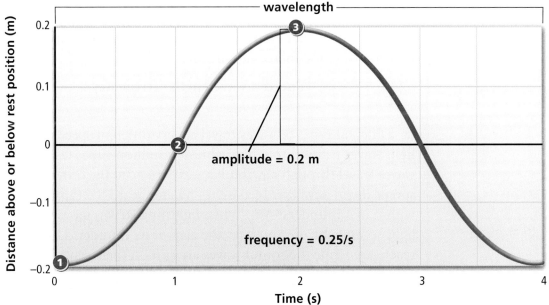

amplitude = 0.2 m

frequency = 0.25/s

wavelength

Distance above or below rest position (m)

Time (s)

READING VISUALS How many seconds does it take for one wave to pass? How much of the wave passes in one second?

INVESTIGATE Frequency

How can you change frequency?

PROCEDURE

1. Tie 3 washers to a string. Tape the string to the side of your desk so that it can swing freely. The swinging washers can model wave action.

2. Pull the washers slightly to the side and let go. Find the frequency by counting the number of complete swings that occur in 1 minute.

3. Make a table in your notebook to record both the length of the string and the frequency.

4. Shorten the string by moving and retaping it. Repeat for 5 different lengths. Keep the distance you pull the washers the same each time.

WHAT DO YOU THINK?

• How did changing the length of the string affect the frequency?

• How does this model represent a wave? How does it differ from a wave?

CHALLENGE How could you vary the amplitude of this model? Predict how changing the amplitude would affect the frequency.

SKILL FOCUS
Collecting data

MATERIALS
• 3 metal washers
• piece of string
• tape
• stopwatch
• meter stick

TIME
30 minutes

Wave speed can be measured.

In addition to amplitude, wavelength, and frequency, a wave's speed can be measured. One way to find the speed of a wave is to time how long it takes for a wave to get from one point to another. Another way to find the speed of a wave is to calculate it. The speed of any wave can be determined when both the frequency and the wavelength are known, using the following formula:

$$\textbf{Speed} = \textbf{wavelength} \cdot \textbf{frequency}$$
$$S = \lambda f$$

Different types of waves travel at very different speeds. For example, light waves travel through air almost a million times faster than sound waves travel through air. You have experienced the difference in wave speeds if you have ever seen lightning and heard the thunder that comes with it in a thunderstorm. When lightning strikes far away, you see the light seconds before you hear the clap of its thunder. The light waves reach you while the sound waves are still on their way.

How fast do you think water waves can travel? Water waves travel at different speeds. You can calculate the speed using wavelength and frequency.

REMINDER

The symbol λ represents wavelength.

Suppose you wish to calculate the speed of an ocean wave with a wavelength of 16 meters and a frequency of 0.31 wave per second. When working through the problem in the example below, it is helpful to think of the frequency as

$$f = 0.31 \text{ (wave)/s}$$

even though the units for frequency are just 1/second. You can think of wavelengths as "meters per wave," or

$$\lambda = 16 \text{ m/(wave)}$$

RESOURCE CENTER
CLASSZONE.COM

Find out more about wave speed.

Calculating Wave Speed

▶ **Sample Problem**

An ocean wave has a wavelength of 16 meters and a frequency of 0.31 wave per second. What is the speed of the wave?

What do you know? wavelength = 16 m,

frequency = $0.31 \dfrac{\text{(wave)}}{\text{s}}$

What do you want to find out? Speed

Write the formula: $S = \lambda f$

Substitute into the formula: $S = 16 \dfrac{\text{m}}{\text{(wave)}} \cdot 0.31 \dfrac{\text{(wave)}}{\text{s}}$

Calculate and simplify: $16 \dfrac{\text{m}}{\text{(wave)}} \cdot 0.31 \dfrac{\text{(wave)}}{\text{s}} = 5 \dfrac{\text{m}}{\text{s}}$

Check that your units agree: Unit is m/s. Unit for speed is m/s. Units agree.

Answer: $S = 5$ m/s

▶ **Practice the Math**

1. In a stormy sea, 2 waves pass a fixed point every second, and the waves are 10 m apart. What is the speed of the waves?

2. In a ripple tank, the wavelength is 0.1 cm, and 10 waves occur each second. What is the speed of the waves (in cm/s)?

1.2 Review

KEY CONCEPTS

1. Make a simple diagram of a wave, labeling amplitude, frequency, and wavelength. For frequency, you will need to indicate a span of time, such as one second.

2. What two measurements of a wave do you need to calculate its speed?

CRITICAL THINKING

3. **Observe** Suppose you are watching water waves pass under the end of a pier. How can you figure out their frequency?

4. **Calculate** A wave has a speed of 3 m/s and a frequency of 6 (wave)/s. What is its wavelength?

⬥ CHALLENGE

5. **Apply** Imagine you are on a boat in the middle of the sea. You are in charge of recording the properties of passing ocean waves into the ship's logbook. What types of information could you record? How would this information be useful? Explain your answer.

CHAPTER INVESTIGATION

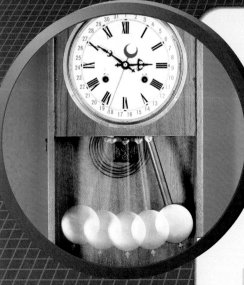

Wavelength

OVERVIEW AND PURPOSE The pendulum on a grandfather clock keeps time as it swings back and forth at a steady rate. The swings of a pendulum can be recorded as a wave with measurable properties. How do the properties of the pendulum affect the properties of the waves it produces? In this investigation you will use your understanding of wave properties to
- construct a pendulum and measure the waves it produces, and
- determine how the length of the pendulum affects the wavelength of the waves.

▶ Problem

How does changing the length of a pendulum affect the wavelength?

▶ Hypothesize

Write a hypothesis in "If . . . , then . . . , because . . ." form to answer the problem question.

▶ Procedure

MATERIALS
- 1/2 sheet white paper
- tape
- scissors
- string
- meter stick
- fine sand
- graduated cylinder
- 2 sheets colored construction paper

1 Make a data table like the one shown on the sample notebook page.

2 Make a cone with the half-sheet of paper by rolling it and taping it as shown. The hole in the bottom of the cone should be no larger than a pea.

3 Cut a hole in each side of the cone and tie the ends of the string to the cone to make a pendulum.

4 Hold the string on the pendulum so that the distance from your fingers holding the string to the bottom of the cone is 20 cm.

5 Cover the bottom of the cone with your fingertip. While you hold the cone, have your partner pour about 40 mL of sand into the cone.

6 Hold the pendulum about 5 cm above the construction paper as shown. Pull the pendulum from the bottom to one side of the construction paper. Be careful not to move the pendulum at the top, or to pull the pendulum over the edge of the paper.

7 Let the pendulum go while your partner gently pulls the paper forward so that the sand makes waves on the paper. Be sure to pull the paper at a steady rate. Let the remaining sand pile up on the end of the paper.

8 Measure the wavelength from crest to crest or trough to trough. Record the wavelength in your table.

9 Run two more trials, repeating steps 5–8. Be sure to pull the paper at the same speed for each trial. Calculate the average wavelength over all three trials, and record it in your table.

10 Repeat steps 4–8, changing the length of the pendulum to 30 cm and then to 40 cm.

▶ Observe and Analyze [Write It Up]

1. **RECORD OBSERVATIONS** Draw the setup of your procedure. Be sure your data table is complete.

2. **IDENTIFY VARIABLES AND CONSTANTS** Identify the variables and constants that affected the wave produced by the moving pendulum. List them in your notebook.

3. **ANALYZE** What patterns can you find in your data? For example, do the numbers increase or decrease as you read down each column?

▶ Conclude [Write It Up]

1. **INFER** Answer your problem question.

2. **INTERPRET** Compare your results with your hypothesis. Do your data support your hypothesis?

3. **IDENTIFY LIMITS** What possible limitations or sources of error could have affected your results?

4. **APPLY** Suppose you were examining the tracing made by a seismograph, a machine that records an earthquake wave. What would happen if you increased the speed at which the paper ran through the machine? What do you think the amplitude of the tracing represents?

▶ INVESTIGATE Further

CHALLENGE Revise your experiment to change one variable other than the length of the pendulum. Run a new trial, changing the variable you choose but keeping everything else constant. How did changing the variable affect the wave produced?

Wavelength

Problem How does changing the length of a pendulum affect the wavelength?

Hypothesize

Observe and Analyze

Table 1. Wavelengths Produced by Pendulums

Pendulum Length (cm)	Trial 1	Trial 2	Trial 3	Average Wavelength (cm)
20				
30				
40				

Conclude

1.3 Waves behave in predictable ways.

◀ BEFORE, you learned	▶ NOW, you will learn
• Waves transfer energy	• How waves change as they encounter a barrier
• Amplitude, wavelength, and frequency can be measured	• What happens when waves enter a new medium
	• How waves interact with other waves

VOCABULARY

reflection p. 25
refraction p. 25
diffraction p. 26
interference p. 27

EXPLORE Reflection

How do ripples reflect?

PROCEDURE

① Put a few drops of food coloring into the pan of water.

② Dip the pencil in the water at one end of the pan to make ripples in the water.

③ Observe the ripples as they reflect off the side of the pan. Draw a sketch of the waves reflecting.

WHAT DO YOU THINK?

• What happens when the waves reach the side of the pan?
• Why do you think the waves behave as they do?

MATERIALS
• wide pan, half full of water
• food coloring
• pencil

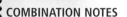

COMBINATION NOTES
Use combination notes in your notebook to describe how waves interact with materials.

Waves interact with materials.

You have read that mechanical waves travel through a medium like air, water, or the ground. In this section, you will read how the motion of waves changes when they encounter a new medium. For instance, when an ocean wave rolls into a ship or a sound wave strikes a solid wall, the wave encounters a new medium.

When waves interact with materials in these ways, they behave predictably. All waves, from water waves to sound waves and even light waves, show the behaviors that you will learn about next. Scientists call these behaviors reflection, refraction, and diffraction.

 What behaviors do all waves have in common?

Reflection

What happens to water waves at the end of a swimming pool? The waves cannot travel through the wall of the pool. Instead, the waves bounce off the pool wall. The bouncing back of a wave after it strikes a barrier is called **reflection.**

Remember what you have learned about forces. A water wave, like all waves, transfers energy. When the water wave meets the wall of the pool, it pushes against the wall. The wall applies an equal and opposite force on the water, sending the wave back in another direction. In the illustration on the right, you can see water waves reflecting off a barrier.

Sound and light waves reflect too. Sound waves reflecting off the walls of a canyon produce an echo. Light waves reflecting off smooth metal behind glass let you see an image of yourself in the mirror. The light waves bounce off the metal just as the water waves bounce off the pool wall. You will learn more about how sound and light waves reflect in the next chapters.

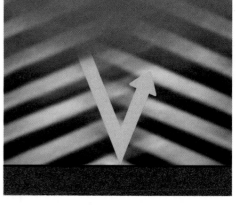

Reflection Water waves move in predictable ways. Here waves are shown from above as they reflect off a barrier.

 How would you define *reflection* in your own words?

Refraction

Sometimes, a wave does not bounce back when it encounters a new medium. Instead, the wave continues moving forward. When a wave enters a new medium at an angle, it bends, or refracts. **Refraction** is the bending of a wave as it enters a new medium at an angle other than 90 degrees. Refraction occurs because waves travel at different speeds in different mediums. Because the wave enters the new medium at an angle, one side of the wave enters the new medium before the rest of the wave. When one side of a wave speeds up or slows down before the other side, it causes the wave to bend.

You have probably noticed the refraction of light waves in water. Objects half-in and half-out of water look broken or split. Look at the photograph of the straw in the glass. What your eyes suggest—that the straw is split—is not real, is it? You are seeing the refraction of light waves caused by the change of medium from air to water. You will learn more about the refraction of light waves in Chapter 4.

Refraction Light waves refract as they pass from air to water, making this straw look split.

Diffraction

You have seen how waves reflect off a barrier. For example, water waves bounce off the side of a pool. But what if the side of the pool had an opening in it? Sometimes, waves interact with a partial barrier, such as a wall with an opening. As the waves pass through the opening, they spread out, or diffract. **Diffraction** is the spreading out of waves through an opening or around the edge of an obstacle. Diffraction occurs with all types of waves.

Look at the photograph on the right. It shows water waves diffracting as they pass through a small gap in a barrier. In the real world, ocean waves diffract through openings in cliffs or rock formations.

Similarly, sound waves diffract as they pass through an open doorway. Turn on a TV or stereo, and walk into another room. Listen to the sound with the door closed and then open. Then try moving around the room. You can hear the sound wherever you stand because the waves spread out, or diffract, through the doorway and reflect from the walls.

Diffraction through an opening

INVESTIGATE Diffraction

How can you make a wave diffract?

PROCEDURE

1. Put a few drops of food coloring into the container of water.
2. Experiment with quick motions of the ruler to set off waves in the container.
3. Place the block on its side in the center of the container. Set the bag of sand on the block to hold it down. Predict how the waves will interact with the barrier you have added.
4. Make another set of waves, and observe how they interact with the barrier.

WHAT DO YOU THINK?

- How did you make the waves diffract?
- How did your observations compare with your prediction?

CHALLENGE How could you change the experiment to make the effect of the diffraction more obvious?

SKILL FOCUS
Predicting

MATERIALS
- wide pan of water
- food coloring
- ruler
- wooden block
- bag of sand

TIME
20 minutes

Diffraction also occurs as waves pass the edge of an obstacle. The photograph at the right shows water waves diffracting as they pass an obstacle. Ocean waves also diffract in this way as they pass large rocks in the water.

Light waves diffract around the edge of an obstacle too. The edges of a shadow appear fuzzy because of diffraction. The light waves spread out, or diffract, around the object that is making the shadow.

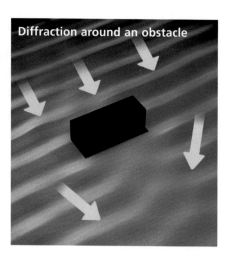

Diffraction around an obstacle

 CHECK YOUR READING Describe what happens when waves diffract.

Waves interact with other waves.

Just as waves sometimes interact with new mediums, they can also interact with other waves. Two waves can add energy to or take away energy from each other in the place where they meet. **Interference** is the meeting and combining of waves.

Waves Adding Together

Suppose two identical waves coming from opposite directions come together at one point. The waves' crests and troughs are aligned briefly, which means they join up exactly. When the two waves merge into a temporary, larger wave, their amplitudes are added together. When the waves separate again, they have their original amplitudes and continue in their original directions.

The adding of two waves is called constructive interference. It builds up, or constructs, a larger wave out of two smaller ones. Look at the diagram at the right to see what happens in constructive interference.

Because the waves in the example joined together perfectly, the amplitude of the new wave equals the combined amplitudes of the 2 original waves. For example, if the crest of a water wave with an amplitude of 1 meter (3.3 ft) met up with the crest of another wave with an amplitude of 1 meter (3.3 ft), there would be a 2 meter (6.6 ft) crest in the spot where they met.

Constructive Interference

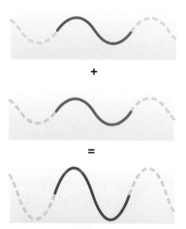

When two wave crests with amplitudes of 1 m each combine, a wave with an amplitude of 2 m is formed.

Waves Canceling Each Other Out

Imagine again that two very similar waves come together. This time, however, the crest of one wave joins briefly with the trough of the other. The energy of one wave is subtracted from the energy of the other. The new wave is therefore smaller than the original wave. This process is called destructive interference. Look at the diagram below to see what happens in destructive interference.

For example, if a 2-meter (6.6 ft) crest met up with a 1-meter (3.3 ft) trough, there would be a temporary crest of only 1 meter (3.3 ft) where they met. If the amplitudes of the two original waves are identical, the two waves can cancel each other out completely!

When identical waves meet, they are usually not aligned. Instead, the crests meet up with crests in some places and troughs in others. As a result, the waves add in some places and subtract in others. The photograph on the left shows a pattern resulting from waves both adding and subtracting on the surface of a pond. Have you ever listened to music on stereo speakers that were placed at a distance from each other? The music may have sounded loud in some places and soft in others, as the sound waves from the two speakers interfered with each other.

Wave interference produces this pattern on a pond as two sets of waves interact.

Destructive Interference

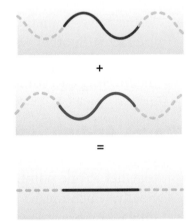

When a 1 m wave crest meets a 1 m wave trough, the amplitudes cancel each other out. A wave with an amplitude of 0 m is formed where they meet.

CHECK YOUR READING Summarize in your own words what happens during interference.

1.3 Review

KEY CONCEPTS

1. Explain what happens when waves encounter a medium that they cannot travel through.

2. Describe a situation in which waves would diffract.

3. Describe two ways that waves are affected by interference.

CRITICAL THINKING

4. **Synthesize** Explain how reflection and diffraction can happen at the same time in a wave.

5. **Compare** How is interference similar to net force? How do you think the two concepts might be related? **Hint:** Think about how forces are involved in wave motion.

CHALLENGE

6. **Predict** Imagine that you make gelatin in a long, shallow pan. Then you scoop the gelatin out of one end of the pan and add icy cold water to the exact same depth as the gelatin. Now suppose you set off waves at the water end. What do you think will happen when the waves meet the gelatin?

Tsunamis!

Tsunamis (tsu-NAH-mees) are among the most powerful waves on Earth. They can travel fast enough to cross the Pacific Ocean in less than a day! When they reach shore, these powerful waves strike with enough force to destroy whole communities.

What Causes Tsunamis?

Tsunamis are caused by an undersea volcanic eruption, an earthquake, or even a landslide. This deep-sea event sends out a series of waves. Surprisingly, if you were out at sea, you would not even notice these powerful waves. The reason has to do with the physics of waves—their velocity, wavelength, and amplitude.

A tsunami generated by a powerful earthquake struck Japan in 1983. The photograph above shows a scene before the tsunami struck. What changes do you see in the picture below showing the scene after the tsunami struck?

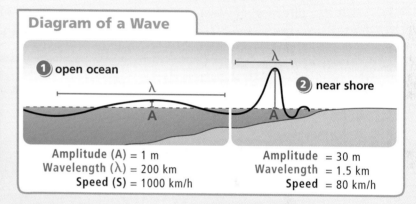

Diagram of a Wave

① open ocean

λ

A

② near shore

λ

A

Amplitude (A) = 1 m	Amplitude = 30 m
Wavelength (λ) = 200 km	Wavelength = 1.5 km
Speed (S) = 1000 km/h	Speed = 80 km/h

The Changing Wave

① On the open ocean, the waves of a tsunami are barely visible. The amplitude of the waves is less than a few meters, but the energy of the waves extends to the sea floor. The tsunami's wavelength is extremely long—up to 200 kilometers (120 mi). These long, low waves can travel as fast as a jet—almost 1000 kilometers per hour (600 mi/h).

② Near shore, the waves slow down as they approach shallow water. As their velocity drops, their wavelengths get shorter, but their amplitude gets bigger. All the energy that was spread out over a long wave in deep water is now compressed into a huge wave that can reach a height of more than 30 meters (100 ft).

Individual tsunami waves may arrive more than an hour apart. Many people have lost their lives returning home between waves, making the fatal mistake of thinking the danger was over.

EXPLORE

1. **VISUALIZE** Look at **②** on the diagram. How tall is 30 meters (100 ft)? Find a 100-foot building or structure near you to visualize the shore height of a tsunami.

2. **CHALLENGE** Use library or Internet resources to prepare a chart on the causes and effects of a major tsunami event.

Chapter Review

the **BIG** idea

Waves transfer energy and interact in predictable ways.

CONTENT REVIEW
CLASSZONE.COM

◄ KEY CONCEPTS SUMMARY

1.1 Waves transfer energy.

Transverse Wave

direction of disturbance

direction of wave

transfer of energy

Longitudinal Wave

direction of disturbance

direction of wave

transfer of energy

VOCABULARY
wave p. 9
medium p. 11
mechanical wave p. 11
transverse wave p. 13
longitudinal wave p. 14

1.2 Waves have measurable properties.

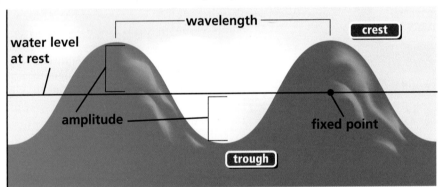

Frequency is the number of waves passing a fixed point in a certain amount of time.

VOCABULARY
crest p. 17
trough p. 17
amplitude p. 17
wavelength p. 17
frequency p. 17

1.3 Waves behave in predictable ways.

Reflection

Refraction

Diffraction

VOCABULARY
reflection p. 25
refraction p. 25
diffraction p. 26
interference p. 27

Reviewing Vocabulary

Draw a word triangle for each of the terms below. On the bottom row, write the term and your own definition of it. Above that, write a sentence in which you use the term correctly. At the top, draw a small picture to show what the term looks like. A sample is completed for you.

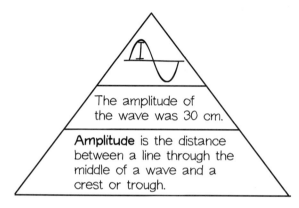

The amplitude of the wave was 30 cm.

Amplitude is the distance between a line through the middle of a wave and a crest or trough.

1. transverse wave

2. diffraction

3. frequency

4. medium

5. crest

6. interference

7. reflection

8. trough

9. refraction

10. wavelength

Reviewing Key Concepts

Multiple Choice *Choose the letter of the best answer.*

11. The direction in which a transverse wave travels is
  a. the same direction as the disturbance
  b. toward the disturbance
  c. from the disturbance downward
  d. at right angles to the disturbance

12. An example of a longitudinal wave is a
  a. water wave
  b. stadium wave
  c. sound wave
  d. rope wave

13. Which statement best defines a wave medium?
  a. the material through which a wave travels
  b. a point halfway between the crest and trough of a wave
  c. the distance from one wave crest to the next
  d. the speed at which waves travel in water

14. As you increase the amplitude of a wave, you also increase the
  a. frequency   **c.** speed
  b. wavelength   **d.** energy

15. To identify the amplitude in a longitudinal wave, you would measure areas of
  a. reflection   **c.** crests
  b. compression   **d.** refraction

16. Which statement describes the relationship between frequency and wavelength?
  a. When frequency increases, wavelength increases.
  b. When frequency increases, wavelength decreases.
  c. When frequency increases, wavelength remains constant.
  d. When frequency increases, wavelength varies unpredictably.

17. For wave refraction to take place, a wave must
  a. increase in velocity
  b. enter a new medium
  c. increase in frequency
  d. merge with another wave

18. Which setup in a wave tank would best enable you to demonstrate diffraction?
  a. water only
  b. water and sand
  c. water and food coloring
  d. water and a barrier with a small gap

19. Two waves come together and interact to form a new, smaller wave. This process is called
  a. destructive interference
  b. constructive interference
  c. reflective interference
  d. positive interference

Use the diagram below to answer the next two questions.

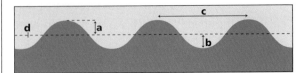

20. What two letters in the diagram measure the same thing? What do they both measure?

21. In the diagram above, what does the letter c measure?

Use the diagram below to answer the next three questions. The diagram shows waves passing a fixed point.

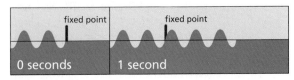

22. At 0 seconds, no waves have passed. How many waves have passed after 1 second?

23. What is being measured in the diagram?

24. How would you write the measurement taken in the diagram?

25. EVALUATE Do you think the following is an accurate definition of medium? Explain your answer.

A **medium** is any solid through which waves travel.

26. APPLY Picture a pendulum. The pendulum is swinging back and forth at a steady rate. How could you make it swing higher? How is swinging a pendulum like making a wave?

27. PREDICT What might happen to an ocean wave that encounters a gap or hole in a cliff along the shore?

28. EVALUATE Do you think *interference* is an appropriate name for the types of wave interaction you read about in Section 1.3? Explain your answer.

Using Math in Science

29. At what speed is the wave below traveling if it has a frequency of 2/s?

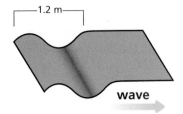

30. An ocean wave has a wavelength of 9 m and a frequency of 0.42/s. What is the wave's speed?

31. Suppose a sound wave has a frequency of 10,000/s. The wave's speed is 340 m/s. Calculate the wavelength of this sound wave.

32. A water wave is traveling at a speed of 2.5 m/s. The wave has a wavelength of 4 m. Calculate the frequency of this water wave.

the BIG idea

33. INTERPRET Look back at the photograph at the start of the chapter on pages 6–7. How does this photograph illustrate a transfer of energy?

34. SYNTHESIZE Describe three situations in which you can predict the behavior of waves.

35. SUMMARIZE Write a paragraph summarizing this chapter. Use the big idea from page 6 as the topic sentence. Then write an example from each of the key concepts listed under the big idea.

UNIT PROJECTS

If you are doing a unit project, make a folder for your project. Include in your folder a list of the resources you will need, the date on which the project is due, and a schedule to track your progress. Begin gathering data.

Interpreting Diagrams

Study the illustration below and then answer the questions.

The illustration below shows a wave channel, a way of making and studying water waves. The motor moves the rod, which moves the paddle back and forth. The movement of the paddle makes waves, which move down the length of the channel. The material behind the paddle absorbs the waves generated in that direction.

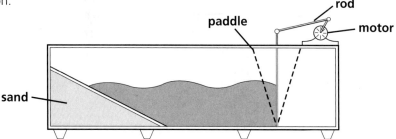

1. An experimenter can adjust the position of the rod on the arm of the motor. Placing it closer to the motor makes shallower waves. Placing it farther from the motor makes deeper waves.
   What property of waves does this affect?

   a. amplitude

   b. direction

   c. frequency

   d. wavelength

2. By changing motor speeds, an experimenter can make the paddle move faster or slower. What property of waves does this affect?

   a. amplitude

   b. direction

   c. trough depth

   d. wavelength

3. Sand is piled up in the channel at the end of the tank opposite the motor. When waves pass over this sand, their wavelengths shorten. Assuming that the speed of the waves stays the same, their frequency

   a. stays the same

   b. increases

   c. decreases

   d. cannot be predicted

4. Suppose there was no sand at the end of the tank opposite the paddle. In that case, the waves would hit the glass wall. What would they do then?

   a. stop

   b. reflect

   c. refract

   d. diffract

Extended Response

Answer the two questions below in detail.

5. Suppose temperatures in one 10-day period were as follows: 94°, 96°, 95°, 97°, 95°, 98°, 99°, 97°, 99°, and 98°. Make a simple line graph of the data. In what ways is the series of temperatures similar to a wave, and in what ways does it differ?

6. Lydia and Bill each drop a ball of the same size into the same tank of water but at two different spots. Both balls produce waves that spread across the surface of the water. As the two sets of waves cross each other, the water forms high crests in some places. What can you say about both waves? Explain your answer.

CHAPTER
2 Sound

the **BIG** idea

Sound waves transfer energy through vibrations.

> How is this guitar player producing sound?

Key Concepts

SECTION
2.1 Sound is a wave.
Learn how sound waves are produced and detected.

SECTION
2.2 Frequency determines pitch.
Learn about the relationship between the frequency of a sound wave and its pitch.

SECTION
2.3 Intensity determines loudness.
Learn how the energy of a sound wave relates to its loudness.

SECTION
2.4 Sound has many uses.
Learn how sound waves are used to detect objects and to make music.

Internet Preview

CLASSZONE.COM

Chapter 2 online resources: Content Review, two Visualizations, three Resource Centers, Math Tutorial, Test Practice

EXPLORE (the BIG idea)

What Gives a Sound Its Qualities?

Tap your finger lightly on a table. Then tap it hard. Try scratching the table with your finger. Now, place your head on the table so that your ear is flat against its surface. Tap the table again.

Observe and Think
How did the sounds differ each time? What did you feel?

How Does Size Affect Sound?

Hang three large nails of different sizes from the edge of a table so that they are not touching. Tap each nail with a metal spoon to make it vibrate. Listen to the sounds that are made by tapping each nail.

Observe and Think Which nail produced the highest sound? the lowest? How does the size of a vibrating object affect its sound?

Internet Activity: Sound

Go to **ClassZone.com** to discover how particles move as sound waves move through the air.

Observe and Think
How are the sound waves in the animation similar to the waves you have already learned about?

NSTA
scilinks.org
SCiLINKS

What Is Sound? **Code: MDL028**

Getting Ready to Learn

◀ CONCEPT REVIEW

- A wave is a disturbance that transfers energy from one place to another.
- Mechanical waves are waves that travel through matter.

◀ VOCABULARY REVIEW

medium p. 11

longitudinal wave p. 14

amplitude p. 17

wavelength p. 17

frequency p. 17

 CONTENT REVIEW
CLASSZONE.COM
Review concepts and vocabulary.

▶ TAKING NOTES

OUTLINE

As you read, copy the headings on your paper in the form of an outline. Then add notes in your own words that summarize what you have read.

VOCABULARY STRATEGY

Place each vocabulary term at the center of a **description wheel** diagram. Write some words on the spokes describing it.

See the Note-Taking Handbook on pages R45–R51.

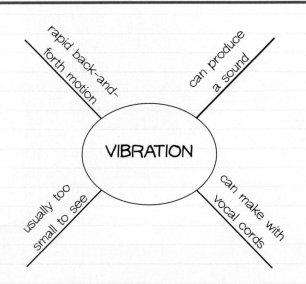

SCIENCE NOTEBOOK

I. Sound is a type of mechanical wave.
   A. How sound waves are produced
      1.
      2.
      3.
   B. How sound waves are detected
      1.
      2.
      3.

rapid back-and-forth motion

can produce a sound

VIBRATION

usually too small to see

can make with vocal cords

Sound is a wave.

 BEFORE, you learned

- Waves transfer energy
- Waves have wavelength, amplitude, and frequency

NOW, you will learn

- How sound waves are produced and detected
- How sound waves transfer energy
- What affects the speed of sound waves

VOCABULARY

sound p. 37
vibration p. 37
vacuum p. 41

EXPLORE Sound

What is sound?

PROCEDURE

1. Tie the middle of the string to the spoon handle.

2. Wrap the string ends around your left and right index fingers. Put the tips of these fingers gently in your ears and hold them there.

3. Stand over your desk so that the spoon dangles without touching your body or the desk. Then move a little to make the spoon tap the desk lightly. Listen to the sound.

MATERIALS

- piece of string
- large metal spoon

WHAT DO YOU THINK?

- What did you hear when the spoon tapped the desk?
- How did sound travel from the spoon to your ears?

Sound is a type of mechanical wave.

In the last chapter, you read that a mechanical wave travels through a material medium. Such mediums include air, water, and solid materials. Sound is an example of a mechanical wave. **Sound** is a wave that is produced by a vibrating object and travels through matter.

The disturbances that travel in a sound wave are vibrations. A **vibration** is a rapid, back-and-forth motion. Because the medium vibrates back and forth in the same direction as the wave travels, sound is a longitudinal wave. Like all mechanical waves, sound waves transfer energy through a medium.

 What do sound waves have in common with other mechanical waves? Your answer should include the word *energy*.

How Sound Waves Are Produced

READING **TiP**

When you see the word *push* or *pull,* think of force.

The disturbances in a sound wave are vibrations that are usually too small to see. Vibrations are also required to start sound waves. A vibrating object pushes and pulls on the medium around it and sends out waves in all directions.

You have a sound-making instrument within your own body. It is the set of vocal cords within the voice box, or larynx, in your throat. Put several of your fingers against the front of your throat. Now hum. Do you feel the vibrations of your vocal cords?

Your vocal cords relax when you breathe to allow air to pass in and out of your windpipe. Your vocal cords tense up and draw close together when you are about to speak or sing. The illustration below shows how sound waves are produced by the human vocal cords.

❶ Your muscles push air up from your lungs and through the narrow opening between the vocal cords.

❷ The force of the air causes the vocal cords to vibrate.

❸ The vibrating vocal cords produce sound waves.

CHECK YOUR READING How do human vocal cords produce sound waves?

How Vocal Cords Produce Sound

Sound waves are produced by vibrations.

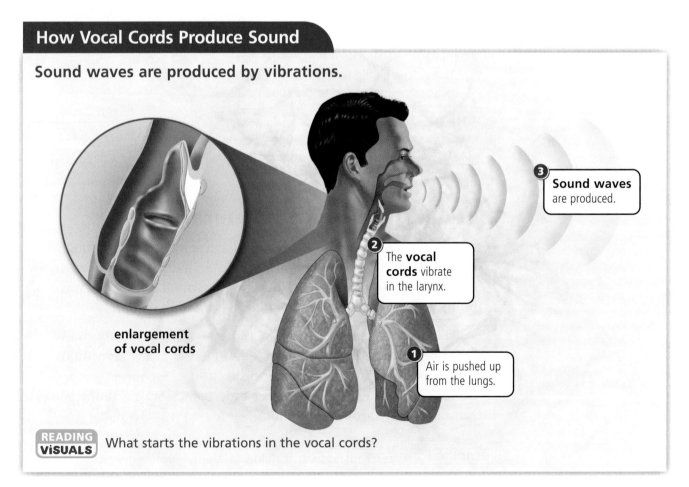

enlargement of vocal cords

❸ **Sound waves** are produced.

❷ The **vocal cords** vibrate in the larynx.

❶ Air is pushed up from the lungs.

READING VISUALS What starts the vibrations in the vocal cords?

How Sound Waves Are Detected

The shape of a human ear helps it collect sound waves. Picture a satellite dish. It collects radio waves from satellites. Your ear works in much the same way. Actually, what we typically call the ear is only the outer section of the ear. The illustration below shows the main parts of the human ear.

1 Your outer ear collects sound waves and reflects them into a tiny tube called the ear canal. At the end of the ear canal is a thin, skin-like membrane stretched tightly over the opening, called the eardrum. When sound waves strike the eardrum, they make it vibrate.

2 The middle ear contains three tiny, connected bones called the hammer, anvil, and stirrup. These bones carry vibrations from the eardrum to the inner ear.

3 One of the main parts of the inner ear, the cochlea (KAWK-lee-uh), contains about 30,000 hair cells. Each of these cells has tiny hairs on its surface. The hairs bend as a result of the vibrations. This movement triggers changes that cause the cell to send electrical signals along nerves to your brain. Only when your brain receives and processes these signals do you actually hear a sound.

> **READING TiP**
>
> As you read each numbered description here, match it to the number on the illustration below.

How the Ear Detects Sound

Sound waves are detected in the human ear, beginning with vibrations of the eardrum.

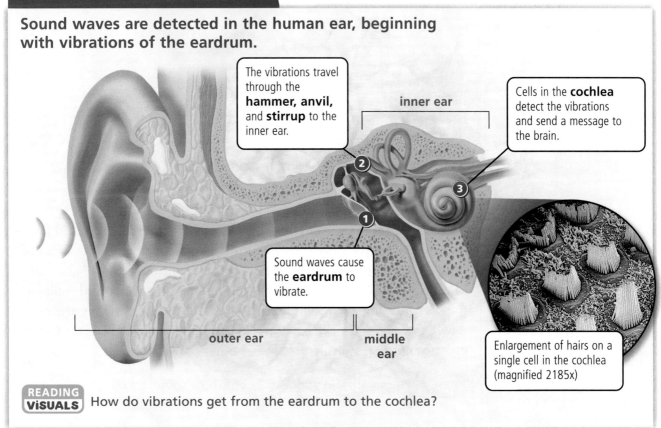

The vibrations travel through the **hammer, anvil,** and **stirrup** to the inner ear.

inner ear

Cells in the **cochlea** detect the vibrations and send a message to the brain.

2

3

1

Sound waves cause the **eardrum** to vibrate.

outer ear

middle ear

Enlargement of hairs on a single cell in the cochlea (magnified 2185x)

READING VISUALS How do vibrations get from the eardrum to the cochlea?

Sound waves vibrate particles.

You can see the motion of waves in water. You can even ride them with a surfboard. But you cannot see air. How, then, can you picture sound waves moving through air? Sound waves transfer the motion of particles too small to see from one place to another.

For example, think about a drum that has been struck. What happens between the time the drum is struck and the sound is heard?

- The drum skin vibrates rapidly. It pushes out and then in, over and over again. Of course, this happens very, very fast. The vibrating drum skin pushes against nearby particles in the air. The particles in the air become bunched together, or compressed.

- When the drum skin pushes the opposite way, a space opens up between the drum's surface and the particles. The particles rush back in to fill the space.

- The back-and-forth movement, or vibration, of the particles is the disturbance that travels to the listener. Both the bunched up areas, or compressions, and the spaces between the compressions are parts of the wave.

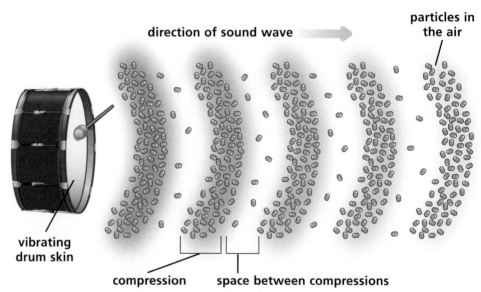

direction of sound wave

particles in the air

vibrating drum skin

compression   space between compressions

Notice that the waves consist of repeating patterns of compressions and spaces between the compressions. The compressions are areas of high air pressure. The spaces between the compressions are areas of low air pressure. The high- and low-pressure air pushes and pulls on the surrounding air, which then pushes and pulls on the air around that. Soon a sound wave has traveled through the air and has transferred kinetic energy from one place to another.

REMINDER
Kinetic energy is the energy of motion.

CHECK YOUR READING Summarize in your own words how sound travels through air.

In the middle 1600s, scientists began to do experiments to learn more about air. They used pumps to force the air out of enclosed spaces to produce a vacuum. A **vacuum** is empty space. It has no particles—or very, very few of them. Robert Boyle, a British scientist, designed an experiment to find out if sound moves through a vacuum.

Boyle put a ticking clock in a sealed jar. He pumped some air out of the jar and still heard the clock ticking. Then he pumped more air out. The ticking grew quieter. Finally, when Boyle had pumped out almost all the air, he could hear no ticking at all. Boyle's experiment demonstrated that sound does not travel through a vacuum.

The photograph at the right shows equipment that is set up to perform an experiment similar to Boyle's. A bell is placed in a sealed jar and powered through the electrical connections at the top. The sound of the loudly ringing bell becomes quieter as air is pumped out through the vacuum plate.

Sound is a mechanical wave. It can move only through a medium that is made up of matter. Sound waves can travel through air, solid materials, and liquids, such as water, because all of these mediums are made up of particles. Sound waves cannot travel through a vacuum.

Sound Experiment

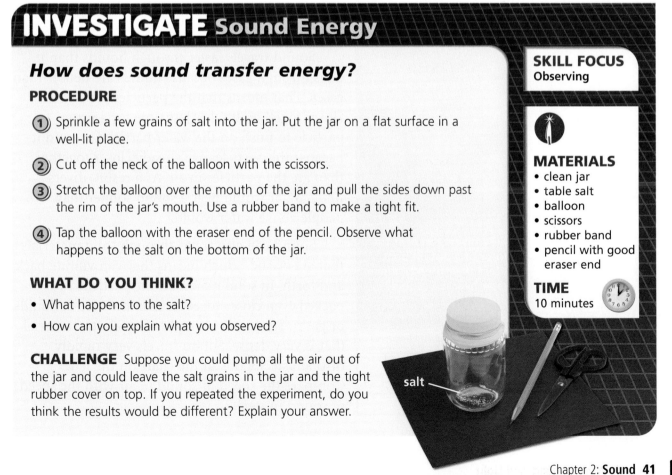

connections

sealed jar

bell

vacuum plate

INFER As air is pumped out of the jar, the sound of the bell becomes quieter. Why do you think the bell is suspended?

 CHECK YOUR READING How did Boyle's experiment show that sound cannot travel through a vacuum?

INVESTIGATE Sound Energy

How does sound transfer energy?

PROCEDURE

1. Sprinkle a few grains of salt into the jar. Put the jar on a flat surface in a well-lit place.

2. Cut off the neck of the balloon with the scissors.

3. Stretch the balloon over the mouth of the jar and pull the sides down past the rim of the jar's mouth. Use a rubber band to make a tight fit.

4. Tap the balloon with the eraser end of the pencil. Observe what happens to the salt on the bottom of the jar.

WHAT DO YOU THINK?

- What happens to the salt?

- How can you explain what you observed?

CHALLENGE Suppose you could pump all the air out of the jar and could leave the salt grains in the jar and the tight rubber cover on top. If you repeated the experiment, do you think the results would be different? Explain your answer.

SKILL FOCUS
Observing

MATERIALS
- clean jar
- table salt
- balloon
- scissors
- rubber band
- pencil with good eraser end

TIME
10 minutes

salt

The speed of sound depends on its medium.

Suppose you are in the baseball stands during an exciting game. A pitch flies from the mound toward home plate, and you see the batter draw back, swing, and hit the ball high. A split second later you hear the crack of the bat meeting the ball. You notice that the sound of the hit comes later than the sight. Just how fast does sound travel?

Sound travels more slowly than light, and it does not always travel at the same speed. Two main factors affect the speed of sound: the material that makes up the medium—such as air or water—and the temperature. If we know the medium and the temperature, however, we can predict the speed of sound.

 CHECK YOUR READING Which two factors affect the speed of sound?

The Effect of the Material

You have probably heard sounds in more than one medium. Think about the medium in which you most often hear sound—air. You listen to a radio or a compact disk player. You hear the siren of a fire truck. These sound waves travel through air, a mixture of gases.

Now think about going swimming. You dip below the water's surface briefly. Someone jumps into the water nearby and splashes water against the pool wall. You hear strange underwater sounds. These sound waves travel through water, a liquid.

Sound travels faster through liquids than it does through gases because liquids are denser than gases. That means that the particles are packed closer together. It takes less time for a water particle to push on the water particles around it because the particles are already closer together than are the particles in air. As a result, divers underwater would hear a sound sooner than people above water would.

Sound can also travel through solid materials that are elastic, which means they can vibrate back and forth. In solid materials, the particles are packed even closer together than they are in liquids or gases. Steel is an example of an elastic material that is very dense. Sound travels very rapidly through steel. Look at the chart on the left. Compare the speed of sound in air with the speed of sound in steel.

These divers can hear the motor of a distant boat before their friends above water hear it.

Materials and Sound Speeds

Medium	State	Speed of Sound
Air (20°C)	Gas	344 m/s (769 mi/h)
Water (20°C)	Liquid	1,400 m/s (3,130 mi/h)
Steel (20°C)	Solid	5,000 m/s (11,200 mi/h)

The Effect of Temperature

Sound also travels faster through a medium at higher temperatures than at lower ones. Consider the medium of air, a mixture of gases. Gas particles are not held tightly together as are particles in solids. Instead, the gas particles bounce all around. The higher the temperature, the more the gas particles wiggle and bounce. It takes less time for particles that are already moving quickly to push against the particles around them than it takes particles that are moving slowly. Sound, therefore, travels faster in hot air than in cold air.

Look at the picture of the snowboarders. The sound waves they make by yelling will travel more slowly through air than similar sounds made on a hot day. If you could bear to stand in air at a temperature of 100°C (212°F—the boiling point of water) and listen to the same person yelling, you might notice that the sound of the person's voice reaches you faster.

These snowboarders' shouts reach their friends more slowly in this cold air than they would in hot air.

Temperature and Sound Speeds

Medium	Temperature	Speed of Sound
Air	0°C (32°F)	331 m/s (741 mi/h)
Air	100°C (212°F)	386 m/s (864 mi/h)

The chart on the right shows the speed of sound in air at two different temperatures. Compare the speed of sound at the temperature at which water freezes with the speed of sound at the temperature at which water boils. Sound travels about 17 percent faster in air at 100°C than in air at 0°C.

 CHECK YOUR READING What is the difference between the speed of sound in air at 0°C and at 100°C?

2.1 Review

KEY CONCEPTS

1. Describe how sound waves are produced.
2. Describe how particles move as energy is transferred through a sound wave.
3. Explain how temperature affects the speed of sound.

CRITICAL THINKING

4. **Predict** Would the sound from a distant train travel faster through air or through steel train tracks? Explain.
5. **Evaluate** Suppose an audience watching a science fiction movie hears a loud roar as a spaceship explodes in outer space. Why is this scene unrealistic?

△ CHALLENGE

6. **Evaluate** A famous riddle asks this question: If a tree falls in the forest and there is no one there to hear it, is there any sound? What do you think? Give reasons for your answer.

EXTREME SCIENCE

RESOURCE CENTER
CLASSZONE.COM

Find out more about
supersonic aircraft.

This photograph may actually show the wake
of a sonic boom. It was taken on a very humid
day, and water vapor may have condensed in
the low-pressure part of the sound wave.

Boom Notes

- The pilot of an airplane cannot
  hear the sonic boom because
  the sound waves are behind
  the plane.

- Lightning heats particles in the
  air so rapidly that they move
  faster than the speed of sound
  and cause a shock wave, which
  is what makes the boom of
  thunder. If a lightning strike
  is very close, you will hear a
  sharp crack.

- Large meteors enter the atmosphere fast enough to make a
  sonic boom.

SURPASSING THE SPEED OF SOUND

Sonic Booms

Airplanes traveling faster than the speed of sound can produce an
incredibly loud sound called a sonic boom. The sonic boom from
a low-flying airplane can rattle and even break windows!

How It Works

Breaking the Barrier

The sound waves produced by
this airplane begin to pile up and
produce a pressure barrier.

This airplane has broken
through the pressure barrier
and has produced a loud boom.

When an airplane reaches extremely high speeds, it actually catches
up to its own sound waves. The waves start to pile up and form a
high-pressure area in front of the plane. If the airplane has enough
acceleration, it breaks through the barrier, making a sonic boom.
The airplane gets ahead of both the pressure barrier and the sound
waves and is said to be traveling at supersonic speeds—speeds faster
than the speed of sound.

Boom and It's Gone

If an airplane that produces a boom is flying very high, it may be
out of sight by the time the sonic boom reaches a hearer on the
ground. To make a sonic boom, a plane must be traveling faster
than about 1240 kilometers per hour (769 mi/h)! The sound does
not last very long—about one-tenth of a second for a small fighter
plane to one-half second for a supersonic passenger plane.

EXPLORE

1. **PREDICT** Specially designed cars have traveled faster than
   the speed of sound. Would you expect them to produce a
   sonic boom?

2. **CHALLENGE** The space shuttles produce sonic booms when
   they are taking off and landing, but not while they are
   orbiting Earth, even though they are moving much faster
   than 1240 km/h. Can you explain why?

Frequency determines pitch.

◄ BEFORE, you learned	▶ NOW, you will learn
• Sound waves are produced by vibrations	• How the frequency of a wave affects the way it sounds
• Frequency measures the number of waves passing a fixed point per second	• How sound quality differs from pitch
	• How the Doppler effect works

VOCABULARY

pitch p. 45
hertz p. 46
ultrasound p. 46
resonance p. 48
Doppler effect p. 50

EXPLORE Pitch

Why does the sound change?

PROCEDURE

1. Hold the ruler flat on the edge of a desk so that it sticks out about 25 centimeters beyond the edge.

2. With your free hand, push the tip of the ruler down and then let it go. As the ruler vibrates, slide it back onto the desk. Listen to the sounds the ruler makes.

WHAT DO YOU THINK?

• What happened to the sound as you slid the ruler back onto the desk?
• Describe the motion of the ruler.

MATERIALS
ruler

Pitch depends on the frequency of a sound wave.

VOCABULARY
Remember to add a description wheel in your notebook for each new term.

When you listen to music, you hear both high and low sounds. The characteristic of highness or lowness of a sound is called **pitch.** The frequency of a sound wave determines the pitch of the sound you hear. Remember that frequency is the number of waves passing a fixed point in a given period of time. A high-frequency wave with short wavelengths, such as that produced by a tiny flute, makes a high-pitched sound. A low-frequency wave with long wavelengths, such as the one produced by the deep croak of a tuba, makes a low-pitched sound. An object vibrating very fast produces a high-pitched sound, while an object vibrating slower produces a lower-pitched sound.

 CHECK YOUR READING   How is frequency related to pitch?

High and Low Frequencies

Frequency is a measure of how often a wave passes a fixed point. One complete wave can also be called a cycle. The unit for measuring frequency, and also pitch, is the hertz. A **hertz** (Hz) is one complete wave, or cycle, per second. For example, a wave with a frequency of 20 hertz has 20 cycles per second. In a wave with a frequency of 100 hertz, 100 waves pass a given point every second. The diagram below shows how frequency and pitch are related.

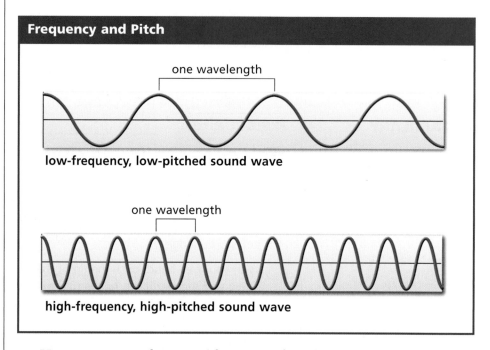

Frequency and Pitch

one wavelength

low-frequency, low-pitched sound wave

one wavelength

high-frequency, high-pitched sound wave

Human ears can hear a wide range of pitches. Most people with good hearing can hear sounds in the range of 20 hertz to 20,000 hertz. The note of middle C on a piano, for example, has a frequency of 262 hertz.

Sound waves with wavelengths below 20 hertz are called infrasound. People cannot hear sounds in this range. Infrasound waves have a very long wavelength and can travel great distances without losing much energy. Elephants may use infrasound to communicate over long distances. Some of the waves that elephants use travel through the ground instead of the air, and they may be detected by another elephant up to 32 kilometers (about 20 miles) away.

The highest frequency that humans can hear is 20,000 hertz. Sound waves in the range above 20,000 hertz are called **ultrasound.** Though people cannot hear ultrasound, it is very useful. Later in this chapter, you will learn about some of the uses of ultrasound. Many animals can hear sound waves in the ultrasound range. The chart on page 47 shows the hearing ranges of some animals.

READING TiP

The prefix *infra* means "below," and the prefix *ultra* means "beyond."

CHECK YOUR READING   What is the range of frequencies that humans can hear?

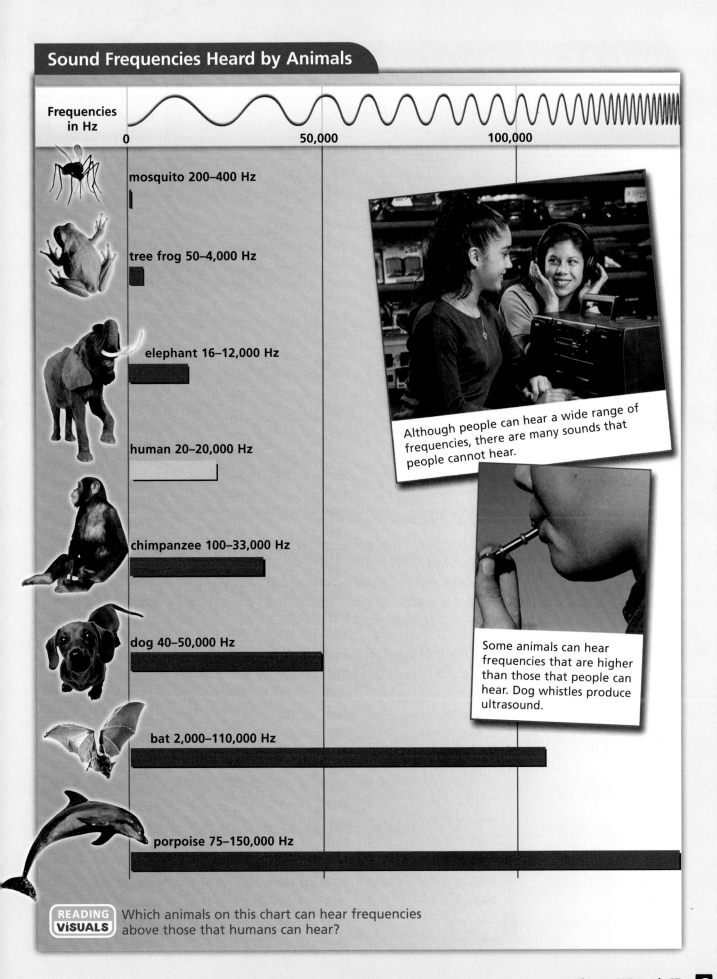

Sound Frequencies Heard by Animals

Frequencies in Hz

0   50,000   100,000

mosquito 200–400 Hz

tree frog 50–4,000 Hz

elephant 16–12,000 Hz

human 20–20,000 Hz

chimpanzee 100–33,000 Hz

dog 40–50,000 Hz

bat 2,000–110,000 Hz

porpoise 75–150,000 Hz

Although people can hear a wide range of frequencies, there are many sounds that people cannot hear.

Some animals can hear frequencies that are higher than those that people can hear. Dog whistles produce ultrasound.

READING ViSUALS Which animals on this chart can hear frequencies above those that humans can hear?

INVESTIGATE Sound Frequency

How is frequency related to pitch?

PROCEDURE

1. Stretch the rubber bands around the open box.

2. Pull one of the rubber bands tightly across the open part of the box so that it vibrates with a higher frequency than the looser rubber band. Tape the rubber band in place.

3. Pluck each rubber band and listen to the sound it makes.

WHAT DO YOU THINK?

• Which rubber band produces a sound wave with a higher pitch?

• How is frequency related to pitch?

CHALLENGE Suppose you are tuning a guitar and want to make one of the strings sound higher in pitch. Do you tighten or loosen the string? Explain your answer.

SKILL FOCUS
Inferring

MATERIALS
• 2 rubber bands of different sizes
• small open box
• tape

TIME
20 minutes

Natural Frequencies

You have read that sound waves are produced by vibrating objects. Sound waves also cause particles in the air to vibrate as they travel through the air. These vibrations have a frequency, or a number of cycles per second. All objects have a frequency at which they vibrate called a natural frequency.

You may have seen a piano tuner tap a tuning fork against another object. The tuner does this to make the fork vibrate at its natural frequency. He or she then listens to the pitch produced by the tuning fork's vibrations and tunes the piano string to match it. Different tuning forks have different frequencies and can be used to tune instruments to different pitches.

When a sound wave with a particular frequency encounters an object that has the same natural frequency, constructive interference takes place. The amplitude of the sound from the vibrating object adds together with the amplitude of the initial sound wave. The strengthening of a sound wave in this way is called **resonance.** When a tuning fork is struck, a nearby tuning fork with the same natural frequency will also begin to vibrate because of resonance.

 How is natural frequency related to resonance?

Sound Quality

Have you ever noticed that two singers can sing exactly the same note, or pitch, and yet sound very different? The singers produce sound waves with their vocal cords. They stretch their vocal cords in just the right way to produce sound waves with a certain frequency. That frequency produces the pitch that the note of music calls for. Why, then, don't the singers sound exactly the same?

Each musical instrument and each human voice has its own particular sound, which is sometimes called the sound quality. Another word for sound quality is timbre (TAM-buhr). Timbre can be explained by the fact that most sounds are not single waves but are actually combinations of waves. The pitch that you hear is called the fundamental tone. Other, higher-frequency pitches are called overtones. The combination of pitches is the main factor affecting the quality of a sound.

Another factor in sound quality is the way in which a sound starts and stops. Think about a musician who is crashing cymbals. The cymbals' sound blasts out suddenly. A sound produced by the human voice, on the other hand, starts much more gently.

CHECK YOUR READING What are two factors that affect sound quality? Which sentences above tell you?

The illustration below shows oscilloscope (uh-SIHL-uh-SKOHP) screens. An oscilloscope is a scientific instrument that tracks an electrical signal. The energy of a sound wave is converted into a signal and displayed on an oscilloscope screen. The screens below show sound wave diagrams made by musicians playing a piano and a clarinet. Both of these musical instruments are producing the same note, or pitch. Notice that the diagrams look slightly different from each other. Each has a different combination of overtones, producing a unique sound quality.

Both oscilloscope images at left show diagrams of sound waves of the same pitch produced on two different instruments. The waves, however, have different sound qualities.

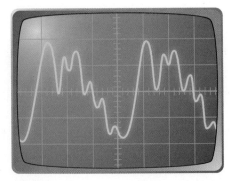

piano

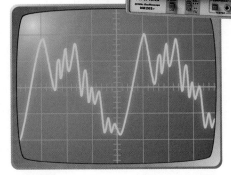

clarinet

The motion of the source of a sound affects its pitch.

Sometimes in traffic, a screeching siren announces that an ambulance must pass through traffic. Drivers slow down and pull over to the side, leaving room for the ambulance to speed by. Suppose you are a passenger in one of these cars. What do you hear?

When the ambulance whizzes past you, the pitch suddenly seems to drop. The siren on the ambulance blasts the same pitches again and again. What has made the difference in what you hear is the rapid motion of the vehicle toward you and then away from you. The motion of the source of a sound affects its pitch.

The Doppler Effect

DESCRIPTION WHEEL
Make a description wheel in your notebook for the Doppler effect.

In the 1800s an Austrian scientist named Christian Doppler hypothesized about sound waves. He published a scientific paper about his work. In it, he described how pitch changes when a sound source moves rapidly toward and then away from a listener. Doppler described the scientific principle we notice when a siren speeds by. The **Doppler effect** is the change in perceived pitch that occurs when the source or the receiver of a sound is moving.

Before long, a Dutch scientist learned of Doppler's work. In 1845 he staged an experiment to test the hypothesis that Doppler described. In the experiment, a group of trumpet players were put on a train car. Other musicians were seated beside the railroad track. Those musicians had perfect pitch—that is, the ability to identify a pitch just by listening to it. The train passed by the musicians while the trumpeters on the train played their instruments. The musicians recorded the pitches they heard from one moment to the next. At the end of the demonstration, the musicians reported that they had heard the pitch of the trumpets fall as the train passed. Their experiment showed that the Doppler effect exists.

CHECK YOUR READING How does the motion of a sound's source affect its pitch?

To listeners outside a train, the sound made by the train seems higher in pitch while it approaches them than while it speeds away.

The Doppler Effect

The perceived pitch of a sound changes as the source of the sound moves toward or away from the hearer.

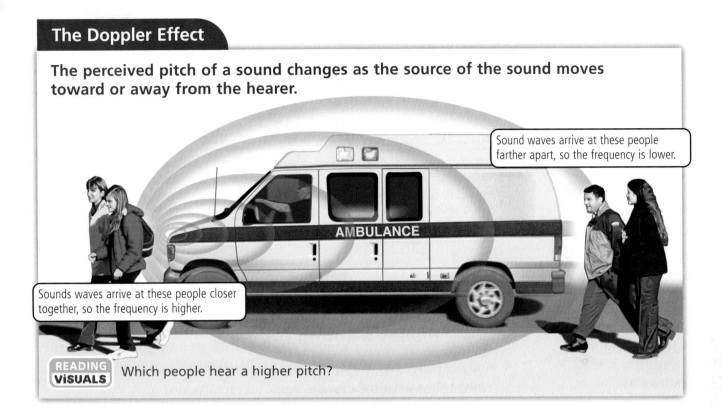

Sound waves arrive at these people farther apart, so the frequency is lower.

Sounds waves arrive at these people closer together, so the frequency is higher.

READING VISUALS Which people hear a higher pitch?

Frequency and Pitch

Again imagine sitting in a car as an ambulance approaches. The siren on the ambulance continually sends out sound waves. As the ambulance pulls closer to you, it catches up with the sound waves it is sending out. As a result, the sound waves that reach your ears are spaced closer together. The frequency, and therefore the pitch, is higher when it reaches you. As the ambulance continues, it gets farther and farther away from you, while the sound waves still move toward you. Now the waves arrive farther and farther apart. As the frequency decreases, you hear a lower pitch.

VISUALIZATION
CLASSZONE.COM

Explore the Doppler effect.

2.2 Review

KEY CONCEPTS

1. Describe what is different about the sound waves produced by a low note and a high note on a musical instrument.

2. Explain why two people singing the same pitch do not sound exactly the same.

3. How does perceived pitch change as a sound source passes a listener?

CRITICAL THINKING

4. **Apply** How could you produce vibrations in a tuning fork without touching it? Explain your answer.

5. **Predict** Suppose you could view the waves produced by a high-pitched and a low-pitched voice. Which wave would display the greater number of compressions in 1 s? Why?

◆ CHALLENGE

6. **Infer** Offer a possible explanation for why no one noticed the Doppler effect before the 1800s.

KEY CONCEPT

2.3 Intensity determines loudness.

◀ **BEFORE,** you learned

- Sound waves are produced by vibrations
- Frequency determines the pitch of a sound
- Amplitude is a measure of the height of a wave crest

▶ **NOW,** you will learn

- How the intensity of a wave affects its loudness
- How sound intensity can be controlled
- How loudness can affect hearing

VOCABULARY

intensity p. 52
decibel p. 52
amplification p. 55
acoustics p. 55

THINK ABOUT

What makes a sound louder?

A drum player has to play softly at some times and loudly at others. Think about what the drummer must do to produce each type of sound. If you could watch the drummer in the photograph in action, what would you see? How would the drummer change the way he moves the drumsticks to make a loud, crashing sound? What might he do to make a very soft sound?

Intensity depends on the amplitude of a sound wave.

OUTLINE
Make an outline for this heading. Remember to include main ideas and details.

I. Main idea
  A. Supporting idea
    1. Detail
    2. Detail
  B. Supporting idea

Earlier you read that all waves carry energy. The more energy a sound wave carries, the more intense it is and the louder it will sound to listeners. The **intensity** of a sound is the amount of energy its sound wave has. A unit called the **decibel** (dB) is used to measure sound intensity. The faint rustling of tree leaves on a quiet summer day can hardly be heard. Some of the softest sounds measure less than 10 decibels. On the other hand, the noise from a jet taking off or the volume of a TV set turned all the way up can hurt your ears. Very loud sounds measure more than 100 decibels. Remember that amplitude is related to wave energy. The greater the amplitude, the more intensity a sound wave has and the louder the sound will be.

 CHECK YOUR READING How is energy related to loudness?

INVESTIGATE Loudness

How is amplitude related to loudness?

PROCEDURE

① Cut a notch in the middle of both ends of the cardboard. Stretch the rubber band around the cardboard so that it fits into the notches as shown.

② Mark lines on the cardboard at one and four centimeters away from the rubber band.

③ Slide the pencils under the rubber band at each end.

④ Pull the rubber band to the one-centimeter line and let it go so that it vibrates with a low amplitude. Notice the sound it makes. Pull the rubber band to the four-centimeter line and let it go again. This time the amplitude is higher. Notice the sound it makes this time.

WHAT DO YOU THINK?

• How did the loudness of the sounds compare?

• How is amplitude related to loudness?

CHALLENGE Using what you learned from experimenting with the rubber band, explain why swinging a drumstick harder on a drum would make a louder sound than swinging a drumstick lightly.

The drummer varies the loudness of a sound by varying the energy with which he hits the drum. Loudness is also affected by the distance between the source and the listener.

Have you ever wondered why sound gradually dies out over distance? Think about someone walking away from you with a radio. When the radio is close, the radio seems loud. As the person walks away, the sound grows fainter and fainter. Sound waves travel in all directions from their source. As the waves travel farther from the radio, their energy is spread out over a greater area. This means that their intensity is decreased. The sound waves with lower intensities are heard as quieter sounds.

Other forces can take energy away from sound waves, too. Forces can act within the medium of a sound wave to decrease the intensity of the waves. This effect on sound is probably a good thing. Imagine what the world would be like if every sound wave continued forever!

Approximate Sound Intensities

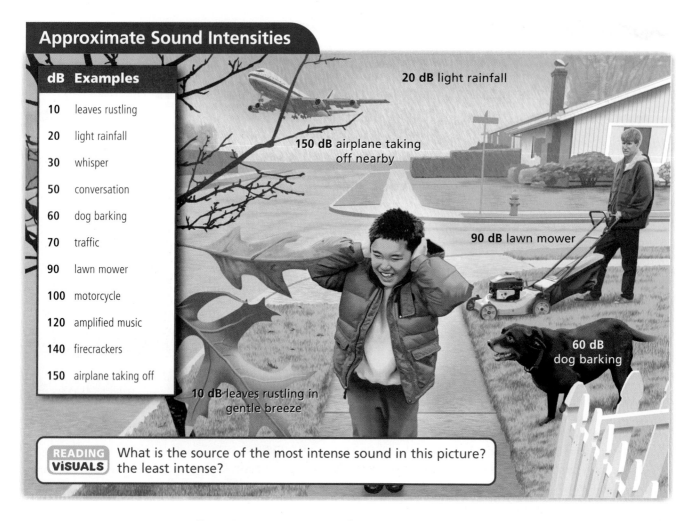

dB	Examples
10	leaves rustling
20	light rainfall
30	whisper
50	conversation
60	dog barking
70	traffic
90	lawn mower
100	motorcycle
120	amplified music
140	firecrackers
150	airplane taking off

20 dB light rainfall

150 dB airplane taking off nearby

90 dB lawn mower

60 dB dog barking

10 dB leaves rustling in gentle breeze

READING VISUALS What is the source of the most intense sound in this picture? the least intense?

The intensity of sound can be controlled.

REMINDER

Remember, amplitude is related to wave energy.

Over time and distance, a sound wave gets weaker and weaker until the sound becomes undetectable. The pitch, however, does not typically change as the sound grows weaker. In other words, even as the amplitude decreases, the frequency stays the same.

Sometimes it is desirable to change sound intensity without changing the pitch and quality of a sound. We can do this by adding energy to or taking energy away from a sound wave. As you have already seen, intensity is the amount of energy in a sound wave. Changing the intensity of a sound wave changes its amplitude.

Sound intensity can be controlled in many ways. Mufflers on cars and trucks reduce engine noise. Have you ever heard a car with a broken muffler? You were probably surprised at how loud it was. Burning fuel in an engine produces hot gases that expand and make a very loud noise. A muffler is designed to absorb some of the energy of the sound waves and so decrease their amplitude. As a result, the intensity of the sound you hear is much lower than it would be without the muffler.

CHECK YOUR READING How could you change the intensity of a sound without changing the pitch?

Amplification

In addition to being reduced, as they are in a muffler, sound waves can be amplified. The word *amplify* may remind you of *amplitude,* the measure of the height of a wave's crest. These words are related. To amplify something means to make it bigger. **Amplification** is the increasing of the strength of an electrical signal. It is often used to increase the intensity of a sound wave.

When you listen to a stereo, you experience the effects of amplification. Sound input to the stereo is in the form of weak electrical signals from a microphone. Transistors in an electronic circuit amplify the signals. The electrical signals are converted into vibrations in a coil in your stereo's speaker. The coil is attached to a cone, which also vibrates and sends out sound waves. You can control the intensity of the sound waves by adjusting your stereo's volume.

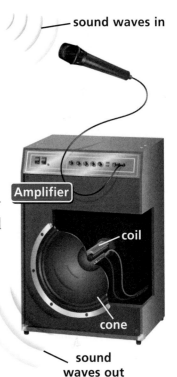

sound waves in

Amplifier

coil

cone

sound waves out

Acoustics

The scientific study of sound is called **acoustics** (uh-KOO-stihks). Acoustics involves both how sound is produced and how it is received and heard by humans and animals.

Acoustics also refers to the way sound waves behave inside a space. Experts called acoustical engineers help design buildings to reduce unwanted echoes. An echo is simply a reflected sound wave. To control sound intensity, engineers design walls and ceilings with acoustical tiles. The shapes and surfaces of acoustical tiles are designed to absorb or redirect some of the energy of sound waves.

The pointed tiles in this sound-testing room are designed to absorb sound waves and prevent any echoes.

The shapes and surfaces in this concert hall direct sound waves to the audience.

READING VISUALS COMPARE AND CONTRAST Imagine sound waves reflecting off the surfaces in the two photographs above. How do the reflections differ?

Intense sound can damage hearing.

healthy hair cells

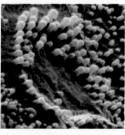

damaged hair cells

When a train screeches to a stop in a subway station, the sound of the squealing brakes echoes off the tunnel walls. Without thinking about it, you cover your ears with your hands. This response helps protect your ears from possible damage.

In the first section of this chapter, you read about the main parts of the human ear. The part of the inner ear called the cochlea is lined with special cells called hair cells. As you have seen, these cells are necessary for hearing.

The hair cells are extremely sensitive. This sensitivity makes hearing possible, but it also makes the cells easy to damage. Continual exposure to sounds of 90 dB or louder can damage or destroy the cells. This is one reason why being exposed to very loud noises, especially for more than a short time, is harmful to hearing.

 CHECK YOUR READING How do high-intensity sounds damage hearing?

RESOURCE CENTER
CLASSZONE.COM

Find out more about sound and protecting your hearing.

Using earplugs can prevent damage from too much exposure to high-intensity sounds such as amplified music. The intensity at a rock concert is between 85 and 120 dB. Ear protection can also protect the hearing of employees in factories and other noisy work sites. In the United States, there are laws that require employers to reduce sounds at work sites to below 90 dB or to provide workers with ear protection.

Even a brief, one-time exposure to an extremely loud noise can destroy hair cells. Noises above 130 dB are especially dangerous. Noises above 140 dB are even painful. It is best to avoid such noises altogether. If you find yourself exposed suddenly to such a noise, covering your ears with your hands may be the best protection.

2.3 Review

KEY CONCEPTS

1. Explain how the terms *intensity, decibel,* and *amplitude* are related.

2. Describe one way in which sound intensity can be controlled.

3. How do loud sounds cause damage to hearing?

CRITICAL THINKING

4. **Synthesize** A wind chime produces both soft and loud sounds. If you could see the waves, how would they differ?

5. **Design an Experiment** How could you demonstrate that sound dies away over distance? Suppose you could use three volunteers, a radio, and a tape recorder.

CHALLENGE

6. **Apply** Which of these acoustical designs would be best for a concert hall? Why?
a. bare room with hard walls, floor, and ceiling
b. room padded with sound-absorbing materials such as acoustical tile
c. room with some hard surfaces and some sound padding

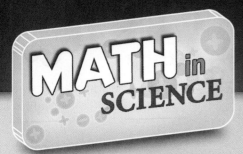

MATH TUTORIAL
CLASSZONE.COM

Click on Math Tutorial for more help with interpreting line graphs.

SKILL: INTERPRETING GRAPHS

Measuring Hearing Loss

An audiogram is a graph that can be used to determine if a patient has hearing loss. The vertical axis shows the lowest intensity, in decibels, that the patient can hear for each frequency tested. Notice that intensity is numbered from top to bottom on an audiogram.

To determine the lowest intensity heard at a given frequency, find the frequency on the horizontal axis. Follow the line straight up until you see the data points, shown as ✱ for the right ear and ● for the left ear. Look to the left to find the intensity. For example, the lowest intensity heard in both ears at 250 Hz is 10 dB.

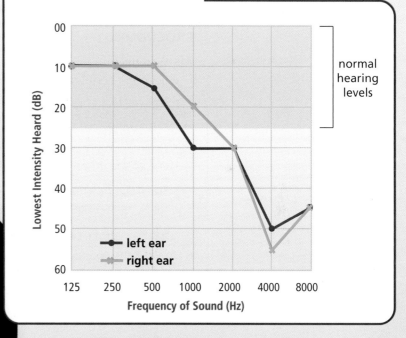

Audiogram for Patient A

Use the graph to answer the following questions.

1. What is the lowest intensity heard in the patient's left ear at 1000 Hz? the right ear at the same frequency?

2. At which frequencies are the data points for both ears within normal hearing levels?

3. Data points outside the normal hearing levels indicate hearing loss. At which frequencies are the data points for both ears outside the normal levels?

CHALLENGE A dip in the graph at 3000 to 4000 Hz is a sign that the hearing loss was caused by exposure to loud noises. The patient is referred to a specialist for further testing. Should Patient A get further testing? Why or why not?

This air traffic ground controller wears ear protection to prevent hearing loss.

KEY CONCEPT
Sound has many uses.

BEFORE, you learned	NOW, you will learn
• Sound waves are produced by vibrations • Sound waves have amplitude, frequency, and wavelength	• How ultrasound is used • How musical instruments work • How sound can be recorded and reproduced

VOCABULARY

echolocation p. 59
sonar p. 59

EXPLORE Echoes

How can you use sound to detect an object?

PROCEDURE

1. Tape the two cardboard tubes onto your desk at a right angle as shown.

2. Put your ear up to the end of one of the tubes. Cover your other ear with your hand.

3. Listen as your partner whispers into the outside end of the other tube.

4. Stand the book upright where the tubes meet. Repeat steps 2 and 3.

MATERIALS

• 2 cardboard tubes
• tape
• book

WHAT DO YOU THINK?

• How did the sound change when you added the book?
• How can an echo be used to detect an object?

Ultrasound waves are used to detect objects.

A ringing telephone, a honking horn, and the sound of a friend's voice are all reminders of how important sound is. But sound has uses that go beyond communication. For example, some animals and people use reflected ultrasound waves to detect objects. Some animals, such as bats, use the echoes of ultrasound waves to find food. People use ultrasound echoes to detect objects underwater or even to produce images of the inside of the body.

 Other than communication, what are three uses of sound?

Echolocation

Sending out ultrasound waves and interpreting the returning sound echoes is called **echolocation** (*echo + location*). Bats flying at night find their meals of flying insects by using echolocation. They send out as many as 200 ultrasound squeaks per second. By receiving the returning echoes, they can tell where prey is and how it is moving. They can also veer away from walls, trees, and other big objects.

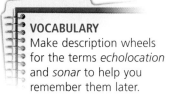

VOCABULARY
Make description wheels for the terms *echolocation* and *sonar* to help you remember them later.

sound waves emitted by bat

sound waves reflected off prey

A number of animals that live in water use echolocation, too. Dolphins, toothed whales, and porpoises produce ultrasound squeaks or clicks. They listen to the returning echo patterns to find fish and other food in the water.

Sonar

People use the principles of echolocation to locate objects underwater. During World War I (1914–1918), scientists developed instruments that used sound waves to locate enemy submarines. Instruments that use echolocation to locate objects are known as **sonar.** Sonar stands for "sound navigation and ranging." The sonar machines could detect sounds coming from submarine propellers. Sonar devices could also send out ultrasound waves and then use the echoes to locate underwater objects. The information from the echoes could then be used to form an image on a screen.

Later, people found many other uses for sonar. Fishing boats use sonar to find schools of fish. Oceanographers—scientists who study the ocean—use it to map the sea floor. People have even used sonar to find ancient sunken ships in deep water.

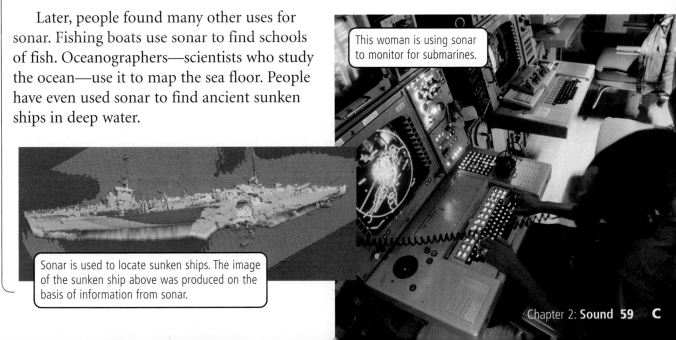

This woman is using sonar to monitor for submarines.

Sonar is used to locate sunken ships. The image of the sunken ship above was produced on the basis of information from sonar.

Medical Uses of Ultrasound

Ultrasound has many uses in medicine. Because ultrasound waves are not heard by humans, ultrasound can be used at very high intensities. For example, high-intensity vibrations from ultrasound waves are used to safely break up kidney stones in patients. The energy transferred by ultrasound waves is also used to clean medical equipment.

One of the most important medical uses of ultrasound is the ultrasound scanner. This device relies on the same scientific principle as sonar. It sends sound waves into a human body and then records the waves that are reflected from inside the body. Information from these echoes forms a picture on a screen. The ultrasound scanner is used to examine internal organs such as the heart, pancreas, bladder, ovaries, and brain. Doppler ultrasound is a technology that can detect the movement of fluids through the body and is used to examine blood flow.

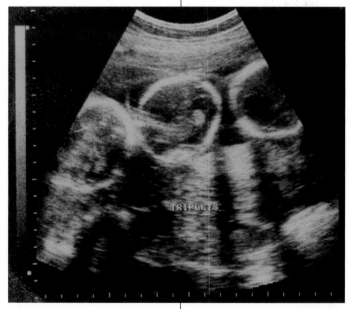

The image of these triplets was produced by reflected ultrasound waves.

CHECK YOUR READING How is an ultrasound scanner similar to sonar?

One of the most well-known uses of ultrasound is to check on the health of a fetus during pregnancy. Problems that are discovered may possibly be treated early. The scan can also reveal the age and gender of the fetus and let the expecting parents know if they will be having twins or triplets. Ultrasound is safer than other imaging methods, such as the x-ray, which might harm the development of the fetus.

Sound waves can produce music.

Why are some sounds considered noise and other sounds considered music? Music is sound with clear pitches or rhythms. Noise is random sound; that means it has no intended pattern.

Musical instruments produce pitches and rhythms when made to vibrate at their natural frequencies. Some musical instruments have parts that vibrate at different frequencies to make different pitches. All of the pitches, together with the resonance of the instrument itself, produce its characteristic sound. The three main types of musical instruments are stringed, wind, and percussion. Some describe electronic instruments as a fourth type of musical instrument. Look at the illustration on the next page to learn more about how each type of musical instrument works.

How Musical Instruments Work

The way a musical instrument vibrates when it is played determines the sound it produces.

Stringed Instruments

Stringed instruments, such as the guitar, are played by plucking the strings. The plucking starts the vibrations that produce sound waves.

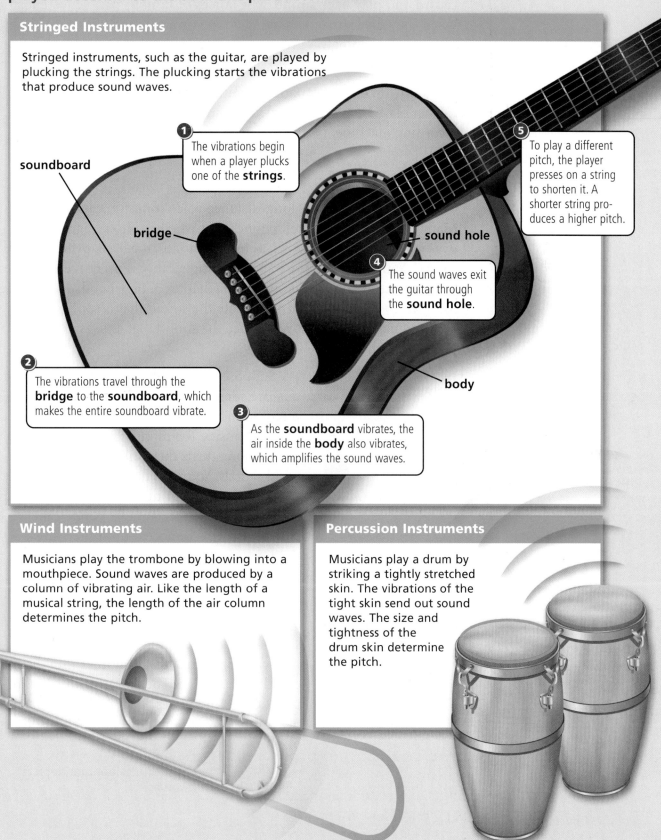

soundboard

1 The vibrations begin when a player plucks one of the **strings**.

5 To play a different pitch, the player presses on a string to shorten it. A shorter string produces a higher pitch.

bridge

sound hole

4 The sound waves exit the guitar through the **sound hole**.

2 The vibrations travel through the **bridge** to the **soundboard**, which makes the entire soundboard vibrate.

3 As the **soundboard** vibrates, the air inside the **body** also vibrates, which amplifies the sound waves.

body

Wind Instruments

Musicians play the trombone by blowing into a mouthpiece. Sound waves are produced by a column of vibrating air. Like the length of a musical string, the length of the air column determines the pitch.

Percussion Instruments

Musicians play a drum by striking a tightly stretched skin. The vibrations of the tight skin send out sound waves. The size and tightness of the drum skin determine the pitch.

Sound can be recorded and reproduced.

For most of human history, people had no way to send their voices farther than they could shout. Nor could people before the 1800s record and play back sound. The voices of famous people were lost when they died. Imagine having a tape or a compact disk recording of George Washington giving a speech!

Then in the late 1800s, two inventions changed the world of sound. In 1876, the telephone was invented. And in 1877, Thomas Edison played the first recorded sound on a phonograph, or sound-recording machine.

The Telephone

The telephone has made long-distance voice communication possible. Many people today use cell phones. But whether phone signals travel over wires or by microwaves, as in cell phones, the basic principles are similar. You will learn more about the signal that is used in cell phones when you read about microwaves in Chapter 3. In general, a telephone must do two things. It must translate the sound that is spoken into it into a signal, and it must reproduce the sound that arrives as a signal from somewhere else.

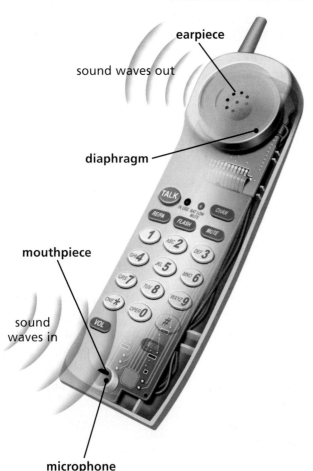

earpiece

sound waves out

diaphragm

mouthpiece

sound waves in

microphone

Suppose you are phoning your best friend to share some news. You speak into the mouthpiece. Sound waves from your voice cause a thin disk inside the mouthpiece to vibrate. A microphone turns these vibrations into electrical signals. Your handset sends these signals over wire to a switching station. Computers in the switching station connect phone callers and keep them connected until they finish their conversation.

Your friend receives the news by listening to the earpiece on his handset. There the process is more or less reversed. The electrical signals that arrive in the earpiece are turned into vibrations that shake another thin disk called a diaphragm. The vibrating diaphragm produces sound waves. The sound your friend hears is a copy of your voice, though it sounds like the real you.

CHECK YOUR READING What part of a telephone detects sound waves?

Recorded Sound

Sound occurs in real time, which means it is here for a moment and then gone. That is why Thomas Edison's invention of the phonograph—a way to preserve sound—was so important.

Edison's phonograph had a needle connected to a diaphragm that could pick up sound waves. The vibrations transferred by the sound waves were sent to a needle that cut into a piece of foil. The sound waves were translated into bumps along the grooves cut into the foil. These grooves contained all the information that was needed to reproduce the sound waves. Look at the image on top at the right to view an enlargement of record grooves. To play back the sound, Edison used another needle to track along the grooves etched in the foil. Later, phonographs were developed that changed sound waves into electrical signals that could be amplified.

Most people today listen to music on audio tapes or CDs. Tape consists of thin strips of plastic coated with a material that can be magnetized. Sounds that have been turned into electrical signals are stored on the tape as magnetic information. A CD is a hard plastic disc that has millions of microscopic pits arranged in a spiral. The bottom photograph at the right shows an enlargement of pits on the surface of a CD. These pits contain the information that a CD player can change into electrical signals, which are then turned into sound waves.

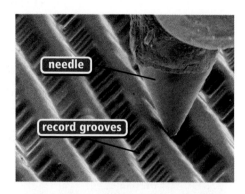

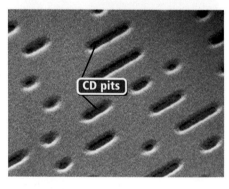

The images above were taken by a scanning electron micrograph (SEM). Both the record grooves (top) and CD pits (bottom) store all of the information needed to reproduce sound.

 CHECK YOUR READING   Describe three devices on which sound is recorded.

2.4 Review

KEY CONCEPTS

1. Describe one medical use of ultrasound.

2. How are vibrations produced by each of the three main types of musical instruments?

3. How does a telephone record and reproduce sound?

CRITICAL THINKING

4. **Model** Draw a simple diagram to show how telephone communication works. Begin your diagram with the mouthpiece and end with the earpiece.

5. **Classify** The pitch of a musical instrument is changed by shortening the length of a vibrating column of air. What type of instrument is it?

⬤ CHALLENGE

6. **Synthesize** How is the earpiece of a telephone similar to the amplifier you read about in Section 3? Look again at the diagram of the amplifier on page 55 to help you find similarities.

CHAPTER INVESTIGATION

Build a Stringed Instrument

DESIGN — YOUR OWN —

OVERVIEW AND PURPOSE

People make music by plucking strings, blowing through tubes, and striking things. Part of each musical instrument vibrates to produce sounds that form the building blocks of music. In this lab, you will use what you have learned about sound to

- make a simple stringed instrument and see how the vibrating string produces sounds and
- change the design so that your stringed instrument produces more than one pitch.

▶ Problem

Write It Up

How does the length of a string affect the pitch of the sound it produces when plucked?

▶ Hypothesize

Write It Up

Write a hypothesis to explain how changing the length of the string affects the pitch of sound that is produced. Your hypothesis should take the form of an "If . . . , then . . . , because . . ." statement. Complete steps 1–3 before writing your hypothesis.

▶ Procedure

MATERIALS
- book
- 3–5 rubber bands
- 2 pencils
- ruler
- shoebox
- scissors

1. Make a data table like the one shown. Try out the following idea for a simple stringed instrument. Stretch a rubber band around a textbook. Put two pencils under the rubber band to serve as bridges.

2. Put the bridges far apart at either end of the book. Find the string length by measuring the distance between the two bridges. Record this measurement in your **Science Notebook.** Pluck the rubber band to make it vibrate. Watch it vibrate and listen to the sound it makes.

3. Move the bridges closer together. What effect does this have on the length of the string? Measure and record the new length. How does this affect the tone that is produced? Record your observations.

4. Make a musical instrument based on the principles you just identified. Begin by stretching rubber bands of the same weight or thickness over the box.

5. If necessary, reinforce the box with an extra layer of cardboard or braces so that it can withstand the tension of the rubber bands without collapsing.

6. Place pencils under the rubber bands at each end of the box. Arrange one pencil at an angle so that each string is a different length. Record the length of each string and your observations of the sounds produced. Experiment with the placement of the bridges.

7. You might also try putting one bridge at the center of the box and plucking on either side of it. How does this affect the range of pitches your instrument produces?

8. Experiment with the working model to see how you can vary the sounds. Try this variation: cut a hole in the center of the box lid. Put the lid back on the box. Replace the rubber bands and bridges. How does the hole change the sound quality?

▶ Observe and Analyze

Write It Up

1. **RECORD OBSERVATIONS** Draw a picture of your completed instrument design. Be sure your data table is complete.

2. **ANALYZE** Explain what effect moving the bridges farther apart or closer together has on the vibrating string.

3. **SYNTHESIZE** Using what you have learned from this chapter, write a paragraph that explains how your instrument works. Be sure to describe how sound waves of different frequencies and different intensities can be produced on your instrument.

▶ Conclude

1. **INTERPRET** Answer the question posed in the problem.

2. **ANALYZE** Compare your results with your hypothesis. Did your results support your hypothesis?

3. **EVALUATE** Describe any difficulties with or limitations of the materials that you encountered as you made your instrument.

4. **APPLY** Based on your experiences, how would you explain the difference between music and noise?

▶ INVESTIGATE Further

CHALLENGE Stringed instruments vary the pitch of musical sounds in several other ways. In addition to the length of the string, pitch depends on the tension, weight, and thickness of the string. Design an experiment to test one of these variables. How does it alter the range of sounds produced by your stringed instrument?

Build a Stringed Instrument

Problem How does the length of a string affect the pitch of the sound it produces when plucked?

Hypothesize

Observe and Analyze

Simple instrument: initial string length _____
Simple instrument: new string length _____

Table 1. Stringed Instrument Sound Observations

Stringed Instrument Designs	Length of Strings (cm)	Observations About Pitch and Sound Quality
Bridges at each end		
Bridge in middle		
After adding sound hole		

Conclude

Chapter Review

the **BIG** idea

Sound waves transfer energy through vibrations.

CONTENT REVIEW
CLASSZONE.COM

◄ **KEY CONCEPTS SUMMARY**

2.1 Sound is a wave.

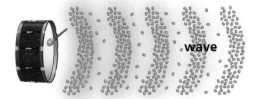

disturbance ➡

wave

Sound is a longitudinal wave that travels through a material medium, such as air.

VOCABULARY
sound p. 37
vibration p. 37
vacuum p. 41

2.2 Frequency determines pitch.

A sound wave with a lower frequency and longer wavelength is perceived to have a lower pitch.

A sound wave with a higher frequency and shorter wavelength is perceived to have a higher pitch.

VOCABULARY
pitch p. 45
hertz p. 46
ultrasound p. 46
resonance p. 48
Doppler effect p. 50

2.3 Intensity determines loudness.

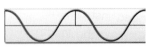

A sound wave with a lower amplitude and energy is perceived as a softer sound.

A sound wave with a higher amplitude and energy is perceived as a louder sound.

VOCABULARY
intensity p. 52
decibel p. 52
amplification p. 55
acoustics p. 55

2.4 Sound has many uses.

Human uses of sound:
sonar
ultrasound
music
telephone
recording

Bats use sound to locate objects.

VOCABULARY
echolocation p. 59
sonar p. 59

Reviewing Vocabulary

Copy and complete the chart below by using vocabulary terms from this chapter.

Property of Wave	Unit of Measurement	Characteristic of Sound
Frequency	**1.**	**2.**
3.	**4.**	loudness

Make a frame for each of the vocabulary words listed below. Write the word in the center. Decide what information to frame it with. Use definitions, examples, descriptions, parts, or pictures. An example is shown.

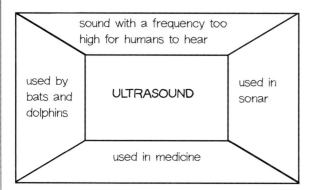

sound with a frequency too high for humans to hear

used by bats and dolphins

ULTRASOUND

used in sonar

used in medicine

5. resonance **8.** acoustics

6. Doppler effect **9.** echolocation

7. amplification **10.** sonar

Reviewing Key Concepts

Multiple Choice *Choose the letter of the best answer.*

11. Sound is a mechanical wave, so it always
   a. travels through a vacuum
   b. has the same amplitude
   c. is made by a machine
   d. travels through matter

12. Which unit is a measure of sound frequency?
   a. hertz
   b. decibel
   c. amp
   d. meter

13. In which of the following materials would sound waves move fastest?
   a. water
   b. cool air
   c. hot air
   d. steel

14. Which of the following effects is caused by amplification?
   a. wavelength increases
   b. amplitude increases
   c. frequency decreases
   d. decibel measure decreases

15. The frequency of a sound wave determines its
   a. pitch
   b. loudness
   c. amplitude
   d. intensity

16. As sound waves travel away from their source, their
   a. intensity increases
   b. energy increases
   c. intensity decreases
   d. frequency decreases

17. A telephone mouthpiece changes sound waves into
   a. electric signals
   b. vibrations
   c. CD pits
   d. grooves on a cylinder

Short Answer *Look at the diagrams of waves below. For the next two items, choose the wave diagram that best fits the description, and explain your choice.*

a.   **b.**   **c.**

18. the sound of a basketball coach blowing a whistle during practice

19. the sound of a cow mooing in a pasture

Thinking Critically

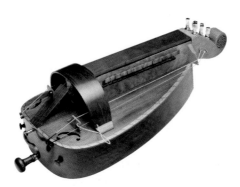

Look at the photograph of an instrument above. Write a short answer to the next two questions.

20. HYPOTHESIZE How might sound waves be produced using the instrument in the photograph?

21. APPLY How might a person playing the instrument in the photograph vary the intensity?

22. COMMUNICATE Two people are singing at the same pitch, yet they sound different. Explain why.

23. SEQUENCE Copy the following sequence chart on your paper. Write the events in the correct sequence on the chart.

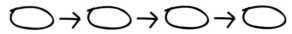

Events

a. Sound waves race out from the wind chime.

b. Forces in air gradually weaken the chime sound.

c. A breeze makes a wind chime vibrate.

d. A person nearby hears the wind chime.

24. COMPARE AND CONTRAST Write a description of the similarities and differences between each of the following pairs of terms: frequency—amplitude; intensity—amplitude; pitch—quality; fundamental tone—overtones.

Using Math in Science

Read the line graph below showing freeway noise levels at a toll collector's booth. Use the data in the graph to answer the next four questions.

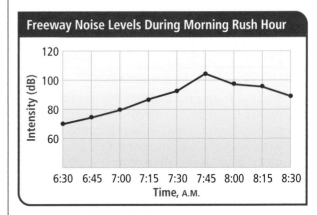

25. Which is the noisiest quarter-hour?

26. Estimate the loudest level of sound that the toll collector is exposed to.

27. If ear protection should be worn for a sound level above 90 dB, should the toll collector wear hearing protection? If so, during which times?

28. Describe how you could turn the line graph into a bar graph. Would the bar graph be as informative? Explain your answer.

the BIG idea

29. ANALYZE Look back at the picture at the start of the chapter on pages 34–35. How are sound waves being produced?

30. SUMMARIZE Write a paragraph summarizing this chapter. Use the Big Idea on page 34 as your topic sentence. Write examples of each key concept listed on page 34.

UNIT PROJECTS

Check your schedule for your unit project. How are you doing? Be sure that you've placed data or notes from your research in your project folder.

Analyzing Experiments

*Read the following description of the way scientists study animals' hearing.
Then answer the questions below.*

Scientists test the hearing ranges of a human by making a sound and asking the person to say whether it was heard. This cannot be done with animals. Scientists use different methods to find animals' hearing ranges. In some experiments, they train animals—by rewarding them with food or water—to make specific behaviors when they hear a sound. Another method is to study an animal's nervous system for electrical reactions to sounds.

Researchers have found that dogs and cats can hear a wide range of sounds. Both dogs and cats can hear much higher frequencies than humans can. Lizards and frogs can only hear sounds in a much narrower range than humans can. Elephants can hear a wider range than lizards and frogs but not as wide a range as dogs and cats. Elephants can hear the lowest frequency sounds of all these animals.

1. What type of behavior would be best for scientists to train animals to make as a signal that they hear a sound?
   a. a typical motion that the animal makes frequently
   b. a motion that is difficult for the animal to make
   c. a motion the animal makes rarely but does make naturally
   d. a complicated motion of several steps

2. According to the passage, which animals can hear sounds with the highest frequencies?
   a. cats
   b. elephants
   c. frogs
   d. lizards

3. The high-pitched sounds of car brakes are sometimes more bothersome to pet dogs than they are to their owners. Based on the experimental findings, what is the best explanation for that observation?
   a. The dogs hear high-intensity sounds that their owners cannot hear.
   b. The dogs hear low-intensity sounds that their owners cannot hear.
   c. The dogs hear low-frequency sounds that their owners cannot hear.
   d. The dogs hear high-frequency sounds that their owners cannot hear.

4. Which animal hears sounds with the longest wavelengths?
   a. cat
   b. dog
   c. elephant
   d. frog

Extended Response

Answer the two questions below in detail. Include some of the terms from the word box in your answer. Underline each term you use in your answer.

| amplitude | distance | Doppler effect |
| frequency | pitch | wavelength |

5. Suppose you are riding in a car down the street and pass a building where a fire alarm is sounding. Will the sound you hear change as you move up to, alongside, and past the building? Why or why not?

6. Marvin had six glass bottles that held different amounts of water. He blew air into each bottle, producing a sound. How would the sounds produced by each of the six bottles compare to the others? Why?

3 Electromagnetic Waves

the **BIG** idea

Electromagnetic waves transfer energy through radiation.

How does this phone stay connected?

Key Concepts

SECTION
3.1 Electromagnetic waves have unique traits.
Learn how electromagnetic waves differ from mechanical waves.

SECTION
3.2 Electromagnetic waves have many uses.
Learn about the behaviors and uses of different types of electromagnetic waves.

SECTION
3.3 The Sun is the source of most visible light.
Learn about the natural and artificial production of light.

SECTION
3.4 Light waves interact with materials.
Learn how light waves behave in a material medium.

Internet Preview

CLASSZONE.COM

Chapter 3 online resources: Content Review, Simulation, Visualization, two Resource Centers, Math Tutorial, Test Practice.

What Melts the Ice Cubes?

Put an ice cube in each of two sandwich bags, and place the bags in sunlight. Cover one with a sheet of white paper, and cover the other with a sheet of black paper. Lift the sheets of paper every five minutes and observe the cubes. Continue until they are melted.

Observe and Think
What did you notice about the way the ice cubes melted? How can you explain what you observed?

What Is White Light Made Of?

Use the shiny side of a compact disk (CD) to reflect light from the Sun onto a sheet of white paper. If bright sunlight is not available, use a flashlight. Try holding the CD at different angles and at different distances from the paper.

Observe and Think
What did you see on the paper? Where do you think that what you observed came from?

Internet Activity:
Electromagnetic Waves

Go to **ClassZone.com** to explore images of the Sun based on different wavelengths.

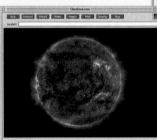

Observe and Think
Why can we see only some of the waves coming from the Sun?

NSTA
scilinks.org
SCI*LINKS*

Light and Color **Code: MDL029**

Getting Ready to Learn

◀ CONCEPT REVIEW

- A wave is a disturbance that transfers energy.
- Mechanical waves have a medium.
- Waves can be measured.
- Waves react to a change in medium.

◀ VOCABULARY REVIEW

mechanical wave p. 11
wavelength p. 17
frequency p. 17
reflection p. 25
field *See Glossary.*

 CONTENT REVIEW
CLASSZONE.COM
Review concepts and vocabulary.

▶ TAKING NOTES

SUPPORTING MAIN IDEAS

Make a chart to show main ideas and the information that supports them. Copy each blue heading. Below each heading, add supporting information, such as reasons, explanations, and examples.

VOCABULARY STRATEGY

Write each new vocabulary term in the center of a **frame game** diagram. Decide what information to frame it with. Use examples, descriptions, parts, sentences that use the term in context, or pictures. You can change the frame to fit each term.

See the Note-Taking Handbook on pages R45–R51.

SCIENCE NOTEBOOK

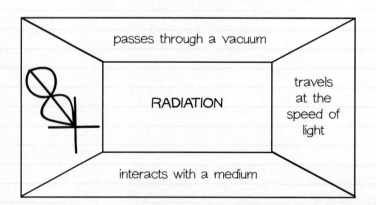

MAIN IDEA
Electromagnetic waves have unique properties.

→ EM waves are disturbances in a field rather than in a medium.

→ EM waves can travel through a vacuum.

→ EM waves travel at the speed of light.

passes through a vacuum

RADIATION

travels at the speed of light

interacts with a medium

Electromagnetic waves have unique traits.

◀ BEFORE, you learned	**▶ NOW,** you will learn
• Waves transfer energy • Mechanical waves need a medium to travel	• How electromagnetic waves differ from mechanical waves • Where electromagnetic waves come from • How electromagnetic waves transfer energy

VOCABULARY

electromagnetic
  wave p. 73
radiation p. 75

EXPLORE Electromagnetic Waves

How does the signal from a remote control travel?

PROCEDURE

1. Turn the TV on and off using the remote control.

2. Work with a partner to try to turn on the TV by aiming the remote control at the mirror.

MATERIALS

• TV with remote control unit
• mirror with stand

WHAT DO YOU THINK?

How did you have to position the remote control and the mirror in order to operate the TV? Why do you think this worked?

VOCABULARY
Create a frame game diagram for the term *electromagnetic wave.*

An electromagnetic wave is a disturbance in a field.

Did you know that you are surrounded by thousands of waves at this very moment? Waves fill every cubic centimeter of the space around you. They collide with or pass through your body all the time.

Most of these waves are invisible, but you can perceive many of them. Light is made up of these waves, and heat can result from them. Whenever you use your eyes to see, or feel the warmth of the Sun on your skin, you are detecting their presence. These waves also allow radios, TVs, and cell phones to send or receive information over long distances. These waves have the properties shared by all waves, yet they are different from mechanical waves in important ways. This second type of wave is called an electromagnetic wave. An **electromagnetic wave** (ih-LEHK-troh-mag-NEHT-ihk) is a disturbance that transfers energy through a field. Electromagnetic waves are also called EM (EE-EHM) waves.

A field is an area around an object where the object can apply a force—a push or a pull—to another object without touching it. You have seen force applied through a field if you have ever seen a magnet holding a card on the door of a refrigerator. The magnet exerts a pull on the door, even though it does not touch the door. The magnet exerts a force through the magnetic field that surrounds the magnet. When a disturbance occurs in an electric or magnetic field rather than in a medium, the wave that results is an electromagnetic wave.

How EM Waves Form

VISUALIZATION
CLASSZONE.COM

Learn more about the nature of EM waves.

EM waves occur when electrically charged atomic particles move. Charged particles exert an electric force on each other, so they have electric fields. A moving charged particle creates a magnetic force, so a moving charge also has a magnetic field around it.

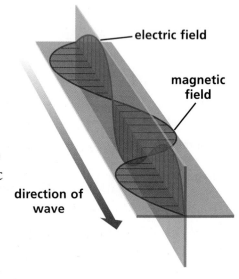

electric field

magnetic field

direction of wave

When electrically charged particles move quickly, they can start a disturbance of electric and magnetic fields. The fields vibrate at right angles to each other, as shown in the diagram above. The EM wave travels in the form of these vibrating fields. As you read in Chapter 1, waves have the properties of wavelength and frequency. In an EM wave, both the electric and the magnetic fields have these properties.

 What are the two types of fields that make up an EM wave?

Sources of EM Waves

Many of the EM waves present in Earth's environment come from the Sun. The Sun's high temperature allows it to give off countless EM waves. Other stars give off as many EM waves as the Sun, but because these bodies are so far away, fewer of their EM waves reach Earth. In addition to the Sun, technology is a source of EM waves that humans use for a wide variety of purposes.

EM waves from the Sun provide most of the energy for the environment on Earth. Some of the energy goes into Earth's surface, which then gives off EM waves of different wavelengths.

 What are two sources of EM waves on Earth?

Electromagnetic waves can travel in a vacuum.

Energy that moves in the form of EM waves is called **radiation** (RAY-dee-AY-shuhn). Radiation is different from the transfer of energy through a medium by a mechanical wave. A mechanical wave must vibrate the medium as it moves, and this uses some of the wave's energy. Eventually, every mechanical wave will give up all of its energy to the medium and disappear. An EM wave can travel without a material medium—that is, in a vacuum or space empty of matter—and does not lose energy as it moves. In theory, an EM wave can travel forever.

READING TiP

EM waves are also called rays. The words *radiation* and *radiate* come from the Latin word *radius,* which means "ray" or "spoke of a wheel."

How EM Waves Travel in a Vacuum

Because they do not need a medium, EM waves can pass through outer space, which is a near vacuum. Also, because they do not give up energy in traveling, EM waves can cross the great distances that separate stars and galaxies. For example, rays from the Sun travel about 150 million kilometers (93 million mi) to reach Earth. Rays from the most distant galaxies travel for billions of years before reaching Earth.

Usually, EM waves spread outward in all directions from the source of the disturbance. The waves then travel until something interferes with them. The farther the waves move from their source, the more they spread out. As they spread out, there are fewer waves in a given area and less energy is transferred. Only a very small part of the energy radiated from the Sun is transferred to Earth. But that energy is still a great amount—enough to sustain life on the planet.

The Speed of EM Waves in a Vacuum

In a vacuum, EM waves travel at a constant speed, and they travel very fast—about 300,000 kilometers (186,000 mi) per second. In 1 second, an EM wave can travel a distance greater than 7 times the distance around Earth. Even at this speed, rays from the Sun take about 8 minutes to reach Earth. This constant speed is called the speed of light. The vast distances of space are often measured in units of time traveled at this speed. For example, the Sun is about 8 light-minutes away from Earth. The galaxy shown in the photograph is 60 million light-years from Earth.

The light and other EM waves from this galaxy took approximately 60 million years to reach Earth.

CHECK YOUR READING How are EM waves used to measure distances in space?

Electromagnetic waves can interact with a material medium.

When EM waves encounter a material medium, they can interact with it in much the same way that mechanical waves do. They can transfer energy to the medium itself. Also, EM waves can respond to a change of medium by reflecting, refracting, or diffracting, just as mechanical waves do. When an EM wave responds in one of these ways, its direction changes. When the direction of the wave changes, the direction in which the energy is transferred also changes.

Transferring Energy

REMINDER

Potential energy comes from position or form; kinetic energy comes from motion.

A mechanical wave transfers energy in two ways. As it travels, the wave moves potential energy from one place to another. It also converts potential energy into kinetic energy by moving the medium back and forth.

In a vacuum, EM waves transfer energy only by moving potential energy from one place to another. But when EM waves encounter matter, their energy can be converted into many different forms.

CHECK YOUR READING In what form do EM waves transfer energy in a vacuum?

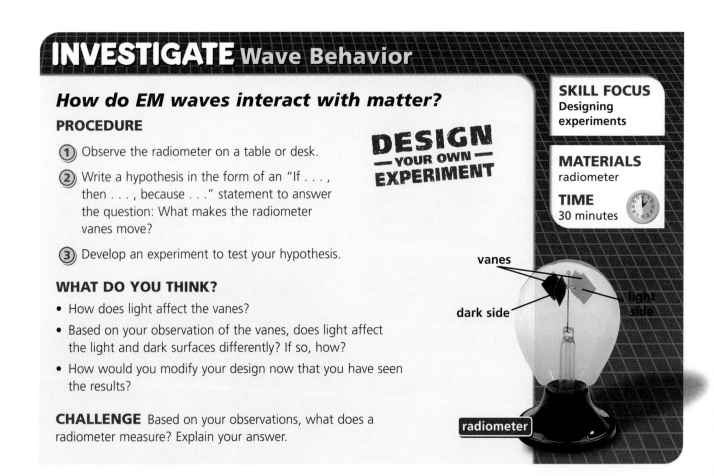

INVESTIGATE Wave Behavior

How do EM waves interact with matter?

PROCEDURE

DESIGN
— YOUR OWN —
EXPERIMENT

① Observe the radiometer on a table or desk.

② Write a hypothesis in the form of an "If . . . , then . . . , because . . ." statement to answer the question: What makes the radiometer vanes move?

③ Develop an experiment to test your hypothesis.

WHAT DO YOU THINK?

- How does light affect the vanes?
- Based on your observation of the vanes, does light affect the light and dark surfaces differently? If so, how?
- How would you modify your design now that you have seen the results?

CHALLENGE Based on your observations, what does a radiometer measure? Explain your answer.

SKILL FOCUS
Designing experiments

MATERIALS
radiometer

TIME
30 minutes

vanes

dark side

light side

radiometer

Converting Energy from One Form to Another

How EM waves interact with a medium depends on the type of the wave and the nature of the material. For example, a microwave oven uses a type of EM wave called microwaves. Microwaves pass through air with very little interaction. However, they reflect off the oven's fan and sides. But when microwaves encounter water, such as that inside a potato, their energy is converted into thermal energy. As a result, the potato gets cooked, but the oven remains cool.

❶ A device on the oven produces microwaves and sends them toward the reflecting fan.

❷ Microwaves are reflected in many directions by the blades of the fan and then again by the sides of the oven.

❸ Microwaves move through the air without transferring energy to the air.

❹ Microwaves transfer energy to the water molecules inside the potato in the form of heat, cooking the potato.

EM waves usually become noticeable and useful when they transfer energy to a medium. You do not observe the microwaves in a microwave oven. All you observe is the potato cooking. In the rest of this chapter, you will learn about different types of EM waves, including microwaves, and about how people use them.

CHECK YOUR READING How does microwave cooking depend on reflection?

Review

KEY CONCEPTS

1. How are EM waves different from mechanical waves?

2. What are two sources of EM waves in Earth's environment?

3. How can EM waves transfer energy differently in a material medium as compared to a vacuum?

CRITICAL THINKING

4. **Predict** What would happen to an EM wave that never came into contact with matter?

5. **Infer** What might be one cause of uneven heating in a microwave oven?

⬤ CHALLENGE

6. **Synthesize** EM waves can interact with a medium. How might this fact be used to make a device for detecting a particular type of EM radiation?

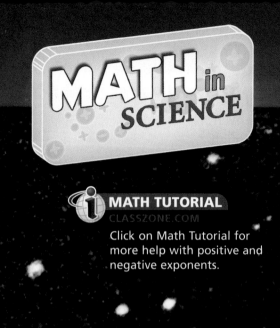

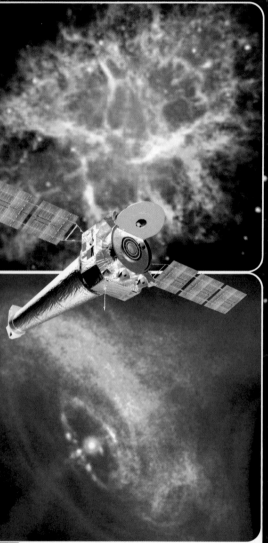

The top photograph shows a visible-light image of the Crab Nebula. The bottom photograph shows the same nebula as it appears at higher x-ray frequencies.

MATH in SCIENCE

MATH TUTORIAL
CLASSZONE.COM

Click on Math Tutorial for more help with positive and negative exponents.

EM Frequencies

The Chandra X-Ray Observatory in the photograph is a space telescope that detects high-frequency EM waves called x-rays. A wave's frequency is the number of peaks that pass a given point in 1 second. EM frequencies usually run from about 100 Hz to about 1 trillion trillion Hz. If written in standard form (using zeros), 1 trillion trillion would look like this:

1,000,000,000,000,000,000,000,000

Because this number is hard to read, it would be helpful to write it more simply. Using exponents, 1 trillion trillion can be written as 10^{24}.

Exponents can also be used to simplify very small numbers. For example, the wavelength of a wave with a frequency of 10^{24} Hz is about one ten-thousandth of one trillionth of a meter. That number can be written in standard form as **0.000,000,000,000,000,1 m.** Using exponents, the number can be written more simply as 10^{-16} **m.**

Examples

Large Numbers

To write a multiple of 10 in exponent form, just count the zeros. Then, use the total as the exponent.

(1) 10,000 has 4 zeros.

(2) 4 is the exponent.

ANSWER 10^4 is the way to write 10,000 using exponents.

Decimals

To convert a decimal into exponent form, count the number of places to the right of the decimal point. Then, use the total with a negative sign as the exponent.

(1) 0.000,001 has 6 places to the right of the decimal point.

(2) Add a negative sign to make the exponent –6.

ANSWER 10^{-6} is the way to write 0.000,001 using exponents.

Answer the following questions.

Write each number using an exponent.
1. 10,000,000   3. 100,000   5. 10,000,000,000
2. 0.000,01   4. 0.0001   6. 0.000,000,001

Write the number in standard form.
7. 10^8 9. 10^{11} 11. 10^{17}
8. 10^{-8} 10. 10^{-12} 12. 10^{-15}

CHALLENGE Using exponents, multiply 10^2 by 10^3. Explain how you got your result.

3.2 Electromagnetic waves have many uses.

◀ **BEFORE, you learned**

- EM waves transfer energy through fields
- EM waves have measurable properties
- EM waves interact with matter

▶ **NOW, you will learn**

- How EM waves differ from one another
- How different types of EM waves are used

VOCABULARY

electromagnetic spectrum p. 80
radio waves p. 82
microwaves p. 83
visible light p. 84
infrared light p. 84
ultraviolet light p. 85
x-rays p. 86
gamma rays p. 86

EXPLORE Radio Waves

How can you make radio waves?

PROCEDURE

1. Tape one end of one length of wire to one end of the battery. Tape one end of the second wire to the other end of the battery.

2. Wrap the loose end of one of the wires tightly around the handle of the fork.

3. Turn on the radio to the AM band and move the selector past all stations until you reach static.

4. Hold the fork close to the radio. Gently pull the free end of wire across the fork's prongs.

MATERIALS

- two 25 cm lengths of copper wire
- C or D battery
- electrical tape
- metal fork
- portable radio

WHAT DO YOU THINK?

- What happens when you stroke the prongs with the wire?
- How does changing the position of the dial affect the results?

EM waves have different frequencies.

It might seem hard to believe that the same form of energy browns your toast, brings you broadcast television, and makes the page you are now reading visible. Yet EM waves make each of these events possible. The various types of EM waves differ from each other in their wavelengths and frequencies.

The frequency of an EM wave also determines its characteristics and uses. Higher-frequency EM waves, with more electromagnetic vibrations per second, have more energy. Lower-frequency EM waves, with longer wavelengths, have less energy.

▼ **REMINDER**

Remember that frequency is the number of waves that pass a given point per second. The shorter the wavelength, the higher the frequency.

The Electromagnetic Spectrum

RESOURCE CENTER
CLASSZONE.COM

Learn more about
the electromagnetic
spectrum.

The range of all EM frequencies is known as the **electromagnetic spectrum** (SPEHK-truhm), or EM spectrum. The spectrum can be represented by a diagram like the one below. On the left are the waves with the longest wavelengths and the lowest frequencies and energies. Toward the right, the wavelengths become shorter, and the frequencies and energies become higher. The diagram also shows different parts of the spectrum: radio waves, microwaves, infrared light, visible light, ultraviolet light, x-rays, and gamma rays.

The EM spectrum is a smooth, gradual progression from the lowest frequencies to the highest. Divisions between the different parts of the spectrum are useful, but not exact. As you can see from the diagram below, some of the sections overlap.

The Electromagnetic Spectrum

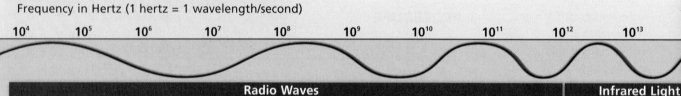

Frequency in Hertz (1 hertz = 1 wavelength/second)

10^4 10^5 10^6 10^7 10^8 10^9 10^{10} 10^{11} 10^{12} 10^{13}

Radio Waves   Infrared Light

Microwaves

This woman is speaking on the radio. **Radio waves** are used for radio and television broadcasts. They are also used for cordless phones, garage door openers, alarm systems, and baby monitors.

Not all astronomy involves visible light. Telescopes like the one above pick up **microwaves** from space. Microwaves are also used for radar, cell phones, ovens, and satellite communications.

The amount of **infrared light** a object gives off depends on its temperature. Above, different colors indicate different amour of infrared light.

Measuring EM Waves

Because all EM waves move at the same speed in a vacuum, the frequency of an EM wave can be determined from its wavelength. EM wavelengths run from about 30 kilometers for the lowest-frequency radio waves to trillionths of a centimeter for gamma rays. EM waves travel so quickly that even those with the largest wavelengths have very high frequencies. For example, a low-energy radio wave with a wavelength of 30 kilometers has a frequency of 10,000 cycles per second.

EM wave frequency is measured in hertz (Hz). One hertz equals one cycle per second. The frequency of the 30-kilometer radio wave mentioned above would be 10,000 Hz. Gamma ray frequencies reach trillions of trillions of hertz.

SUPPORTING MAIN IDEAS
Write details that support the main idea that EM waves form a spectrum based on frequency.

CHECK YOUR READING Why is wavelength all you need to know to calculate EM wave frequency in a vacuum?

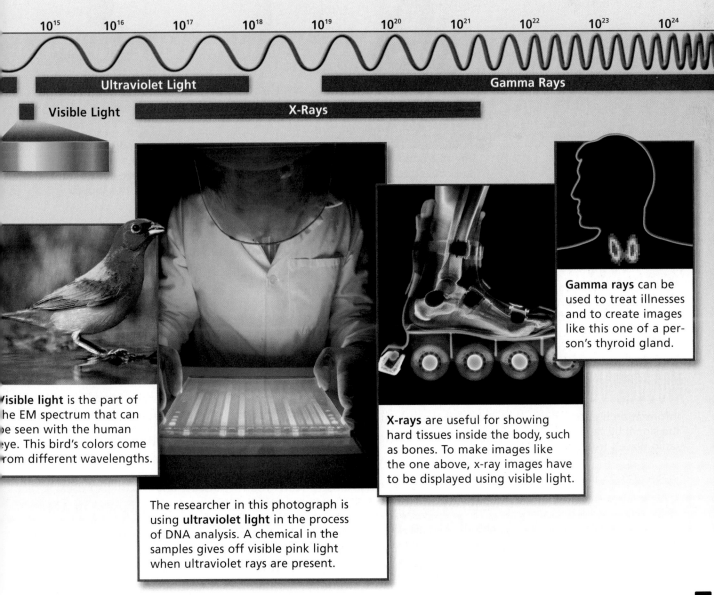

10^{15} 10^{16} 10^{17} 10^{18} 10^{19} 10^{20} 10^{21} 10^{22} 10^{23} 10^{24}

Ultraviolet Light

Gamma Rays

Visible Light

X-Rays

Gamma rays can be used to treat illnesses and to create images like this one of a person's thyroid gland.

Visible light is the part of the EM spectrum that can be seen with the human eye. This bird's colors come from different wavelengths.

X-rays are useful for showing hard tissues inside the body, such as bones. To make images like the one above, x-ray images have to be displayed using visible light.

The researcher in this photograph is using **ultraviolet light** in the process of DNA analysis. A chemical in the samples gives off visible pink light when ultraviolet rays are present.

Radio waves and microwaves have long wavelengths and low frequencies.

Radio waves are EM waves that have the longest wavelengths, the lowest frequencies, and the lowest energies. Radio waves travel easily through the atmosphere and many materials. People have developed numerous technologies to take advantage of the properties of radio waves.

Radio Waves

Radio was the first technology to use EM waves for telecommunication, which is communication over long distances. A radio transmitter converts sound waves into radio waves and broadcasts them in different directions. Radio receivers in many locations pick up the radio waves and convert them back into sound waves.

1 Sound waves enter the microphone and are converted into electrical impulses.

2 The electrical impulses are converted into radio waves and broadcast by the transmitter.

3 The radio waves reach a radio receiver and are converted back into sound.

Different radio stations broadcast radio waves at different frequencies. To pick up a particular station, you have to tune your radio to the frequency for that station. The numbers you see on the radio—such as 670 or 99.5—are frequencies.

Simply transmitting EM waves at a certain frequency is not enough to send music, words, or other meaningful sounds. To do that, the radio transmitter must attach information about the sounds to the radio signal. The transmitter attaches the information by modulating—that is, changing—the waves slightly. Two common ways of modulating radio waves are varying the amplitude of the waves and varying the frequency of the waves. Amplitude modulation is used for AM radio, and frequency modulation is used for FM radio.

You might be surprised to learn that broadcast television also uses radio waves. The picture part of a TV signal is transmitted using an AM signal. The sound part is transmitted using an FM signal.

AM Signal

Information is encoded in the signal by varying the radio wave's amplitude.

FM Signal

Information is encoded in the signal by varying the radio wave's frequency.

 CHECK YOUR READING What two properties of EM waves are used to attach information to radio signals?

Microwaves

A type of EM waves called microwaves comes next on the EM spectrum. **Microwaves** are EM waves with shorter wavelengths, higher frequencies, and higher energy than other radio waves. Microwaves get their name from the fact that their wavelengths are generally shorter than those of radio waves. Two important technologies that use microwaves are radar and cell phones.

READING TiP

As you read about the different categories of EM waves, refer to the diagram on pages 80 and 81.

Radar The term *radar* stands for "radio detection and ranging." Radar came into wide use during World War II (1939–1945) as a way of detecting aircraft and ships from a distance and estimating their locations. Radar works by transmitting microwaves, receiving reflections of the waves from objects the waves strike, and converting these patterns into visual images on a screen. Today, radar technology is used to control air traffic at airports, analyze weather conditions, and measure the speed of a moving vehicle.

Radar led to the invention of the microwave oven. The discovery that microwaves could be used to cook food was made by accident when microwaves melted a candy bar inside a researcher's pocket.

Cell Phones A cell phone is actually a radio transmitter and receiver that uses microwaves. Cell phones depend on an overlapping network of cells, or areas of land several kilometers in diameter. Each cell has at its center a tower that sends and receives microwave signals. The tower connects cell phones inside the cell to each other or to the regular wire-based telephone system. These two connecting paths are shown below.

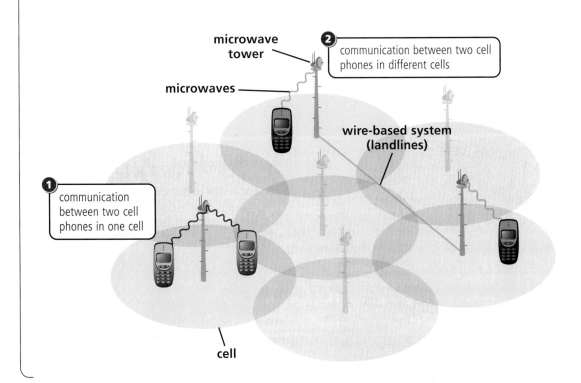

microwave tower

microwaves

2 communication between two cell phones in different cells

wire-based system (landlines)

1 communication between two cell phones in one cell

cell

Infrared, visible, and ultraviolet light have mid-range wavelengths and frequencies.

Visible light is the part of the EM spectrum that human eyes can see. It lies between 10^{14} Hz and 10^{15} Hz. We perceive the longest wavelengths of visible light as red and the shortest as violet. This narrow band is very small compared with the rest of the spectrum. In fact, visible light is only about 1/100,000 of the complete EM spectrum. The area below visible light and above microwaves is the infrared part of the EM spectrum. Above visible light is the ultraviolet part of the spectrum. You will read more about visible light in the next section.

READING TiP

Infrared means "below red." *Ultraviolet* means "beyond violet."

Infrared Light

The **infrared light** part of the spectrum consists of EM frequencies between microwaves and visible light. Infrared radiation is the type of EM wave most often associated with heat. Waves in this range are sometimes called heat rays. Although you cannot see infrared radiation, you can feel it as warmth coming from the Sun, a fire, or a radiator. Infrared lamps are used to provide warmth in bathrooms and to keep food warm after it is cooked. Infrared rays also help to cook food—for example, in a toaster or over charcoal.

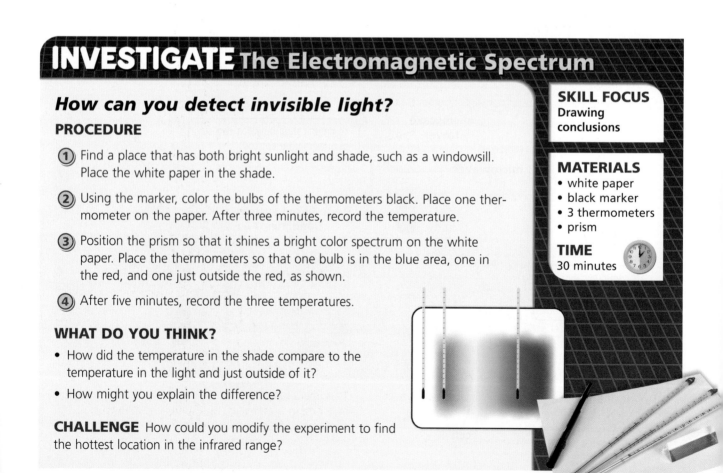

INVESTIGATE The Electromagnetic Spectrum

How can you detect invisible light?

PROCEDURE

1. Find a place that has both bright sunlight and shade, such as a windowsill. Place the white paper in the shade.

2. Using the marker, color the bulbs of the thermometers black. Place one thermometer on the paper. After three minutes, record the temperature.

3. Position the prism so that it shines a bright color spectrum on the white paper. Place the thermometers so that one bulb is in the blue area, one in the red, and one just outside the red, as shown.

4. After five minutes, record the three temperatures.

WHAT DO YOU THINK?

- How did the temperature in the shade compare to the temperature in the light and just outside of it?

- How might you explain the difference?

CHALLENGE How could you modify the experiment to find the hottest location in the infrared range?

SKILL FOCUS
Drawing conclusions

MATERIALS
- white paper
- black marker
- 3 thermometers
- prism

TIME
30 minutes

Some animals, such as pit viper snakes, can actually see infrared light. Normally, human beings cannot see infrared light. However, infrared scopes and cameras convert infrared radiation into visible wavelengths. They do this by representing different levels of infrared radiation with different colors of visible light. This technology can create useful images of objects based on the objects' temperatures.

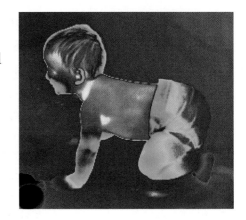

In this infrared image, warmer areas appear red and orange, while cooler ones appear blue, green, and purple.

 How do human beings perceive infrared radiation?

Ultraviolet Light

The **ultraviolet light** part of the EM spectrum consists of frequencies above those of visible light and partially below those of x-rays. Because ultraviolet (UV) light has higher frequencies than visible light, it also carries more energy. The waves in this range can damage your skin and eyes. Sunblock and UV-protection sunglasses are designed to filter out these frequencies.

Ultraviolet light has beneficial effects as well. Because it can damage cells, UV light can be used to sterilize medical instruments and food by killing harmful bacteria. In addition, UV light causes skin cells to produce vitamin D, which is essential to good health. Ultraviolet light can also be used to treat skin problems and other medical conditions.

Like infrared light, ultraviolet light is visible to some animals. Bees and other insects can see higher frequencies than people can. They see nectar guides—marks that show where nectar is located—that people cannot see with visible light. The photographs below show how one flower might look to a person and to a bee.

This photograph shows the flower as it appears in visible light.

This photograph shows the flower as it might appear to a bee in ultraviolet light. Bees are able to see nectar guides in the UV range.

X-rays and gamma rays have short wavelengths and high frequencies.

At the opposite end of the EM spectrum from radio waves are x-rays and gamma rays. Both have very high frequencies and energies. **X-rays** have frequencies from about 10^{16} Hz to 10^{21} Hz. **Gamma rays** have frequencies from about 10^{19} Hz to more than 10^{24} Hz. Like other EM waves, x-rays and gamma rays are produced by the Sun and by other stars. People have also developed technologies that use these EM frequencies.

X-rays allow us to see inside the body.

X-rays pass easily through the soft tissues of the body, but many are absorbed by denser matter such as bone. If photographic film is placed behind the body and x-rays are aimed at the film, only the x-rays that pass through the body will expose the film. This makes x-ray images useful for diagnosing bone fractures and finding dense tumors. But too much exposure to x-rays can damage tissue. Even in small doses, repeated exposure to x-rays can cause cancer over time. When you have your teeth x-rayed, you usually wear a vest made out of lead for protection. Lead blocks high-frequency radiation.

Gamma rays have the highest frequencies and energies of any EM waves. Gamma rays are produced by some radioactive substances as well as by the Sun and other stars. Gamma rays can penetrate the soft and the hard tissues of the body, killing normal cells and causing cancer cells to develop. If carefully controlled, this destructive power can be beneficial. Doctors can also use gamma rays to kill cancer cells and fight tumors.

3.2 Review

KEY CONCEPTS

1. What two properties of EM waves change from one end of the EM spectrum to the other?

2. Describe two uses for microwave radiation.

3. How are EM waves used in dentistry and medicine?

CRITICAL THINKING

4. **Infer** Why do you think remote controls for TVs, VCRs, and stereos use infrared light rather than ultraviolet light?

5. **Apply** For a camera to make images of where heat is escaping from a building in winter, what type of EM wave would it need to record?

⬥ CHALLENGE

6. **Synthesize** When a person in a car is talking on a cell phone, and the car moves from one cell to another, the conversation continues without interruption. How might this be possible?

Are Cell Phones Harmful?

In 1993, a man appearing on a popular television talk show claimed that cell phone radiation had caused his wife's brain cancer. Since that time, concerned scientists have conducted more than a dozen studies. None of them have shown clear evidence of a connection between cell phones and cancer. However, researchers have made a number of experimental observations.

▶ Experimental Observations

Here are some results from scientists' investigations.

1. Substances that cause cancer work by breaking chemical bonds in DNA.
2. Only EM radiation at ultraviolet frequencies and above can break chemical bonds.
3. Microwave radiation may make it easier for molecules called free radicals to damage DNA bonds.
4. Other factors such as psychological stress may cause breaks in DNA bonds.
5. Performing multiple tasks like driving and talking on the phone reduces the brain's ability to perform either task.
6. Exposing the brain to microwave radiation may slow reaction times.

▶ Hypotheses

Here are some hypotheses that could be used for further research.

A. Microwaves from cell phones can break DNA bonds.
B. Cell phones may contribute to cancer.
C. Holding and talking into a cell phone while driving increases a person's risk of having an accident.
D. Worrying about cell phones may be a health risk.

Talking on a cell phone while driving may increase the risk of accidents.

▶ Determining Relevance

On Your Own On a piece of paper, write down each hypothesis. Next to the hypothesis write each observation that you think is relevant. Include your reasons.

As a Group Discuss how each observation on your list is or is not relevant to a particular hypothesis.

CHALLENGE Based on the observations listed above, write a question that you think would be a good basis for a further experiment. Then explain how the answer to this question would be helpful.

KEY CONCEPT

The Sun is the source of most visible light.

◀ **BEFORE**, you learned

- Visible light is part of the EM spectrum
- EM waves are produced both in nature and by technology

▶ **NOW**, you will learn

- How visible light is produced by materials at high temperatures
- How some living organisms produce light
- How humans produce light artificially

VOCABULARY

incandescence p. 89
luminescence p. 89
bioluminescence p. 89
fluorescence p. 91

THINK ABOUT

Why is light important?

This railroad worm has eleven pairs of green lights on its sides and a red light on its head. The animal probably uses these lights for illumination and to frighten away predators. Almost every living organism, including humans, depends on visible light. Think of as many different ways as you can that plants, animals, and people use light. Then, think of all the sources of visible light that you know of, both natural and artificial. Why is light important to living organisms?

Light comes from the Sun and other natural sources.

RESOURCE CENTER
CLASSZONE.COM

Learn more about visible light.

It is hard to imagine life without light. Human beings depend on vision in countless ways, and they depend on light for vision. Light is the only form of EM radiation for which human bodies have specialized sensory organs. The human eye is extremely sensitive to light and color and the many kinds of information they convey.

Most animals depend on visible light to find food and to do other things necessary for their survival. Green plants need light to make their own food. Plants, in turn, supply food directly or indirectly for nearly all other living creatures. With very few exceptions, living creatures depend on light for their existence.

CHECK YOUR READING How is plants' use of light important to animals?

Most of the visible light waves in the environment come from the Sun. The Sun's high temperature produces light of every wavelength. The production of light by materials at high temperatures is called **incandescence** (IHN-kuhn-DEHS-uhns). When a material gets hot enough, it gives off light by glowing or by bursting into flames.

Other than the Sun, few natural sources of incandescent light strongly affect life on Earth. Most other stars give off as much light as the Sun, or even more, but little light from stars reaches Earth because they are so far away. Lightning produces bright, short-lived bursts of light. Fire, which can occur naturally, is a lower-level, longer-lasting source of visible light. The ability to make and use fire was one of the first light technologies, making it possible for human beings to see on a dark night or inside a cave.

 CHECK YOUR READING Why does little light reach Earth from stars other than the Sun?

Some living things produce visible light.

Many organisms produce their own visible light, which they use in a variety of ways. They produce this light through luminescence. **Luminescence** is the production of light without the high temperatures needed for incandescence. The production of light by living organisms is called **bioluminescence.** Bioluminescent organisms produce light from chemical reactions rather than from intense heat. Bioluminescence enables organisms to produce light inside their tissues without being harmed.

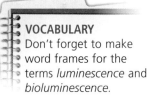 **VOCABULARY** Don't forget to make word frames for the terms *luminescence* and *bioluminescence.*

Bioluminescent organisms include insects, worms, fish, squid, jellyfish, bacteria, and fungi. Some of these creatures have light-producing organs that are highly complex. These organs might include light-producing cells but also reflectors, lenses, and even color filters.

The firefly, a type of beetle, uses bioluminescence to attract mates. A chemical reaction in its abdomen allows the firefly to glow at specific intervals. The pattern of glowing helps fireflies of the same species identify each other at night. Most often, the male flashes a signal while flying, and the female responds with a flash. After they have identified each other, the fireflies may continue to exchange flashes until the male has located the female.

The process of bioluminescence is very efficient. Almost all of the energy released by the chemical reactions of bioluminescence is converted into light. Very little heat is produced. Researchers in lighting technology wanted for years to imitate this efficiency, and that became possible with the development of light-emitting diodes (LEDs). LEDs produce little heat, converting almost all of the incoming electrical energy into light.

 CHECK YOUR READING How is bioluminescence different from incandescence?

A female firefly responds to a male's signal.

Human technologies produce visible light.

Human beings invented the first artificial lighting when they learned to make and control fire. For most of human history, people have made light with devices that use fire in some form, such as oil lamps, candles, and natural gas lamps. After the discovery of electricity, people began to make light through a means other than fire. However, the technique of using a very hot material as a light source stayed the same until the invention of fluorescent lighting. In recent years, "cool" lighting has become much more common.

INVESTIGATE Artificial Lighting

Is all artificial light the same?

Many types of artificial light sources are available. These sources differ in the amount of light they produce, the way the light beams are directed, and the characteristics of the light itself.

DESIGN — YOUR OWN — EXPERIMENT

PROCEDURE

1. Design a procedure to discover and record differences among several different types of artificial lighting. Your procedure should test how different colored materials appear in different types of lighting. You should compare the results with how these materials appear in direct sunlight.

2. Write up your experiment and carry it out.

WHAT DO YOU THINK?

- What differences did you discover among bulbs of different types and sizes?
- How would you improve your design if you were to repeat your experiment?

SKILL FOCUS
Designing experiments

MATERIALS
Artificial lighting with a variety of bulb types and sizes

TIME
30 minutes

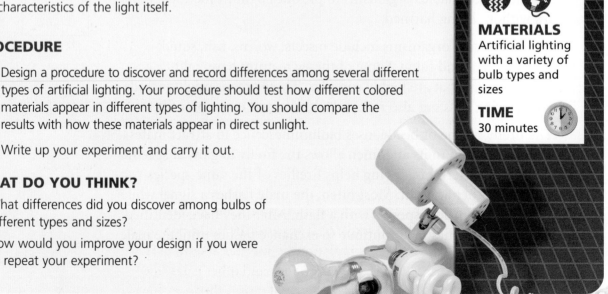

Incandescent and Fluorescent Lighting

The development of the electric light bulb in the late 1800s made light available at a touch. An ordinary light bulb is a sealed glass tube with a thin tungsten wire running through it. This wire is called a filament. When electrical current passes through the filament, the tungsten gets hotter and begins to glow. Because these light bulbs use high temperatures to produce light, they are called incandescent bulbs.

Tungsten can become very hot—about 3500 degrees Celsius (6300°F)—without melting. At such high temperatures, tungsten gives off a bright light. However, the tungsten filament also produces much infrared radiation. In fact, the filament produces more infrared light than visible light. As a result, incandescent bulbs waste a lot of energy that ends up as heat. At such high temperatures, tungsten also slowly evaporates and collects on the inside of the bulb. Eventually, the filament weakens and breaks, and the bulb burns out.

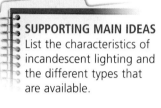

SUPPORTING MAIN IDEAS
List the characteristics of incandescent lighting and the different types that are available.

 CHECK YOUR READING What causes ordinary light bulbs to burn out?

Since the 1980s, halogen (HAL-uh-juhn) bulbs have come into wide use. Halogen bulbs have several advantages over ordinary incandescent bulbs. They contain a gas from the halogen group. This gas combines with evaporating tungsten atoms and deposits the tungsten back onto the filament. As a result, the filament lasts longer. The filament can also be raised to a higher temperature without damage, so it produces more light. Halogen bulbs, which are made of quartz, resist heat better than glass.

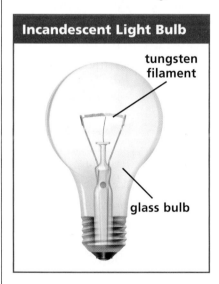

Incandescent Light Bulb

tungsten filament

glass bulb

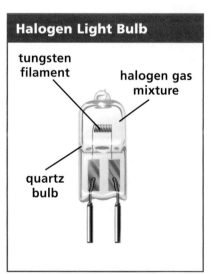

Halogen Light Bulb

tungsten filament

halogen gas mixture

quartz bulb

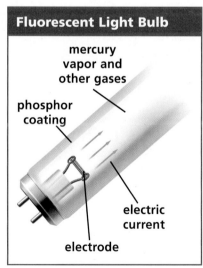

Fluorescent Light Bulb

mercury vapor and other gases

phosphor coating

electric current

electrode

Many electric lights in use today are fluorescent. **Fluorescence** (flu-REHS-uhns) occurs when a material absorbs EM radiation of one wavelength and gives off EM radiation of another. Fluorescent bulbs are filled with a mixture of mercury vapor and other gases that give off ultraviolet light when an electric current passes through them.

The insides of the bulbs are coated with a powder called phosphor that fluoresces. Phosphor absorbs ultraviolet light and gives off visible light. Because fluorescent lighting is cool and does not waste much energy as heat, it is more efficient and more economical than incandescent lighting.

 Why are fluorescent lights more efficient than incandescent lights?

Other Types of Artificial Lighting

LEDs are being used more and more in place of incandescent bulbs.

Like fluorescent lights, many other artificial light sources use a gas in place of a filament. For example, neon lights use gas-filled tubes to produce light. However, instead of ultraviolet light, the gas gives off visible light directly. The colors of neon lights come from the particular mixtures of gases and filters used. Vapor lights, which are commonly used for street lights, work in a similar way. In a vapor light, a material such as sodium is heated until it becomes a gas, or vapor. The vapor responds to an electric current by glowing brightly.

One of fastest-growing types of artificial lighting is the light emitting diode, or LED. LEDs do not involve bulbs, filaments, or gases. Instead, they produce light electronically. A diode is a type of semiconductor—a device that regulates electric current. An LED is a semiconductor that converts electric energy directly into visible light.

LEDs have many advantages over traditional forms of lighting. They produce a very bright light, do not break easily, use little energy, produce little heat, and can last for decades. Some technologists believe that LEDs will eventually replace most traditional forms of artificial lighting.

3.3 Review

KEY CONCEPTS

1. Describe natural, nonliving sources of incandescent light.

2. What advantages does bioluminescence have over incandescence as a way for living organisms to produce light?

3. What are some advantages and disadvantages of artificial incandescent lighting?

CRITICAL THINKING

4. **Classify** Make a chart summarizing the different types of artificial lighting discussed in this section.

5. **Infer** Why do you think moonlight does not warm you, even though the Moon reflects light from the hot Sun?

CHALLENGE

6. **Compare and Contrast** What does LED lighting have in common with bioluminescence? How are the two different?

KEY CONCEPT

Light waves interact with materials.

 BEFORE, you learned

- Mechanical waves respond to a change in medium
- Visible light is made up of EM waves
- EM waves interact with a new medium in the same ways that mechanical waves do

NOW, you will learn

- How the wave behavior of light affects what we see
- How light waves interact with materials
- Why objects have color
- How different colors are produced

VOCABULARY

transmission p. 93
absorption p. 93
scattering p. 95
polarization p. 96
prism p. 97
primary colors p. 98
primary pigments p. 99

EXPLORE Light and Matter

How can a change in medium affect light?

PROCEDURE

① Fill the container with water.

② Add 10 mL (2 tsp) of milk to the water. Put on the lid, and gently shake the container until the milk and water are mixed.

③ In a dark room, shine the light at one side of the container from about 5 cm (2 in.) away. Observe what happens to the beam of light.

WHAT DO YOU THINK?

- What happened to the beam of light from the flashlight?
- Why did the light behave in this way?

MATERIALS

- clear plastic container with lid
- water
- measuring spoons
- milk
- flashlight

Light can be reflected, transmitted, or absorbed.

You have read that EM waves can interact with a material medium in the same ways that mechanical waves do. Three forms of interaction play an especially important role in how people see light. One form is reflection. Most things are visible because they reflect light. The two other forms of interaction are transmission and absorption.

Transmission (trans-MIHSH-uhn) is the passage of an EM wave through a medium. If the light reflected from objects did not pass through the air, windows, or most of the eye, we could not see the objects. **Absorption** (uhb-SAWRP-shun) is the disappearance of an EM wave into the medium. Absorption affects how things look, because it limits the light available to be reflected or transmitted.

VOCABULARY
Don't forget to make word frames for *transmission* and *absorption*.

How Materials Transmit Light

Materials can be classified according to the amount and type of light they transmit.

❶ Transparent (trans-PAIR-uhnt) materials allow most of the light that strikes them to pass through. It is possible to see objects through a transparent material. Air, water, and clear glass are transparent. Transparent materials are used for items such as windows, light bulbs, thermometers, sandwich bags, and clock faces.

❷ Translucent (trans-LOO-suhnt) materials transmit some light, but they also cause it to spread out in all directions. You can see light through translucent materials, but you cannot see objects clearly through them. Some examples are lampshades, frosted light bulbs, frosted windows, sheer fabrics, and notepaper.

❸ Opaque (oh-PAYK) materials do not allow any light to pass through them, because they reflect light, absorb light, or both. Heavy fabrics, construction paper, and ceramic mugs are opaque. Shiny materials may be opaque mainly because they reflect light. Other materials, such as wood and rock, are opaque mainly because they absorb light.

CHECK YOUR READING What is the difference between translucent and opaque materials?

This stained-glass window contains transparent, translucent, and opaque materials.

A light filter is a material that is transparent to some kinds of light and opaque to others. For example, clear red glass transmits red light but absorbs other wavelengths. Examples of light filters are the colored covers on taillights and traffic lights, infrared lamp bulbs, and UV-protected sunglasses. Filters that transmit only certain colors are called color filters.

Scattering

Sometimes fine particles in a material interact with light passing through the material to cause scattering. **Scattering** is the spreading out of light rays in all directions, because particles reflect and absorb the light. Fog or dust in the air, mud in water, and scratches or smudges on glass can all cause scattering. Scattering creates glare and makes it hard to see through even a transparent material. Making the light brighter causes more scattering, as you might have noticed if you have ever tried to use a flashlight to see through fog.

Fine particles, such as those in fog, scatter light and reduce visibility.

Scattering is what makes the sky blue. During the middle of the day, when the Sun is high in the sky, molecules in Earth's atmosphere scatter the blue part of visible light more than they scatter the other wavelengths. This process makes the sky light and blue. It is too bright to see the faint stars beyond Earth's atmosphere. At dawn and dusk, light from the Sun must travel farther through the atmosphere before it reaches your eyes. By the time you see it, the greens and blues are scattered away and the light appears reddish. At night, because there is so little sunlight, the sky is dark and you can see the stars.

SUPPORTING MAIN IDEAS
Be sure to add to your chart the different ways light interacts with materials.

 How does scattering make the sky blue?

Polarization

Polarizing filters reduce glare and make it easier to see objects. **Polarization** (POH-luhr-ih-ZAY-shuhn) is a quality of light in which all of its waves vibrate in the same direction. Remember that EM waves are made of electric and magnetic fields vibrating at right angles to each other. Polarization describes the electric fields of a light wave. When all of the electric fields of a group of light waves vibrate in the same direction, the light is polarized.

Light can be polarized by a particular type of light filter called a polarizing filter. A polarizing filter acts on a light wave's electric field like the bars of a cage. The filter allows through only waves whose electric fields vibrate in one particular direction. Light that passes through the filter is polarized. In the illustration below, these waves are shown in darker yellow.

Light reflecting off the surface of this pond causes glare.

A polarizing filter reduces glare, making it possible to see objects under the water.

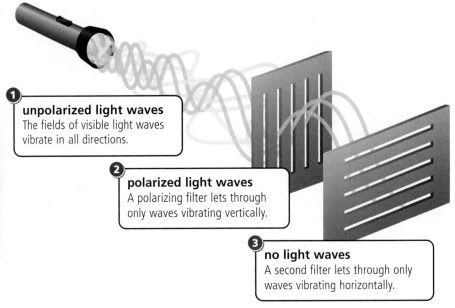

1 unpolarized light waves
The fields of visible light waves vibrate in all directions.

2 polarized light waves
A polarizing filter lets through only waves vibrating vertically.

3 no light waves
A second filter lets through only waves vibrating horizontally.

What do you think happens when polarized light passes into a second polarizing filter? If the direction of the second filter is the same as the first, then all of the light will pass through the second filter. The light will still be polarized. If the second filter is at a right angle to the first, as in the illustration above, then no light at all will pass through the second filter.

Wavelengths determine color.

The section of the EM spectrum called visible light is made up of many different wavelengths. When all of these wavelengths are present together, as in light from the Sun or a light bulb, the light appears white.

Seen individually, different wavelengths appear as different colors of light. This fact can be demonstrated by using a prism. A **prism** is a tool that uses refraction to spread out the different wavelengths that make up white light. The prism bends some of the wavelengths more than others. The lightwaves, bent at slightly different angles, form a color spectrum. The color spectrum could be divided into countless individual wavelengths, each with its own color. However, the color spectrum is usually divided into seven named color bands. In order of decreasing wavelength, the bands are red, orange, yellow, green, blue, indigo, and violet. You see a color spectrum whenever you see a rainbow.

Prisms split light into colors by refracting wavelengths in different amounts.

Color Reflection and Absorption

The color of an object or material is determined by the wavelengths it absorbs and those it reflects. An object has the color of the wavelengths it reflects. A material that reflects all wavelengths of visible light appears white. A material that absorbs all wavelengths of visible light appears black. A green lime absorbs most wavelengths but reflects green, so the lime looks green, as shown below.

1 In this simplified diagram, light of all colors strikes the lime.

2 The lime absorbs all wavelengths except green.

3 The lime reflects mostly green, so it appears green.

The color that an object appears to the eye depends on another factor besides the wavelengths the object absorbs and reflects. An object can reflect only wavelengths that are in the light that shines on it. In white light, a white object reflects all the wavelengths of visible light and appears white. If you shine only red light on a white piece of paper, however, the paper will appear red, not white, because only red light is available to be reflected.

In summary, two factors determine the color of an object: first, the wavelengths that the object itself reflects or absorbs, and second, the wavelengths present in the light that shines on the object.

 CHECK YOUR READING What color band or bands does a red apple absorb? a white flower?

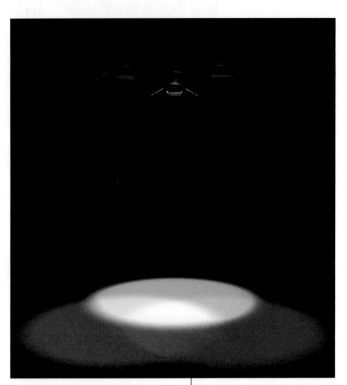

Primary Colors of Light

The human eye can detect only three color bands: red, green, and blue. Your brain perceives these three colors and various mixtures of them as all the colors. These three colors of light, which can be mixed to produce all possible colors, are called **primary colors.** When all three colors are mixed together equally, they appear white, or colorless. Whenever colored light is added to a mixture, specific wavelengths are added. Mixing colors by adding wavelengths is called additive color mixing.

An example of the practical use of primary colors is a color television or computer monitor. The screen is divided into thousands of tiny bundles of red, green, and blue dots, or pixels. A television broadcast or DVD sends signals that tell the monitor which pixels to light up and when to do so. By causing only some pixels to give off light, the monitor can mix the three colors to create an amazing variety of colorful images.

Primary colors of light combine to make the secondary colors yellow, cyan (light blue), and magenta (dark pink).

△ CHECK YOUR READING What does an equal mix of all three primary colors produce?

INVESTIGATE Mixing Colors

What is black ink made of?

PROCEDURE

1. Trim each of the filter papers to a disk about 10 cm (4 in.) in diameter. Make two parallel cuts about 1 cm (.5 in.) apart and 5 cm (2 in.) long from the edge of each disk toward the center. Fold the paper to make a flap at a right angle.

2. Use a different marker to make a dark spot in the middle of the flap on each disk.

3. Fill each of the cups with water. Set one of the disks on top of each cup so that the water covers the end of the flap but does not reach the ink spot.

4. After 15 minutes, examine each of the flaps.

WHAT DO YOU THINK?

- What did you observe about the effects of water on the ink spots?
- How do the three different samples compare?

CHALLENGE Write a hypothesis to explain what you observed about the colors in a black marker.

SKILL FOCUS
Observing

MATERIALS
- 3 coffee filters
- scissors
- 3 brands of black felt-tip marker
- 3 cups
- water

TIME
30 minutes

Primary Pigments

Remember that two factors affect an object's color. One is the wavelengths present in the light that shines on the object. The other is the wavelengths that the object's material reflects or absorbs. Materials can be mixed to produce colors just as light can. Materials that are used to produce colors are called pigments. The **primary pigments** are cyan, yellow, and magenta. You can mix primary pigments just as you can mix primary colors to produce all the colors.

The primary pigment colors are the same as the secondary colors of light. The secondary pigment colors are red, blue, and green—the same as the primary colors of light.

The effect of mixing pigments is different from the effect of mixing light. Remember that a colored material absorbs all wavelengths except those of the color it reflects. Yellow paint absorbs all wavelengths except yellow. Because pigments absorb wavelengths, whenever you mix pigments, you are subtracting wavelengths rather than adding them. Mixing colors by subtracting wavelengths is called subtractive color mixing. When all three primary pigments are mixed together in equal amounts, all wavelengths are subtracted. The result is black—the absence of reflected light.

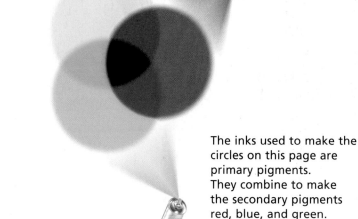

The inks used to make the circles on this page are primary pigments. They combine to make the secondary pigments red, blue, and green.

 CHECK YOUR READING How is mixing pigments different from mixing light?

3.4 Review

KEY CONCEPTS

1. What are some ways in which materials affect how light is transmitted?

2. How does a polarizing filter reduce glare?

3. In order for an object to appear white, which wavelengths must the light contain and the object reflect?

CRITICAL THINKING

4. **Apply** Imagine that you are a firefighter searching a smoke-filled apartment. Would using a stronger light help you see better? Explain your answer.

5. **Predict** Higher-energy EM waves penetrate farthest into a dense medium. What colors are more likely to penetrate to the bottom of a lake?

⬤ CHALLENGE

6. **Synthesize** If you focus a red light, a green light, and a blue light on the same part of a black curtain, what color will the curtain appear to be? Why?

CHAPTER INVESTIGATION

Wavelength and Color

OVERVIEW AND PURPOSE Lighting directors use color filters to change the look of a scene. The color an object appears depends on both the wavelengths of light shining on it and the wavelengths of light it reflects. In this exercise, you will investigate the factors that affect these wavelengths and so affect the color of an object. You will

- make a light box
- study the effect of different colors of light on objects of different colors

Problem

How does the appearance of objects of different colors change in different colors of light?

Hypothesize

Read the procedure below and look at the sample notebook page. Predict what color each object will appear in each color of light. Give a reason for each prediction.

Procedure

1. Draw a data table like the one in the sample **Science Notebook.**

2. Make 3 color filters by cutting a 10 cm (4 in.) square from each color of acetate.

3. Make a 3 cm (1 in.) wide hole in the middle of the top of the box. This will be the viewing hole.

4. Make an 8 cm (3 in.) hole in one end of the box. This will be the light hole.

5. You will observe each of the four colored objects four times—with no filter and with the red, blue, and green filters. Use masking tape to position the filters in the light hole, as shown.

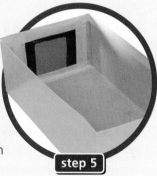
step 5

MATERIALS

- 3 sheets of acetate (red, blue, and green)
- ruler
- scissors
- shoe box
- masking tape
- light source
- 4 solid-colored objects (white, black, red, and yellow)

6 Place the light box on a flat surface near a strong white light source, such as sunlight or a bright lamp. Position the box with the uncovered light hole facing the light source. Place the white object inside the box, look through the eyehole, and observe the object's color. Record your observations.

step 7

7 Use the light box to test each of the combinations of object color and filter shown in the table on the sample notebook page. Record your results.

▶ Observe and Analyze
Write It Up

1. **RECORD OBSERVATIONS** Be sure your data table is complete.

2. **COMPARE** What color did the red object appear to be when viewed with a blue filter? a red filter?

▶ Conclude
Write It Up

1. **INTERPRET** Answer your problem question.

2. **ANALYZE** Compare your results to your predictions. How do the results support your hypothesis?

3. **IDENTIFY VARIABLES** What different variables affected the outcome of your experiment?

4. **INFER** Why do colors of objects appear to change in different types of light?

5. **IDENTIFY LIMITS** What possible limitations or sources of error could have affected your results?

6. **APPLY** If you were going to perform on a stage that was illuminated using several different color filters, what color clothing should you wear in order to look as bright and colorful as possible?

▶ INVESTIGATE Further

CHALLENGE Perform this experiment using different kinds of artificial light. Try it with a low-wattage incandescent bulb, a high-wattage incandescent bulb, a fluorescent bulb, or a full-spectrum bulb. How do different kinds of artificial light affect the colors that objects appear to be?

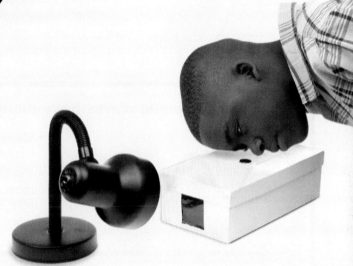

Wavelength and Color

Problem

How does the appearance of objects of different colors change in different colors of light?

Hypothesize

Observe and Analyze

Table 1. Predicted and Observed Colors of Objects with Different Colored Filters

Predicted	no filter	red filter	blue filter	green filter
white object				
black object				
red object				
yellow object				
Observed	no filter	red filter	blue filter	green filter
white object				

Chapter Review

CONTENT REVIEW
CLASSZONE.COM

the BIG idea

Electromagnetic waves transfer energy through radiation.

KEY CONCEPTS SUMMARY

3.1 Electromagnetic waves have unique traits.

- Electromagnetic (EM) waves are made of vibrating electric and magnetic fields.
- EM waves travel at the speed of light through a vacuum.
- EM waves transfer energy and can interact with matter.

VOCABULARY
electromagnetic wave p. 73
radiation p. 75

3.2 Electromagnetic waves have many uses.

- EM waves are grouped by frequency on the EM spectrum.
- The EM spectrum is divided into radio waves, microwaves, infrared light, visible light, ultraviolet light, x-rays, and gamma rays.

VOCABULARY
EM spectrum p. 80
radio waves p. 82
microwaves p. 83
visible light p. 84
infrared light p. 84
ultraviolet light p. 85
x-rays p. 86
gamma rays p. 86

3.3 The Sun is the source of most visible light.

- Most visible light in the environment comes from the Sun.
- Many living organisms produce visible light for their own use.
- Humans produce visible light artificially.

VOCABULARY
incandescence p. 89
luminescence p. 89
bioluminescence p. 89
fluorescence p. 91

3.4 Light waves interact with materials.

- Reflection, transmission, and absorption affect what light we see.
- Light can be scattered and polarized.
- Visible light is made up of many wavelengths.
- The primary colors are red, blue, and green.
- The primary pigments are yellow, cyan, and magenta.

VOCABULARY
transmission p. 93
absorption p. 93
scattering p. 95
polarization p. 96
prism p. 97
primary colors p. 98
primary pigments p. 99

Reviewing Vocabulary

Make a four-square diagram for each of the listed terms. Write the term in the center. Define the term in one square. Write characteristics, examples, and nonexamples in other squares. A sample is shown below.

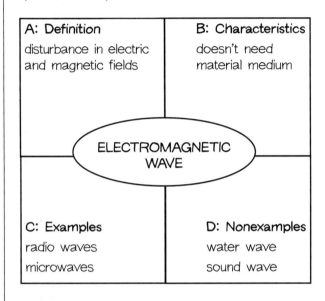

A: Definition	B: Characteristics
disturbance in electric and magnetic fields	doesn't need material medium

ELECTROMAGNETIC WAVE

C: Examples	D: Nonexamples
radio waves microwaves	water wave sound wave

1. gamma rays
2. infrared light
3. transmission
4. absorption
5. pigment
6. radiation
7. bioluminescence
8. EM spectrum
9. incandescence
10. polarization

Reviewing Key Concepts

Multiple Choice *Choose the letter of the best answer.*

11. An electromagnetic wave is a disturbance that transfers energy through a field. In this sense, a disturbance is the same as a
    a. confusion
    b. magnification
    c. vibration
    d. conflict

12. Unlike mechanical waves, EM waves can travel through
    a. a vacuum
    b. water
    c. the ground
    d. air

13. A light year is a measure of
    a. time
    b. distance
    c. speed
    d. wavelength

14. The Sun and a light bulb both produce light through
    a. bioluminescence
    b. incandescence
    c. luminescence
    d. polarization

15. Which of the following types of light bulb converts ultraviolet waves into visible light waves?
    a. incandescent
    b. fluorescent
    c. halogen
    d. tungsten

16. An object seen through translucent material appears less clear than one seen through transparent material because the translucent material
    a. transmits none of the light coming from the object
    b. reflects all the light coming from the object
    c. transmits all the light coming from the object
    d. diffuses some light coming from the object

17. An object appears red because it
    a. reflects light waves of all colors
    b. reflects light waves of red
    c. absorbs light waves of red
    d. transmits light waves of all colors

18. Primary colors of light can combine to make
    a. black light
    b. white light
    c. primary pigments
    d. ultraviolet light

Short Answer *Write a short answer to each question.*

19. What vibrates in an EM wave?

20. How can EM waves be used to measure distance?

21. Describe how microwaves are used in communications.

22. What two properties of an EM wave change as you move from one part of the EM spectrum to another?

23. How does visible light differ from other EM waves? How is it similar?

24. Explain briefly how an incandescent light bulb works.

Thinking Critically

The diagram below shows how far different wavelengths of visible light penetrate into ocean water. Use information from this diagram to answer the next three questions.

25. OBSERVE An EM wave can interact with a material in different ways. Which type of interaction keeps some light waves from reaching the ocean floor?

26. PREDICT How would violet light behave in the same water? Think of where violet is on the color spectrum.

27. SYNTHESIZE How is the apparent color of objects near the ocean floor affected by the interactions shown in the diagram?

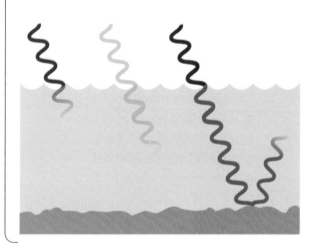

28. ANALYZE Under what circumstances can an EM wave begin to convert some of its electromagnetic energy into other forms of energy?

29. ANALYZE What two things must be true about the light source and the material of an object for you to see an object as red?

30. PREDICT If you shine a blue light on a white object, what color will the object appear to be? What color light would you need to add to make the white object appear white?

31. APPLY Why might incandescent lighting become less common in the future? Explain your reasoning.

32. IDENTIFY CAUSE AND EFFECT Liquid crystal displays like the ones used in some calculators work by polarizing light. Describe how two polarizing filters could cause the numbers on the display panel to appear black.

33. COMPARE AND CONTRAST In what way would a sieve be a good model for a polarizing light filter? In what ways would it not be?

34. CONTRAST In what ways is a fluorescent bulb more efficient than incandescent and halogen bulbs?

35. PREDICT What color will a white object appear to be if you look at it through a blue filter?

the BIG idea

36. ANALYZE Return to the question on page 70. Answer the question again, using what you have learned in the chapter.

37. SUMMARIZE Write a summary of this chapter. Use the Big Idea statement from page 70 as the title for your summary. Use the Key Concepts listed on page 70 as the topic sentences for each paragraph. Provide an example for each key concept.

38. ANALYZE Describe all of the EM wave behaviors and interactions that occur when a radiator warms a kitten.

UNIT PROJECTS

Check your schedule for your unit project. How are you doing? Be sure that you've placed data or notes from your research in your project folder.

Interpreting Diagrams

The diagram below shows part of the electromagnetic (EM) spectrum.
The lower band shows frequency in hertz. The upper band shows part of
the spectrum used by different technologies.

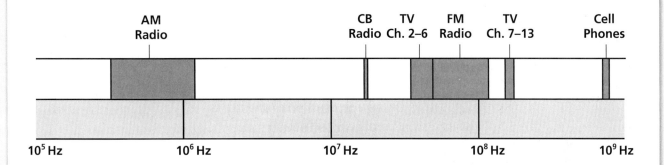

Use the diagram to answer the following questions.

1. Which of the technologies listed below
uses the highest frequencies?

  a. AM radio

  b. CB radio

  c. FM radio

  d. TV channels 2–6

2. If you were receiving a signal at a frequency of
nearly 10^9 Hz, what would you be using?

  a. a CB radio

  b. an AM radio

  c. an FM radio

  d. a cell phone

3. A television station broadcasts its video signal at
10^6 Hz and its audio signal at 10^8 Hz. To receive
the broadcasts, your television would need to use
the technologies of

  a. both AM and FM radio

  b. both CB and AM radio

  c. both CB and FM radio

  d. both CB radio and cell phone transmissions

4. Signals with similar frequencies sometimes interfere
with each other. For this reason, you might expect
interference in which of the following?

  a. lower television channels from cell phones

  b. upper television channels from FM radio

  c. lower television channels from FM radio

  d. upper television channels from cell phones

Extended Response

*Answer the two questions below in detail. Include
some of the terms from the word box. Underline
each term you use in your answer.*

frequency	energy	interaction
field	medium	vacuum

5. What are the similarities and differences between
mechanical waves and electromagnetic waves?

6. What are some advantages and disadvantages of
different types of artificial lighting?

THE STORY OF LIGHT

Light has fascinated people since ancient times. The earliest ideas about light were closely associated with beliefs and observations about vision. Over the centuries, philosophers and scientists developed an increasingly better understanding of light as a physical reality that obeyed the laws of physics.

With increased understanding of the nature and behavior of light has come the ability to use light as a tool. Many applications of light technology have led to improvements in human visual abilities. People can now make images of a wide range of objects that were invisible to earlier generations. The study of light has also led to technologies that do not involve sight at all.

This timeline shows just a few of the many steps on the road to understanding light. The boxes below the timeline show how these discoveries have been applied and developed into new technologies.

400 B.C.
Light Travels in a Straight Line
Observing the behavior of shadows, Chinese philosopher Mo-Ti finds that light travels in a straight line. His discovery helps explain why light passing through a small opening forms an upside-down image.

300 B.C.
Reflection Obeys Law
Greek mathematician Euclid discovers that light striking mirrors obeys the law of reflection. The angle at which light reflects off a mirror is equal to the angle at which it strikes the mirror.

EVENTS

450 B.C.	425 B.C.	400 B.C.	375 B.C.	350 B.C.	325 B.C.	300 B.C.

APPLICATIONS AND TECHNOLOGY

APPLICATION

Camera Obscura

The principle described by Mo-Ti in 400 B.C. led to the development of the camera obscura. When light from an object shines through a small hole into a dark room, an image of the object appears on the far wall. The darkened room is called, in Latin, *camera obscura*. Because light travels in a straight line, the highest points on the object appear at the lowest points on the image; thus, the image appears upside down. Room-sized versions of the camera obscura like the one shown here were a popular attraction in the late 1800s.

1666

White Light Is Made of Colors

British scientist Isaac Newton makes a remarkable discovery. After studying the effects of a prism on white light, Newton realizes that white light is actually made up of different colors. This contradicts the long-held belief that white light is pure light, and that colored light gets its color from the impurities of different materials.

A.D. 1000

Eyes Do Not Shoot Rays

Egyptian mathematician and astronomer Ali Alhazen publishes his *Book of Optics*. A diagram of the eye, from this book, is shown below. Alhazen proves that light travels from objects to the eyes, not the other way around. The previously accepted theory, put forth by Greek philosopher Plato centuries ago, claimed that light travels from the eyes to objects.

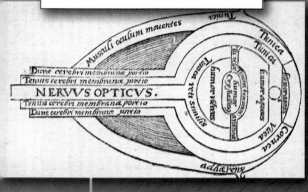

1676

Light Speeds Into Distance

Looking through a telescope, Danish astronomer Olaus Roemer observes one of Jupiter's moons "setting" earlier and earlier as Earth approaches the planet—and later and later as Earth moves farther away. Roemer infers that distance affects the time it takes light to travel from Jupiter to Earth. He estimates the speed of light as 230,000 kilometers per second.

A.D. 1000　　　1025　　　　　　　　　1625　　1650　　1675

TECHNOLOGY

Reflecting Telescopes

Early astronomers such as Galileo used refracting telescopes. These telescopes, which used a lens to gather light, were difficult to focus because of the uneven refraction of different wavelengths. Isaac Newton built the first reflecting telescope, which overcame this difficulty by using a mirror to gather light and focus an image. All major astronomical telescopes, including the Hubble Space Telescope, now use mirrors.

1821
Light Waves Move Like Ripples in a Pond
French physicist Augustin-Jean Fresnel confirms the theory that light waves are transverse waves. Like water waves, light waves vibrate at right angles to the direction of their travel. This theory helps to explain many observed behaviors of light, including diffraction fringes like those surrounding this mountain climber.

1801
Light Makes Waves
British scientist Thomas Young finds that beams of light can interact to produce an interference pattern. He aims light through two slits and observes alternating light and dark bands on a screen. Young concludes that light acts as if it were made up of waves, which contradicts the theory put forth by Newton and others that light is made up of particles.

1887
No Medium Needed
U.S. scientists Albert Michelson and Edward Morley disprove the theory that light, like other waves, must have a medium. The men devise an experiment to detect the effect of ether—material that light supposedly uses to move through space—on a light beam. The experiment shows that no ether exists and therefore that light waves need no medium.

| 1750 | 1775 | 1800 | 1825 | 1850 | 1875 | 1900 |

APPLICATION
Holograms
Holograms are used today to create images for art, communications, and research. A hologram is an interference pattern created by a collision between the two halves of a split laser beam. One half shines on film, and the other half shines on the object. The object reflects this second beam onto the film, where it creates an interference pattern with the first beam. This interference pattern captures a three-dimensional image of the object, as in this hologram of a shark.

TECHNOLOGY
Gravitational Lenses
As part of his theory of relativity, Albert Einstein predicted that light would bend in a gravitational field. His theory was confirmed in 1919. During a solar eclipse, scientists witnessed the bending of light from more distant stars as that light passed near the Sun. Astronomers take advantage of this effect to get a better look at objects deep in space. Sometimes light from a distant object passes through a closer object's gravitational field on its way to Earth. By analyzing images of the object, scientists can learn more about it.

1960
Light Beams Line Up
U.S. inventor Theodore Harold Maiman builds a working laser by stimulating emission of light in a cylinder of ruby crystal. Laser light waves all have the same wavelength, and their peaks occur together.

2001
Light Is Completely Stopped
After slowing light to the speed of a bicycle, Danish physicist Lene Vestergaard Hau brings it to a complete halt in a super-cold medium. Controlling the speed of light could revolutionize computers, communications, and other electronic technology.

RESOURCE CENTER
CLASSZONE.COM

Learn more about current research involving light.

1925   1950   1975   2000

APPLICATION
Lasers in Eye Surgery
For centuries, people have used corrective lenses to help their eyes focus images more clearly. Today, with the help of lasers, doctors can correct the eye itself. Using an ultraviolet laser, doctors remove microscopic amounts of a patient's cornea to change the way it refracts light. As a result, the eye focuses images exactly on the retina. For many nearsighted people, the surgery results in 20/20 vision or better.

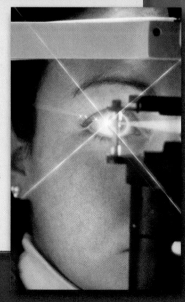

INTO THE FUTURE

Much of our current knowledge in science, from the workings of our bodies to the universe as a whole, is founded upon experiments that used light. Evidence from new light applications will continue to shape our knowledge. In the future, the nature of light, itself, may again come into question as new experiments are performed.

As new light microscopes are developed, scientists will gain more detailed information about how systems within our bodies work, such as how our brain cells interact with each other to perform a complex task. With powerful telescopes, scientists will gain a better understanding of the universe at its beginnings and how galaxies are formed.

Finally, as we continue to study the behavior of light, we may continue to modify its very definition. Sometimes considered a stream of particles, and other times considered waves, light is now understood to have qualities of both particles and waves.

ACTIVITIES

Make a Camera Obscura
Take a small box and paint the interior black. On one side, make a pinhole. On a side next to that one, make a hole about 5 cm in diameter.

On a bright, sunny day, hold the box so that sunlight enters the box through the pinhole. Fit your eye snugly against the larger hole and look inside.

Writing About Science
Lasers are currently used in entertainment, medicine, communication, supermarkets, and so on. Write a prediction about a specific use of lasers in the future. You might describe a new invention.

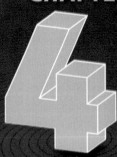

Light and Optics

the **BIG** idea

Optical tools depend on the wave behavior of light.

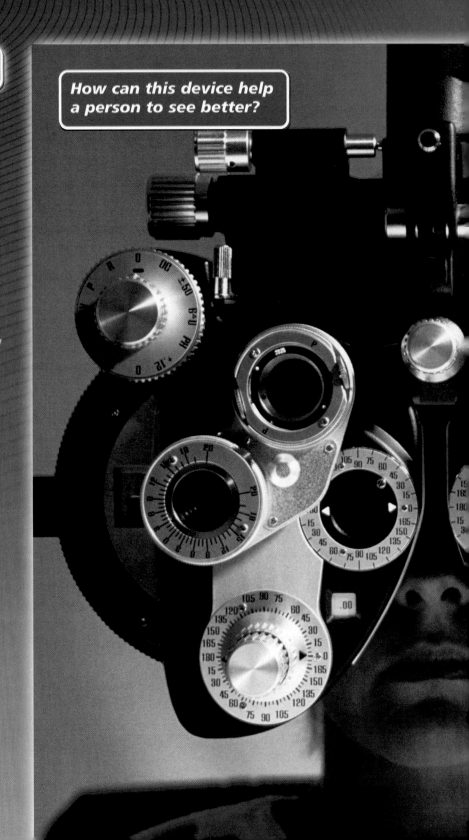

How can this device help a person to see better?

Key Concepts

SECTION
4.1 Mirrors form images by reflecting light.
Learn how mirrors use reflection to create images.

SECTION
4.2 Lenses form images by refracting light.
Learn how lenses use refraction to create images.

SECTION
4.3 The eye is a natural optical tool.
Learn about how eyes work as optical tools.

SECTION
4.4 Optical technology makes use of light waves.
Learn about complex optical tools.

Internet Preview

CLASSZONE.COM

Chapter 4 online resources: Content Review, Simulation, Visualization, three Resource Centers, Math Tutorial, Test Practice.

EXPLORE (the BIG idea)

How Does a Spoon Reflect Your Face?

Look at the reflection of your face in the bowl of a shiny metal spoon. How does your face look? Is it different from what you would expect? Now turn the spoon over and look at your face in the round side. How does your face look this time?

Observe and Think Why do the two sides of the spoon affect the appearance of your face in these ways?

Why Do Things Look Different Through Water?

Fill a clear, round jar with straight, smooth sides with water. Look through the jar at different objects in the room. Experiment with different distances between the objects and the jar and between yourself and the jar.

Observe and Think How does the jar change the way things look? What do you think causes these changes?

Internet Activity: Optics

Go to **ClassZone.com** to learn more about optics.

Observe and Think How does research in optics benefit other areas of scientific investigation?

NSTA scilinks.org **SCI**LINKS

Lenses Code: MDL030

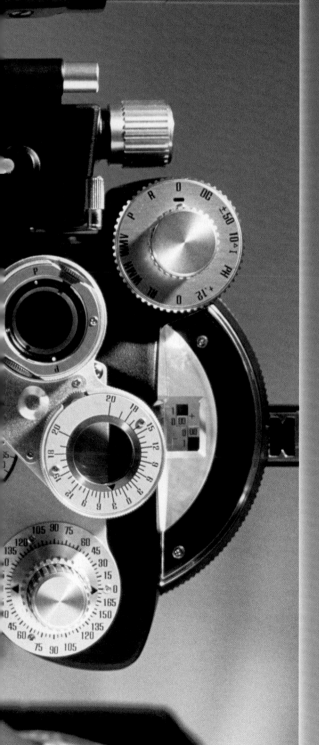

Getting Ready to Learn

◀ CONCEPT REVIEW

- Light tends to travel in a straight line.
- The speed of light is affected by a material medium.
- Reflection and refraction are two ways light interacts with materials.

◀ VOCABULARY REVIEW

reflection p. 25
refraction p. 25
visible light p. 84

CONTENT REVIEW
CLASSZONE.COM
Review concepts and vocabulary.

▶ TAKING NOTES

COMBINATION NOTES

To take notes about a new concept, first make an informal outline of the information. Then make a sketch of the concept and label it so you can study it later.

CHOOSE YOUR OWN STRATEGY

Take notes about new vocabulary terms, using one or more of the strategies from earlier chapters—**four square, description wheel,** or **frame game.** Feel free to mix and match the strategies, or to use an entirely different vocabulary strategy.

See the Note-Taking Handbook on pages R45–R51.

SCIENCE NOTEBOOK

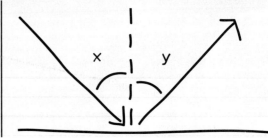

NOTES
The angle of incidence (x) equals the angle of reflection (y).

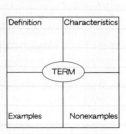

FOUR SQUARE

Definition	Characteristics
TERM	
Examples	Nonexamples

DESCRIPTION WHEEL

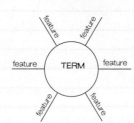

feature feature
feature TERM feature
feature feature

FRAME GAME

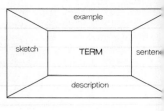

example
sketch TERM senten
description

4.1 Mirrors form images by reflecting light.

 BEFORE, you learned

- EM waves interact with materials
- Light can be reflected

 NOW, you will learn

- About the science of optics
- How light is reflected
- How mirrors form images

VOCABULARY

optics p. 113
law of reflection p. 114
regular reflection p. 114
diffuse reflection p. 114
image p. 115
convex p. 116
concave p. 116
focal point p. 117

EXPLORE Reflection

How does surface affect reflection?

PROCEDURE

1. Tear off a square sheet of aluminum foil. Look at your reflection in the shiny side of the foil.

2. Turn the foil over and look at your reflection in the dull side.

3. Crumple up the piece of foil, then smooth it out again, shiny side up. Again, look at your reflection in the foil.

WHAT DO YOU THINK?
- How did the three reflections differ from one another?
- What might explain these differences?

MATERIALS
aluminum foil

COMBINATION NOTES
Don't forget to include sketches of important concepts in your notebook.

Optics is the science of light and vision.

Optics (AHP-tihks) is the study of visible light and the ways in which visible light interacts with the eye to produce vision. Optics is also the application of knowledge about visible light to develop tools—such as eyeglasses, mirrors, magnifying lenses, cameras, and lasers—that extend vision or that use light in other ways.

Mirrors, lenses, and other optical inventions are called optical tools. By combining optical tools, inventors have developed powerful instruments to extend human vision. For example, the microscope uses a combination of mirrors and lenses to make very small structures visible. Telescopes combine optical tools to extend vision far into space. As you will see, some of the latest optical technology—lasers—use visible light in ways that do not involve human vision at all.

Mirrors use regular reflection.

You have read that when light waves strike an object, they either pass through it or they bounce off its surface. Objects are made visible by light waves, or rays, bouncing off their surfaces. In section 3 you will see how the light waves create images inside the human eye.

Light rays bounce off objects in a very predictable way. For example, look at the diagram on the left below. Light rays from a flashlight strike a mirror at an angle of 60° as measured from the normal, an imaginary line perpendicular to the surface of the mirror. This angle is called the angle of incidence. The angle at which the rays reflect off the mirror, called the angle of reflection, is also 60° as measured from the normal. The example illustrates the **law of reflection,** which states that the angle of reflection equals the angle of incidence. As you can see in the second diagram, holding the flashlight at a different angle changes both the angle of incidence and the angle of reflection. However, the two angles remain equal.

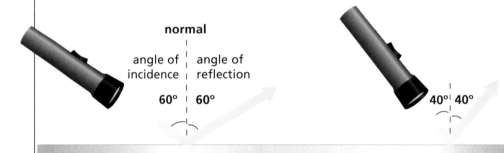

normal

angle of incidence | angle of reflection

60° | 60°

40° | 40°

The angle of reflection equals the angle of incidence.

The light rays striking the mirror bounce back by regular reflection. Rays striking everything else bounce back by diffuse reflection.

If the surface of an object is very smooth, like a mirror, light rays that come from the same direction will bounce off in the same new direction. The reflection of parallel light rays all in the same direction is called **regular reflection.**

If the surface is not very smooth—even if it feels smooth to the touch, like a piece of paper—light rays striking it from the same direction bounce off in many new directions. Each light ray follows the law of reflection, but rays coming from the same direction bounce off different bumps and hollows of the irregular surface. The reflection of parallel light rays in many different directions is called **diffuse reflection.**

How can you use mirrors to see around a corner?

SKILL FOCUS
Analyzing

PROCEDURE

1. To make a periscope, cut two flaps on opposite sides of the carton, one from the top and one from the bottom, as shown in the illustration.

2. Fold each flap inward until it is at a 45-degree angle to the side cuts and tape it into place.

3. Attach a mirror to the outside surface of each of the flaps.

4. Holding the periscope straight up, look through one of the openings. Observe what you can see through the other opening.

WHAT DO YOU THINK?

- Where are the objects you see when you look through the periscope?
- How does the angle of the mirrors affect the path of light through the periscope?

CHALLENGE How would it affect what you see through the periscope if you changed the angle of the mirrors from 45 degrees to 30 degrees? Try it.

MATERIALS
- paper milk or juice carton
- scissors
- tape
- 2 mirrors slightly smaller than the bottom of the carton
- protractor

TIME
30 minutes

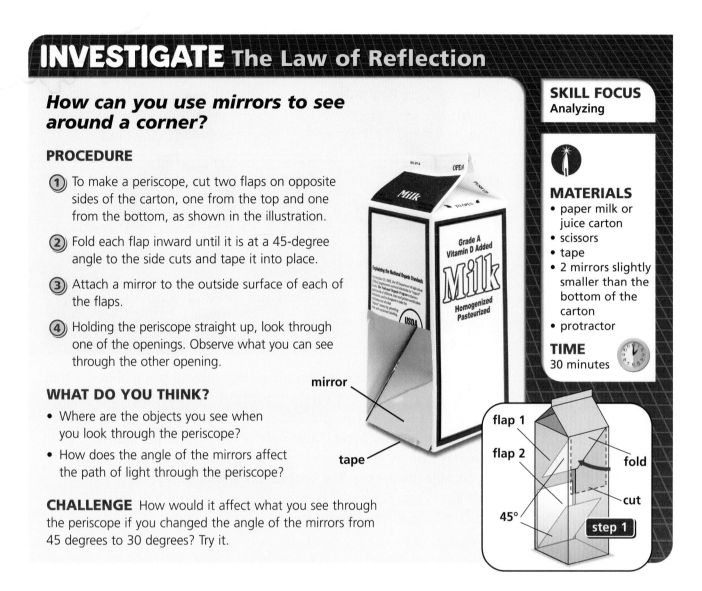

mirror

tape

flap 1

flap 2

fold

cut

45°

step 1

Shape determines how mirrors form images.

When you look in a mirror, you see an image of yourself. An **image** is a picture of an object formed by waves of light. The image of yourself is formed by light waves reflecting off you, onto the mirror, and back toward your eyes. Mirrors of different shapes can produce images that are distorted in certain ways.

VISUALIZATION
CLASSZONE.COM

See reflection in action.

Flat Mirrors

Your image in a flat mirror looks exactly like you. It appears to be the same size as you, and it's wearing the same clothes. However, if you raise your right hand, the image of yourself in the mirror will appear to raise its left hand. That is because you see the image as a person standing facing you. In fact, your right hand is reflected on the right side of the image, and your left on the left side.

CHECK YOUR READING If you wink your left eye while looking in the mirror, which eye in the image of you will wink?

The solid line shows the actual path of light. The broken line shows where the light appears to be coming from.

If you look closely at your image in a mirror, you will notice that it actually appears to be on the far side of the mirror, exactly as far from the mirror as you are. This is a trick of light. The solid yellow arrows in the photograph above show the path of the light rays from the boy's elbow to the mirror and back to his eyes. The light rays reflect off the mirror. The broken line shows the apparent path of the light rays. They appear to his eyes to be coming through the mirror from a spot behind it.

Concave and Convex Mirrors

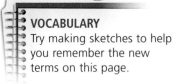

VOCABULARY
Try making sketches to help you remember the new terms on this page.

Unlike light rays hitting a flat mirror, parallel light rays reflecting off a curved mirror do not move in the same direction. A **convex** mirror is curved outward, like the bottom of a spoon. In a convex mirror, parallel light rays move away from each other, as you can see in the diagram below on the left. A **concave** mirror is curved inward toward the center, like the inside of a spoon. Parallel light rays reflecting off a concave mirror move toward each other, as shown on the right.

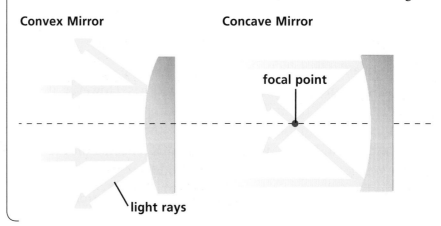

Convex Mirror   Concave Mirror

focal point

light rays

The rays striking a concave mirror cross and then move apart again. The point at which the rays meet is called the **focal point** of the mirror. The distance between the mirror and its focal point depends on the shape of the curve.

The images formed in these mirrors depend on the curve of the mirror's surface and the distance of the object from the mirror. Your image in a curved mirror may appear larger or smaller than you are, and it may even be upside down.

Convex Mirror

Your image in a convex mirror appears smaller than you.

Concave Mirror, Far Away

If you are standing far away, your image in a concave mirror appears upside down and smaller than you.

Concave Mirror, Up Close

If you are standing inside the focal point, your image in a concave mirror appears right-side up and larger.

All rays parallel to a line through the center of the mirror are reflected off the mirror and pass through the mirror's focal point. Rays from the top of the object are reflected downward and those from the bottom are reflected upward.

 CHECK YOUR READING How does your distance from the mirror affect the way your image appears in a concave mirror?

 Review

KEY CONCEPTS

1. Explain the term *optics* in your own words.

2. How is diffuse reflection similar to regular reflection? How is it different?

3. Describe the path that light rays take when they form an image of your smile when you look into a flat mirror.

CRITICAL THINKING

4. **Infer** Imagine seeing your reflection in a polished table top. The image is blurry and hard to recognize. What can you tell about the surface of the table from your observations?

5. **Analyze** Why do images formed by concave mirrors sometimes appear upside down?

CHALLENGE

6. **Synthesize** Draw the letter *R* below as it would appear if you held the book up to (a) a flat mirror and (b) a convex mirror.

R

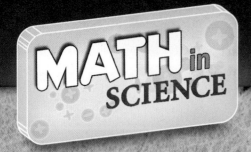

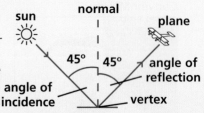

SKILL: MEASURING ANGLES

Send Help!

MATH TUTORIAL
CLASSZONE.COM

Click on Math Tutorial for
more help with measuring
angles.

Survival kits often contain a small mirror that can be used to signal
for help. If you were lost in the desert and saw a search plane overhead, you could use the mirror to reflect sunlight toward the plane
and catch the pilot's attention. To aim your signal, you would use
the law of reflection. The angle
at which a ray of light bounces
off a mirror—the angle of reflection—is always equal to the
angle at which the ray strikes the
mirror—the angle of incidence.

Example

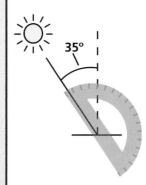

**Measure the angle of incidence using a
protractor as follows:**

(1) Place the center mark of the
protractor over the vertex of the
angle formed by the incident ray
and the normal.

(2) Place the left 0° mark of the
protractor on the incident ray.

(3) Read the number where the normal
crosses the scale (35°).

(4) The angle of incidence is 35°.

ANSWER Therefore, the angle of reflection will be 35°.

**Copy each of the following angles of incidence, extend its
sides, and use a protractor to measure it.**

1.   2.   3.   4.

CHALLENGE Copy the drawing below. Use a protractor to
find the angle of reflection necessary to signal the plane
from point A.

• A

A mirror can
be used to
signal for help.

4.2 Lenses form images by refracting light.

◀ **BEFORE, you learned**

- Waves can refract when they move from one medium to another
- Refraction changes the direction of a wave

▶ **NOW, you will learn**

- How a material medium can refract light
- How lenses control refraction
- How lenses produce images

VOCABULARY

lens p. 121
focal length p. 123

EXPLORE Refraction

How does material bend light?

PROCEDURE

① Place the pencil in the cup, as shown in the photograph. Look at the cup from the side so that you see part of the pencil through the cup.

② Fill the cup one-third full with water and repeat your observations.

③ Gently add oil until the cup is two-thirds full. After the oil settles into a separate layer, observe.

WHAT DO YOU THINK?

- How did the appearance of the pencil change when you added the water? the oil?
- What might explain these changes?

MATERIALS

- clear plastic cup
- pencil
- water
- mineral oil

A medium can refract light.

When sunlight strikes a window, some of the light rays reflect off the surface of the glass. Other rays continue through the glass, but their direction is slightly changed. This slight change in direction is called refraction. Refraction occurs when a wave strikes a new medium—such as the window—at an angle other than 90° and keeps going forward in a slightly different direction.

Refraction occurs because one side of the wave reaches the new medium slightly before the other side does. That side changes speed, while the other continues at its previous speed, causing the wave to turn.

 CHECK YOUR READING How does the motion of a light wave change when it refracts?

Refraction of Light

COMBINATION NOTES
Sketch the ways light is refracted when it moves into a denser medium and into a thinner medium.

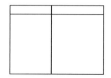

Recall that waves travel at different speeds in different mediums. The direction in which a light wave turns depends on whether the new medium slows the wave down or allows it to travel faster. Like reflection, refraction is described in terms of an imaginary line—called the normal—that is perpendicular to the new surface. If the medium slows the wave, the wave will turn toward the normal. If the new medium lets the wave speed up, the wave will turn away from the normal. The wave in the diagram below turns toward the normal as it slows down in the new medium.

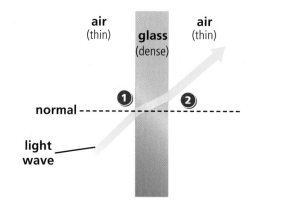

air (thin) glass (dense) air (thin)

normal

light wave

1 Waves moving at an angle into a denser medium turn toward the normal.

2 Waves moving at an angle into a thinner medium turn away from the normal.

Light from the Sun travels toward Earth through the near vacuum of outer space. Sunlight refracts when it reaches the new medium of Earth's upper atmosphere. Earth's upper atmosphere is relatively thin and refracts light only slightly. Denser materials, such as water and glass, refract light more.

By measuring the speed of light in different materials and comparing this speed to the speed of light in a vacuum, scientists have been able to determine exactly how different materials refract light. This knowledge has led to the ability to predict and control refraction, which is the basis of much optical technology.

READING TiP

A dense medium has more mass in a given volume than a thin medium.

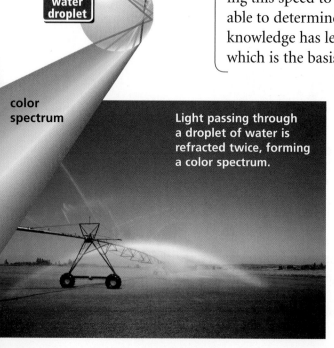

light

water droplet

color spectrum

Light passing through a droplet of water is refracted twice, forming a color spectrum.

Refraction and Rainbows

You've seen rainbows in the sky after a rainstorm or hovering in the spray of a sprinkler. Rainbows are caused by refraction and reflection of light through spherical water drops, which act as prisms. Just as a prism separates the colors of white light, producing the color spectrum, each water drop separates the wavelengths of sunlight to produce a spectrum. Only one color reaches your eye from each drop. Red appears at the top of a rainbow because it is coming from higher drops, while violet comes from lower drops.

Shape determines how lenses form images.

When you look at yourself in a flat mirror, you see your image clearly, without distortions. Similarly, when you look through a plain glass window, you can see what is on the other side clearly. Just as curved mirrors distort images, certain transparent mediums called lenses alter what you see through them. A **lens** is a clear optical tool that refracts light. Different lenses refract light in different ways and form images useful for a variety of purposes.

READING **TiP**

Distort means to change the shape of something by twisting or moving the parts around.

Convex and Concave Lenses

Like mirrors, lenses can be convex or concave. A convex lens is curved outward; a concave lens is curved inward. A lens typically has two sides that are curved, as shown in the illustration below.

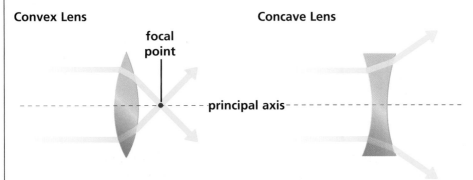

Convex Lens

focal point

principal axis

A convex lens causes parallel light rays to meet at a focal point.

Concave Lens

A concave lens causes parallel light rays to spread out.

Convex Parallel light rays passing through a convex lens are refracted inward. They meet at a focal point on the other side of the lens. The rays are actually refracted twice—once upon entering the lens and once upon leaving it. This is because both times they are entering a new medium at an angle other than 90 degrees. Rays closest to the edges of the lens are refracted most. Rays passing through the center of the lens—along the principal axis, which connects the centers of the two curved surfaces—are not refracted at all. They pass through to the same focal point as all rays parallel to them.

REMINDER

The focal point is the point at which parallel light rays meet after being reflected or refracted.

Concave Parallel light rays that pass through a concave lens are refracted outward. As with a convex lens, the rays are refracted twice. Rays closest to the edges of the lens are refracted most; rays at the very center of the lens pass straight through without being deflected. Because they are refracted away from each other, parallel light rays passing through a concave lens do not meet.

CHECK YOUR READING   Compare what happens to parallel light rays striking a concave mirror with those striking a concave lens.

How a Convex Lens Forms an Image

A convex lens forms an image by refracting light rays. Light rays reflected from an object are refracted when they enter the lens and again when they leave the lens. They meet to form the image.

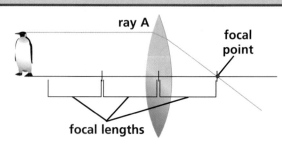

① Light rays reflect off the penguin in all directions, and many enter the lens. Here a single ray (A) from the top of the penguin enters the lens and is refracted downward.

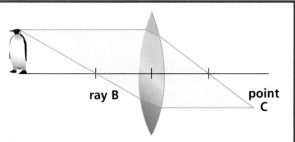

② Another light ray (B) from the top of the penguin passes through the lens at the bottom and meets the first ray at point C. All of the rays from the top of the penguin passing through the lens meet at this point.

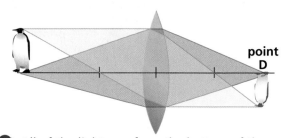

③ All of the light rays from the bottom of the penguin meet at a different point (D). Light rays from all parts of the penguin meet at corresponding points on the image.

READING VISUALS Where do light rays reflected from the middle of the penguin meet?

Images Formed by Lenses

When light rays from an object pass through a lens, an image of the object is formed. The type of image depends on the lens and, for convex lenses, on the distance between the lens and the object.

SIMULATION
CLASSZONE.COM

Work with convex and concave lenses to form images.

Notice the distance between the penguin and the lens in the illustration on page 122. The distance is measured in terms of a **focal length,** which is the distance from the center of the lens to the lens's focal point. The penguin is more than two focal lengths from the camera lens, which means the image formed is upside down and smaller.

If the penguin were between one and two focal lengths away from a convex lens, the image formed would be upside down and larger. Overhead projectors form this type of image, which is then turned right side up by a mirror and projected onto a screen for viewing.

Finally, if an object is less than one focal length from a convex lens, it will appear right side up and larger. In order to enlarge an object so that you can see details, you hold a magnifying lens close to the object. In the photograph, you see a face enlarged by a magnifying lens. The boy's face is less than one focal length from the lens.

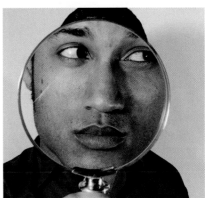

If you look at an object through a concave lens, you'll see an image of the object that is right side up and smaller than the object normally appears. In the case of concave lenses, the distance between the object and the lens does not make a difference in the type of image that is formed. In the next section you'll see how the characteristics of the images formed by different lenses play a role in complex optical tools.

CHECK YOUR READING When will an image formed by a convex lens be upside down?

4.2 Review

KEY CONCEPTS

1. What quality of a material affects how much it refracts light?
2. How does the curve in a lens cause it to refract light differently from a flat piece of glass?
3. How does a camera lens form an image?

CRITICAL THINKING

4. **Infer** You look through a lens and see an image of a building upside down. What type of lens are you looking through?
5. **Make a Model** Draw the path of a light ray moving at an angle from air into water. Write a caption to explain the process.

CHALLENGE

6. Study the diagram on the opposite page. Describe the light rays that would pass through the labeled focal point. Where are they coming from, and how are they related to each other?

CHAPTER INVESTIGATION

Looking at Lenses

OVERVIEW AND PURPOSE Optical tools such as microscopes, telescopes, and eyeglasses use lenses to create images of objects. In this lab, you will use what you have learned about light and lenses to
- experiment with a convex lens to focus images of objects
- determine what makes it possible to focus images of objects.

▶ Procedure

PART A

1. Make a data table like the one shown on the sample notebook page.

2. Draw a stick figure on one index card. Assemble the cards, clay, and lens as shown in the photograph.

3. Position the convex lens so that you can see an enlarged, right-side up image of the stick figure. Measure the distances between the lens and the card, and between the lens and your eye. Record the distances in your data table.

4. Position the lens so that you can see an enlarged, upside down image of the stick figure. Measure the distances between the lens and the object, and between the lens and your eye. Record the distances in your data table.

5. Position the lens so that you can see a reduced, upside down image of the stick figure. Measure the distances between the lens and the object, and between the lens and your eye. Record the distances in your data table.

MATERIALS
- index cards
- marker
- modeling clay
- convex lens
- books
- meter stick
- flashlight
- masking tape
- white poster board

PART B

6 Put an arrow made of tape on the lens of the flashlight as shown.

7 Assemble poster board and clay to make a screen. Arrange the flashlight, lens, and screen as shown below right.

step 6

8 Shine the beam from the flashlight through the lens to form an enlarged, upside down image on the screen. Measure the distances between the lens and the flashlight and between the lens and the screen.

9 Position the light and screen to produce a reduced, upside down image. Measure the distances between the lens and the flashlight and between the lens and the screen.

10 Position the light and screen to produce an enlarged right-side up image.

▶ Observe and Analyze   Write It Up

1. **RECORD OBSERVATIONS** Draw pictures of each setup in steps 3–9 to show what happened. Be sure your data table is complete.

2. **ANALYZE** What was the distance from the lens to the object in step 3? Answer this question for each of the other steps. How do the distances compare?

3. **ANALYZE** What happened when you tried to form the three types of images on the screen? How can you explain these results?

▶ Conclude   Write It Up

1. **ANALYZE** What conclusions can you draw about the relationship between the distances you measured and the type of image that was produced?

2. **IDENTIFY LIMITS** Describe possible sources of error in your procedure or any places where errors might have occurred.

3. **APPLY** What kind of lenses are magnifying glasses? When a magnifying glass produces a sharp clear image, where is the object located in relation to the lens?

step 7

▶ INVESTIGATE Further

CHALLENGE If you were to repeat steps 8 and 9 with a concave lens, you would not be able to focus an image on the screen. Why not?

Looking at Lenses
Observe and Analyze
Table 1. Distances from Lens

Image	Object	Eye
Object enlarged and right-side up		
Object enlarged and upside down		
Object reduced and upside down		
	Flashlight	Screen
Object enlarged and right-side up		
Object enlarged and upside down		
Object reduced and upside down		

Conclude

4.3 The eye is a natural optical tool.

BEFORE, you learned

• Mirrors and lenses focus light to form images
• Mirrors and lenses can alter images in useful ways

NOW, you will learn

• How the eye depends on natural lenses
• How artificial lenses can be used to correct vision problems

VOCABULARY

cornea p. 127
pupil p. 127
retina p. 127

EXPLORE Focusing Vision

How does the eye focus an image?

PROCEDURE

① Position yourself so you can see an object about 6 meters (20 feet) away.

② Close one eye, hold up your index finger, and bring it as close to your open eye as you can while keeping the finger clearly in focus.

③ Keeping your finger in place, look just to the side at the more distant object and focus your eye on it.

④ Without looking away from the more distant object, observe your finger.

WHAT DO YOU THINK?

• How does the nearby object look when you are focusing on something distant?
• What might be happening in your eye to cause this change in the nearby object?

The eye gathers and focuses light.

The eyes of human beings and many other animals are natural optical tools that process visible light. Eyes transmit light, refract light, and respond to different wavelengths of light. Eyes contain natural lenses that focus images of objects. Eyes convert the energy of light waves into signals that can be sent to the brain. The brain interprets these signals as shape, brightness, and color. Altogether, these processes make vision possible.

In this section, you will learn how the eye works. You will also learn how artificial lenses can be used to improve vision.

How Light Travels Through the Human Eye

1 Light enters the eye through the **cornea** (KAWR-nee-uh), a transparent membrane that covers the eye. The cornea acts as a convex lens and does most of the refracting in the eye.

2 The light then continues through the **pupil,** a circular opening that controls how much light enters the eye. The pupil is surrounded by the iris, which opens and closes to change the size of the pupil.

3 Next the light passes through the part of the eye called the lens. The lens is convex on both sides. It refracts light to make fine adjustments for near and far objects. Unlike the cornea, the lens is attached to tiny muscles that contract and relax to control the amount of refraction that occurs and to move the focal point.

4 The light passes through the clear center of the eye and strikes the **retina** (REHT-uhn-uh). The retina contains specialized cells that respond to light. Some of these cells send signals through the optic nerve to the brain. The brain interprets these signals as images.

> **READING TiP**
>
> The word *lens* can refer both to an artificial optical tool and to a specific part of the eye.

How the Human Eye Forms an Image

The cornea and lens together focus a reduced, inverted image on the retina.

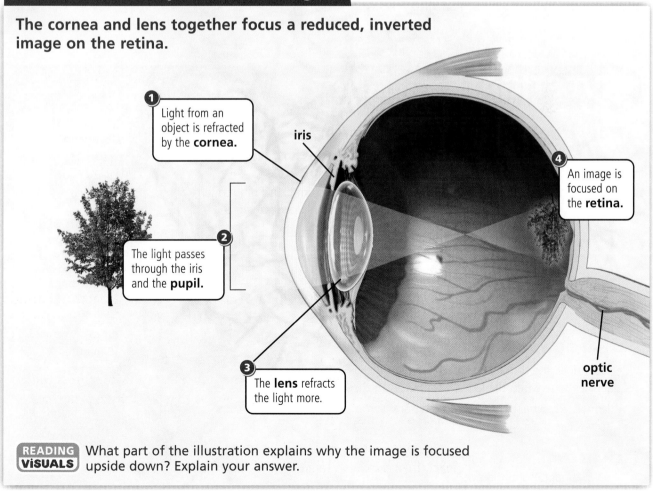

1 Light from an object is refracted by the **cornea.**

iris

4 An image is focused on the **retina.**

2 The light passes through the iris and the **pupil.**

3 The **lens** refracts the light more.

optic nerve

READING VISUALS What part of the illustration explains why the image is focused upside down? Explain your answer.

How the Eye Forms Images

COMBINATION NOTES
Make a chart showing how light interacts with different parts of the eye.

For you to see an object clearly, your eye must focus an image of the object on your retina. The light reflected from each particular spot on the object must converge on a matching point on your retina. Many such points make up an image of an entire object. Because the light rays pass through the lens's focal point, the image is upside down. The brain interprets this upside down image as an object that is right-side up.

For a complete image to be formed in the eye and communicated to the brain, more than the lens and the cornea are needed. The retina also plays an important role. The retina contains specialized cells that detect brightness and color and other qualities of light.

Rod Cells Rod cells distinguish between white and black and shades of gray. Rods respond to faint light, so they help with night vision.

Cone Cells Cone cells respond to different wavelengths of light, so they detect color. There are three types of cones, one for each of the colors red, blue, and green. Cones respond to other colors with combinations of these three, as the screen of a color monitor does. The brain interprets these combinations as the entire color spectrum.

 CHECK YOUR READING Which type of cell in the retina detects color?

INVESTIGATE Vision

How does distance affect vision?

PROCEDURE

1. Arrange the materials as shown so that the lamp shines through the lens onto the plate. The lens should be about $\frac{2}{3}$ a meter from the lamp.

2. Adjust the distance between the plate and the lens until you see a focused image of the bulb on the plate. Measure this distance.

3. Move the lens until it is about a meter and a half from the lamp. Adjust the plate once again to get a focused image, then measure the distance between the plate and the lens.

WHAT DO YOU THINK?

- How does the distance needed between the plate and the lens change when the lamp is farther from the lens?

- How is what happens in the eye different from what you did to refocus the image?

CHALLENGE How could you change the model to make it more like what happens in the eye?

SKILL FOCUS
Observing

MATERIALS
- convex lens
- index card
- modeling clay
- white paper plate
- lamp

TIME
10 minutes

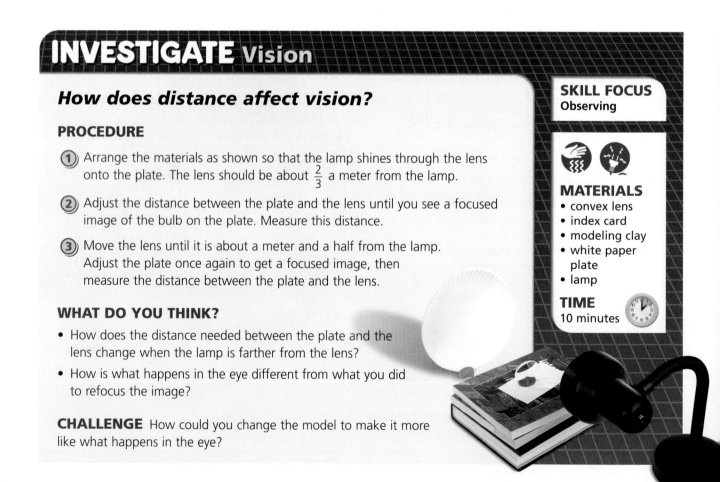

Corrective lenses can improve vision.

What happens when the image formed by the lens of the eye does not fall exactly on the retina? The result is that the image appears blurry. This can occur either because of the shape of the eye or because of how the lens works. Artificial lenses can be used to correct this problem.

Corrective Lenses

A person who is nearsighted cannot see objects clearly unless they are near. Nearsightedness occurs when the lens of the eye focuses the image in front of the retina. The farther away the object is, the farther in front of the retina the image forms. This problem can be corrected with glasses made with concave lenses. The concave lenses spread out the rays of light before they enter the eye. The point at which the rays meet then falls on the retina.

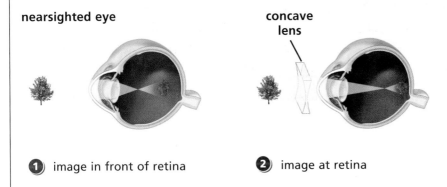

nearsighted eye   **concave lens**

1 image in front of retina   **2** image at retina

Objects are clearer to a farsighted person when the objects are farther away. Farsightedness occurs when the lens of the eye focuses an object's image behind the retina. This condition can result from aging, which may make the lens less flexible. The closer the object is, the farther behind the retina the image forms. Farsightedness can be corrected with glasses made from convex lenses. The convex lenses bend the light rays inward before they enter the eye. The point at which the rays meet then falls on the retina.

READING **TiP**

Nearsighted people can see objects near to them best. *Farsighted* people can see objects better when the objects are farther away.

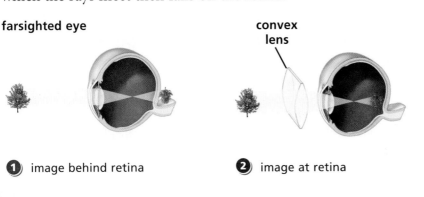

farsighted eye   **convex lens**

1 image behind retina   **2** image at retina

CHECK YOUR READING What kind of lens is used for correcting nearsightedness?

Surgery and Contact Lenses

Wearing glasses is an effective way to correct vision. It is also possible to change the shape of the cornea to make the eye refract properly. The cornea is responsible for two-thirds of the refraction that takes place inside the eye. As you know, the eye's lens changes shape to focus an image, but the shape of the cornea does not ordinarily change.

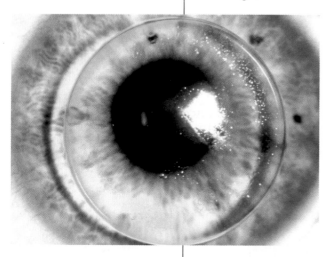

However, using advanced surgical technology, doctors can change the shape of the cornea. By doing this, they change the way light rays focus in the eye so that the image lines up with the retina. To correct for nearsightedness, surgeons remove tissue from the center of the cornea. This flattens the cornea and makes it less convex so that it will refract less. To correct for farsightedness, surgeons remove tissue from around the edges of the cornea. This increases the cornea's curvature to make it refract more. Surgery changes the shape of the cornea permanently and can eliminate the need for eyeglasses.

Contact lenses fit directly onto the cornea, changing the way light is refracted as it enters a person's eye.

Contact lenses also correct vision by changing the way the cornea refracts light. Contact lenses are corrective lenses that fit directly onto the cornea. The lenses actually float on a thin layer of tears. The moisture, the contact lens, and the cornea all function together. The lens of the eye then focuses the light further. Because the change is temporary, contacts, like eyeglasses, can be adapted to new changes in the eye.

 CHECK YOUR READING What are two ways of changing the way the cornea refracts light to correct vision?

4.3 Review

KEY CONCEPTS

1. Where are images focused in an eye with perfect vision?

2. What causes people with nearsightedness to see blurry images of objects at a distance?

3. What kind of lens is used for correcting farsightedness? Why?

CRITICAL THINKING

4. **Make a Model** Draw a diagram to answer the following question: How does a convex lens affect the way a nearsighted eye focuses an image?

5. **Analyze** What distance would an eye doctor need to measure to correct a problem with nearsightedness or farsightedness?

⚠ CHALLENGE

6. **Apply** A person alternates between wearing glasses and wearing contact lenses to correct farsightedness. Are the contact lenses more or less convex than the lenses of the glasses? Explain the reasoning behind your response.

4.4 Optical technology makes use of light waves.

◀ BEFORE, you learned

- Mirrors are optical tools that use reflection
- Lenses are optical tools that use refraction
- The eye is a natural optical tool
- Lenses can correct vision

▶ NOW, you will learn

- How mirrors and lenses can be combined to make complex optical tools
- How optical tools are used to extend natural vision
- How laser light is made and used in optical technology

VOCABULARY

laser p. 135
fiber optics p. 137

EXPLORE Combining Lenses

How can lenses be combined?

PROCEDURE

1. Assemble the lenses, clay, and index cards as shown in the photograph.

2. Line the lenses up so that you have a straight line of sight through them.

3. Experiment with different distances between
   - the lenses
   - the far lens and an object
   - the near lens and your eye
   Find an arrangement that allows you to see a clear image of an object through both lenses.

MATERIALS

- 2 convex lenses
- modeling clay
- 2 index cards

WHAT DO YOU THINK?

- What kind of image could you see? What arrangement or arrangements work best to produce an image?
- How do you think the lenses are working together to focus the image?

Mirrors and lenses can be combined to make more powerful optical tools.

COMBINATION NOTES
As you read this section, make a list of optical tools. Add sketches to help you remember important concepts.

If you know about submarines, then you know how much they depend on their periscopes to see above the water. Periscopes are made by combining mirrors. Lenses can also be combined. In the eye, for example, the cornea and the eye's lens work together to focus an image. Mirrors and lenses can be combined with each other, as they are in an overhead projector. Many of the most powerful and complex optical tools are based on different combinations of mirrors and lenses.

Microscopes

Microscopes are used to see objects that are too small to see well with the naked eye. An ordinary microscope works by combining convex lenses. The lens closer to the object is called the objective. The object is between one and two focal lengths from this lens, so the lens focuses an enlarged image of the object inside the microscope.

The other microscope lens—the one you look through—is called the eyepiece. You use this lens to look at the image formed by the objective. Like a magnifying glass, the eyepiece lens forms an enlarged image of the first image.

Very small objects do not reflect much light. Most microscopes use a lamp or a mirror to shine more light on the object.

 CHECK YOUR READING Which types of images do the lenses in a microscope form?

Telescopes

Telescopes are used to see objects that are too far away to see well with the naked eye. One type of telescope, called a refracting telescope, is made by combining lenses. Another type of telescope, called a reflecting telescope, is made by combining lenses and mirrors.

RESOURCE CENTER
CLASSZONE.COM

Find out more about microscopes and telescopes.

Refracting telescopes combine convex lenses, just as microscopes do. However, the objects are far away from the objective lens instead of near to it. The object is more than two focal lengths from the objective lens, so the lens focuses a reduced image of the object inside the telescope. The eyepiece of a telescope then forms an enlarged image of the first image, just as a microscope does. This second image enlarges the object.

Reflecting telescopes work in the same way that refracting telescopes do. However, there is no objective lens where light enters the telescope. Instead, a concave mirror at the opposite end focuses an image of the object. A small flat mirror redirects the image to the side of the telescope. With this arrangement, the eyepiece does not interfere with light on its way to the concave mirror. The eyepiece then forms an enlarged image of the first image.

Both refracting and reflecting telescopes must adjust for the small amount of light received from distant objects. The amount of light gathered can be increased by increasing the diameter of the objective lens or mirror. Large mirrors are easier and less expensive to make than large lenses. So reflecting telescopes can produce brighter images more cheaply than refracting telescopes.

 CHECK YOUR READING How is a reflecting telescope different from a refracting telescope?

Microscopes and Telescopes

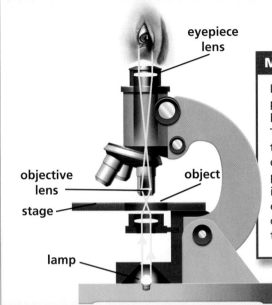

eyepiece lens

objective lens

stage

lamp

object

Microscope

Light from an object passes through a convex lens called an objective. The objective lens focuses the light to form an enlarged image. The eyepiece lens enlarges the image even more. The one-celled algae at right, called diatoms, appear 400 times their normal size.

diatoms

Refracting Telescope

surface of the Moon

The objective lens gathers and focuses light from a distant object to form an image of the object. The eyepiece enlarges the image. The telescope image of the Moon at left shows fine details of the lunar surface.

objective lens

light

eyepiece lens

Reflecting Telescope

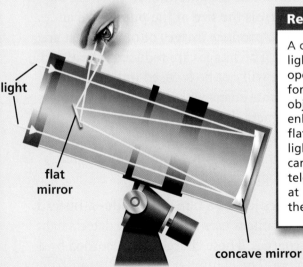

light

flat mirror

concave mirror

A concave mirror gathers light through a wide opening and focuses it to form an image of the object. The eyepiece lens enlarges the image. The flat mirror redirects the light so that the eyepiece can be out of the way. The telescope image of Saturn at right shows details of the planet's rings.

the planet Saturn

READING VISUALS Which type of telescope is similar in construction to a microscope?

INVESTIGATE Optical Tools

How can you make a simple telescope?

Use what you have learned about how a telescope works to build one. Figure out how far apart the two lenses need to be and use that information to construct a working model.

PROCEDURE

① Decide how the lenses should be positioned in relation to an object you select to view.

② Adjust the lenses until you get a clear image.

③ Use the other materials to fix the lenses into place and to make it possible to adjust the distance between them.

WHAT DO YOU THINK?

• How did you end up positioning the lenses in relation to the object?

• Did your telescope work? Why do you think you got this result?

CHALLENGE Is your telescope image upside down or right-side up? How can you explain this observation?

SKILL FOCUS
Making models

MATERIALS
• 2 convex lenses
• 2 cardboard tubes
• duct tape

TIME
30 minutes

Cameras

Most film cameras focus images in the same way that the eye does. The iris of a camera controls the size of the aperture, an opening for light, just as the iris of an eye controls the size of the pupil. Like an eye, a camera uses a convex lens to produce images of objects that are more than two focal lengths away. The images are reduced in size and upside down. In the eye, an image will not be focused unless it falls exactly on the retina. In a camera, an image will not be focused unless it falls exactly on the film. The camera does not change the shape of its lens as the eye does to change the focal point. Instead, the camera allows you to move the lens nearer to or farther away from the film until the object you want to photograph is in focus.

A digital camera focuses images just as a film camera does. Instead of using film, though, the digital camera uses a sensor that detects light and converts it into electrical charges. These charges are recorded by a small computer inside the camera. The computer can then reconstruct the image immediately on the camera's display screen.

READING TiP

The term *digital* is often used to describe technology involving computers. Computers process information digitally, that is, using numbers.

How Cameras Work

A camera focuses an image in the same way as an eye.

film camera

light

lens

iris

aperture

film

READING VISUALS What part of a camera corresponds to the pupil of an eye?

Eye and Camera

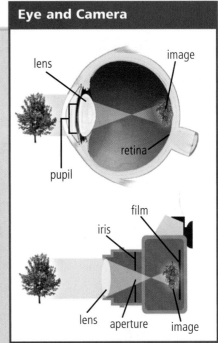

lens

image

pupil

retina

film

iris

lens

aperture

image

Digital Camera

A **digital camera** records images digitally, that is, using a computer.

Lasers use light in new ways.

A **laser** (LAY-zuhr) is a device that produces an intense, concentrated beam of light that is brighter than sunlight. The word *laser* means "light amplification by stimulated emission of radiation." Laser light has many uses. It carries a lot of energy and can be controlled precisely.

Ordinary visible light is made up of many different wavelengths. Even colored light usually contains many different wavelengths. But a laser beam is made up of light waves with a single wavelength and a pure color. In addition, the waves are in phase, which means the peaks are lined up so they match exactly.

REMINDER

The peak of a wave is where it has the greatest energy.

Visible light waves of different wavelengths

Light waves of a single wavelength

Single wavelength waves in phase

Light waves in a laser beam are highly concentrated and exactly parallel. Ordinary light spreads out, growing more faint as it gets farther from its source. Laser light spreads out very little. After traveling 1 kilometer (0.6 mi), a laser beam may have a diameter of only one meter.

Making Laser Light

RESOURCE CENTER
CLASSZONE.COM

Learn more about lasers.

A laser is made in a special tube called an optical cavity. A material that is known to give off a certain wavelength of light, such as a ruby crystal, is placed inside the tube. Next, an energy source, such as a bright flash of light, stimulates the material, causing it to emit, or give off, light waves. Both ends of the crystal are mirrored so that they reflect light back and forth between them. One end is mirrored more than the other. As the light waves pass through the crystal, they cause the material to give off more light waves—all perfectly parallel, all with the same wavelength, and all with their crests and troughs lined up. Eventually the beam becomes concentrated and strong enough to penetrate the less-mirrored end of the crystal. What comes out of the end is a laser beam.

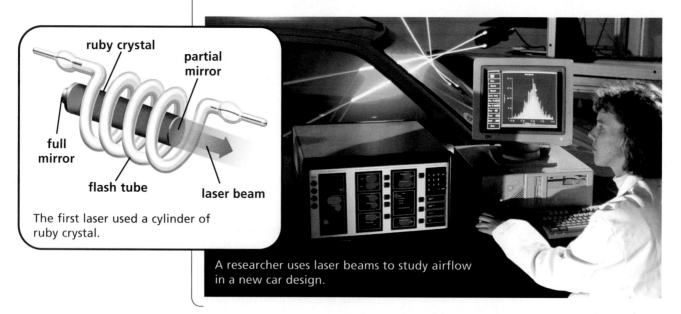

ruby crystal
partial mirror
full mirror
flash tube
laser beam

The first laser used a cylinder of ruby crystal.

A researcher uses laser beams to study airflow in a new car design.

Visual Uses of Lasers

Lasers are used today in an amazing variety of ways. One of these ways is to create devices that do the kind of work the human eye does—detecting and interpreting light waves. For example, surveyors once used telescopes to measure distances and angles. Now lasers can be used to take these measurements more precisely. Lasers are used to read bar codes, to scan images and pages of text, and to create holograms—three-dimensional images that appear to hover in the air. Holograms, which are hard to reproduce, are sometimes used in important documents so that the documents cannot be duplicated.

Fiber Optics

Some laser applications use visible light in ways that have nothing to do with vision. One of the fastest growing technologies is fiber optics. **Fiber optics** is technology based on the use of laser light to send signals through transparent wires called optical fibers. Fiber optics makes use of a light behavior called total internal reflection. Total internal reflection occurs when all of the light inside a medium reflects off the inner surface of the medium.

When light strikes the inner surface of a transparent medium, it may pass through the surface or it may be reflected back into the medium. Which one occurs depends on the angle at which the light hits the surface. For example, if you look through the sides of an aquarium, you can see what is behind it. But if you look at the surface of the water from below, it will act like a mirror, reflecting the inside of the aquarium.

Laser light is very efficient at total internal reflection. It can travel long distances inside clear fibers of glass or other materials. Light always travels in a straight line; however, by reflecting off the sides of the fibers, laser light inside fibers can go around corners and even completely reverse direction.

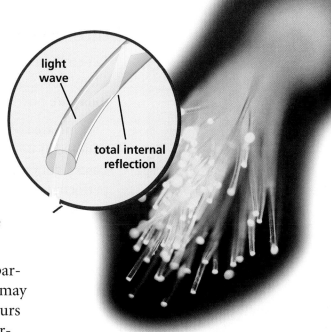

light wave

total internal reflection

optical fibers

 CHECK YOUR READING What is total internal reflection? What questions do you have about this light behavior?

Fiber optics is important in communications, because it can be used to transmit information very efficiently. Optical fibers can carry more signals than a corresponding amount of electrical cable. Optical cables can be used in place of electrical wires for telephone lines, cable television, and broadband Internet connections.

Fiber optics also has visual uses. For example, fiber optics is used in medicine to look inside the body. Using optical cable, doctors can examine organs and diagnose illnesses without surgery or x-rays. Optical fibers can also deliver laser light to specific points inside the body to help surgeons with delicate surgery.

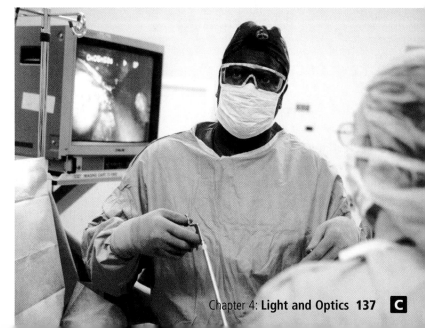

This surgeon uses fiber optics to see inside a patient's body.

Future Uses of Lasers

Research involving new uses of lasers continues at an amazing pace. Many new discoveries and developments in science and technology today are possible only because of lasers.

One area of research in which lasers have made a big impact is nanotechnology—the development of super-tiny machines and tools. Laser light can be controlled very precisely, so scientists can use it to perform extremely fine operations. For example, lasers could be used to cut out parts to make molecule-size motors. Lasers can also be used as "optical tweezers" to handle extremely small objects such as molecules. Scientists are even beginning to use lasers to change the shape of molecules. They do this by varying the laser's wavelength.

Future applications of lasers are also sure to involve new ways of transferring energy. Remember that a wave is a disturbance that transfers energy. Laser light is made up of EM waves. EM waves can move energy over great distances without losing any of it. When EM waves encounter a material medium, their energy can then be converted into other forms and put to use.

One possible future use of lasers is to supply energy to spacecraft. Scientists imagine a day when orbiting space stations will make rockets unnecessary. A cable between the ground and the station will make it possible for a "space elevator" to escape Earth's gravity by climbing up the cable. The elevator will be powered by an Earth-based laser. A device on board the elevator will convert the laser's energy into electrical power.

In this artist's illustration, a space elevator of the future draws power from a laser beam to climb to an orbiting space station.

4.4 Review

KEY CONCEPTS

1. How do refracting and reflecting telescopes use convex lenses and mirrors?

2. What is different about the way a camera focuses images from the way an eye focuses images?

3. How is laser light different from ordinary light?

CRITICAL THINKING

4. **Predict** What would happen to laser light if it passed through a prism?

5. **Analyze** What are two ways reflection is involved in fiber optics?

○ CHALLENGE

6. **Apply** How could the speed of light and a laser beam be used to measure the distance between two satellites?

PHOTOGRAPHER

Optics in Photography

Photographers use the science of optics to help them make the best photographs possible. For example, a portrait photographer chooses the right equipment and lighting to make each person look his or her best. A photographer needs to understand how light reflects, refracts, and diffuses to achieve just the right effect.

Using Reflection

A gold-colored reflector reflects only gold-colored wavelengths of light onto the subject. Photographers use these to fill in shadows and add warmth.

without gold reflector   **with gold reflector**

Using Diffusion

When light is directed toward a curved reflective surface, the light scatters in many directions. This diffused light produces a softer appearance than direct light.

direct light   **diffused light**

Using Refraction

Lenses refract light in different ways. A long lens makes the subject appear closer. A wide-angle lens includes more space around the subject.

long lens

wide-angle lens

EXPLORE

1. **COMPARE** Find photos of people and compare them to the photos above. Which would have been improved by the use of a gold reflector? a long lens? diffused light?

2. **CHALLENGE** Using a disposable camera and a desk lamp, experiment with photography yourself. Try using a piece of paper as a reflector and observe its effects on the photograph. What happens if you use more than one reflector? What happens if you use a different color of paper?

4 Chapter Review

Optical tools depend on the wave behavior of light.

CONTENT REVIEW
CLASSZONE.COM

◀ KEY CONCEPTS SUMMARY

4.1 Mirrors form images by reflecting light.

flat mirror

- Light rays obey the law of reflection.
- Mirrors work by regular reflection.
- Curved mirrors can form images that are distorted in useful ways.

VOCABULARY
optics p. 113
law of reflection p. 114
regular reflection p. 114
diffuse reflection p. 114
image p. 115
convex p. 116
concave p. 116
focal point p. 117

4.2 Lenses form images by refracting light.

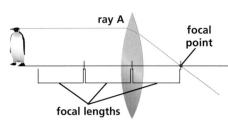
ray A
focal point
focal lengths

- Lenses have curved surfaces that refract parallel light waves in different amounts.
- Convex lenses bend light inward toward a focal point.
- Concave lenses spread light out.
- Lenses form a variety of useful images.

VOCABULARY
lens p. 121
focal length p. 123

4.3 The eye is a natural optical tool.

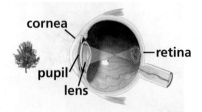
cornea
retina
pupil
lens

- The eyes of humans and many animals use lenses to focus images on the retina.
- The retina detects images and sends information about them to the brain.

VOCABULARY
cornea p. 127
pupil p. 127
retina p. 127

4.4 Optical technology makes use of light waves.

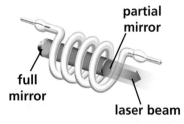
partial mirror
full mirror
laser beam

- Many optical tools are made by combining mirrors and lenses.
- Examples of optical tools include telescopes, microscopes, cameras, and lasers.
- Lasers have a wide variety of uses.

VOCABULARY
laser p. 135
fiber optics p. 137

For each item below, fill in the blank. If the right column is blank, give a brief description or definition. If the left column is blank, give the correct term.

Term	Description
1.	shape like the inside of a bowl
2. convex	
3.	science of light, vision, and related technology
4.	picture of object formed by light rays
5. focal point	
6.	controls the amount of light entering the eye
7.	distance between mirror or lens and place where light rays meet
8. fiber optics	
9. law of reflection	
10.	concentrated, parallel light waves of a single wavelength

Reviewing Key Concepts

Multiple Choice *Choose the letter of the best answer.*

11. What shape is a mirror that reflects parallel light rays toward a focal point?
   a. convex   **c.** concave
   b. flat   **d.** regular

12. According to the law of reflection, a light ray striking a mirror
   a. continues moving through the mirror in the same direction
   b. moves into the mirror at a slightly different angle
   c. bounces off the mirror toward the direction it came from
   d. bounces off the mirror at the same angle it hits

13. Reflecting telescopes focus images using
   a. several mirrors
   b. several lenses
   c. both mirrors and lenses
   d. either a mirror or a lens, but not both

14. Ordinary light differs from laser light in that ordinary light waves
   a. all have the same wavelength
   b. tend to spread out
   c. stay parallel to one another
   d. all have their peaks lined up

15. Nearsighted vision is corrected when lenses
   a. reflect light away from the eye
   b. allow light rays to focus on the retina
   c. allow light to focus slightly past the retina
   d. help light rays reflect regularly

16. Lasers do work similar to that of human vision when they are used to
   a. perform surgery
   b. send phone signals over optical cable
   c. scan bar codes at the grocery store
   d. change the shape of molecules

Short Answer *Write a short answer to each question.*

17. Name one optical tool, describe how it works, and explain some of its uses.

18. How are the images that are produced by a convex mirror different from those produced by a concave mirror?

19. Describe what typically happens to a ray of light from the time it enters the eye until it strikes the retina.

20. How do lenses correct nearsightedness and farsightedness?

21. What does a refracting telescope have in common with a simple microscope?

22. Describe two ways the distance of an object from a lens can affect the appearance of the object's image.

Thinking Critically

INTERPRET *In the four diagrams below, light rays are shown interacting with a material medium. For the next four questions, choose the letter of the diagram that answers the question.*

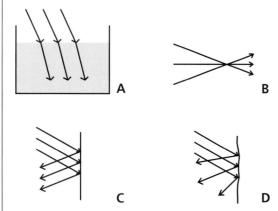

A

B

C

D

23. Which diagram shows regular reflection?

24. Which diagram shows diffuse reflection?

25. Which diagram shows refraction?

26. Which diagram shows light rays converging at a focal point?

COMPARE AND CONTRAST *Copy the chart below. For each pair of terms, write down one way they are alike (compare) and one way they are different (contrast).*

Terms	Compare	Contrast
27. flat mirror, curved mirror		
28. convex lens, concave lens		
29. focal point, focal length		
30. nearsighted, farsighted		
31. simple microscope, refracting telescope		
32. regular reflection, total internal reflection		

33. INFER What is the approximate focal length of the eye's lens? How do you know?

34. ANALYZE Why is laser light used in fiber optics?

35. APPLY In order to increase the magnification of a magnifying glass, would you need to make the convex surfaces of the lens more or less curved?

36. APPLY Describe a possible use for laser light not mentioned in the chapter. What characteristics of laser light does this application make use of?

the **BIG** idea

37. SYNTHESIZE Using what you have learned in this chapter, describe two possible uses of an optical tool like the one shown on pages 110–111. Explain what wave behaviors of light would be involved in these uses. Then explain how these uses could benefit the person in the photo.

38. APPLY Make a sketch of an optical tool that would use three mirrors to make a beam of light return to its source. Your sketch should include:

- the path of light waves through the tool
- labels indicating the names of parts and how they affect the light
- several sentences describing one possible use of the tool

UNIT PROJECTS

Evaluate all the data, results, and information from your project folder. Prepare to present your project.

Interpreting Diagrams

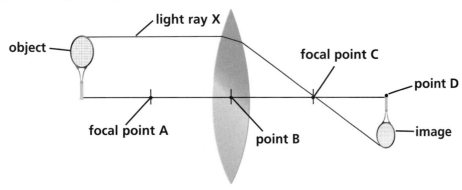

Study the diagram above and then answer the questions that follow.

1. What kind of lens is shown in the diagram?

  a. concave   **c.** flat

  b. convex   **d.** prism

2. What happens to parallel light rays passing through this type of lens?

  a. They become polarized.

  b. They form a rainbow.

  c. They bend inward.

  d. They bend outward.

3. All light rays parallel to light ray X will pass through what point?

  a. point A   **c.** point C

  b. point B   **d.** point D

4. How far is the object in the diagram from the lens?

  a. less than one focal length

  b. one focal length

  c. about two focal lengths

  d. more than three focal lengths

5. Where would you position a screen in order to see the image in focus on the screen?

  a. at point A

  b. at point B

  c. at point C

  d. at point D

Extended Response

Answer the two questions below in detail. Include some of the terms from the word box. Underline each term you use in your answer.

concave	focal point	real image
convex	refraction	virtual image
flat mirror	reflection	magnifying glass

6. What kind of mirror would you use to see what is happening over a broad area? Why?

7. Choose one of the following optical tools and explain how it uses mirrors and/or lenses to form an image: camera, telescope, periscope, microscope.

Ecology

symbiosis

Tickbird
(Buphagus erythrorhynchus)

Impala
(Aepyceros melampus)

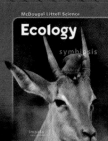

Ecology
Contents Overview

Unit Features

1 Ecosystems and Biomes   6

the **BIG** idea

Matter and energy together support life
within an environment.

2 Interactions Within Ecosystems   42

the **BIG** idea

Living things within an ecosystem interact with
each other and the environment.

3 Human Impact on Ecosystems   78

the **BIG** idea

Humans and human population growth
affect the environment.

ECOSYSTEMS ON FIRE

It may seem strange to set fire to a wilderness preserve, but fire brings health to some ecosystems.

SCIENTIFIC AMERICAN FRONTIERS

View the video "Prairie Comeback" to learn about the restoration of a prairie ecosystem.

An astonishing variety of plants blooms in this prairie in Missouri.

Fire and Life

Intense heat, smoke, the crackling of burning grasses, the crashing of flaming trees—all these characteristics of fire seem threatening. In recent years, forest fires have burned huge areas of forest and have endangered people and property nearby. But even though fire can be destructive, it can also be an agent of life. In fact, scientists are actively using fire to manage ecosystems—areas that contain specific groups of living and nonliving things. Prairies, forests, and woodlands are examples of ecosystems.

The fear of fire has led people to limit fires that are a natural part of some ecosystems. Preventing or putting out smaller fires in a forest ecosystem can mean trouble. Occasional small fires burn small amounts of material and cause only limited damage. Without these smaller fires, burnable materials may build up and lead to the outbreak of a catastrophic fire.

The species of living things in some ecosystems have adaptations that allow them to thrive on fire. In North America trees such as lodgepole pine and jack pine depend upon flames to release seeds from their cones. Cape lilies lying under the forest floor blossom almost immediately after a forest fire. On prairies, flowers such as the rare coastal gayfeather in Texas or the fringed prairie orchid in Illinois benefit from prairie fires.

controlled burn

new growth

Seven months after a controlled burn, light shines on a new patch of wild hyacinth growing at the base of an oak tree.

Observing Patterns

Ecosystems include living things, such as plants and animals, and nonliving things, such as water and soil. Fires affect both the living and the nonliving. The photographs above show part of an oak woodland ecosystem. The photograph on the left shows a burn—a fire set deliberately by humans. The photograph on the right shows the same area seven months later.

Ashes left from fires add nutrients to the soil. Fire also opens space on the forest floor. Areas that were shaded by small trees, plants, and dead branches receive light. Over time, wild hyacinth and other new plants grow around the oak, and new insects and animals move into the area.

View the "Prairie Comeback" segment of your Scientific American Frontiers video to see how understanding ecosystems can help bring a prairie into bloom.

IN THIS SCENE FROM THE VIDEO ▶ a bison grazes on new growth that appears after the prairie is burned.

BRINGING BACK THE PRAIRIE At one time natural events, such as lightning, along with human activity caused regular patterns of fire on the prairie. Bison grazed on tender young plants that grew up after fires, and the plants that weren't eaten by the bison had room to grow. In 1989, an organization called The Nature Conservancy turned the Chapman-Barnard Cattle Ranch in Northeast Oklahoma into the Tall Grass Prairie Restoration Preserve.

Scientists at the preserve are using controlled fire and reintroducing bison to the area. Today there are more than 750 species of plants and animals growing in the preserve.

In tall-grass prairie ecosystems, fire provides similar benefits. Fire burns away overgrown plants, enriches the soil, and clears the way for the growth of new plants. Bison prefer to graze on these new plants that appear after a fire.

A New Understanding

Although some of the benefits provided by ecosystems can't be measured, researchers are starting to measure the financial contributions of ecosystems. Ecosystems may help clean our water, balance gases in the atmosphere, and maintain temperature ranges.

Researchers today are studying these benefits. In fact, a new frontier in ecology, called ecosystem services, is emerging. This new study is gaining the attention of both scientists and economists.

Given our growing awareness of the importance of ecosystems, should humans deliberately set fire to areas in forests or prairies? The answer to this question requires an understanding of interactions among living and nonliving parts of ecosystems. Forest and prairie fires can be dangerous, but properly managed, they provide important benefits to society as well as to the natural world.

UNANSWERED Questions

Understanding the connections within ecosystems raises more questions. In the coming years, people will need to analyze the costs and benefits of ecosystem restoration.

- How will humans balance the need to feed the human population with the cost of destroying ecosystems such as the prairie?
- How can scientists and wildlife managers protect people and property near forests while maintaining forest ecosystems?
- How do ecosystems protect natural resources, such as soil and water?

UNIT PROJECTS

As you study this unit, work alone or with a group on one of the projects listed below. Use the bulleted steps to guide your project.

Build an Ecosystem

Use an aquarium or other container to build an ecosystem.

- Set up your ecosystem. Observe it daily, and record your observations.
- Bring your ecosystem into your classroom, or take photographs and make diagrams of it. Present the record of your observations along with the visual displays.

Conservation Campaign

Find out how much water, paper, and energy are used in a month at your school.

- Describe a plan for conserving resources.
- Present your plan. You might make posters, write announcements, or perform a short skit.

Design a Park

You are part of a group that is planning a park near your school. Your group wants the park to include plants that lived in the area twenty-five years ago.

- Collect information from local museums, park districts, or botanic gardens. You can also visit Web sites sponsored by those organizations.
- Prepare a report and drawing of your park design.

CAREER CENTER
CLASSZONE.COM

Learn more about careers in ecology.

CHAPTER

1

Ecosystems and Biomes

the **BIG** idea

Matter and energy together support life within an environment.

How many living and nonliving things can you identify in this photograph?

Key Concepts

SECTION
1.1 Ecosystems support life.
Learn about different factors that make up an ecosystem.

SECTION
1.2 Matter cycles through ecosystems.
Learn about the water, carbon, and nitrogen cycles.

SECTION
1.3 Energy flows through ecosystems.
Learn how energy moves through living things.

SECTION
1.4 Biomes contain many ecosystems.
Learn about different land and water biomes.

Internet Preview

CLASSZONE.COM

Chapter 1 online resources:
Content Review, Simulation, Visualization, three Resource Centers, Math Tutorial, Test Practice

EXPLORE (the BIG idea)

How Do Plants React to Sunlight?

Move a potted plant so that the Sun shines on it from a different direction. Observe the plant each day for a week.

Observe and Think What change do you observe in the plant? What is it that plants get from the Sun?

What Is Soil?

Get a cupful of soil from outside and funnel it into a clear plastic bottle. Fill the bottle two-thirds full with water and place the bottle cap on tightly. Shake the bottle so that the soil and water mix completely. Place the bottle on a windowsill overnight. Wash your hands.

Observe and Think What has happened to the soil and water mixture? How many different types of material do you observe?

Internet Activity: A Prairie Ecosystem

Go to **ClassZone.com** to discover the types of plants and animals best adapted for tall-grass and short-grass prairies. Learn more about how to keep a prairie thriving.

Observe and Think What do all prairie plants have in common? How do prairie plants differ?

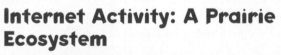
NSTA
scilinks.org
SCiLINKS

Food Chains and Food Webs **Code: MDL001**

Getting Ready to Learn

 CONCEPT REVIEW

- The natural world that surrounds all living things is called the environment.
- Most living things need water, air, food, and living space.
- All living things need a source of energy to stay alive and grow.

 VOCABULARY REVIEW

See Glossary for definitions.

biology	nutrient
energy	photosynthesis
environment	respiration
matter	system

CONTENT REVIEW
CLASSZONE.COM
Review concepts and vocabulary.

▶ **TAKING NOTES**

COMBINATION NOTES

To take notes about a new concept, first make an informal outline of the information. Then make a sketch of the concept and label it so you can study it later.

VOCABULARY STRATEGY

Write each new vocabulary term in the center of a **frame game** diagram. Decide what information to frame the term with. Use examples, descriptions, parts, sentences that use the term in context, or pictures. You can change the frame to fit each item.

See the Note-Taking Handbook on pages R45–R51.

SCIENCE NOTEBOOK

NOTES

Parts of an ecosystem:
- Animals
- Plants
- Soil
- Water
- Light
- Microorganisms

Light
Plants
Animal
Water
Soil

	nonliving factors	
physical or chemical	**ABIOTIC FACTOR**	water, light, soil, temperature
	affected by living factors	

Ecosystems support life.

 BEFORE, you learned

- Living things need to obtain matter and energy from the environment
- The Sun provides Earth with light and heat

 NOW, you will learn

- What factors define an ecosystem
- About living factors in an ecosystem
- About nonliving factors in an ecosystem

VOCABULARY

ecology p. 9
ecosystem p. 9
biotic factor p. 10
abiotic factor p. 10

EXPLORE Your Environment

How much can temperature vary in one place?

PROCEDURE

① Choose three different locations inside your classroom where you can measure temperature.

② Place a thermometer at each location. Wait for at least two minutes. Record the temperatures in your notebook.

③ Compare the data you and your classmates have collected.

WHAT DO YOU THINK?

- Which location was the warmest, and which was the coldest?
- Describe what factors may have affected the temperature at each location.

MATERIALS
- thermometer
- stopwatch

VOCABULARY
Add frame game diagrams for *ecology* and *ecosystem* to your notebook.

Living things depend on the environment.

You wouldn't find a kangaroo in the Arctic and you won't see a polar bear in Australia. Each of these organisms is suited to a certain environment. The kangaroo and the polar bear are able to survive despite the harsh conditions of their surroundings. **Ecology** is the scientific study of how organisms interact with their environment and all the other organisms that live in that environment.

Scientists use the word **ecosystem** to describe a particular environment and all the living things that are supported by it. An ecosystem can be as small as a pond or as large as a desert. What is important in an ecosystem is how the living parts of the ecosystem relate to the nonliving parts.

RESOURCE CENTER
CLASSZONE.COM
Learn more about
ecosystems.

Let's take a look at a pond. A pond ecosystem is more than just water and fish. Plants grow in and around the water, and animals feed on these plants. A variety of tiny microorganisms in the water are food for fish and for each other. These are just a few of the living parts, or **biotic factors** (by-AHT-ihk), of a pond ecosystem. The nonliving parts, or **abiotic factors** (AY-by-AHT-ihk), include the air that supplies oxygen and carbon dioxide, the soil that provides nutrients, the water in the pond, and the sunlight that plants need to grow.

CLASSIFY Name three living and three nonliving factors that are part of this pond ecosystem.

Biotic factors interact with an ecosystem.

Living things depend upon an ecosystem for food, air, and water, as well as other things they need for survival. In turn, living things have an impact on the ecosystem in which they live. Plants, as a biotic factor in land ecosystems, affect other biotic and abiotic parts of ecosystems. Plants are an important source of food. The types of plants found in a particular ecosystem will determine the types of animals that can live there. Plants can affect temperature by blocking sunlight. Plant roots hold soil in place. Even the atmosphere is affected by plants taking in carbon dioxide and releasing oxygen.

Animals, as biotic factors, also affect an ecosystem. A beaver that builds a dam changes the flow of a river and so affects the surrounding landscape. Large herds of cattle can overgraze a grassland ecosystem and cause the soil to erode. In an ocean biome, corals form giant reefs th   food and shelter for marine organisms.

Many abiotic factors affect ecosystems.

Abiotic factors include both the physical and chemical parts of an ecosystem. Physical factors are factors that you can see or feel, such as the temperature or the amount of water or sunlight. Important chemical factors include the minerals and compounds found in the soil and whether the ecosystem's water is fresh or salty. It is the combination of different abiotic factors that determines the types of organisms that an ecosystem will support.

 CHECK YOUR READING List four different abiotic factors that can affect an ecosystem.

Temperature

Temperature is an important abiotic factor in any ecosystem. In a land ecosystem, temperature affects the types of plants that will do well there. The types of plants available for food and shelter, in turn, determine the types of animals that can live there. For example, a tropical rain forest has not only a lot of rain but it has consistently warm temperatures. The wide variety of plants that grow in a tropical rain forest supports a wide variety of monkeys, birds, and other organisms.

Animals are as sensitive to temperature as plants are. Musk oxen with their thick coat of fur can survive in very cold environments, where temperatures of –40°C (–40°F) are normal. The water buffalo, with its light coat, is better suited to warm temperatures. The wild water buffalo lives where temperatures can reach 48°C (118°F).

READING TiP

The word *biotic* means "living." The prefix *a-* in *abiotic* means "not," so *abiotic* means "not living."

This musk ox's thick fur keeps it warm in the cold temperatures of northern Canada.

A water buffalo cools itself in a shallow stream during a hot day in India.

 READING VISUALS COMPARE AND CONTRAST How are these animals alike? How are they different?

Chapter 1: **Ecosystems and Biomes** 11 **D**

Light

COMBINATION NOTES
Remember to make notes and diagrams to show how abiotic factors affect biotic factors in an ecosystem.

You can easily understand how abiotic factors work together when you think about sunlight and temperature. Sunlight warms Earth's surface and atmosphere. In addition, energy from sunlight supports all life on Earth. The Sun provides the energy that plants capture and use to produce food in a process called photosynthesis. The food produced by plants, and other photosynthetic organisms, feeds almost all the other living things found on Earth.

The strength of sunlight and the amount of sunlight available in a land ecosystem determine the types of plants in that ecosystem. A desert ecosystem will have plants like cacti, which can survive where sunlight is very strong. Meanwhile, mosses and ferns grow well on the forest floor, where much of the light is blocked by the trees above.

Light is a factor in ocean ecosystems as well. The deeper the water is, the less light there is available. In the shallow water near the shore, photosynthetic organisms can survive at the surface and on the ocean floor. In the open ocean, light is available for photosynthetic organisms only in the first hundred meters below the surface.

Soil

Soil, which is a mixture of small rock and mineral particles, is an important abiotic factor in land ecosystems. Organisms within the soil break down the remains of dead plants and animals. This process of decay provides important raw materials to the living plants and animals of an ecosystem.

The size of soil particles affects how much air and water the soil can hold.

decayed leaves

roots

earthworm

Different ecosystems have different types of soil. The characteristics of the soil in an ecosystem affect plant growth. Soils that have a lot of decaying, or organic, matter can hold water well and allow air to reach the plant roots. Sandy soils usually do not hold water well because the water flows through too easily. Clay soil, which has small, tightly packed particles, will not allow water to move through easily at all. Minerals in the soil also affect plant growth.

 Explain how soil can affect plant life in an ecosystem.

Water

Another important abiotic factor in land ecosystems is the amount of water available to support life. All living things need water to carry out life processes. Plants need water as well as sunlight for photosynthesis. Animals need water to digest food and release the energy stored in the food. Look at the photograph to see the effect that an underground water source has on an otherwise dry, desert ecosystem. Trees could not survive there without a plentiful supply of water.

Ecosystems that have a lot of water can support a large number of different types of plants. These different types of plants can then support a large number of different types of animals. Tropical rain forests, the wettest of all ecosystems on land, are also the most diverse. Desert ecosystems, which are the driest land ecosystems, have far fewer types of plants and animals. The types and number of living things in a land ecosystem will always be related to the amount of fresh water available for its inhabitants.

INFER An oasis forms in the desert when underground water comes to the surface. How can you identify the boundary of this oasis?

1.1 Review

KEY CONCEPTS

1. Draw a diagram of an ecosystem near where you live. Label the factors "biotic" or "abiotic."

2. Give two examples of how plants and animals affect their environment.

3. Describe how temperature, light, and soil affect an ecosystem.

CRITICAL THINKING

4. **Predict** Think of a forest ecosystem. Now imagine that a large volcanic eruption throws large amounts of dust and ash into the air, blocking out sunlight. How might the forest ecosystem be affected if the sunlight is blocked for a day? For a year?

⬤ CHALLENGE

5. **Apply** Think of how you fit into your local environment. List ways in which you interact with biotic and abiotic factors within your ecosystem.

CHAPTER INVESTIGATION

Soil Samples

OVERVIEW AND PURPOSE Nonliving, or abiotic, factors all have an effect on soil. The quality of the soil affects how well plants grow in a particular environment. In this investigation, you will

- observe and record how water travels through three soil samples
- predict how different types of soil would affect plant growth

▶ Problem

How does soil type affect how water moves through soil?

▶ Hypothesize

You should complete steps 1–5 in the procedure before writing your hypothesis. Write a hypothesis to explain how water moves through certain types of soil. Your hypothesis should take the form of an "If . . . , then . . . , because . . ." statement.

▶ Procedure

MATERIALS
- 3 pieces of paper
- spoon
- 50 mL each of clay, coarse sand, loam
- hand lens
- toothpick
- eyedropper
- water
- 3 pieces of filter paper
- 3 plastic funnels
- 3 large beakers
- small beaker
- stopwatch

1 Make a data table in your **Science Notebook** like the one shown on page 15.

2 Label three sheets of paper "Clay," "Sand," and "Loam." Carefully place a spoonful of each sample on the appropriately labeled paper.

3 Carefully examine each of the soils, with and without the hand lens. Describe the color of each, and record the information in your data table.

4. Use a toothpick to separate the particles of each sample of soil. Record the size of the particles in the data table.

5. Put a small amount of each soil sample in the palm of your hand. Add a drop of water and mix the soil around with your finger. Write a description of the texture of each sample in your data table. Be sure to wash your hands after you finish. After you have recorded your observations, write your hypothesis.

6. Fold each piece of filter paper to form cones as shown in the diagram. Place one filter inside each funnel. Place one funnel in each large beaker. Measure 50 mL of each soil sample and place the sample in one of the funnels.

7. Measure 150 mL of water and pour it into the funnel containing the clay. Start the stopwatch when the water begins to drip out of the funnel. Stop the watch when the water stops dripping. Record the time in seconds in the data table.

8. Repeat step 7 for the sand and the loam. When you have finished with the activity, dispose of the materials according to your teacher's directions, and wash your hands.

Observe and Analyze

1. **INTERPRET DATA** Through which soil sample did the water move the fastest? The slowest?

2. **OBSERVE** What type of changes occurred in the soil as the water was added?

Conclude

1. **INTERPRET** Compare your results with your hypothesis. Does your data support your hypothesis?

2. **IDENTIFY LIMITS** What sources of error could have affected this investigation?

3. **EVALUATE** Based on your observations, what can account for the differences in the times recorded for the three soil samples?

4. **PREDICT** Based on your results, which of the soil samples would you expect to be the best type of soil in which to grow plants? Explain.

▶ INVESTIGATE Further

CHALLENGE Design an experiment in which you test which of the three soil samples is best for growing plants. Include a materials list, hypothesis, and procedure for your experiment.

Soil Samples
Table 1. Soil Characteristics

Characteristics	Clay	Sand	Loam
Color			
Particle size			
Texture			
Time for water to stop dripping (sec)			

Matter cycles through ecosystems.

◀ **BEFORE,** you learned	▶ **NOW,** you will learn
• Ecosystems support life • Living and nonliving factors interact in an ecosystem • Temperature, light, soil, and water are important nonliving factors in ecosystems	• How matter is exchanged between organisms and their environment • About the water, carbon, and nitrogen cycles

VOCABULARY

cycle p. 16
water cycle p. 17
carbon cycle p. 18
nitrogen cycle p. 19

EXPLORE The Water Cycle

Do plants release water?

PROCEDURE

(1) Cover a branch of the plant with a plastic bag. Tape the bag firmly around the stem.

(2) Water the plant and place it in a sunny window or under a lamp. Wash your hands.

(3) Check the plant after ten minutes, at the end of class, and again the next day.

WHAT DO YOU THINK?
• What do you see inside the plastic bag?
• What purpose does the plastic bag serve?

MATERIALS
• 1 small potted plant
• 1 clear plastic bag
• tape
• water

All ecosystems need certain materials.

Explore cycles in nature.

Living things depend on their environment to meet their needs. You can think of those needs in terms of the material, or matter, required by all living things. For example, all organisms take in water and food in order to survive. All of the materials an organism takes in are returned to the ecosystem, while the organism lives or after it dies.

The movement of matter through the living and nonliving parts of an ecosystem is a continuous process, a cycle. A **cycle** is a series of events that happens over and over again. Matter in an ecosystem may change form, but it never leaves the ecosystem, so the matter is said to cycle through the ecosystem. Three of the most important cycles in ecosystems involve water, carbon, and nitrogen.

Water Cycle

Different processes combine to move water through the environment.

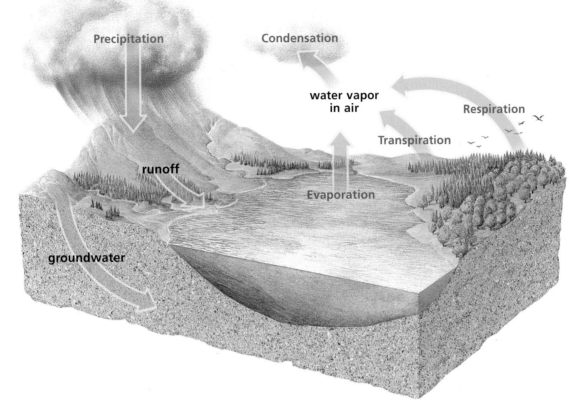

Water cycles through ecosystems.

Water is stored on Earth's surface in lakes, rivers, and oceans. Water is found underground, filling the spaces between soil particles and cracks in rocks. Large amounts of water are stored in glaciers and polar ice sheets. Water is also part of the bodies of living things. But water is not just stored, it is constantly moving. The movement of water through the environment is called the **water cycle.**

Water is made up of just two elements: oxygen and hydrogen. As water moves through an ecosystem, it changes in physical form, moving back and forth between gas, liquid, and solid. Water in the atmosphere is usually in gaseous form—water vapor. Water that falls to Earth's surface is referred to as precipitation. For precipitation to occur, water vapor must condense—it must change into a liquid or solid. This water can fall as rain, snow, sleet, mist, or hail.

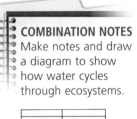

COMBINATION NOTES
Make notes and draw a diagram to show how water cycles through ecosystems.

△ CHECK YOUR READING   What are the three physical forms of water in the water cycle?

Water returns to the atmosphere when heated, changing back into vapor, a process called evaporation. Living things also release water vapor. Animals release water vapor when they breathe, or respire. Plants release water vapor through a process called transpiration.

Carbon cycles through ecosystems.

Carbon is an element found in all living things. Carbon moves through Earth's ecosystems in a cycle referred to as the **carbon cycle.** It is through carbon dioxide gas found in Earth's atmosphere that carbon enters the living parts of an ecosystem.

Plants use carbon dioxide to produce sugar—a process called photosynthesis. Sugars are carbon compounds that are important building blocks in food and all living matter. Food supplies the energy and materials living things need to live and grow. To release the energy in food, organisms break down the carbon compounds—a process called respiration. Carbon is released and cycled back into the atmosphere as carbon dioxide. When living things die and decay, the rest of the carbon that makes up living matter is released.

CHECK YOUR READING Name three ways that living things are part of the carbon cycle.

Earth's oceans contain far more carbon than the air does. In water ecosystems—lakes, rivers, and oceans—carbon dioxide is dissolved in water. Algae and certain types of bacteria are the photosynthetic organisms that produce food in these ecosystems. Marine organisms, too, release carbon dioxide during respiration. Carbon is also deposited on the ocean floor when organisms die.

READING TiP

Notice that photosynthesis is a process that brings carbon into living matter and respiration is a process that releases carbon.

Carbon Cycle

Different processes combine to move carbon through the environment.

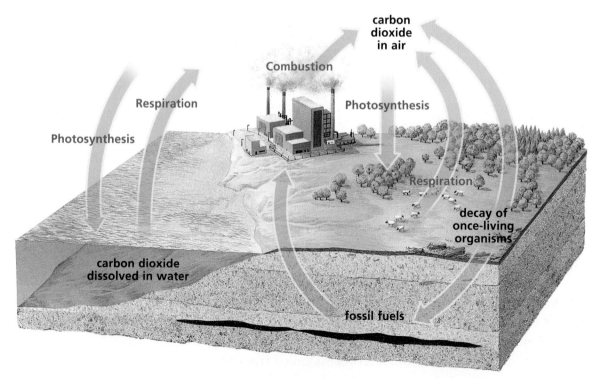

What is one form in which carbon is stored on the ocean floor?

PROCEDURE

1. Use the mortar and pestle to crush the seashell into a powder.
2. Pour the powder into a small beaker.
3. Add enough white vinegar to cover the powder.

WHAT DO YOU THINK?

- What happens when white vinegar is added to the crushed shell?
- What is the material produced in the reaction and where did it come from originally?

CHALLENGE What type of reaction have you observed?

SKILL FOCUS
Observing

MATERIALS
- mortar and pestle
- whole seashell or fragments
- small beaker
- white vinegar

TIME
15 minutes

Large amounts of carbon are stored underground. The remains of plants and animals buried for millions of years decay slowly and change into fossil fuels, such as coal and oil. The carbon in fossil fuels returns to ecosystems in a process called combustion. As humans burn fossil fuels to release energy, dust particles and gases containing carbon are also released into the environment.

Nitrogen cycles through ecosystems.

Nitrogen is another element important to life that cycles through Earth in the **nitrogen cycle.** Almost four-fifths of the air you breathe is clear, colorless nitrogen gas. Yet, you cannot get the nitrogen you need to live from the air. All animals must get nitrogen from plants.

Plants cannot use pure nitrogen gas either. However, plants can absorb certain compounds of nitrogen. Plants take in these nitrogen compounds through their roots, along with water and other nutrients. So how does the nitrogen from the atmosphere get into the soil? One source is lightning. Every lightning strike breaks apart, or fixes, pure nitrogen, changing it into a form that plants can use. This form of nitrogen falls to the ground when it rains.

Nitrogen Cycle

Different processes combine to move nitrogen through the environment.

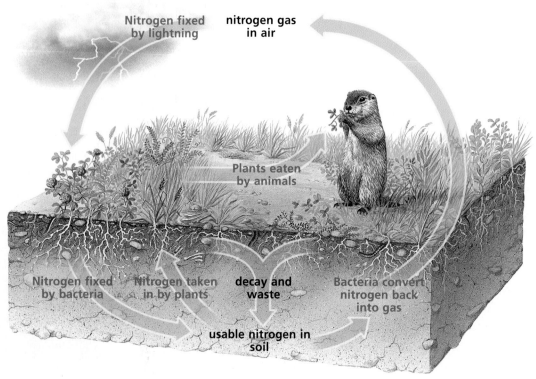

Nitrogen fixed by lightning

nitrogen gas in air

Plants eaten by animals

Nitrogen fixed by bacteria

Nitrogen taken in by plants

decay and waste

Bacteria convert nitrogen back into gas

usable nitrogen in soil

VISUALIZATION
CLASSZONE.COM

Watch the nitrogen cycle in action.

A far greater source of nitrogen is nitrogen-fixing bacteria. These bacteria live in the oceans as well as the soil. Some even attach themselves to the roots of certain plants, like alfalfa or soybeans. When organisms die, decomposers in the ocean or soil break them down. Nitrogen in the soil or water is used again by living things. A small amount is returned to the atmosphere by certain bacteria that can break down nitrogen compounds into nitrogen gas.

1.2 Review

KEY CONCEPTS

1. Draw a diagram of the water cycle. Show three ways in which water moves through the cycle.

2. Summarize the main parts of the carbon cycle.

3. Explain two ways that nitrogen gas in the atmosphere is changed into nitrogen compounds that plants can use.

CRITICAL THINKING

4. **Predict** When people burn fossil fuels, carbon dioxide gas is added to the atmosphere. How might increased carbon dioxide affect plant growth?

5. **Compare and Contrast** Review the nitrogen and carbon cycles. How are these two cycles similar and different?

⬥ CHALLENGE

6. **Apply** Draw a cycle diagram that shows how water is used in your household. Include activities that use water, sources of water, and ways that water leaves your house.

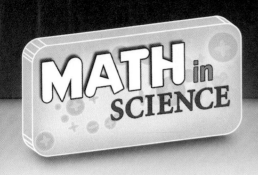
 MATH TUTORIAL
CLASSZONE.COM
Click on Math Tutorial for more help with adding integers.

This iceberg is made up of fresh water, which freezes at 0°C. The surrounding ocean is salt water, which doesn't freeze at 0°C.

Temperature and the Water Cycle

Changes in temperature help water move through the environment. At freezing temperatures—below 32°F or 0°C for sea-level environments—water can begin to become solid ice. Ice starts to melt when the temperature rises above freezing, causing the water to become liquid again. Temperature change also causes water to become vapor, or gas, within the air.

Example

Suppose you are waiting for winter to come so you can skate on a small pond near your house. The weather turns cold. One day the temperature is 25°C, then the next day the air temperature drops by 35°C. What temperature is the air? If the air stays below 0°C, some of the water will begin to freeze.

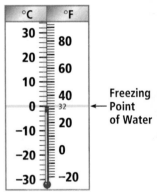

(1) Write a verbal model:
25 degrees + a 35-degree drop = what temperature?

(2) Write an equation. Use negative and positive integers:
$25 + (-35) = ?$

(3) Solve the equation:
$25 - 35 = -10$

ANSWER $-10°C$.

Answer the following questions.

1. A container of water is left out over night, when the temperature is $-18°C$. In the morning, the air temperature rises by 8°C. What temperature is the air? What will happen to the water?

2. An ice block sits in a field where the air is 0°C. The air temperature rises by 16°C, then it drops by 8°C. What temperature is the air in the field now? What will happen to the ice?

3. What happens to a block of ice after the temperature in the air follows this pattern: $-6 + 17 + 10 + 18 + (-5)$? What temperature has the air reached?

CHALLENGE Use a thermometer to measure the temperature of the air outside and indoors in degrees Celsius. Write two addition equations that show the temperature change between the two locations. One equation should show a rise, and one should show a drop.

KEY CONCEPT

1.3 Energy flows through ecosystems.

◀ **BEFORE, you learned**	▶ **NOW, you will learn**
• Matter cycles continuously through an ecosystem • Living things are part of the water, carbon, and nitrogen cycles	• How living things move energy through an ecosystem • How feeding relationships are important in ecosystems • How the amount of energy changes as it flows through an ecosystem

VOCABULARY

producer p. 23
consumer p. 24
decomposer p. 25
food chain p. 26
food web p. 26
energy pyramid p. 28

EXPLORE Energy

How can you observe energy changing form?

PROCEDURE

1. Mark and cut a spiral pattern in a square piece of paper.

2. Cut a 15-cm piece of thread and tape one end to the center of the spiral.

3. Adjust the lamp to shine straight at the ceiling. Turn the lamp on.

4. Hold the spiral by the thread and let it hang 10 cm above the light bulb. CAUTION: Don't let the paper touch the bulb!

WHAT DO YOU THINK?
• What do you see happen to the spiral?
• In what sense has the energy changed form?

MATERIALS
• paper
• marker
• scissors
• thread
• tape
• desk lamp

Living things capture and release energy.

Everything you do—running, reading, and working—requires energy. The energy you use is chemical energy, which comes from the food you eat. When you go for a run, you use up energy. Some of that energy is released to the environment as heat, as you sweat. Eventually, you will need to replace the energy you've used.

Energy is vital to all living things. Most of that energy comes either directly or indirectly from the Sun. To use the Sun's energy, living things must first capture that energy and store it in some usable form. Because energy is continuously used by the activities of living things, it must be continuously replaced in the ecosystem.

Producers

All of these producers capture energy from sunlight.

Plants

This tomato plant uses energy from the Sun to produce food.

The food is used as a source of energy and material for the plant and all the organisms that eat the plant.

READING VISUALS What process do all of these producers have in common?

Seaweed

Seaweed is a producer found in Earth's oceans and coastal zones.

Phytoplankton

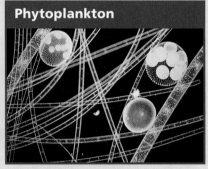

The most numerous producers are tiny organisms that live in water called phytoplankton.

Producers

A **producer** is an organism that captures energy and stores it in food as chemical energy. The producers of an ecosystem make energy available to all the other living parts of an ecosystem. Most energy enters ecosystems through photosynthesis. Plants, and other photosynthetic organisms, take water and carbon dioxide from their environment and use energy from the Sun to produce sugars. The chemical energy stored in sugars can be released when sugars are broken down.

VOCABULARY
Remember to add a frame game for *producers* to your notebook.

○ **CHECK YOUR READING** How does energy enter into the living parts of an ecosystem?

Plants are the most common producers found in land ecosystems. In water ecosystems, most food is produced by photosynthetic bacteria and algae. A few examples of producers that use photosynthesis are shown in the photographs above.

The Sun provides most of the energy that is stored in food. One exception is the unusual case of a type of bacteria that lives in the deep ocean, where there is no sunlight. These bacteria produce food using heated chemicals released from underwater vents. This process is called chemosynthesis. Whether producers use photosynthesis or chemosynthesis, they do just as their name suggests—they produce food for themselves and for the rest of the ecosystem.

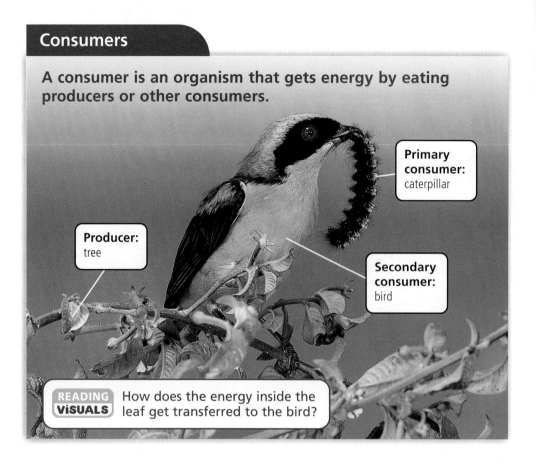

Consumers

A consumer is an organism that gets energy by eating producers or other consumers.

Producer:
tree

Primary consumer:
caterpillar

Secondary consumer:
bird

READING VISUALS How does the energy inside the leaf get transferred to the bird?

Consumers

Organisms that cannot produce their own food must get their food from other sources. **Consumers** are organisms that get their energy by eating, or consuming, other organisms. To understand how energy flows through an ecosystem, you have to study feeding relationships. A feeding relationship starts with a producer, followed by one and often many more consumers.

 CHECK YOUR READING Describe the producer-consumer relationship in terms of energy.

Consumers are classified by their position in a feeding relationship. In a meadow ecosystem, animals such as antelopes and grasshoppers feed on grasses. They are primary consumers because they are the first link between the producers and the rest of the consumers in an ecosystem. The wolves that eat the antelopes and the meadowlarks that eat the grasshoppers are secondary consumers. There are also tertiary consumers, like the prairie falcon that eats the meadowlark. Ecosystems also have special consumers called scavengers, like the vulture, which is a consumer that feeds on dead animals.

In the photograph above, energy enters the ecosystem through the tree, which is the producer. The caterpillar that gets its energy by feeding on the leaves is the first, or primary, consumer. The bird that gets its energy by feeding on the caterpillar is a secondary consumer.

READING TiP

Primary is a word that means "first in order," *secondary* means "second in order," and *tertiary* means "third in order."

Decomposers

If you've been for a hike through a forest, or a walk through a park, you have seen the interaction of producers and consumers. Tall trees and leafy shrubs are home to many insects and the birds that feed upon the insects. Also important to the maintenance of an ecosystem are decomposers, a group of organisms that often go unseen. **Decomposers** are organisms that break down dead plant and animal matter into simpler compounds.

mushrooms

Fungi, such as these mushrooms, are decomposers.

You can think of decomposers as the clean-up crew of an ecosystem. In a forest, consumers such as deer and insects eat a tiny fraction of the leaves on trees and shrubs. The leaves that are left on the forest floor, as well as dead roots and branches, are eventually digested by fungi and bacteria living in the soil. Decomposers also break down animal remains, including waste materials. A pinch of soil may contain almost half a million fungi and billions of bacteria.

The energy within an ecosystem gets used up as it flows from organism to organism. Decomposers are the organisms that release the last bit of energy from once-living matter. Decomposers also return matter to soil or water where it may be used again and again.

INVESTIGATE Decomposers

Where do decomposers come from?

PROCEDURE

1. Carefully use scissors to cut an opening across the middle of the bottle.

2. Place a handful of stones in the bottom of the bottle for drainage, and add enough soil to make a layer 10 cm deep.

3. Place some leaves and fruit slices on top of the soil.

4. Seal the cut you made with tape. Mark the date on the tape.

5. Add water through the top of the bottle to moisten the soil, and put the cap on the bottle. Wash your hands.

6. Observe the fruit slices each day for two weeks. Record your observations. Keep the soil moist.

October 3

WHAT DO YOU THINK?

- What do you observe happening to the fruit slices?
- Where do the decomposers in your bottle come from?

CHALLENGE Predict what would happen if you used potting soil instead of soil from outside.

SKILL FOCUS
Observing

MATERIALS
- clear soda bottle with cap
- scissors
- stones
- garden soil
- leaves
- slices of fruit
- masking tape
- marker
- water

TIME
30 minutes

Models help explain feeding relationships.

COMBINATION NOTES
Remember to take notes and draw a diagram for *food chain* and *food web*.

You have learned how energy is captured by producers and moved through ecosystems by consumers and decomposers. Scientists use two different models to show the feeding relationships that transfer energy from organism to organism. These models are food chains and food webs.

Food Chain

A chain is made of links that are connected one by one. Scientists use the idea of links in a chain as a model for simple feeding relationships. A **food chain** describes the feeding relationship between a producer and a single chain of consumers in an ecosystem.

The illustration in the white box on page 27 shows a wetland food chain. The first link in the chain is a cattail, a primary producer that captures the Sun's energy and stores it in food. The second link is a caterpillar, a primary consumer of the cattail. The frog is the next link, a secondary consumer that eats the caterpillar. The final link is a heron, a tertiary consumer that eats the frog. Energy is captured and released at each link in the chain. The arrows represent the flow of energy from organism to organism. You can see that some of the energy captured by the cattail makes its way through a whole chain of other organisms in the ecosystem.

Food Web

A **food web** is a model of the feeding relationships between many different consumers and producers in an ecosystem. A food web is more like a spiderweb, with many overlapping and interconnected food chains. It is a better model for the complex feeding relationships in an ecosystem, which usually has many different producers, with many primary and secondary consumers.

READING TiP

Notice that the food chain described above is also a part of the food web described here. Follow the blue arrows in the diagram on page 27.

The illustration on page 27 also shows a wetland food web. You can see that the feeding relationships can go in several directions. For example, the food web shows that ruddy ducks eat bulrushes, which are producers. That makes ruddy ducks primary consumers. Ruddy ducks are also secondary consumers because they eat snails. A food web shows how one consumer can play several roles in an ecosystem.

CHECK YOUR READING What is the difference between a food chain and a food web?

Both food chains and food webs show how different organisms receive their energy. They also show how different organisms depend on one another. If one organism is removed from the food web or food chain, it may affect many other organisms in the ecosystem.

Energy Flows Through Ecosystems

Energy is transferred from one organism to the next as organisms eat or are eaten.

A Wetland Food Chain

Flow of Energy
Energy flow starts at the bottom. Arrows represent energy moving from an organism that is eaten to the organism that eats it.

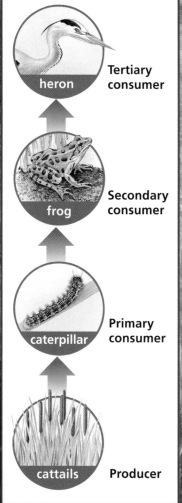

heron — **Tertiary consumer**

frog — **Secondary consumer**

caterpillar — **Primary consumer**

cattails — **Producer**

Decomposers
These tiny organisms recycle dead and decayed material.

A Wetland Food Web

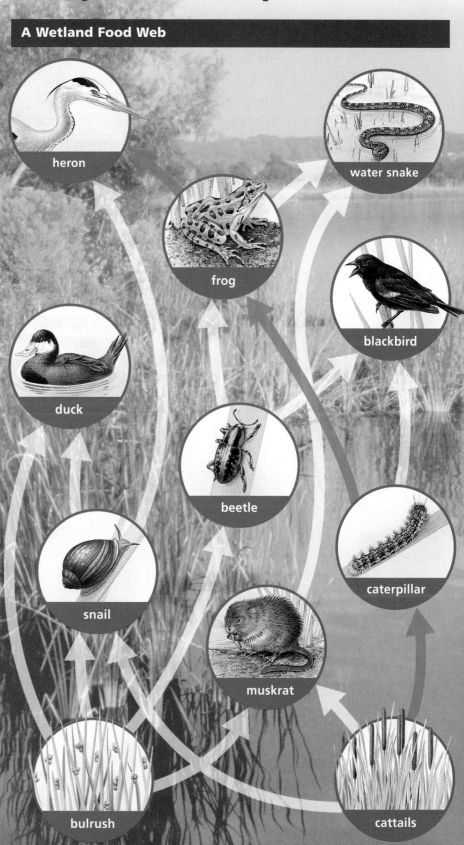

heron

water snake

frog

blackbird

duck

beetle

caterpillar

snail

muskrat

bulrush

cattails

Available energy decreases as it moves through an ecosystem.

Another way to picture the flow of energy in an ecosystem is to use an energy pyramid. An **energy pyramid** is a model that shows the amount of energy available at each feeding level of an ecosystem. The first level includes the producers, the second level the primary consumers, and so on. Because usable energy decreases as it moves from producers to consumers, the bottom level is the largest. The available energy gets smaller and smaller the farther up the pyramid you go.

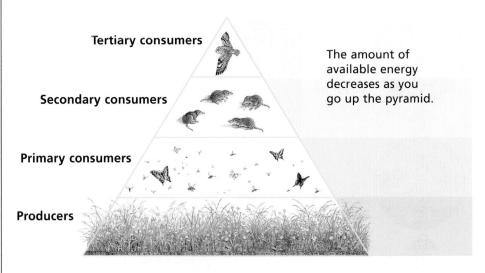

Tertiary consumers

Secondary consumers

Primary consumers

Producers

The amount of available energy decreases as you go up the pyramid.

READING TiP

Refer to the diagram above as you read the text. It is because available energy decreases at each level that the diagram takes the shape of a pyramid.

In the pyramid shown here, plants are the producers. They capture energy from sunlight, use some of it, then store the rest as food. The plants are eaten by insects, which also use some of the energy before being eaten by shrews. The shrews use energy before being eaten by the owl. You can see that it takes a lot of sunlight to support the producers and consumers in a food web that feeds an owl.

1.3 Review

KEY CONCEPTS

1. Describe the role of producers, consumers, and decomposers in an ecosystem.

2. Explain why a food web provides a better model of an ecosystem than a food chain does.

3. Explain how the amount of available energy changes as energy moves up a food chain.

CRITICAL THINKING

4. **Apply** Draw a food chain and a food web for an ecosystem near your home.

5. **Predict** Imagine that muskrats are removed from a wetland ecosystem. Predict what would happen both to producers and to secondary consumers.

⬤ CHALLENGE

6. **Synthesize** Explain how the carbon cycle is related to a food web. Describe how energy and matter move through the food web and the carbon cycle.

Biomagnification

Matter moves through living things in an ecosystem. Some of it is used up, some of it is stored. Sometimes, a toxic, or poisonous, material can get into a food chain and be stored. Biomagnification is the process by which matter becomes concentrated in living things.

Moving up the Food Chain

DDT provides one example of the effects of biomagnification in an ecosystem. DDT is a chemical that was widely used to kill plant-eating insects. Some chemicals break down over time, but DDT does not. DDT collected in water and soil, was absorbed by living things, and moved up the food chain. The diagram shows how DDT became magnified in a wetland ecosystem. It entered through tiny organisms called zooplankton, which absorbed DDT from the water.

1 The concentration of DDT in zooplankton was about 800 times greater than in the environment.

2 Minnows fed on zooplankton. DDT was magnified 31 times, so the concentration of DDT in minnows was 24,800 times greater than in the environment: 800 x 31 = 24,800.

3 Trout ate minnows. DDT was magnified 1.7 times, so the concentration of DDT in trout was 42,160 times greater than in the environment.

4 Gulls ate trout. DDT was magnified 4.8 times, so the concentration of DDT in gulls was over 200,000 times greater than in the environment.

DDT is especially harmful to large birds such as osprey and eagles. The chemical made the shells of the eggs of these large birds so thin that the eggs did not survive long enough to hatch.

Moving up the Food Chain

This diagram shows how DDT moved up a food chain in Long Island Sound. The color in each circle below represents a certain level of DDT.

1 Zooplankton

2 Minnows

3 Trout

4 Gull

CHALLENGE Even though DDT was effective, some insects were not harmed by DDT. Predict what might happen to the numbers of those insects as a result of DDT use.

1.4 Biomes contain many ecosystems.

BEFORE, you learned

- Feeding relationships describe how energy flows through ecosystems
- The amount of available energy decreases as it flows through ecosystems

NOW, you will learn

- How biomes vary by region and by the plant life they support
- How different ecosystems make up a biome
- About the different land and water biomes on Earth

VOCABULARY

biome p. 30
coniferous p. 32
deciduous p. 33
estuary p. 36

THINK ABOUT

What do this plant's characteristics suggest about its environment?

A plant's overall shape and form help it to survive in its environment. Look closely at this plant in the photograph. Describe its shape. Does it have leaves? a stem? flowers? Look at the surrounding area. What do your observations suggest about the environment in general?

Regions of Earth are classified into biomes.

COMBINATION NOTES
Remember to take notes and draw a diagram for each of the six land biomes described in the text.

If you could travel along the 30° latitude line, either north or south of the equator, you'd notice an interesting pattern. You would see deserts give way to grasslands and grasslands give way to forests. Across Earth, there are large geographic areas that are similar in climate and that have similar types of plants and animals. Each of these regions is classified as a **biome** (BY-ohm). There are six major land biomes on Earth, as shown on the map on page 31.

Climate is an important factor in land biomes. Climate describes the long-term weather patterns of a region, such as average yearly rainfall and temperature ranges. Climate also affects soil type. Available water, temperature, and soil are abiotic factors important in ecosystems. The fact that the abiotic factors of a particular biome are similar helps to explain why the ecosystems found in these biomes are similar. Biomes represent very large areas, which means that there will be many ecosystems within a biome.

Each land biome is characterized by a particular climate, the quality of the soil, and the plant life found there.

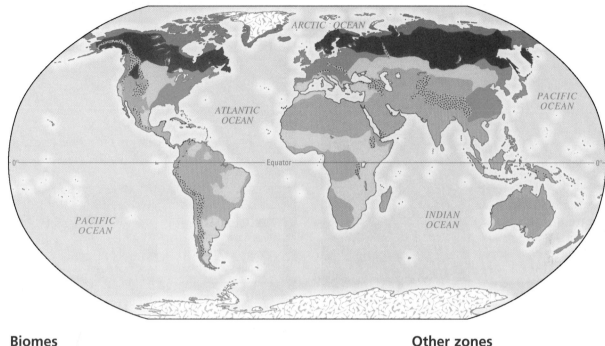

Biomes

🟦 Tundra   🟦 Desert   🟦 Temperate Forest

🟦 Taiga   🟦 Grassland   🟦 Tropical Forest

Other zones

🟦 Mountain Zones

🟦 Polar Ice

Taiga and Tundra

If you go to the northernmost regions of Earth, you will find two biomes—tundra and taiga—that are characterized by long cold winters and short cool summers. In the Arctic tundra, temperatures can go as low as –50°C, with a high of about 18°C. Temperature ranges in the taiga (TY-guh) are similar, –40°C to 20°C.

snowy owl

The tundra doesn't get much precipitation, less than 25 centimeters each year. Yet the area is wet because cold temperatures keep the water from evaporating. One of the important characteristics of tundra is permafrost, a deep layer of permanently frozen soil that lies just below the surface soil. Permafrost prevents trees from taking root in the tundra. Plants of the tundra are small and include mosses, grasses, and woody shrubs. Organisms called lichens also do well in the tundra.

The producers of tundra ecosystems support rodents, caribou, and musk oxen. Grizzly bears, white fox, and snowy owls are predators found there. Migrating birds come to nest in the tundra, feeding on insects that mature in summer.

Tundra Only small plants and lichens grow in the tundra because the soil below the surface is frozen.

Taiga Evergreen trees grow in the taiga, where the ground is cold but not frozen.

Even though the temperatures of the taiga are similar to those of the tundra, the taiga has more precipitation, 30 to 60 centimeters a year. The effect of this is that there is more snow on the ground, which insulates the soil below, keeping it from permanently freezing.

Taiga ecosystems are characterized by evergreen trees called **coniferous** (koh-NIHF-uhr-uhs) trees. These trees have needlelike leaves that produce food all year long. This is an advantage in taiga ecosystems because decomposers work slowly in the cold, so the soil is low in nutrients. The wood and leaves of these trees feed insects and their seeds feed birds and squirrels. Taiga ecosystems support deer, elk, snowshoe hares, and beavers. Predators include lynx, owls, bears, and wolves.

Desert and Grassland

collared lizard

Deserts and grasslands are biomes found toward the middle latitudes. You can see from the map on page 31 that a desert biome often leads into a grassland biome. What deserts and grasslands have in common is that they do not get enough precipitation to support trees.

Some deserts are cold and some deserts are hot, but all deserts are characterized by their dry soil. Less than 25 centimeters of rain falls each year in a desert. Desert plants, like the cactus, and desert animals, like the collared lizard, can get by on very little water. Small burrowing animals like the kangaroo rat and ground squirrel are part of desert ecosystems. Desert predators include snakes, owls, and foxes.

Grassland ecosystems develop in areas of moderate rainfall, generally from 50 to 90 centimeters each year. There is enough rain to support grasses, but too little rain to support forests. Periodic wildfires and droughts keep smaller shrubs and tree seedlings from growing. Summers in grassland ecosystems are warm, up to 30°C, but winters are cold.

Grasses do well in large open areas. The more rain a grassland ecosystem gets, the higher the grasses grow. These ecosystems support seed-eating rodents that make their burrows in the grassland soil. There are also large grazing animals, like bison, wild horses, gazelle, and zebra. Predators include wolves, tigers, and lions.

Desert Plants of the desert are adapted to survive in dry soil. Many must also survive high daytime temperatures.

Grassland Grasslands receive enough rain to support grasses. Wildfires keep shrubs and trees from growing.

Temperate Forest and Tropical Forest

Trees need more water than smaller plants, shrubs, and grasses. So forest biomes are usually located in regions where more water is available. The taiga is a forest biome. There the coniferous trees survive on smaller amounts of precipitation because the cold weather limits evaporation. Across the middle latitudes, temperate forests grow where winters are short and 75 to 150 centimeters of precipitation fall each year. Near the equator, there are no winters. There, tropical forests grow where 200 to 450 centimeters of rain fall each year.

Most temperate forests are made up of deciduous trees, sometimes referred to as broadleaf trees. **Deciduous** (dih-SIHJ-oo-uhs) trees drop their leaves as winter approaches and then grow new leaves in spring.

Temperate Forest
Temperate forests contain many trees with leaves that change color and fall as winter approaches.

Tropical Forest
Tropical forests are warm enough that trees stay green during the entire year.

The most common broadleaf trees in North American deciduous forests are oak, birch, beech, and maple. Temperate forests support a wide variety of animals. Animals like mice, chipmunks, squirrels, raccoons, and deer live off seeds, fruit, and insects. Predators include wolves, bobcats, foxes, and mountain lions.

Most temperate forests in North America are deciduous. However, the wet winters and dry summers in the Pacific Northwest support forests made up mostly of coniferous trees—redwoods, spruce, and fir. These forests are referred to as temperate rain forests. The largest trees in the United States are found in these temperate rain forests.

Tropical forests are located near the equator, where the weather is warm all year, around 25°C. The tropical rain forest is the wettest land biome, with a rainfall of 250 to 400 centimeters each year. The trees tend to have leaves year round. This provides an advantage because the soil is poor in nutrients. High temperatures cause materials to break down quickly, but there are so many plants the nutrients get used up just as quickly.

More types of animals, plants, and other organisms live in the tropical rain forest than anywhere else on Earth. The trees grow close together and support many tree-dwelling animals like monkeys, birds, insects, and snakes. There are even plants, like orchids and vines, that grow on top of the trees.

 CHECK YOUR READING How does the variety of plants in a biome affect the variety of animals in a biome?

How can you graph climate data for your area?

PROCEDURE

1. Gather local data on the average monthly precipitation and the average monthly temperature for a 12-month period.

2. On graph paper, mark off 12 months along the *x*-axis. Make a *y*-axis for each side of the graph, marking one "Temperature (°C)" and the other "Precipitation (mm)."

3. Plot the average precipitation for each month as a bar graph.

4. Plot the average temperature for each month as a line graph.

WHAT DO YOU THINK?

- How much precipitation did the area receive overall?
- What is the temperature range for the area?

CHALLENGE Collect data for the same location, going back 10, 20, and 30 years ago. Graph the data for each of these and compare these graphs to your original graph. Has the climate in your area changed? How might severe changes in climate affect the plant and animal life in your area?

SKILL FOCUS
Graphing data

MATERIALS
- graph data
- 2 colored pencils

TIME
20 minutes

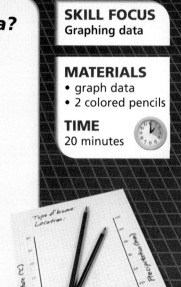

Water covers most of Earth's surface.

Close to three-quarters of Earth's surface is covered by water. Water, or aquatic, biomes can be divided into two broad categories: freshwater biomes and saltwater biomes. Plants have a role as producers in the water biomes that are closely surrounded by land—in ponds and streams and wetlands, and in coastal areas. The food chains of deepwater ecosystems depend on tiny photosynthetic microorganisms called phytoplankton.

leopard frog

Freshwater Biomes

The ecosystems of freshwater biomes are affected by the qualities of the landscape in which they are found. For example, the running water of streams and rivers results from differences in elevation. In shallow rivers, green algae and plants grow in from the banks, providing food for insects and snails that feed fish, salamanders, turtles, and frogs. Plants in a freshwater biome, like a stream or river, may take root in the soil under the water if the water is not too deep or moving too fast. Phytoplankton are not part of river ecosystems because of the moving water.

Aquatic Biomes

Freshwater biomes include the still water of lakes, the running water of rivers, and estuaries where fresh and salt waters mix.

Lakes and Ponds

Estuaries

Rivers and Streams

Ponds and lakes have still water. Ponds are shallow and support many plants as producers. The deeper lakes depend much more on phytoplankton. Ponds and lakes support many different insects, shell-fish, snakes, fish, and the land animals that feed off them.

○ **CHECK YOUR READING** Name two types of freshwater biomes.

Estuaries are water ecosystems that mark a transition between freshwater and saltwater biomes. An **estuary** is the lower end of a river that feeds into the ocean, where fresh water and salt water mix. Marshes and wetlands are two types of estuaries. Estuaries are sometimes referred to as the nurseries of the sea because so many marine animals travel into the calm waters of an estuary to reproduce. Seaweed, marsh grasses, shellfish, and birds all thrive in estuaries.

Marine Biomes

Marine biomes are saltwater biomes. The three general marine biomes are coastal ocean, open ocean, and deep ocean. Beaches are part of the coastal ocean biome. Tidal pools also form along the coast as the tide comes in and goes out and the conditions constantly change. Organisms like crabs and clams are able to survive the ever-changing conditions to thrive in coastal areas.

Organisms in the open ocean receive less sunlight than in the coastal ocean, and the temperatures are colder. Many types of fish and

RESOURCE CENTER
CLASSZONE.COM

Find out more about land and aquatic biomes.

Coastal

Marine biomes include rocky and sandy shores as well as the open ocean and the deep waters below, where little or no light can reach.

Open Ocean

Deep Ocean

other marine animals and floating seaweed live in the upper ocean. There are no plants in the open ocean. The producers at the bottom of the food chain are different types of phytoplankton.

The deep-ocean regions are much colder and darker than the upper ocean. In the deep ocean there is no sunlight available for photosynthesis. The animals in the deep ocean either feed on each other or on material that falls down from upper levels of the ocean. Many organisms in deep ocean biomes can only be seen with a microscope.

1.4 Review

KEY CONCEPTS

1. In biomes located on land, abiotic factors are used to classify the different biome types. What are these abiotic factors?

2. Name a characteristic type of plant for each of the six land biomes.

3. Name six different aquatic biomes.

CRITICAL THINKING

4. **Predict** If an ecosystem in the grassland biome started to receive less and less rainfall every year, what new biome would be established?

5. **Infer** Name some abiotic factors that affect aquatic biomes and ecosystems.

⬥ CHALLENGE

6. **Apply** Use the map on page 31 to list the following four biomes in the order you would find them moving from the equator to the poles.
   • desert
   • taiga
   • tropical Forest
   • tundra

the **BIG** idea

Matter and energy together support life within an environment.

 **CONTENT REVIEW**
CLASSZONE.COM

KEY CONCEPTS SUMMARY

1.1 Ecosystems support life.

Ecosystems are made up of living things (biotic) and nonliving things (abiotic).

plants   animals   temperature   Sun   soil   water

Biotic Factors   **Abiotic Factors**

VOCABULARY
ecology p. 9
ecosystem p. 9
biotic factor p. 10
abiotic factor p. 10

1.2 Matter cycles through ecosystems.

Water, carbon, and nitrogen are materials that are necessary for life. They move through ecosystems in continuous cycles.

VOCABULARY
cycle p. 16
water cycle p. 17
carbon cycle p. 18
nitrogen cycle p. 19

1.3 Energy flows through ecosystems.

Producers are the basis of feeding relationships in ecosystems.

cattails   caterpillar   frog

Producer   **Primary consumer**   **Secondary consumer**

Food chains and food webs help show how energy moves through living things.

VOCABULARY
producer p. 23
consumer p. 24
decomposer p. 25
food chain p. 26
food web p. 26
energy pyramid p. 28

1.4 Biomes contain many ecosystems.

Ecosystems of land biomes
• are affected by climate
• are affected by conditions of the soil
• are characterized by types of plants

Ecosystems of water biomes
• can be freshwater or saltwater
• are affected by landscape if freshwater
• are affected by depth if marine

VOCABULARY
biome p. 30
coniferous p. 32
deciduous p. 33
estuary p. 36

Reviewing Vocabulary

Write a statement describing how the terms in each pair are similar and different.

1. biotic, abiotic

2. producer, consumer

3. food chain, food web

The table shows the meanings of word roots that are used in many science terms.

Root	Meaning
bio–	life
ecos–	house
–ogy	study of

Use the information in the table to write definitions for the following terms.

4. ecology

5. biome

6. ecosystem

Reviewing Key Concepts

Multiple Choice *Choose the letter of the best answer.*

7. Which best describes the components of an ecosystem?
   - **a.** light, water, soil, and temperature
   - **b.** autotrophs and heterotrophs
   - **c.** biotic and abiotic factors
   - **d.** producers, consumers, and decomposers

8. What is the primary source of energy for most ecosystems?
   - **a.** water
   - **b.** nitrogen
   - **c.** soil
   - **d.** sunlight

9. What is the process by which the water in rivers, lakes, and oceans is converted to a gas and moves into the atmosphere?
   - **a.** precipitation
   - **b.** evaporation
   - **c.** condensation
   - **d.** transpiration

10. The process called nitrogen fixation is essential for life on Earth. Which of the following is an example of nitrogen fixation?
    - **a.** Plants take in nitrogen gas from the atmosphere.
    - **b.** Animals take in nitrogen gas from the atmosphere.
    - **c.** Water absorbs nitrogen.
    - **d.** Bacteria convert nitrogen gas into a form that plants can use.

11. Which organism is a decomposer?
    - **a.** vulture
    - **b.** sunflower
    - **c.** musk ox
    - **d.** fungus

12. How are decomposers important in an ecosystem?
    - **a.** They make atmospheric nitrogen available to plants in a usable form.
    - **b.** They convert organic matter into more complex compounds.
    - **c.** They are an important source of food for scavengers.
    - **d.** They break down organic matter into simpler compounds.

13. What factor is least important in determining the plant life in a biome?
    - **a.** average annual rainfall
    - **b.** average annual temperature
    - **c.** the type of soil
    - **d.** the type of animals living there

Short Answer *Write a short answer to each question.*

14. Write a paragraph to describe how carbon dioxide gas in the atmosphere can become part of the carbon compounds found inside animals.

15. Write a paragraph to explain how the amount of available energy changes as you move from producers to consumers in a food web.

16. Write a paragraph to describe one important way in which the flow of energy through ecosystems is different from the cycling of matter.

Thinking Critically

Use the diagram to answer the next four questions.

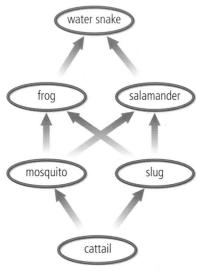

17. CONNECT What does the diagram above represent and how does it relate to energy in an ecosystem?

18. CLASSIFY Identify each of the animals in the diagram above as a producer, primary consumer, or secondary consumer or tertiary consumer.

19. APPLY Another animal that is found in many wetlands ecosystems is the shrew. The shrew eats salamanders and slugs and is eaten by water snakes. Copy the diagram above and show how you would add the shrew to the diagram.

20. CONNECT Use the diagram above to make an energy pyramid. If only one-tenth of the energy available at each level is passed on to the next higher level, how much of the energy in a cattail is transferred to a salamander?

21. SYNTHESIZE Why would it be difficult to show a decomposer as part of an energy pyramid?

22. RANK Arrange the following list of biomes according to the relative amounts of precipitation in each, going from the least amount to the most: grassland, desert, deciduous forest, taiga, tropical rain forest.

23. SYNTHESIZE Why are plants but not animals considered an important factor in classifying a land biome?

24. SUMMARIZE Draw a diagram that illustrates aquatic biomes. On your diagram label the following: freshwater river, freshwater lake, estuary, coastal zone, open ocean zone. How do abiotic factors differ among these biomes?

25. COMPARE AND CONTRAST In what ways is your home like an ecosystem? In what ways is it different?

26. APPLY Describe a change in an abiotic factor that affected living factors in an ecosystem near you.

the BIG idea

27. CLASSIFY Look again at the photograph on pages 6–7. Now that you have finished the chapter, how would you change or add details to your answer to the question on the photograph?

28. SYNTHESIZE Write one or more paragraphs describing how matter and energy together support life in an ecosystem. You may use examples from one specific ecosystem if you wish. In your description, use each of the following terms. Underline each term in your answer.

ecosystem	decomposer
food web	nitrogen cycle
producer	carbon cycle
primary consumer	secondary consumer

UNIT PROJECTS

If you are doing a unit project, make a folder for your project. Include in your folder a list of the resources you will need, the date on which the project is due, and a schedule to track your progress. Begin gathering data.

Interpreting Graphs

Choose the letter of the best response.

The graphs below show average monthly temperature and precipitation for one year in Staunton, Virginia, an area located in a temperate deciduous forest biome.

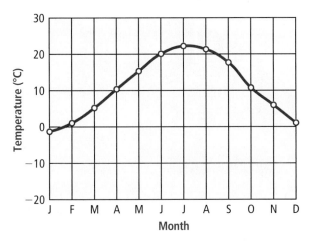

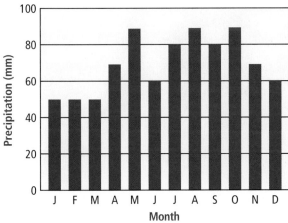

SOURCE: NASA

1. What was the average temperature during July?
   a. 20°
   b. 10°
   c. 23°
   d. 0°

2. Which months had the most precipitation?
   a. January, February, March
   b. May, August, October
   c. July, August, September
   d. December, January, February

3. What were conditions during May?
   a. warm and moist
   b. warm and dry
   c. cool and moist
   d. cool and dry

4. Which temperature is closest to the average temperature for the year shown?
   a. about 16°
   b. about 0°
   c. about 20°
   d. about 10°

5. How much precipitation would you estimate fell as snow in the year shown?
   a. less than 50 mm
   b. between 50 and 100 mm
   c. between 100 and 200 mm
   d. over 200 mm

Extended Response

6. Most of the United States is part of a temperate deciduous forest biome. The deciduous forest biome has four seasons. Trees in this biome lose their leaves yearly. Use this information, as well as the information in the graphs, to describe the seasons in the temperate deciduous forest biome.

7. Write a paragraph in which you describe a typical ecosystem in your city or town. In your answer include biotic factors such as plants, animals, and other organisms. Also include abiotic factors such as light, temperature, soil, and water. Finish your description by saying how you and other humans affect the ecosystem.

2 Interactions Within Ecosystems

the BIG idea

Living things within an ecosystem interact with each other and the environment.

Key Concepts

Internet Preview

CLASSZONE.COM

Chapter 2 online resources: Content Review, Simulation, two Resource Centers, Math Tutorial, Test Practice

How do living things interact?

EXPLORE (the BIG idea)

How Do Living Things Interact Where You Live?

Take your notebook outside. Observe how different living things interact. Record your observations.

Observe and Think Do the interactions you see benefit both living things or just one? Do they involve just animals or plants and animals?

How Many Roles Can a Living Thing Have in an Ecosystem?

While you are outside, choose an organism within your view and think about how it fits into the ecosystem.

Observe and Think In what way does the organism fit into feeding relationships in the ecosystem? What are some other roles the organism plays?

Internet Activity: Carrying Capacity

Go to **ClassZone.com** to simulate the carrying capacity of an area for a population of deer.

Observe and Think What factors other than available food might affect the carrying capacity for a popuation of deer?

NSTA scilinks.org
SCI*LINKS*

Populations and Communities **Code: MDL002**

Getting Ready to Learn

◀ CONCEPT REVIEW

- Ecosystems support life.
- Different ecosystems make up a biome.

◀ VOCABULARY REVIEW

producer p. 23 **food chain** p. 26
consumer p. 24 **food web** p. 26
interaction *See Glossary.*

CONTENT REVIEW
CLASSZONE.COM
Review concepts and vocabulary.

▶ TAKING NOTES

OUTLINE

As you read, copy the headings on your paper in the form of an outline. Then add notes in your own words that summarize what you read.

VOCABULARY STRATEGY

Write each new vocabulary term in the center of a **four square** diagram. Write notes in the squares around each term. Include definition, some characteristics, and some examples of the term. If possible, write some things that are not examples of the terms.

See the Note-Taking Handbook on pages R45–R51.

SCIENCE NOTEBOOK

I. Groups of living things interact within ecosystems.
  A. Organisms occupy specific living areas.
    1. populations: same species in one area
    2. habitat and niche: place where organisms live; role of organisms
    3. community: several populations living together

Definition	Characteristics
where something lives	supplies shelter and food
HABITAT	
Examples	Nonexamples
a tree is a habitat for a bird	(you won't always use this square)

2.1 Groups of living things interact within ecosystems.

BEFORE, you learned

- Abiotic and biotic factors interact in an ecosystem
- Matter and energy necessary for life move through the environment

NOW, you will learn

- How groups of organisms interact in an ecosystem
- About levels of organization in an ecosystem
- About living patterns of different groups of organisms

VOCABULARY

species p. 45
population p. 46
habitat p. 46
niche p. 47
community p. 48

EXPLORE Counting Animals

How can you use a grid to estimate the number of animals in an area?

PROCEDURE

(1) Mark off an area on the graph paper as shown. Count the number of large squares in that area.

(2) Use a handful of rice to represent a group of animals. Spread the rice evenly within the area you marked. Count the number of "animals" inside one large square.

(3) Use a calculator to multiply the counts from steps 1 and 2. This will give you an estimate of the total number of "animals." Check your answer by counting all the grains of rice.

WHAT DO YOU THINK?

- How close was your estimate to the actual number?
- What would prevent a scientist from making an actual count of animals in an area?

MATERIALS

- handful of rice
- large-grid graph paper
- marker
- calculator

Organisms occupy specific living areas.

On a walk through the woods, you may see many different plants and animals. These organisms, like all living things, depend on their environment to meet their needs. The particular types of living things you see will depend on the characteristics of the area you are visiting.

Scientists group living things according to their shared characteristics. The smallest grouping is the species. Scientists consider organisms to be members of the same **species** (SPEE-sheez) if the organisms are so similar that they can produce offspring that can also produce offspring. Members of a species can successfully reproduce.

READING TiP

The terms *species, specific,* and *special* come from the same Latin root meaning "kind." A species is a kind, or type, of organism.

Galápagos Island Populations

A population is a group of the same organisms that live in the same area.

Cacti	Crabs	Iguanas

Populations

Scientists use the term **population** to mean a group of organisms of the same species that live in a particular area. In a way, this is similar to the population of people who live in a particular city or town. You can then think of those people who live in different cities or towns as belonging to different populations. It is the boundary of an area that defines a population. In the study of ecology, members of the same species that live in different areas belong to different populations.

A biological population can be a group of animals or a group of plants. It can be a group of bacteria or fungi or any other living thing. Populations of many different species will be found living in the same area. For example, the photographs above show different populations of organisms that all live in the same place—on one of the Galápagos Islands. The island has a population of cacti, a population of crabs, and a population of iguanas.

 CHECK YOUR READING What is the difference between a species and a population?

Habitats and Niches

The Galápagos Islands are a small group of volcanic islands, off the coast of South America, that are famous for their unusual plant and animal life. These islands are the **habitat**—the physical location—where these plants and animals live. Island habitats have certain physical characteristics that describe them, including the amount of precipitation, a range of temperatures, and the quality of the soil. Different habitats have different characteristics.

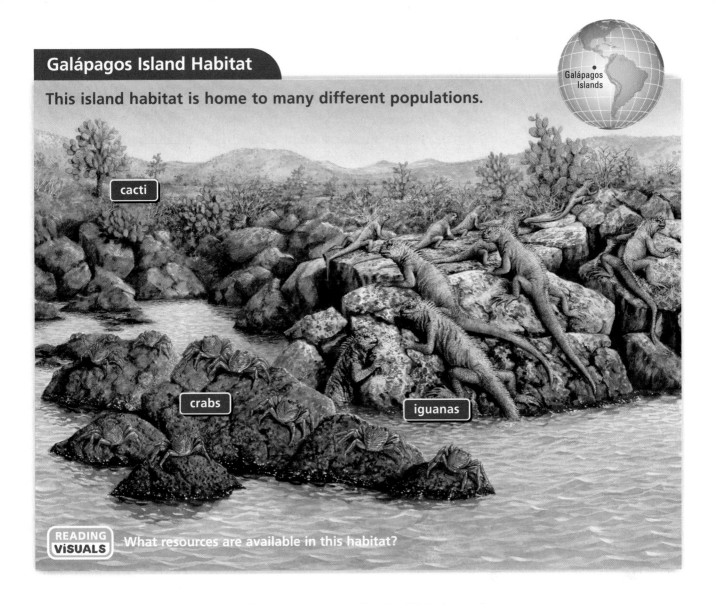

Galápagos Island Habitat

This island habitat is home to many different populations.

Galápagos Islands

cacti

crabs

iguanas

READING VISUALS What resources are available in this habitat?

A habitat is filled with different species, each of which depends on the habitat's resources to meet its needs. The characteristics of a habitat determine the species of plants that can grow there. The species of plants found in a habitat, in turn, determine the species of animals and other organisms that will do well there.

Different populations within a habitat interact. They are part of the flow of energy and matter through an ecosystem. For example, in the Galápagos Island scene above, the cacti capture the Sun's energy and store fresh water. They also provide food for the iguana, who eats the cactus leaves. The cactus is a producer and the iguana is a primary consumer. The crabs of the Galápagos are secondary consumers that feed on other shellfish. Each of these organisms has a role to play in the habitat, a role which is referred to as its **niche** (nihch).

The niche an organism fills in a habitat is not limited to its place in a food web. Plants provide nesting sites as well as food. The droppings left behind by animals fertilize soil and often spread seed. Generally, no two species will fill exactly the same niche in a habitat.

Communities

Take a mental tour of your school. Note that you share space with people who do many different things—students, teachers, custodians, librarians, counselors, and many others. They all work together and help each other. We often say that a school is a community.

Scientists use the term *community* in a slightly different way. A biological **community** is a group of populations that live in a particular area and interact with one another. Cacti, iguanas, and crabs are part of the Galápagos Island community. This community also includes populations of tortoises, finches, fleas, bacteria, and many other species.

 How is a school community similar to a community of living things?

The environment can be organized into five levels.

OUTLINE
Add the different levels of the environment to your outline. Make sure to explain each term in the supporting details.

The five terms—biome, ecosystem, community, population, and organism—describe the environment at different levels.

1. **Biome** A biome describes in very general terms the climate and types of plants that are found in similar places around the world.

2. **Ecosystem** Within each biome are many ecosystems. Inside an ecosystem, living and nonliving factors interact to form a stable system. An ecosystem is smaller than a biome and includes only organisms and their local environment.

3. **Community** A community is made up of the living components of the ecosystem. In a community, different plants, animals, and other organisms interact with each other.

4. **Population** A population is a group of organisms of the same species that live in the same area.

5. **Organism** An organism is a single individual animal, plant, fungus, or other living thing. As the picture on page 49 shows, an organism plays a part in each level of the environment.

Patterns exist in populations.

Members of a population settle themselves into the available living space in different ways, forming a pattern. Populations may be crowded together, be spread far apart, or live in small groups. A population may also show a pattern over time. The number of individuals in the population may rise and fall, depending on the season or other conditions, or as a result of interactions with other organisms.

Levels in the Environment

Organisms living in an African savannah illustrate the different levels of the environment.

Grassland

1 **Biome**
The African savannah is part of a grassland biome.

2 **Ecosystem**
The community of organisms, along with water, soil, and other abiotic factors, make up an ecosystem.

3 **Community**
Populations of wildebeests, gazelles, lions, and grasses share the same living areas and resources. These and other populations form a savannah community.

4 **Population**
Gazelles travel together in herds looking for areas to graze in. The total number of gazelles in an ecosystem is called a population of gazelles.

5 **Organism**
The gazelle lives in various grassland habitats in eastern Africa and fills a particular niche.

READING VISUALS Describe the gazelle's place in each level of the environment.

Patterns in Living Space

The patterns formed by a population often show how the population meets its needs. For example, in California's Mojave desert the pale soil is dotted with dark-green shrubs called creosote bushes. A surprising thing about the bushes is their even spacing. No human shaped this habitat, however. The bushes are the same distance from each other because the roots of each bush release a toxin, a type of poison, that prevents the roots of other bushes from growing.

The distribution of animals in a habitat is often influenced by how they meet their needs. Animals must be able to reach their food supply and have places to raise their young. If you put up bird houses for bluebirds on your property, they must be spaced at least a hundred meters apart. Bluebirds need a large area of their own around their nest in order to collect enough insects to feed their young.

READING TiP

As you read this paragraph, note the pattern of wilde-beests and elephants in the photograph.

Sometimes, the particular pattern of individuals in a living space helps a population survive. Herring swim in schools, with the individual fish spaced close together. Wildebeests roam African grasslands in closely packed herds. These animals rely on the group for their safety. Even if one member of the group is attacked, many more will survive.

CHECK YOUR READING What are some reasons for the spacing patterns observed in different populations?

elephant

wildebeest

READING VISUALS COMPARE AND CONTRAST How would you describe the spacing of these elephants and wildebeests?

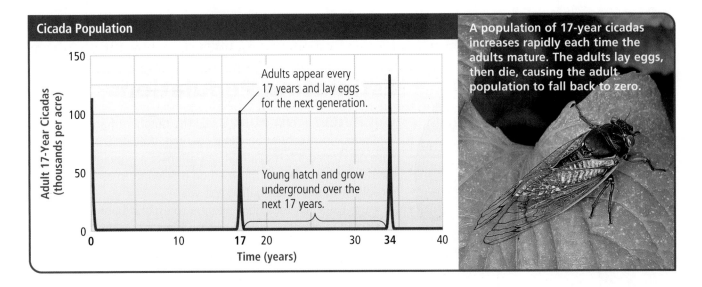

Cicada Population

Adult 17-Year Cicadas (thousands per acre)

Adults appear every 17 years and lay eggs for the next generation.

Young hatch and grow underground over the next 17 years.

Time (years)

A population of 17-year cicadas increases rapidly each time the adults mature. The adults lay eggs, then die, causing the adult population to fall back to zero.

Patterns in Time

At a spring picnic, you would rarely see the wasps called yellow jackets. At a fall picnic, however, they swarm to the food. This is an example of a population whose size changes with time. In spring, the queen wasp lays eggs and new wasps hatch. She continues to lay eggs all summer and the population grows. When winter comes, all the wasps except the queen die, and the population decreases.

Many birds that nest in North America in summer fly south to Central and South America in winter. There they find enough food and good nesting sites. In North America, this seasonal pattern leads to small bird populations in winter and large ones in summer.

The graph above shows an unusual pattern of population growth. Certain species of cicadas appear only every 17 years. Because no other species can rely on these insects as their main source of food, the cicadas survive long enough to lay eggs when they do appear.

2.1 Review

KEY CONCEPTS

1. What are two characteristics of a population?

2. Order these terms from the simplest to the most complex: biome, community, ecosystem, organism, population.

3. How do the terms *habitat* and *niche* relate to each other?

CRITICAL THINKING

4. **Apply** Choose a biological community in your region. Describe some of the populations that make up that community.

5. **Infer** How might the seasonal patterns of insect populations relate to the seasonal patterns of bird populations?

⬤ CHALLENGE

6. **Apply** The Explore activity on page 45 shows one way in which scientists sample a population to determine its total size. Would this method work for estimating the size of a population of 17-year cicadas? Why or why not?

CHAPTER INVESTIGATION

Estimating Populations

OVERVIEW AND PURPOSE The number of animals in a wild population cannot be easily counted. Wildlife biologists have developed a formula that can estimate a population's size by using small samples. This method is referred to as mark and recapture. In this investigation you will

- use the mark-recapture method to estimate population size
- test the effectiveness of the mark-recapture method by simulating an outbreak of disease in a population

▶ Problem

How effective is the mark-recapture method in estimating population size?

▶ Hypothesize

Write a hypothesis to explain how you will use a sudden change in population size to determine the effectiveness of the mark-recapture method. Your hypothesis should take the form of an "If . . . , then . . . , because . . ." statement.

MATERIALS
- paper bag
- white kidney beans
- 2 colored markers
- calculator

▶ Procedure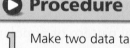

1. Make two data tables in your **Science Notebook,** like the ones shown on page 53.

2. From your teacher, obtain a paper bag containing a "population" of white kidney beans.

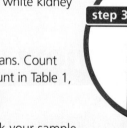
step 3

3. Remove a small handful of beans. Count the sample and record the count in Table 1, under First Capture Total.

4. Use a colored marker to mark your sample population. Return the beans to the bag, and gently shake the bag to mix all the beans.

5. Remove and count a second sample of beans. Record the count in Table 1, under Recapture Total.

6. Count the number of beans from this sample that were marked from the first capture. Record this number in Table 1, under Recapture Marked. Return all the beans to the bag.

7 Use a calculator and the following formula to estimate the population size. Record the estimate in Table 1 as the Calculated Population Estimate.

$$\frac{\text{First Capture Total} \times \text{Recapture Total}}{\text{Recapture Marked}} = \text{Population Estimate}$$

8 Disease strikes. Remove a small handful of beans from the bag. Count the beans, and record this count in Table 2, under Killed by Disease. Set these beans aside.

9 Repeat steps 3–7 to mark and recapture your survivor population. This time use a different colored marker to mark your sample population, and only include the beans marked in the second color in your counts.

10 Fill in Data Table 2 for the survivor population. Use the formula from step 7 to calculate your estimate of the survivor population.

11 Once you have calculated your estimate of survivors, dump out the paper bag and count all the beans that were inside. Record this count in Table 2, under Actual Survivors Total.

▶ Observe and Analyze | Write It Up |

1. **CALCULATE** From Table 2 add together the number of actual survivors and the number killed by disease. Put this in Table 1, under Actual Population Total.

2. **CALCULATE** Find the percentage of the population affected by disease using the following formula:

$$\frac{\text{Killed by disease} \times 100}{\text{Actual Population Total}} = \text{Percentage affected}$$

▶ Conclude | Write It Up |

1. **INFER** How did the estimated number of beans compare with the actual number?

2. **IDENTIFY LIMITS** What aspects of this investigation most likely would not be possible in a natural habitat? Why not?

3. **EVALUATE** Compare your results with your hypothesis. Do your data support your hypothesis?

▶ INVESTIGATE Further

CHALLENGE Determine if using larger samples of a population gives better population estimates. Get another bag of unmarked beans from your teacher. Use a spreadsheet program, if available, to record your data and calculate the results.

Estimating Populations
Table 1. Population sampling before disease

First Capture Total	Recapture Total	Recapture Marked	Calculated Population Estimate	Actual Population Total

Table 2. Population sampling after disease

Survivors First Capture Total	Survivors Recapture Total	Survivors Recapture Marked	Calculated Survivors Estimate	Killed by Disease	Actual Survivors Total

Organisms can interact in different ways.

◁ BEFORE, you learned	▷ NOW, you will learn
• Different populations live together in a habitat • Different species fill different niches in a habitat • There are patterns in the ways organisms interact with each other and their environment	• About different types of interactions in an ecosystem • How some species benefit from interactions • How some species are harmed by interactions

VOCABULARY

predator p. 55
prey p. 55
competition p. 55
cooperation p. 57
symbiosis p. 58
mutualism p. 58
commensalism p. 59
parasitism p. 59

THINK ABOUT

What are some of the ways people interact?

People in a community interact with each other in many ways. An interaction is the way a person behaves toward or responds to another person. This photo-

graph shows groups of people at a soccer game. There are players from two teams and fans who are watching the game. How would you describe the interactions among the people in this photograph?

Organisms interact in different ways.

The photograph above shows how members of a human community both compete and cooperate. Different members of the populations of a biological community also compete and cooperate. They not only share a habitat, but they also share the resources in that habitat. How different organisms interact depends on their relationship to each other.

A robin in a meadow finds a caterpillar and swallows it. This is one obvious way organisms in an ecosystem interact—one eats, and the other gets eaten. Organisms also compete. The robin may have to compete with a flicker to get the caterpillar. And organisms can cooperate. Ants work together to build a nest, collect food, and defend their colony.

 CHECK YOUR READING Name three ways organisms may interact with each other in an ecosystem.

Predator and Prey

Many interactions between organisms in an ecosystem involve food. A food chain shows the feeding relationships between different species. There are producers and consumers. Another way to look at a food chain is through the interactions of predators and prey. The **predator** is an animal that eats another. The **prey** is an animal that is eaten by a predator. In a food chain, an organism can be both predator and prey. A meadowlark that feeds on a grasshopper is, in turn, eaten by a prairie falcon.

▼ REMINDER

A *producer* is an organism that makes its own food; a *consumer* is an organism that eats another organism for food.

Predators can affect how members of their prey populations are distributed. Herring move together in a school and wildebeests travel in herds to protect themselves. It is the sick or older members of the population that will most likely be eaten by predators. Species of prey may also have adaptations that relate to the behavior of predators. This is true of cicadas and their long reproductive cycles.

Prey populations, in turn, affect the location and number of predator populations. For example some birds are predators feeding on insects. One factor that may affect movement of birds from one location to another is the availability of insects.

Competition

In a team game, two teams compete against each other with the same goal in mind—to win the game. In a biological community, competition is for resources, not wins. **Competition** is the struggle between individuals or different populations for a limited resource.

In an ecosystem, competition may occur within the same species. Individual plants compete with each other for light, space, and nutrients. For example, creosote bushes compete with other creosote bushes for the same water supply. The toxins produced by the roots of one creosote bush prevent other creosote bushes from growing.

Competition also occurs between members of different species. In the tropical rain forests of Indonesia, vines called strangler figs compete with trees for water, light, and nutrients. The vine attaches itself to a host tree. As it grows, the vine surrounds and eventually kills the tree by blocking out sunlight and using up available water and nutrients.

INFER Do you think a strangler fig could survive on its own?

host tree

strangler fig

Competition

Competition between species
Two different species, hyenas and vultures, compete for the remains of a dead animal.

Competition within species Two male deer lock horns as they battle over territory.

Competition occurs between species and within species. For example, vultures and hyenas will compete over the food left in the remains of a dead animal. Wolves will compete with one another over territory. A wolf will mark its territory by urinating on trees and so warn off other wolves. Animals also compete over territory by fighting, using threatening sounds, and putting on aggressive displays.

Competition within species often occurs during the mating season. Male birds use mating songs and displays of feathers to compete for the attention of females. Male hippopotamuses fight to attract female hippopotamuses. Male crickets chirp to attract female crickets.

CHECK YOUR READING What sorts of resources do plants and animals compete for?

READING TIP

Compare and contrast the meanings of *competition* and *coexistence*.

Competition does not occur between all populations that share the same resources. Many populations can coexist in a habitat—different species can live together without causing harm to one another. Many different populations of plants coexist in a forest. Maple trees, beech trees, and birch trees can live side by side and still have enough water, nutrients, and sunlight to meet their needs.

INVESTIGATE Species Interactions

How do predator-prey populations interact?

Use these rules for predator-prey interaction for each round. If a predator card touches three or more prey cards, remove the prey cards touched. If the predator card does not touch at least three prey cards, remove the predator card and leave the prey cards. Predator cards are large, prey cards are small.

PROCEDURE

(1) Use masking tape to mark a boundary on a table top.

(2) Scatter five prey cards into the area. Take a predator card and toss it, trying to get it to land on the prey.

(3) According to the rules above, remove the predators and prey that have "died." Record the number of predators and prey that have

"survived." This represents one generation.

(4) Double the populations of predators and prey—they have "reproduced."

(5) Scatter the prey cards into the area and then toss the predator cards as before. Repeat steps 3 and 4 for a total of 15 rounds (generations).

WHAT DO YOU THINK?

• How does the size of the prey population affect the predator population?

• How might the size of a habitat affect the interaction of predators and prey?

CHALLENGE Use graph paper and colored pencils to make a graph of your results. Or use a spreadsheet program if one is available to you.

predator

prey

Cooperation

Not all interactions in an ecosystem involve competition. **Cooperation** is an interaction in which organisms work in a way that benefits them all. Some predators cooperate when they hunt. Although individual lions may hunt on their own, they also hunt in packs to kill large prey.

Killer whales also cooperate when they hunt. The whales swim in packs called pods. The pod swims in circles around a school of fish, forcing the fish close together so they are easier to catch. Pod members may also take turns chasing a seal until it gets tired and is easily killed. The pod may even work together to attack larger species of whales.

Ants, bees, and termites are social insects. Members of a colony belong to different groups, called castes, and have different responsibilities. Some groups gather food while others defend the colony. Other animals, like apes and monkeys, live in family groups. Members of the family cooperate to care for their young.

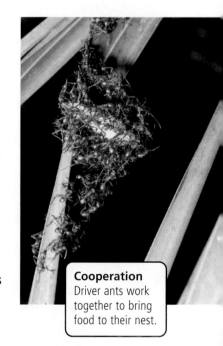

Cooperation
Driver ants work together to bring food to their nest.

The survival of one species might depend on another species.

OUTLINE
Add a sentence about *symbiosis* to your outline and define the three types of symbiosis in the supporting details.

You have learned that many different organisms live together in a habitat. The fact that organisms live together forces them to interact in different ways. For example, an organism preys upon another for food. Or perhaps there is competition among organisms over resources such as food, water, and territory.

The actions of different organisms can be so closely related that the survival of one species depends on the action or presence of another. In such a relationship, at least one of the species is getting a resource that it needs to survive. Benefits of the relationship may include food, reproductive help, or protection.

The relationship between individuals of two different species who live together in a close relationship is called **symbiosis** (SIHM-bee-OH-sihs). This word means "living together." A symbiotic relationship may affect the partners in different ways.

- Both species benefit from the relationship.
- One species benefits while the other is not affected.
- One species benefits while the other is harmed.

Here are some examples for each of the three types of symbiosis.

Both Species Benefit

Mutualism The interaction between the hummingbird and the flower benefits both.

Stroll through a garden on a sunny day and notice the bees buzzing from flower to flower. Look closely at a single bee and you may see yellow pollen grains sticking to its hairy body. The relationship between the flower and the bee is an example of **mutualism** (MYOO-choo-uh-LIHZ-uhm)—an interaction between two species that benefits both. The bees get food in the form of nectar, and the flowers get pollen from other flowers, which they need to make seeds.

Many plants rely on mutualism to reproduce. The pollen needed to make seeds must be spread from flower to flower. The birds and insects that feed on the nectar in these flowers transfer pollen from one flower to the next. The seeds produced are then moved to new ground by animals that eat the seeds or the fruits that hold the seeds. This form of mutualism doesn't benefit the individual flower but instead ensures the survival of the species.

In some cases, mutualism is necessary for the survival of the organisms themselves. For example, termites are able to live off a food that most animals cannot digest: wood. The termites, in fact, can't digest wood either. However, they have living in their guts tiny single-celled organisms, protozoans, that can break the wood down into digestible components. The protozoans get a safe place to live, and the termites can take advantage of a plentiful food source.

RESOURCE CENTER
CLASSZONE.COM

Explore symbiotic relationships.

 CHECK YOUR READING Describe how a bee and a flower benefit from a symbiotic relationship.

One Species Benefits

Commensalism (kuh-MEHN-suh-LIHZ-uhm) is a relationship between two species in which one species benefits while the other is not affected. Orchids and mosses are plants that can have a commensal relationship with trees. The plants grow on the trunks or branches of trees. They get the light they need as well as nutrients that run down along the tree. As long as these plants do not grow too heavy, the tree is not affected.

Commensal relationships are very common in ocean ecosystems. Small fish called remoras use a type of built-in suction cup to stick to a shark's skin and hitch a ride. When the shark makes a kill, the remora eats the scraps. The shark makes no attempt to attack the remora. The remora benefits greatly from this commensal relationship; the shark is barely affected.

Not all commensal relationships involve food. Some fish protect themselves by swimming among the stinging tentacles of a moon jellyfish. The fish benefit from the relationship because the tentacles keep them safe from predators. The jellyfish is not helped or hurt by the presence of the fish. As in this example, it is common in commensal relationships for the species that benefits to be smaller than the species it partners with.

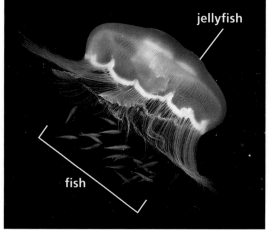

jellyfish

fish

Commensalism The interaction between the jellyfish and the fish benefits the fish only.

One Species Is Harmed

There is one symbiotic relationship in which a small partner can harm a much larger host. **Parasitism** (PAR-uh-suh-TIHZ-uhm) is a relationship between two species in which one species benefits while the species it depends on, its host, is harmed. Parasites are often tiny organisms that feed off, and weaken, their hosts. Ticks, lice, and mites are external parasites that live on or attach to their host's skin. Other parasites, like tapeworms and ringworms, are internal parasites that live inside their hosts.

Symbiotic Relationships

Mutualism
Both species benefit from the relationship.

Commensalism
One species benefits while the other is not affected.

Parasitism
One species benefits while the other is harmed.

Parasitism
Mistletoe is a plant that takes nourishment from a tree, causing damage to the tree.

Mutualism
Aphids are insects that provide ants with a sweet liquid. Ants live alongside the aphids, protecting them from predators.

Commensalism
Lichens benefit from living on a tree, but the tree is not harmed.

Parasitism
Ticks are animals that attach to their hosts, feeding on the host's blood.

Mutualism
Nitrogen-fixing bacteria get their nourishment from the roots of certain plants, providing the plants with nitrogen in return.

Commensalism
Mice do well living near humans, living off the food scraps humans leave behind.

The relationship between cowbirds and warblers is an unusual type of association called nest or brood parasitism. Female cowbirds never build their own nests or rear their own young. Instead, they lay their eggs in warbler nests. Although nest parasitism does not harm the host warbler, it does harm the warbler species because either warblers eggs do not hatch, or the chicks do not survive. The warbler species is often harmed because cowbirds push most warbler eggs from the nest in order to make room for their own eggs. Once the cowbird chicks hatch, their larger size helps them to outcompete the smaller warbler chicks for food, so that the host's chicks starve.

Parasitism The larger cowbird chick is cared for by a warbler at the expense of the smaller warbler chick.

 How is parasitism different from commensalism?

Interactions in an ecosystem are complex.

Different types of symbiosis occur throughout an ecosystem and often overlap. They may occur in the same locations, and the same species might be involved in more than one symbiotic relationship. The illustration on page 60 shows different symbiotic relationships that may occur in a backyard.

Symbiosis is just one of many interactions that take place in an ecosystem. The yard may have a garden, with individual tomato plants competing for water and nutrients; it may have ants cooperating to maintain a successful colony. An ecosystem is more than just a collection of biotic and abiotic factors. Interactions within an ecosystem help explain how resources are shared and used up and how energy flows through the system.

2.2 Review

KEY CONCEPTS

1. Name two ways in which members of the same species interact.

2. In what ways do members of different species interact?

3. Give an example of each type of symbiotic relationship: mutualism, commensalism, and parasitism.

CRITICAL THINKING

4. **Apply** Think of a biological community near you, and give an example of how one population has affected another.

5. **Compare and Contrast** Explain how symbiotic relationships are similar to and different from predator-prey interactions.

CHALLENGE

6. **Synthesize** Mutualism is more common in tropical ecosystems such as rain forests and coral reefs than in other ecosystems. Why do you think this is so?

Think SCIENCE

Where Are the Salamanders?

At the Cottonwood Lake Study Area in rural Stutsman County, North Dakota, U.S. Fish and Wildlife Service biologists have been studying wetland ecosystems for more than 30 years. Salamanders are one of the most abundant species in these wetlands. But in May 2000, the researchers started noticing sick salamanders in one wetland. By July, most salamanders had died. What killed them?

▶ Observations

a. In the past, cold winter weather and food shortages have killed salamanders at Cottonwood Lake.

b. The sick salamanders had discolored skin and enlarged livers.

c. The previous year, leopard frogs in a nearby wetland were found dying from a contagious fungal infection.

d. A viral disease has killed tiger salamanders elsewhere in the West.

e. Both large, well-fed salamanders and small, poorly nourished salamanders died.

This barred tiger salamander can be found in many wetlands in the Great Plains.

▶ Inferences

The following statements are possible inferences:

a. A food shortage caused salamanders to starve.

b. The fungal disease that killed leopard frogs also killed the salamanders

c. Salamanders were killed by a viral disease.

▶ Evaluate Inferences

On Your Own Which of the inferences are supported by the observations? Write the observations that support each of the inferences you identify.

As a Group Discuss your decisions. Come up with a list of reasonable inferences.

CHALLENGE What further observations would you make to test any of these inferences?

2.3 Ecosystems are always changing.

◀ **BEFORE, you learned**

- Populations in an ecosystem interact in different ways
- Organisms can benefit from interactions in an ecosystem
- Organisms can be harmed by interactions in an ecosystem

▶ **NOW, you will learn**

- How different factors affect the size of a population
- How biological communities get established
- How biological communities change over time

VOCABULARY

limiting factor p. 64
carrying capacity p. 65
succession p. 66
pioneer species p. 66

EXPLORE Population Growth

How does sugar affect the growth of yeast?

PROCEDURE

1. Use a marker to label the cups A, B, C. Pour 150 mL of warm water into each cup. Mark the water level with the marker.

2. Add 1/2 teaspoon of dry yeast to each plastic cup and stir.

3. Add 1/4 teaspoon of sugar to cup B. Add 1 teaspoon of sugar to cup C. Stir.

4. Wait 15 minutes. Measure the height of the foam layer that forms in each cup.

WHAT DO YOU THINK?

- Which cup had the most foam, which cup had the least?
- Describe the effect of sugar on a population of yeast.

MATERIALS

- 3 clear plastic cups
- warm water
- sugar
- dry yeast
- measuring spoons
- measuring cup
- stirring rod
- marker
- ruler

Populations change over time.

You may have a strong memory of a park you visited as a little child. You remember collecting pine cones, listening to woodpeckers, and catching frogs. Then you visit again, years later, and the park has changed. Maybe more land has been added, there are more birds and trees. Or maybe the area around the park has been developed. There seem to be fewer woodpeckers, and you can't find any frogs. The community has changed. There are a lot of factors that affect the populations within a biological community. Some have to do with the organisms themselves. Others relate to the habitat.

Population Growth and Decline

One factor that obviously affects population size is how often organisms reproduce. Birth rate is a measure of the number of births in an animal population. It can also be a measure of the stability of an ecosystem. For example, black bears reproduce once every two years. If there is not enough food available, however, the female bear's reproductive cycle is delayed, and the bear population does not grow.

Predator-prey interactions also affect population size. The graphs show how an increase in the moose population—the prey—in Isle Royale National Park was followed by an increase in the island's population of wolves—the predators. The wolves preyed upon the moose, the moose population decreased, then the wolf population decreased.

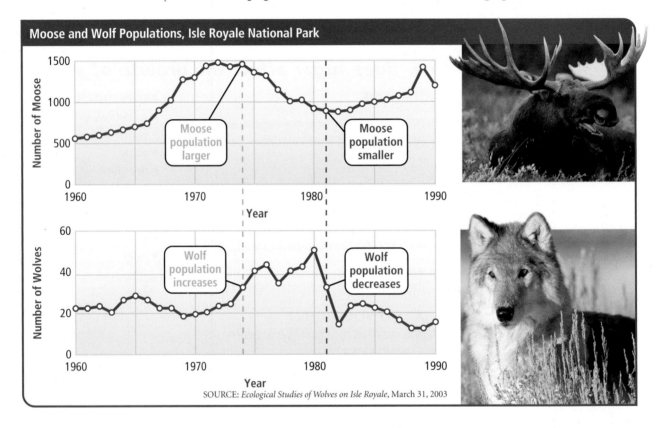

Moose and Wolf Populations, Isle Royale National Park

Moose population larger

Moose population smaller

Wolf population increases

Wolf population decreases

SOURCE: *Ecological Studies of Wolves on Isle Royale*, March 31, 2003

READING **TiP**

Note in the graphs above that it can take some time for the size of one population to affect the size of the other.

Any factor or condition that limits the growth of a population in an ecosystem is called a **limiting factor.** A large population of predators will limit the population of prey; a small population of prey will limit the population of predators. Too much or too little of any biotic or abiotic factor—like food, water, or light—makes an ecosystem unstable and brings about change.

A lack of nutrients in the soil is a limiting factor for plants. That is why farmers fertilize their crops. That same fertilizer, if it runs off into a lake, can increase the population of algae, another photosynthetic organism. A large population of algae can cover a lake with scum and use up oxygen needed by fish. This then limits the fish population.

What effect does spacing have upon a population of plants?

DESIGN
— YOUR OWN —
EXPERIMENT

Using the materials listed, design an experiment to test this hypothesis: "If plants grow too close together, the health of the population will be affected because the individual plants do not get enough of the nutrients and water that they need."

PROCEDURE

① Decide how to use the seeds, cups, and soil to test the hypothesis.

② Write up your experimental procedure. Include safety tips.

WHAT DO YOU THINK?

• What are the variables in your experiment?

• What evidence would you expect to see if your hypothesis is true?

CHALLENGE Conduct your experiment. Note that seeds must be planted near the top of the soil. A good measure for this is the tip of a pencil. Measure and record the growth of the seedlings. Allow the seedlings to grow for two weeks before drawing your conclusions.

SKILL FOCUS
Designing experiments

MATERIALS
• paper cups
• potting soil
• radish seeds
• water
• pencil
• ruler

TIME
20 minutes

Maintaining a Balance

Living things have certain minimum requirements for food, water, and living space. When a population reaches a state where it can no longer grow, the population has reached its **carrying capacity,** the maximum number of individuals that an ecosystem can support. You can see on page 64 that the graph for the moose population does appear to peak around 1500. Even if there were no wolves on the island of Isle Royale, the population of moose would still be limited because there is only so much food and space available.

 Explain the term *carrying capacity*.

VOCABULARY
Remember to make a four square diagram for *carrying capacity* in your notebook. Try to use *limiting factor* in your diagram.

An ecosystem's carrying capacity is different for each population. A meadow ecosystem will support many more bees and ants than bluebirds, for example. Isle Royale supports many more moose than wolves. The moose is a primary consumer of plants. It is at a lower level of the energy pyramid than the wolf, a secondary consumer.

Biotic factors can be limiting factors. These factors include the interactions between populations, such as competition, predation, and parasitism. Abiotic factors, such as temperature, availability of water or minerals, and exposure to wind, are also limiting.

Ecosystems change over time.

Take a walk in a New Hampshire woods and you may see the remains of old stone walls scattered about. A hundred years ago this land was mostly farmland. The farms were abandoned. And now, new trees have grown where farm animals once grazed.

Succession (suhk-SEHSH-uhn) is the gradual change in an ecosystem in which one biological community is replaced by another. The change from field to forest is an example of succession. Over time the grasses of open farmland are slowly replaced by small plants and shrubs, then trees.

Primary Succession

READING TiP

Succeed and *succession* come from the same Latin root word, *succedere*, meaning to go up or to follow after.

Very few places on Earth are without some form of life. Even when a lava flow covers an area or a glacier retreats and leaves behind an empty and barren environment, plants will move into the area and bring it back to life. These are examples of primary succession, the establishment of a new biological community.

Pioneer species are the first living things to move into a barren environment. In the illustration below, moss and lichen move in after a glacier retreats. There is little or no topsoil. Moss and lichen are common pioneers because they have tiny rootlike structures that can take hold on exposed rock.

Primary Succession

Primary succession can occur after a glacier retreats, when little topsoil is present.

1 Moss and lichen grow on rock with little or no soil. These pioneer species break apart the surface rock.

2 Over time, the rock breaks down further, forming soil. Larger plants take root. These support populations of animals.

3 Coniferous trees take root in a deep layer of soil. A diversity of plants and animals are supported in this habitat.

As the pioneers grow, they gradually weaken the rock surface. The rock breaks down and weathers over time. Decaying plant matter adds nutrients, forming soil. Now a variety of small plants and shrubs can take root. These plants, in turn, support insects, birds, and small rodents. Eventually there is enough soil to support coniferous trees. Forests grow, providing a stable habitat for larger animals.

RESOURCE CENTER
CLASSZONE.COM
Learn more about succession.

Secondary Succession

Secondary succession takes place after a major disturbance to the biological community in a stable ecosystem. Despite the disturbance, the soil remains. A community can be disturbed by a natural event, like fire or flood, or it can be disturbed by human activity. A forest cleared or farmland abandoned can lead to secondary succession.

The illustration below shows secondary succession following a forest fire. The damage, as bad as it is, is surface damage. Below the surface, seeds and plant roots survive. After a time, grasses and small shrubs grow up among the decaying remains of the original plants. Birds, insects, and rodents return. Alder trees take root—alders are trees that put nutrients into the soil. Over time, a variety of trees and plants grow, providing food for a variety of animals.

CHECK YOUR READING What is the difference between primary and secondary succession?

Secondary Succession

Secondary succession occurs if soil remains after a disturbance, such as a forest fire.

① Plants at the surface are burned; however, below the surface seeds and some plant roots survive.

② Grasses and small shrubs sprout among the charred trees and vegetation. Smaller animals return.

③ Deciduous trees like elm and maple grow and mature. A forest habitat is reestablished. More animals are supported.

Patterns of Change

All types of ecosystems go through succession. Succession can establish a forest community, a wetland community, a coastal community, or even an ocean community. Succession can happen over tens or hundreds of years. The pattern is the same, however. First a community of producers is established. These are followed by decomposers and consumers, then more producers, then more decomposers and consumers. Over time, a stable biological community develops.

In a way, the establishment of a biological community is like planting a garden. You first prepare the soil. Perhaps you add compost. This adds organic matter and nutrients to the soil, which helps the soil hold water. With the right preparation, your vegetables and flowers should grow well.

Pioneer species can function in one of two ways in an ecological succession. They can help other species to grow or they can prevent species from getting established.

READING TiP

As you read about the two ways plant species function in succession, think in terms of cooperation and competition.

- Some plant species function a bit like gardeners. Trees such as alders have nitrogen-fixing bacteria on their roots that improve the nutrient content of the soil and allow other tree seedlings to grow. Pioneering species may also stabilize the soil, shade the soil surface, or add nutrients to the soil when they die and decay.

- Other plant species produce conditions that keep out other plants. The plants may release chemicals that keep other plants from taking root. Or a new species may outcompete other species by using up resources or better resisting a disease.

Such interactions between living things help to determine succession in an ecosystem.

2.3 Review

KEY CONCEPTS

1. Describe three factors that could limit the size of a population in a habitat.

2. List two natural disturbances and two human-made disturbances that can lead to succession.

3. What role do pioneer species play in succession?

CRITICAL THINKING

4. **Infer** How and why would secondary succession in a tundra habitat differ from secondary succession in a rainforest habitat?

5. **Predict** Suppose you are clearing an area in your yard to construct a small pond. Sketch the stages of succession that would follow this disturbance.

○ CHALLENGE

6. **Synthesize** Imagine you are the wildlife manager for a forest preserve that supports both moose and wolves. What types of information should you collect to determine the carrying capacity for each species?

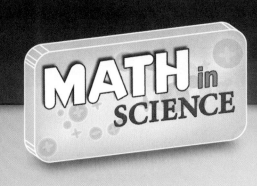

MATH in SCIENCE

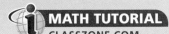
MATH TUTORIAL
CLASSZONE.COM

Click on Math Tutorial for more help with multiplying fractions and whole numbers.

Birth Rates and Populations

Ecologists pay careful attention to the yearly birth rates of endangered species. A birth rate is usually expressed as a fraction. It is the number of births divided by the number of adult females. A 2/5 birth rate for a population means that there are 2 births for every 5 adult females.

Example

Suppose at a national park in Borneo, there is a 2/5 birth rate among orangutans. There are 150 adult females in the park. Estimate how many young will be born. To find out, multiply the fraction by the number of adult females.

(1) Multiply the numerator of the fraction by the whole number.

$$150 \text{ females} \times \frac{2 \text{ births}}{5 \text{ females}} = \frac{150 \times 2}{5} = \frac{300}{5}$$

(2) Divide by the denominator.

$$\frac{300}{5} = 300 \div 5 = 60$$

ANSWER 60 young

Answer the following questions.

1. In 2001, there were about 72 adult female right whales. Scientists observing the whales reported a 1/3 birth rate. About how many right whales were born in 2001?

2. Giant pandas are severely endangered. Currently about 140 giant pandas live in captivity, in zoos and parks. About 3/5 of these were born in captivity. How many is that?

3. The orangutan population of the world has decreased sharply. At one time there were over 100,000 ranging across Asia. Now there may be 21,000, of which, 2/3 live in Borneo. About how many orangutans live in Borneo?

CHALLENGE Suppose 1/1 is given as the desired birth rate to save an endangered population. If the population is currently at 4 births per 20 adult females, by how many times does the rate need to increase to reach the desired rate?

2 Chapter Review

the BIG idea

Living things within an ecosystem interact with each other and the environment.

CONTENT REVIEW
CLASSZONE.COM

◀ KEY CONCEPTS SUMMARY

(2.1) Groups of living things interact within ecosystems.

- Members of the same species form a population within a habitat.

- Each species has a distinct role within a habitat. This is its niche.

Population of Crabs

Island Habitat for Crabs

VOCABULARY
species p. 45
population p. 46
habitat p. 46
niche p. 47
community p. 48

(2.2) Organisms can interact in different ways.

Organisms within a community interact with each other in many ways. Some are predators, some are prey. Some compete with one another, some cooperate. Some species form symbiotic relationships with other species:

Mutualism
benefits both

Commensalism
benefits one, other unaffected

Parasitism
benefits one, harms other

VOCABULARY
predator p. 55
prey p. 55
competition p. 55
cooperation p. 57
symbiosis p. 58
mutualism p. 58
commensalism p. 59
parasitism p. 59

(2.3) Ecosystems are always changing.

Primary Succession

In a barren area, a new community is established with pioneer species, like mosses, that do well with little or no soil. Mosses eventually give way to coniferous trees.

Secondary Succession

When a disturbance damages a community but soil remains, the community gets reestablished from seeds and roots left behind. Grasses grow, then small shrubs, and eventually trees.

VOCABULARY
limiting factor p. 64
carrying capacity p. 65
succession p. 66
pioneer species p. 66

Reviewing Vocabulary

Draw a Venn diagram for each pair of terms. Put shared characteristics in the overlap area, put differences to the outside. A sample diagram is provided.

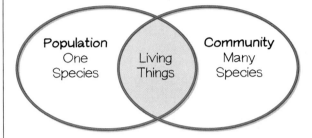

Population
One
Species

Living
Things

Community
Many
Species

1. habitat, niche

2. mutualism, commensalism

3. mutualism, parasitism

4. competition, cooperation

5. primary succession, secondary succession

Reviewing Key Concepts

Multiple Choice *Choose the letter of the best answer.*

6. What is carrying capacity?
   a. the largest population an ecosystem can support
   b. the smallest population an ecosystem can support
   c. the number of species an ecosystem can support
   d. the number of habitats in an ecosystem

7. A new species of bird moves into a habitat. The birds feed on a particular caterpillar, so that the resulting population of butterflies is small. What can be said of the relationship between the birds and the butterflies?
   a. The birds and the butterflies have a commensal relationship.
   b. The birds and butterflies compete.
   c. The birds are a limiting factor for the butterflies.
   d. The birds and butterflies cooperate.

8. Certain types of worms live in the mud at the bottom of lakes. What does the mud represent for the worm?
   a. an ecosystem
   b. a niche
   c. a community
   d. a habitat

9. What is a pioneer species?
   a. a species that travels within an ecosystem
   b. a species that is among the first to move into an area after a natural disaster
   c. a species that depends upon animal life
   d. a species that cannot return after a natural disaster

10. Which is an example of competition within the same species?
    a. whales in a pod
    b. wildebeests in a herd
    c. creosote bushes in a desert
    d. birds that fly south

11. Which is an example of parasitism?
    a. dog and tick
    b. termite and protozoans
    c. shark and remora
    d. flower and hummingbird

12. Which is an example of secondary succession?
    a. succession after a forest fire
    b. succession after a large volcanic lava flow devastates an area
    c. succession after a glacier retreats, leaving bare rock
    d. succession after a hurricane washes away all the sand from a beach

Short Answer *Write a short answer to each question.*

13. Put the terms in order, starting with the term that includes the largest number of individuals and ending with the group containing the fewest individuals: community, population, ecosystem, biome.

14. List four ways in which members of the same species can cooperate with each other.

15. Describe three different types of symbiosis.

Thinking Critically

The data in the table below come from the records of a Canadian trading company that, in the late 1800s, bought lynx and hare pelts from hunters and trappers. The Canadian lynx and varying hare share the same habitat. The lynx relies on the hare as a food source. Use the table to answer the next three questions.

Year	Lynx	Hare
1	2	30
2	15	55
3	65	90
4	75	160
5	100	200
6	95	140
7	75	80
8	40	35
9	20	3
10	3	4
11	30	40
12	55	95

16. ANALYZE How would you describe the pattern that emerges between the two populations in years 1–7? How does the pattern change in years 8–10?

17. EVALUATE The data on the lynx and hare pelts have been used to suggest the sizes of the lynx and hare populations. Is this a reasonable approach to take? Why or why not?

18. ANALYZE Scientists have observed that hare populations will go through cycles of increasing and decreasing populations even when the lynx is not part of the habitat. How would you explain this observation?

19. APPLY A forest has pine trees, along with oak trees and birch trees. All the trees provide shelter and food for different animals in the habitat. Do these trees occupy the same niche? Explain.

20. INFER Explain why low-growing plants like mosses are eventually replaced by shrubs, and shrubs replaced by trees, in both primary and secondary successions.

21. PROVIDE EXAMPLES List three human activities that could lead to secondary succession.

22. ANALYZE Creosote bushes in the Mojave desert are spread out, so that each plant is about an equal distance from another. Write a short paragraph to describe the interaction of the creosote bushes, using the terms from the table.

competition	population pattern
limiting factor	community

23. APPLY How might building homes in a wooded area affect carrying capacity of different populations in the area?

the BIG idea

24. SUMMARIZE Look again at the photograph on pages 42–43. How would you change or add details to your answer to the question on the photograph?

25. APPLY Imagine that you are an ecologist from another galaxy who arrives on Earth. Describe a human community using the terms that an Earth ecologist would use to describe a natural community. Your description should include at least three examples of interactions between individuals (whether the same or different species). Identify the biotic or abiotic factors that serve as limiting factors to human population growth. Also state whether you think the human population is at or below its carrying capacity—and why.

UNIT PROJECTS

By now you should have completed the following items for your unit project.

• questions that you have asked about the topic

• schedule showing when you will complete each step of your project

• list of resources including Web sites, print resources, and materials

Understanding Symbiosis

*Read the following description of the strangler fig and the relationship it has
with other species in a rain forest. Then answer the questions that follow.*

Strangler figs are part of many symbiotic relationships in a rain-forest
ecosystem. In some cases, the symbiotic relationship benefits both the fig
and an animal. Fig wasps lay their eggs in the fruit of the strangler fig and,
in turn, pollinate it. Many birds feed on the fruit of the strangler fig and, in
doing so, spread the seeds of the plant. The fig does not benefit from its
interactions with all species. For example, certain butterflies feed on juice
from the fruit without affecting the tree in any way.

The symbiotic relationship that gives the strangler fig its name is that
between the strangler fig and its host tree. Birds drop seeds onto the top of a
tree, and vines of the fig grow downward. Eventually, the vines of the strangler fig touch the ground and join with the roots of the host tree. The host
tree is harmed because the leaves of the strangler fig block sunlight and its
vines take root, using up nutrients the host tree needs.

1. Which feeding relationship is a form of mutualism
in which both species benefit?
   a. the strangler fig and its host tree
   b. the strangler fig and the butterflies
   c. the strangler fig and the birds
   d. the strangler fig and the fig wasp
2. Which symbiotic relationship is a form of parasitism in which one species benefits and the other
is harmed?
   a. the strangler fig and its host tree
   b. the strangler fig and the butterflies
   c. the strangler fig and the birds
   d. the strangler fig and the fig wasp

3. Which symbiotic relationship is a commensal relationship in which one species benefits without
affecting the other?
   a. the strangler fig and its host tree
   b. the strangler fig and the butterflies
   c. the strangler fig and the birds
   d. the strangler fig and the fig wasp

4. Which word best describes the interaction
between the strangler fig and its host?
   a. coexistence
   b. cooperation
   c. competition
   d. community

Extended Response

5. Strangler figs attach to trees that are sometimes
cut for lumber. Write a paragraph that describes
how removal of the host trees would affect these
populations.
   • butterflies
   • birds
   • wasps
   • strangler figs

6. Write a paragraph describing some of the different
roles played by a strangler fig in the rain forest.
Use the vocabulary terms listed below in your
answer.

habitat	niche	populations
community	ecosystem	

TIMELINES in Science

WILDERNESS CONSERVATION

The idea of wilderness conservation would have seemed strange to anyone living before the 1800s. The wilderness was vast and much of the wildlife in it dangerous to humans.

In the late 1800s, as smoke from railroads and factories rose in American skies, scientists, artists, even presidents began the work of setting aside land as parks and reservations to protect natural landscapes. Forestry, unpracticed in the U.S. before the 1890s, became a priority of the federal government as the new century dawned. Industries learned to harvest and nurture forests rather than clearing them. Next came the protection of animal species along with a call to control the pollution and depletion caused by human activity.

1872

National Parks Protect Resources

On March 1, 1872, President Ulysses S. Grant signs a law declaring Yellowstone's 2 million acres in northwest Wyoming as the country's first national park. Yellowstone serves as a model, and by 1887, about 45 million acres of forest have been set aside.

EVENTS

1870

APPLICATIONS and TECHNOLOGY

TECHNOLOGY

Seeing the Wilderness

Developments in photography in 1839, and its spread during the Civil War, led to adventurous mobile photographers in the late 1800s. In the early 1860s Mathew Brady and other photographers took mobile studios to the battlefields to bring war news to the public. By the late 1860s and early 1870s the wagonload shrank to a pack load. In 1871, William Henry Jackson balanced his tripod in Yellowstone, as the official photographer of the region's first U.S. Geological Survey.

1898
U.S. Division of Forestry Formed

Gifford Pinchot becomes the first chief of the Division of Forestry. Pinchot warns lumberers to abandon clear-cutting, urging them to practice forestry, a more scientific approach. Pinchot instructs lumberers "to have trees harvested when they are ripe."

1892
Sierra Club Founded

The Sierra Club is formed to help people explore and enjoy the mountains of the Pacific region. The Club's goal, with John Muir the unanimous choice for President, is to help people and government preserve the forests of the Sierra Nevada.

1916
National Park Service (NPS) Founded

The system of protected forests grows so big that a federal agency is formed to oversee it. Stephen Mather serves as its first director. Today the NPS employs 20,000 staff; has 90,000 volunteers; and oversees 83.6 million acres.

1880   1890   1900   1910

APPLICATION

Protecting Animal Species

Fashions of the 1890s used feathers, furs, even whole birds. Out of concern for the extinction of many birds, including the Carolina para-keet and the heath hen, a movement to stop wearing rare feathers began at small tea parties. The U.S. Congress enacted the Lacey Act in 1900 to restore endangered species of game and wild birds. The land-mark act became the first in a century of laws protecting animals. The Migratory Bird Treaty of 1918, the Bald Eagle Act of 1940, and the Endangered Species Act of 1973 set animal conservation as a national priority. The Endangered Species Act met its strongest test in protecting the northern spotted owl, whose entire range—in California, Oregon, Washington, and Canada—is protected.

1951
Nature Conservancy Established
The Nature Conservancy is formed to preserve plants, animals, and natural communities that represent Earth's biological diversity.

1963
Glen Canyon Destroyed
Completion of the Glen Canyon dam causes flooding in Glen Canyon, an immense area north of the Grand Canyon. Many groups fight to close the dam, but it is too late. The canyon is destroyed as Lake Powell forms.

1962
Silent Spring *Breaks Silence*
Biologist and science writer Rachel Carson publishes *Silent Spring.* Chemical pesticides have been widely used and publicized, but Carson uses scientific evidence to show that many of these chemicals harm people and the environment.

1968
Grand Canyon Dam Plans Squashed
Plans to dam the Grand Canyon are withdrawn as a result of public outcry. Recalling what happened to Glen Canyon, organizers ran national newspaper ads in 1966 making the public aware of plans to dam the Canyon.

1950   1960   1970

TECHNOLOGY
Maps to Save the Wilderness
Land and wildlife conservation has benefited from computer-based mapping technology called global information systems (GIS). GIS compiles satellite photographs, temperature readings, and other information into a central set of data. Scientists enter distributions of animals and overlay these data on existing maps. The resulting GIS maps show the gap in an animal's range and the quality of its habitat. Government efforts to restore the habitat of the endangered San Joaquin Kit Fox relied on GIS maps.

1980 to present
Reservation vs. Resource

In 1980, Congress expands the Arctic National Wildlife Refuge (ANWR) to more than twice its 1960 size. In 2001, President George W. Bush proposes limited oil drilling within the range. Today, debate continues over how to manage its resources and wildlife.

 RESOURCE CENTER
CLASSZONE.COM

Read more about current conservation efforts.

1990   **2000**

APPLICATION

Selling a Service

In New York City in 1996, the water department spent $1.5 billion to protect natural watersheds rather than build a $6 billion water treatment plant. In 2001, a group of scientists met to promote the value that ecosystems bring to society—benefits that include pest control, air purification, and water treatment. For example, dragonflies can eat 300 mosquitoes in a single day. Toads and bats can eat a thousand or more mosquitoes in a single day or night.

INTO THE FUTURE

Society has long put a price on natural resources—minerals, water, timber, and so on. But how much is an ecosystem worth? Communities have begun to look at the dollar values of "ecosystem services," the ongoing activities in nature that keep our environment healthy. Data is needed on ecosystem processes. Such data can be compared to the services of human-made treatment plants and agriculture.

Other questions arise with protecting species. Many species, such as wild turkeys and bald eagles, once endangered have come back in great numbers. When a protected species thrives it may endanger another species or bump up against the human landscape and human activity. How can managers of resources set priorities?

ACTIVITIES

Ecosystem Services Proposal

What services to the human population are provided by your local ecosystem? Choose one service and describe how natural processes and interactions within the ecosystem provide the benefits you've identified. What processes are involved?

Write a proposal for protecting the ecosystem. Include a comparison of the estimated cost of protecting the ecosystem and the cost of human services that provide a similar benefit.

Writing Project: The Story Behind the News

Research one of the events described on the timeline. Then write the story behind that event.

Human Impact on Ecosystems

How have humans affected this landscape?

the **BIG** idea

Humans and human population growth affect the environment.

Key Concepts

SECTION

3.1 Human population growth presents challenges.
Learn how the increasing human population must share land and resources and dispose of its wastes.

SECTION

3.2 Human activities affect the environment.
Learn how humans may affect natural resources, air and water quality, and biodiversity.

SECTION

3.3 People are working to protect ecosystems.
Learn about federal, local, and scientific efforts to improve resource use and protect ecosystems.

Internet Preview

CLASSZONE.COM

Chapter 3 online resources: Content Review, Visualization, four Resource Centers, Math Tutorial, Test Practice

EXPLORE (the BIG idea)

How Many Is Six Billion?

Use a piece of paper, scissors, and some tape to make a box that measures 1 cm by 1 cm by 1 cm. Fill the box with rice. Use the number of grains of rice in 1 cm³ to calculate the volume of 6,000,000,000 grains of rice.

Observe and Think How many grains of rice are in a cubic centimeter? Do 6 billion grains take up more or less space than you expected?

How Easily Does Polluted Water Move Through Plants?

Place a few drops of food coloring in a half cup of water. Take a leafy stalk of celery and make a fresh cut across the bottom. Place the celery in the water overnight.

Observe and Think What do you observe about the celery and its leaves? What do your observations suggest about plants growing near polluted water?

Internet Activity: The Environment

Go to **ClassZone.com** to explore the effects of human activities on the environment.

Observe and Think How are people working to protect the environment?

Population Growth **Code: MDL003**

Getting Ready to Learn

◀ CONCEPT REVIEW

- Both living and nonliving factors affect ecosystems.
- Populations can grow or decline over time.
- Matter and energy move through the environment.

◀ VOCABULARY REVIEW

species p. 45

habitat p. 46

See Glossary for definitions.

diversity, urban

CONTENT REVIEW
CLASSZONE.COM

Review concepts and vocabulary.

▶ TAKING NOTES

SUPPORTING MAIN IDEAS

Make a chart to show main ideas and the information that supports them. Copy each blue heading; then add supporting information, such as reasons, explanations, and examples.

VOCABULARY STRATEGY

Think about a vocabulary term as a **magnet word** diagram. Write the other terms or ideas related to that term around it.

See the Note-Taking Handbook on pages R45–R51.

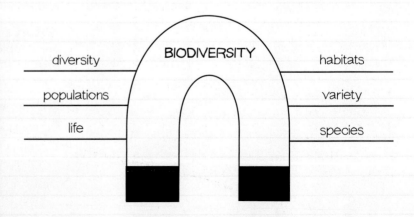

SCIENCE NOTEBOOK

Human populations can put pressure on ecosystems.

Humans produce waste that must be disposed of.

Resources must be shared among a growing human population.

Human population centers are expanding.

diversity   BIODIVERSITY   habitats

populations   variety

life   species

KEY CONCEPT

Human population growth presents challenges.

◀ **BEFORE**, you learned

- Populations have boundaries and are affected by limiting factors
- Living things form communities

▶ **NOW**, you will learn

- How a growing human population puts pressure on ecosystems
- How sharing resources can be difficult

VOCABULARY

natural resource p. 84
population density p. 86

EXPLORE Sharing Resources

How can you model resource distribution?

PROCEDURE

1. You will work in a group of several classmates. One member of your group gets a bag of objects from your teacher.

2. Each object in the bag represents a necessary resource. Divide the objects so that each member of the group gets the resources he or she needs.

3. After 10 minutes, you may trade resources with other groups.

WHAT DO YOU THINK?

- Did you get a fair share of your group's objects?
- How does the number of people in each group affect the outcome?
- Was the job made easier when trading occurred across groups?

MATERIALS
bag containing an assortment of objects

SUPPORTING MAIN IDEAS
Make a chart to show information that supports the first main idea presented: *The human population is increasing.*

The human population is increasing.

According to the United Nations, on October 12, 1999, Earth's human population reached 6 billion. Until 300 years ago, it had never grown beyond a few hundred million people. Only 200 years ago, the population reached 1 billion. So the increase to 6 billion people has occurred in a very short time. About one-third of all humans alive today are 14 years old or younger. Partly for this reason, experts predict Earth's population will keep growing—to 9 billion or more by the year 2050.

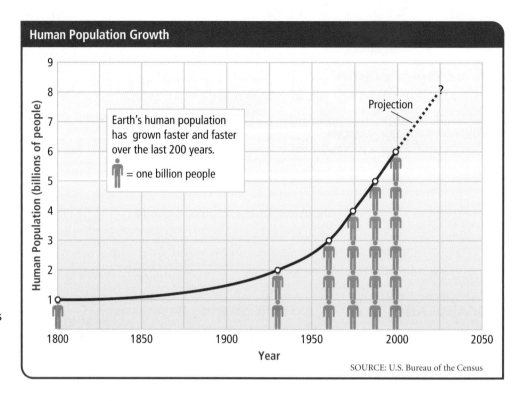

Human Population Growth

Human Population (billions of people)

Earth's human population has grown faster and faster over the last 200 years.

 = one billion people

Projection

Year

SOURCE: U.S. Bureau of the Census

PREDICT The graph shows actual population growth through 2000. Predict how the population will grow in the future.

The graph above shows how the human population has grown in the last 200 years. You can see from the way the graph gets noticeably steeper after 1950 how quickly the population has increased in just the last 50 years. It is not just the number of babies being born that contributes to Earth's large human population. People are living longer as a result of improving health care and nutrition.

The dotted line on the graph shows a projection, which helps us predict what the population would be if it continues to grow at the rate it is growing today. However, remember that an ecosystem has a carrying capacity for any given population. At some point, Earth will reach its carrying capacity for the human population. Today, many people think that our planet is close to—if not already at—its carrying capacity for humans.

CHECK YOUR READING How might Earth's carrying capacity affect human population growth?

Human populations can put pressure on ecosystems.

VISUALIZATION
CLASSZONE.COM

Examine how the human population has grown.

If your family has guests for the weekend, you may find that you run out of hot water for showers or do not have enough milk for everyone's breakfast. The resources that would ordinarily be enough for your family are no longer enough.

You read in Chapter 2 that resources such as food, water, and space can be limiting factors for biological populations. These same resources limit Earth's human population. As the human population grows, it uses more resources—just as your weekend visitors used more of your home's resources. The activities of the growing human population are putting pressure on Earth's ecosystems.

▼ REMINDER

A *limiting factor* is something that prevents a population from continuing to grow.

Pressures of Waste Disposal

As Earth's human population grows, so does the amount of waste produced by humans. Humans, like all living things, produce natural waste. Often, the water that carries this waste is treated to remove harmful chemicals before being cycled back to the environment. However, some of these materials still make it into lakes, rivers, and oceans, harming these ecosystems.

Much of the waste material produced by humans is the result of human activity. Some of this waste is garbage, or food waste. The rest of it is trash, or nonfood waste. In the United States, huge amounts of trash are thrown out each year. Most garbage and trash ends up in landfills.

Landfills take up a lot of space. The Fresh Kills Landfill in Staten Island, New York, is 60 meters (197 ft) high and covers an area as big as 2200 football fields. Decomposing trash and garbage can release dangerous gases into the air as well as harmful chemicals into the ground. Liners, which are layers of plastic or packed clay, are used to keep chemicals from leaking into surrounding land and water.

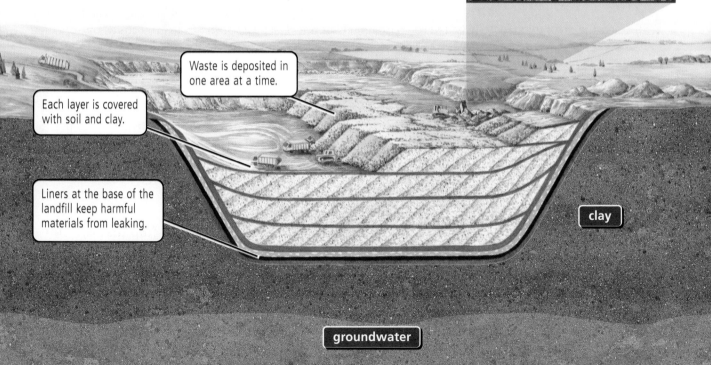

Waste is deposited in one area at a time.

Each layer is covered with soil and clay.

Liners at the base of the landfill keep harmful materials from leaking.

clay

groundwater

Another way to get rid of trash and garbage is to incinerate it—burn it. The problem with incineration is that it releases harmful gases and chemicals into the air. To prevent the release of these harmful substances, incinerator smokestacks have filters. To prevent further environmental contamination, used filters must be disposed of safely.

Pressures on Resources

You have seen that a growing human population puts pressure on ecosystems by the amount of waste it leaves behind. Human populations also put pressure on ecosystems by what they take away. Humans depend on the environment for resources. A **natural resource** is any type of material or energy that humans use to meet their needs. Natural resources that humans take from their environment include water, food, wood, stone, metal, and minerals.

Clean fresh water is an important resource. Only 3 percent of Earth's water supply is fresh water—and two-thirds of that small amount is locked up in polar ice caps, glaciers, and permanent snow. As the human population grows, sharing this important resource will become more difficult.

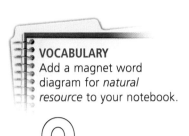

VOCABULARY
Add a magnet word diagram for *natural resource* to your notebook.

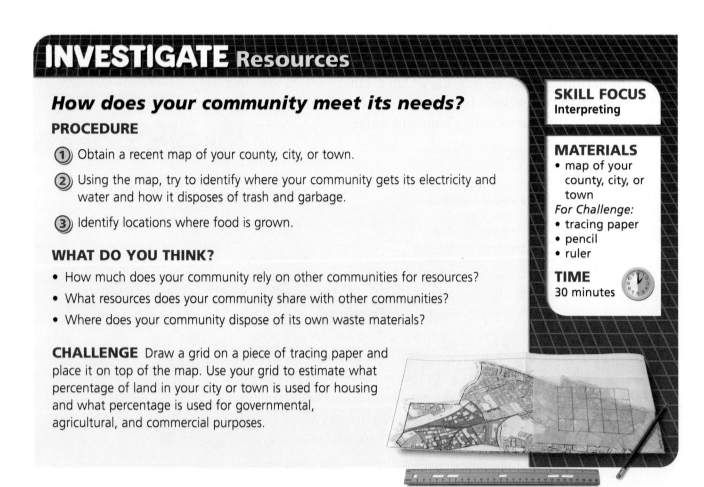

INVESTIGATE Resources

How does your community meet its needs?

PROCEDURE

1. Obtain a recent map of your county, city, or town.
2. Using the map, try to identify where your community gets its electricity and water and how it disposes of trash and garbage.
3. Identify locations where food is grown.

WHAT DO YOU THINK?

- How much does your community rely on other communities for resources?
- What resources does your community share with other communities?
- Where does your community dispose of its own waste materials?

CHALLENGE Draw a grid on a piece of tracing paper and place it on top of the map. Use your grid to estimate what percentage of land in your city or town is used for housing and what percentage is used for governmental, agricultural, and commercial purposes.

SKILL FOCUS
Interpreting

MATERIALS
- map of your county, city, or town

For Challenge:
- tracing paper
- pencil
- ruler

TIME
30 minutes

Case Study: The Colorado River

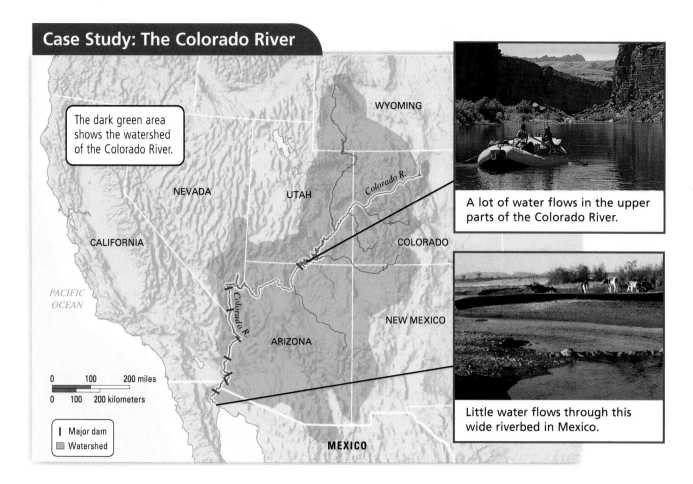

The dark green area shows the watershed of the Colorado River.

WYOMING

NEVADA

UTAH

Colorado R.

CALIFORNIA

COLORADO

PACIFIC OCEAN

Colorado R.

NEW MEXICO

ARIZONA

| 0 | 100 | 200 miles |
| 0 | 100 | 200 kilometers |

▮ Major dam
▨ Watershed

MEXICO

A lot of water flows in the upper parts of the Colorado River.

Little water flows through this wide riverbed in Mexico.

A case study that involves the Colorado River shows how a growing human population puts pressures on natural resources. This example also shows that sharing resources isn't easy. The watershed of this major Western river extends into seven U.S. states and parts of Mexico. The watershed includes all the smaller rivers and streams that flow into the Colorado River. In a region where little rain falls each year, these streams and rivers are an important source of water for drinking and agriculture.

As the West was settled, people in the downstream states of California, Arizona, and Nevada worried that the people in the upstream states of Colorado, Utah, Wyoming, and New Mexico would drain too much water from the river. In 1922 the seven states signed an agreement that divided the water between the two groups.

Problems with this agreement soon became apparent. First, the needs of Native American and Mexican populations were not considered. Second, the dams and channels built to prevent floods and transport water harmed river ecosystems. And third, the seven states planned to use more water than the river usually holds. As a result, the river often runs nearly dry at its mouth, in Mexico.

READING TiP

As you read about the Colorado River, refer to the map above to see where the river flows and the states that use the Colorado River's water.

○ **CHECK YOUR READING** List three problems that developed after people made a plan to share Colorado River water.

Pressures of Urban Growth

CLASSZONE.COM

Learn more about urban expansion.

Until recently, the majority of Earth's population was spread out, so the population density was low. **Population density** is the measure of the number of people in a given area. Generally, the lower the population density, the less pressure there is on the environment.

Today, about half of the world's population lives in urban, or city, areas. People are attracted to these areas to live and to work. Over time, suburban areas around a city develop as more and more people look for a place to live. In cities, buildings are spaced close together, so the population density is high. A large number of people in a small area changes the landscape. The local environment can no longer support the number of people living there, and so resources must come from outside.

CHECK YOUR READING How does population density in a city differ from the population density of a suburb?

In recent years, some people have raised concern over the dramatic growth in and around urban areas. Los Angeles; Houston; Atlanta; and Washington, D.C. are all cities that have rapidly expanded. Another urban area that has experienced dramatic growth is Las Vegas, Nevada. The images below show the effects of increasing

Las Vegas, 1972

The darker colors distinguish the developed land of Las Vegas from the surrounding desert.

Las Vegas, 1997

city center

Over 25 years, the city expanded in all directions. The population went from 273,000 to 1,124,000.

population density around the city between 1972 and 1997. Located in the middle of the desert, Las Vegas depends upon the Colorado River for water and electrical energy. As the population grows, so does the need for natural resources.

Pressures of Expanding Land Use

An increasing demand for resources in a particular area is one consequence of urban growth. But as communities around cities expand onto surrounding land, the environment is affected. Natural habitats, such as forests, are destroyed. Because forests cycle carbon through the environment, cutting down trees affects the carbon cycle. Soil that was held in place by tree roots may wash into lakes and rivers.

INFER What do you think this ecosystem looked like a hundred years ago? two hundred years ago?

Another consequence of widespread development is the loss of productive farmland. Development replaces more than 2.5 million acres of farmland each year in the United States. This means less land is available locally to produce food for the growing population. The result is that food is often transported great distances.

Unlike compact city development, widespread suburban development also increases the need for residents to have cars. This is because most people in suburban areas live farther from where they work, shop, or go to school. A greater number of cars decreases the air quality in communities and requires additional road construction, which can interrupt natural habitats and endanger wildlife.

 CHECK YOUR READING Describe some ways that development harms natural ecosystems.

Review

KEY CONCEPTS

1. Identify four pressures placed on ecosystems by an increasing human population.

2. Give an example that shows how resources can be difficult to share.

CRITICAL THINKING

3. **Apply** Describe an example of sharing resources that occurs in your home.

4. **Infer** How would a city's population density change if the city increased in area and the number of people in it remained the same?

CHALLENGE

5. **Evaluate** Imagine that you lived along the Colorado River. What information would you need if you wanted to evaluate a water-sharing agreement?

Ecology in Urban Planning

Urban planners design and locate buildings, transportation systems, and green spaces in cities. One important thing they consider is how their proposal for development will affect the ecosystem. With the help of ecology, urban planners can balance the needs of humans and the environment.

❶ GATHERING DATA Urban planners use maps to gather information about the layout of a city, where populations of plants and animals exist, and where water and land resources are located.

❷ ANALYZING DATA Scientists help urban planners determine how the location and density of buildings, roads, or parks can affect natural habitats.

❸ APPLYING DATA By understanding the ecosystem, urban planners can develop areas to support different needs.

This habitat is left untouched because it supports rare migrating birds. Development would disturb the ecosystem and put the birds at risk.

This area has a stable population of native species. Park benches and trails encourage human recreation in well defined areas.

EXPLORE

1. **APPLY** Both ecologists and urban planners have to understand the ways that biotic and abiotic factors are interconnected. List some biotic and abiotic factors in a human community.

2. **CHALLENGE** Use the Internet to find out more about the planning board or planning office in your community. Is your community growing? In what ways? What are some decisions that planners are helping to make?

3.2 Human activities affect the environment.

◀ **BEFORE, you learned**

- Human populations are increasing
- Human population growth causes problems

▶ **NOW, you will learn**

- How natural resources are classified
- How pollution affects the environment
- How a loss of diversity affects the environment

VOCABULARY

pollution p. 91
biodiversity p. 91

THINK ABOUT

How do you use water?

Think of the number of times you use water every day. Like all living things, you need water. In fact, more than half of the material that makes up your body is water.

No matter where you live, most of the time you can turn on a faucet and clean water flows out the spout. You use water when you take a shower, fix a snack, or wash a dish. If you've ever lost water service to your home, you've probably been reminded how much you depend upon it. No doubt about it, our need for water is serious.

SUPPORTING MAIN IDEAS
Make a chart to show information that supports the main idea: *Humans use many resources.*

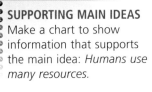

Humans use many resources.

Throughout history, people around the world have relied on natural resources for survival. Ancient civilizations used stone to create tools and weapons. And wood was an important fuel for cooking and keeping warm. Today, humans continue to rely on the environment and have discovered additional resources to meet their needs. In Section 3.1 you read about sharing natural resources. Scientists classify these resources into two categories:

- renewable resources
- nonrenewable resources

Renewable Resources

RESOURCE CENTER
CLASSZONE.COM

Find out more about
natural resources.

Two hundred years ago, most small towns in the Northeastern part of the United States included farm fields, pasture, and woods. The wooded areas that weren't farmed were used as wood lots. The wood from these lots supplied firewood for towns and was often exported for income.

Trees are an example of a renewable resource—a resource that can be used over and over again. Energy from sunlight is another important renewable resource. Because the Sun is expected to supply energy for another five billion years, energy from sunlight is considered essentially unlimited. As you read earlier in your study of the water cycle, water can be classified as a renewable resource. Renewable resources can be replaced naturally or by humans in a short amount of time, but they may run out if they are overused or managed poorly.

CHECK YOUR READING Give three examples of renewable resources. Explain why each one is considered renewable.

Nonrenewable Resources

Nonrenewable resources are resources that cannot be replaced. In some cases, they may be replenished by natural processes, but not quickly enough for human purposes. Nonrenewable resources are often underground, making them more difficult to reach. But technology has enabled humans to locate and remove nonrenewable resources from places that used to be impossible to reach.

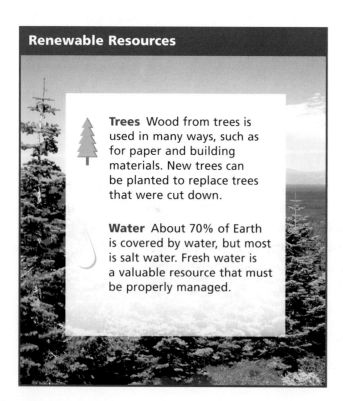

Renewable Resources

Trees Wood from trees is used in many ways, such as for paper and building materials. New trees can be planted to replace trees that were cut down.

Water About 70% of Earth is covered by water, but most is salt water. Fresh water is a valuable resource that must be properly managed.

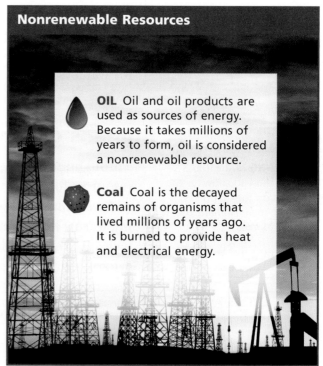

Nonrenewable Resources

OIL Oil and oil products are used as sources of energy. Because it takes millions of years to form, oil is considered a nonrenewable resource.

Coal Coal is the decayed remains of organisms that lived millions of years ago. It is burned to provide heat and electrical energy.

Coal, petroleum, and natural gas are nonrenewable resources that are removed from underground by mining or drilling. Also called fossil fuels, they are the main energy source for heating, industry, and transportation and are used to make many products. Many minerals, like copper and gold, are also considered nonrenewable resources.

Pollution endangers biodiversity.

As you walk along a city street, you may smell exhaust or see litter. These are examples of pollution. **Pollution** is the addition of harmful substances to the environment. Many of the ways humans use natural resources cause pollution to be released into the soil, air, and water. Pollutants include chemicals, bacteria, and dirt. Even materials that are ordinarily not harmful can cause pollution when they build up in one location.

As pollution becomes common in an ecosystem, living things may be threatened. Plant and animal populations may decrease and biodiversity may decline. **Biodiversity** is the number and variety of life forms within an ecosystem. Healthy ecosystems support a variety of species. An ecosystem with a variety of organisms can recover more easily from disturbances than an ecosystem that has fewer species.

VOCABULARY
Don't forget to add magnet diagrams for the words *pollution* and *biodiversity.*

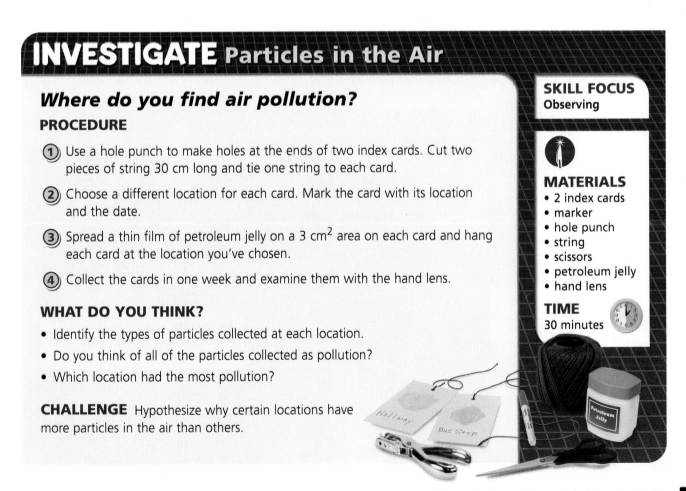

INVESTIGATE Particles in the Air

Where do you find air pollution?

PROCEDURE

1. Use a hole punch to make holes at the ends of two index cards. Cut two pieces of string 30 cm long and tie one string to each card.

2. Choose a different location for each card. Mark the card with its location and the date.

3. Spread a thin film of petroleum jelly on a 3 cm^2 area on each card and hang each card at the location you've chosen.

4. Collect the cards in one week and examine them with the hand lens.

WHAT DO YOU THINK?

- Identify the types of particles collected at each location.
- Do you think of all of the particles collected as pollution?
- Which location had the most pollution?

CHALLENGE Hypothesize why certain locations have more particles in the air than others.

SKILL FOCUS
Observing

MATERIALS
- 2 index cards
- marker
- hole punch
- string
- scissors
- petroleum jelly
- hand lens

TIME
30 minutes

Air Quality

Air quality affects entire ecosystems. For example, in 1980, Mount St. Helens erupted on the West Coast of the United States. Hot ash was blown 15 miles up into the air. Three days later some of that ash reached the East Coast. Although natural events occasionally release air pollutants, human activities pollute every day.

READING TiP

Pollute and *pollutant* are in the same word family as pollution.

Today in the United States, motor vehicles, factories, and power plants are the main sources of air pollution. The fossil fuels they burn release sulfur dioxide, nitrogen dioxide, and carbon monoxide into the air. These pollutants affect humans and animals and are the main cause of acid rain, a serious problem affecting ecosystems.

CHECK YOUR READING What air pollutants contribute to acid rain problems in the United States?

Acid rain occurs when air pollutants such as sulfur dioxide and nitrogen dioxide mix with water in the atmosphere to form acid droplets of rain, ice, snow, or mist. Just as the wind carried ash from Mount St. Helens, wind can carry these droplets for very long distances before they fall as rain.

Acid rain has been very harmful in areas without rich soil to help correct the rain's acidity. In New York's Adirondack Mountains, acid rain has killed all the fish in some lakes. The photograph below shows the impact of acid rain on trees in the Adirondacks. Where acid rain falls, it damages leaves and soil. This damage destroys both habitats and food sources for many animals, eventually reducing biodiversity.

Acid-Rain Damage

A close look at the branch reveals that some of the needles are turning brown.

Air Quality Spruce trees in the Adirondacks show damage caused when pollutants in the air mix with rain.

Water Quality

Water quality is another factor that affects biodiversity in ecosystems. Forty years ago, newspaper headlines announced that Lake Erie was "dead" because of pollution. Almost every living thing in the lake had died. Lake Erie suffered for years from pollution by neighborhoods, industries, and farms along its banks. Rivers that emptied into the lake also carried pollution with them.

The pollution found in Lake Erie is common in communities across the United States. Chemicals or waste that drain off of farm fields, animal feedlots, and landfills all cause water pollution. So do oil spills, soil erosion, and the discharging of wastewater from towns and industries.

 CHECK YOUR READING Name four different sources of water pollution.

Like air pollution, water pollution affects entire ecosystems. One river that suffers from heavy pollution is the Duwamish River in Washington. Over 600 million gallons of untreated waste and storm water drain off the land into the river. As a result, large amounts of bacteria and harmful chemicals contaminate the water, killing fish and putting humans at risk.

When fish and amphibians in aquatic ecosystems are exposed to pollution, the entire food web is affected. If fish become scarce, some birds may no longer find enough food. The bird population may decrease as birds die or move to a new habitat. The result is that biodiversity in the ecosystem decreases.

Water Quality A scientist tests the water of the Duwamish River after chemicals were released into the river.

Chemical Pollution

Pollution that flows into aquatic ecosystems can harm—even kill—organisms like these fish.

Pollution Across Systems

As you have learned, pollution can be spread among ecosystems by abiotic factors. For example, wind carried ash from Mount St. Helens to different ecosystems. Wind also carries acid rain to forest ecosystems. Pollution can also move between air and water. For example, some chemical pollutants can run off land and into a body of water. These pollutants, like the water itself, can evaporate from the water's surface and cycle into the air, moving into the atmosphere.

① Runoff containing harmful chemicals flows into this pond.

② The chemicals evaporate into the air from the surface of the water.

Habitat loss endangers biodiversity.

Scientists know that an ecosystem with many different species of plants and animals can withstand the effects of flooding, drought, and disease more effectively than an ecosystem with fewer species. But for biodiversity to be maintained, a habitat must be able to support a large number of different species. If living space is limited or a food source is removed, then the number of species in a biological community will be reduced.

Removing Habitat

One way human activities affect habitats is by reducing the amounts of natural resources available to living things. When this occurs, populations that rely on those resources are less likely to survive. For example, if you trim all the dead branches off the trees in your yard and remove them, insects that live in rotting wood will not settle in your yard. As a result, woodpeckers that may have nested in the area will lose their source of food. By removing this food source, you might affect the biodiversity in your backyard.

Now consider altering an ecosystem much larger than your backyard. Instead of removing a single resource, imagine removing a large area of land that is a habitat to many different species. Disturbing habitats removes not only food but space, shelter, and protection for living things.

Removing Habitat

A clear-cut forest provides a dramatic example of habitat loss.

Forest Habitat The forest provides food and shelter for many organisms.

Deforestation Removing all the trees from an area removes habitat that other species depend on.

Because of land development, forests that once stretched for hundreds of miles have been fragmented, or broken apart into small patches. Organisms that depend on trees cannot live in woods that have large areas that have been clear-cut. Their habitat is removed or reduced so there is a greater risk of attack by predators. Skunks, raccoons, and crows, which eat the eggs of forest songbirds, will not travel deep into large forests. However, they can reach nests more easily when forests are broken into small areas.

 CHECK YOUR READING Why is biodiversity important and how can human activities affect it?

Changing Habitat

Another kind of habitat loss occurs when humans move species into new habitats, either on purpose or by accident. Some species, when released in a new place, successfully compete against the native species, crowding them out. Over time, these species, called invasive species, may replace the native species.

One example of an invasive plant is purple loosestrife. In the 1800s loosestrife from Europe was brought to the United States to use as a garden plant and medicinal herb. One loosestrife plant can make about 2 million seeds a year. These seeds are carried long distances by wind, water, animals, and humans. Loosestrife sprouts in wetlands, where it can fill in open-water habitat or replace native plants such as goldenrod. Most ducks and fish do not feed on purple loosestrife.

Habitat loss occurs when purple loosestrife fills in open water or crowds out goldenrod.

Invasive Species Purple loosestrife fills in wetlands and crowds out native species, disturbing organisms that rely on native species for food or living space.

Native Species Goldenrod is a native species that is a food source for many wetland populations.

When the native plants that wetland animals depend on are crowded out by loosestrife, the animals disappear, too.

Scientists estimate that Earth supports more than 10 million different species. They also estimate that thousands of species are threatened, and over a hundred species of plants and animals become extinct every year. By protecting biodiversity we can help ecosystems thrive and even recover more quickly after a natural disturbance such as a hurricane. And biodiversity directly benefits humans. For example, many medications are based on natural compounds from plants that only grow in certain types of ecosystems.

3.2 Review

KEY CONCEPTS

1. List some renewable and nonrenewable resources that you need to survive.

2. Describe two ways in which pollution can move through ecosystems.

3. Explain what scientists mean by *biodiversity*.

CRITICAL THINKING

4. **Explain** Under some circumstances, valuable natural resources can be considered pollutants. Explain this statement, giving two examples.

5. **Compare** Identify two natural habitats in your area, one with high biodiversity and one with low biodiversity. Describe the biodiversity of each.

◢ CHALLENGE

6. **Hypothesize** When lakes are polluted by acid rain, the water appears to become clearer, not cloudier. Why do you think this is the case?

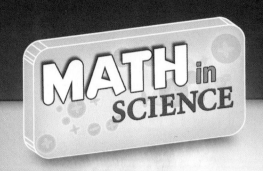

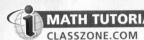
MATH TUTORIAL
CLASSZONE.COM
Click on Math Tutorial for more help with finding the volume of a rectangular prism.

How Much Water?

When you take a 10-minute shower, you are using about 190 liters of water. How much is that? Liters are a metric unit of capacity— the amount of liquid that can fit into a container of a certain size. The liter is based on a metric unit of volume. One liter is equal to 1000 cubic centimeters.

Example

A rectangular tank holds the amount of water used for a 10-minute shower. The dimensions of the tank are 250 cm × 40 cm × 19 cm. What is the volume of the tank?

Volume = **length** × **width** × height

$$V = l \times w \times h$$

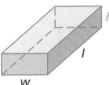

(1) Use the formula for volume.
Replace variables with actual dimensions.

$V = 250$ cm × 40 cm × 19 cm

(2) Calculate by multiplying.

$(250 \times 40) \times 19$

$10{,}000 \quad \times 19 = 190{,}000$

(3) Check units:
cm × cm × cm = cm³ (cubic centimeters)

ANSWER 250 cm × 40 cm × 19 cm = 190,000 cm³

Find the following volumes or dimensions.

1. Brushing your teeth with the water running uses the water in a tank 14 cm by 45 cm by 12 cm. Sketch an aquarium that holds exactly this amount. Label the dimensions. What is the volume?

2. If you turn off the water while you brush, you use only about half as much water. Sketch a rectangular tank that holds this volume. Label the dimensions. What is the volume?

3. A typical toilet flush uses the water in a 50 cm by 20 cm by 20 cm space. Find the volume in cubic centimeters. Sketch a model of this volume.

CHALLENGE An Olympic swimming pool is 50 m by 25 m by 3 m. What is its volume? There are approximately 5678 cubic meters of water in the water tower shown. How many Olympic pools of water would it take to fill the tower?

3.3 People are working to protect ecosystems.

◀ **BEFORE, you learned**

- Human activities produce pollutants
- Human activity is depleting some natural resources

▶ **NOW, you will learn**

- About some of the laws that have been passed to help protect the environment
- About efforts that are being made to conserve natural resources

VOCABULARY

conservation p. 99
sustainable p. 102

EXPLORE Environmental Impacts

What happens when soil is compressed?

PROCEDURE

① Fill two pots with 1 cup each of potting soil.

② Compress the soil in the second pot by pushing down hard upon it with your hand.

③ Pour 1 cup of water into the first pot. Start the stopwatch as soon as you start pouring. Stop the watch as soon as all the water has been absorbed. Record the time.

④ Pour 1 cup of water into the second pot and again record how long it takes for the water to be absorbed. Wash your hands.

MATERIALS

- 2 plant pots with trays
- measuring cups
- potting soil
- water
- stopwatch

WHAT DO YOU THINK?

- What effect does compressing the soil have upon how quickly the water is absorbed?
- What might happen to water that is not absorbed quickly by soil?

Environmental awareness is growing.

SUPPORTING MAIN IDEAS
Make a chart to list some of the activities that show that environmental awareness is growing.

As people moved westward across grassy plains and steep mountain ranges of the United States, many believed our nation's resources were endless. Midwestern prairies were converted to farmland. Forests were clear-cut for lumber. Land was mined for coal.

By the 1800s, foresters and naturalists began to take interest in preserving the wild areas they saw rapidly disappearing. In 1872 our nation's outlook started to change when Yellowstone, the world's first national park, was established. It wasn't long before conservation of wild places became a goal. **Conservation** is the process of saving or protecting a natural resource.

The movement to protect our environment grew rapidly in the 1960s. *Silent Spring,* a book that raised public awareness of the effect of harmful chemicals in the environment, sparked debate about serious pollution problems. As local efforts for environmental protection grew, the United States government responded. Throughout the 1970s important laws were passed to preserve and protect the environment. Today small groups of citizens, along with local and national government efforts, protect America's natural resources.

 List three events in the history of the environmental movement in the United States.

 **RESOURCE CENTER**
CLASSZONE.COM

Discover how people help ecosystems recover.

Volunteers work to clean up a stream.

Local Efforts

Maybe you have heard the expression "Think globally, act locally." It urges people to consider the health of the entire planet and to take action in their own communities. Long before federal and state agencies began enforcing environmental laws, individuals were coming together to protect habitats and the organisms that depend on them. These efforts are often referred to as grassroots efforts. They occur on a local level and are primarily run by volunteers.

Often the efforts of a few citizens gather the support and interest of so many people that they form a larger organization. These groups work to bring about change by communicating with politicians, publishing articles, or talking to the news media. Some groups purchase land and set it aside for preservation.

Federal Efforts

You have probably heard of the Endangered Species Act or the Clean Air Act. You might wonder, though, exactly what these laws do. The United States government works with scientists to write laws that ensure that companies and individuals work together to conserve natural resources and maintain healthy ecosystems.

In the late 1960s the National Environmental Policy Act, known as NEPA, made the protection of natural ecosystems a national goal. Several important laws followed. For example, the Clean Air Act and Clean Water Act improved the control of different kinds and amounts of pollutants that can be put into the air and water. The Environmental Protection Agency (EPA) enforces all federal environmental laws.

CHECK YOUR READING Identify two federal environmental laws.

Over the past decades, chemical waste from factories has piled up in landfills and polluted water sources. These wastes can threaten ecosystems and human health. In 1980, citizen awareness of the dangers led to the Superfund Program. The goal of the program is to identify dangerous areas and to clean up the worst sites.

Helping Endangered Species

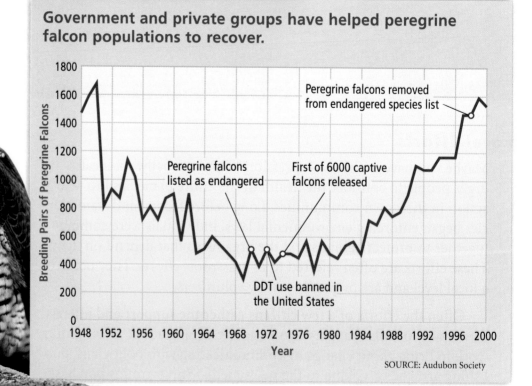

Government and private groups have helped peregrine falcon populations to recover.

Peregrine falcons listed as endangered

First of 6000 captive falcons released

Peregrine falcons removed from endangered species list

DDT use banned in the United States

Breeding Pairs of Peregrine Falcons

Year

SOURCE: Audubon Society

Ecosystem Recovery

A growing awareness of the importance of healthy ecosystems is inspiring restoration projects.

Wetland

Restoration efforts in Galveston Bay, Texas, focus on bringing back the sea-grass meadows near the coast.

Volunteers help replant sea grass around Galveston Island State Park. Sea grass is a major habitat for birds, fish, and crabs and helps prevent erosion by holding bottom sediments in place.

Desert

Members of a restoration group work to restore desert plants and soil in Red Rock Canyon State Park, California.

1 A power auger is used to break up severely compacted soil and prepare it for planting.

2 Seedlings of native species, like the saltbush, are grown off site. Once they reach a more mature size, they are brought in to be planted.

3 Plastic cones are used to protect plants from being disturbed by severe weather or predators.

Federal agencies oversee the Superfund Program and other environmental laws. In addition to federal laws protecting the environment, there are state laws. Companies must follow all the laws that apply in each state where they do business. The same company may need to follow different laws in different states.

The United States is just one of many countries learning to deal with the effects of their human population on the environment. Dozens of countries have already met to discuss concerns about clear-cutting, water pollution, and endangered species. At this international level, the United Nations Environment Programme encourages sound environmental practices worldwide.

INFER At this Superfund site, the chemical cadmium pollutes the soil. Why does this worker need to wear a face mask?

Conserving resources protects ecosystems.

Around the world, individuals and companies are expressing more interest in **sustainable** practices—ways of living and doing business that use natural resources without using them up. Sustainable development allows people to enjoy a high quality of life while limiting harm to ecosystems. Developing new technologies, reducing resource use, and creating less waste are three ways to practice sustainability.

 CHECK YOUR READING What are sustainable practices?

Improving Resource Use

As you read in Chapter 2, many different interactions take place in ecosystems. Some organisms form close relationships with one other and their environment. Humans are like other organisms. We depend on the environment to help meet our requirements for life. Because many of the resources we rely on are limited, businesses and governments are changing the way they manage farms, forests, and energy resources. They are adopting sustainable practices.

Some farmers are practicing sustainable methods that protect land and provide nutritious food. Nearly one-third of U.S. farms practice conservation tillage, a method that involves planting seeds without plowing the soil. This technique can cut soil erosion by more than 90 percent. Organic farmers reject fertilizers and pesticides made from fossil fuels. Instead they use natural fertilizers, like compost, and natural pest controls, like ladybugs, which eat aphids.

Forestry practices are also changing. Cutting selectively instead of clear-cutting reduces soil erosion and encourages rapid regrowth. The U.S. Forest Service has adopted an ecosystem-management approach that tries to balance the need for timber with the need to conserve soil and water and preserve wildlife and biodiversity.

CHECK YOUR READING Give two examples of sustainable practices.

Energy companies are also promoting sustainability by developing alternative energy sources that do not come from fossil fuels. By the time you buy your first car, it may run on fuel cells, and the electricity in your house may be generated by a solar power plant.

Commercial geothermal power plants are a renewable energy source that uses the heat of molten rock in the Earth's interior. Geothermal power already supplies electricity to households in New Zealand, Japan, the United States, and elsewhere.

The energy of falling or flowing water can also be used to generate electricity in a hydropower plant. Commercial hydropower plants generate over half of the alternative energy used in the United States. Like solar and geothermal power, hydropower releases no pollutants. But hydropower often requires dams, which are expensive to build and can flood wildlife habitats and interfere with fish migration.

Wind is another source of energy that is clean and renewable. Large open areas with relatively constant winds are used as wind farms. Wind turbines are spread across these farms and convert the energy of moving air into electricity. Wind-generating capacity has increased steadily around the world in just the last ten years.

Solar Energy These mirrors collect and concentrate sunlight, which will be used to generate electricity.

INFER What benefits do people get from using mass transit? Why might some people be reluctant to use mass transit?

READING TiP

The prefix *re–* means *again*, so to *recycle* a resource is to use it again.

Reducing Waste and Pollution

Perhaps you are one of the many students who take a bus to school. Buses and trains are examples of mass transit, which move large groups of people at the same time. When you travel by mass transit, you are working to reduce waste and pollution. The photograph to the left shows a light rail train that carries commuters from downtown Portland, Oregon, into suburbs an hour away. In Portland, mass transit like this light rail helps reduce traffic congestion, air pollution, and noise pollution.

Another way to reduce pollution is by carpooling. Many states encourage carpools by reducing tolls or reserving highway lanes for cars carrying more than one person. Traffic is also reduced when workers telecommute, or work from home, using computers and telephones. Of course a telecommuter uses energy at home. But there are many ways to reduce home energy use. You can install compact fluorescent light bulbs, which use less electricity than a regular light bulb. And you can choose energy-efficient appliances.

CHECK YOUR READING How does mass transit benefit the environment?

Most homes are heated with oil or natural gas, two nonrenewable resources. To use less of these resources, you lower your thermostat in winter or add insulation around doors and windows to keep heat inside. Many power companies offer a free energy audit, to show how you can use less energy at home.

Recycling is a fairly new idea in human communities, but if you think about it, it's what biological communities have always done to reduce waste and pollution. Resources are used again and again as they move through the water, nitrogen, and carbon cycles. Materials

These students are participating in a local recycling program.

that people now commonly recycle include glass, aluminum, certain types of plastic, office paper, newspaper, and cardboard.

Sometimes materials are recycled into the same product. Cans and glass bottles are melted down to make new cans and bottles. Materials can also be recycled into new products. Your warm fleece jacket might be made from recycled soda bottles. The cereal box on your breakfast table might be made from recycled paper.

 CHECK YOUR READING Name three things people can do at home that reduce waste and pollution.

Think globally, act locally.

Visitors to an ocean beach may find signs like the one on the right. Such signs remind people that small actions—like protecting the nests of sandpipers—make a difference in the preservation of ecosystems.

The challenges facing society are great. Providing Earth's growing population with clean water and air and with energy for warmth and transportation are only some of the many tasks. Scientists continue to learn about the interactions in ecosystems and how important ecosystems are to humans. As you have read about the interactions in ecosystems, you have probably realized that humans—including you—have a large effect on the natural world.

In the coming years, protection of ecosystems will remain a major challenge. By thinking globally, you will be able to understand the effects of society's decisions about resources, development, and transportation. By acting locally you can become involved in efforts to reduce the use of limited resources and to restore ecosystems.

3.3 Review

KEY CONCEPTS

1. List at least five ways that you can reduce your use of natural resources.

2. Describe three ways that resources can be managed in a sustainable way.

CRITICAL THINKING

3. **Infer** Controlling air and water pollution and protecting endangered species usually require the involvement of the federal government. Why can't state or local governments do this on their own?

CHALLENGE

4. **Apply** Explain how efforts to protect endangered species relate to restoration of ecosystems.

Cleaning Oil Spills

DESIGN —YOUR OWN—

OVERVIEW AND PURPOSE

One example of a harmful effect of human activity is an oil spill. You've probably heard about oil spills in the news. Damage to an oil-carrying ship or barge can cause thick black oil to spill into the water. The oil floats on the water, and waves can carry the oil to shore. Oil gets caught on sand and living things that are part of a coastal ecosystem. These spills are especially difficult to clean up. In this investigation you will

- simulate an oil spill and test the effectiveness of various materials used to remove oil
- evaluate materials and processes used to clean up oil spills

MATERIALS
- small beaker
- 40 mL vegetable oil
- turmeric
- spoon
- aluminum baking pan
- sand
- large beaker
- water
- sponge
- dish soap
- rubbing alcohol
- paper towels
- cotton balls
- cotton rag
- cornstarch
- yarn
- feather
- seaweed

▶ Problem
Write It Up

What materials are effective at removing oil spilled near a coastal ecosystem?

▶ Hypothesize
Write It Up

Write a hypothesis to propose a material or materials that might best remove oil from a coastal area. Your hypothesis should take the form of an "If . . . , then . . . , because . . ." statement.

▶ Procedure

1. Measure out 40 mL of vegetable oil in a small beaker. Stir in turmeric to make the oil yellow.

2. Pour sand into one end of the pan as shown to model a beach.

3. Carefully pour enough water into the pan so that it forms a model ocean at least 2 cm deep. Try not to disturb the sand pile.

4. Use the yellow-colored oil to model an oil spill. Pour the oil onto the slope of the sand so that it runs off into the water.

step 4

5 Test the materials for effectiveness in removing the oil from the sand and the water.

6 Place the feather and the seaweed on the beach or in the water, where the oil is. Test materials for effectiveness in removing oil from the feather and seaweed.

7 Make a table in your **Science Notebook** like the one below. Record your observations on the effectiveness of each material.

8 Using your observations from step 7, design a process for removing oil from sand and water. This process may involve several materials and require a series of steps.

▶ Observe and Analyze   Write It Up

1. **RECORD** Write up your procedure for cleaning oil from sand and water. You may want to include a diagram.

2. **EVALUATE** What, if any, difficulties did you encounter in carrying out this experiment?

▶ Conclude   Write It Up

1. **INTERPRET** How do your results compare with your hypothesis? Answer the problem statement.

2. **EVALUATE** Which materials were most useful for cleaning the water? Were they the same materials that were most useful for cleaning the sand?

3. **EVALUATE** Suppose you are trying to clean oil off of living things, such as a bird or seaweed. What process would you use?

4. **IDENTIFY LIMITS** In which ways did this demonstration fail to model a real oil spill?

▶ INVESTIGATE Further

CHALLENGE Explain how the observations you made in this investigation might be useful in designing treatments for an actual oil spill.

Cleaning Oil Spills

Problem What material or method is most effective in containing or cleaning up oil spills?

Hypothesis

Observations

	water	sand	feather	seaweed
paper towel				
cotton				

Chapter Review

the BIG idea

Humans and human population growth affect the environment.

CONTENT REVIEW
CLASSZONE.COM

 KEY CONCEPTS SUMMARY

3.1 Human population growth presents challenges.

As the population continues to grow, there is a greater demand for natural resources. Cities and countries share many resources. Increasing populations put pressure on ecosystems.

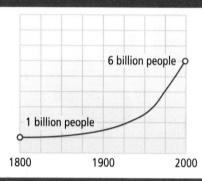

6 billion people

1 billion people

1800   1900   2000

VOCABULARY
natural resource p. 84
population
 density p. 86

3.2 Human activities affect the environment.

Pollution and habitat loss make it difficult for plants and animals to survive. Without the necessary resources, biodiversity of living things decreases, and ecosystems become less stable.

Pollution   **Habitat Loss**

VOCABULARY
pollution p. 91
biodiversity p. 91

3.3 Humans are working to protect ecosystems.

Working at local and governmental levels, humans are helping ecosystems recover.

Laws protect endangered species.

Researchers are investigating alternative resources.

VOCABULARY
conservation p. 99
sustainable p. 102

Reviewing Vocabulary

Place each vocabulary term at the center of a description wheel diagram. Write some words describing it on the spokes.

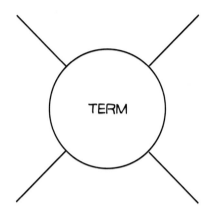

TERM

1. population density

2. natural resources

3. pollution

4. biodiversity

5. sustainable

6. conservation

Reviewing Key Concepts

Multiple Choice *Choose the letter of the best answer.*

7. In 2000, how big was Earth's human population?
  a. 1 billion   **c.** 6 billion
  b. 3 billion   **d.** 9 billion

8. Experts predict that by the year 2050, Earth's population will reach what number?
  a. 3 billion   **c.** 9 billion
  b. 6 billion   **d.** 12 billion

9. Which statement best explains why Earth's population has grown very rapidly in the last 100 years?
  a. On average, women are having children at an older age.
  b. People live longer because of improved health care and nutrition.

  c. Global warming has enabled farmers to grow more food.
  d. More land has been developed for housing.

10. Which of the four natural resources listed is likely to be used up the soonest?
  a. petroleum   **c.** sunlight
  b. water   **d.** wood

11. Which of the following is an example of increasing biodiversity?
  a. A forest is clear-cut for its wood, leaving land available for new uses.
  b. New species of animals and plants appear in a wildlife preserve.
  c. A new species of plant outcompetes all of the others around a lake.
  d. A cleared rain forest results in a change to a habitat.

12. Which represents a sustainable practice?
  a. conservation tillage and use of natural fertilizers
  b. more efficient removal of oil
  c. allowing unlimited use of water for higher fees
  d. restocking a lake with fish every year

13. What environmental problem does the Superfund Program address?
  a. habitat loss
  b. land development
  c. biodiversity
  d. pollution

Short Answer *Write a short answer to each question.*

14. List four ways increased human population density affects ecosystems.

15. Three ways that humans dispose of waste are landfills, incineration, and wastewater treatment plants. List one advantage and one disadvantage of each.

16. Write a paragraph to describe how an increase in population density affects land development.

Thinking Critically

Use the graph to answer the next three questions.

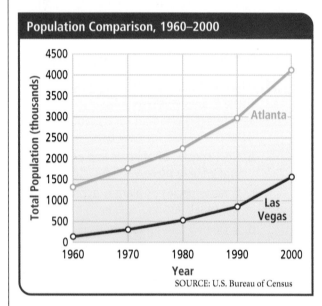

Population Comparison, 1960–2000

Total Population (thousands) vs Year (1960–2000)

Atlanta

Las Vegas

SOURCE: U.S. Bureau of Census

17. COMPARE AND CONTRAST Describe the population size and rate of growth for the cities of Atlanta and Las Vegas. Would you expect the population of Las Vegas to ever get bigger than that of Atlanta based on the data supplied?

18. EVALUATE Is it possible to determine from the data shown whether the population density is higher in Atlanta than Las Vegas? What other information would you need?

19. CONNECT Atlanta is located in a temperate-forest biome and Las Vegas is located in a desert biome. How might the characteristics of these biomes affect the carrying capacity of the human populations in these cities?

20. PREDICT If states in the U.S. used less water from the Colorado River, how would the depth of the river in Mexico be affected?

21. COMPARE AND CONTRAST Explain why trees are generally considered a renewable resource. Now describe circumstances under which they could be considered a nonrenewable resource.

22. CLASSIFY Sort the resources below into the correct categories:

Resource	Renewable	Nonrenewable
Water		
Coal		
Soil		
Wood		
Copper		
Petroleum		
Aluminum		
Sunlight		

23. CALCULATE A compact fluorescent bulb uses less energy than a regular bulb. It is estimated that a coal-burning power plant would release 72 kilograms more carbon dioxide (CO_2) a year to power one regular bulb than it would to power one fluorescent bulb. If you replace five regular bulbs with five compact bulbs, how much less CO_2 would be released in a 10-year period?

the **BIG** idea

24. PROVIDE EXAMPLES Look again at the photograph on pages 78–79. How would you change or add details to your answer to the question on the photograph?

25. APPLY You are on the town council of a community located on a small island. The council has decided to make a brochure for the town's citizens. In your brochure, describe the island habitat. Include information about natural resources, such as water and soil. List the plants and animals that live there. Establish four rules that the community should follow to preserve the local habitat.

UNIT PROJECTS

Evaluate the materials in your project folder. Finish your project and get ready to present it to your class.

Analyzing Data

Nowhere is the impact of human population growth more obvious than in the growth of urbanized areas. Buildings, parking lots, and roads are replacing forests, farmland, and wetlands. The table below shows the growth of urbanized areas around 10 cities in the United States during a 20-year period.

1. What patterns can you see in the way information is presented from the top of the table to the bottom?

  a. Cities are arranged alphabetically.

  b. Cities are arranged by growth in population over 20 years.

  c. Cities are arranged by the growth in land area over 20 years.

  d. Cities are arranged by size of urban area.

2. How would you describe the change in the land around Atlanta between 1970 and 1990?

  a. In 1990, more land was used for farming.

  b. The number of buildings and roads increased.

  c. The urbanized area decreased.

  d. Natural habitats for birds increased.

3. Which type of graph would be best for displaying the data in the table?

  a. a bar graph

  b. a circle graph

  c. a line graph

  d. a double bar graph

4. How many square kilometers around Philadelphia were affected by urbanization between 1970 and 1990?

  a. 1116 km^2 **c.** 1068 km^2

  b. 1166 km^2 **d.** 1020 km^2

Growth in land area, 1970–1990

Location	Growth in Land Area (Km^2)
Atlanta, GA	1816
Houston, TX	1654
New York City–N.E. New Jersey	1402
Washington, D.C.–MD–VA	1166
Philadelphia, PA	1068
Los Angeles, CA	1020
Dallas–Fort Worth, TX	964
Tampa–St. Petersburg–Clearwater, FL	929
Phoenix, AZ	916
Minneapolis–Saint Paul, MN	885

SOURCE: U.S. Bureau of Census data on Urbanized Areas

Extended Response

5. Write a paragraph to describe how a rural area would change if the land were developed and the area became more urban. Use the vocabulary words listed below in your answer.

population density	biodiversity
renewable resources	nonrenewable resources

6. If you were an urban designer working for a small city that expected to expand rapidly in the next 10 years, what recommendations would you make to the city council on how the land should be developed?

UNIT E

Space Science

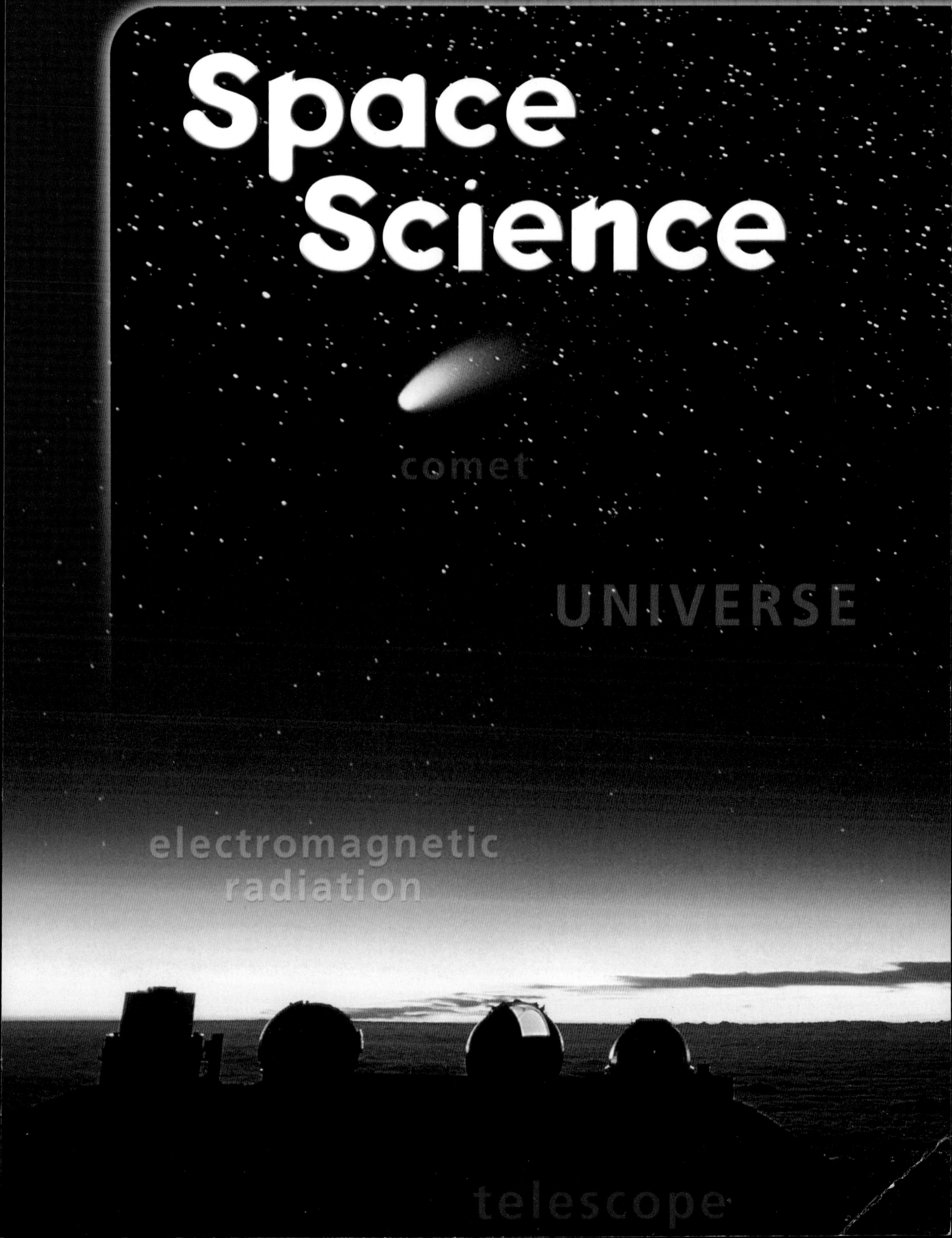
comet
UNIVERSE
electromagnetic radiation
telescope

Space Science
Contents Overview

Unit Features

1 Exploring Space   6

the BIG idea

People develop and use technology
to explore and study space.

2 Earth, Moon, and Sun   40

the BIG idea

Earth and the Moon move in predictable
ways as they orbit the Sun.

3 Our Solar System   76

the BIG idea

Planets and other objects form a
system around our Sun.

4 Stars, Galaxies, and the Universe   112

the BIG idea

Our Sun is one of billions of stars
in one of billions of galaxies in the
universe.

DANGER
from the Sky

How can astronomers find out whether a large object from space is going to strike our planet?

SCIENTIFIC AMERICAN FRONTIERS

View the video segment "Big Dish" to learn how astronomers use the largest radio telescope on Earth.

The streak of light in the photograph above was produced by a tiny particle from space burning up in Earth's atmosphere. Shown to the left is Barringer Crater in Arizona.

Collisions in Space

In the summer of 1994, telescopes all over the world were aimed at Jupiter. For the first time in history, astronomers had warning of a collision in space. Jupiter's gravity had split a comet named Shoemaker-Levy 9 into more than 20 large pieces. As the rocky objects collided with Jupiter's atmosphere, they exploded spectacularly.

Astronomers have found evidence of impacts closer to home. The craters that cover much of the Moon's surface were caused by collisions with space objects billions of years ago. In 1953 an astronomer even caught on film the bright flash of an object hitting the Moon. Other solid bodies in space also have impact craters. Little evidence of impacts remains on Earth because its surface is always changing. Fewer than 200 craters are still visible.

Earth's atmosphere protects us from collisions with small objects, which burn up in the air. However, when a large object strikes Earth, the atmosphere can spread the effects of the impact far beyond the crater. A large collision may throw dust high into the air, where it can be carried around the globe. The dust can block sunlight for months and sharply lower global temperatures.

About 65 million years ago, a large space object struck Earth. The dust from this collision can be found around the world in a layer of rock that was forming at the time. At about the same time, most species of organisms died out, including the dinosaurs. Many scientists think that the collision caused this global devastation.

The Risk of a Major Collision

When will the next space object hit Earth? A collision is probably occurring as you read this sentence. Tiny particles hit Earth's atmosphere all the time. Some of these particles have enough mass to make it through the atmosphere. Objects that reach Earth's surface are called meteorites. Most meteorites splash harmlessly into the ocean or hit unpopulated areas. Every few years a meteorite damages a home or other property. However, there is no known case of a meteorite's killing a person.

Collisions that cause widespread damage happen less often because the solar system contains fewer large objects. In 1908 a large object from space exploded above a remote region of Russia. The explosion knocked down trees across an area more than half the size of Rhode Island. Even this impact was small in comparison with major collisions that affect the entire world. Such collisions happen on average about twice every million years. Events that kill off many species occur even less often.

Tracking Asteroids

Although Earth is unlikely to have a major collision with a space object anytime soon, the danger is too great to ignore. Scientists are using telescopes to find large, rocky space objects called asteroids. After locating an asteroid, they use computer models to predict its path centuries into the future. Scientists expect that by 2008 they will have found almost all of the asteroids that could cause global devastation on Earth.

Locating objects that may threaten life on Earth is just the first step. Scientists also want to

SCIENTIFIC AMERICAN FRONTIERS

View the "Big Dish" segment of your *Scientific American Frontiers* video to learn how astronomers are using the giant Arecibo radio telescope to explore the universe.

IN THIS SCENE FROM THE VIDEO ▶

You see a close-up of the Arecibo telescope's dome and one of its antennas.

EXPLORING ASTEROIDS An asteroid's crashing into Earth may seem like the subject of a science fiction movie. Yet asteroids pose a real danger to humans. Some asteroids could cause widespread destruction if they struck our planet.

Astronomers are tracking these asteroids to determine how close they will pass to Earth in the future.

Asteroids are too faint to be viewed clearly with optical telescopes on Earth. However, radio telescopes can provide detailed images of asteroids. Inside the dome of the Arecibo telescope is the world's most powerful radar transmitter. The transmitter can bounce a beam of radio waves off the telescope's dish to reach an asteroid millions of miles away. The telescope picks up returning signals, which are converted into images.

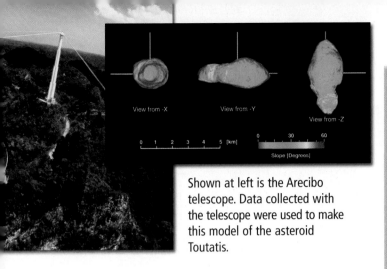

Shown at left is the Arecibo telescope. Data collected with the telescope were used to make this model of the asteroid Toutatis.

learn about the characteristics of asteroids. The Arecibo telescope in Puerto Rico is an important tool for studying asteroids. The largest radio dish in the world, it allows scientists to determine the motions and shapes of asteroids. Computer models and tests with real materials provide additional information about the mass, materials, and structure of each asteroid.

If scientists ever find an asteroid headed toward Earth, these studies may help us change the asteroid's course safely. Remember the comet that struck Jupiter in many pieces? If an asteroid broke apart before reaching Earth, pieces hitting different locations could cause even more damage than a single impact. Before using a bomb or laser to change the course of an asteroid, governments must make sure that the asteroid will not break apart. Fortunately, scientists would have decades to study a dangerous asteroid and figure out what action to take.

UNANSWERED Questions

Scientists are learning about the risk of an asteroid's colliding with Earth. The more we learn about collisions in space, the more questions we have.

- What methods can be used to change the course of an asteroid that threatens Earth?

- How can we make sure that an asteroid will not break apart because of our efforts to change its course?

- How many smaller but still dangerous objects may be headed toward Earth?

UNIT PROJECTS

As you study this unit, work alone or with a group on one of these projects.

Observe the Sky

Choose a space object or part of the distant sky to observe over a month. Keep an observation journal of what you see and think.

- Pay special attention to any changes relative to other objects in the sky.

- Look up information or construct tools to help you observe.

- Copy your best drawings for a display board. Explain your observations.

Multimedia Presentation

The Arecibo telescope is not used only for studying asteroids. Prepare a multimedia presentation on other research that is being carried out with the giant radio telescope.

- Find information about the research from Internet sites and other sources.

- Prepare both audio and visual components for your presentation.

Map a Space Object

Use a large potato to represent a newly explored space object. Draw lines of latitude and longitude. Then identify features, and make a flat map.

- Use roller-ball pens to mark poles, an equator, and lines of longitude and latitude. Try not to pierce the potato's skin.

- Do the potato's eyes seem like craters or volcanoes? Decide how to name the different types of features.

- Make a flat map of the space object.

CAREER CENTER
CLASSZONE.COM

Learn about careers in astronomy.

Exploring Space

the **BIG** idea

People develop and use technology to explore and study space.

What challenges must be overcome in space exploration?

Key Concepts

SECTION

Some space objects are visible to the human eye.
Learn about views of space from Earth and about the arrangement of the universe.

SECTION

Telescopes allow us to study space from Earth.
Learn how astronomers gather information about space from different kinds of radiation.

SECTION

Spacecraft help us explore beyond Earth.
Learn how astronauts and instruments provide information about space.

SECTION

Space exploration benefits society.
Learn about the benefits of space exploration.

Internet Preview

CLASSZONE.COM

Chapter 1 online resources: Content Review, Simulation, Visualization, two Resource Centers, Math Tutorial, Test Practice

Why Does the Sun Appear to Move Around Earth?

Stand in front of a floor lamp, and turn around slowly. Notice how the lamp moves within your field of vision.

Observe and Think
Why did the lamp seem to move?

What Colors Are in Sunlight?

In bright sunlight, hold a clear plastic pen over a box. Move the pen until a rainbow pattern appears.

Observe and Think
What colors did you see? What might have caused them to appear?

Internet Activity: Universe

Go to **ClassZone.com** to simulate moving through different levels of scale in the universe.

Observe and Think How much of the universe could you see without a telescope?

NSTA
scilinks.org
SCi*LINKS*

Space Probes Code: MDL057

Getting Ready to Learn

◀ CONCEPT REVIEW

- There are more stars in the sky than anyone can easily count.
- Telescopes magnify the appearance of distant objects in the sky.
- Once an invention exists, people are likely to think up new ways of using it.

◀ VOCABULARY REVIEW

See Glossary for definitions.

data

energy

gravity

technology

CONTENT REVIEW
CLASSZONE.COM
Review concepts and vocabulary.

▶ TAKING NOTES

MAIN IDEA WEB

Write each new blue heading, or main idea, in the center box. In the boxes around it, take notes about important terms and details that relate to the main idea.

VOCABULARY STRATEGY

Think about a vocabulary term as a **magnet word** diagram. Write the other terms or ideas related to that term around it.

See the Note-Taking Handbook on pages R45–R51.

SCIENCE NOTEBOOK

The constellations change position in the night sky as Earth rotates.

Polaris is located straight over the North Pole.

The sky seems to turn as Earth rotates.

Polaris can help you figure out direction and location.

ORBIT

path around another object

influence of gravity

Moon orbits Earth

planets orbit Sun

space telescopes

satellites

Some space objects are visible to the human eye.

◀ **BEFORE, you learned**

- Earth is one of nine planets that orbit the Sun
- The Moon orbits Earth
- Earth turns on its axis every 24 hours

▶ **NOW, you will learn**

- How the universe is arranged
- How stars form patterns in the sky
- How the motions of bodies in space appear from Earth

VOCABULARY

orbit p. 10
solar system p. 10
galaxy p. 10
universe p. 10
constellation p. 12

EXPLORE Distance

How far is the Moon from Earth?

PROCEDURE

1. Tie one end of the string around the middle of the tennis ball. The tennis ball will represent Earth.

2. Wrap the string 9.5 times around the tennis ball, and make a mark on the string at that point. Wrap the aluminum foil into a ball around the mark. The foil ball will represent the Moon.

3. Stretch out the string to put the model Moon and Earth at the right distance compared to their sizes.

MATERIALS

- tennis ball
- aluminum foil (5 cm strip)
- string (250 cm)
- felt marker

WHAT DO YOU THINK?

- How does the scale model compare with your previous idea of the distance between Earth and the Moon?
- How many Earths do you estimate would fit between Earth and the Moon?

We see patterns in the universe.

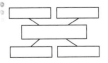

MAIN IDEA WEB
Record details about patterns in space.

For most of history, people had very limited knowledge of space. They saw planets and stars as points of light in the night sky. However, they did not know how far those bodies were from Earth or from each other. Early observers made guesses about planets and stars on the basis of their appearance and the ways they seemed to move in the sky. Different peoples around the world connected the patterns they saw in the sky with stories about imaginary beings.

We still have much to learn about the universe. Within the last few hundred years, however, new tools and scientific theories have greatly increased our knowledge. In this chapter you will learn about the arrangement of planets and stars. You will also learn about the ways in which astronomers explore and study space.

Arrangement of the Universe

If you look up at the sky on a clear night, you will see only a tiny fraction of the planets and stars that exist. The number of objects in the universe and the distances between them are greater than most people can imagine. Yet these objects are not spread around randomly. Gravity causes objects in space to be grouped together in different ways.

The images on page 11 show some basic structures in the universe. Like a camera lens zooming out, the images provide views of space at different levels of size.

READING **TiP**

The word *orbit* can be a noun or a verb.

❶ Earth Our planet's diameter is about 13,000 kilometers (8000 mi). This is almost four times the diameter of the Moon, which orbits Earth. An **orbit** is the path of an object in space as it moves around another object because of gravity.

❷ Solar System Earth and eight other major planets orbit the Sun. The Sun, the planets, and various smaller bodies make up the **solar system.** The Sun is about 100 times greater in diameter than Earth. You could fit more than 4000 bodies the size of the Sun between the Sun and the solar system's outermost planet at its average distance from the Sun. The Sun is one of countless stars in space. Astronomers have detected planets orbiting some of these other stars.

❸ The Milky Way Our solar system and the stars you can see with your bare eyes are part of a galaxy called the Milky Way. A **galaxy** is a group of millions or billions of stars held together by their own gravity. If the solar system were the size of a penny, the Milky Way would stretch from Chicago to Dallas. Most stars in the Milky Way are so far away that our galaxy appears to us as a hazy band of light.

❹ The Universe The **universe** is everything—space and all the matter and energy in it. The Milky Way is just one of many billions of galaxies in the universe. These galaxies extend in all directions.

Astronomers study space at each of these different levels. Some focus on planets in the solar system. Other astronomers study distant galaxies. To learn how the universe formed, astronomers even study the smallest particles that make up all matter.

CHECK YOUR READING What is the relationship between the solar system and the Milky Way?

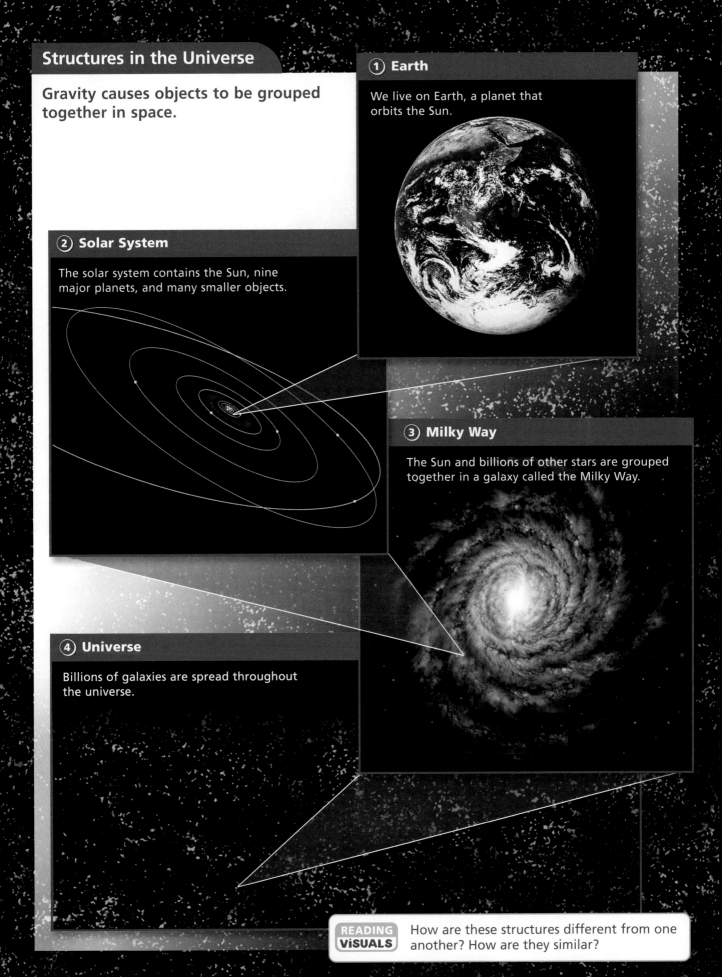

Structures in the Universe

Gravity causes objects to be grouped together in space.

① Earth

We live on Earth, a planet that orbits the Sun.

② Solar System

The solar system contains the Sun, nine major planets, and many smaller objects.

③ Milky Way

The Sun and billions of other stars are grouped together in a galaxy called the Milky Way.

④ Universe

Billions of galaxies are spread throughout the universe.

READING VISUALS How are these structures different from one another? How are they similar?

Constellation Patterns

The stars of a constellation are often far apart from one another, but they appear grouped together when viewed from Earth.

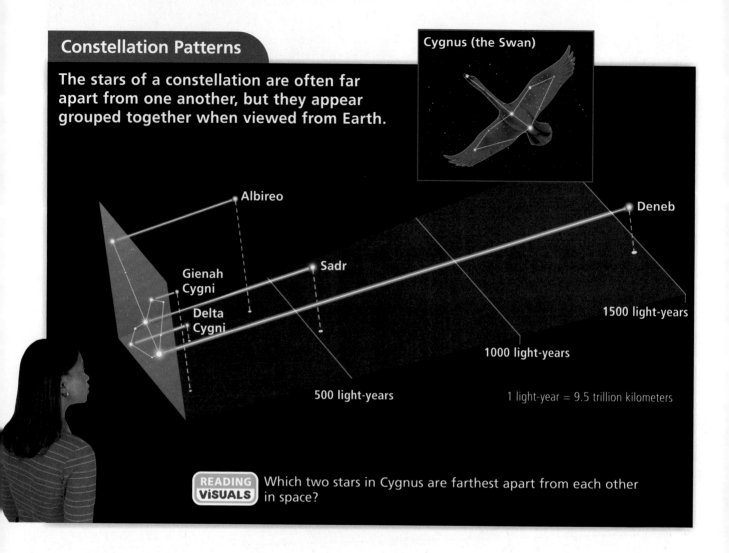

Cygnus (the Swan)

Albireo

Deneb

Gienah Cygni

Sadr

Delta Cygni

1500 light-years

1000 light-years

500 light-years

1 light-year = 9.5 trillion kilometers

READING VISUALS Which two stars in Cygnus are farthest apart from each other in space?

Constellations

VISUALIZATION
CLASSZONE.COM

View images of the night sky taken throughout the year.

If you want to find a particular place in the United States, it helps to know the name of the state it is in. Astronomers use a similar system to describe the locations of objects in the sky. They have divided the sky into 88 areas named for the constellations.

A **constellation** is a group of stars that form a pattern in the sky. In the constellation Cygnus, for example, a group of bright stars form the shape of a flying swan. Any other objects in that area of the sky, such as galaxies, are said to be located in Cygnus, even if they are not parts of the swan pattern. The ancient Greeks named many of the constellations for animals and imaginary beings.

Unlike the planets in the solar system, the stars in a constellation are usually not really close to each other. They seem to be grouped together when viewed from Earth. But as the illustration above shows, you would not see the same pattern in the stars if you viewed them from another angle.

 CHECK YOUR READING What relationship exists among the stars in a constellation?

The sky seems to turn as Earth rotates.

You cannot see all of the constellations at once, because Earth blocks half of space from your view. However, you can see a parade of constellations each night as Earth rotates. As some constellations slowly come into view over the eastern horizon, others pass high in the sky above you, and still others set at the western horizon. Throughout the ages, many peoples have observed these changes and used them to help in navigation and measuring time.

If you extended the North Pole into space, it would point almost exactly to a star called Polaris, or the North Star. If you were standing at the North Pole, Polaris would be directly over your head. As Earth rotates through the night, the stars close to Polaris seem to move in circles around it. Although not the brightest star in the sky, Polaris is fairly bright and easy to find. You can use Polaris to figure out direction and location.

The stars in this image were photographed over several hours to show how they move across the night sky.

 CHECK YOUR READING What causes constellations to change positions during the night?

INVESTIGATE Constellation Positions

How does time of day affect the positions of constellations?

PROCEDURE

1. Cut out both diagrams on the Constellation Wheel Sheet and assemble them as shown.

2. Rotate the wheel so that the current month is aligned with 9 P.M. Observe the positions of the constellations.

3. Align the current month with other times to determine how the positions of the constellations change during the night.

WHAT DO YOU THINK?

- How do the positions of the constellations change during the night?
- In which direction does the northern sky seem to turn?

CHALLENGE Earth's rotation makes the sky seem to turn. What does the model tell you about the direction of Earth's rotation?

SKILL FOCUS
Analyzing

MATERIALS
- Constellation Wheel Sheet
- scissors
- brass fastener

TIME
20 minutes

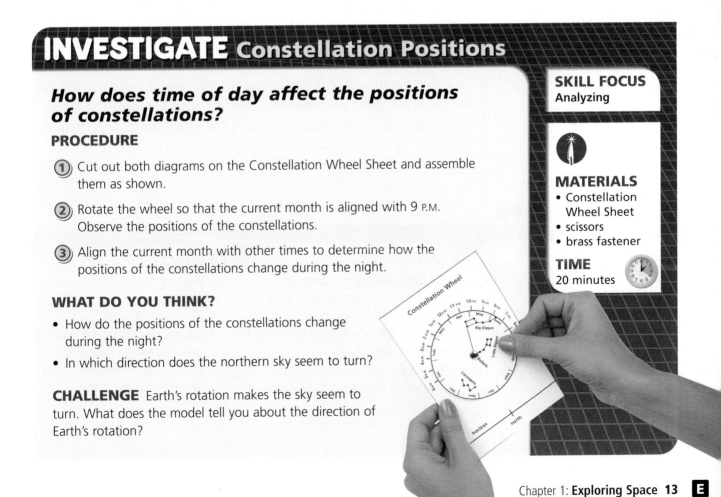

The movements of planets and other nearby objects are visible from Earth.

A jet plane travels at a greater speed and altitude than a bird. Yet if a bird and a plane flew overhead at the same time, you might think that the bird was faster. You would have this impression because the farther away a moving object is from you, the less it seems to move.

Stars are always moving, but they are so far away that you cannot see their movements. Observers have seen the same constellation patterns for thousands of years. Only over a much longer period does the motion of stars gradually change constellation patterns.

By contrast, the Moon moves across the star background a distance equal to its width every hour as it orbits Earth. The Moon is our closest neighbor. The planets are farther away, but you can see their gradual movements among the constellations over a period of weeks or months.

Planet comes from a Greek word that means "wanderer." Ancient Greek astronomers used this term because they noticed that planets move among the constellations. It is easiest to see the movements of Venus and Mars, the two planets closest to Earth. They change their positions in the sky from night to night.

The apparent movement of the sky led early astronomers to believe that Earth was at the center of the universe. Later astronomers discovered that Earth and the other planets orbit the Sun. The time-line on pages 72–75 introduces some of the astronomers who helped discover how planets really move in the solar system.

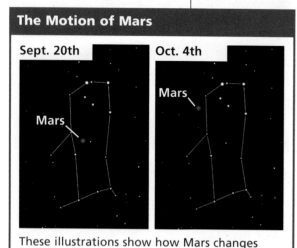

The Motion of Mars

Sept. 20th

Mars

Oct. 4th

Mars

These illustrations show how Mars changes positions in the constellation Gemini over a period of two weeks.

1.1 Review

KEY CONCEPTS

1. What are the basic structures in which objects are grouped together in space?

2. What is a constellation?

3. How does Earth's rotation affect our view of stars?

CRITICAL THINKING

4. **Compare and Contrast** How is the grouping of stars in a constellation different from the grouping of planets in the solar system?

5. **Apply** The planet Jupiter is farther than Mars from Earth. Which planet seems to move faster when viewed from Earth? Explain.

○ CHALLENGE

6. **Predict** Suppose that you are standing at the North Pole on a dark night. If you keep turning clockwise at the same speed as Earth's rotation, how would your movement affect your view of the stars?

Telescopes allow us to study space from Earth.

◄ **BEFORE,** you learned

- Objects in the universe are grouped together in different ways
- The motions of planets and other nearby objects are visible from Earth

▶ **NOW,** you will learn

- About light and other forms of radiation
- How astronomers gather information about space

VOCABULARY

electromagnetic radiation p. 15
spectrum p. 16
wavelength p. 16
telescope p. 17

EXPLORE Distortion of Light

How can light become distorted?

PROCEDURE

① Place a white sheet of paper behind a glass filled with plain water. Shine a flashlight through the glass, and observe the spot of light on the paper.

② Pour a spoonful of salt into the water. Stir the water, and observe the spot of light.

WHAT DO YOU THINK?

- How did the spot of light change after you mixed the salt into the water?
- How could Earth's atmosphere cause similar changes in light from space?

MATERIALS
- flashlight
- glass filled with water
- sheet of white paper
- spoon
- salt

Light and other forms of radiation carry information about space.

VOCABULARY
Add a magnet word diagram for *electromagnetic radiation* to your notebook.

When you look at an object, your eyes are gathering light from that object. Visible light is a form of **electromagnetic radiation** (ih-LEHK-troh-mag-NEHT-ihk), which is energy that travels across distances as certain types of waves. There are other forms of electromagnetic radiation that you cannot see directly, such as radio waves and x-rays. Scientists have developed instruments to detect these other forms.

Electromagnetic radiation travels in all directions throughout space. Almost everything we know about the universe has come from our study of radiation. Astronomers can often learn about the size, distance, and movement of an object by studying its radiation. Radiation can also reveal what an object is made of and how it has changed.

The Electromagnetic Spectrum

The different forms of electromagnetic radiation vary in their wavelengths.

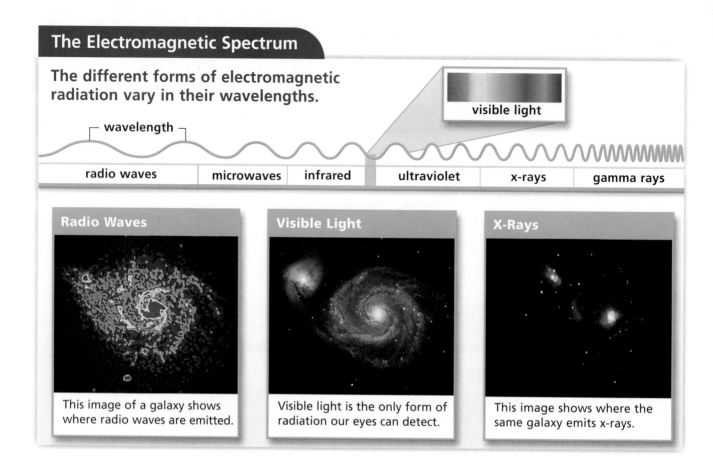

visible light

wavelength

| radio waves | microwaves | infrared | ultraviolet | x-rays | gamma rays |

Radio Waves
This image of a galaxy shows where radio waves are emitted.

Visible Light
Visible light is the only form of radiation our eyes can detect.

X-Rays
This image shows where the same galaxy emits x-rays.

READING TiP

A prism is a transparent object that is used to separate the wavelengths of light.

If you shine a flashlight through a prism, the beam of white light will separate into a range of colors called a **spectrum** (SPEHK-truhm). The colors that make up visible light are red, orange, yellow, green, blue, indigo, and violet. These are the colors in a rainbow, which appears when light spreads out as it passes through raindrops.

In a spectrum, the colors of visible light appear in the order of their wavelengths. **Wavelength** is the distance between one wave peak and the next wave peak. Red light has the longest wavelength. Violet light has the shortest.

As you can see in the illustration above, visible light is just a tiny part of a larger spectrum called the electromagnetic spectrum. The electromagnetic spectrum includes all the forms of electromagnetic radiation. Notice that the wavelength of infrared radiation is longer than the wavelength of visible light but not as long as the wavelength of microwaves or radio waves. The wavelength of ultraviolet radiation is shorter than the wavelength of visible light but not as short as the wavelength of x-rays or gamma rays.

CHECK YOUR READING How is visible light different from other forms of electromagnetic radiation?

Astronomers use telescopes to collect information about space.

A **telescope** is a device that gathers electromagnetic radiation. If you have ever looked through a telescope, it was probably one that gathers visible light. Such telescopes provide images that are much clearer than what is seen with the naked eye. Images from other types of telescopes show radiation that your eyes cannot detect. Each form of radiation provides different information about objects in space.

Astronomers usually record images from telescopes electronically, which allows them to use computers to analyze images. Different colors or shades in an image reveal patterns of radiation. For example, in the right-hand image on page 16, the colors yellow and red indicate where the galaxy is emitting large amounts of x-rays.

Most types of telescopes gather radiation with a glass lens or a reflecting surface, such as a mirror. Larger lenses and reflecting surfaces produce brighter and more detailed images. You can magnify an image from a telescope to any size. However, enlarging an image will not bring out any more details of an object. If the image is fuzzy at a small size, it will remain fuzzy no matter how much it is enlarged.

Visible-Light, Infrared, and Ultraviolet Telescopes

There are two types of visible-light telescopes: reflecting telescopes and refracting telescopes. Reflecting telescopes can also be built to gather infrared or ultraviolet radiation.

- **Reflecting Telescope** This type of telescope has a curved mirror that gathers light. The image comes into focus in front of the mirror. Many reflecting telescopes have a second mirror that reflects the image to recording equipment or to a lens called an eyepiece.

- **Refracting Telescope** This type of telescope has an objective lens, or curved piece of glass, at one end of a long tube. The lens gathers light and focuses it to form an image near the other end of the tube. An eyepiece magnifies this image.

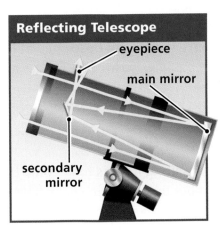

Reflecting Telescope

eyepiece

main mirror

secondary mirror

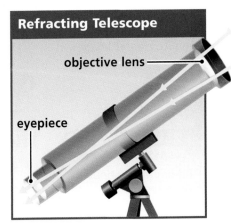

Refracting Telescope

objective lens

eyepiece

Most powerful visible-light telescopes are built on mountaintops in rural areas. Rural areas offer a much better view of the night sky than cities do, because the many electric lights in cities make dim space objects hard to see. By locating telescopes on mountaintops, astronomers reduce problems caused by Earth's atmosphere. The atmosphere interferes with light coming in from space. In fact, movements of the air are what make stars appear to twinkle. At high altitudes there is less air above the ground to interfere with light.

Radio Telescopes

Radio Telescope

Radio telescopes show where radio waves are being emitted by objects in space. A radio telescope has a curved metal surface, called a dish, that gathers radio waves and focuses them onto an antenna. The dish works in the same way as the main mirror of a reflecting telescope. Some radio telescopes have dishes made of metal mesh rather than solid metal.

Because radio waves are so long, a single radio telescope must be very large to produce useful images. To improve the quality of images, astronomers often aim a group of radio telescopes at the same object. Signals from the telescopes are combined and then converted into an image. Groups of radio telescopes, like the Very Large Array in New Mexico, can show more detail than even the largest single dish.

Signals from these radio telescopes in New Mexico can be combined to produce clearer images.

Unlike visible-light telescopes, radio telescopes are not affected by clouds or bad weather. They even work well in daylight. In addition, radio telescopes can be located at low altitudes because most radio waves pass freely through Earth's atmosphere.

CHECK YOUR READING What is the function of the dish in a radio telescope?

RESOURCE CENTER
CLASSZONE.COM
Find out more about telescopes.

Telescopes in Space

Many exciting images have come from the Hubble Space Telescope and other telescopes in space. The Hubble telescope is a reflecting telescope. It was placed in orbit around Earth in 1990. Astronomers operate it from the ground, although astronauts have visited it to make repairs and improvements. The telescope sends images and measurements back to Earth electronically.

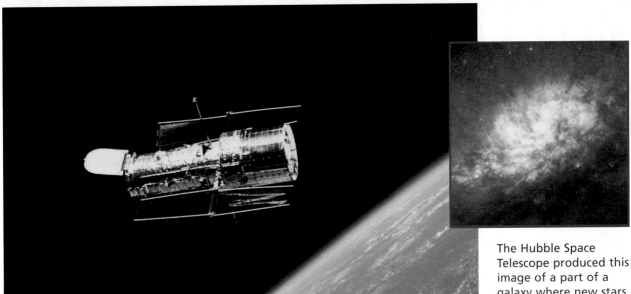

The Hubble Space Telescope produced this image of a part of a galaxy where new stars are appearing.

Because the Hubble telescope is located in space, Earth's atmosphere does not interfere with light from objects the telescope is aimed at. This lack of interference allows it to obtain clearer images than ground-based telescopes with much larger mirrors. In addition to collecting visible light, the Hubble telescope produces images of ultraviolet and infrared radiation.

The Hubble Space Telescope is part of a group of telescopes that orbit Earth. The telescopes allow astronomers to gain information from the full range of electromagnetic radiation. The Compton Gamma-Ray Observatory was sent into orbit in 1991. The Chandra X-Ray Observatory was launched eight years later. These telescopes were placed in space because Earth's atmosphere blocks most x-rays and gamma rays.

 CHECK YOUR READING   Why does the Hubble telescope produce clearer images than a telescope of the same size on Earth?

1.2 Review

KEY CONCEPTS

1. How are visible light, radio waves, and other forms of electromagnetic radiation different from each other?

2. What function do mirrors serve in reflecting telescopes?

3. Why are some telescopes placed on mountains or in orbit around Earth?

CRITICAL THINKING

4. **Compare and Contrast** What are the similarities and differences between refracting telescopes and reflecting telescopes?

5. **Analyze** Why would it be difficult to build radio telescopes if they did not work well at low altitudes?

CHALLENGE

6. **Analyze** Why might astronomers use different types of telescopes to obtain images of the same object in space?

Observing Spectra

OVERVIEW AND PURPOSE Visible light is made up of different colors that can be separated into a rainbow band called a spectrum. Astronomers gain information about the characteristics of stars by spreading their light into spectra (*spectra* is the plural form of *spectrum*). A spectroscope is a device that produces spectra. In most spectroscopes, diffraction gratings are used to separate light into different colors. The colors with the longest wavelengths appear farthest from the slit in a spectroscope. The colors with the shortest wavelengths appear closest to the slit. In this investigation you will

- build a spectroscope and observe the spectra of three different light sources
- identify ways in which the spectra of light sources differ

MATERIALS
- shoebox with lid
- ruler
- scissors
- diffraction grating
- tape
- index card
- pencils or markers in a variety of colors
- incandescent light
- fluorescent light
for Challenge:
- cellophane in several colors

▶ Procedure

1 Cut a hole measuring 3 cm by 1.5 cm in each end of a shoebox. Make sure that the holes line up.

2 On the inside of the box, tape a piece of diffraction grating over one of the holes. Handle the diffraction grating by its edges so that you do not get finger-prints on it.

step 1

3 Cut an index card in half, and tape the halves over the outside of the other hole as shown. Leave a very narrow slit between the two halves of the index card.

4 Put the lid on the shoebox. Then turn off the overhead lights in the classroom.

5 Look through the hole covered with the diffraction grating, aiming the spectroscope's slit at the sky through a window. **Caution:** *Never look directly at the Sun.* Observe the spectrum you see to the left of the slit.

step 5

6 Repeat step 5 while aiming the spectroscope at an incandescent light and then at a fluorescent light.

▶ Observe and Analyze
Write It Up

1. **RECORD OBSERVATIONS** For each light source, draw in your data table the spectrum you see to the left of the slit. Describe the colors and patterns in the spectrum, and label the light source.

2. **IDENTIFY LIMITS** What problems, if any, did you experience in observing the spectra? Why was it important to turn off overhead lights for this activity?

▶ Conclude
Write It Up

1. **COMPARE AND CONTRAST** How did the spectra differ from one another? Did you notice any stripes of color that were brighter or narrower than other colors in the same spectrum? Did you notice any lines or spaces separating colors?

2. **ANALYZE** The shorter the wavelength of a color, the closer it appears to the slit in a spectroscope. On the basis of your observations, which color has the shortest wavelength? Which color has the longest wavelength?

3. **INFER** How might the spectra look different if the slit at the end of the spectroscope were curved instead of a straight line?

▶ INVESTIGATE Further

CHALLENGE Cover the slit on your spectroscope with a piece of colored cellophane. Aiming the spectroscope at a fluorescent light or another light source, observe and draw the resulting spectrum. Then repeat with cellophane of other colors. List the colors that each piece of cellophane transmitted. Did these results surprise you? If so, why?

Observing Spectra
Observe and Analyze
Table 1. Spectra of Different Light Sources

Light Source	Drawing	Description

Conclude

Spacecraft help us explore beyond Earth.

◀ **BEFORE, you learned**

- The motions of planets and other nearby objects are visible from Earth
- Light and other forms of radiation carry information about the universe

▶ **NOW, you will learn**

- How astronauts explore space near Earth
- How different types of spacecraft are used in exploration

VOCABULARY

satellite p. 23
space station p. 24
lander p. 28
probe p. 29

EXPLORE Viewing Space Objects

How do objects appear at different distances?

PROCEDURE

① Crumple the paper into a ball and place it on your desk.

② Sketch the ball at the same time as another student sketches it. One of you should sketch it from a distance of 1 m. The other should sketch it from 5 m away.

WHAT DO YOU THINK?

- How do the details in the two drawings compare?
- What details might be easier to see on a planet if you were orbiting the planet?

MATERIALS
- paper
- pencils

Astronauts explore space near Earth.

RESOURCE CENTER
CLASSZONE.COM

Learn more about space exploration.

Space travel requires very careful planning. Astronauts take everything necessary for survival with them, including air, water, and food. Spacecraft need powerful rockets and huge fuel tanks to lift all their weight upward against Earth's gravity. The equipment must be well designed and maintained, since any breakdown can be deadly.

Once in space, astronauts must get used to a special environment. People and objects in an orbiting spacecraft seem to float freely unless they are fastened down. This weightless condition occurs because they are falling in space at the same rate as the spacecraft. In addition, to leave their airtight cabin, astronauts must wear special protective suits. Despite these conditions, astronauts have managed to perform experiments and make important observations about space near Earth.

Moon Missions

For about a decade, much of space exploration was focused on a race to the Moon. This race was driven by rivalry between the United States and the Soviet Union, which included Russia. In 1957 the Soviet Union launched the first artificial satellite to orbit Earth. A **satellite** is an object that orbits a more massive object. The Soviet Union also sent the first human into space in 1961. Although the United States lagged behind in these early efforts, it succeeded in sending the first humans to the Moon.

Preparation Many steps had to be taken before astronauts from the United States could visit the Moon. The National Aeronautics and Space Administration (NASA) sent spacecraft without crews to the Moon to find out whether it was possible to land on its surface. NASA also sent astronauts into space to practice important procedures.

Landings The NASA program to reach the Moon was called Apollo. During early Apollo missions, astronauts tested spacecraft and flew them into orbit around the Moon. On July 20, 1969, crew members from *Apollo 11* became the first humans to walk on the Moon's surface. NASA achieved five more Moon landings between 1969 and 1972. During this period, the Soviet Union sent spacecraft without crews to get samples of the Moon's surface.

Scientific Results The Apollo program helped scientists learn about the Moon's surface and interior. Much of the information came from 380 kilograms (weighing 840 lb) of rock and soil that astronauts brought back to Earth. These samples are still being studied.

Powerful booster rockets were used to launch the Apollo spacecraft. Beginning with *Apollo 15*, astronauts rode in lunar roving vehicles to explore greater areas of the Moon's surface.

Orbiting Earth

A **space station** is a satellite in which people can live and work for long periods. The United States and the Soviet Union launched the first space stations in the early 1970s. After the breakup of the Soviet Union in 1991, the Russian space agency and NASA began to act as partners rather than rivals. Russian and U. S. astronauts carried out joint missions aboard *Mir* (meer), the Russian space station.

The *Mir* missions helped prepare for the International Space Station (ISS). The United States, Russia, and 15 other nations are working together to build the ISS. When completed, it will cover an area about as large as two football fields. The ISS is too large to launch into space in one piece. Instead, sections of the space station are being launched separately and assembled in orbit over a period of years.

Construction of the ISS began in 1998. The first three-member crew arrived at the station in 2000. In addition to constructing the station, crew members make observations of Earth and perform experiments. Some experiments are much more effective when they are performed in space, where gravity affects them differently. For example, scientists can grow cell tissue more easily in space than they can on Earth. Research on cell tissue grown in space may increase our understanding of cancer and other diseases.

International Space Station

Each section of the space station has a specific function.

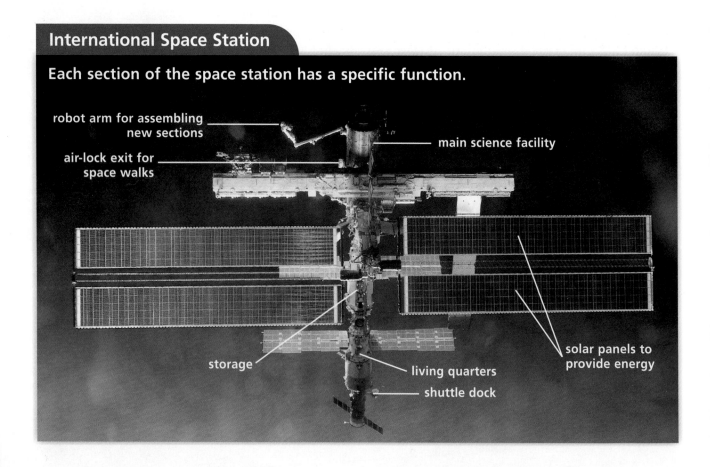

- robot arm for assembling new sections
- air-lock exit for space walks
- main science facility
- storage
- living quarters
- shuttle dock
- solar panels to provide energy

Research and technological advances from the space station may lay the groundwork for new space exploration. ISS crew members study how living in space affects the human body over long periods. This research may provide useful information for future efforts to send astronauts to other planets.

Most crews have flown to the ISS aboard space shuttles. Unlike earlier spacecraft, a space shuttle can be used again and again. At the end of a mission, it reenters Earth's atmosphere and glides down to a runway. The large cargo bay of a space shuttle can carry satellites, equipment, and laboratories.

NASA has launched space shuttles more than 100 times since 1981. Space shuttles are much more sophisticated than the Apollo spacecraft that carried astronauts to the Moon. However, space travel remains a dangerous activity.

Two booster rockets and an external fuel tank are needed to lift a space shuttle into orbit.

 CHECK YOUR READING Why might some researchers choose to perform experiments aboard a space station rather than on Earth?

INVESTIGATE Launch Planning

How does Earth's rotation affect launches of spacecraft?

SKILL FOCUS
Identifying variables

PROCEDURE

1. Tightly wad 14 sheets of paper into balls, and place the balls in a small bucket.

2. Stand 1.5 m away from a large bucket placed on a desk. Try tossing 7 balls into the bucket.

3. While turning slowly, try tossing the remaining 7 balls into the bucket.

WHAT DO YOU THINK?

- How much more difficult was it to toss the paper balls into the bucket while you were turning than when you were standing still?

- Why does Earth's rotation make launching rockets into space more complicated?

CHALLENGE How would you design an experiment to show the variables involved in a launch from Earth toward another rotating body in space, such as the Moon?

MATERIALS
- paper
- small bucket
- large bucket

TIME
10 minutes

Spacecraft carry instruments to other worlds.

Currently, we cannot send humans to other planets. One obstacle is that such a trip would take years. A spacecraft would need to carry enough air, water, and other supplies needed for survival on the long journey. Another obstacle is the harsh conditions on other planets, such as extreme heat and cold. Some planets do not even have surfaces to land on.

Because of these obstacles, most research in space is accomplished through the use of spacecraft without crews aboard. These missions pose no risk to human life and are less expensive than missions involving astronauts. The spacecraft carry instruments that test the compositions and characteristics of planets. Data and images are sent back to Earth as radio signals. Onboard computers and radio signals from Earth guide the spacecraft.

Spacecraft have visited all the major planets in our solar system except Pluto. NASA has also sent spacecraft to other bodies in space, such as comets and moons. Scientists and engineers have designed different types of spacecraft to carry out these missions.

CHECK YOUR READING What questions do you still have about space exploration?

Flybys

The first stage in space exploration is to send out a spacecraft that passes one or more planets or other bodies in space without orbiting them. Such missions are called flybys. After a flyby spacecraft leaves Earth's orbit, controllers on Earth can use the spacecraft's small rockets to adjust its direction. Flyby missions may last for decades. However, because a spacecraft flies by planets quickly, it can collect data and images from a particular planet only for a brief period.

As a flyby spacecraft passes a planet, the planet's gravity can be used to change the spacecraft's speed or direction. During the flyby of the planet, the spacecraft can gain enough energy to propel it to another planet more quickly. This method allowed *Voyager 2* to fly past Saturn, Uranus, and Neptune, even though the spacecraft left Earth with only enough energy to reach Jupiter.

Many complex mathematical calculations are needed for a flyby mission to be successful. Experts must take into account Earth's rotation and the positions of the planets that the spacecraft will pass. The period of time when a spacecraft can be launched is called a launch window.

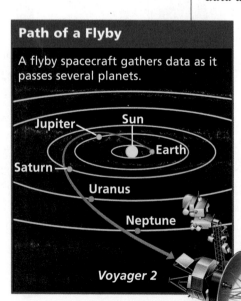

Path of a Flyby

A flyby spacecraft gathers data as it passes several planets.

Jupiter · Sun · Earth · Saturn · Uranus · Neptune

Voyager 2

Orbiters

The second stage in space exploration is to study a planet over a long period of time. Spacecraft designed to accomplish this task are called orbiters. As an orbiter approaches its target planet, rocket engines are fired to slow the spacecraft down. The spacecraft then goes into orbit around the planet.

In an orbiter mission, a spacecraft orbits a planet for several months to several years. Since an orbiter remains near a planet for a much longer period of time than a flyby spacecraft, it can view most or all of the planet's surface. An orbiter can also keep track of changes that occur over time, such as changes in weather and volcanic activity.

Orbiters allow astronomers to create detailed maps of planets. Most orbiters have cameras to photograph planet surfaces. Orbiters may also carry other instruments, such as a device for determining the altitudes of surface features or one for measuring temperatures in different regions.

Some orbiters are designed to explore moons or other bodies in space instead of planets. It is also possible to send a spacecraft to orbit a planet and later move it into orbit around one of the planet's moons.

REMINDER

Remember that objects orbit, or move around, other objects in space because of the influence of gravity.

CHECK YOUR READING What is the main difference between a flyby spacecraft and an orbiter?

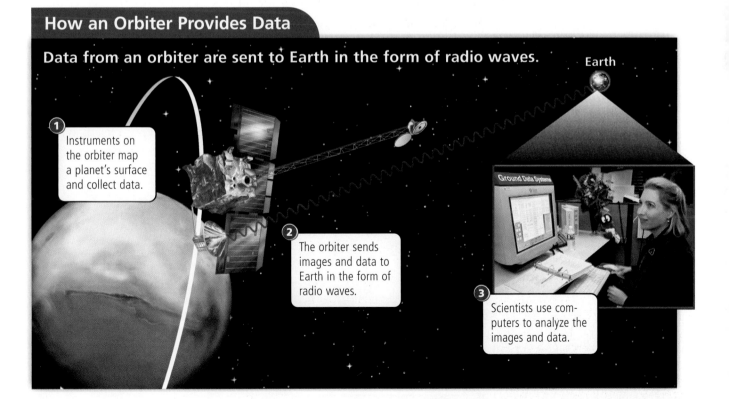

How an Orbiter Provides Data

Data from an orbiter are sent to Earth in the form of radio waves.

Earth

1. Instruments on the orbiter map a planet's surface and collect data.

2. The orbiter sends images and data to Earth in the form of radio waves.

Ground Data Systems

3. Scientists use computers to analyze the images and data.

Landers and Probes

The third stage in space exploration is to land instruments on a planet or to send instruments through its atmosphere. Such a mission can tell us more about the features and properties of a planet. It can also provide clues to what the planet was like in the past.

A **lander** is a craft designed to land on a planet's surface. After a lander touches down, controllers on Earth can send it commands to collect data. Landers have been placed successfully on the Moon, Venus, and Mars. Some have operated for months or years at a time.

The images taken by a lander are more detailed than those taken by an orbiter. In addition to providing close-up views of a planet's surface, a lander can measure properties of the planet's atmosphere and surface. A lander may have a mechanical arm for gathering soil and rock samples. It may also contain a small vehicle called a rover, which can explore beyond the landing site.

1 The spacecraft slows down as it moves through the atmosphere.

Landing Sequence

Parachutes and air bags can be used to slow a lander as it descends to a planet's surface.

2 A parachute opens, and the lander is lowered from the spacecraft. Air bags are inflated shortly before landing.

3 The lander bounces on the surface and rolls to a stop.

4 The air bags are deflated and pulled back.

5 A rover from the lander begins to move across the surface.

One of the most successful space missions was that of *Mars Pathfinder*, which landed on Mars in 1997. *Mars Pathfinder* and its rover sent back thousands of photographs. These images provided evidence that water once flowed over the surface of Mars. Unfortunately, another lander, sent two years later, failed to work after it reached Mars.

Some spacecraft are designed to work only for a short time before they are destroyed by conditions on a planet. The term **probe** is often used to describe a spacecraft that drops into a planet's atmosphere. As the probe travels through the atmosphere, its instruments identify gases and measure properties such as pressure and temperature. Probes are especially important for exploring the deep atmospheres of giant planets, such as Jupiter.

 CHECK YOUR READING What is the difference between a probe and a lander?

Combining Missions

A lander or a probe can work in combination with an orbiter. For example, in 1995 the orbiter *Galileo* released a probe into Jupiter's atmosphere as it began orbiting the planet. The probe sent data back to the orbiter for nearly an hour before it was destroyed. The orbiter passed the data on to Earth. *Galileo* continued to orbit Jupiter for eight years.

Future space missions may involve even more complex combinations of spacecraft. Planners hope to send groups of landers to collect soil and rock samples from the surface of Mars. A rocket will carry these samples to an orbiter. The orbiter will then bring the samples to Earth for study.

Review

KEY CONCEPTS

1. Why are space stations important for scientific research?
2. How is information sent between Earth and a spacecraft?
3. What are the three main stages in exploring a planet?

CRITICAL THINKING

4. **Analyze** Why is most space exploration accomplished with spacecraft that do not have astronauts on board?
5. **Infer** Why is it important to map a planet's surface before planning a lander mission?

CHALLENGE

6. **Predict** Early space exploration was influenced by political events, such as the rivalry between the United States and the Soviet Union. What circumstances on Earth might interfere with future space missions?

MATH in SCIENCE

MATH TUTORIAL
CLASSZONE.COM
Click on Math Tutorial for more help with powers and exponents.

Distances in Space

Astronomers often deal with very large numbers. For example, the planet Venus is about 100 million kilometers from the Sun. Written out, 100 million is 100,000,000. To use fewer zeros and to make the number easier to write and read, you could write 100 million as 10^8, which is the same value in exponent form.

Example

PROBLEM Write 1000 km, using an exponent.

To find the exponent of a number, you can write the number as a product. For example,

$$1000 \text{ km} = 10 \times 10 \times 10 \text{ km}$$

This product has 3 factors of 10. When whole numbers other than zero are multiplied together, each number is a factor of the product. To write a product that has a repeated factor, you can use an exponent. The exponent is the number of times the factor is repeated. With factors of 10, you can also determine the exponent by counting the zeros in the given number.

There are 3 zeros in 1000.   The factor 10 is repeated 3 times.

$$1000 = 10 \times 10 \times 10$$

ANSWER The exponent form of 1000 km is 10^3 km.

Write each distance, using an exponent.

1. 10,000 km

2. 1,000,000 km

3. 100,000,000,000 km

4. 10,000,000,000,000 km

5. 100,000,000,000,000,000 km

6. 10 km

CHALLENGE The galaxy shown on this page is about 10^{18} kilometers across. Write the value of 10^{18} without using an exponent.

Galaxy M83, which is roughly the same size as the Milky Way, has a diameter of about 10^{18} kilometers.

1.4 Space exploration benefits society.

 BEFORE, you learned

- Light and other radiation carry information about space
- Astronauts explore space near Earth

NOW, you will learn

- How space exploration has helped us to learn more about Earth
- How space technology is used on Earth

VOCABULARY

impact crater p. 32

THINK ABOUT

How does Earth look from space?

This photograph of Earth over the Moon was taken by the crew of *Apollo 8*. The Apollo missions provided the first images of our planet as a whole. What do you think we can learn about Earth from photographs taken from space?

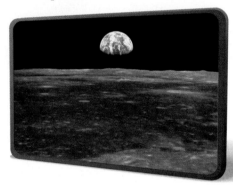

Space exploration has given us new viewpoints.

 **MAIN IDEA WEB**
Record in your notes important information that space exploration has provided about Earth.

Space exploration enriches us in many ways. Throughout history, the study of stars and planets has inspired new ideas. As we meet the challenges of space exploration, we gain valuable technology. Space exploration is also an exciting adventure.

Space science has advanced knowledge in other scientific fields, such as physics. For example, observations of the Moon and other bodies in space helped scientists understand how gravity works. Scientists figured out that the same force that causes an object to fall to the ground causes the Moon to orbit Earth.

Finally, the study of other worlds can teach us about our own. Earth has changed considerably since its formation. By comparing Earth with different worlds, scientists can learn more about the history of Earth's surface features and atmosphere.

 CHECK YOUR READING Identify some benefits of space exploration.

Formation of a Crater

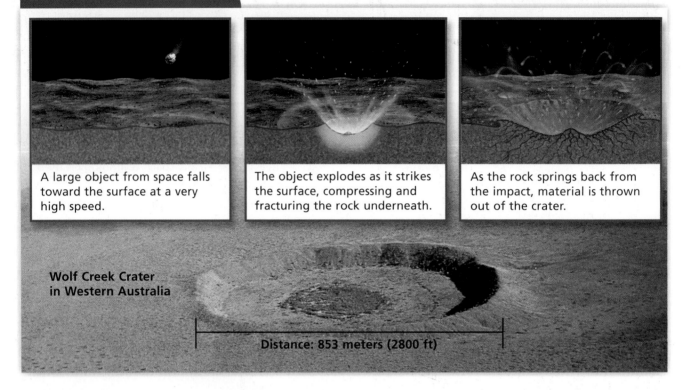

A large object from space falls toward the surface at a very high speed.

The object explodes as it strikes the surface, compressing and fracturing the rock underneath.

As the rock springs back from the impact, material is thrown out of the crater.

Wolf Creek Crater in Western Australia

Distance: 853 meters (2800 ft)

Surface Features

Exploration of other worlds has helped us learn about the impacts of space objects. When an object strikes the surface of a larger object in space, it explodes and leaves behind a round pit called an **impact crater.** The illustration above shows how an impact crater forms.

Earth has little evidence of impacts because its surface is constantly being worn down by wind and water and altered by forces beneath the surface. However, impact craters remain on the Moon, Mercury, and many other bodies that have no wind or liquid water.

Atmosphere

We are also learning about Earth's atmosphere from space exploration. Earth's temperature allows liquid water to remain on the surface. Mars and Venus, the planets closest to Earth, have no liquid water on their surfaces. By comparing Earth with those planets, we can see how liquid water has affected the development of Earth's atmosphere.

Another area of study involves the energy Earth receives from the Sun. Many scientists think that small changes visible on the Sun's surface can affect weather on Earth. These changes may have caused periods of cooling in Earth's atmosphere.

CHECK YOUR READING   What have scientists learned about Earth's past from studying bodies in space?

INVESTIGATE Weathering

How does weather affect evidence of impacts on Earth?

PROCEDURE

1. Fill a shoebox lid halfway with sand, and smooth the surface with a ruler.

2. Create three craters by dropping a golf ball into the sand from a height of 70 cm. Remove the ball carefully. Leave the lid inside the classroom.

3. Repeat steps 1 and 2 outdoors, leaving the lid in an area where it will be exposed to the weather.

4. Check both lids after 24 hours. Observe changes in each one.

WHAT DO YOU THINK?

- How did the craters in the sand that you left outdoors differ in appearance from the craters in the sand that remained inside?
- What aspect of weather caused any differences you observed?

CHALLENGE What natural processes besides weather can affect evidence of impacts from space objects on Earth?

SKILL FOCUS
Predicting

MATERIALS
- 2 shoebox lids
- sand
- meter stick
- golf ball

TIME
30 minutes

Space technology has practical uses.

Space exploration has done more than increase our knowledge. It has also provided us with technology that makes life on Earth easier. Each day you probably benefit from some material or product that was developed for the space program.

Satellite Views of Earth

One of the most important benefits of space exploration has been the development of satellite technology. Satellites collect data from every region of our planet. The data are sent to receivers on Earth and converted into images. Scientists have learned from the space program how to enhance such images to gain more information.

Weather satellites show conditions throughout Earth's atmosphere. Images and data from weather satellites have greatly improved weather forecasting. Scientists can now provide warnings of dangerous storms long before they strike populated areas.

Other satellites collect images of Earth's surface to show how it is being changed by natural events and human activity. Satellite data are also used for wildlife preservation, conservation of natural resources, and mapping.

Technology Spinoffs

Have you ever come up with a new way to use something that was designed for a different purpose? NASA often creates advanced technology to meet the special demands of space travel. Many spinoffs of technology from the space program can be found in homes, offices, schools, and hospitals.

Everything on a spacecraft must be as small and lightweight as possible because the heavier a spacecraft is, the more difficult it is to launch. Design techniques developed to meet this need have improved devices used on Earth, such as tools for diagnosing diseases and devices that help people overcome disabilities.

NASA designers helped develop a system that allows this boy to communicate by using eye movements.

Materials and parts on a spacecraft have to endure harsh conditions, such as extreme heat and cold. Many new homes and buildings contain fire-resistant materials developed for the space program. Firefighters wear protective suits made from fabric originally used in space suits. NASA has also helped design devices that allow firefighters to avoid injury from inhaling smoke.

Humans need a safe environment in spacecraft and space stations. NASA has developed systems for purifying air, water, and food. These systems now help protect people on Earth as well as in space.

1.4 Review

KEY CONCEPTS

1. How has space exploration helped us learn about impacts of space objects on Earth?
2. How do satellites provide images of Earth's surface and atmosphere?
3. Give two examples of technology we use on Earth that is a result of space exploration.

CRITICAL THINKING

4. **Infer** Hurricanes form in the middle of the ocean. Why would satellites be useful in tracking hurricanes?
5. **Apply** What space-technology spinoffs might be used in a school?

⬤ CHALLENGE

6. **Predict** It takes over a year for a spacecraft to reach Mars and return to Earth. If astronauts ever travel to Mars, they will need a spacecraft that can recycle air and water. How might such technology be adapted for use on Earth?

How Earth's Gravity Affects Plants

One of the most important issues in biology is understanding how plants grow. By applying the results of research on this issue, American farmers now grow twice as much food as they did 50 years ago.

One aspect of plant growth is the direction in which plants grow. After a plant sprouts from a seed, some of its cells form a shoot that grows upward. Other cells grow downward, becoming roots. How does this happen? Biologists think that plants usually respond to signals from the Sun and from the force of gravity.

Gravity and Plant Growth

To test the importance of sunlight, biologists can grow plants in the dark on Earth. Testing the impact of gravity, though, is more difficult. In 1997, a space shuttle carried moss plants into space. The plants grew for two weeks in microgravity, an environment in which objects are almost weightless. When the shuttle returned the plants to Earth, biologists studied how they had grown.

Prediction

Biologists had predicted that the moss would grow randomly. They expected that without signals from sunlight or the force of gravity, the moss would grow in no particular pattern.

Results

The biologists were surprised by what they saw. The moss had not grown randomly. Instead, the plants had spread out in a clear pattern. Each plant had formed a clockwise spiral.

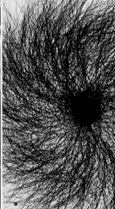

The left-hand photograph shows moss growing on Earth. The right-hand photograph shows the same variety of moss growing in space. How do the mosses differ?

Significance

The moss experiment may be important for future space exploration. Can plants provide the food and oxygen that astronauts will need on long voyages to other planets? Experiments with moss are among the first steps in finding out.

EXPLORE

1. **PROVIDE EXAMPLES** Make a list of other spiral formations that occur in nature. Discuss why spirals may be common.

2. **CHALLENGE** Use library or Internet resources to learn about other experiments that test the effects of microgravity on plants and seeds.

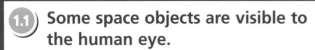

the **BIG** idea

People develop and use technology to explore and study space.

◀ KEY CONCEPTS SUMMARY

1.1 **Some space objects are visible to the human eye.**

- Gravity causes objects in space to be grouped together in different ways.
- Stars form patterns in the sky.
- The sky seems to turn as Earth rotates.

VOCABULARY
orbit p. 10
solar system p. 10
galaxy p. 10
universe p. 10
constellation p. 12

1.2 **Telescopes allow us to study space from Earth.**

Each form of electromagnetic radiation provides different information about objects in space. Astronomers use different types of telescopes to gather visible light and other forms of radiation.

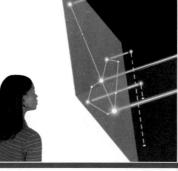

VOCABULARY
electromagnetic radiation p. 15
spectrum p. 16
wavelength p. 16
telescope p. 17

1.3 **Spacecraft help us explore beyond Earth.**

Astronauts can explore space near Earth. Spacecraft without crews carry instruments to other worlds. A flyby mission usually provides data from several bodies in space. Orbiters, landers, and probes gather data from one planet or body.

VOCABULARY
satellite p. 23
space station p. 24
lander p. 28
probe p. 29

1.4 **Space exploration benefits society.**

Space exploration has taught us about Earth's development. It has also provided technology that has important uses on Earth.

VOCABULARY
impact crater p. 32

Reviewing Vocabulary

Write a definition of each word. Use the meaning of the underlined word part to help you.

Word	Root Meaning	Definition
EXAMPLE <u>satellite</u>	person of lesser rank	an object that orbits a more massive object
1. <u>orbit</u>	circle	
2. <u>solar</u> system	Sun	
3. <u>uni</u>verse	one	
4. constell<u>ation</u>	star	
5. electro-magnetic <u>radiation</u>	to emit rays	
6. <u>spect</u>rum	to look at	
7. <u>probe</u>	test	
8. impact <u>crater</u>	bowl	

Reviewing Key Concepts

Multiple Choice *Choose the letter of the best answer.*

9. Stars in a galaxy are held together by
   a. light   **c.** gravity
   b. radiation   **d.** satellites

10. Astronomers use constellations to
   a. locate objects in the sky
   b. calculate the distances of objects
   c. calculate the masses of objects
   d. classify spectra

11. Stars rise and set in the night sky because
   a. Earth orbits the Sun
   b. Earth rotates
   c. the North Pole points toward Polaris
   d. the stars are moving in space

12. In the electromagnetic spectrum, different forms of radiation are arranged according to their
   a. colors   **c.** wavelengths
   b. distances   **d.** sizes

13. Astronomers often locate telescopes on mountains to
   a. lessen the interference of Earth's atmosphere
   b. save money on land
   c. keep their discoveries secret
   d. get closer to space objects

14. A reflecting telescope gathers light with a
   a. lens   **c.** refractor
   b. eyepiece   **d.** mirror

15. What was the goal of the Apollo program?
   a. to view Earth from space
   b. to explore the Sun
   c. to explore the Moon
   d. to explore other planets

16. Which type of mission produces detailed maps of a planet?
   a. flyby   **c.** lander
   b. orbiter   **d.** probe

17. What causes an impact crater to form on a planet's surface?
   a. Gravity pulls soil and rock downward.
   b. Wind and water wear away the surface.
   c. Forces beneath the surface push upward.
   d. An object from space strikes the surface.

Short Answer *Write a short answer to each question.*

18. Why is it easier to see the motions of planets than to see the motions of stars?

19. How do astronomers obtain most of their information about space?

20. How does the size of a telescope's main lens or mirror affect its performance?

21. Why have lightweight materials been developed for space travel?

Thinking Critically

Copy the Venn diagram below, and use it to help you answer the next two questions.

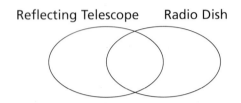

Reflecting Telescope   Radio Dish

22. COMPARE AND CONTRAST Fill in the Venn diagram to show similarities and differences between a reflecting telescope and a radio dish.

23. APPLY Suppose that you live in an area that has frequent storms. Which would be more suitable for your location, a reflecting telescope or a radio dish? Explain.

24. COMPARE AND CONTRAST What are the similarities and differences between visible light and radio waves?

25. HYPOTHESIZE Many of the constellations named by ancient peoples are now hard to see from populated areas. Why might it have been easier to see them hundreds or thousands of years ago?

26. ANALYZE What may be the advantages of electronically recording an image from a telescope instead of looking at the object directly through the telescope's eyepiece?

27. SYNTHESIZE Suppose it became possible to send astronauts to explore a nearby planet. What concerns would need to be taken into account before deciding whether to send a spacecraft with astronauts or a spacecraft with no crew aboard?

28. COMPARE AND CONTRAST Compare and contrast the development of the International Space Station with the Apollo missions to the Moon.

29. ANALYZE If you were designing a medical device to be implanted in a patient's body, why might you seek help from designers of space technology?

30. EVALUATE Do you think that the United States should continue to maintain its own space program, or should it combine its space program with the programs of other nations? Explain.

31. SEQUENCE Astronomers have learned that some stars other than the Sun have planets orbiting them. Imagine that you are planning a program to explore one of these planet systems. Copy the chart below. Use the chart to identify stages in the exploration of the system and to describe what would occur during each stage.

Stage of Exploration	Description

the **BIG** idea

32. PROVIDE EXAMPLES Look again at the photograph on pages 6–7. Now that you have finished the chapter, how would you change your response to the question on the photograph?

33. EVALUATE In the United States billions of dollars are spent each year on space exploration. Do you think that this expense is justified? Why or why not?

UNIT PROJECTS

If you are doing a unit project, make a folder for your project. Include in your folder a list of the resources you will need, the date on which the project is due, and a schedule to track your progress. Begin gathering data.

Analyzing a Star Map

Use the star map to answer the next five questions.

1. Constellations are represented on the map as dots that are

a. surrounded by planets

b. grouped in a spiral pattern

c. connected by lines

d. scattered in a random pattern

2. How would a map showing the same portion of the sky two hours later compare with the map above?

a. Almost all the space objects would have changed position noticeably.

b. No space objects would have changed position.

c. Only the moon would have changed position.

d. Only the planets would have changed position.

3. Why would the map for two hours later be different from this map?

a. The Moon is rotating on its axis.

b. Earth is rotating on its axis.

c. The solar system is part of the Milky Way.

d. The planets move in relation to the stars.

4. A map showing the same portion of the sky exactly one year later would look very similar to this map. What would probably be different?

a. the shapes of the constellations

b. the names of the constellations

c. the positions of the Moon and the planets

d. the radiation of the stars

5. Which statement best describes the location of the stars shown on the map?

a. They are outside the solar system but within the Milky Way galaxy.

b. They are within the solar system.

c. They are outside the Milky Way galaxy but within the universe.

d. They are outside the universe.

Extended Response

Answer the two questions below in detail. Include some of the terms shown in the word box. In your answer, underline each term you use.

electromagnetic radiation	solar system
Milky Way	radio waves
universe	visible light

6. What is the relationship between Earth, our solar system, the Milky Way, and the universe?

7. What do visible-light telescopes and radio telescopes have in common? How are they different?

Earth, Moon, and Sun

the **BIG** idea

Earth and the Moon move in predictable ways as they orbit the Sun.

Key Concepts

SECTION
2.1 **Earth rotates on a tilted axis and orbits the Sun.**
Learn what causes day and night and why there are seasons.

SECTION
2.2 **The Moon is Earth's natural satellite.**
Learn about the structure and motion of Earth's Moon.

SECTION
2.3 **Positions of the Sun and Moon affect Earth.**
Learn about phases of the Moon, eclipses, and tides.

Internet Preview

CLASSZONE.COM

Chapter 2 online resources:
Content Review, two
Visualizations, two Resource
Centers, Math Tutorial,
Test Practice

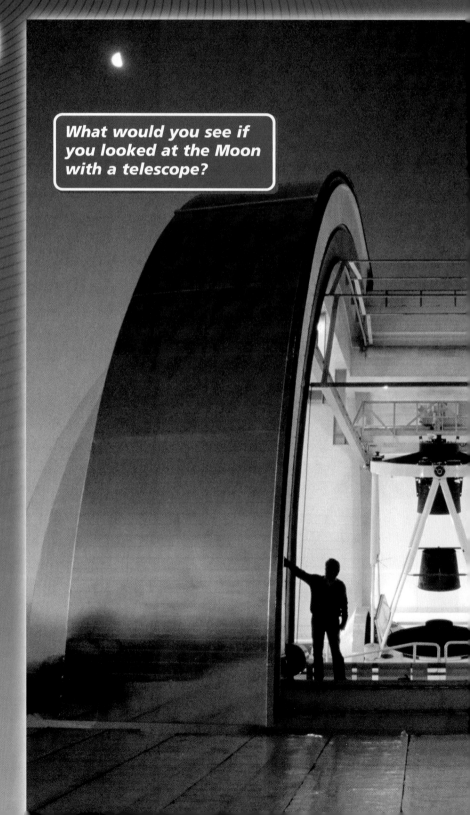

What would you see if you looked at the Moon with a telescope?

EXPLORE (the BIG idea)

How Do Shadows Move?

Place a small sticky note on a window that sunlight shines through. At several different times of day, sketch the location of the note's shadow in the room.

Observe and Think
Does the shadow move in a clockwise or counterclockwise direction? Does the shadow's distance from the window change?

What Makes the Moon Bright?

On a day when you see the Moon in the sky, compare it with a round object. Hold the object in line with the Moon. Make sure that your hand does not block the sunlight. Notice the part of the object that is bright.

Observe and Think
How does the sunlight on the object compare with the light on the Moon?

Internet Activity: Seasons

Go to **ClassZone.com** to explore seasons. Find out how sunlight affects the temperature in different places at different times of year.

Observe and Think
Does the picture show Earth in June or in December?

NSTA
scilinks.org
SCiLINKS

The Moon Code: MDL058

Getting Ready to Learn

◀ CONCEPT REVIEW

- The sky seems to turn as Earth rotates.
- The motions of nearby space objects are visible from Earth.
- Light and other radiation carry information about space.

◀ VOCABULARY REVIEW

orbit p. 10
electromagnetic radiation p. 15
satellite p. 23
See Glossary for definitions.
force, gravity, mass

ⓘ CONTENT REVIEW
CLASSZONE.COM
Review concepts and vocabulary.

▶ TAKING NOTES

COMBINATION NOTES

To take notes about a new concept, first make an informal outline of the information. Then make a sketch of the concept and label it so you can study it later.

VOCABULARY STRATEGY

Write each new vocabulary term in the center of a **frame game** diagram. Decide what information to frame the term with. Use examples, descriptions, pictures, or sentences in which the term is used in context. You can change the frame to fit each term.

See the Note-Taking Handbook on pages R45–R51.

SCIENCE NOTEBOOK

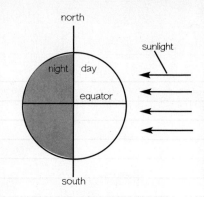

NOTES

Earth turns.
- It turns on an imaginary axis.
  - Poles are ends of axis.
  - Equator is halfway.
- Rotation takes 24 hours.
- Sun shines on one side only.
  - Light side is daytime.
  - Dark side is night.

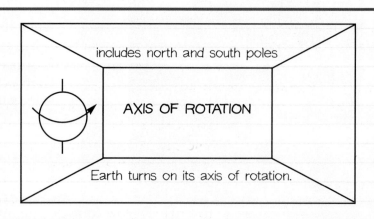

includes north and south poles

AXIS OF ROTATION

Earth turns on its axis of rotation.

KEY CONCEPT

Earth rotates on a tilted axis and orbits the Sun.

 BEFORE, you learned

- Stars seem to rise, cross the sky, and set because Earth turns
- The Sun is very large and far from Earth
- Earth orbits the Sun

NOW, you will learn

- Why Earth has day and night
- How the changing angles of sunlight produce seasons

VOCABULARY

axis of rotation p. 44
revolution p. 45
season p. 46
equinox p. 46
solstice p. 46

EXPLORE Time Zones

What time is it in Iceland right now?

PROCEDURE

① Find your location and Iceland on the map. Identify the time zone of each.

② Count the number of hours between your location and Iceland. Add or subtract that number of hours from the time on your clock.

MATERIAL
time zone map

WHAT DO YOU THINK?

- By how much is Iceland's time earlier or later than yours?
- Why are clocks set to different times?

Earth's rotation causes day and night.

When astronauts explored the Moon, they felt the Moon's gravity pulling them down. Their usual "down"—Earth—was up in the Moon's sky.

As you read this book, it is easy to tell which way is down. But is down in the same direction for a person on the other side of Earth? If you both pointed down, you would be pointing toward each other. Earth's gravity pulls objects toward the center of Earth. No matter where you stand on Earth, the direction of down will be toward Earth's center. There is no bottom or top. Up is out toward space, and down is toward the center of the planet.

As Earth turns, so do you. You keep the same position with respect to what is below your feet, but the view above your head changes.

 In what direction does gravity pull objects near Earth?

The directions north, south, east, and west are based on the way the planet rotates, or turns. Earth rotates around an imaginary line running through its center called an **axis of rotation.** The ends of the axis are the north and south poles. Any location on the surface moves from west to east as Earth turns. If you extend your right thumb and pretend its tip is the North Pole, then your fingers curve the way Earth rotates.

At any one time, about half of Earth is in sunlight and half is dark. However, Earth turns on its axis in 24 hours, so locations move through the light and darkness in that time. When a location is in sunlight, it is daytime there. When a location is in the middle of the sunlit side, it is noon. When a location is in darkness, it is night there, and when the location is in the middle of the unlit side, it is midnight,

> The globe and the flat map show the progress of daylight across Earth in two ways. This location is experiencing sunrise.

noon

midnight

night moves westward

CHECK YOUR READING If it is noon at one location, what time is it at a location directly on the other side of Earth?

INVESTIGATE Rotation

What causes day and night?

In this model the lamp represents the Sun, and your head represents Earth. The North Pole is at the top of your head. You will need to imagine locations on your head as if your head were a globe.

PROCEDURE

1. Face the lamp and hold your hands to your face as shown in the photograph. Your hands mark the horizon. For a person located at your nose, the Sun would be high in the sky. It would be noon.

2. Face away from the lamp. Determine what time it would be at your nose.

3. Turn to your left until you see the lamp along your left hand.

4. Continue turning to the left, through noon, until you just stop seeing the lamp.

WHAT DO YOU THINK?

- What times was it at your nose in steps 2, 3, and 4?
- When you face the lamp, what time is it at your right ear?

CHALLENGE How can a cloud be bright even when it is dark on the ground?

SKILL FOCUS
Making models

MATERIALS
lamp

TIME
15 minutes

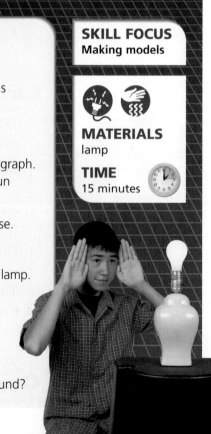

Earth's tilted axis and orbit cause seasons.

Just as gravity causes objects near Earth to be pulled toward Earth's center, it also causes Earth and other objects near the Sun to be pulled toward the Sun's center. Fortunately, Earth does not move straight into the Sun. Earth moves sideways, at nearly a right angle to the Sun's direction. Without the Sun's gravitational pull, Earth would keep moving in a straight line out into deep space. However, the Sun's pull changes Earth's path from a straight line to a round orbit about 300 million kilometers (200,000,000 mi) across.

Just as a day is the time it takes Earth to rotate once on its axis, a year is the time it takes Earth to orbit the Sun once. In astronomy, a **revolution** is the motion of one object around another. The word *revolution* can also mean the time it takes an object to go around once.

Earth's rotation and orbit do not quite line up. If they did, Earth's equator would be in the same plane as Earth's orbit, like a tiny hoop and a huge hoop lying on the same tabletop. Instead, Earth rotates at about a 23° angle, or tilt, from this lined-up position.

READING TiP

Use the second vowel in each word to help you remember that an object rot<u>a</u>tes on its own <u>a</u>xis, but rev<u>o</u>lves around another <u>o</u>bject.

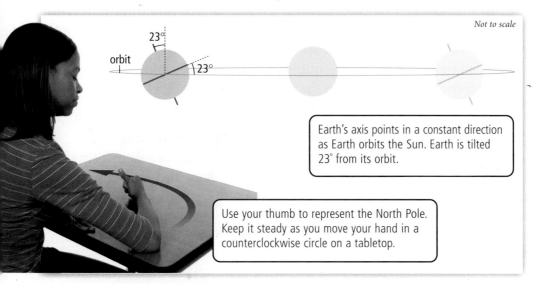

Not to scale

orbit — 23°

Earth's axis points in a constant direction as Earth orbits the Sun. Earth is tilted 23° from its orbit.

Use your thumb to represent the North Pole. Keep it steady as you move your hand in a counterclockwise circle on a tabletop.

As Earth moves, its axis always points in the same direction in space. You could model Earth's orbit by moving your right fist in a circle on a desktop. You would need to point your thumb toward your left shoulder and keep it pointing that way while moving your hand around the desktop.

Earth's orbit is not quite a perfect circle. In January, Earth is about 5 million kilometers closer to the Sun than it is in July. You may be surprised to learn that this distance makes only a tiny difference in temperatures on Earth. However, the combination of Earth's motion around the Sun with the tilt of Earth's axis does cause important changes of temperature. Turn the page to find out how.

July

153,000,000 km

148,000,000 km

January *Not to scale*

Earth's orbit is almost a circle. Earth's distance from the Sun varies by only about 5,000,000 km—about 3%—during a year.

Seasonal Patterns

Most locations on Earth experience **seasons,** patterns of temperature changes and other weather trends over the course of a year. Near the equator, the temperatures are almost the same year-round. Near the poles, there are very large changes in temperatures from winter to summer. The temperature changes occur because the amount of sunlight at each location changes during the year. The changes in the amount of sunlight are due to the tilt of Earth's axis.

Look at the diagram on page 47 to see how the constant direction of Earth's tilted axis affects the pattern of sunlight on Earth at different times of the year. As Earth travels around the Sun, the area of sunlight in each hemisphere changes. At an **equinox** (EE-kwuh-NAHKS), sunlight shines equally on the northern and southern hemispheres. Half of each hemisphere is lit, and half is in darkness. As Earth moves along its orbit, the light shifts more into one hemisphere than the other. At a **solstice** (SAHL-stihs), the area of sunlight is at a maximum in one hemisphere and a minimum in the other hemisphere. Equinoxes and solstices happen on or around the 21st days of certain months of the year.

1 **September Equinox** When Earth is in this position, sunlight shines equally on the two hemispheres. You can see in the diagram that the North Pole is at the border between light and dark. The September equinox marks the beginning of autumn in the Northern Hemisphere and of spring in the Southern Hemisphere.

2 **December Solstice** Three months later, Earth has traveled a quarter of the way around the Sun, but its axis still points in the same direction into space. The North Pole seems to lean away from the direction of the Sun. The solstice occurs when the pole leans as far away from the Sun as it will during the year. You can see that the North Pole is in complete darkness. At the same time, the opposite is true in the Southern Hemisphere. The South Pole seems to lean toward the Sun and is in sunlight. It is the Southern Hemisphere's summer solstice and the Northern Hemisphere's winter solstice.

3 **March Equinox** After another quarter of its orbit, Earth reaches another equinox. Half of each hemisphere is lit, and the sunlight is centered on the equator. You can see that the poles are again at the border between day and night.

4 **June Solstice** This position is opposite the December solstice. Earth's axis still points in the same direction, but now the North Pole seems to lean toward the Sun and is in sunlight. The June solstice marks the beginning of summer in the Northern Hemisphere. In contrast, it is the winter solstice in the Southern Hemisphere.

 CHECK YOUR READING In what month does winter begin in the Southern Hemisphere?

Seasons

Earth's orbit and steady, tilted axis produce seasons.

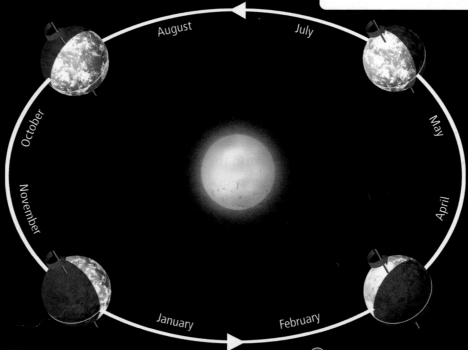

① September Equinox Half of the sunlight is in each hemisphere. The strongest sunlight is on the equator.

④ June Solstice More than half of the Northern Hemisphere is in sunlight. The strongest sunlight is north of the equator, so the Northern Hemisphere grows warmer.

August

July

October

May

November

April

January

February

Not to scale

② December Solstice Less than half of the Northern Hemisphere is in sunlight. The strongest sunlight is south of the equator, so the Southern Hemisphere grows warmer.

③ March Equinox Half of the sunlight is in each hemisphere. The strongest sunlight is on the equator.

View from the Sun

If you could stand on the Sun and look at Earth, you would see different parts of Earth at different times of year.

fall — spring —
① September Equinox

winter — summer —
② December Solstice

spring — fall —
③ March Equinox

summer — winter —
④ June Solstice

The equinoxes and solstices mark the beginnings of seasons in the two hemispheres. Warmer seasons occur when more of a hemisphere is in sunlight.

READING VISUALS Look at the poles to help you see how each hemisphere is lit. When is the South Pole completely in sunlight?

Angles of Sunlight

RESOURCE CENTER
CLASSZONE.COM

Learn more about seasons.

You have seen that seasons change as sunlight shifts between hemispheres during the year. On the ground, you notice the effects of seasons because the angle of sunlight and the length of daylight change over the year. The effects are greatest at locations far from the equator. You may have noticed that sunshine seems barely warm just before sunset, when the Sun is low in the sky. At noon the sunshine seems much hotter. The angle of light affects the temperature.

When the Sun is high in the sky, sunlight strikes the ground at close to a right angle. The energy of sunlight is concentrated. Shadows are short. You may get a sunburn quickly when the Sun is at a high angle. When the Sun is low in the sky, sunlight strikes the ground at a slant. The light is spread over a greater area, so it is less concentrated and produces long shadows. Slanted light warms the ground less.

Near the equator, the noonday Sun is almost overhead every day, so the ground is warmed strongly year-round. In the middle latitudes, the noon Sun is high in the sky only during part of the year. In winter the noon Sun is low and warms the ground less strongly.

 CHECK YOUR READING How are temperatures throughout the year affected by the angles of sunlight?

Sun Height and Shadows

Winter Solstice, 12 P.M.	Spring Equinox, 12 P.M.	Summer Solstice, 12 P.M.

Winter shadows are long because sunlight is spread out. The Sun appears low in the sky even at noon.

location on Earth

Spring and fall shadows are of medium length, and the noon Sun appears higher in the sky.

Summer shadows are short because the light is concentrated in a small area. The noon Sun appears high in the sky.

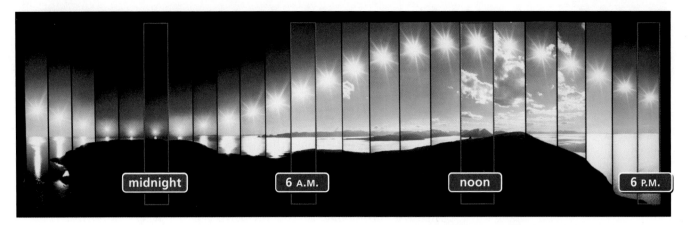

midnight | 6 A.M. | noon | 6 P.M.

Near the pole in the summer, the Sun stays above the horizon, so there is no night. This series of photographs was taken over the course of a day.

Lengths of Days

Seasonal temperatures depend on the amount of daylight, too. In Chicago, for example, the summer Sun heats the ground for about 15 hours a day, but in winter there may be only 9 hours of sunlight each day. The farther you get from the equator, the more extreme the changes in day length become. As you near one of the poles, summer daylight may last for 20 hours or more.

Very close to the poles, the Sun does not set at all for six months at a time. It can be seen shining near the horizon at midnight. Tourists often travel far north just to experience the midnight Sun. At locations near a pole, the Sun sets on an equinox and then does not rise again for six months. Astronomers go to the South Pole in March to take advantage of the long winter night, which allows them to study objects in the sky without the interruption of daylight.

Very near the equator, the periods of daylight and darkness are almost equal year-round—each about 12 hours long. Visitors who are used to hot weather during long summer days might be surprised when a hot, sunny day ends suddenly at 6 P.M. At locations away from the equator, daylight lasts 12 hours only around the time of an equinox.

READING TIP

Equinox means "equal night"—daylight and nighttime are equal in length.

2.1 Review

KEY CONCEPTS

1. What causes day and night?
2. What happens to Earth's axis of rotation as Earth orbits the Sun?
3. How do the areas of sunlight in the two hemispheres change over the year?

CRITICAL THINKING

4. **Apply** If you wanted to enjoy longer periods of daylight in the summertime, would you head closer to the equator or farther from it? Why? *closer*

5. **Compare and Contrast** How do the average temperatures and the seasonal changes at the equator differ from those at the poles?

⚠ CHALLENGE

6. **Infer** If Earth's axis were tilted so much that the North Pole sometimes pointed straight at the Sun, how would the hours of daylight be affected at your location?

CHAPTER INVESTIGATION

Modeling Seasons

OVERVIEW AND PURPOSE Why is the weather in North America so much colder in January than in July? You might be surprised to learn that it has nothing to do with Earth's distance from the Sun. In fact, Earth is closest to the Sun in January. In this lab, you will model the cause of seasons as you
- orient a light source at different angles to a surface
- determine how the angles of sunlight at a location change as Earth orbits the Sun

▶ Problem

Write It Up

How does the angle of light affect the amount of solar energy a location receives at different times of year?

▶ Hypothesize

Write It Up

After performing step 3, write a hypothesis to explain how the angles of sunlight affect the amounts of solar energy your location receives at different times of year. Your hypothesis should take the form of an "If . . . , then . . . , because . . ." statement.

MATERIALS
- graph paper
- flashlight
- meter stick
- protractor
- globe
- stack of books
- sticky note

▶ Procedure

PART A

1. Mark an X near the center of the graph paper. Shine the flashlight onto the paper from about 30 cm straight above the X—at an angle of 90° to the surface. Observe the size of the spot of light.

2. Shine the flashlight onto the X at different angles. Keep the flashlight at the same distance. Write down what happens to the size of the spot of light as you change angles.

3. Repeat step 2, but observe just one square near the X. Write down what happens to the brightness of the light as you change the angle. The brightness shows how much energy the area receives from the flashlight.

4. Think about the temperatures at different times of year at your location, then write your hypothesis.

step 2

90°

PART B

5 Set up the globe, books, and flashlight as shown in the photograph. Point the globe's North Pole to the right. This position represents solstice A.

solstice A

6 Find your location on the globe. Place a folded sticky note onto the globe at your location as shown in the photograph. Rotate the globe on its axis until the note faces toward the flashlight.

7 The flashlight beam represents noonday sunlight at your location. Use the protractor to estimate the angle of the light on the surface.

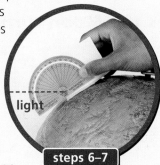

light

steps 6–7

8 Move the globe to the left side of the table and the flashlight and books to the right side of the table. Point the North Pole to the right. This position represents solstice B.

9 Repeat step 7 for solstice B.

solstice B

▶ Observe and Analyze
Write It Up

1. RECORD Draw the setup of your materials in each part of the investigation. Organize your notes.

2. ANALYZE Describe how the angle of the flashlight in step 2 affected the area of the spot of light. Which angle concentrated the light into the smallest area?

3. EVALUATE At which angle did a square of the graph paper receive the most energy?

4. COMPARE Compare the angles of light in steps 7 and 9. In which position was the angle of light closer to 90°?

▶ Conclude
Write It Up

1. EVALUATE How did the angle of sunlight at your location differ at the two times of year? At which position is sunlight more concentrated at your location?

2. APPLY The amount of solar energy at a location affects temperature. Which solstice—A or B—represents the summer solstice at your location?

3. INTERPRET Do your results support your hypothesis? Explain why or why not.

▶ INVESTIGATE Further

CHALLENGE What happens in the other hemisphere at the two times of year? Use the model to find out.

Modeling Seasons

Problem How does the angle of light affect the amount of solar energy a location receives at different times of year?

Hypothesize

Observe and Analyze

Table 1. Solstices A and B

	Solstice A	Solstice B
Drawing		
Angle of light (°)		
Observations		

Conclude

2.2 The Moon is Earth's natural satellite.

BEFORE, you learned

- Earth turns as it orbits the Sun
- The day side of Earth is the part in sunlight
- The Moon is the closest body to Earth

NOW, you will learn

- How the Moon moves
- What the Moon's dark-colored and light-colored features are
- About the inside structure of the Moon

VOCABULARY

mare p. 53

EXPLORE The Moon's Motion

How much does the Moon turn?

PROCEDURE

1. Draw a circle to represent the Moon's orbit with Earth at the center. The compass represents the Moon.

2. Move the compass around the circle. Keep the side of the compass marked *E* always facing Earth.

3. Observe the positions of the *E* and the compass needle at several positions on the circle.

WHAT DO YOU THINK?
What does the model tell you about the Moon's motion?

MATERIALS
- paper
- magnetic compass

The Moon rotates as it orbits Earth.

When you look at the disk of the Moon, you may notice darker and lighter areas. Perhaps you have imagined them as features of a face or some other pattern. People around the world have told stories about the animals, people, and objects they have imagined while looking at the light and dark areas of the Moon. As you will read in this chapter, these areas tell a story to scientists as well.

The pull of gravity keeps the Moon, Earth's natural satellite, in orbit around Earth. Even though the Moon is Earth's closest neighbor in space, it is far away compared to the sizes of Earth and the Moon.

The Moon's diameter is about 1/4 Earth's diameter, and the Moon is about 30 Earth diameters away.

Earth   Moon

The distance between Earth and the Moon is roughly 380,000 kilometers (240,000 mi) —about a hundred times the distance between New York and Los Angeles. If a jet airliner could travel in space, it would take about 20 days to cover a distance that huge. Astronauts, whose spaceships traveled much faster than jets, needed about 3 days to reach the Moon.

You always see the same pattern of dark-colored and light-colored features on the Moon. Only this one side of the Moon can be seen from Earth. The reason is that the Moon, like many other moons in the solar system, always keeps one side turned toward its planet. This means that the Moon turns once on its own axis each time it orbits Earth.

 CHECK YOUR READING Why do you see only one side of the Moon?

The Moon's craters show its history.

The half of the Moon's surface that constantly faces Earth is called the near side. The half that faces away from Earth is called the far side. Much of the Moon's surface is light-colored. Within the light-colored areas are many small, round features. There are also dark-colored features, some of which cover large areas. Much of the near side of the Moon is covered with these dark-colored features. In contrast, the far side is mostly light-colored with just a few of the darker features.

Just as on Earth, features on the Moon are given names to make it easier to discuss them. The names of the larger surface features on the Moon are in the Latin language, because centuries ago scientists from many different countries used Latin to communicate with one another. Early astronomers thought that the dark areas might be bodies of water, so they used the Latin word for "sea." Today, a dark area on the Moon is still called a lunar **mare** (MAH-ray). The plural form is *maria* (MAH-ree-uh).

The maria are not bodies of water, however. All of the features that can be seen on the Moon are different types of solid or broken rock. The Moon has no air, no oceans, no clouds, and no life.

Moon

The side of the Moon that constantly faces Earth has large, dark areas called maria.

Mass 1% of Earth's mass
Diameter 27% of Earth's diameter
Average distance from Earth 380,000 km
Orbits in 27.3 Earth days
Rotates in 27.3 Earth days

READING TiP

Lunar means "having to do with the Moon." The word comes from *luna*, the Latin word for the Moon.

Craters and Maria

The light-colored areas of the Moon are higher—at greater altitudes—than the maria, so they are called the lunar highlands. The ground of the lunar highlands is rocky, and some places are covered with a powder made of finely broken rock.

The highlands have many round features, called impact craters, that formed when small objects from space hit the Moon's surface. Long ago, such collisions happened more often than they do today. Many impact craters marked the surfaces of the Moon, Earth, and other bodies in space. On Earth, however, most craters have been worn away by water and wind. On the dry, airless Moon, impact craters from a long time ago are still visible.

Long ago, some of the largest craters filled with molten rock, or lava, that came from beneath the Moon's surface. The lava filled the lowest areas and then cooled, forming the large, flat plains called maria. Smaller impacts have continued to occur, so the dark plains of the maria do contain some craters. Most of the large maria are on the near side of the Moon. However, the widest and deepest basin on the Moon is on the far side, near the Moon's south pole.

CHECK YOUR READING How did the maria form? List the steps.

Lunar Map

Light-colored highlands and dark maria form a familiar pattern on the near side of the Moon and a very different pattern on the far side.

Near Side

The Moon's near side has many large, dark-colored maria.

Mare Imbrium

Mare Crisium

Crater Tycho

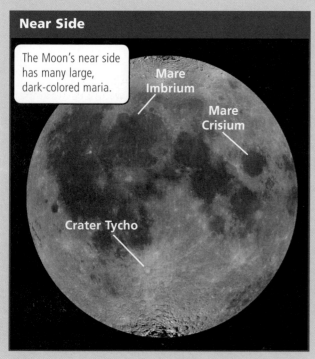

Far Side

The Moon's far side consists mostly of light-colored highlands.

Mare Moscoviense

Crater Tsiolkovskiy

Mare Orientale

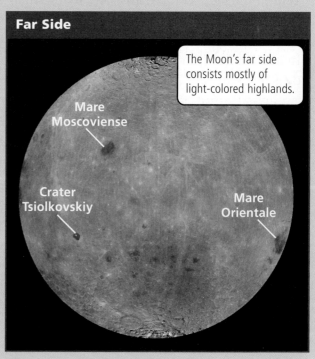

INVESTIGATE Moon Features

How did the Moon's features form?

In this model, you will use a paper towel to represent the Moon's surface and gelatin to represent molten rock from inside the Moon.

PROCEDURE

1. Pour about 1 cm of partly cooled liquid gelatin into the cup.

2. Hold the paper towel by bringing its corners together. Push the towel into the cup until the center of the towel touches the bottom of the cup. Open the towel slightly.

3. Place the cup in the bowl of ice, and allow the gelatin time to solidify.

WHAT DO YOU THINK?

- What part of the towel did the gelatin affect?
- When you look down into the cup, what can the smooth areas tell you about heights?

CHALLENGE Early astronomers thought there might be oceans on the Moon. How does your model lava resemble an ocean?

Moon Rocks

Moon rocks have different ages. Some of the surface rock of the Moon is about 4.5 billion years old—as old as the Moon itself. This very old rock is found in the lunar highlands. The rock in the maria is younger because it formed from lava that solidified later, 3.8–3.1 billion years ago. These two main types of rock and their broken pieces cover most of the Moon's surface. Astronauts explored the Moon and brought back samples of as many different types of material as they could.

Impacts from space objects leave craters, and they also break the surface material into smaller pieces. This breaking of material is called weathering, even though it is not caused by wind and water. Weathered material on the Moon forms a type of dry, lifeless soil. The lunar soil is more than 15 meters (50 ft) deep in some places. Impacts can also toss lunar soil into different places, compact it into new rocks, or melt it and turn it into a glassy type of rock.

The dark-colored rock that formed from lava is called basalt (buh-SAWLT). Lunar basalt is similar to the rock deep beneath Earth's oceans. The basalt of the lunar maria covers large areas but is often only a few hundred meters in depth. However, the basalt can be several kilometers deep at the center of a mare, a depth similar to that of Earth's oceans.

Almost 400 kg (weighing more than 800 lb) of Moon rocks and soil were collected and brought back to Earth by astronauts.

highland rock

basalt

The Moon has layers.

COMBINATION NOTES
Remember to take notes and make diagrams when you read about new ideas and terms.

Scientists on Earth have analyzed the lunar rocks and soil to determine their ages and materials. These results told scientists a story about how the Moon changed over time. During an early stage of the Moon's history, impacts happened often and left craters of many different sizes. That stage ended about 3.8 billion years ago, and impacts have happened much less often since then. The highland rocks and soil come from the original surface and impacts. Shortly after the impacts slowed, lava flooded the low-lying areas and formed the maria. Then the flooding stopped. During the last 3 billion years, the Moon has gained new impact craters from time to time but has remained mostly unchanged.

Structure

The Moon's interior resembles Earth's interior in several ways.

Scientists have used information from lunar rocks and other measurements to figure out what is inside the Moon. Beneath its thin coating of crushed rock, the Moon has three layers—a crust, a mantle, and a core. As on Earth, the crust is the outermost layer. It averages about 70 kilometers (about 40 mi) thick and contains the least dense type of rock.

Beneath the crust is a thick mantle that makes up most of the Moon's volume. The mantle is made of dense types of rock that include the elements iron and magnesium. The basalt on the lunar surface contains these same elements, so scientists infer that the material of the basalt came from the mantle.

In the middle of the Moon is a small core, approximately 700 kilometers (400 mi) across. Although dense, it makes up only a tiny fraction of the Moon's mass. Scientists have less information about the core than the mantle because material from the core did not reach the Moon's surface. The core seems to consist of iron and other metals.

CHECK YOUR READING What are your own questions about the Moon?

Formation

Scientists develop models to help them understand their observations, such as the observed similarities and differences between Earth and the Moon. The two objects have similar structures and are made of similar materials. However, the materials are in different proportions. The Moon has more materials like Earth's crust and mantle and less material like Earth's core.

Scientists have used these facts to develop models of how the Moon formed. A widely accepted model of the Moon's origin involves a giant collision. In this model, an early version of Earth was hit by a

Formation of the Moon

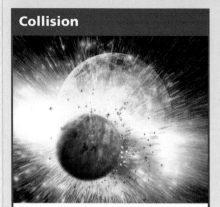

Collision

An early version of Earth is struck by a slightly smaller space body.

Re-Forming

The many pieces pull each other into orbits. Most of the material forms a new version of Earth.

Earth and Moon

The Moon forms from material that orbits the new version of Earth.

smaller space body. Much of the material from both bodies, especially the cores, combined to form a new version of Earth. The energy of the collision also threw material out, away from Earth. Bits of material from the crusts and mantles of both bodies went into orbit around the new Earth. Much of this orbiting material clumped together and became the Moon. Computer simulations of these events show that the Moon may have formed quickly—perhaps within just one year.

Evidence from fossils and rocks on Earth show that, whether the Moon formed from a giant collision or in some other way, it was once much closer to Earth than it is today. The Moon has been moving slowly away from Earth. It now moves 3.8 centimeters (1.5 in.) farther from Earth each year. However, this change is so slow that you will not notice any difference in your lifetime.

2.2 Review

KEY CONCEPTS

1. How many times does the Moon rotate on its axis during one trip around Earth?

2. What are the dark spots and the light areas on the Moon called?

3. Describe the Moon's layers.

CRITICAL THINKING

4. **Compare and Contrast** How are the Moon's dark-colored areas different from its light-colored areas?

5. **Draw Conclusions** How have the Moon rocks that astronauts brought back to Earth helped scientists understand the history of the Moon?

⬥ CHALLENGE

6. **Analyze** Scientists use indirect methods to learn about the cores of Earth and the Moon. Imagine you have several Styrofoam balls, some with steel balls hidden inside. Without breaking a ball open, how might you tell whether it contains a steel ball?

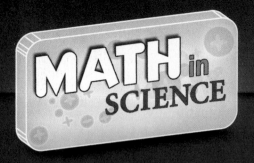

MATH TUTORIAL

Click on Math Tutorial for more help with line graphs.

Graphing Sunlight

The location of the Moon and the Sun in the sky depend on your location on Earth and when you look. In summer, the noon Sun is at a greater angle above the horizon—closer to 90°—than it is in winter. In summer, the Sun rises earlier and sets later than in winter. Longer days and steeper angles of sunlight combine to make summer days much warmer than winter days. Plot the data for Washington, D.C. (latitude 39° N) to see the changing patterns of sunlight.

Washington, D.C.

Month	Sunlight Each Day (h)	Angle of Sun at Noon (°)
Jan.	9.9	31.4
Feb.	11.0	40.8
Mar.	12.2	51.6
Apr.	13.5	63.2
May	14.5	71.4
June	14.9	74.6
July	14.5	71.4
Aug.	13.5	63.0
Sept.	12.2	51.6
Oct.	11.0	40.2
Nov.	9.9	31.1
Dec.	9.5	27.7

This is a series of images of the Sun photographed at exactly the same time of day every few days over most of a year. The bottom of the photograph is from just one of the days and includes a stone circle calendar.

Example

You can make a double line graph to see patterns in the data. Use a colored pencil to label the second *y*-axis.

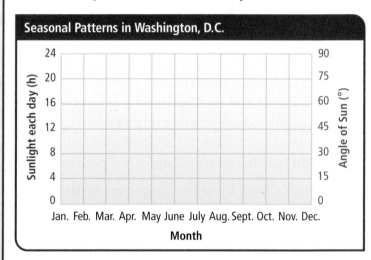

Seasonal Patterns in Washington, D.C.

(1) Copy all three graph axes onto graph paper.

(2) Use the *y*-axis on the left to plot the data for the hours of daylight. Draw line segments to connect the points.

(3) Use the *y*-axis on the right and a colored pencil to plot the data for the angle of the Sun. Draw line segments to connect the points.

Answer the following questions.

1. During which time period do days get shorter?

2. About how many degrees higher in the sky is the noon Sun in June than in December? About how many more hours of sunlight are there each day in June than in December?

3. Does the angle of the Sun change more quickly between June and July or between September and October? How can you tell?

CHALLENGE Copy the axes again, then graph the data your teacher gives you for a location near the North Pole. Use your graphs to compare daylight patterns at the two latitudes.

2.3 Positions of the Sun and Moon affect Earth.

 BEFORE, you learned

- The Moon orbits Earth
- Sunlight shines on Earth and the Moon

 NOW, you will learn

- Why the Moon has phases
- What causes eclipses
- Why Earth's oceans have tides

VOCABULARY

eclipse p. 63
umbra p. 63
penumbra p. 63

THINK ABOUT

Have you seen the Moon in daylight?

Many people think that the Moon is visible only at night. This idea is not surprising, because the Moon is the brightest object in the sky at night. In the daytime the Moon is only as bright as a tiny, thin cloud. It is easy to miss, even in a cloudless blue sky. You can see the Moon sometimes in the day-time, sometimes at night, often at both times, and sometimes not at all. Why does the Moon sometimes disappear from view?

Phases are different views of the Moon's sunlit half.

COMBINATION NOTES
Use the blue heading to start a new set of notes.

What you see as moonlight is really light from the Sun reflected by the Moon's surface. At any time, sunlight shines on half of the Moon's surface. Areas where sunlight does not reach look dark, just as the night side of Earth looks dark from space. As the Moon turns on its axis, areas on the surface move into and out of sunlight.

When you look at the Moon, you see a bright shape that is the lit part of the near side of the Moon. The unlit part is hard to see. Lunar phases are the patterns of lit and unlit portions of the Moon that you see from Earth. It takes about a month for the Moon to orbit Earth and go through all the phases.

 CHECK YOUR READING Why do you sometimes see only part of the near side of the Moon?

The Moon's position in its monthly orbit determines how it appears from Earth. The diagram on page 61 shows how the positions of the Moon, the Sun, and Earth affect the shapes you see in the sky.

Waxing Moon

First Week The cycle begins with a new moon. From Earth, the Moon and the Sun are in the same direction. If you face a new moon, you face the Sun. Your face and the far side of the Moon are in sunlight. The near side of the Moon is unlit, so you do not see it. During a new moon, there appears to be no Moon.

As the Moon moves along its orbit, sunlight begins falling on the near side. You see a thin crescent shape. During the first week, the Moon keeps moving farther around, so more of the near side becomes lit. You see thicker crescents as the Moon waxes, or grows.

Second Week When half of the near side of the Moon is in sunlight, the Moon has completed one-quarter of its cycle. The phase is called the first quarter, even though you might describe the shape as a half-moon. You can see in the diagram that the Moon is 90 degrees—at a right angle—from the Sun. If you face the first-quarter moon when it is high in the sky, sunlight will shine on the right side of your head and the right side of the Moon.

You see more of the Moon as it moves along its orbit during the second week. The phase is called gibbous (GIHB-uhs) when the near side is more than half lit but not fully lit. The Moon is still waxing, so the phases during the second week are called waxing gibbous moons.

 CHECK YOUR READING Why does the Moon sometimes seem to have a crescent shape?

Waning Moon

Third Week Halfway through its cycle, the whole near side of the Moon is in sunlight—a full moon. You might think of it as the second quarter. Viewed from Earth, the Moon and the Sun are in opposite directions. If you face a full moon at sunset, sunlight from behind you lights the back of your head and the near side of the Moon.

As the Moon continues around during the third week, less and less of the near side is in sunlight. The Moon seems to shrink, or wane, so these phases are called waning gibbous moons.

Fourth Week When the near side is again only half in sunlight, the Moon is three-quarters of the way through its cycle. The phase is called the third quarter. The Moon is again 90 degrees from the Sun. If you face the third-quarter moon when it is high in the sky, sunlight will shine on the left side of your head and the left side of the Moon.

The appearance of the Moon depends on the positions of the Sun, Moon, and Earth.

If you could watch the Moon from high above its pole, you would always see half the Moon in sunlight and half in darkness.

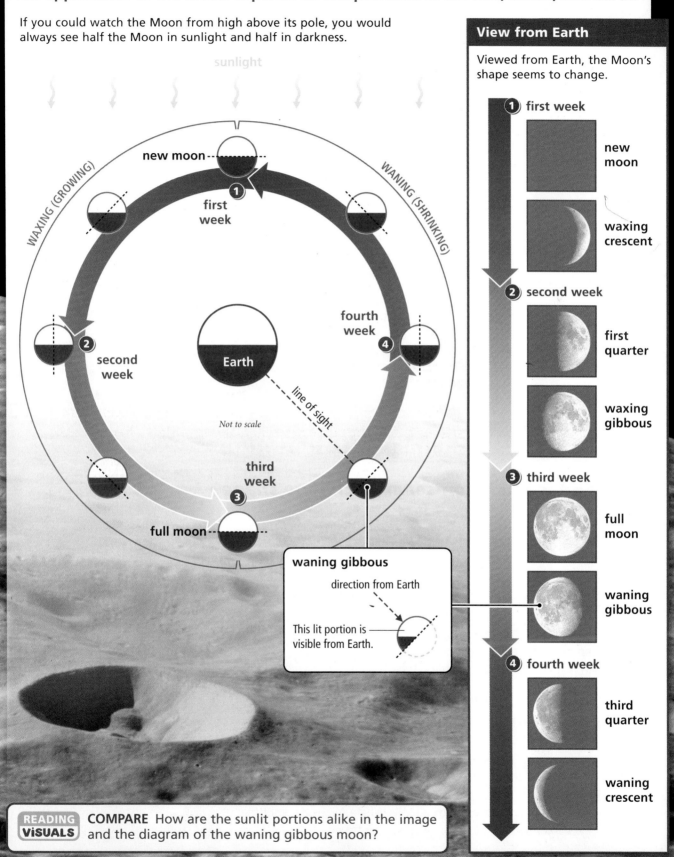

View from Earth

Viewed from Earth, the Moon's shape seems to change.

① **first week**
- new moon
- waxing crescent

② **second week**
- first quarter
- waxing gibbous

③ **third week**
- full moon
- waning gibbous

④ **fourth week**
- third quarter
- waning crescent

waning gibbous
direction from Earth
This lit portion is visible from Earth.

sunlight

WAXING (GROWING)

WANING (SHRINKING)

new moon
first week ①

second week ②

Earth

line of sight

Not to scale

third week ③

full moon

fourth week ④

READING VISUALS **COMPARE** How are the sunlit portions alike in the image and the diagram of the waning gibbous moon?

As the Moon continues to move around Earth during the fourth week, less and less of the near side is in sunlight. The waning crescent moon grows thinner and thinner. At the end of the fourth week, the near side is again unlit, and the new moon begins a new cycle.

Crescent and Gibbous Moons

Think through the waxing lunar phases again. The Moon waxes from new to crescent to gibbous during the first half of its cycle. Then it wanes from full to gibbous to crescent during the second half of its cycle.

The amount of the Moon that you see from Earth depends on the angle between the Moon and the Sun. When this angle is small, you see only a small amount of the Moon. Crescent moons occur when the Moon appears close to the Sun in the sky. As a result, they are visible most often in the daytime or around the time of sunrise or sunset. When the angle between the Sun and the Moon is large, you see a large amount of the Moon. Gibbous and full moons appear far from the Sun in the sky. You may see them in the daytime, but you are more likely to notice them at night.

 CHECK YOUR READING What shape does the Moon appear to be when it is at a small angle to the Sun?

INVESTIGATE Phases of the Moon

Why does the Moon seem to change shape?
PROCEDURE

1. Place the ball on the stick, which will act as a handle. The ball will represent the Moon, and your head will represent Earth.

2. Hold the ball toward the light, then move it to your left until you see a bright edge. Draw what you see.

3. Move the ball farther around until half of what you see is lit. Draw it.

4. Keep moving the ball around to your left until the side you see is fully lit, then half lit, then lit only a little bit. Each time, face the ball and draw it.

WHAT DO YOU THINK?
- In step 2, which side of the ball was lit? Explain why.
- How are your drawings like the photographs of the Moon's phases? Label each drawing with the name of the corresponding lunar phase.

CHALLENGE When the Moon is a crescent, sometimes you can dimly see the rest of the Moon if you look closely. Where might the light that makes the darker part of the Moon visible come from?

SKILL FOCUS
Making models

MATERIALS
- foam ball
- stick
- lamp

TIME
20 minutes

Shadows in space cause eclipses.

Sunlight streams past Earth and the Moon, lighting one side of each body. Beyond each body is a long, thin cone of darkness where no sunlight reaches—a shadow in space. The two bodies are far apart, so they usually miss each other's shadow as the Moon orbits Earth. However, if the Moon, the Sun, and Earth line up exactly, a shadow crosses Earth or the Moon. An **eclipse** occurs when a shadow makes the Sun or the Moon seem to grow dark. In a lunar eclipse, the Moon darkens. In a solar eclipse, the Sun seems to darken.

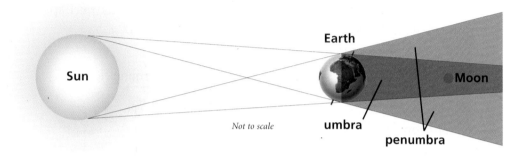

Sun   Earth   Moon

Not to scale   umbra   penumbra

Lunar Eclipses

The Moon becomes dark during a lunar eclipse because it passes through Earth's shadow. There are two parts of Earth's shadow, as you can see in the diagram above. The **umbra** is the darkest part. Around it is a spreading cone of lighter shadow called the **penumbra.**

Just before a lunar eclipse, sunlight streaming past Earth produces a full moon. Then the Moon moves into Earth's penumbra and becomes slightly less bright. As the Moon moves into the umbra, Earth's dark shadow seems to creep across and cover the Moon. The entire Moon can be in darkness because the Moon is small enough to fit entirely within Earth's umbra. After an hour or more, the Moon moves slowly back into the sunlight that is streaming past Earth.

A total lunar eclipse occurs when the Moon passes completely into Earth's umbra. If the Moon misses part or all of the umbra, part of the Moon stays light and the eclipse is called a partial lunar eclipse.

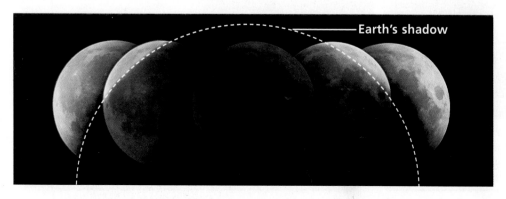

Earth's shadow

The Moon starts getting dark on one side as it passes into Earth's umbra. Even when the Moon is completely within Earth's umbra, some red sunlight, bent by Earth's atmosphere, may still reach the Moon.

Solar Eclipses

In a solar eclipse, the Sun seems to darken because the Moon's shadow falls onto part of Earth. Imagine that you are in the path of a solar eclipse. At first, you see a normal day. You cannot see the dark Moon moving toward the Sun. Then part of the Sun seems to disappear as the Moon moves in front of it. You are in the Moon's penumbra. After several hours of growing darkness, the Moon covers the Sun's disk completely. The sky becomes as dark as night, and you may see constellations. In place of the Sun is a black disk—the new moon—surrounded by a pale glow. You are in the Moon's umbra, the darkest part of the shadow, experiencing a total solar eclipse. After perhaps a minute, the Sun's bright surface starts to appear again.

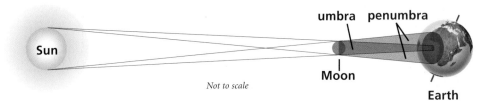

umbra penumbra

Sun

Moon

Not to scale

Earth

A solar eclipse occurs when the Moon passes directly between Earth and the Sun. As you can see in the diagram above, the side of the Moon that faces Earth is unlit, so solar eclipses occur only during new moons.

If you could watch a solar eclipse from space, it might seem more like a lunar eclipse. You would see the Moon's penumbra, with the dark umbra in the center, move across Earth's daylight side. However, the Moon is smaller than Earth, so it casts a smaller shadow. As you can see in the diagram above, the Moon's umbra covers only a fraction of Earth's surface at a time.

June 21, 2001, Eclipse

total eclipse

In this time-lapse photograph, the Sun's disk appears darker as the Moon passes in front. When the Moon is exactly in front of the Sun, the sky grows as dark as night.

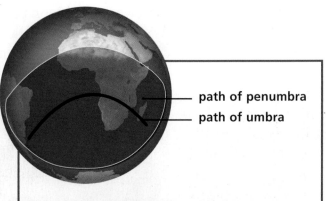

path of penumbra
path of umbra

Path of June 21, 2001, Eclipse Only locations along the thin central path of the shadow experience a total eclipse. Other locations experience a partial eclipse.

Only locations in the path of the Moon's shadow experience a solar eclipse. Some people travel thousands of miles to be in the thin path of the Moon's umbra so that they can experience a total solar eclipse. Locations near the path of the umbra get an eclipse that is less than total. If only the penumbra moves over your location, you experience a partial solar eclipse. The Moon covers just part of the Sun.

Bright light from the Sun's disk can damage your eyes if you look directly at it. The Sun is unsafe to look at even when the Moon covers most of the Sun's disk. If you have the chance to experience a solar eclipse, use a safe method to view the Sun.

CHECK YOUR READING Where is the Moon during a solar eclipse? Find a way to remember the difference between the two types of eclipses.

COMBINATION NOTES
Remember to make notes about new ideas.

The Moon's gravity causes tides on Earth.

If you have spent time near an ocean, you may have experienced the usual pattern of tides. At first, you might see dry sand that slopes down to the ocean. Then, waves creep higher and higher onto the sand. The average water level rises slowly for about 6 hours. The highest level is called high tide. Then the water level slowly drops for about 6 hours. The lowest level is called low tide. Then the water level rises and falls again. The entire pattern—two high tides and two low tides—takes a little more than 24 hours.

In areas with tides, the water generally reaches its lowest level twice a day and its highest level twice a day.

CHECK YOUR READING How many high tides do you expect per day?

Tides occur because the Moon's gravity changes the shape of Earth's oceans. The Moon pulls on different parts of Earth with different amounts of force. It pulls hardest on the side of Earth nearest it, a little less hard on the center of Earth, and even less hard on the farthest side of Earth. If Earth were flexible, it would be pulled into a football shape. Earth's crust is hard enough to resist being pulled into a different shape, but Earth's oceans do change shape.

Cause of Tides

The Moon's gravity changes the shape of Earth's oceans.

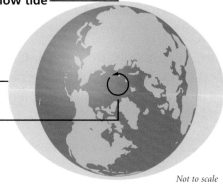

low tide

high tide

rotation of Earth

Moon

Not to scale

The diagram above shows what would happen if Earth were covered with a thick layer of water. The Moon's pull produces a bulge of thicker ocean water on the side of Earth nearest the Moon. Another bulge of water is produced on the side of Earth farthest from the Moon because the Moon pulls the center of Earth away from that side. The layer of water is thinnest in the middle, between the bulges.

A location moves past different thicknesses of water as Earth turns on its axis. As a result, the water level there rises and falls. The thickest water produces the highest level, which is high tide. A quarter of a rotation—6 hours—later, the location has moved to the thinnest layer of water, or low tide. Another high tide and low tide complete the cycle. Because the Moon is orbiting while Earth is turning, the cycle takes a little longer than the 24 hours in a day.

 CHECK YOUR READING Why does a cycle of tides take about 24 hours?

2.3 Review

KEY CONCEPTS

1. When the Moon is full, where is it in its orbit around Earth?

2. Where is the Moon in its orbit at the time of a solar eclipse?

3. If it is high tide where you are, is the tide high or low on the side of Earth directly opposite you?

CRITICAL THINKING

4. **Apply** If you were on the Moon's near side during a new moon, how much of the side of Earth facing you would be sunlit?

5. **Predict** If Earth did not turn, how would the pattern of tides be affected?

⬥ CHALLENGE

6. **Predict** Would we see lunar phases if the Moon did not rotate while it orbits Earth?

ARCHAEOLOGIST

Astronomy in Archaeology

In order to understand how people lived and thought long ago, archaeologists study the buildings and other physical remains of ancient cultures. Archaeologists often think about what needs people had in order to figure out how they used the things they built. For example, people needed to know the time of year in order to decide when to plant crops, move to a different location for winter, or plan certain ceremonies.

Archaeologists can use their knowledge about objects in the sky to hypothesize about the purpose of an ancient structure. They can also use knowledge and models from astronomy to test their hypotheses. For example, archaeologists found some structures at Chimney Rock that were built at times of special events in the sky.

Antikythera Computer

A device with gears and dials was found in an ancient Greek shipwreck. While examining the device, a scientist noticed terms, patterns, and numbers from astronomy. These observations led him to form a hypothesis that ancient Greeks used the instrument to calculate the positions of the Sun, Moon, and other bodies in space. Gamma-ray images of the instrument's interior later supported this hypothesis.

Chimney Rock

Chimney Rock, in Colorado, is topped by two natural pillars of rock. The Moon appears to rise between the pillars under special circumstances that happen about every 18 years. Near the pillars are ruins of buildings of the Anasazi people. In order to construct the buildings and live here, the builders had to haul materials and water much farther than was usual. Some archaeologists hypothesize that the Anasazi built here in order to watch or celebrate special events in the sky.

Stonehenge

Stonehenge is an arrangement of stones in Britain. The first stones were placed there around 3100 B.C. The way that the Sun and Moon line up with the stones has led some archaeologists to think that they were designed to help people predict solstices and eclipses. Solstices tell people the time of year, so Stonehenge has sometimes been called a calendar.

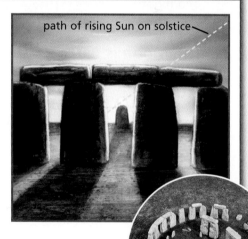
path of rising Sun on solstice

Stonehenge as seen from above

EXPLORE

1. **COMPARE** How is each archaeological example related to astronomy?
2. **CHALLENGE** Make a list of five print or television advertisements that feature the Sun or other objects in the sky. Bring in copies of the advertisements if you can. Why might the advertisers have chosen these objects?

Ruins of buildings were found on a high, narrow ridge at Chimney Rock.

2 Chapter Review

the BIG idea

Earth and the Moon move in predictable ways as they orbit the Sun.

CONTENT REVIEW
CLASSZONE.COM

◄ KEY CONCEPTS SUMMARY

2.1 Earth rotates on a tilted axis and orbits the Sun.

Earth's rotation in sunlight causes day and night.

The changing angles of sunlight on Earth cause seasons.

VOCABULARY
axis of rotation p. 44
revolution p. 45
season p. 46
equinox p. 46
solstice p. 46

2.2 The Moon is Earth's natural satellite.

Dark-colored maria formed from lava-filled craters.

Light-colored highlands are old and cratered.

The Moon's near side always faces Earth.

crust
mantle
core

VOCABULARY
mare p. 53

2.3 Positions of the Sun and Moon affect Earth.

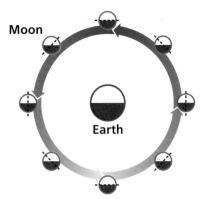

Moon

Earth

Lunar phases are different views of the Moon's sunlit half.

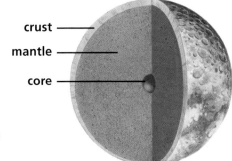

penumbra

umbra

Shadows cause eclipses.

The Moon's gravity causes tides as Earth turns.

VOCABULARY
eclipse p. 63
umbra p. 63
penumbra p. 63

Reviewing Vocabulary

Use words and diagrams to show the relationship between the terms in each the following pairs. Underline the two terms in each answer.

1. revolution, rotation

2. revolution, season

3. solstice, equinox

4. mare, impact crater

5. eclipse, umbra

6. umbra, penumbra

Reviewing Key Concepts

Multiple Choice *Choose the letter of the best answer.*

7. How long does it take Earth to turn once on its axis of rotation?

   a. an hour   **c.** a month
   b. a day   **d.** a year

8. How long does it take Earth to orbit the Sun?

   a. an hour   **c.** a month
   b. a day   **d.** a year

9. About how long does it take the Moon to revolve once around Earth?

   a. an hour   **c.** a month
   b. a day   **d.** a year

10. Why is it hotter in summer than in winter?

    a. Earth gets closer to and farther from the Sun.
    b. Sunlight strikes the ground at higher angles.
    c. Earth turns faster in some seasons.
    d. Earth revolves around the Sun more times in some seasons.

11. The dark maria on the Moon formed from

    a. dried-up seas
    b. finely-broken rock
    c. large shadows
    d. lava-filled craters

12. The lunar highlands have more impact craters than the maria, so scientists know that the highlands

    a. are older than the maria
    b. are younger than the maria
    c. are flatter than the maria
    d. are darker than the maria

13. Why is just one side of the Moon visible from Earth?

    a. The Moon does not rotate on its axis as it orbits Earth.
    b. The Moon rotates once in the same amount of time that it orbits.
    c. Half of the Moon is always unlit by the Sun.
    d. Half of the Moon does not reflect light.

14. Why does the Moon seem to change shape from week to week?

    a. Clouds block part of the Moon.
    b. The Moon moves through Earth's shadow.
    c. The Moon is lit in different ways.
    d. Different amounts of the dark-colored side of the Moon face Earth.

15. Which words describe the different shapes that the Moon appears to be?

    a. waning and waxing
    b. waning and crescent
    c. waxing and gibbous
    d. crescent and gibbous

16. During a total eclipse of the Moon, the Moon is

    a. in Earth's umbra
    b. in Earth's penumbra
    c. between Earth and the Sun
    d. casting a shadow on Earth

Short Answer *Write a short answer to each question.*

17. What motion produces two high tides in a day? Explain your answer.

18. How are the structure of the Moon and the structure of Earth similar?

Thinking Critically

Use the lunar map below to answer the next four questions.

Near Side

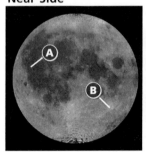

Far Side

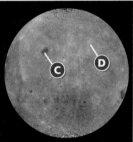

19. **APPLY** Which points are at higher elevations? Explain how you know.

20. **COMPARE** During a first-quarter moon, will point A, point B, both, or neither be in sunlight? **Hint:** Use the diagram on page 61.

21. **INFER** During a total lunar eclipse, which points will be in darkness?

22. **INFER** During a total solar eclipse, the Moon is new. Which points will be in darkness?

23. **CONNECT** Use your knowledge of the motions of Earth and the Moon to determine how long it takes the Moon to travel once around the Sun.

24. **ANALYZE** Which two parts of the Moon have important chemical elements in common? Choose from the following: core, mantle, crust, maria, highlands.

25. **APPLY** If it is noon for you, what time is it for someone directly on the opposite side of Earth?

26. **CLASSIFY** On what part or parts of Earth are winter and summer temperatures the most different from each other?

27. **APPLY** If it is the winter solstice in New York, what solstice or equinox is it in Sydney, Australia, in the Southern Hemisphere?

28. **PREDICT** If Earth stayed exactly the same distance from the Sun throughout the year, would the seasons be different? Explain what you think would happen.

29. **PREDICT** If Earth's axis were not tilted with respect to the orbit, would the seasons be different? Explain what you think would happen.

30. **PROVIDE EXAMPLES** How do the positions of the Sun and the Moon affect what people do? Give three examples of the ways that people's jobs or other activities are affected by the positions of the Sun, the Moon, or both.

31. **PREDICT** Which shape of the Moon are you most likely to see during the daytime? **Hint:** Compare the directions of the Sun and Moon from Earth in the diagram on page 61.

32. **CLASSIFY** What types of information have scientists used to make inferences about the Moon's history?

———— **South Pole**

33. **ANALYZE** The photograph above shows the side of Earth in sunlight at a particular time. The location of the South Pole is indicated. Was the photograph taken in March, in June, in September, or in December?

the BIG idea

34. **APPLY** Look again at the photograph on pages 40–41. Now that you have finished the chapter, how would you change your response to the question on the photograph?

35. **SYNTHESIZE** If you were an astronaut in the middle of the near side of the Moon during a full moon, how would the ground around you look? How would Earth, high in your sky, look? Describe what is in sunlight and what is in darkness.

UNIT PROJECTS

If you need to do an experiment for your unit project, gather the materials. Be sure to allow enough time to observe results before the project is due.

Analyzing a Diagram

The sketches show the phases of the Moon one week apart. The diagram shows the Moon's orbit around Earth. Use the diagram and the sketches to answer the questions below.

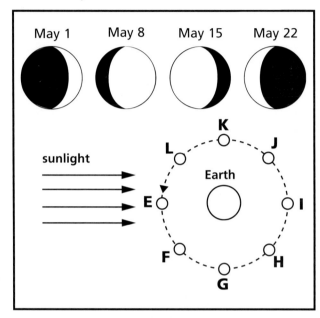

May 1 May 8 May 15 May 22

sunlight

K
L   J
Earth
E   I
F   H
G

1. At which letter on the diagram might a full moon occur?

a. E   **c.** I
b. G   **d.** J

2. Which letter on the diagram shows the position of the Moon on May 8?

a. E   **c.** G
b. F   **d.** H

3. Approximately when was the Moon full?

a. May 4   **c.** May 18
b. May 11   **d.** May 29

4. At which letter on the diagram might a solar eclipse occur?

a. E   **c.** I
b. H   **d.** L

5. How much of the sunlit part of the Moon was visible from Earth on May 8?

a. None of the sunlit part was visible.
b. About one-quarter of the sunlit part was visible.
c. About three-quarters of the sunlit part was visible.
d. All of the sunlit part was visible.

6. Which of these sketches show Earth's shadow on the Moon?

a. those for May 1 and May 22
b. those for May 8 and May 15
c. all 4 of them
d. none of them

7. Which factor is most directly responsible for determining how often a full moon appears?

a. the size of the Moon
b. the size of Earth
c. how quickly the Moon orbits Earth
d. how quickly the Moon turns on its axis

Extended Response

Answer the two questions below in detail. A diagram may help you to answer.

8. The Moon was once much closer to Earth. What effect do you think that this distance had on eclipses?

9. What do you think would happen to tides on Earth if Earth stopped rotating? Why?

TIMELINES in Science

THE STORY OF ASTRONOMY

Around the year A.D. 140, an astronomer named Ptolemy wrote down his ideas about the motion of bodies in space. Ptolemy shared the view of many Greek astronomers that the Sun, the Moon, and the planets orbit Earth in perfect circles. The Greeks had observed that planets sometimes seem to reverse direction in their motion across the sky. Ptolemy explained that the backward movements are smaller orbits within the larger orbits. For 1400 years, Europeans accepted this Earth-centered model. In the mid-1500s, however, astronomers began to challenge and then reject Ptolemy's ideas.

The timeline shows a few events in the history of astronomy. Scientists have developed special tools and procedures to study objects in the sky. The boxes below the timeline show how technology has led to new knowledge about space and how that knowledge has been applied.

1543

Sun Takes Center Stage

Nicolaus Copernicus, a Polish astronomer, proposes that the planets orbit the Sun rather than Earth. His Sun-centered model shocks many because it conflicts with the traditional belief that Earth is the center of the universe.

EVENTS

| 1500 | 1520 | 1540 | 1560 |

APPLICATIONS AND TECHNOLOGY

APPLICATION

Navigating by Sunlight and Starlight

For thousands of years, sailors studied the sky to find their way at sea. Because the Sun and stars move in predictable ways, sailors used them to navigate across water. During the 1400s, sailors began to use a device called a mariner's astrolabe to observe the positions of the Sun and stars. Later devices allowed sailors to make more accurate measurements.

This mariner's astrolabe was made in the 1600s.

1609

Scientist Pinpoints Planet Paths

German astronomer Johannes Kepler concludes that the orbits of planets are not circles but ellipses, or flattened circles. Kepler, formerly the assistant of Tycho Brahe, reached his conclusion by studying Brahe's careful observations of the motions of planets.

1863

Stars and Earth Share Elements

English astronomer William Huggins announces that stars are made of hydrogen and other elements found on Earth. Astronomers had traditionally believed that stars were made of a unique substance. Huggins identified the elements in stars by studying their spectra.

1687

Laws of Gravity Revealed

English scientist Isaac Newton explains that gravity causes planets to orbit the Sun. His three laws of motion explain how objects interact on Earth as well as in space.

1600   1620   1640   1660   1680   1860

TECHNOLOGY

Viewing Space

The telescope was probably invented in the early 1600s, when an eyeglass maker attached lenses to both ends of a tube. Soon afterward, Italian scientist Galileo Galilei copied the invention and used it to look at objects in space. Galileo's telescope allowed him to study features never seen before, such as mountains on the Moon. Most astronomers now use telescopes that gather visible light with mirrors rather than lenses. There are also special telescopes that gather other forms of electromagnetic radiation.

1912
Cycles of Stars Are Key to Distances
Certain types of stars, called Cepheid variables, get brighter and then dimmer in a regular cycle. Astronomer Henrietta Leavitt finds that brighter stars have longer cycles. This discovery will allow the distances to these stars to be calculated.

1916
Time, Space, and Mass Are Connected
The general theory of relativity expands Newton's theory of gravitation. Albert Einstein shows that mass affects time and space. According to this theory, gravity will affect the light we receive from objects in space.

1929
Big Is Getting Bigger
Edwin Hubble has already used Cepheid variables to show that some objects in the sky are actually distant galaxies. Now he finds that galaxies are generally moving apart, at rates that increase with distance. Many astronomers conclude that the universe is expanding.

| 1880 | 1900 | 1920 | 1940 | 1960 |

TECHNOLOGY

Colliding Particles Give Details About the Start of the Universe

Scientists think that all matter and energy was in an extremely hot, dense state and then exploded rapidly in an event called the big bang. Some scientists are attempting to re-create some of the conditions that existed during the first billionth of a second after the big bang. They use devices called particle accelerators to make tiny particles move almost at the speed of light. When the particles crash into each other, they produce different types of particles and radiation. Scientists use what they learn from the particles and the radiation to develop models of conditions at the beginning of the universe.

1998

Fast Is Getting Faster

Two groups of astronomers studying exploding stars called supernovae come to the same remarkable conclusion. Not only is the universe expanding, but the rate of expansion is increasing. In the diagram below, the rate of expansion is shown by the distances between rings and between galaxies.

The expanding universe

Present

Expansion slows down

Expansion speeds up

Big Bang

Farthest supernova

~15 billion years

RESOURCE CENTER
CLASSZONE.COM
Learn more about current advances in astronomy.

1980   2000

TECHNOLOGY

Measuring the Big Bang

In 1965 two researchers noticed radio waves that came from all directions instead of from just one direction, like a signal from a space object. They inferred that the radiation was left over from the big bang. In 1989 and again in 2001, NASA launched spacecraft to study the radiation. Data gathered using these telescopes in space are still being used to test different models of the big bang, including the arrangement of matter in the universe. In this map of the sky, red and yellow show the areas that were hottest after the big bang.

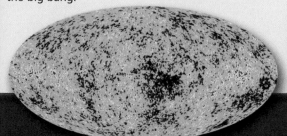

INTO THE FUTURE

Throughout history, people have learned about the universe from visible light and other radiation. New and better measurements have been made as technologies improved. Better and more complex models are filling in details that cannot be measured directly. In the future, improvements will continue. Computers, telescopes in space, and other instruments will allow astronomers to collect better data and make better models.

Some matter in the universe does not give off or reflect any detectable radiation. This is called dark matter. Astronomers infer its existence from its effects on matter that is detected. In the future, astronomers hope to determine what dark matter is, exactly where it is, and how it moves in the universe. In a similar way, astronomers will learn more about why the universe is expanding faster with time and what energy is involved in this acceleration.

ACTIVITIES

Reliving History

Some early astronomers observed the Moon in order to develop and test their ideas about space. For two weeks or more, make frequent observations of the Moon and keep your notes, sketches, and thoughts in a notebook. You might look for the Moon at a certain time each day or night or perhaps record the direction in which the Moon sets. A newspaper may list the times of moonrise and moonset for your location.

Compare your observations and thoughts with those of other students. You might also find out what people in other cultures thought of the patterns of change they saw in the Moon.

Writing About Science

Choose one of these famous astronomers and research his or her story. Write a biographical profile or an imaginary interview with that person.

Our Solar System

the **BIG** idea

Planets and other objects form a system around our Sun.

Key Concepts

SECTION

Planets orbit the Sun at different distances.
Learn about the sizes and the distances of objects in the solar system and about its formation.

SECTION

The inner solar system has rocky planets.
Learn about the processes that shape Earth and other planets.

SECTION

The outer solar system has four giant planets.
Learn about the largest planets.

SECTION

Small objects are made of ice and rock.
Learn about moons, asteroids, and comets.

Internet Preview

CLASSZONE.COM

Chapter 3 online resources: Content Review, Visualization, two Resource Centers, Math Tutorial, Test Practice

This image shows Jupiter with one of its large moons. How big are these objects compared with Earth?

EXPLORE (the BIG idea)

How Big Is Jupiter?

Measure 1.4 mL of water (about 22 drops) into an empty 2 L bottle to represent Earth. Use a full 2 L bottle to represent Jupiter. Lift each one.

Observe and Think How big is Jupiter compared with Earth? Using this scale, you would need more than nine hundred 2 L bottles to represent the Sun. How big is the Sun compared with Jupiter?

How Round Is an Orbit?

Tie a loop 10 cm long in a piece of string. Place two thumbtacks 2 cm apart in the center of a piece of paper. Loop the string around the thumbtacks and use a pencil to draw an oval the shape of Pluto's orbit. Remove one thumbtack. The remaining thumbtack represents the Sun.

Observe and Think How would you describe the shape of this orbit? How different is it from a circle?

Internet Activity: Spacing

Go to **ClassZone.com** to take a virtual spaceflight through the solar system. Examine distances between planets as your virtual spaceship travels at a constant speed.

Observe and Think What do you notice about the relative distances of the planets?

NSTA
scilinks.org
SCiLINKS

The Solar System **Code: MDL059**

Getting Ready to Learn

◁ CONCEPT REVIEW

- The planets we see are much closer than the stars in constellations.
- The Sun, the planets, and smaller bodies make up the solar system.
- Scientists observe different types of electromagnetic radiation from space objects.

◁ VOCABULARY REVIEW

orbit p. 10

solar system p. 10

satellite p. 23

impact crater p. 32

axis of rotation p. 44

CONTENT REVIEW
CLASSZONE.COM
Review concepts and vocabulary.

▷ TAKING NOTES

MAIN IDEA AND DETAILS

Make a two-column chart. Write **main ideas,** such as those in the blue headings, in the column on the left. Write **details** about each of those main ideas in the column on the right.

VOCABULARY STRATEGY

Draw a **word triangle** diagram for each new vocabulary term. In the bottom row write and define the term. In the middle row, use the term correctly in a sentence. At the top, draw a small picture to help you remember the term.

See the Note-Taking Handbook on pages R45–R51.

SCIENCE NOTEBOOK

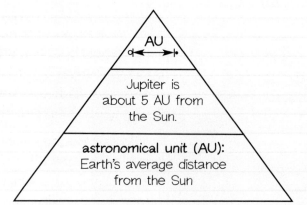

MAIN IDEAS	DETAIL NOTES
1. Planets have different sizes and distances.	1. Objects in the solar system • Sun • planets • moons • comets and asteroids
2.	2.

AU

Jupiter is about 5 AU from the Sun.

astronomical unit (AU): Earth's average distance from the Sun

3.1 Planets orbit the Sun at different distances.

 BEFORE, you learned

- Earth orbits the Sun
- The Moon is Earth's natural satellite
- The Moon's features tell us about its history

 NOW, you will learn

- What types of objects are in the solar system
- About sizes and distances in the solar system
- How the solar system formed

VOCABULARY

astronomical unit (AU) p. 81

ellipse p. 81

EXPLORE Planet Formation

How do planets form?

PROCEDURE

① Fill the bowl about halfway with water.

② Stir the water quickly, using a circular motion, and then remove the spoon.

③ Sprinkle wax pieces onto the swirling water.

WHAT DO YOU THINK?

- In what direction did the wax move?
- What else happened to the wax?

MATERIALS

- bowl
- water
- spoon
- wax pieces

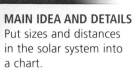

MAIN IDEA AND DETAILS
Put sizes and distances in the solar system into a chart.

Planets have different sizes and distances.

You may have seen some planets in the sky without realizing it. They are so far from Earth that they appear as tiny dots of light in the darkened sky. If you have seen something that looks like a very bright star in the western sky in the early evening, you have probably seen the planet Venus. Even if you live in a city, you may have seen Mars, Jupiter, or Saturn but thought that you were seeing a star. Mercury is much more difficult to see. You need a telescope to see three of the planets in our solar system—Uranus, Neptune, and Pluto.

Like the Moon, planets can be seen because they reflect sunlight. Planets do not give off visible light of their own. Sunlight is also reflected by moons and other objects in space, called comets and asteroids. However, these objects are usually too far away and not bright enough to see without a telescope.

 Why do planets look bright?

Objects in the Solar System

The sizes of objects in the solar system range from very small to very large.

asteroids

Sun
On this scale,
the Sun is about
a meter across.

Mars

Saturn

Earth

Saturn's moons

Venus

Mercury

Jupiter's moons

Neptune

Neptune's moons

Jupiter

Uranus's
moons

Uranus

0   20,000   40,000 kilometers

Objects smaller than about 100 kilometers
are represented as dots.

comets

Pluto

Distances of Planets

Sun Venus Mars   Jupiter   Saturn   Uranus

Mercury Earth   asteroids

0   2   4 AU

Objects in the solar system have very different sizes. An asteroid may be as small as a mountain, perhaps 1/1000 Earth's diameter. In contrast, the largest planets are about 10 Earth diameters across. The Sun's diameter is about 100 times Earth's. If the planets were the sizes shown on page 80, the Sun would be about a meter across.

Distances

The distances between most objects in space are huge in comparison with the objects' diameters. If Earth and the Sun were the sizes shown on page 80, they would be more than 100 meters from each other.

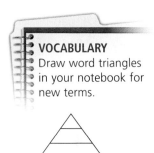

VOCABULARY
Draw word triangles in your notebook for new terms.

Astronomers understand huge distances by comparing them with something more familiar. One **astronomical unit,** or AU, is Earth's average distance from the Sun. An AU is about 150 million kilometers (93 million mi). Mercury is less than 0.5 AU from the Sun, Jupiter is about 5 AU from the Sun, and Pluto gets nearly 50 AU from the Sun at times. You can use the diagram at the bottom of pages 80–81 to compare these distances. However, the planets are not arranged in a straight line—they move around the Sun.

You can see that the planets are spaced unevenly. The first four planets are relatively close together and close to the Sun. They define a region called the inner solar system. Farther from the Sun is the outer solar system, where the planets are much more spread out.

CHECK YOUR READING What are the two regions of the solar system?

Orbits

More than 99 percent of all the mass in the solar system is in the Sun. The gravitational pull of this huge mass causes planets and most other objects in the solar system to move around, or orbit, the Sun.

The shape of each orbit is an **ellipse**—a flattened circle or oval. A circle is a special type of ellipse, just as a square is a special type of rectangle. Most of the planets' orbits are very nearly circles. Only one planet—Pluto—has an orbit that looks a little flattened instead of round.

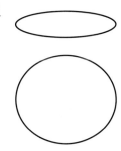

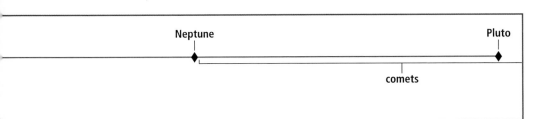

Neptune

Pluto

comets

INVESTIGATE Distances

How far apart are the planets?

PROCEDURE

①　Mark one sheet from the end of the roll of paper as the location of the Sun. Mark an X and write the word *Sun* with dots rather than lines.

②　Use the Distance Table data sheet to mark the distances for the rest of the solar system. Count sheets and estimate tenths of a sheet as necessary. Re-roll or fold the paper neatly.

③　Go to a space where you can unroll the paper. Compare the distances of planets as you walk along the paper and back again.

WHAT DO YOU THINK?

• How does the distance between Earth and Mars compare with the distance between Saturn and Uranus?

• How would you use the spacing to sort the planets into groups?

CHALLENGE If it took two years for the *Voyager 2* spacecraft to travel from Earth to Jupiter, about how long do you think it took for *Voyager 2* to travel from Jupiter to Neptune?

The solar system formed from a swirling cloud of gas and dust.

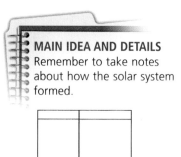

MAIN IDEA AND DETAILS
Remember to take notes about how the solar system formed.

The planets orbit the Sun in similar ways. Their paths are almost in a flat plane, like the rings of a target. They all orbit the Sun in the same direction—counterclockwise as seen from above Earth's North Pole. Most of the planets rotate on their axes in this direction, too. Many other objects in the solar system also orbit and rotate in this same direction. These similar motions have given scientists clues about how the solar system formed.

According to the best scientific model, the solar system formed out of a huge cloud of different gases and specks of dust. The cloud flattened into a disk of whirling material. Most of the mass fell to the center and became a star—the Sun. At the same time, tiny bits of dust and frozen gases in the disk stuck together into clumps. The clumps stuck together and became larger. Large clumps became planets. They moved in the same direction that the flat disk was turning.

Not all the clumps grew big enough to be called planets. However, many of these objects still orbit the Sun the same way that planets orbit. Some of the objects close to the Sun are like rocks or mountains in space and are called asteroids. Other objects, farther from the Sun, are more like enormous snowballs or icebergs. They are called comets.

Formation of the Solar System

The Sun and other objects formed out of material in a flat disk.

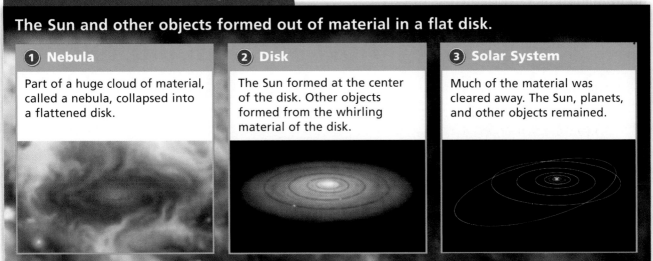

1 Nebula

Part of a huge cloud of material, called a nebula, collapsed into a flattened disk.

2 Disk

The Sun formed at the center of the disk. Other objects formed from the whirling material of the disk.

3 Solar System

Much of the material was cleared away. The Sun, planets, and other objects remained.

Some objects orbit planets instead of orbiting the Sun directly, so they are considered moons. You will read more about asteroids, comets, and moons in Section 3.4.

You can tell a little bit about the size of an object in space from its shape. Lumpy objects are usually much smaller than round objects. As a space object starts to form, the clumps come together from many directions and produce an uneven shape. The gravity of each part affects every other part. The pieces pull each other closer together. When an object has enough mass, this pulling becomes strong enough to make the object round. Any parts that would stick far out are pulled in toward the center until the object becomes a sphere.

CHECK YOUR READING Why do planets and large moons have a spherical shape?

3.1 Review

KEY CONCEPTS

1. What are the types of space objects in the solar system?

2. Why is the unit of measurement used for the distances of planets from the Sun different from the unit used for their sizes?

3. How did planets and other objects in the solar system form out of material in a disk?

CRITICAL THINKING

4. **Analyze** Why do the planets all orbit in one direction?

5. **Infer** Which of the two moons below has more mass? Explain why you think so.

CHALLENGE

6. **Apply** Could you model all the sizes of objects in the solar system by using sports balls? Explain why or why not.

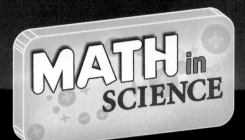

MATH TUTORIAL
CLASSZONE.COM

Click on Math Tutorial for more help with the percent equation.

How Much Would You Weigh on Other Worlds?

When astronauts walked on the Moon, they felt much lighter than they felt when they were on Earth. Neil Armstrong's total mass—about 160 kilograms with space suit and backpack—did not change. However, the Moon did not pull as hard on him as Earth did, so he weighed less on the Moon. At the surface, the Moon's gravitational pull is only 17% of Earth's gravitational pull. You can use percentages to calculate Neil Armstrong's weight on the Moon.

Example

On Earth, with his heavy space suit and backpack, Neil Armstrong weighed about 1600 newtons (360 lb). To calculate his weight on the Moon, find 17% of 1600 newtons.

"Of" means "multiply."	17% of 1600 N = 17% × 1600 N
Change the percent to a decimal fraction.	= 0.17 × 1600 N
Simplify.	= 272 N

ANSWER With his suit and backpack, Neil Armstrong weighed about 270 newtons on the Moon.

Use the percentages in the table to answer the following questions.

1. A backpack weighs 60 newtons (13 lb) on Earth. **(a)** How much would it weigh on Jupiter? **(b)** How much would it weigh on Jupiter's moon Io?

2. **(a)** How much would a student weighing 500 newtons (110 lb) on Earth weigh on Saturn? **(b)** on Venus?

3. On which planet or moon would you be lightest?

CHALLENGE A pencil weighs 0.3 newtons (1 oz) on Earth. How much would it weigh on the Moon? If an astronaut let go of the pencil on the Moon, would the pencil fall? Explain.

Percent of Weight on Earth	
Planet or Moon	**%**
Mercury	38
Venus	91
Earth	100
Moon (Earth)	17
Mars	38
Jupiter	236
Io (Jupiter)	18
Europa (Jupiter)	13
Ganymede (Jupiter)	15
Callisto (Jupiter)	13
Saturn	92
Titan (Saturn)	14
Uranus	89
Neptune	112
Triton (Neptune)	8.0
Pluto	6.7
Charon (Pluto)	2.8

This picture of Buzz Aldrin on the Moon was taken by Neil Armstrong, who can be seen reflected in Aldrin's helmet.

3.2 The inner solar system has rocky planets.

◀ BEFORE, you learned	▶ NOW, you will learn
• Planets are closer together in the inner solar system than in the outer solar system	• How four processes change the surfaces of solid planets
• Planets formed along with the Sun	• How atmospheres form and then affect planets
• Gravity made planets round	• What the planets closest to the Sun are like

VOCABULARY

terrestrial planet p. 85
tectonics p. 86
volcanism p. 86

EXPLORE Surfaces

How does a planet's mantle affect its surface?

PROCEDURE

① Dampen a paper towel and place it on top of two blocks to model a crust and a mantle.

② Move one block. Try different amounts of motion and different directions.

WHAT DO YOU THINK?
• What happened to the paper towel?
• What landforms like this have you seen?

MATERIALS
• 2 blocks
• paper towel
• newspaper

The terrestrial planets have rocky crusts.

Scientists study Earth to learn about other planets. They also study other planets to learn more about Earth. The **terrestrial planets** are Mercury, Venus, Earth, and Mars—the four planets closest to the Sun. They all have rocky crusts and dense mantles and cores. Their insides, surfaces, and atmospheres formed in similar ways and follow similar patterns. One planet—Earth—can be used as a model to understand the others. In fact, the term *terrestrial* comes from *terra*, the Latin word for Earth.

Earth

Most of Earth's rocky surface is hidden by water. More details about Earth and other planets are listed in the Appendix at the back of this book.

Mass 6×10^{24} kg
Diameter 12,800 km
Average distance from Sun 1 AU

Orbits in 365 days
Rotates in 24 hours

Processes and Surface Features

All terrestrial planets have layers. Each planet gained energy from the collisions that formed it. This energy heated and melted the planet's materials. The heaviest materials were metals, which sank to the center and formed a core. Lighter rock formed a mantle around the core. The lightest rock rose to the surface and cooled into a crust.

Four types of processes then shaped each planet's rocky crust. The processes acted to different extents on each planet, depending on how much the crust and inside of the planet cooled.

READING TiP

Compare what you read about each type of feature with the pictures and diagrams on page 87.

1 Tectonics Earth's crust is split into large pieces called tectonic plates. These plates are moved by Earth's hot mantle. Mountains, valleys, and other features form as the plates move together, apart, or along each other. The crusts of other terrestrial planets are not split into plates but can be twisted, wrinkled up, or stretched out by the mantle. **Tectonics** is the processes of change in a crust due to the motion of hot material underneath. As a planet cools, the crust gets stiffer and the mantle may stop moving, so this process stops.

2 Volcanism A second process, called **volcanism,** occurs when molten rock moves from a planet's hot interior onto its surface. The molten rock is called lava when it reaches the surface through an opening called a volcano. On Earth, lava often builds up into mountains. Volcanoes are found on Earth, Venus, and Mars. Lava can also flow onto large areas and cool into flat plains like the lunar maria. When the inside of a planet cools enough, no more molten rock reaches the surface.

3 Weathering and Erosion You have read about weathering on Earth and the Moon. Weather or small impacts break down rocks. The broken material is moved by a group of processes called erosion. The material may form dunes, new layers of rock, or other features. On Earth, water is important for weathering and erosion. However, similar things happen even without water. Wind can carry sand grains that batter at rocks and form new features. Even on a planet without air, rock breaks down from being heated in the daylight and cooled at night. The material is pulled downhill by gravity.

RESOURCE CENTER
CLASSZONE.COM

Find out more about impact craters on Earth and other space objects.

4 Impact Cratering A small object sometimes hits a planet's surface so fast that it causes an explosion. The resulting impact crater is often ten times larger than the object that produced it. On Earth, most craters have been erased by other processes. Impact craters are easier to find on other planets. If a planet or part of a planet is completely covered with impact craters, then the other processes have not changed the surface much in billions of years.

CHECK YOUR READING What processes affect the surfaces of terrestrial planets?

Features of Rocky Planets

The processes that shape features on a planet's surface can be divided into four types. The features can tell you different things about the planet.

① Tectonics

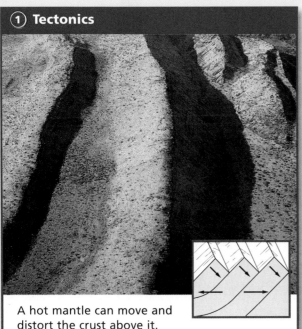

A hot mantle can move and distort the crust above it.
This system of mountains and valleys on **Earth** formed as the crust was stretched.

② Volcanism

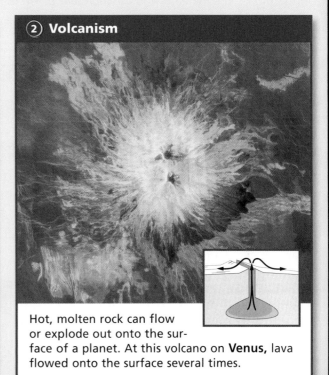

Hot, molten rock can flow or explode out onto the surface of a planet. At this volcano on **Venus,** lava flowed onto the surface several times.

③ Weathering and Erosion

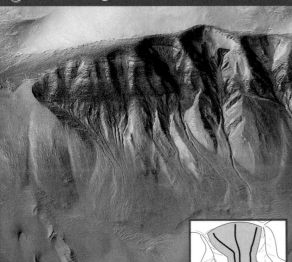

Rock can be broken down and moved. In this region of **Mars,** material broken from a cliff was moved by erosion into new slopes and dunes.

④ Impact Cratering

A small space object can hit a planet's surface and leave a crater. Because the other processes on **Mercury** are weak, newer craters can be seen on a background of older, more eroded craters.

READING VISUALS Which two processes happen because of hot material beneath the surface?

INVESTIGATE Layers

How do the layers inside of planets form?

In this model, the materials you use represent different rocks and metals that make up the solid planets.

PROCEDURE

1. Put pieces of gelatin into the container until it is about one-quarter full.

2. Mix in a spoonful each of sand and wax. Use the spoon to break the gelatin into small pieces as you mix. Remove the spoon.

3. Place the container in a bowl of hot tap water (about 70°C) and observe what happens as the gelatin melts.

WHAT DO YOU THINK?

- What happened to each of the materials when the gelatin melted?
- How do the results resemble the core, mantle, and crust of Earth and other planets?

CHALLENGE How might you improve this model?

Atmospheres

Atmospheres on terrestrial planets mainly formed from gases that poured out of volcanoes. If a planet's gravity is strong enough, it pulls the gases in and keeps them near the surface. If a planet's gravity is too weak, the gases expand into outer space and are lost.

Venus, Earth, and Mars each had gravity strong enough to hold heavy gases such as carbon dioxide. However, the lightest gases—hydrogen and helium—escaped into outer space. The atmospheres of Venus and Mars are mostly carbon dioxide.

An atmosphere can move energy from warmer places to cooler places. This movement of heat energy makes temperatures more uniform between a planet's day side and its night side and between its equator and its poles. An atmosphere can also make a planet's whole surface warmer by slowing the loss of energy from the surface.

After Earth formed, its atmosphere of carbon dioxide kept the surface warm enough for water to be liquid. Oceans covered most of Earth's surface. The oceans changed the gases of the atmosphere, and living organisms caused even more changes. Earth's atmosphere is now mostly nitrogen with some oxygen.

 Why is the solid Earth surrounded by gases?

Craters cover the surface of Mercury.

Mercury, like the Moon, has smooth plains and many craters. The processes at work on Earth also affected Mercury.

Tectonics Long, high cliffs stretch across Mercury's surface. Scientists think that Mercury's huge core of iron shrank when it cooled long ago. The crust wrinkled up, forming cliffs, as the planet got a little smaller.

Volcanism Parts of the surface were covered with lava long ago. Large, smooth plains formed. The plains are similar to lunar maria.

Weathering and Erosion Small impacts and temperature changes have broken rock. Gravity has moved broken material downhill.

Impact Cratering Round features cover much of the surface. These craters show that the other processes have not changed Mercury's surface very much for a long time.

Mercury has the longest cycle of day and night of the terrestrial planets—three months of daylight and three months of darkness. There is no atmosphere to move energy from the hot areas to the cold areas. In the long daytime, it can get hotter than 420°C (about 800°F)—hot enough to melt lead. During the long, cold night, the temperature can drop lower than –170°C (about –280°F).

—no data

Mercury

This map of Mercury was made from many images taken by one spacecraft. The blank patches show areas that were not mapped by the spacecraft.

Mass 6% of Earth's mass

Diameter 38% of Earth's diameter

Average distance from Sun 0.39 AU

Orbits in 88 Earth days

Rotates in 59 Earth days

CHECK YOUR READING How is Mercury similar to the Moon?

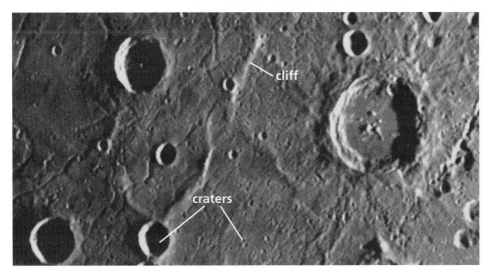

cliff

craters

Craters of all sizes cover Mercury's surface, but there are also flat lava plains and cliffs from long ago.

MAIN IDEA AND DETAILS
When you see a new heading, remember to take notes about important ideas.

Volcanoes shape the surface of Venus.

The planet Venus is only a little smaller than Earth and orbits a little closer to the Sun. As a result, Venus is sometimes called Earth's sister planet. However, Venus is different from Earth in important ways.

Venus takes about eight months to turn just once on its axis. Unlike most other planets, Venus rotates and orbits in opposite directions. The rotation and orbit together produce very long days and nights—two months of daylight followed by two months of darkness.

The atmosphere of Venus is very dense. Air pressure on Venus is 90 times that on Earth. Venus's atmosphere is mostly carbon dioxide. This gas slows the loss of energy and makes the surface very hot. The ground temperature on Venus is about 470°C (about 870°F). The atmosphere of Venus moves energy around so well that the long nights are as hot as the days and the poles are as hot as the equator. In addition, there are droplets of sulfuric acid, a corrosive chemical, in the atmosphere. These droplets form thick white clouds that completely cover the planet and hide the surface.

Like Mercury, Venus is affected by the same four types of processes that change Earth's surface. Scientists think that tectonics and volcanism may still be changing Venus's surface today.

Tectonics Patterns of cracks and cliffs have formed as movements of the hot mantle have stretched, wrinkled, and twisted the surface.

Volcanism Most of the surface of Venus has been covered with lava in the last billion years or so. Volcanoes and flat lava plains are found all over the surface.

Thick clouds make it impossible to see Venus's surface in visible light. This inset shows a map of Venus that scientists made using radio waves.

Venus

Venus is nearly the size of Earth but has a thicker atmosphere and is much hotter than Earth. The surface is rocky, as you can see in the image below.

Mass 82% of Earth's mass
Diameter 95% of Earth's diameter
Average distance from Sun 0.72 AU

Orbits in 225 Earth days
Rotates in 243 Earth days

weathered and eroded rock

spacecraft

Weathering and Erosion Venus is too hot to have liquid water, and the winds do not seem to move much material. Erosion may be slower on Venus than on Earth.

Impact Cratering Round craters mark the surface here and there. Older craters have been erased by the other processes. Also, Venus's thick atmosphere protects the surface from small impacts.

 Why is Venus not covered with craters?

Erosion changes the appearance of Mars.

Mars is relatively small, with a diameter about half that of Earth. The orange color of some of the surface comes from molecules of iron and oxygen—rust. Mars has two tiny moons. They were probably once asteroids that were pulled into orbit around Mars.

Surface of Mars

The same processes that affect the other terrestrial planets affect Mars.

Tectonics Valleys and raised areas formed on Mars as the mantle moved. One huge system of valleys, called Valles Marineris, is long enough to stretch across the United States.

Volcanism Most of the northern hemisphere has smooth plains of cooled lava. Several volcanoes are higher than any mountain on Earth. The lava must have built up in the same spot for a long time, so scientists have inferred that the crust of Mars has cooled more than Earth's crust. On Earth, the tectonic plates move, so chains of smaller volcanoes form instead of single larger volcanoes.

Weathering and Erosion Fast winds carry sand that breaks down rocks. Wind and gravity move the broken material, forming new features such as sand dunes. There are also landforms that look like the results of gigantic flash floods that happened long ago.

Impact Cratering Round craters cover much of the southern hemisphere of Mars. Many craters are very old and eroded. A few impact craters on the volcanoes make scientists think that the volcanoes have not released lava for a long time.

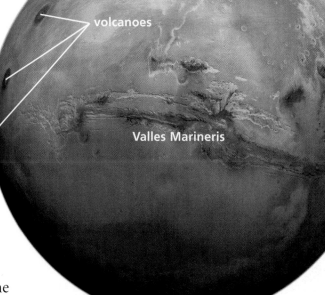

Mars

The atmosphere of Mars is thin but causes weathering and erosion.

Mass 11% of Earth's mass
Diameter 53% of Earth's diameter
Average distance from Sun 1.5 AU
Orbits in 1.9 Earth years
Rotates in 25 hours

volcanoes

Valles Marineris

red dust carried by wind

distant hills

weathered and eroded rock

The sky of Mars is made red by dust that the wind picks up and carries to new places.

Gases and Water on Mars

The atmosphere of Mars is mostly carbon dioxide. The air pressure is only about 1 percent of the air pressure on Earth. The gas is not dense enough to keep the surface warm or to move much energy from cold areas to warmer areas. Therefore, temperatures may reach almost 20°C (about 60°F) in the daytime and −90°C (−130°F) at night. The large differences in temperature produce fast winds. The winds cause gigantic dust storms that sometimes cover most of the planet.

Like Earth, Mars has polar caps that grow in winter and shrink in summer. However, the changing polar caps of Mars are made mostly of frozen carbon dioxide—dry ice. The carbon dioxide of the atmosphere can also form clouds, fog, and frost on the ground.

There is no liquid water on the surface of Mars today. Any water would quickly evaporate or freeze. However, there were floods in the past, and there is still frozen water in the ground and in one polar cap. Water is important for life and will also be needed to make rocket fuel if humans are ever to make trips to Mars and back.

 CHECK YOUR READING In what ways is Mars different from Earth?

3.2 Review

KEY CONCEPTS

1. What are the four types of processes that shape planets' surfaces? For each, give one example of a feature that the process can produce.

2. How can an atmosphere affect the temperature of a planet's surface?

3. Which terrestrial planet has the oldest, least-changing surface?

CRITICAL THINKING

4. **Compare and Contrast** Make a chart with columns for the four types of processes and for an atmosphere. Fill out a row for each planet.

5. **Apply** If a planet had a surface with craters but no other features, what could you say about the inside of the planet?

◖ CHALLENGE

6. **Infer** Describe how a hot mantle can affect a planet's atmosphere. **Hint**: Which of the four processes is involved?

dark hills

light stripes

0   0.5   1.0 kilometers

What Shapes the Surface of Mars?

Many features on Mars, when seen close up, look a lot like features found on Earth. Astronomers use their knowledge of the four types of processes that affect the terrestrial planets to hypothesize about the features on Mars. Using what you know about the processes, make your own hypotheses to explain the features in the image to the left.

▶ Results of Research

- Small objects hit the surface, producing craters.
- Volcanoes erupt, creating mountains and flows of lava.
- The mantle moves the crust, producing mountains and valleys.
- Wind, water, and gravity move material on the surface, eroding some places and building up others.

▶ Observations

- Dark, raised triangles point roughly east.
- Patterns of light stripes run mostly north-south between the dark hills.
- The features are inside a huge impact crater.

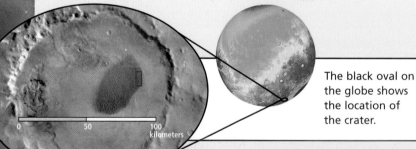

The large image shows details of the area in the red rectangle.

0   50   100
kilometers

The black oval on the globe shows the location of the crater.

▶ Form a Hypothesis

On Your Own Consider one or more processes that might produce the hills and stripes seen in the image at left.

As a Group With a small group discuss possible hypotheses to explain the formation of these features. See if the group can agree on which one is most reasonable.

CHALLENGE Create a model that you can use to test your hypothesis. What will you use to represent the surface of Mars and the forces acting on it?

3.3 The outer solar system has four giant planets.

◀ **BEFORE**, you learned

- Planets formed along with the Sun
- Vast distances separate planets
- The gravity of a terrestrial planet may be strong enough to hold the heavier gases

▶ **NOW**, you will learn

- About the four giant planets in the solar system
- What the atmospheres of giant planets are like
- About the rings of giant planets

VOCABULARY

gas giant p. 94
ring p. 97

THINK ABOUT

What is Jupiter like inside?

Most of Jupiter's huge mass is hidden below layers of clouds. Scientists learn about Jupiter by studying its gravity, its magnetic field, its motions, and its radiation. Scientists also use data from other space bodies to make models, from which they make predictions. Then they observe Jupiter to test their predictions. What might it be like under Jupiter's clouds?

VOCABULARY
Remember to draw a word triangle when you read a new term.

The gas giants have very deep atmospheres.

You have already read about the four rocky planets in the inner solar system, close to the Sun. Beyond Mars stretches the outer solar system, where the four largest planets slowly orbit the Sun. The **gas giants**— Jupiter, Saturn, Uranus (YUR-uh-nuhs), and Neptune—are made mainly of hydrogen, helium, and other gases.

When you think of gases, you probably think of Earth's air, which is not very dense. However, the giant planets are so large and have such large amounts of these gases that they have a lot of mass. The huge gravitational force from such a large mass is enough to pull the gas particles close together and make the atmosphere very dense. Inside the giant planets, the gases become more dense than water. The outermost parts are less dense and more like Earth's atmosphere.

CHECK YOUR READING Why are the gas giants dense inside?

The atmosphere of a giant planet is very deep. Imagine traveling into one. At first, the atmosphere is thin and very cold. There may be a haze of gases. A little lower is a layer of clouds that reflect sunlight, just like clouds on Earth. There are strong winds and other weather patterns. Lower down, it is warmer and there are layers of clouds of different materials. As you go farther, the atmosphere gradually becomes dense enough to call a liquid. It also gets thousands of degrees hotter as you get closer to the center of the planet. The materials around you become more and more dense until they are solid. Scientists think that each of the four gas giants has a solid core, larger than Earth, deep in its center.

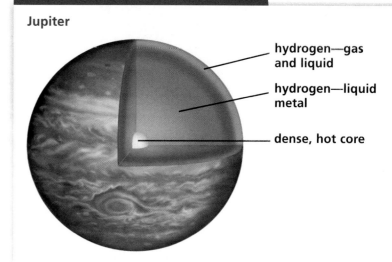

Interior of a Giant Planet

Jupiter

— hydrogen—gas and liquid

— hydrogen—liquid metal

— dense, hot core

Jupiter is a world of storms and clouds.

Jupiter is the largest planet in the solar system. It is more than 10 times larger than Earth in diameter and more than 1200 times larger in volume. A jet plane that could circle Earth in about 2 days would take 23 days to circle Jupiter. If you could weigh the planets on a cosmic scale, all the other planets put together would weigh less than half as much as Jupiter.

Jupiter is more than five times farther from the Sun than Earth is. It moves more slowly through space than Earth and has a greater distance to travel in each orbit. Jupiter takes 12 Earth years to go once around the Sun.

Even though it is big, Jupiter takes less than 10 hours to turn once on its axis. This fast rotation produces fast winds and stormy weather. Like Earth, Jupiter has bands of winds that blow eastward and westward, but Jupiter has many more bands than Earth does.

Jupiter

Jupiter's colorful stripes are produced by clouds at different levels in Jupiter's deep atmosphere.

Mass 318 Earth masses
Diameter 11 Earth diameters
Average distance from Sun 5.2 AU
Orbits in 12 Earth years
Rotates in 9.9 hours

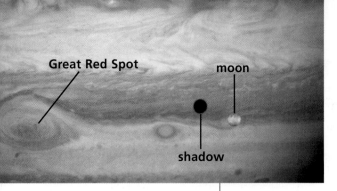

Great Red Spot

moon

shadow

This image shows one of Jupiter's moons casting a shadow on Jupiter. If you were in that shadow, you would experience a solar eclipse.

Stripes of cold clouds form along the bands. The clouds look white because they are made of crystals that reflect sunlight. The crystals in these high white clouds are frozen ammonia rather than frozen water, as on Earth. Between Jupiter's white bands of clouds, you can see down to the next layer. The lower clouds are brown or red and made of different chemicals. Sometimes there are clear patches in the brown clouds, where the next layer of bluish clouds shows through.

CHECK YOUR READING What are Jupiter's white stripes?

Storms can form between bands of winds that blow in opposite directions. Because Jupiter has no land to slow the storms, they can last for a long time. The largest of these storms is the Great Red Spot, which is twice as wide as Earth and at least 100 years old. Its clouds rise even higher than the white ammonia-ice clouds. Scientists are trying to find out which chemicals produce the spot's reddish color.

Saturn has large rings.

REMINDER

Density is the amount of mass in a given volume. An object of low density can still have a great total mass if it has a large volume.

The sixth planet from the Sun is Saturn. Saturn is only a little smaller than Jupiter, but its mass is less than one-third that of Jupiter. Because there is less mass, the gravitational pull is weaker, so the gas particles can spread out more. As a result, Saturn has a much lower density than Jupiter. The storms and stripes of clouds form deeper in Saturn's atmosphere than in Jupiter's, so the details are harder to see.

Saturn

Saturn has an average density less than that of liquid water on Earth. The diameter of Saturn's ring system is almost as great as the distance from Earth to the Moon.

Mass 95 Earth masses

Diameter 9 Earth diameters

Average distance from Sun 9.5 AU

Orbits in 29 Earth years

Rotates in 11 hours

Saturn was the first planet known to have rings. A planetary **ring** is a wide, flat zone of small particles that orbit a planet. All four gas giants have rings around their equators. Saturn's rings are made of chunks of water ice the size of a building or smaller. Larger chunks, considered to be tiny moons, orbit within the rings. Saturn's main rings are very bright. The outermost ring is three times as wide as the planet, but it is usually too faint to see. Saturn's rings have bright and dark stripes that change over time.

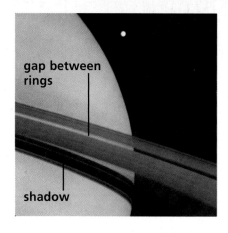

gap between rings

shadow

Sunlight shines from the upper right of this image. The rings cast shadows on Saturn's clouds.

You can use Saturn's rings to see the planet's seasons. Like Earth's axis of rotation, Saturn's axis is tilted. The angle is 27 degrees. When the image on this page was taken, sunlight shone more on the northern hemisphere, so the north side of the rings was bright. The shadow of the rings fell on the southern hemisphere. Winter started in Saturn's northern hemisphere in May 2003 and will last more than seven Earth years. Saturn is almost ten times farther from the Sun than Earth is, so Saturn takes almost 30 Earth years to go around the Sun once.

INVESTIGATE Giant Planets

Why do Saturn's rings seem to change size?

PROCEDURE

1. Poke the stick through the plate and cut off the plate's rim. Shape the clay onto both sides of the plate to make a model of a planet with rings.

2. Model Saturn's orbit for your partner. Stand between your partner and the classroom clock. Point one end of the stick at the clock. Hold the model at the same height as your partner's eyes. Have your partner watch the model with just one eye open.

3. Move one step counterclockwise around your partner and point the stick at the clock again. Make sure the model is as high as your partner's eyes. Your partner may need to turn to see the model.

4. Continue taking steps around your partner and pointing the stick at the clock until you have moved the model all the way around your partner.

5. Switch roles with your partner and repeat steps 2, 3, and 4.

WHAT DO YOU THINK?

- How did your view of the rings change as the model planet changed position?

- How many times per orbit do the rings seem to vanish?

CHALLENGE How do Saturn's axis and orbit compare with those of Earth?

SKILL FOCUS
Observing

MATERIALS
- ice-cream stick
- disposable plate
- scissors
- clay

TIME
20 minutes

Uranus and Neptune are extremely cold.

The seventh and eighth planets from the Sun are Uranus and Neptune. These planets are similar in size—both have diameters roughly one-third that of Jupiter. Unlike Jupiter and Saturn, Uranus and Neptune are only about 15 percent hydrogen and helium. Most of the mass of each planet is made up of heavier gases, such as methane, ammonia, and water. As a result, Uranus and Neptune are more dense than Jupiter.

Uranus looks blue-green, and Neptune appears deep blue. The color comes from methane gas, which absorbs certain colors of light. Each planet has methane gas above a layer of white clouds. Sunlight passes through the gas, reflects off the clouds, then passes through the gas again on its way out. The gas absorbs the red, orange, and yellow parts of sunlight, so each planet's bluish color comes from the remaining green, blue, and violet light that passes back out of the atmosphere.

Uranus is a smooth blue-green in visible light. The small infrared image shows that the pole facing the Sun is warmer than the equator.

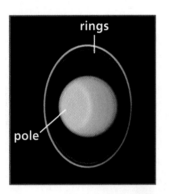

rings

pole

Uranus

Uranus is about twice Saturn's distance from the Sun. The farther a planet is from the Sun, the more slowly it moves along its orbit. The greater distance also results in a larger orbit, so it takes Uranus 84 Earth years to travel around the Sun.

Like the other gas giants, Uranus has a system of rings and moons around its equator. The ring particles and moons orbit Uranus in the same direction as the planet's spin. Unlike the other planets, Uranus has an axis of rotation that is almost in the plane of its orbit. As a result, Uranus seems to spin on its side. During a solstice, one pole of Uranus points almost straight toward the Sun.

Some scientists think that there was a large collision early in Uranus's history. The result left the planet and its system spinning at an unusual angle.

Uranus

Each pole of Uranus experiences more than 40 years of sunlight and then more than 40 years of darkness as the planet orbits the Sun.

Mass 15 Earth masses   **Orbits in** 84 Earth years

Diameter 4 Earth diameters   **Rotates in** 17 hours

Average distance from Sun 19 AU

Neptune

Neptune orbits about 10 AU farther from the Sun than Uranus, so you would expect it to be colder. However, Neptune has about the same outside temperature as Uranus because it is hotter inside.

Uranus is usually one smooth color, but light and dark areas often appear on Neptune. Clouds of methane ice crystals can form high enough in the atmosphere of Neptune to look white.

Storm systems can appear in darker shades of blue than the rest of the planet. One storm, seen during the flyby of the *Voyager 2* spacecraft in 1989, was named the Great Dark Spot. Unlike the huge storm on Jupiter, the Great Dark Spot did not stay at the same latitude. It moved toward Neptune's equator. The winds there may have broken up the storm. Images of Neptune obtained a few years later with the Hubble Space Telescope showed no sign of the Great Dark Spot.

○ **CHECK YOUR READING** What are the white patches often seen on Neptune?

Neptune

Neptune has a large moon that orbits in a direction opposite to Neptune's rotation. Scientists think a giant collision might have occurred in Neptune's past.

Mass 17 Earth masses
Diameter 4 Earth diameters
Average distance from Sun 30 AU
Orbits in 164 Earth years
Rotates in 16 hours

High clouds cast shadows on the layer below.

cloud

shadow

3.3 Review

KEY CONCEPTS

1. Which planet has a greater mass than all the other planets put together?

2. What do you see instead of a solid surface when you look at an image of a giant planet?

3. Which planets have rings?

CRITICAL THINKING

4. **Compare and Contrast** Why do Jupiter and Saturn show a lot of white, while Uranus and Neptune are more blue in color?

5. **Analyze** Most of Saturn is much less dense than most of Earth. Yet Saturn's mass is much greater than Earth's mass. How can this be so?

○ CHALLENGE

6. **Apply** If Uranus had areas of ice crystals high in its atmosphere, how would its appearance change?

KEY CONCEPT
Small objects are made of ice and rock.

 BEFORE, you learned

- Smaller bodies formed with the Sun and planets
- Planets in the inner solar system consist of rock and metal
- The outer solar system is cold

 NOW, you will learn

- About Pluto and the moons of the giant planets
- How asteroids and comets are similar and different
- What happens when tiny objects hit Earth's atmosphere

VOCABULARY

asteroid p. 103
comet p. 104
meteor p. 105
meteorite p. 105

THINK ABOUT

Do small space bodies experience erosion?

Very small bodies in space often have potato-like shapes. Some are covered with dust, boulders, and craters. Solar radiation can break down material directly or

by heating and cooling a surface. Broken material can slide downhill, even on a small asteroid. What other processes do you think might act on small and medium-sized bodies in space?

Pluto and most objects in the outer solar system are made of ice and rock.

READING TiP

The name of Earth's satellite is the Moon, but the word *moon* is also used to refer to other satellites.

The materials in a space body depend on where it formed. The disk of material that became the solar system was cold around the outside and hottest in the center, where the Sun was forming. Far from the center, chemicals such as carbon dioxide, ammonia, and water were frozen solid. These ices became part of the material that formed bodies in the outer solar system. Bodies that formed near the center of the solar system are made mostly of rock and metal. Bodies that formed far from the center are mostly ice with some rock and a little metal.

Some of the bodies had enough mass to become rounded. Some even melted and formed cores, mantles, and crusts. Many of these bodies have mountains and valleys, volcanoes, and even winds and clouds. The processes at work on Earth also affect other space bodies.

CHECK YOUR READING What do the proportions of ice, rock, and metal show about a space object?

Pluto and Charon

Many space bodies of ice and rock orbit the Sun at the distance of Neptune and beyond. Since 1992, scientists have been using sophisticated equipment to find and study these bodies. However, one body has been known since 1930. Because Pluto was discovered decades before the other objects, it is considered one of the nine major planets.

Pluto is the smallest of the nine planets. It is smaller than the Moon. Pluto's mass is less than 0.3 percent of Earth's mass, so its gravitational pull is weak. However, Pluto is round and probably has a core, mantle, and crust. Pluto also has a thin atmosphere. No spacecraft has passed close to Pluto, so scientists do not have clear images of the planet's surface.

 CHECK YOUR READING Why do scientists know less about Pluto than about other planets?

Pluto's moon, Charon, has a diameter half that of Pluto and a mass about 15 percent of Pluto's. Because Pluto and Charon orbit each other, they are sometimes called a double planet. Just as the Moon always has the same side facing Earth, Pluto and Charon always keep the same sides turned toward each other.

Pluto and Charon also move together around the Sun. Pluto's path around the Sun is not as round as the orbits of the rest of the planets, so its distance from the Sun changes a lot as it orbits. Pluto gets closer to the Sun than Neptune's distance of 30 AU. At the other side of its orbit, Pluto is about 50 AU from the Sun. Pluto's orbit is at an angle with respect to Neptune's, as you can see in the diagram below, so the two paths do not cross and the planets will not collide.

Pluto

This map of Pluto's surface shows only bright and dark areas because Pluto is very distant from Earth and no spacecraft has been close enough to see Pluto's surface in detail.

Mass 0.2% Earth's mass
Diameter 18% Earth's diameter
Average distance from Sun 40 AU
Orbits in 248 Earth years
Rotates in 6 Earth days

Pluto and Charon's orbit

Neptune's orbit

As Pluto and Charon travel along their orbit, they sometimes get closer to the Sun than Neptune does.

Moons of Gas Giants

RESOURCE CENTER
CLASSZONE.COM

Learn more about the different moons of giant planets.

Each giant planet has a system of moons. Six of the moons are larger than Pluto. Their features are formed by the same processes that shape the terrestrial planets. Saturn's largest moon, Titan, has a dense atmosphere of nitrogen, as Earth does, although a haze hides Titan's surface. Neptune's largest moon, Triton, has a thin atmosphere and ice volcanoes. Jupiter has four large moons—Io, Europa, Ganymede, and Callisto. Io (EYE-oh) is dotted with volcanoes, which continue to erupt, so Io has few impact craters. Europa (yu-ROH-puh) has long ridges where the crust has been pushed and pulled by the material beneath it. The outer two moons have craters over most of their surfaces.

The other moons of the gas giants are all smaller than Pluto, with diameters ranging from about 1600 kilometers (1000 mi) down to just a few kilometers. The smallest moons have irregular shapes, and some may be bodies that were captured into orbit.

CHECK YOUR READING What processes are at work on the largest moons?

Some Moons of Gas Giants

Moons in the outer solar system are shaped by the same processes that produce features on the terrestrial planets.

Saturn's moon **Titan** has a dense atmosphere of cold nitrogen gas. A thick haze hides this moon's surface.

haze

Jupiter's moon **Europa** has a crust of frozen water shaped by tectonics. Warm material below has broken the crust into many pieces.

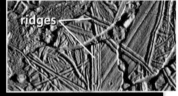

ridges

Neptune's moon **Triton** has dark streaks that show where ice volcanoes have erupted. Winds in the thin atmosphere blow material to one side of an eruption.

ice volcano

streak

Jupiter's moon **Io** has a surface constantly being changed by volcanoes. New material covers the surface and then changes color over time.

volcano (color added)

 READING VISUALS Which images show volcanoes?

Asteroids and comets orbit the Sun.

Objects called asteroids and comets formed along with the Sun, planets, and moons. These objects still orbit the Sun at different distances. Most of the objects are much smaller than planets and had too little mass to become round. The objects that formed far from the Sun are made mostly of ice, with some rock and metal. The objects that formed closer to the Sun, where it was warmer, have little or no ice.

MAIN IDEA AND DETAILS
Remember to take notes to help you study later.

Asteroids

Small, solid, rocky bodies that orbit close to the Sun are called **asteroids.** They range from almost 1000 kilometers (600 mi) in diameter down to a kilometer or less. Except for the largest, their gravity is too weak to pull them into round spheres. Therefore, most asteroids have irregular shapes. Some asteroids are the broken pieces of larger, rounded asteroids.

Most asteroids have paths that keep them between the orbits of Mars and Jupiter. This huge region is called the asteroid belt, and contains more than 10,000 asteroids. However, the asteroids are so far apart that spacecraft from Earth have passed completely through the belt without danger of collision. The mass of all the asteroids put together is estimated to be less than the mass of our Moon.

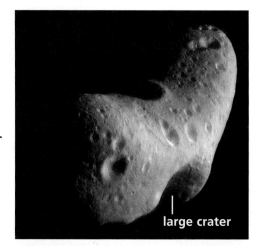

large crater

This asteroid is small compared with a planet, but it is large compared with a person. The large crater at the bottom is about the size of a small city.

The surfaces of asteroids are covered with craters, broken rock, and dust. Even though asteroids are far apart, smaller objects do hit them from time to time. Impacts from very long ago are still visible because most asteroids are not massive enough to have formed cores, mantles, and crusts. Therefore, they do not have volcanism or tectonics to erase the craters. Most asteroids do not have atmospheres, so their surfaces change only when impacts happen or when gravity pulls material downhill.

 CHECK YOUR READING   Why do asteroids have craters?

Some asteroids have collided with Earth in the past. The collisions left impact craters, some of which can still be seen today. Scientists have found evidence that an asteroid 10 kilometers (6 mi) in diameter hit Earth 65 million years ago. A cloud of dust from the collision spread around the world and probably affected surface temperatures. Many forms of life, including dinosaurs, died off at about that time, and the impact may have been part or all of the reason. Today astronomers are working to study all asteroids larger than 1 kilometer (0.6 mi) in diameter to determine whether any could hit Earth.

Comets

Sometimes, a fuzzy spot appears in the night sky. It grows from night to night as it changes position against the background stars. The fuzzy spot is a cloud of material, called a coma (KOH-muh), around a small space object. An object that produces a coma is called a **comet.** A comet without its coma is a small, icy object that is difficult to see even with a powerful telescope. Scientists use the number of comets that have become visible to infer that vast numbers of comets exist.

Comets formed far from the Sun, so they are made of different ices as well as rock and some metal. Their orbits are usually more oval than the paths of planets. A comet's orbit may carry it from regions far beyond Pluto's orbit to the inner solar system.

When a comet gets close to the Sun, solar radiation warms the surface and turns some of the ice into gas. A coma forms as the gas moves outward, often carrying dust with it. High-speed particles and radiation from the Sun push this material into one or more tails that can stretch for millions of kilometers. A comet's tails point away from the Sun no matter which way the comet is moving. The coma and tails look bright because sunlight shines on them, even though they may be less dense than Earth's atmosphere.

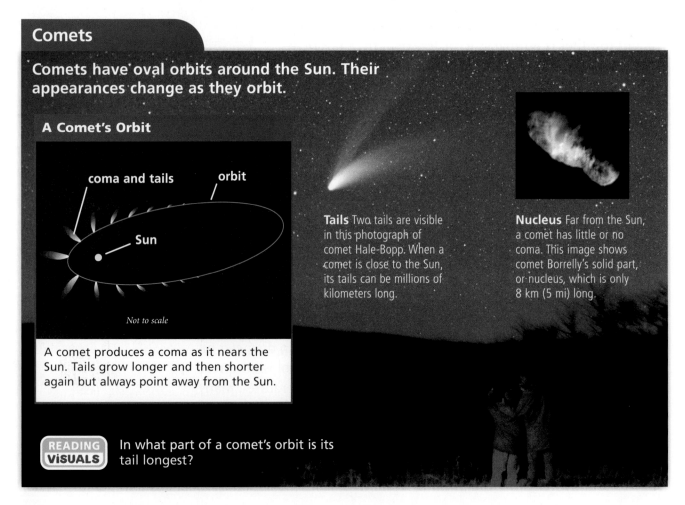

Comets

Comets have oval orbits around the Sun. Their appearances change as they orbit.

A Comet's Orbit

coma and tails   orbit

Sun

Not to scale

A comet produces a coma as it nears the Sun. Tails grow longer and then shorter again but always point away from the Sun.

Tails Two tails are visible in this photograph of comet Hale-Bopp. When a comet is close to the Sun, its tails can be millions of kilometers long.

Nucleus Far from the Sun, a comet has little or no coma. This image shows comet Borrelly's solid part, or nucleus, which is only 8 km (5 mi) long.

READING VISUALS In what part of a comet's orbit is its tail longest?

Most comets are too faint to be noticed easily from Earth. Many years can go by between appearances of bright comets, such as the one in the photograph on page 104.

in the photograph on page 104.

 CHECK YOUR READING What makes a comet visible?

Meteors and Meteorites

Earth collides constantly with particles in space. Earth orbits the Sun at about 100,000 kilometers per hour (70,000 mi/h), so these particles enter Earth's thin upper atmosphere at very high speeds. The particles and the air around them become hot enough to glow, producing brief streaks of light called **meteors.** You may be able to see a few meteors per hour on a clear, dark night. Several times during the year, Earth passes through a stream of orbiting particles left by a comet. In the resulting meteor shower, you can see many meteors per hour.

A meteor produced by a particle from a comet may last less than a second. Bits of rock or metal from asteroids may produce brighter, longer-lasting meteors. Rarely, a very bright meteor, called a fireball, lights up the sky for several seconds.

An object with greater mass, perhaps 10 grams or more, may not be destroyed by Earth's atmosphere. A **meteorite** is a space object that reaches Earth's surface. The outside of a meteorite is usually smooth from melting, but the inside may still be frozen. Most meteorites come from the asteroid belt, but a few are rocky fragments that have been blasted into space from the Moon and Mars.

This piece of iron is part of a huge meteorite. The energy of the impact melted the metal and changed its shape.

 CHECK YOUR READING What is the difference between a meteor and a meteorite?

3.4 Review

KEY CONCEPTS

1. How are Pluto and most moons of the gas giant planets similar?
2. List two differences between asteroids and comets.
3. What causes meteors?

CRITICAL THINKING

4. **Apply** Of the four types of processes that shape terrestrial worlds, which also shape the surfaces of moons of giant planets?
5. **Compare and Contrast** How is a comet different from a meteor?

⚠ CHALLENGE

6. **Predict** What do you think Pluto would look like if its orbit brought it close to the Sun?

CHAPTER INVESTIGATION

Exploring Impact Craters

DESIGN — YOUR OWN — **EXPERIMENT**

OVERVIEW AND PURPOSE Nearly 50,000 years ago, an asteroid plummeted through Earth's atmosphere and exploded near what is now Winslow, Arizona. The photograph at left shows the resulting impact crater, which is about 1.2 kilometers (0.7 mi) wide. Most of the other craters on Earth have been erased. However, some planets and most moons in the solar system have surfaces that are covered with craters. In this investigation you will

- use solid objects to make craters in a flour surface
- determine how one variable affects the resulting crater

▶ Problem

How does one characteristic of an impact or a colliding object affect the resulting crater?

▶ Hypothesize

Complete steps 1–5 before writing your problem statement and hypothesis. Once you have identified a variable to test, write a hypothesis to explain how changing this variable will affect the crater. Your hypothesis should take the form of an "If . . . , then . . . , because . . ." statement.

▶ Procedure

MATERIALS
- newspapers
- container
- flour
- colored powder
- several objects
- meter stick
- ruler
- balance

1. Place the container on newspapers and add flour to a depth of 2–4 cm. Stir the flour to break up any lumps, and then smooth the surface with a ruler. Sprinkle the top with colored powder.

2. Drop an object into the flour from waist height, then carefully remove it without disturbing the flour. Use the diagram to identify the various parts of the impact crater you made.

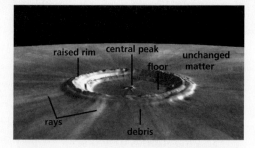

raised rim   central peak   unchanged matter
floor
rays   debris

3. To help you design your experiment, try several cratering methods. Make each new crater in a different location in the container. If your container becomes too full of craters, stir the flour, smooth it, and sprinkle on more colored powder.

4. Design an experiment to test the effects of a variable. Choose just one variable to change—the height, the size or mass of the object, or perhaps the fluffiness of the flour. Determine how much you need to change your variable in order to get results different enough to see.

5. Experiment to find some part of the crater that is affected by changing your variable, such as the depth, the size of the blanket of debris, or the number of rays. Design your experiment so that you measure the part of the crater that changes the most.

6. Write a specific problem statement by completing the question, How does _____ affect _____? Write a hypothesis to answer your problem statement.

7. Perform your experiment. Do not change any factors except your chosen variable.

8. Make several trials for each value of your variable, because there are some factors you cannot control.

9. Record measurements and other observations and make drawings as you go along.

▶ Observe and Analyze

Write It Up

1. **RECORD** Use a diagram to show how you measure the craters. Organize your data into a table. Include spaces for averages.

2. **IDENTIFY VARIABLES** List the variables and constants. The independent variable is the factor that you changed. The dependent variable is affected by this change. Use these definitions when you graph your results.

3. **CALCULATE** Determine averages by adding all of your measurements at each value of your independent variable, then dividing the sum by the number of measurements.

4. **GRAPH** Make a line graph of your average results. Place the independent variable on the horizontal axis and the dependent variable on the vertical axis. Why should you use a line graph instead of a bar graph for these data?

▶ Conclude

Write It Up

1. **ANALYZE** Answer your problem statement. Do your data support your hypothesis?

2. **EVALUATE** Did you identify a trend in your results? Is your experiment a failure if you did not identify a trend? Why or why not?

3. **IDENTIFY LIMITS** How would you modify the design of your experiment now that you have seen the results?

4. **APPLY** What do you think would happen if a colliding object hit water instead of land?

▶ INVESTIGATE Further

CHALLENGE How do the craters in this model differ from real impact craters? Design, but do not attempt, an experiment to simulate the cratering process more realistically.

Exploring Impact Craters
Problem How does _____ affect _____?
Hypothesize
Observe and Analyze
Table 1. Data and Averages

Conclude

Chapter Review

the BIG idea

Planets and other objects form a system around our Sun.

CONTENT REVIEW
CLASSZONE.COM

◀ KEY CONCEPTS SUMMARY

 Planets orbit the Sun at different distances.

The planets have different sizes and distances from the Sun. The solar system formed from a disk of dust and gas. Massive objects became round.

inner solar system
Mercury, Venus, Earth, Mars, asteroids

outer solar system
Jupiter, Saturn, Uranus, Neptune, Pluto, comets

VOCABULARY
astronomical unit
 (AU) p. 81
ellipse p. 81

 The inner solar system has rocky planets.

- The terrestrial planets are round and have layers.
- Atmospheres came from volcanoes and impacts.
- Four processes produce surface features.

         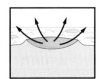

tectonics   volcanism   weathering   impact cratering
                                   and erosion

VOCABULARY
terrestrial planet p. 85
tectonics p. 86
volcanism p. 86

 The outer solar system has four giant planets.

- The gas giants have very dense, deep atmospheres with layers of clouds.
- All four giant planets have ring systems.

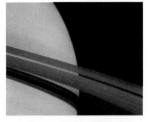

Close-up of Saturn's rings

VOCABULARY
gas giant p. 94
ring p. 97

Small objects are made of ice and rock.

- Objects in the inner solar system are rocky.
- Pluto and most other objects in the outer solar system are made of ice and rock.
- Rocky asteroids and icy comets orbit the Sun and produce tiny fragments that may become meteors.

The asteroid Eros

VOCABULARY
asteroid p. 103
comet p. 104
meteor p. 105
meteorite p. 105

Reviewing Vocabulary

Make a Venn diagram for each pair of terms. Put an important similarity in the overlapping part. Use the rest of the diagram to show an important difference.

Example:

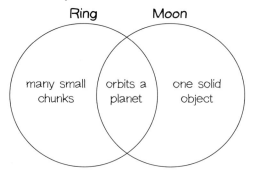

Ring   Moon

many small chunks | orbits a planet | one solid object

1. terrestrial planet, gas giant

2. volcanism, impact cratering

3. erosion, tectonics

4. asteroid, comet

5. meteor, meteorite

6. comet, meteor

Reviewing Key Concepts

Multiple Choice *Choose the letter of the best answer.*

7. Even though orbits are ellipses, what shape is a typical planet's orbit most like?
   a. a short rectangle
   b. an egg-shape with a pointy end
   c. a long, narrow oval
   d. a circle

8. How is a moon different from a planet?
   a. A moon is smaller than any planet.
   b. A moon is less massive than any planet.
   c. A moon is in orbit around a planet.
   d. A moon is unable to have an atmosphere.

9. Which of these appears in Earth's atmosphere?
   a. a moon   **c.** a meteor
   b. an asteroid   **d.** a comet

10. How did planets and other objects in the solar system form?
    a. After the Sun formed, it threw off hot pieces that spun and cooled.
    b. The Sun captured objects that formed in other places in the galaxy.
    c. Two stars collided, and the broken pieces went into orbit around the Sun.
    d. Material in a disk formed large clumps as the Sun formed in the center of the disk.

11. Which process occurs only when a small space object interacts with a larger space body?
    a. tectonics   **c.** erosion
    b. volcanism   **d.** impact cratering

12. Which processes occur because a planet or another space body is hot inside?
    a. tectonics and volcanism
    b. volcanism and erosion
    c. erosion and impact cratering
    d. impact cratering and tectonics

13. What do all four gas giants have that terrestrial planets do not have?
    a. atmospheres   **c.** moons
    b. solid surfaces   **d.** rings

14. What are the white stripes of Jupiter and the white spots of Neptune?
    a. clouds high in the atmosphere
    b. smoke from volcanoes
    c. continents and islands
    d. holes in the atmosphere

Short Answer *Write a short answer to each question.*

15. The solid part of a comet is small in comparison with a planet. However, sometimes a comet appears to be larger than the Sun. What makes it seem so large?

16. Why do all nine major planets orbit the Sun in the same direction?

Use the image of Jupiter's moon Ganymede to answer the next five questions.

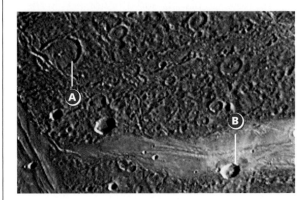

17. OBSERVE Which crater, A or B, is more eroded? Explain why you think so.

18. COMPARE AND CONTRAST Describe the differences between the surface in the upper half of the image and the long, triangular area near the bottom of the image.

19. INFER Explain which area of the surface, the smooth part or the heavily cratered part, is probably older.

20. APPLY The lighter area was produced by tectonic processes and may have been covered with molten material. What can you infer about the inside of this moon?

21. SEQUENCE A crack runs through part of crater A. Explain how you can tell whether the crack or the crater formed first. **Hint:** Think about what would have happened if the other feature had formed first.

22. PREDICT Suppose the Moon were hotter inside. How might its surface be different?

23. IDENTIFY CAUSE Mercury's surface is not as hot as Venus's, even though Mercury is closer to the Sun. In addition, the night side of Mercury gets very cold, while the night side of Venus is about as hot as the day side. Why are the temperature patterns on these two planets so different?

24. EVALUATE Would it be easier to design a lander mission for the surface of Venus or the surface of Mercury? Explain your reasoning.

25. INFER Some comets orbit in a direction opposite to that of the planets. Why might this make some scientists wonder if they formed with the rest of the solar system?

26. HYPOTHESIZE Scientists calculate the mass of a planet from the effects of its gravity on other objects, such as moons. However, Mercury and Venus have no moons. What other objects in space could have been used to determine the planets' masses?

27. COMPARE AND CONTRAST Images of Earth from space show white clouds above darker land and water. In what ways are they like and unlike images of Jupiter?

Earth   **Jupiter**

28. ANALYZE Scientists sometimes use round numbers to compare quantities. For example, a scientist might say that the Sun's diameter is about 100 times Earth's diameter, even though she knows that the precise value is 109 times. Why might she use such an approximation?

the BIG idea

29. APPLY Look back at pages 76–77. Think about the answer you gave to the question about the large image of a planet and moon. How would you answer this question differently now?

30. SYNTHESIZE Ice is generally less dense than rock, which is generally less dense than metal. Use what you know about materials in the solar system to estimate whether a moon of Mars, a moon of Uranus, or the planet Mercury should be the least dense.

UNIT PROJECTS

Check your schedule for your unit project. How are you doing? Be sure that you have placed data or notes from your research in your project folder.

Interpreting a Passage

Read the following passage. Then answer the questions that follow.

Life in Extreme Environments

Could living organisms survive in the crushing, hot atmosphere of Venus? Could they thrive on a waterless asteroid or get their energy from tides in the dark ocean that might be beneath the surface of Europa? Scientists are looking for answers to these questions right here on Earth. They study extremophiles, which are life forms that can survive in extreme environments—very high or low temperatures or other difficult conditions. These environments have conditions similar to those on other planets, and those on moons, asteroids, and comets.

Scientists have found tiny organisms that grow in the scalding water of hot vents on the ocean floor, deep inside rock, and in miniature ponds within glaciers. Scientists have also found organisms that were dormant because they were frozen solid for thousands of years but that were still capable of living and growing after warming up. By studying extremophiles, scientists learn more about the conditions needed to support life.

Choose from the following four environments to answer each of the next three questions.

- the dark ocean that might be underneath Europa's surface
- the flood channels on Mars, which have been dry and frozen for a long time
- the very hot, high-pressure environment of Venus
- the dry rock of an asteroid that alternately heats and cools

1. Some organisms survive deep underwater, where photosynthesis does not occur because little or no sunlight reaches those depths. Which environment can these organisms teach about?

   a. under Europa's surface   **c.** Venus

   b. Martian flood channels   **d.** an asteroid

2. Some organisms survive in very deep cracks in rocks, where they are protected from changing temperatures. Where else might scientists look for these types of organisms?

   a. under Europa's surface   **c.** Venus

   b. Martian flood channels   **d.** an asteroid

3. Where might scientists look for tiny organisms that are dormant but that might revive if given warmth and water?

   a. under Europa's surface   **c.** Venus

   b. Martian flood channels   **d.** an asteroid

4. Where, outside Earth, should scientists look for tiny ponds of water within solid ice?

   a. the other terrestrial planets

   b. the gas giants

   c. small space objects in the inner solar system

   d. small space objects in the outer solar system

Extended Response

Answer the two questions in detail.

5. A class was given a sample of ordinary dormant, dry yeast that had been exposed to an extreme environment. Describe ways the students might test the yeast to see if it remained undamaged, or even survived, the conditions.

6. Imagine that scientists have found extremophiles in clouds of frozen water crystals high in Earth's atmosphere. How might this discovery affect a search for organisms on the gas giants?

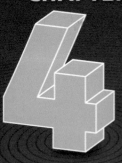

4

Stars, Galaxies, and the Universe

the **BIG** idea

Our Sun is one of billions of stars in one of billions of galaxies in the universe.

What could be present in the light and dark areas in this galaxy?

Key Concepts

SECTION

4.1 **The Sun is our local star.**
Learn how the Sun produces energy and about the Sun's layers and features.

SECTION

4.2 **Stars change over their life cycles.**
Learn how stars form and change.

SECTION

4.3 **Galaxies have different sizes and shapes.**
Learn how galaxies are classified.

SECTION

4.4 **The universe is expanding.**
Learn about the formation and expansion of the universe.

Internet Preview

CLASSZONE.COM

Chapter 4 online resources:
Visualization, Simulation,
three Resource Centers,
Math Tutorial, Test Practice

EXPLORE (the BIG idea)

How Can Stars Differ?

Look at the sky at night and find three stars that differ in appearance. Try to identify the locations of these stars, using the star maps in the Appendix at the back of this book.

Observe and Think
How did the characteristics of the stars differ?

How Do Galaxies Move Apart?

Blow air into a balloon until it is partially inflated. Use a felt-tip pen to make 12 dots on the round end. Then stand in front of a mirror and observe the dots as you completely inflate the balloon.

Observe and Think What caused the dots to move apart? What might cause galaxies to move apart in the universe?

Internet Activity: Galaxy Shapes

Go to **ClassZone.com** to explore the different shapes of galaxies in the universe.

Observe and Think How do the types of galaxies differ from one another?

NSTA
scilinks.org
SCiLINKS

The Sun Code: MDL060

Getting Ready to Learn

◀ CONCEPT REVIEW

- Electromagnetic radiation carries information about space.
- Our solar system is in the Milky Way galaxy.
- A galaxy is a group of millions or billions of stars.

◀ VOCABULARY REVIEW

solar system p. 10

galaxy p. 10

universe p. 10

electromagnetic radiation p. 15

wavelength p. 16

CONTENT REVIEW
CLASSZONE.COM
Review concepts and vocabulary.

▶ TAKING NOTES

CHOOSE YOUR OWN STRATEGY

Take notes using one or more of the strategies from earlier chapters—**main idea web, combination notes,** or **main idea and details.** Feel free to mix and match the strategies, or use an entirely different note-taking strategy.

VOCABULARY STRATEGY

Place each vocabulary term at the center of a **description wheel** diagram. Write some words describing it on the spokes.

See the Note-Taking Handbook on pages R45–R51.

SCIENCE NOTEBOOK

Main Idea Web

Combination Notes

Main Idea and Details

very low density

seen only during eclipse

extends outward several million km

CORONA

outer layer of Sun's atmosphere

uneven shape

The Sun is our local star.

BEFORE, you learned

- There are different wavelengths of electromagnetic radiation
- The Sun provides light in the solar system

NOW, you will learn

- How the Sun produces energy
- How energy flows through the Sun's layers
- About solar features and solar wind

VOCABULARY

fusion p. 116
convection p. 116
corona p. 116
sunspot p. 118
solar wind p. 119

EXPLORE Solar Atmosphere

How can blocking light reveal dim features?

PROCEDURE

1. Unbend the paper clip and use it to make a tiny hole in the center of the card.

2. Turn on the lamp, and briefly try to read the writing on the bulb.

3. Close one eye, and hold the card in front of your other eye. Through the hole, try to read the writing on the bulb.

WHAT DO YOU THINK?

- How did looking through the hole affect your view of the writing?
- How might a solar eclipse affect your view of the Sun's dim outermost layer?

MATERIALS

- small paper clip
- index card
- lamp with 45-watt bulb

The Sun produces energy from hydrogen.

MAIN IDEA AND DETAILS
You could record information about the Sun by using a main idea and details table.

The Sun is the only star in our solar system. Astronomers have been able to study the Sun in more detail than other stars because it is much closer to Earth. As a result, they have learned a great deal about its size and composition and the way it produces energy.

The Sun is far larger than any of the planets. It contains 99.9 percent of the mass of the entire solar system. For comparison, imagine that Earth had the mass of a sparrow; then the Sun would have the mass of an elephant.

The Sun consists mostly of hydrogen gas. Energy is produced when hydrogen in the Sun's interior turns into helium. This energy is the source of light and warmth that make life possible on Earth.

Energy flows through the Sun's layers.

Although the Sun is made entirely of gas, it does have a structure. Energy produced in the center of the Sun flows out through the Sun's layers in different forms, including visible light.

The Sun's Interior

The Sun's interior generally becomes cooler and less dense as you move away from the center.

REMINDER

Remember that radiation is energy that travels across distances as electromagnetic waves.

1 Core The center of the Sun, called the core, is made of very dense gas. Temperatures reach about 15 million degrees Celsius. Under these extreme conditions, some hydrogen particles collide and combine to form helium in a process called **fusion.** The process releases energy that travels through the core by radiation.

2 Radiative Zone Energy from the core moves by radiation through a thick layer called the radiative zone. Although this layer is very hot and dense, conditions in the radiative zone are not extreme enough for fusion to occur.

3 Convection Zone In the convection zone, energy moves mainly by convection. **Convection** is the transfer of energy from place to place by the motion of heated gas or liquid. Rising currents of hot gas in the convection zone carry energy toward the Sun's surface.

 CHECK YOUR READING   Where does the Sun's energy come from?

The Sun's Atmosphere

SIMULATION
CLASSZONE.COM

View the Sun at different wavelengths.

The Sun's outer layers are called its atmosphere. These layers are much less dense than the interior. The atmosphere generally becomes hotter and less dense as you move outward.

4 Photosphere Visible light moves by radiation out into space from the photosphere. It takes about eight minutes for the light to reach Earth. Since the photosphere is the layer you see in photographs of the Sun, it is often called the Sun's surface. Convection currents beneath the photosphere cause it to have a bumpy texture.

5 Chromosphere The chromosphere is the thin middle layer of the Sun's atmosphere. It gives off a pinkish light.

6 Corona The Sun's outermost layer is called the **corona.** The corona, which varies in shape, extends outward several million kilometers. Both the chromosphere and the corona are much hotter than the photosphere. However, they have such low densities that you can see their light only during a total eclipse of the Sun, when the Moon blocks the much brighter light from the photosphere.

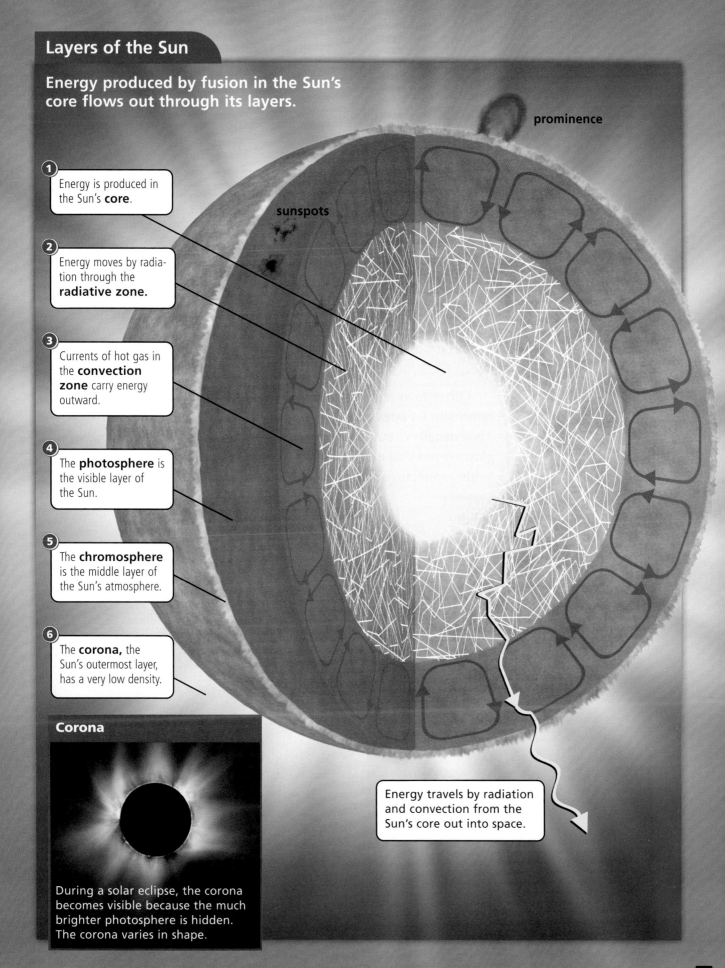

Layers of the Sun

Energy produced by fusion in the Sun's core flows out through its layers.

prominence

sunspots

1 Energy is produced in the Sun's **core**.

2 Energy moves by radiation through the **radiative zone**.

3 Currents of hot gas in the **convection zone** carry energy outward.

4 The **photosphere** is the visible layer of the Sun.

5 The **chromosphere** is the middle layer of the Sun's atmosphere.

6 The **corona,** the Sun's outermost layer, has a very low density.

Energy travels by radiation and convection from the Sun's core out into space.

Corona

During a solar eclipse, the corona becomes visible because the much brighter photosphere is hidden. The corona varies in shape.

Features on the Sun

Astronomers have observed features on the Sun that vary over time. Near the Sun's surface there are regions of magnetic force called magnetic fields. These magnetic fields get twisted into different positions as the Sun rotates. Features appear on the surface in areas where strong magnetic fields are located.

Sunspots are spots on the photosphere that are cooler than surrounding areas. Although they appear dark, sunspots are actually bright. They only seem dim because the rest of the photosphere is so much brighter.

Sunspot activity follows a pattern that lasts about 11 years. At the peak of the cycle, dozens of sunspots may appear. During periods of low activity, there may not be any sunspots.

Sunspots move across the Sun's surface as it rotates. Astronomers first realized that the Sun rotates when they noticed this movement. Because the Sun is not solid, some parts rotate faster than others.

Other solar features include flares and prominences (PRAHM-uh-nuhn-sihz). Flares are eruptions of hot gas from the Sun's surface. They usually occur near sunspots. Prominences are huge loops of glowing gas that extend into the corona. They occur where magnetic fields connecting sunspots soar into the outer atmosphere.

 CHECK YOUR READING How are sunspots different from other areas of the photosphere?

Solar Features

Features on the Sun appear in areas where a magnetic field is strong.

Sunspots

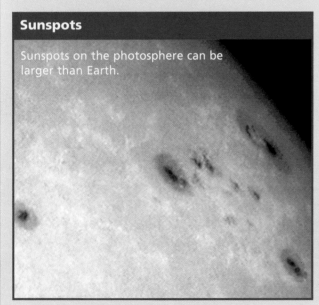

Sunspots on the photosphere can be larger than Earth.

Prominences

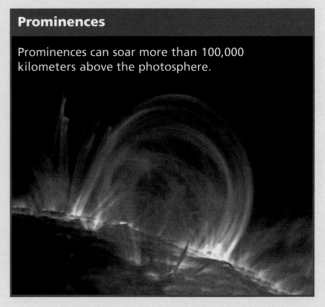

Prominences can soar more than 100,000 kilometers above the photosphere.

Solar Wind

Material in the Sun's corona is continually streaming out into space. The electrically charged particles that flow out in all directions from the corona are called the **solar wind.** The solar wind extends throughout our solar system.

This circular green aurora occurred over Alaska when particles from the solar wind entered the atmosphere.

Most of the solar wind flowing toward Earth is safely guided around the planet by Earth's magnetic field. When solar-wind particles do enter the upper atmosphere, they release energy, which can produce beautiful patterns of glowing light in the sky. Such displays of light are called auroras (uh-RAWR-uhz), or the northern and southern lights. Auroras often occur near the poles.

Earth's atmosphere usually prevents charged particles from reaching the surface. However, during the peak of the sunspot cycle, flares and other kinds of solar activity release strong bursts of charged particles into the solar wind. These bursts, called magnetic storms, can disrupt electric-power delivery across large regions by causing surges in power lines. They can also interfere with radio communication.

Magnetic storms are much more harmful above the protective layers of Earth's atmosphere. Bursts of particles in the solar wind can damage or destroy orbiting satellites. The solar wind also poses a danger to astronauts during space flights.

  What causes auroras to form?

4.1 Review

KEY CONCEPTS

1. How does the Sun produce energy?
2. How does energy move from the Sun's core to the photosphere?
3. How does the solar wind normally affect Earth?

CRITICAL THINKING

4. **Analyze** Why is the core the only layer of the Sun where energy is produced?
5. **Compare and Contrast** Make a diagram comparing sunspots, flares, and prominences.

△ CHALLENGE

6. **Infer** A communications satellite stops working while in orbit, and a surge in an electric power line causes blackouts in cities across a large region. What probably happened in the Sun's atmosphere shortly before these events?

CHAPTER INVESTIGATION

Temperature, Brightness, and Color

OVERVIEW AND PURPOSE Think of the metal heating surface on a hot plate. How can you tell whether the hot plate is fully heated? Is the metal surface brighter or dimmer than when it is just starting to get warm? Does the color of the surface change as the hot plate gets hotter? You may already have an idea of how temperature, brightness, and color are related—at least when it comes to heated metal. Do the same relationships apply to electric lights? to stars? This investigation is designed to help you find out. You will

- construct a wax photometer to compare the brightnesses and colors of different light sources
- determine how the temperature of a light source affects its brightness and color

▶ Problem

How are brightness and color related to temperature?

▶ Hypothesize

Write a hypothesis to explain how brightness and color are related to temperature. Your hypothesis should take the form of an "If . . . , then . . . , because . . ." statement.

▶ Procedure

1. An instrument called a photometer makes it easier to compare the brightnesses and colors of different light sources. Assemble the wax photometer as shown on page 121. The aluminum foil between the wax blocks should be folded so that the shiny side faces out on both sides.

2. Hold the photometer so that you can see both blocks. Bring it to different locations in the classroom, and observe how the brightnesses and colors of the blocks change as the two sides of the photometer are exposed to different light conditions.

3. Tape a piece of copper wire to each end of a battery, and connect the wires to a light-bulb holder. The battery will provide electricity to heat up the wire inside a light bulb.

MATERIALS

- 2 paraffin blocks
- aluminum foil
- 2 rubber bands
- 2 light-bulb holders
- 2 miniature light bulbs
- 3 AA batteries
- 4 pieces of uninsulated copper wire 15 cm long
- masking tape
for Challenge:
- incandescent lamp
- dimmer switch

step 3

4. Tape the negative terminal, or flat end, of one battery to the positive terminal of another battery. Tape a piece of copper wire to each end, and connect the wires to a light-bulb holder. Because two batteries will provide electricity to the bulb in this holder, the wire in the bulb will be hotter than the wire in the bulb powered by one battery.

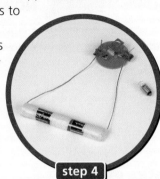
step 4

5. With the room darkened, insert a bulb into each light-bulb holder. If the bulb connected to two batteries does not light up, you may need to press the two batteries together with your fingers.

6. Place the photometer halfway between the two light bulbs. Compare the brightnesses of the two light sources. Record your observations in your **Science Notebook.**

7. Move the photometer closer to the cooler bulb until both sides of the photometer are equally bright. Compare the colors of the two light sources. Record your observations in your **Science Notebook**. To avoid draining the batteries, remove the bulbs from the holders when you have completed this step.

step 6

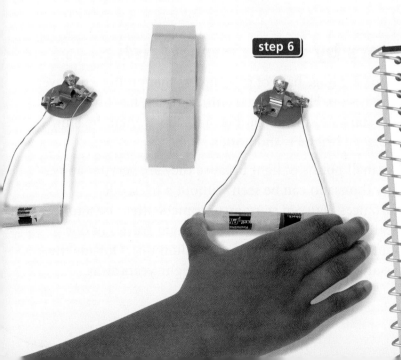

▶ Observe and Analyze
Write It Up

1. **RECORD OBSERVATIONS** Draw the setup of your photometer and light sources. Be sure your data table is complete with descriptions of brightness and color.

2. **IDENTIFY** Identify the variables in this experiment. List them in your **Science Notebook.**

▶ Conclude
Write It Up

1. **INTERPRET** Answer the question in the problem. Compare your results with your hypothesis.

2. **ANALYZE** How does distance affect your perception of the brightness of an object?

3. **APPLY** Judging by the results of the investigation, would you expect a red star or a yellow star to be hotter? Explain why.

▶ INVESTIGATE Further

CHALLENGE Connect an incandescent lamp to a dimmer switch. Write a procedure to show how you would use a photometer to show the relationship between the color and the temperature of the bulb as it fades from brightest to dimmest. Then carry out your procedure.

Temperature, Brightness, and Color
Observe and Analyze
Table 1. Properties of Light from Two Sources

	Cooler Bulb (one battery)	Warmer Bulb (two batteries)
Brightness		
Color		

Chapter 4: **Stars, Galaxies, and the Universe** 121 **E**

Stars change over their life cycles.

◀ BEFORE, you learned

- The Sun is our local star
- The other stars are outside our solar system
- There are huge distances between objects in the universe

▶ NOW, you will learn

- How stars are classified
- How stars form and change

VOCABULARY

light-year p. 122
parallax p. 123
nebula p. 125
main sequence p. 126
neutron star p. 126
black hole p. 126

EXPLORE Characteristics of Stars

How does distance affect brightness?

PROCEDURE

① In a darkened room, shine a flashlight onto a dark surface from 30 cm away while your partner shines a flashlight onto the surface from the same distance. Observe the two spots of light.

② Move one of the flashlights back 15 cm and then another 15 cm. Compare the two spots of light each time you move the flashlight.

MATERIALS
- 2 flashlights
- meter stick
- dark surface

WHAT DO YOU THINK?
- How did distance affect the brightness of the light on the dark surface?
- How does the distance of a star from Earth affect our view of it?

MAIN IDEA WEB
A main idea web would be a good choice for taking notes about the characteristics of stars.

We classify stars by their characteristics.

Like our Sun, all stars are huge balls of glowing gas that produce or have produced energy by fusion. However, stars differ in size, brightness, and temperature. Some stars are smaller, fainter, and cooler than the Sun. Others are much bigger, brighter, and hotter.

Stars look like small points of light because they are very far away. At most, only a few thousand can be seen without a telescope. To describe the distances between stars, astronomers often use a unit called the light-year. A **light-year** is the distance light travels in one year, which is about 9.5 trillion kilometers (6 trillion mi). Outside the solar system, the star closest to Earth is about 4 light-years away.

Brightness and Distance

If you look at stars, you will probably notice that some appear to be brighter than others. The amount of light a star gives off and its distance from Earth determine how bright it appears to an observer. A star that gives off a huge amount of light can appear faint if it is far away. On the other hand, a star that gives off much less light can appear bright if it is closer to Earth. Therefore, to determine the true brightness of a star, astronomers must measure its distance from Earth.

One way astronomers measure distance is by using **parallax,** which is the apparent shift in the position of an object when viewed from different locations. Look at an object with your right eye closed. Now quickly open it and close your left eye. The object will seem to move slightly because you are viewing it from a different angle. The same kind of shift occurs when astronomers view stars from different locations.

To measure the parallax of a star, astronomers plot the star's position in the sky from opposite sides of Earth's orbit around the Sun. They then use the apparent shift in position and the diameter of Earth's orbit to calculate the star's distance.

 CHECK YOUR READING What factors affect how bright a star appears from Earth?

INVESTIGATE Parallax

How does the distance of an object affect parallax?

PROCEDURE

1. Stand 1 m away from a classmate. Have the classmate hold up a meter stick at eye level.

2. With your left eye closed, hold a capped pen up close to your face. Look at the pen with your right eye, and line it up with the zero mark on the meter stick. Then open your left eye and quickly close your right eye. Observe how many centimeters the pen seems to move. Record your observation.

3. Repeat step 2 with the pen held at arm's length and then with the pen held at half your arm's length. Record your observation each time.

WHAT DO YOU THINK?

• How many centimeters did the pen appear to move each time you observed it?

• How is parallax affected when you change the distance of the pen from you?

CHALLENGE How could you use this method to estimate distances that you cannot measure directly?

SKILL FOCUS
Measuring

MATERIALS
• meter stick
• capped pen

TIME
10 minutes

Size

It is hard to get a sense of how large stars are from viewing them in the sky. Even the Sun, which is much closer than any other star, is far larger than its appearance suggests. The diameter of the Sun is about 100 times greater than that of Earth. A jet plane flying 800 kilometers per hour (500 mi/h) would travel around Earth's equator in about two days. If you could travel around the Sun's equator at the same speed, the trip would take more than seven months.

Some stars are much larger than the Sun. Giant and supergiant stars range from ten to hundreds of times larger. A supergiant called Betelgeuse (BEET-uhl-JOOZ) is more than 600 times greater in diameter than the Sun. If Betelgeuse replaced the Sun, it would fill space in our solar system well beyond Earth's orbit. Because giant and supergiant stars have such huge surface areas to give off light, they are very bright. Betelgeuse is one of the brightest stars in the sky, even though it is 522 light-years away.

There are also stars much smaller than the Sun. Stars called white dwarfs are about 100 times smaller in diameter than the Sun, or roughly the size of Earth. White dwarfs cannot be seen without a telescope.

A star the size of the Sun
Diameter = 1.4 million kilometers (900,000 mi)

White dwarf
1/100 the Sun's diameter

Giant star
10–100 times the Sun's diameter

Supergiant star
100–1000 times the Sun's diameter

Color and Temperature

If you observe stars closely, you may notice that they vary slightly in color. Most stars look white. However, a few appear slightly blue or red. The differences in color are due to differences in temperature.

You can see how temperature affects color by heating up metal. For example, if you turn on a toaster, the metal coils inside will start to glow a dull red. As they get hotter, the coils will turn a brighter orange. The illustration on page 125 shows changes in the color of a metal bar as it heats up.

Like the color of heated metal, the color of a star indicates its temperature. Astronomers group stars into classes by color and surface temperature. The chart on page 125 lists the color and temperature range of each class of star. The coolest stars are red. The hottest stars are blue-white. Our Sun—a yellow, G-class star—has a surface temperature of about 6000°C.

Stars of every class give off light that is made up of a range of colors. Astronomers can spread a star's light into a spectrum to learn about the star's composition. The colors and lines in a spectrum reveal which gases are present in the star's outer layers.

 CHECK YOUR READING How does a star's temperature affect its appearance?

Color and Temperature

Objects that radiate light change color as they heat up.

Classification of Stars		
Class	Color	Surface Temperature (°C)
O	blue-white	above 25,000
B	blue-white	10,000–25,000
A	white	7500–10,000
F	yellow-white	6000–7500
G	yellow	5000–6000
K	orange	3500–5000
M	red	below 3500

Stars are classified according to their colors and temperatures. The Sun is a G-class star.

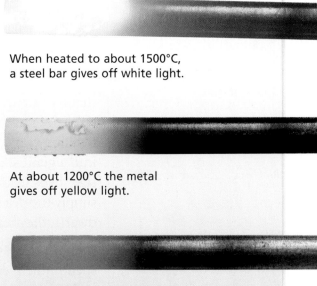

When heated to about 1500°C, a steel bar gives off white light.

At about 1200°C the metal gives off yellow light.

A steel bar glows red when heated to about 600°C.

Stars have life cycles.

Although stars last for very long periods, they are not permanent. Like living organisms, stars go through cycles of birth, maturity, and death. The life cycle of a star varies, depending on the mass of the star. Higher-mass stars develop more quickly than lower-mass stars. Toward the end of their life cycles, higher-mass stars also behave differently from lower-mass stars.

Stars form inside a cloud of gas and dust called a **nebula** (NEHB-yuh-luh). Gravity pulls gas and dust closer together in some regions of a nebula. As the matter contracts, it forms a hot, dense sphere. The sphere becomes a star if its center grows hot and dense enough for fusion to occur.

When a star dies, its matter does not disappear. Some of it may form a nebula or move into an existing one. There, the matter may eventually become part of new stars.

Colors have been added to this photograph of the Omega Nebula in order to bring out details.

CHECK YOUR READING How is gravity involved in the formation of stars?

Stages in the Life Cycles of Stars

RESOURCE CENTER
CLASSZONE.COM

Learn more about life
cycles of stars.

The diagram on page 127 shows the stages that stars go through in their life cycles. Notice that the length of a cycle and the way a star changes depend on the mass of the star at its formation.

Lower-Mass Stars The stage in which stars produce energy through the fusion of hydrogen into helium is called the **main sequence.** Because they use their fuel slowly, lower-mass stars can remain in the main-sequence stage for billions of years. The Sun has been a main-sequence star for 4.6 billion years and will remain one for about another 5 billion years. When a lower-mass star runs out of hydrogen, it expands into a giant star, in which helium fuses into carbon. Over time a giant star sheds its outer layers and becomes a white dwarf. A white dwarf is simply the dead core of a giant star. Although no fusion occurs in white dwarfs, they remain hot for billions of years.

Higher-Mass Stars Stars more than eight times as massive as our Sun spend much less time in the main-sequence stage because they use their fuel rapidly. After millions of years, a higher-mass star expands to become a supergiant star. In the core of a supergiant, fusion produces heavier and heavier elements. When an iron core forms, fusion stops and gravity causes the core to collapse. Then part of the core bounces outward, and the star erupts in an explosion called a supernova.

For a brief period, a supernova can give off as much light as a galaxy. The outer layers of the exploded star shoot out into space, carrying with them heavy elements that formed inside the star. Eventually this matter may become part of new stars and planets.

Neutron Stars and Black Holes

The collapsed core of a supergiant star may form an extremely dense body called a **neutron star.** Neutron stars measure only about 20 kilometers (12 mi) in diameter, but their masses are one to three times that of the Sun.

Neutron stars emit little visible light. However, they strongly emit other forms of radiation, such as x-rays. Some neutron stars emit beams of radio waves as they spin. These stars are called pulsars because they seem to pulse as the beams rotate.

Sometimes a supernova leaves behind a core with a mass more than three times that of the Sun. In such a case, the core does not end up as a neutron star. Instead, it collapses even further, forming an invisible object called a **black hole.** The gravity of a black hole is so strong that no form of radiation can escape from it.

A pulsar emits beams of radio waves as it spins rapidly. The pulsar seems to pulse as the beams rotate toward and away from Earth.

 CHECK YOUR READING How do lower-mass stars differ from higher-mass stars after the main-sequence stage?

Life Cycles of Stars

A star forms inside a cloud of gas and dust called a nebula.
The life cycle of a star depends on its mass.

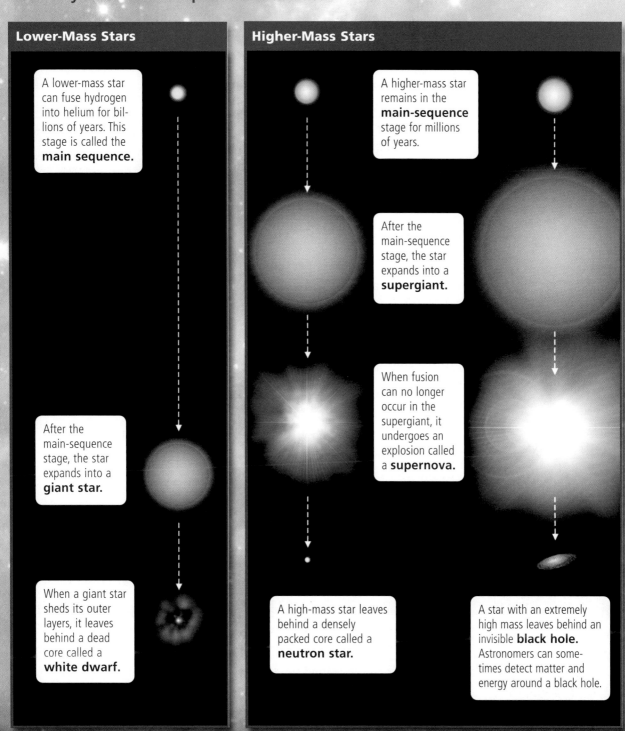

Lower-Mass Stars

A lower-mass star can fuse hydrogen into helium for billions of years. This stage is called the **main sequence.**

After the main-sequence stage, the star expands into a **giant star.**

When a giant star sheds its outer layers, it leaves behind a dead core called a **white dwarf.**

Higher-Mass Stars

A higher-mass star remains in the **main-sequence** stage for millions of years.

After the main-sequence stage, the star expands into a **supergiant.**

When fusion can no longer occur in the supergiant, it undergoes an explosion called a **supernova.**

A high-mass star leaves behind a densely packed core called a **neutron star.**

A star with an extremely high mass leaves behind an invisible **black hole.** Astronomers can sometimes detect matter and energy around a black hole.

READING VISUALS How do the stars shown in this illustration differ in the main-sequence stage of their life cycles?

Star Systems

Unlike our Sun, most stars do not exist alone. Instead, they are grouped with one or more companion stars. The stars are held together by the force of gravity between them. A binary star system consists of two stars that orbit each other. A multiple star system consists of more than two stars.

In many star systems, the stars are too close together to be seen individually. However, astronomers have developed ways of detecting such systems. For example, in a binary star system, one of the stars may orbit in front of the other when viewed from Earth. The star that orbits in front will briefly block some of the other star's light, providing a clue that more than one star is present. The illustration at right shows a binary star system that can be detected this way. Sometimes astronomers can also figure out whether a star is really a star system by studying its spectrum.

Star systems are an important source of information about star masses. Astronomers cannot measure the mass of a star directly. However, they can figure out a star's mass by observing the effect of the star's gravity on a companion star.

Binary Star System

Some binary star systems appear to dim briefly when one star orbits in front of the other and blocks some of its light.

When neither star is in front of the other, the star system appears to give off more light.

CHECK YOUR READING Why are star systems important to astronomers?

4.2 Review

KEY CONCEPTS

1. Why must astronomers figure out a star's distance to calculate its actual brightness?

2. How are color and temperature related in stars?

3. How does a star's mass affect its life cycle?

CRITICAL THINKING

4. **Analyze** Some of the brightest stars are red supergiants. How can stars with cooler red surfaces be so bright?

5. **Infer** Will the Sun eventually become a black hole? Why or why not?

◯ CHALLENGE

6. **Infer** At what stage in the life cycle of the Sun will it be impossible for life to exist on Earth? Explain.

Brightness and Temperature of Stars

MATH TUTORIAL
CLASSZONE.COM
Click on Math Tutorial for more help with scatter plots.

A star's brightness, or luminosity, depends on the star's surface temperature and size. If two stars have the same surface temperature, the larger star will be more luminous. The Hertzsprung-Russell (H-R) diagram below is a scatter plot that shows the relative temperatures and luminosities of various stars.

Example

Describe the surface temperature and luminosity of Spica.

(1) Surface temperature: Without drawing on the graph, imagine a line extending from Spica down to the temperature axis. Spica is one of the hottest stars.

(2) Luminosity: Imagine a line extending from Spica across to the luminosity axis. Spica has a high luminosity.

ANSWER Spica is one of the hottest and most luminous stars.

Use the diagram to answer the questions.

1. Describe the surface temperature and luminosity of Proxima Centauri.

2. Compare the surface temperature and luminosity of the Sun with the surface temperature and luminosity of Betelgeuse.

3. Compare the surface temperature and luminosity of the red dwarfs with the surface temperature and luminosity of the blue supergiants.

CHALLENGE When an old red giant star loses its outer atmosphere, all that remains is the very hot core of the star. Because the core is small, it does not give off much light. What kind of star does the red giant star become after it loses its outer atmosphere? How can you tell from the diagram?

Hertzsprung-Russell (H-R) Diagram

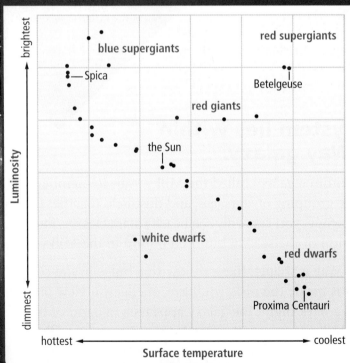

4.3 Galaxies have different sizes and shapes.

 BEFORE, you learned

- Our solar system is part of a galaxy called the Milky Way
- Stars change over their life cycles

NOW, you will learn

- About the size and shape of the Milky Way
- How galaxies are classified
- About the centers of galaxies

VOCABULARY

quasar p. 133

EXPLORE The Milky Way

Why does the Milky Way look hazy?

PROCEDURE

1. Use a white gel pen to make 50 small dots close together on a piece of black paper.

2. Tape the paper to a wall, and move slowly away from it until you have difficulty seeing the individual dots.

WHAT DO YOU THINK?

- At what distance did the dots become hazy?
- Why might some of the stars in the Milky Way appear hazy from Earth?

MATERIALS
- white gel pen
- black paper
- tape

COMBINATION NOTES
You could record information about the Milky Way in a combination notes table.

Our solar system lies within the Milky Way galaxy.

The Sun lies within a galaxy called the Milky Way. Remember that a galaxy is a huge grouping of stars, gas, and dust held together by gravity. Without a telescope, you can only see nearby stars clearly. Those stars are a tiny fraction of the several hundred billion in the Milky Way.

The Milky Way is shaped like a disk with a bulge in the center. Because Earth is inside the disk, you have an edge-on view of part of the galaxy. On a dark night, the galaxy appears as a band of blended starlight. The Milky Way got its name from the hazy, or milky, appearance of this band of stars. You cannot see the center of the galaxy because it is hidden by dust.

 CHECK YOUR READING Why can't we see all of the Milky Way from Earth?

The Milky Way

When you look at the Milky Way, it appears as a band of hazy light.

Illustration of Side View

disk — Sun's location — bulge

The Milky Way is about 100,000 light-years in diameter.

The disk of the Milky Way measures more than 100,000 light-years in diameter. The bulge of densely packed stars at the center is located about 26,000 light-years from the Sun. A large but very faint layer of stars surrounds the disk and bulge. In addition to stars, the Milky Way contains clouds of gas and dust called nebulae.

The stars and nebulae in the Milky Way orbit the galaxy's center at very high speeds. However, the galaxy is so large that the Sun takes about 250 million years to complete one orbit.

INVESTIGATE Galaxy Shapes

How can you classify galaxies according to shape?

PROCEDURE

1. Cut out the photographs of galaxies on the Galaxy Photo Sheet.

2. Sort the galaxies into different groups according to their shapes. You may need a group for galaxies that do not fit in other groups.

WHAT DO YOU THINK?

• How many groups did you sort the galaxies into?

• Describe each group briefly, and list which galaxies you put in each group.

CHALLENGE What is the connection between the apparent shape of a galaxy and the galaxy's relationship to the viewer? **Hint:** Think about how an edge-on view of a compact disc differs from a view of it lying flat on a table.

SKILL FOCUS
Classifying

MATERIALS
• Galaxy Photo Sheet
• scissors

TIME
15 minutes

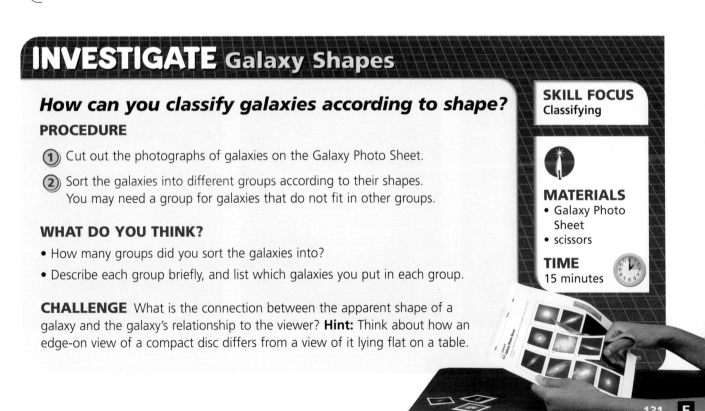

Galaxies vary in appearance.

Galaxies differ greatly in size. Some contain as few as a hundred million stars, but the biggest have more than a trillion stars. Galaxies also vary in shape. Astronomers have classified galaxies into three main types based on their shape.

 CHECK YOUR READING What are two ways in which galaxies can differ from one another?

Types of Galaxies

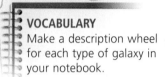

The three main types of galaxies are spiral, elliptical, and irregular. Most galaxies are either spiral or elliptical.

Spiral galaxies have arms of stars, gas, and dust that curve away from the center of the galaxy in a spiral pattern. The Milky Way is a spiral galaxy. Like the Milky Way, other spiral galaxies are disk-shaped and have a central bulge. Most of the stars in the disk and the bulge are old stars. However, the dense spiral arms within the disk contain many young, bright stars.

Elliptical galaxies are shaped like spheres or eggs. Unlike spiral galaxies, elliptical galaxies have almost no dust or gas between stars, and all of their stars are old.

Irregular galaxies are faint galaxies without a definite shape. They are smaller than the other types of galaxies and have many fewer stars.

Galaxies sometimes collide with other galaxies. These collisions can cause changes in their shapes. The Extreme Science feature on page 134 describes such collisions.

Spiral Galaxy

Elliptical Galaxy

Irregular Galaxy

Centers of Galaxies

Most large galaxies seem to have supermassive black holes at their centers. The mass of a supermassive black hole can be millions or even billions of times greater than that of the Sun. At the center of the Milky Way, for example, is a black hole with a mass about three million times that of the Sun.

Like all black holes, a supermassive black hole is invisible. Astronomers can identify the presence of a black hole by the behavior of matter around it. The gravity of a supermassive black hole is so strong that it draws in a huge whirlpool of gas from nearby stars. As gases are pulled toward the black hole, they become compressed and extremely hot, so they give off very bright light. The motions of stars orbiting the black hole can also reveal its presence.

If the center of a galaxy is very bright, it may look like a star from a great distance. The very bright centers of some distant galaxies are called **quasars.** *Quasar* is a shortened form of *quasi-stellar,* which means "seeming like a star." The galaxy surrounding a quasar is often hard to see because the quasar is so much brighter than it.

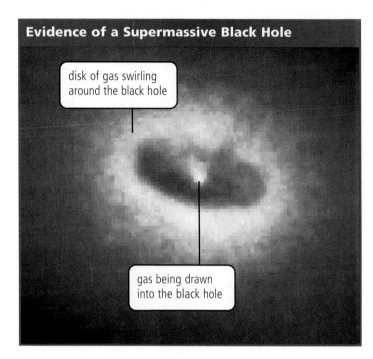

Evidence of a Supermassive Black Hole

disk of gas swirling around the black hole

gas being drawn into the black hole

 CHECK YOUR READING How can astronomers detect the presence of a supermassive black hole at the center of a galaxy?

Review

KEY CONCEPTS

1. What is the shape of the Milky Way?

2. Why does the Milky Way look like a hazy band of stars in the sky?

3. What keeps the stars in galaxies from moving apart?

CRITICAL THINKING

4. **Compare and Contrast** Make a diagram showing similarities and differences among the three main types of galaxies.

5. **Infer** How might our view of the Milky Way be different if the Sun were located inside the central bulge?

CHALLENGE

6. **Predict** If two spiral galaxies collide, what might eventually happen to the supermassive black holes at their centers?

EXTREME SCIENCE

When Galaxies Collide

A small galaxy is moving through our galaxy, the Milky Way, right now!

- The small galaxy may be destroyed by the collision, but the Milky Way is not in danger.
- The same galaxy seems to have moved through the Milky Way ten times before.
- Other galaxies may also be moving through the Milky Way.

Not to Worry!

Galaxies containing many billions of stars are colliding all the time. What are the chances that their stars will crash into one another? The chances are very small, because there is so much empty space between stars.

Galactic Cannibals

When galaxies collide, a larger galaxy can "eat up" a smaller one.

- The stars of the smaller galaxy become part of the larger one.
- The collision of two spiral galaxies may form a new elliptical galaxy.

Bent Out of Shape

Sometimes galaxies pass very close to each other without actually colliding. In these near misses, gravity can produce some interesting new shapes. For example, the Tadpole Galaxy (left) has a long tail of dust and gas pulled out by the gravity of a passing galaxy.

Model Galaxies

Astronomers use computer simulations to predict how the stars and gas in galaxies are affected by a collision. To understand galaxy collisions better, they then compare the simulations with images of actual galaxies.

EXPLORE

1. **PREDICT** Draw the shape of the new galaxy that the two in the photograph on the left might form.

2. **CHALLENGE** Look at online images and simulations of galaxy collisions. Make a chart showing how these collisions can differ.

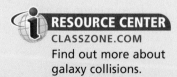

RESOURCE CENTER
CLASSZONE.COM
Find out more about galaxy collisions.

Come back in a few billion years and you may see that these two spiral galaxies have become one elliptical galaxy.

4.4 The universe is expanding.

- Galaxies contain millions or billions of stars
- Electromagnetic radiation carries information about space

▶ **NOW,** you will learn

- How galaxies are moving apart in the universe
- What scientists are discovering about the development of the universe

VOCABULARY

Doppler effect p. 136
big bang p. 138

EXPLORE Large Numbers

How much is a billion?

PROCEDURE

MATERIALS
- book
- ruler
- calculator

1. Guess how thick a billion-page book would be. Write down your guess.

2. Count how many sheets of paper in a book add up to a millimeter in thickness. Multiply by 2 to calculate the number of pages.

3. Then divide 1 billion (1,000,000,000) by that number to determine how many millimeters thick the book would be. Divide your result by 1,000,000 to convert to kilometers.

WHAT DO YOU THINK?
- How thick would a billion-page book be?
- How close was your guess?

Galaxies are moving farther apart in the universe.

COMBINATION NOTES
You could record information about the expansion of the universe in a combination notes table.

The universe is unbelievably huge. It consists of all space, energy, and matter. The Milky Way is just one of about 100 billion galaxies. These galaxies occur in groups that together form superclusters. Between the superclusters are huge areas of nearly empty space.

Because the universe is so huge, you might think that the most distant regions of the universe are very different from space near Earth. However, by looking at the spectra of light from stars and galaxies, astronomers have determined that the same elements are found throughout the universe. Scientific observations also indicate that the same physical forces and processes operate everywhere.

Looking Back in Time

When we look far out into space, we see galaxies by the light they gave off long ago. This light has traveled millions or even billions of years before reaching telescopes on Earth. The Andromeda Galaxy, for example, is the closest large galaxy. The light of its stars takes over 2 million years to reach Earth. When we view this galaxy through a telescope, we are seeing what happened in it 2 million years ago. To see what is happening there now, we would have to wait 2 million years for the light to arrive.

Light from the Andromeda Galaxy takes 2 million years to reach Earth.

As astronomers look at galaxies farther and farther away, they see how the universe looked at different times in the past. These views are like photographs in an album that show someone at various stages of life. Astronomers can see how the universe has developed over billions of years.

CHECK YOUR READING Why can astronomers learn about the past by looking at distant galaxies?

The Motion of Galaxies

Have you ever noticed that the sound of an ambulance siren changes as it travels toward and then away from you? The pitch of the siren seems to be higher as the ambulance approaches. As the ambulance passes you and starts moving away, the pitch of the siren seems to get lower. The shifting pitch of the siren is an example of the **Doppler effect,** which is a change in the observed wavelength or frequency of a wave that occurs when the source of the wave or the observer is moving.

The Doppler effect occurs with light as well as sound. If a galaxy is moving toward Earth, the light we receive will seem compressed to shorter wavelengths. This change is called a blue shift because the light shifts toward the blue end of the spectrum. If a galaxy is moving away from Earth, the light we receive will seem stretched to longer wavelengths. This change is called a red shift because the light shifts toward the red end of the spectrum.

In the early 1900s, astronomers discovered that light from distant galaxies is stretched to longer wavelengths. This fact indicates that the galaxies are moving apart. By analyzing the spectra of galaxies, astronomers also discovered that the galaxies are moving apart faster the farther away they are. These observations led astronomers to conclude that the universe has been expanding throughout its history.

Evidence of an Expanding Universe

The Doppler effect can show how galaxies are moving in relation to Earth.

moving away

moving toward

Earth

Light from a galaxy moving away from Earth will seem stretched to longer wavelengths.

Light from a galaxy moving toward Earth will seem compressed to shorter wavelengths.

READING VISUALS What do the arrows on the light waves indicate?

The illustration of raisin-bread dough rising will help you imagine this expansion. Suppose you were a raisin. You would observe that all the other raisins are moving away from you as the dough expands. The raisins are being moved apart by the expanding dough. Furthermore, you would observe that distant raisins are moving away faster than nearby raisins. They move away faster because there is more dough expanding between you and those raisins.

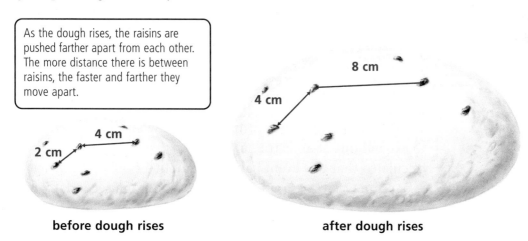

As the dough rises, the raisins are pushed farther apart from each other. The more distance there is between raisins, the faster and farther they move apart.

8 cm

4 cm

4 cm

2 cm

before dough rises

after dough rises

Like the dough that expands and moves raisins apart, space in the universe is expanding and moving galaxies apart. The universe does not expand into anything, since there is nothing outside the universe. Rather, the universe itself is expanding.

CHECK YOUR READING How are galaxies moving in relation to each other?

INVESTIGATE Galaxies

How does the universe expand?

PROCEDURE

1. Spread the cut rubber band against the ruler without stretching it. Mark off every centimeter for 6 centimeters.

2. Align the first mark on the rubber band with the 1-centimeter mark on the ruler and hold it in place tightly. Stretch the rubber band so that the second mark is next to the 3-centimeter mark on the ruler.

3. Observe how many centimeters each mark has moved from its original location against the ruler.

WHAT DO YOU THINK?

- How far did each mark on the rubber band move from its original location?

- What does this activity demonstrate about the expansion of the universe?

CHALLENGE How could you calculate the rates at which the marks moved when you stretched the rubber band?

SKILL FOCUS
Measuring

MATERIALS
- thick rubber band cut open
- ballpoint pen
- ruler

TIME

20 minutes

Scientists are investigating the origin of the universe.

After astronomers learned that galaxies are moving apart, they developed new ideas about the origin of the universe. They concluded that all matter was once merged together and then the universe suddenly began to expand. The evidence for this scientific theory is so strong that almost all astronomers now accept it.

The **big bang** is the moment in time when the universe started to expand out of an extremely hot, dense state. Astronomers have calculated that this event happened about 14 billion years ago. The expansion was very rapid. In a tiny fraction of a second, the universe may have expanded from a size much smaller than a speck of dust to the size of our solar system.

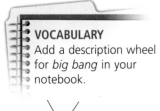

VOCABULARY
Add a description wheel for *big bang* in your notebook.

Evidence of the Big Bang

Evidence for the big bang comes from various sources. One important source of evidence is microwave radiation. Astronomers predicted in 1948 that the universe would still be filled with microwaves emitted shortly after the big bang. In 1965 researchers detected this kind of radiation streaming through space in all directions.

Besides the presence of microwave radiation and the motions of galaxies, scientists have found other evidence of the big bang by observing space. For example, images of very distant galaxies provide information about the universe's development. Additional evidence of the big bang has come from experiments and computer models.

Development of the Universe

Immediately after the big bang, the universe was incredibly dense and hot—much hotter than the core of the Sun. Matter and energy behaved very differently than they do under present conditions. As the universe rapidly expanded, it went through a series of changes.

Scientists do not fully understand what conditions were like in the early universe. However, they are gaining a clearer picture of how the universe developed. One way that scientists are learning about this development is by performing experiments in particle accelerators. These huge machines expose matter to extreme conditions.

Scientists have found that the earliest stages in the universe's development occurred in a tiny fraction of a second. However, it took about 300,000 years for the first elements to form. Stars, planets, and galaxies began to appear within the next billion years. Some evidence suggests that the first stars formed only a few hundred million years after the big bang.

This Hubble telescope image of very distant galaxies has helped scientists learn what the universe was like about 13 billion years ago.

 What happened to the universe shortly after the big bang?

4.4 Review

KEY CONCEPTS

1. How are distant regions of the universe similar to space near Earth?

2. What does the Doppler effect indicate about the motion of galaxies?

3. How do scientists explain the origin of the universe?

CRITICAL THINKING

4. **Apply** If a star 100 light-years from Earth is beginning to expand into a giant star, how long will it take for astronomers to observe this development? Explain.

5. **Analyze** Why do scientists need to perform experiments to learn about the earliest stages of the universe?

⚫ CHALLENGE

6. **Infer** Galaxy A and galaxy B both give off light that appears stretched to longer wavelengths. The light from galaxy B is stretched to even longer wavelengths than the light from galaxy A. What can you infer from these data?

the BIG idea

Our Sun is one of billions of stars in one of billions of galaxies in the universe.

CONTENT REVIEW
CLASSZONE.COM

◀ KEY CONCEPTS SUMMARY

4.1 The Sun is our local star.

The Sun produces energy from hydrogen. Energy flows through the Sun's layers. Features appear on the Sun's surface.

interior layers

atmosphere

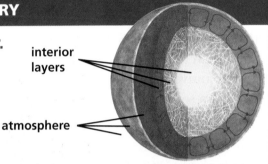

VOCABULARY
fusion p. 116
convection p. 116
corona p. 116
sunspot p. 118
solar wind p. 119

4.2 Stars change over their life cycles.

Stars vary in brightness, size, color, and temperature. The development of a star depends on the mass of the star. Most stars are grouped with one or more companion stars.

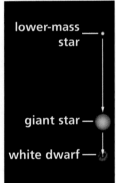

lower-mass star

giant star

white dwarf

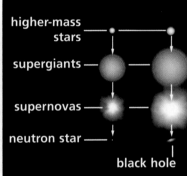

higher-mass stars

supergiants

supernovas

neutron star

black hole

VOCABULARY
light-year p. 122
parallax p. 123
nebula p. 125
main sequence p. 126
neutron star p. 126
black hole p. 126

4.3 Galaxies have different sizes and shapes.

Our galaxy, the Milky Way, is a spiral galaxy. Galaxies can also be elliptical or irregular. Irregular galaxies have no definite shape.

Spiral Galaxy

Elliptical Galaxy

Irregular Galaxy

VOCABULARY
quasar p. 133

4.4 The universe is expanding.

Galaxies are moving farther apart in the universe. Scientists are investigating the origin and development of the universe.

VOCABULARY
Doppler effect p. 136
big bang p. 138

Reviewing Vocabulary

Make a frame for each of the vocabulary words listed below. Write the word in the center. Decide what information to frame it with. Use definitions, examples, descriptions, parts, or pictures. An example is shown below.

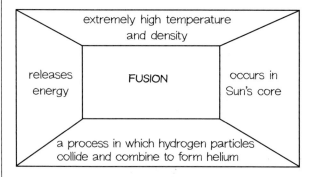

extremely high temperature and density

releases energy

FUSION

occurs in Sun's core

a process in which hydrogen particles collide and combine to form helium

1. convection
2. corona
3. sunspot
4. solar wind
5. nebula
6. black hole
7. Doppler effect
8. big bang

Reviewing Key Concepts

Multiple Choice *Choose the letter of the best answer.*

9. Which layer do you usually see in photographs of the Sun?
   a. convection zone
   b. photosphere
   c. chromosphere
   d. corona

10. Which statement is true of sunspots?
    a. They are permanent features on the Sun's surface.
    b. They are caused by solar wind.
    c. They are where fusion occurs.
    d. They are cooler than surrounding areas.

11. Which unit is usually used to describe the distances of stars?
    a. astronomical units
    b. light-years
    c. kilometers
    d. miles

12. Which example best shows the relationship between color and temperature?
    a. A rainbow forms when sunlight strikes raindrops.
    b. A flashlight beam looks red when passed through a red plastic filter.
    c. A chemical light-stick glows a yellow-green color.
    d. A metal rod in a fireplace changes in color from red to orange.

13. How do lower-mass stars differ from higher-mass stars?
    a. They develop more quickly.
    b. They develop more slowly.
    c. They end up as black holes.
    d. They have too little mass to produce energy.

14. Which term describes the Milky Way?
    a. spiral galaxy
    b. elliptical galaxy
    c. irregular galaxy
    d. quasar

15. The Doppler effect is used to determine
    a. the number of stars in a galaxy
    b. the number of galaxies in the universe
    c. the size of the universe
    d. whether a galaxy is moving toward or away from Earth

16. What is the big bang?
    a. the collision of galaxies
    b. the formation of the solar system
    c. the beginning of the universe's expansion
    d. the time when stars began to form

Short Answer *Write a short answer to each question.*

17. Why can't we see the Sun's corona under normal conditions?

18. How do astronomers use parallax to calculate a star's distance?

19. Where do heavy elements, such as iron, come from?

20. How can astronomers tell whether a black hole exists in the center of a galaxy?

The table below shows the distances of some galaxies and the speeds at which they are moving away from the Milky Way. Use the table to answer the next three questions.

Galaxy	Distance (million light-years)	Speed (kilometers per second)
NGC 7793	14	241
NGC 6946	22	336
NGC 2903	31	472
NGC 6744	42	663

21. COMPARE AND CONTRAST How do the speed and distance of NGC 7793 compare with the speed and distance of NGC 2903?

22. ANALYZE What general pattern do you see in these data?

23. APPLY What would you estimate to be the speed of a galaxy located 60 million light-years away? **Hint:** Notice the pattern between the first and third rows and the second and fourth rows in the chart.

24. INFER Why might the solar wind have a stronger effect on inner planets than on outer planets in the solar system?

25. PREDICT The core of a particular star consists almost entirely of helium. What will soon happen to this star?

26. ANALYZE Planets shine by reflected light. Why do some planets in our solar system appear brighter than stars, even though the stars give off their own light?

27. IDENTIFY CAUSE A star dims for a brief period every three days. What could be causing it to dim?

28. COMPARE AND CONTRAST Describe the similarities and differences between the life cycles of lower-mass stars and higher-mass stars.

29. EVALUATE If you wanted to study a neutron star, would you use a visible-light telescope or an x-ray telescope? Explain why.

30. INFER Suppose that astronomers find evidence of iron and other heavy elements in a galaxy. On the basis of this evidence, what can you assume has already occurred in that galaxy?

31. ANALYZE Why did the discovery that galaxies are moving farther apart help scientists conclude that all matter was once merged together?

32. PREDICT What changes do you predict will happen in the universe over the next 10 billion years?

33. COMPARE AND CONTRAST The photographs above show a spiral galaxy and an elliptical galaxy. What similarities and differences do you see in these two types of galaxies?

the BIG idea

34. INFER Look again at the photograph on pages 112–113. Now that you have finished the chapter, how would you change your response to the question on the photograph? What else might be present?

35. SYNTHESIZE Think of a question that you still have about the universe. What information would you need to answer the question? How might you obtain this information?

UNIT PROJECTS

Evaluate all the data, results, and information in your project folder. Prepare to present your project.

Analyzing a Chart

Use the chart and diagram to answer the next six questions.

Classification of Stars

Class	Color	Surface Temperature (°C)
O	blue-white	above 25,000
B	blue-white	10,000–25,000
A	white	7500–10,000
F	yellow-white	6000–7500
G	yellow	5000–6000
K	orange	3500–5000
M	red	below 3500

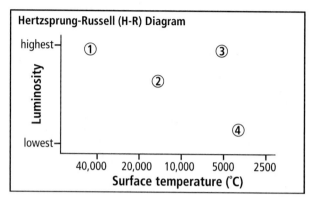

1. Which class of star has the lowest surface temperature?

a. O **c.** G
b. B **d.** M

2. Which class of star has the highest surface temperature?

a. O **c.** G
b. B **d.** M

3. What would be the color of a star with a surface temperature of 8000°C?

a. blue-white **c.** orange
b. white **d.** red

4. Toward the end of their life cycles, very massive stars expand in size, and their surface temperature becomes lower. Which of the following is an example of this change?

a. A white star becomes a blue-white star.

b. A blue-white star becomes a red star.

c. A red star becomes a blue-white star.

d. A yellow star becomes a yellow-white star.

5. The H-R diagram above shows the surface temperatures and luminosities, or true brightnesses, of four stars. Which of the stars is a type O?

a. 1 **c.** 3
b. 2 **d.** 4

6. Which two stars on the H-R diagram have the most similar surface temperatures?

a. 1 and 2 **c.** 2 and 3
b. 1 and 3 **d.** 3 and 4

Extended Response

Answer the two questions below in detail.

7. Why is looking at a star in the night sky like seeing back into time?

8. How could you use two flashlights to demonstrate the concept that the apparent brightness of a star is affected by its distance from Earth? You can include a diagram as part of your answer.

Student Resource Handbooks

Scientific Thinking Handbook

Making Observations

An **observation** is an act of noting and recording an event, characteristic, behavior, or anything else detected with an instrument or with the senses.

Observations allow you to make informed hypotheses and to gather data for experiments. Careful observations often lead to ideas for new experiments. There are two categories of observations:

- **Quantitative observations** can be expressed in numbers and include records of time, temperature, mass, distance, and volume.

- **Qualitative observations** include descriptions of sights, sounds, smells, and textures.

EXAMPLE

A student dissolved 30 grams of Epsom salts in water, poured the solution into a dish, and let the dish sit out uncovered overnight. The next day, she made the following observations of the Epsom salt crystals that grew in the dish.

To determine the mass, the student found the mass of the dish before and after growing the crystals and then used subtraction to find the difference.

The student measured several crystals and calculated the mean length. (To learn how to calculate the mean of a data set, see page R36.)

Table 1. Observations of Epsom Salt Crystals

Quantitative Observations	Qualitative Observations
• mass = 30 g	• Crystals are clear.
• mean crystal length = 0.5 cm	• Crystals are long, thin, and rectangular.
• longest crystal length = 2 cm	• White crust has formed around edge of dish.

Photographs or sketches are useful for recording qualitative observations.

 Epsom salt crystals

MORE ABOUT OBSERVING

- Make quantitative observations whenever possible. That way, others will know exactly what you observed and be able to compare their results with yours.

- It is always a good idea to make qualitative observations too. You never know when you might observe something unexpected.

Predicting and Hypothesizing

A **prediction** is an expectation of what will be observed or what will happen. A **hypothesis** is a tentative explanation for an observation or scientific problem that can be tested by further investigation.

EXAMPLE

Suppose you have made two paper airplanes and you wonder why one of them tends to glide farther than the other one.

1. Start by asking a question.

2. Make an educated guess. After examination, you notice that the wings of the airplane that flies farther are slightly larger than the wings of the other airplane.

3. Write a prediction based upon your educated guess, in the form of an "If . . . , then . . ." statement. Write the independent variable after the word *if,* and the dependent variable after the word *then.*

4. To make a hypothesis, explain why you think what you predicted will occur. Write the explanation after the word *because.*

---

1. Why does one of the paper airplanes glide farther than the other?

2. The size of an airplane's wings may affect how far the airplane will glide.

3. Prediction: If I make a paper airplane with larger wings, then the airplane will glide farther.

> To read about independent and dependent variables, see page R30.

4. Hypothesis: If I make a paper airplane with larger wings, then the airplane will glide farther, because the additional surface area of the wing will produce more lift.

> Notice that the part of the hypothesis after *because* adds an explanation of why the airplane will glide farther.

MORE ABOUT HYPOTHESES

• The results of an experiment cannot prove that a hypothesis is correct. Rather, the results either support or do not support the hypothesis.

• Valuable information is gained even when your hypothesis is not supported by your results. For example, it would be an important discovery to find that wing size is not related to how far an airplane glides.

• In science, a hypothesis is supported only after many scientists have conducted many experiments and produced consistent results.

Inferring

An **inference** is a logical conclusion drawn from the available evidence and prior knowledge. Inferences are often made from observations.

EXAMPLE

A student observing a set of acorns noticed something unexpected about one of them. He noticed a white, soft-bodied insect eating its way out of the acorn.

The student recorded these observations.

Observations

- There is a hole in the acorn, about 0.5 cm in diameter, where the insect crawled out.
- There is a second hole, which is about the size of a pinhole, on the other side of the acorn.
- The inside of the acorn is hollow.

Here are some inferences that can be made on the basis of the observations.

Inferences

- The insect formed from the material inside the acorn, grew to its present size, and ate its way out of the acorn.
- The insect crawled through the smaller hole, ate the inside of the acorn, grew to its present size, and ate its way out of the acorn.
- An egg was laid in the acorn through the smaller hole. The egg hatched into a larva that ate the inside of the acorn, grew to its present size, and ate its way out of the acorn.

When you make inferences, be sure to look at all of the evidence available and combine it with what you already know.

MORE ABOUT INFERENCES

Inferences depend both on observations and on the knowledge of the people making the inferences. Ancient people who did not know that organisms are produced only by similar organisms might have made an inference like the first one. A student today might look at the same observations and make the second inference. A third student might have knowledge about this particular insect and know that it is never small enough to fit through the smaller hole, leading her to the third inference.

Identifying Cause and Effect

In a **cause-and-effect relationship,** one event or characteristic is the result of another. Usually an effect follows its cause in time.

There are many examples of cause-and-effect relationships in everyday life.

Cause	Effect
Turn off a light.	Room gets dark.
Drop a glass.	Glass breaks.
Blow a whistle.	Sound is heard.

Scientists must be careful not to infer a cause-and-effect relationship just because one event happens after another event. When one event occurs after another, you cannot infer a cause-and-effect relationship on the basis of that information alone. You also cannot conclude that one event caused another if there are alternative ways to explain the second event. A scientist must demonstrate through experimentation or continued observation that an event was truly caused by another event.

EXAMPLE

Make an Observation

Suppose you have a few plants growing outside. When the weather starts getting colder, you bring one of the plants indoors. You notice that the plant you brought indoors is growing faster than the others are growing. You cannot conclude from your observation that the change in temperature was the cause of the increased plant growth, because there are alternative explanations for the observation. Some possible explanations are given below.

- The humidity indoors caused the plant to grow faster.

- The level of sunlight indoors caused the plant to grow faster.

- The indoor plant's being noticed more often and watered more often than the outdoor plants caused it to grow faster.

- The plant that was brought indoors was healthier than the other plants to begin with.

To determine which of these factors, if any, caused the indoor plant to grow faster than the outdoor plants, you would need to design and conduct an experiment.

See pages R28–R35 for information about designing experiments.

Recognizing Bias

Television, newspapers, and the Internet are full of experts claiming to have scientific evidence to back up their claims. How do you know whether the claims are really backed up by good science?

Bias is a slanted point of view, or personal prejudice. The goal of scientists is to be as objective as possible and to base their findings on facts instead of opinions. However, bias often affects the conclusions of researchers, and it is important to learn to recognize bias.

When scientific results are reported, you should consider the source of the information as well as the information itself. It is important to critically analyze the information that you see and read.

SOURCES OF BIAS

There are several ways in which a report of scientific information may be biased. Here are some questions that you can ask yourself:

1. **Who is sponsoring the research?**

   Sometimes, the results of an investigation are biased because an organization paying for the research is looking for a specific answer. This type of bias can affect how data are gathered and interpreted.

2. **Is the research sample large enough?**

   Sometimes research does not include enough data. The larger the sample size, the more likely that the results are accurate, assuming a truly random sample.

3. **In a survey, who is answering the questions?**

   The results of a survey or poll can be biased. The people taking part in the survey may have been specifically chosen because of how they would answer. They may have the same ideas or lifestyles. A survey or poll should make use of a random sample of people.

4. **Are the people who take part in a survey biased?**

   People who take part in surveys sometimes try to answer the questions the way they think the researcher wants them to answer. Also, in surveys or polls that ask for personal information, people may be unwilling to answer questions truthfully.

SCIENTIFIC BIAS

It is also important to realize that scientists have their own biases because of the types of research they do and because of their scientific viewpoints. Two scientists may look at the same set of data and come to completely different conclusions because of these biases. However, such disagreements are not necessarily bad. In fact, a critical analysis of disagreements is often responsible for moving science forward.

Identifying Faulty Reasoning

Faulty reasoning is wrong or incorrect thinking. It leads to mistakes and to wrong conclusions. Scientists are careful not to draw unreasonable conclusions from experimental data. Without such caution, the results of scientific investigations may be misleading.

EXAMPLE

Scientists try to make generalizations based on their data to explain as much about nature as possible. If only a small sample of data is looked at, however, a conclusion may be faulty. Suppose a scientist has studied the effects of the El Niño and La Niña weather patterns on flood damage in California from 1989 to 1995. The scientist organized the data in the bar graph below.

The scientist drew the following conclusions:

1. The La Niña weather pattern has no effect on flooding in California.

2. When neither weather pattern occurs, there is almost no flood damage.

3. A weak or moderate El Niño produces a small or moderate amount of flooding.

4. A strong El Niño produces a lot of flooding.

Flood and Storm Damage in California

Estimated damage (millions of dollars)

■ Weak–moderate El Niño
■ Strong El Niño

Starting year of season
(July 1–June 30)

SOURCE: *Governor's Office of Emergency Services, California*

For the six-year period of the scientist's investigation, these conclusions may seem to be reasonable. However, a six-year study of weather patterns may be too small of a sample for the conclusions to be supported. Consider the following graph, which shows information that was gathered from 1949 to 1997.

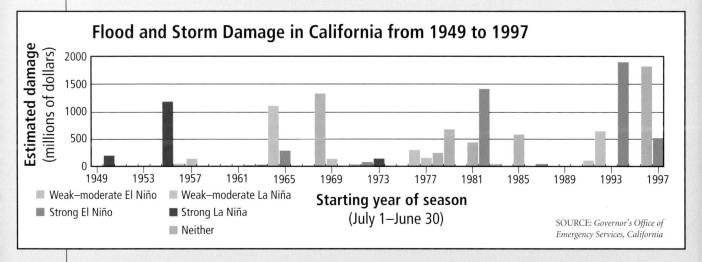

Flood and Storm Damage in California from 1949 to 1997

Estimated damage (millions of dollars)

■ Weak–moderate El Niño   ■ Weak–moderate La Niña
■ Strong El Niño   ■ Strong La Niña
■ Neither

Starting year of season
(July 1–June 30)

SOURCE: *Governor's Office of Emergency Services, California*

The only one of the conclusions that all of this information supports is number 3: a weak or moderate El Niño produces a small or moderate amount of flooding. By collecting more data, scientists can be more certain of their conclusions and can avoid faulty reasoning.

Analyzing Statements

To **analyze** a statement is to examine its parts carefully. Scientific findings are often reported through media such as television or the Internet. A report that is made public often focuses on only a small part of research. As a result, it is important to question the sources of information.

Evaluate Media Claims

To **evaluate** a statement is to judge it on the basis of criteria you've established. Sometimes evaluating means deciding whether a statement is true.

Reports of scientific research and findings in the media may be misleading or incomplete. When you are exposed to this information, you should ask yourself some questions so that you can make informed judgments about the information.

1. **Does the information come from a credible source?**

   Suppose you learn about a new product and it is stated that scientific evidence proves that the product works. A report from a respected news source may be more believable than an advertisement paid for by the product's manufacturer.

2. **How much evidence supports the claim?**

   Often, it may seem that there is new evidence every day of something in the world that either causes or cures an illness. However, information that is the result of several years of work by several different scientists is more credible than an advertisement that does not even cite the subjects of the experiment.

3. **How much information is being presented?**

   Science cannot solve all questions, and scientific experiments often have flaws. A report that discusses problems in a scientific study may be more believable than a report that addresses only positive experimental findings.

4. **Is scientific evidence being presented by a specific source?**

   Sometimes scientific findings are reported by people who are called experts or leaders in a scientific field. But if their names are not given or their scientific credentials are not reported, their statements may be less credible than those of recognized experts.

Differentiate Between Fact and Opinion

Sometimes information is presented as a fact when it may be an opinion. When scientific conclusions are reported, it is important to recognize whether they are based on solid evidence. Again, you may find it helpful to ask yourself some questions.

1. What is the difference between a fact and an opinion?

A **fact** is a piece of information that can be strictly defined and proved true. An **opinion** is a statement that expresses a belief, value, or feeling. An opinion cannot be proved true or false. For example, a person's age is a fact, but if someone is asked how old they feel, it is impossible to prove the person's answer to be true or false.

2. Can opinions be measured?

Yes, opinions can be measured. In fact, surveys often ask for people's opinions on a topic. But there is no way to know whether or not an opinion is the truth.

HOW TO DIFFERENTIATE FACT FROM OPINION

Human Activities and the Environment

Unfortunately, human use of fossil fuels is one of the most significant developments of the past few centuries. Humans rely on fossil fuels, a non-renewable energy resource, for more than 90 percent of their energy needs.

This careless misuse of our planet's resources has resulted in pollution, global warming, and the destruction of fragile ecosystems. For example, oil pipelines carry more than one million barrels of oil each day across tundra regions. Transporting oil across such areas can only result in oil spills that poison the land for decades.

Opinions

Notice words or phrases that express beliefs or feelings. The words *unfortunately* and *careless* show that opinions are being expressed.

Opinion

Look for statements that speculate about events. These statements are opinions, because they cannot be proved.

Facts

Statements that contain statistics tend to be facts. Writers often use facts to support their opinions.

Lab Handbook

Safety Rules

Before you work in the laboratory, read these safety rules twice. Ask your teacher to explain any rules that you do not completely understand. Refer to these rules later on if you have questions about safety in the science classroom.

Directions

- Read all directions and make sure that you understand them before starting an investigation or lab activity. If you do not understand how to do a procedure or how to use a piece of equipment, ask your teacher.
- Do not begin any investigation or touch any equipment until your teacher has told you to start.
- Never experiment on your own. If you want to try a procedure that the directions do not call for, ask your teacher for permission first.
- If you are hurt or injured in any way, tell your teacher immediately.

Dress Code

goggles

apron

gloves

- Wear goggles when
  — using glassware, sharp objects, or chemicals
  — heating an object
  — working with anything that can easily fly up into the air and hurt someone's eye
- Tie back long hair or hair that hangs in front of your eyes.
- Remove any article of clothing—such as a loose sweater or a scarf—that hangs down and may touch a flame, chemical, or piece of equipment.
- Observe all safety icons calling for the wearing of eye protection, gloves, and aprons.

Heating and Fire Safety

fire safety

heating safety

- Keep your work area neat, clean, and free of extra materials.
- Never reach over a flame or heat source.
- Point objects being heated away from you and others.
- Never heat a substance or an object in a closed container.
- Never touch an object that has been heated. If you are unsure whether something is hot, treat it as though it is. Use oven mitts, clamps, tongs, or a test-tube holder.
- Know where the fire extinguisher and fire blanket are kept in your classroom.
- Do not throw hot substances into the trash. Wait for them to cool or use the container your teacher puts out for disposal.

Electrical Safety

electrical safety

- Never use lamps or other electrical equipment with frayed cords.
- Make sure no cord is lying on the floor where someone can trip over it.
- Do not let a cord hang over the side of a counter or table so that the equipment can easily be pulled or knocked to the floor.
- Never let cords hang into sinks or other places where water can be found.
- Never try to fix electrical problems. Inform your teacher of any problems immediately.
- Unplug an electrical cord by pulling on the plug, not the cord.

Chemical Safety

chemical safety

poison

fumes

- If you spill a chemical or get one on your skin or in your eyes, tell your teacher right away.
- Never touch, taste, or sniff any chemicals in the lab. If you need to determine odor, waft. Wafting consists of holding the chemical in its container 15 centimeters (6 in.) away from your nose, and using your fingers to bring fumes from the container to your nose.
- Keep lids on all chemicals you are not using.
- Never put unused chemicals back into the original containers. Throw away extra chemicals where your teacher tells you to.
- Pour chemicals over a sink or your work area, not over the floor.
- If you get a chemical in your eye, use the eyewash right away.
- Always wash your hands after handling chemicals, plants, or soil.

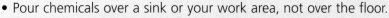

Wafting

Glassware and Sharp-Object Safety

sharp objects

- If you break glassware, tell your teacher right away.
- Do not use broken or chipped glassware. Give these to your teacher.
- Use knives and other cutting instruments carefully. Always wear eye protection and cut away from you.

Animal Safety

- Never hurt an animal.
- Touch animals only when necessary. Follow your teacher's instructions for handling animals.
- Always wash your hands after working with animals.

Cleanup

disposal

- Follow your teacher's instructions for throwing away or putting away supplies.
- Clean your work area and pick up anything that has dropped to the floor.
- Wash your hands.

Using Lab Equipment

Different experiments require different types of equipment. But even though experiments differ, the ways in which the equipment is used are the same.

Beakers

- Use beakers for holding and pouring liquids.

- Do not use a beaker to measure the volume of a liquid. Use a graduated cylinder instead. (See page R16.)

- Use a beaker that holds about twice as much liquid as you need. For example, if you need 100 milliliters of water, you should use a 200- or 250-milliliter beaker.

Test Tubes

- Use test tubes to hold small amounts of substances.

- Do not use a test tube to measure the volume of a liquid.

- Use a test tube when heating a substance over a flame. Aim the mouth of the tube away from yourself and other people.

- Liquids easily spill or splash from test tubes, so it is important to use only small amounts of liquids.

Test-Tube Holder

- Use a test-tube holder when heating a substance in a test tube.

- Use a test-tube holder if the substance in a test tube is dangerous to touch.

- Make sure the test-tube holder tightly grips the test tube so that the test tube will not slide out of the holder.

- Make sure that the test-tube holder is above the surface of the substance in the test tube so that you can observe the substance.

Test-Tube Rack

- Use a test-tube rack to organize test tubes before, during, and after an experiment.

- Use a test-tube rack to keep test tubes upright so that they do not fall over and spill their contents.

- Use a test-tube rack that is the correct size for the test tubes that you are using. If the rack is too small, a test tube may become stuck. If the rack is too large, a test tube may lean over, and some of its contents may spill or splash.

Forceps

- Use forceps when you need to pick up or hold a very small object that should not be touched with your hands.

- Do not use forceps to hold anything over a flame, because forceps are not long enough to keep your hand safely away from the flame. Plastic forceps will melt, and metal forceps will conduct heat and burn your hand.

Hot Plate

- Use a hot plate when a substance needs to be kept warmer than room temperature for a long period of time.

- Use a hot plate instead of a Bunsen burner or a candle when you need to carefully control temperature.

- Do not use a hot plate when a substance needs to be burned in an experiment.

- Always use "hot hands" safety mitts or oven mitts when handling anything that has been heated on a hot plate.

Microscope

Scientists use microscopes to see very small objects that cannot easily be seen with the eye alone. A microscope magnifies the image of an object so that small details may be observed. A microscope that you may use can magnify an object 400 times—the object will appear 400 times larger than its actual size.

Eyepiece Objects are viewed through the eyepiece. The eyepiece contains a lens that commonly magnifies an image 10 times.

Coarse Adjustment This knob is used to focus the image of an object when it is viewed through the low-power lens.

Fine Adjustment This knob is used to focus the image of an object when it is viewed through the high-power lens.

Low-Power Objective Lens This is the smallest lens on the nosepiece. It magnifies an image approximately 10 times.

Arm The arm supports the body above the stage. Always carry a microscope by the arm and base.

Stage Clip The stage clip holds a slide in place on the stage.

Base The base supports the microscope.

Body The body separates the lens in the eyepiece from the objective lenses below.

Nosepiece The nosepiece holds the objective lenses above the stage and rotates so that all lenses may be used.

High-Power Objective Lens This is the largest lens on the nosepiece. It magnifies an image approximately 40 times.

Stage The stage supports the object being viewed.

Diaphragm The diaphragm is used to adjust the amount of light passing through the slide and into an objective lens.

Mirror or Light Source Some microscopes use light that is reflected through the stage by a mirror. Other microscopes have their own light sources.

VIEWING AN OBJECT

1. Use the coarse adjustment knob to raise the body tube.

2. Adjust the diaphragm so that you can see a bright circle of light through the eyepiece.

3. Place the object or slide on the stage. Be sure that it is centered over the hole in the stage.

4. Turn the nosepiece to click the low-power lens into place.

5. Using the coarse adjustment knob, slowly lower the lens and focus on the specimen being viewed. Be sure not to touch the slide or object with the lens.

6. When switching from the low-power lens to the high-power lens, first raise the body tube with the coarse adjustment knob so that the high-power lens will not hit the slide.

7. Turn the nosepiece to click the high-power lens into place.

8. Use the fine adjustment knob to focus on the specimen being viewed. Again, be sure not to touch the slide or object with the lens.

MAKING A SLIDE, OR WET MOUNT

1 Place the specimen in the center of a clean slide.

2 Place a drop of water on the specimen.

3 Place a cover slip on the slide. Put one edge of the cover slip into the drop of water and slowly lower it over the specimen.

4 Remove any air bubbles from under the cover slip by gently tapping the cover slip.

5 Dry any excess water before placing the slide on the microscope stage for viewing.

Spring Scale (Force Meter)

- Use a spring scale to measure a force pulling on the scale.

- Use a spring scale to measure the force of gravity exerted on an object by Earth.

- To measure a force accurately, a spring scale must be zeroed before it is used. The scale is zeroed when no weight is attached and the indicator is positioned at zero.

- Do not attach a weight that is either too heavy or too light to a spring scale. A weight that is too heavy could break the scale or exert too great a force for the scale to measure. A weight that is too light may not exert enough force to be measured accurately.

Graduated Cylinder

- Use a graduated cylinder to measure the volume of a liquid.

- Be sure that the graduated cylinder is on a flat surface so that your measurement will be accurate.

- When reading the scale on a graduated cylinder, be sure to have your eyes at the level of the surface of the liquid.

- The surface of the liquid will be curved in the graduated cylinder. Read the volume of the liquid at the bottom of the curve, or meniscus (muh-NIHS-kuhs).

- You can use a graduated cylinder to find the volume of a solid object by measuring the increase in a liquid's level after you add the object to the cylinder.

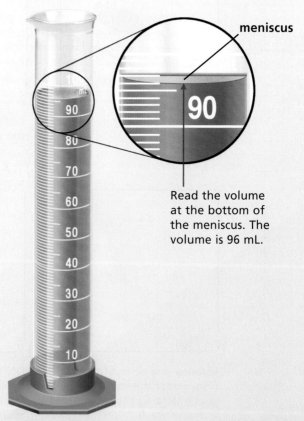

meniscus

Read the volume at the bottom of the meniscus. The volume is 96 mL.

Metric Rulers

- Use metric rulers or meter sticks to measure objects' lengths.

- Do not measure an object from the end of a metric ruler or meter stick, because the end is often imperfect. Instead, measure from the 1-centimeter mark, but remember to subtract a centimeter from the apparent measurement.

- Estimate any lengths that extend between marked units. For example, if a meter stick shows centimeters but not millimeters, you can estimate the length that an object extends between centimeter marks to measure it to the nearest millimeter.

- **Controlling Variables** If you are taking repeated measurements, always measure from the same point each time. For example, if you're measuring how high two different balls bounce when dropped from the same height, measure both bounces at the same point on the balls—either the top or the bottom. Do not measure at the top of one ball and the bottom of the other.

EXAMPLE

How to Measure a Leaf

1. Lay a ruler flat on top of the leaf so that the 1-centimeter mark lines up with one end. Make sure the ruler and the leaf do not move between the time you line them up and the time you take the measurement.

2. Look straight down on the ruler so that you can see exactly how the marks line up with the other end of the leaf.

3. Estimate the length by which the leaf extends beyond a marking. For example, the leaf below extends about halfway between the 4.2-centimeter and 4.3-centimeter marks, so the apparent measurement is about 4.25 centimeters.

4. Remember to subtract 1 centimeter from your apparent measurement, since you started at the 1-centimeter mark on the ruler and not at the end. The leaf is about 3.25 centimeters long (4.25 cm – 1 cm = 3.25 cm).

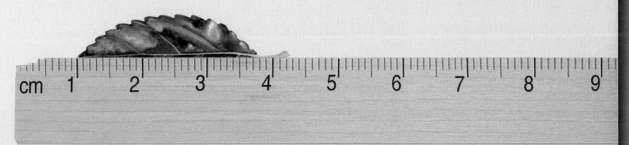

Triple-Beam Balance

This balance has a pan and three beams with sliding masses, called riders. At one end of the beams is a pointer that indicates whether the mass on the pan is equal to the masses shown on the beams.

1. Make sure the balance is zeroed before measuring the mass of an object. The balance is zeroed if the pointer is at zero when nothing is on the pan and the riders are at their zero points. Use the adjustment knob at the base of the balance to zero it.

2. Place the object to be measured on the pan.

3. Move the riders one notch at a time away from the pan. Begin with the largest rider. If moving the largest rider one notch brings the pointer below zero, begin measuring the mass of the object with the next smaller rider.

4. Change the positions of the riders until they balance the mass on the pan and the pointer is at zero. Then add the readings from the three beams to determine the mass of the object.

300 g	position of largest rider
90 g	position of middle rider
+ 3 g	position of smallest rider
393 g	mass of beaker

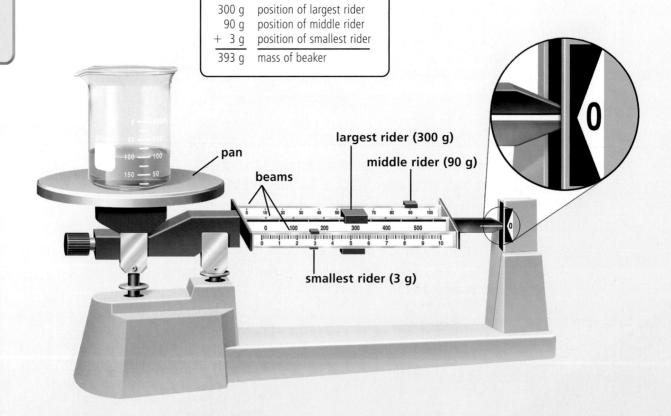

pan

beams

largest rider (300 g)

middle rider (90 g)

smallest rider (3 g)

Double-Pan Balance

This type of balance has two pans. Between the pans is a pointer that indicates whether the masses on the pans are equal.

1. Make sure the balance is zeroed before measuring the mass of an object. The balance is zeroed if the pointer is at zero when there is nothing on either of the pans. Many double-pan balances have sliding knobs that can be used to zero them.

2. Place the object to be measured on one of the pans.

3. Begin adding standard masses to the other pan. Begin with the largest standard mass. If this adds too much mass to the balance, begin measuring the mass of the object with the next smaller standard mass.

4. Add standard masses until the masses on both pans are balanced and the pointer is at zero. Then add the standard masses together to determine the mass of the object being measured.

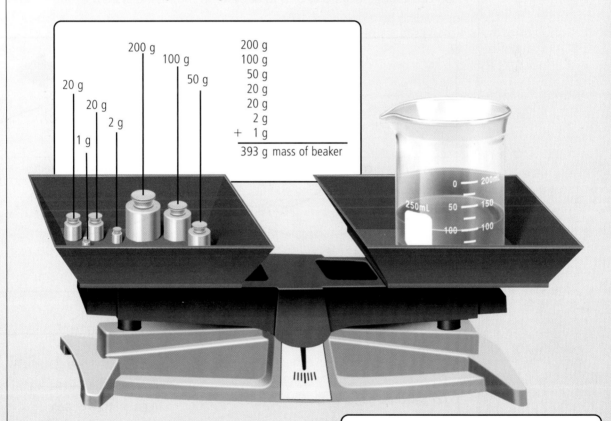

200 g
100 g
50 g
20 g
20 g
2 g
+ 1 g
393 g mass of beaker

Never place chemicals or liquids directly on a pan. Instead, use the following procedure:

1. Determine the mass of an empty container, such as a beaker.

2. Pour the substance into the container, and measure the total mass of the substance and the container.

3. Subtract the mass of the empty container from the total mass to find the mass of the substance.

The Metric System and SI Units

Scientists use International System (SI) units for measurements of distance, volume, mass, and temperature. The International System is based on multiples of ten and the metric system of measurement.

Basic SI Units		
Property	**Name**	**Symbol**
length	meter	m
volume	liter	L
mass	kilogram	kg
temperature	kelvin	K

SI Prefixes		
Prefix	**Symbol**	**Multiple of 10**
kilo-	k	1000
hecto-	h	100
deca-	da	10
deci-	d	$0.1 \left(\frac{1}{10}\right)$
centi-	c	$0.01 \left(\frac{1}{100}\right)$
milli-	m	$0.001 \left(\frac{1}{1000}\right)$

Changing Metric Units

You can change from one unit to another in the metric system by multiplying or dividing by a power of 10.

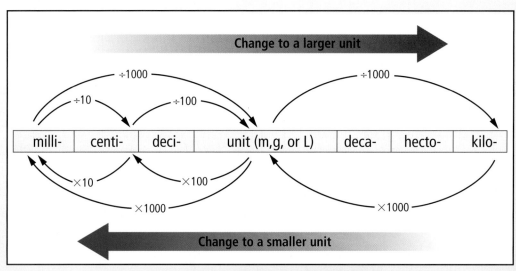

Example

Change 0.64 liters to milliliters.

(1) Decide whether to multiply or divide.

(2) Select the power of 10.

ANSWER 0.64 L = 640 mL

Change to a smaller unit by multiplying.

$$mL \longleftarrow \times 1000 \longrightarrow L$$

$$0.64 \times 1000 = 640.$$

Example

Change 23.6 grams to kilograms.

(1) Decide whether to multiply or divide.

(2) Select the power of 10.

ANSWER 23.6 g = 0.0236 kg

Change to a larger unit by dividing.

$$g \longrightarrow \div 1000 \longrightarrow kg$$

$$23.6 \div 1000 = 0.0236$$

LAB HANDBOOK

Temperature Conversions

Even though the kelvin is the SI base unit of temperature, the degree Celsius will be the unit you use most often in your science studies. The formulas below show the relationships between temperatures in degrees Fahrenheit (°F), degrees Celsius (°C), and kelvins (K).

$$°C = \frac{5}{9}(°F - 32)$$

$$°F = \frac{9}{5}°C + 32$$

$$K = °C + 273$$

See page R42 for help with using formulas.

Examples of Temperature Conversions

Condition	Degrees Celsius	Degrees Fahrenheit
Freezing point of water	0	32
Cool day	10	50
Mild day	20	68
Warm day	30	86
Normal body temperature	37	98.6
Very hot day	40	104
Boiling point of water	100	212

Converting Between SI and U.S. Customary Units

Use the chart below when you need to convert between SI units and U.S. customary units.

SI Unit	From SI to U.S. Customary			From U.S. Customary to SI		
Length	When you know	multiply by	to find	When you know	multiply by	to find
kilometer (km) = 1000 m	kilometers	0.62	miles	miles	1.61	kilometers
meter (m) = 100 cm	meters	3.28	feet	feet	0.3048	meters
centimeter (cm) = 10 mm	centimeters	0.39	inches	inches	2.54	centimeters
millimeter (mm) = 0.1 cm	millimeters	0.04	inches	inches	25.4	millimeters
Area	When you know	multiply by	to find	When you know	multiply by	to find
square kilometer (km^2)	square kilometers	0.39	square miles	square miles	2.59	square kilometers
square meter (m^2)	square meters	1.2	square yards	square yards	0.84	square meters
square centimeter (cm^2)	square centimeters	0.155	square inches	square inches	6.45	square centimeters
Volume	When you know	multiply by	to find	When you know	multiply by	to find
liter (L) = 1000 mL	liters	1.06	quarts	quarts	0.95	liters
	liters	0.26	gallons	gallons	3.79	liters
	liters	4.23	cups	cups	0.24	liters
	liters	2.12	pints	pints	0.47	liters
milliliter (mL) = 0.001 L	milliliters	0.20	teaspoons	teaspoons	4.93	milliliters
	milliliters	0.07	tablespoons	tablespoons	14.79	milliliters
	milliliters	0.03	fluid ounces	fluid ounces	29.57	milliliters
Mass	When you know	multiply by	to find	When you know	multiply by	to find
kilogram (kg) = 1000 g	kilograms	2.2	pounds	pounds	0.45	kilograms
gram (g) = 1000 mg	grams	0.035	ounces	ounces	28.35	grams

Precision and Accuracy

When you do an experiment, it is important that your methods, observations, and data be both precise and accurate.

low precision

precision,
but not accuracy

precision and
accuracy

Precision

In science, **precision** is the exactness and consistency of measurements. For example, measurements made with a ruler that has both centimeter and millimeter markings would be more precise than measurements made with a ruler that has only centimeter markings. Another indicator of precision is the care taken to make sure that methods and observations are as exact and consistent as possible. Every time a particular experiment is done, the same procedure should be used. Precision is necessary because experiments are repeated several times and if the procedure changes, the results will change.

EXAMPLE

Suppose you are measuring temperatures over a two-week period. Your precision will be greater if you measure each temperature at the same place, at the same time of day, and with the same thermometer than if you change any of these factors from one day to the next.

Accuracy

In science, it is possible to be precise but not accurate. **Accuracy** depends on the difference between a measurement and an actual value. The smaller the difference, the more accurate the measurement.

EXAMPLE

Suppose you look at a stream and estimate that it is about 1 meter wide at a particular place. You decide to check your estimate by measuring the stream with a meter stick, and you determine that the stream is 1.32 meters wide. However, because it is hard to measure the width of a stream with a meter stick, it turns out that you didn't do a very good job. The stream is actually 1.14 meters wide. Therefore, even though your estimate was less precise than your measurement, your estimate was actually more accurate.

Making Data Tables and Graphs

Data tables and graphs are useful tools for both recording and communicating scientific data.

Making Data Tables

You can use a **data table** to organize and record the measurements that you make. Some examples of information that might be recorded in data tables are frequencies, times, and amounts.

EXAMPLE

Suppose you are investigating photosynthesis in two elodea plants. One sits in direct sunlight, and the other sits in a dimly lit room. You measure the rate of photosynthesis by counting the number of bubbles in the jar every ten minutes.

1. Title and number your data table.
2. Decide how you will organize the table into columns and rows.
3. Any units, such as seconds or degrees, should be included in column headings, not in the individual cells.

Table 1. Number of Bubbles from Elodea

Time (min)	Sunlight	Dim Light
0	0	0
10	15	5
20	25	8
30	32	7
40	41	10
50	47	9
60	42	9

Always number and title data tables.

The data in the table above could also be organized in a different way.

Table 1. Number of Bubbles from Elodea

Light Condition	Time (min)						
	0	10	20	30	40	50	60
Sunlight	0	15	25	32	41	47	42
Dim light	0	5	8	7	10	9	9

Put units in column heading.

Making Line Graphs

You can use a **line graph** to show a relationship between variables. Line graphs are particularly useful for showing changes in variables over time.

EXAMPLE

Suppose you are interested in graphing temperature data that you collected over the course of a day.

Table 1. Outside Temperature During the Day on March 7

	Time of Day						
	7:00 A.M.	9:00 A.M.	11:00 A.M.	1:00 P.M.	3:00 P.M.	5:00 P.M.	7:00 P.M.
Temp (°C)	8	9	11	14	12	10	6

1. Use the vertical axis of your line graph for the variable that you are measuring—temperature.

2. Choose scales for both the horizontal axis and the vertical axis of the graph. You should have two points more than you need on the vertical axis, and the horizontal axis should be long enough for all of the data points to fit.

3. Draw and label each axis.

4. Graph each value. First find the appropriate point on the scale of the horizontal axis. Imagine a line that rises vertically from that place on the scale. Then find the corresponding value on the vertical axis, and imagine a line that moves horizontally from that value. The point where these two imaginary lines intersect is where the value should be plotted.

5. Connect the points with straight lines.

Be sure to add a number and a title to your graph.

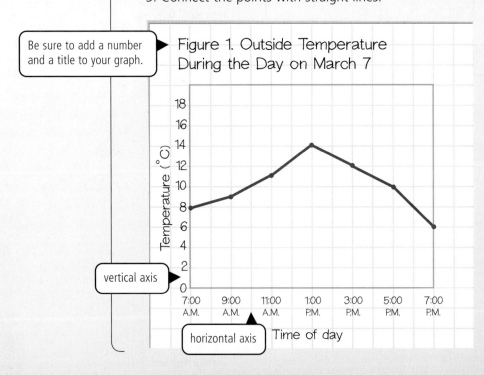

Figure 1. Outside Temperature During the Day on March 7

vertical axis

horizontal axis   Time of day

Making Circle Graphs

You can use a **circle graph,** sometimes called a pie chart, to represent data as parts of a circle. Circle graphs are used only when the data can be expressed as percentages of a whole. The entire circle shown in a circle graph is equal to 100 percent of the data.

EXAMPLE

Suppose you identified the species of each mature tree growing in a small wooded area. You organized your data in a table, but you also want to show the data in a circle graph.

1. To begin, find the total number of mature trees.

    $56 + 34 + 22 + 10 + 28 = 150$

2. To find the degree measure for each sector of the circle, write a fraction comparing the number of each tree species with the total number of trees. Then multiply the fraction by 360°.

    Oak: $\frac{56}{150} \times 360° = 134.4°$

3. Draw a circle. Use a protractor to draw the angle for each sector of the graph.

4. Color and label each sector of the graph.

5. Give the graph a number and title.

Table 1. Tree Species in Wooded Area

Species	Number of Specimens
Oak	56
Maple	34
Birch	22
Willow	10
Pine	28

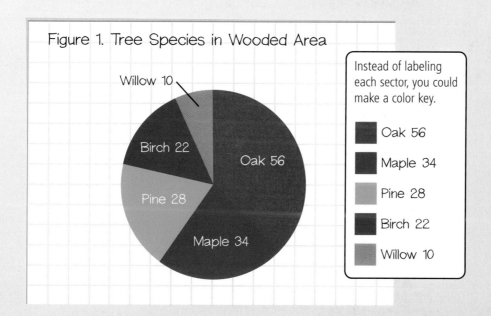

Figure 1. Tree Species in Wooded Area

Instead of labeling each sector, you could make a color key.

- Oak 56
- Maple 34
- Pine 28
- Birch 22
- Willow 10

Bar Graph

A **bar graph** is a type of graph in which the lengths of the bars are used to represent and compare data. A numerical scale is used to determine the lengths of the bars.

EXAMPLE

To determine the effect of water on seed sprouting, three cups were filled with sand, and ten seeds were planted in each. Different amounts of water were added to each cup over a three-day period.

Table 1. Effect of Water on Seed Sprouting

Daily Amount of Water (mL)	Number of Seeds That Sprouted After 3 Days in Sand
0	1
10	4
20	8

1. Choose a numerical scale. The greatest value is 8, so the end of the scale should have a value greater than 8, such as 10. Use equal increments along the scale, such as increments of 2.

2. Draw and label the axes. Mark intervals on the vertical axis according to the scale you chose.

3. Draw a bar for each data value. Use the scale to decide how long to make each bar.

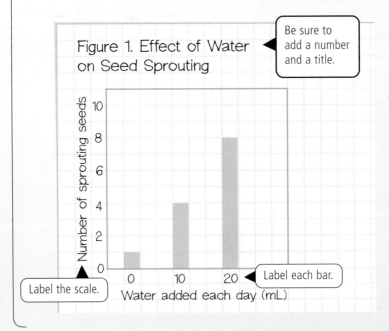

Figure 1. Effect of Water on Seed Sprouting

Be sure to add a number and a title.

Label the scale.

Label each bar.

Double Bar Graph

A **double bar graph** is a bar graph that shows two sets of data. The two bars for each measurement are drawn next to each other.

EXAMPLE

The seed-sprouting experiment was done using both sand and potting soil. The data for sand and potting soil can be plotted on one graph.

1. Draw one set of bars, using the data for sand, as shown below.
2. Draw bars for the potting-soil data next to the bars for the sand data. Shade them a different color. Add a key.

Table 2. Effect of Water and Soil on Seed Sprouting

Daily Amount of Water (mL)	Number of Seeds That Sprouted After 3 Days in Sand	Number of Seeds That Sprouted After 3 Days in Potting Soil
0	1	2
10	4	5
20	8	9

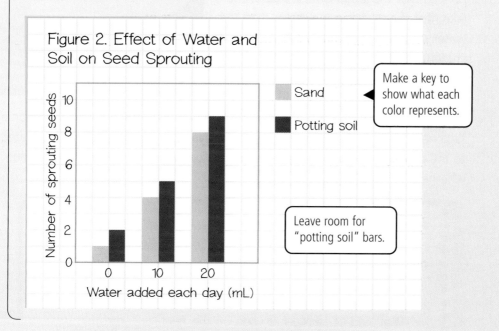

Figure 2. Effect of Water and Soil on Seed Sprouting

Make a key to show what each color represents.

Leave room for "potting soil" bars.

Designing an Experiment

Use this section when designing or conducting an experiment.

Determining a Purpose

Don't forget to learn as much as possible about your topic before you begin.

You can find a purpose for an experiment by doing research, by examining the results of a previous experiment, or by observing the world around you. An **experiment** is an organized procedure to study something under controlled conditions.

1. Write the purpose of your experiment as a question or problem that you want to investigate.

2. Write down research questions and begin searching for information that will help you design an experiment. Consult the library, the Internet, and other people as you conduct your research.

EXAMPLE

Middle school students observed an odor near the lake by their school. They also noticed that the water on the side of the lake near the school was greener than the water on the other side of the lake. The students did some research to learn more about their observations. They discovered that the odor and green color in the lake came from algae. They also discovered that a new fertilizer was being used on a field nearby. The students inferred that the use of the fertilizer might be related to the presence of the algae and designed a controlled experiment to find out whether they were right.

Problem
How does fertilizer affect the presence of algae in a lake?

Research Questions
- Have other experiments been done on this problem? If so, what did those experiments show?
- What kind of fertilizer is used on the field? How much?
- How do algae grow?
- How do people measure algae?
- Can fertilizer and algae be used safely in a lab? How?

Research
As you research, you may find a topic that is more interesting to you than your original topic, or learn that a procedure you wanted to use is not practical or safe. It is OK to change your purpose as you research.

Writing a Hypothesis

A **hypothesis** is a tentative explanation for an observation or scientific problem that can be tested by further investigation. You can write your hypothesis in the form of an "If . . . , then . . . , because . . ." statement.

Hypothesis

If the amount of fertilizer in lake water is increased, then the amount of algae will also increase, because fertilizers provide nutrients that algae need to grow.

Hypotheses
For help with hypotheses, refer to page R3.

Determining Materials

Make a list of all the materials you will need to do your experiment. Be specific, especially if someone else is helping you obtain the materials. Try to think of everything you will need.

Materials

- 1 large jar or container
- 4 identical smaller containers
- rubber gloves that also cover the arms
- sample of fertilizer-and-water solution
- eyedropper
- clear plastic wrap
- scissors
- masking tape
- marker
- ruler

Determining Variables and Constants

EXPERIMENTAL GROUP AND CONTROL GROUP

An experiment to determine how two factors are related always has two groups—a control group and an experimental group.

1. Design an experimental group. Include as many trials as possible in the experimental group in order to obtain reliable results.

2. Design a control group that is the same as the experimental group in every way possible, except for the factor you wish to test.

Experimental Group: two containers of lake water with one drop of fertilizer solution added to each

Control Group: two containers of lake water with no fertilizer solution added

> Go back to your materials list and make sure you have enough items listed to cover both your experimental group and your control group.

VARIABLES AND CONSTANTS

Identify the variables and constants in your experiment. In a controlled experiment, a **variable** is any factor that can change. **Constants** are all of the factors that are the same in both the experimental group and the control group.

1. Read your hypothesis. The **independent variable** is the factor that you wish to test and that is manipulated or changed so that it can be tested. The independent variable is expressed in your hypothesis after the word *if*. Identify the independent variable in your laboratory report.

2. The **dependent variable** is the factor that you measure to gather results. It is expressed in your hypothesis after the word *then*. Identify the dependent variable in your laboratory report.

> **Hypothesis**
> If the amount of fertilizer in lake water is increased, then the amount of algae will also increase, because fertilizers provide nutrients that algae need to grow.

Table 1. Variables and Constants in Algae Experiment

Independent Variable	Dependent Variable	Constants
Amount of fertilizer in lake water	Amount of algae that grow	• Where the lake water is obtained • Type of container used • Light and temperature conditions where water will be stored

> Set up your experiment so that you will test only one variable.

MEASURING THE DEPENDENT VARIABLE

Before starting your experiment, you need to define how you will measure the dependent variable. An **operational definition** is a description of the one particular way in which you will measure the dependent variable.

Your operational definition is important for several reasons. First, in any experiment there are several ways in which a dependent variable can be measured. Second, the procedure of the experiment depends on how you decide to measure the dependent variable. Third, your operational definition makes it possible for other people to evaluate and build on your experiment.

EXAMPLE 1

An operational definition of a dependent variable can be qualitative. That is, your measurement of the dependent variable can simply be an observation of whether a change occurs as a result of a change in the independent variable. This type of operational definition can be thought of as a "yes or no" measurement.

Table 2. Qualitative Operational Definition of Algae Growth

Independent Variable	Dependent Variable	Operational Definition
Amount of fertilizer in lake water	Amount of algae that grow	Algae grow in lake water

A qualitative measurement of a dependent variable is often easy to make and record. However, this type of information does not provide a great deal of detail in your experimental results.

EXAMPLE 2

An operational definition of a dependent variable can be quantitative. That is, your measurement of the dependent variable can be a number that shows how much change occurs as a result of a change in the independent variable.

Table 3. Quantitative Operational Definition of Algae Growth

Independent Variable	Dependent Variable	Operational Definition
Amount of fertilizer in lake water	Amount of algae that grow	Diameter of largest algal growth (in mm)

A quantitative measurement of a dependent variable can be more difficult to make and analyze than a qualitative measurement. However, this type of data provides much more information about your experiment and is often more useful.

Writing a Procedure

Write each step of your procedure. Start each step with a verb, or action word, and keep the steps short. Your procedure should be clear enough for someone else to use as instructions for repeating your experiment.

> If necessary, go back to your materials list and add any materials that you left out.

Controlling Variables
The same amount of fertilizer solution must be added to two of the four containers.

Controlling Variables
All four containers must receive the same amount of light.

Procedure

1. Put on your gloves. Use the large container to obtain a sample of lake water.

2. Divide the sample of lake water equally among the four smaller containers.

3. Use the eyedropper to add one drop of fertilizer solution to two of the containers.

4. Use the masking tape and the marker to label the containers with your initials, the date, and the identifiers "Jar 1 with Fertilizer," "Jar 2 with Fertilizer," "Jar 1 without Fertilizer," and "Jar 2 without Fertilizer."

5. Cover the containers with clear plastic wrap. Use the scissors to punch ten holes in each of the covers.

6. Place all four containers on a window ledge. Make sure that they all receive the same amount of light.

7. Observe the containers every day for one week.

8. Use the ruler to measure the diameter of the largest clump of algae in each container, and record your measurements daily.

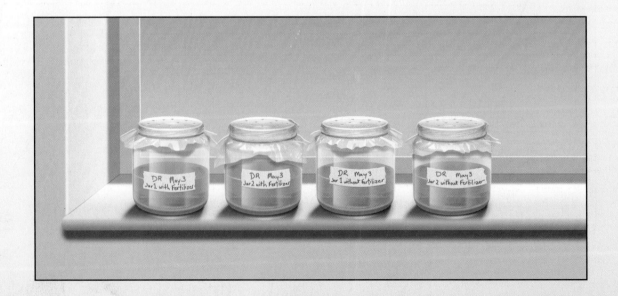

Recording Observations

Once you have obtained all of your materials and your procedure has been approved, you can begin making experimental observations. Gather both quantitative and qualitative data. If something goes wrong during your procedure, make sure you record that too.

Observations
For help with making qualitative and quantitative observations, refer to page R2.

For more examples of data tables, see page R23.

Table 4. Fertilizer and Algae Growth

Date and Time	Experimental Group		Control Group		
	Jar 1 with Fertilizer (diameter of algae in mm)	Jar 2 with Fertilizer (diameter of algae in mm)	Jar 1 without Fertilizer (diameter of algae in mm)	Jar 2 without Fertilizer (diameter of algae in mm)	Observations
5/3 4:00 P.M.	0	0	0	0	condensation in all containers
5/4 4:00 P.M.	0	3	0	0	tiny green blobs in jar 2 with fertilizer
5/5 4:15 P.M.	4	5	0	3	green blobs in jars 1 and 2 with fertilizer and jar 2 without fertilizer
5/6 4:00 P.M.	5	6	0	4	water light green in jar 2 with fertilizer
5/7 4:00 P.M.	8	10	0	6	water light green in jars 1 and 2 with fertilizer and in jar 2 without fertilizer
5/8 3:30 P.M.	10	18	0	6	cover off jar 2 with fertilizer
5/9 3:30 P.M.	14	23	0	8	drew sketches of each container

Notice that on the sixth day, the observer found that the cover was off one of the containers. It is important to record observations of unintended factors because they might affect the results of the experiment.

Use technology, such as a microscope, to help you make observations when possible.

Drawings of Samples Viewed Under Microscope on 5/9 at 100x

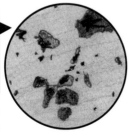
Jar 1 with Fertilizer

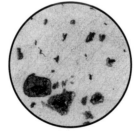
Jar 2 with Fertilizer

Jar 1 without Fertilizer

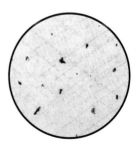
Jar 2 without Fertilizer

Summarizing Results

To summarize your data, look at all of your observations together. Look for meaningful ways to present your observations. For example, you might average your data or make a graph to look for patterns. When possible, use spreadsheet software to help you analyze and present your data. The two graphs below show the same data.

EXAMPLE 1

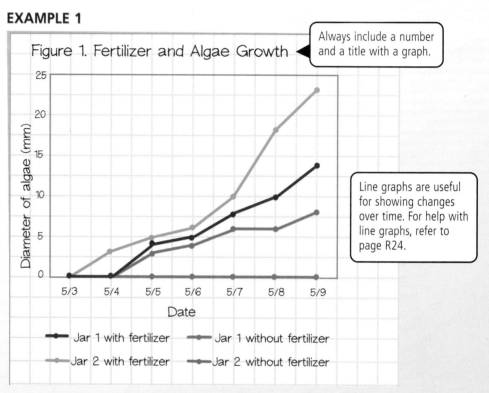

Always include a number and a title with a graph.

Line graphs are useful for showing changes over time. For help with line graphs, refer to page R24.

EXAMPLE 2

Bar graphs are useful for comparing different data sets. This bar graph has four bars for each day. Another way to present the data would be to calculate averages for the tests and the controls, and to show one test bar and one control bar for each day.

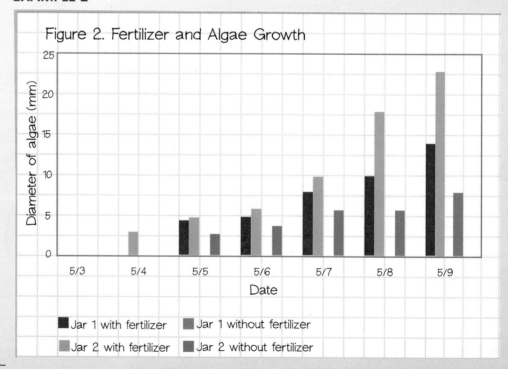

LAB HANDBOOK

Drawing Conclusions

RESULTS AND INFERENCES

To draw conclusions from your experiment, first write your results. Then compare your results with your hypothesis. Do your results support your hypothesis? Be careful not to make inferences about factors that you did not test.

For help with making inferences, see page R4.

Results and Inferences

The results of my experiment show that more algae grew in lake water to which fertilizer had been added than in lake water to which no fertilizer had been added. My hypothesis was supported. I infer that it is possible that the growth of algae in the lake was caused by the fertilizer used on the field.

Notice that you cannot conclude from this experiment that the presence of algae in the lake was due only to the fertilizer.

QUESTIONS FOR FURTHER RESEARCH

Write a list of questions for further research and investigation. Your ideas may lead you to new experiments and discoveries.

Questions for Further Research

- What is the connection between the amount of fertilizer and algae growth?
- How do different brands of fertilizer affect algae growth?
- How would algae growth in the lake be affected if no fertilizer were used on the field?
- How do algae affect the lake and the other life in and around it?
- How does fertilizer affect the lake and the life in and around it?
- If fertilizer is getting into the lake, how is it getting there?

Math Handbook

Describing a Set of Data

Means, medians, modes, and ranges are important math tools for describing data sets such as the following widths of fossilized clamshells.

13 mm   25 mm   14 mm   21 mm   16 mm   23 mm   14 mm

Mean

The **mean** of a data set is the sum of the values divided by the number of values.

> #### Example
>
> To find the mean of the clamshell data, add the values and then divide the sum by the number of values.
>
> $$\frac{13 \text{ mm} + 25 \text{ mm} + 14 \text{ mm} + 21 \text{ mm} + 16 \text{ mm} + 23 \text{ mm} + 14 \text{ mm}}{7} = \frac{126 \text{ mm}}{7} = 18 \text{ mm}$$
>
> **ANSWER** The mean is 18 mm.

Median

The **median** of a data set is the middle value when the values are written in numerical order. If a data set has an even number of values, the median is the mean of the two middle values.

> #### Example
>
> To find the median of the clamshell data, arrange the values in order from least to greatest. The median is the middle value.
>
> 13 mm   14 mm   14 mm   16 mm   21 mm   23 mm   25 mm
>
> **ANSWER** The median is 16 mm.

Mode

The **mode** of a data set is the value that occurs most often.

Example

To find the mode of the clamshell data, arrange the values in order from least to greatest and determine the value that occurs most often.

13 mm   14 mm   14 mm   16 mm   21 mm   23 mm   25 mm

ANSWER The mode is 14 mm.

A data set can have more than one mode or no mode. For example, the following data set has modes of 2 mm and 4 mm:

2 mm   2 mm   3 mm   4 mm   4 mm

The data set below has no mode, because no value occurs more often than any other.

2 mm   3 mm   4 mm   5 mm

Range

The **range** of a data set is the difference between the greatest value and the least value.

Example

To find the range of the clamshell data, arrange the values in order from least to greatest.

13 mm   14 mm   14 mm   16 mm   21 mm   23 mm   25 mm

Subtract the least value from the greatest value.

13 mm is the least value.
25 mm is the greatest value.

25 mm − 13 mm = 12 mm

ANSWER The range is 12 mm.

Using Ratios, Rates, and Proportions

You can use ratios and rates to compare values in data sets. You can use proportions to find unknown values.

Ratios

A **ratio** uses division to compare two values. The ratio of a value a to a nonzero value b can be written as $\frac{a}{b}$.

Example

The height of one plant is 8 centimeters. The height of another plant is 6 centimeters. To find the ratio of the height of the first plant to the height of the second plant, write a fraction and simplify it.

$$\frac{8 \text{ cm}}{6 \text{ cm}} = \frac{4 \times \overset{1}{\cancel{2}}}{3 \times \underset{1}{\cancel{2}}} = \frac{4}{3}$$

ANSWER The ratio of the plant heights is $\frac{4}{3}$.

You can also write the ratio $\frac{a}{b}$ as "a to b" or as $a : b$. For example, you can write the ratio of the plant heights as "4 to 3" or as 4 : 3.

Rates

A **rate** is a ratio of two values expressed in different units. A unit rate is a rate with a denominator of 1 unit.

Example

A plant grew 6 centimeters in 2 days. The plant's rate of growth was $\frac{6 \text{ cm}}{2 \text{ days}}$. To describe the plant's growth in centimeters per day, write a unit rate.

Divide numerator and denominator by 2: $\quad \dfrac{6 \text{ cm}}{2 \text{ days}} = \dfrac{6 \text{ cm} \div 2}{2 \text{ days} \div 2}$

You divide 2 days by 2 to get 1 day, so divide 6 cm by 2 also.

Simplify: $\quad = \dfrac{3 \text{ cm}}{1 \text{ day}}$

ANSWER The plant's rate of growth is 3 centimeters per day.

Proportions

A **proportion** is an equation stating that two ratios are equivalent. To solve for an unknown value in a proportion, you can use cross products.

Example

If a plant grew 6 centimeters in 2 days, how many centimeters would it grow in 3 days (if its rate of growth is constant)?

Write a proportion:	$\dfrac{6 \text{ cm}}{2 \text{ days}} = \dfrac{x}{3 \text{ days}}$
Set cross products:	$6 \text{ cm} \cdot 3 = 2x$
Multiply 6 and 3:	$18 \text{ cm} = 2x$
Divide each side by 2:	$\dfrac{18 \text{ cm}}{2} = \dfrac{2x}{2}$
Simplify:	$9 \text{ cm} = x$

ANSWER The plant would grow 9 centimeters in 3 days.

Using Decimals, Fractions, and Percents

Decimals, fractions, and percentages are all ways of recording and representing data.

Decimals

A **decimal** is a number that is written in the base-ten place value system, in which a decimal point separates the ones and tenths digits. The values of each place is ten times that of the place to its right.

Example

A caterpillar traveled from point *A* to point *C* along the path shown.

A   **36.9 cm**   B   **52.4 cm**   C

ADDING DECIMALS To find the total distance traveled by the caterpillar, add the distance from *A* to *B* and the distance from *B* to *C*. Begin by lining up the decimal points. Then add the figures as you would whole numbers and bring down the decimal point.

```
  36.9 cm
+ 52.4 cm
  89.3 cm
```

ANSWER The caterpillar traveled a total distance of 89.3 centimeters.

Example continued

SUBTRACTING DECIMALS To find how much farther the caterpillar traveled on the second leg of the journey, subtract the distance from *A* to *B* from the distance from *B* to *C*.

$$\begin{array}{r} 52.4 \text{ cm} \\ -\ 36.9 \text{ cm} \\ \hline 15.5 \text{ cm} \end{array}$$

ANSWER The caterpillar traveled 15.5 centimeters farther on the second leg of the journey.

Example

A caterpillar is traveling from point *D* to point *F* along the path shown. The caterpillar travels at a speed of 9.6 centimeters per minute.

D   **E**   **33.6 cm**   **F**

MULTIPLYING DECIMALS You can multiply decimals as you would whole numbers. The number of decimal places in the product is equal to the sum of the number of decimal places in the factors.

For instance, suppose it takes the caterpillar 1.5 minutes to go from *D* to *E*. To find the distance from *D* to *E*, multiply the caterpillar's speed by the time it took.

> **Align as shown.** ▶

$$\begin{array}{rl} 9.6 & \quad 1 \quad \text{decimal place} \\ \times\ 1.5 & +\ 1 \quad \text{decimal place} \\ \hline 480 & \\ 96 & \\ \hline 14.40 & \quad 2 \quad \text{decimal places} \end{array}$$

ANSWER The distance from *D* to *E* is 14.4 centimeters.

DIVIDING DECIMALS When you divide by a decimal, move the decimal points the same number of places in the divisor and the dividend to make the divisor a whole number.

For instance, to find the time it will take the caterpillar to travel from *E* to *F*, divide the distance from *E* to *F* by the caterpillar's speed.

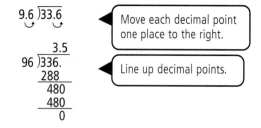

9.6)33.6   ◀ Move each decimal point one place to the right.

$$\begin{array}{r} 3.5 \\ 96\ \overline{)336.} \\ \underline{288} \\ 480 \\ \underline{480} \\ 0 \end{array}$$

◀ Line up decimal points.

ANSWER The caterpillar will travel from *E* to *F* in 3.5 minutes.

Fractions

A **fraction** is a number in the form $\frac{a}{b}$, where b is not equal to 0. A fraction is in **simplest form** if its numerator and denominator have a greatest common factor (GCF) of 1. To simplify a fraction, divide its numerator and denominator by their GCF.

Example

A caterpillar is 40 millimeters long. The head of the caterpillar is 6 millimeters long. To compare the length of the caterpillar's head with the caterpillar's total length, you can write and simplify a fraction that expresses the ratio of the two lengths.

Write the ratio of the two lengths: $\dfrac{\text{Length of head}}{\text{Total length}} = \dfrac{6 \text{ mm}}{40 \text{ mm}}$

Write numerator and denominator as products of numbers and the GCF: $= \dfrac{3 \times 2}{20 \times 2}$

Divide numerator and denominator by the GCF: $= \dfrac{3 \times \overset{1}{\cancel{2}}}{20 \times \underset{1}{\cancel{2}}}$

Simplify: $= \dfrac{3}{20}$

ANSWER In simplest form, the ratio of the lengths is $\frac{3}{20}$.

Percents

A **percent** is a ratio that compares a number to 100. The word *percent* means "per hundred" or "out of 100." The symbol for *percent* is %.

For instance, suppose 43 out of 100 caterpillars are female. You can represent this ratio as a percent, a decimal, or a fraction.

Percent	Decimal	Fraction
43%	0.43	$\dfrac{43}{100}$

Example

In the preceding example, the ratio of the length of the caterpillar's head to the caterpillar's total length is $\frac{3}{20}$. To write this ratio as a percent, write an equivalent fraction that has a denominator of 100.

Multiply numerator and denominator by 5: $\dfrac{3}{20} = \dfrac{3 \times 5}{20 \times 5}$

$= \dfrac{15}{100}$

Write as a percent: $= 15\%$

ANSWER The caterpillar's head represents 15 percent of its total length.

Using Formulas

A **formula** is an equation that shows the general relationship between two or more quantities.

In science, a formula often has a word form and a symbolic form. The formula below expresses Ohm's law.

Word Form

$$\text{Current} = \frac{\text{voltage}}{\text{resistance}}$$

Symbolic Form

$$I = \frac{V}{R}$$

In this formula, I, V, and R are variables. A mathematical **variable** is a symbol or letter that is used to represent one or more numbers.

> The term *variable* is also used in science to refer to a factor that can change during an experiment.

Example

Suppose that you measure a voltage of 1.5 volts and a resistance of 15 ohms. You can use the formula for Ohm's law to find the current in amperes.

Write the formula for Ohm's law: $\quad I = \dfrac{V}{R}$

Substitute 1.5 volts for V and 15 ohms for R: $\quad I = \dfrac{1.5 \text{ volts}}{15 \text{ ohms}}$

Simplify: $\quad I = 0.1 \text{ amp}$

ANSWER The current is 0.1 ampere.

If you know the values of all variables but one in a formula, you can solve for the value of the unknown variable. For instance, Ohm's law can be used to find a voltage if you know the current and the resistance.

Example

Suppose that you know that a current is 0.2 amperes and the resistance is 18 ohms. Use the formula for Ohm's law to find the voltage in volts.

Write the formula for Ohm's law: $\quad I = \dfrac{V}{R}$

Substitute 0.2 amp for I and 18 ohms for R: $\quad 0.2 \text{ amp} = \dfrac{V}{18 \text{ ohms}}$

Multiply both sides by 18 ohms: $\quad 0.2 \text{ amp} \cdot 18 \text{ ohms} = V$

Simplify: $\quad 3.6 \text{ volts} = V$

ANSWER The voltage is 3.6 volts.

Finding Areas

The area of a figure is the amount of surface the figure covers.

Area is measured in square units, such as square meters (m²) or square centimeters (cm²). Formulas for the areas of three common geometric figures are shown below.

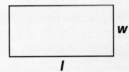

Area = (side length)²
$A = s^2$

Area = length × width
$A = lw$

Area = $\frac{1}{2}$ × base × height
$A = \frac{1}{2}bh$

Example

Each face of a halite crystal is a square like the one shown. You can find the area of the square by using the steps below.

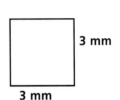

3 mm

3 mm

Write the formula for the area of a square:	$A = s^2$
Substitute 3 mm for s:	$= (3 \text{ mm})^2$
Simplify:	$= 9 \text{ mm}^2$

ANSWER The area of the square is 9 square millimeters.

Finding Volumes

The volume of a solid is the amount of space contained by the solid.

Volume is measured in cubic units, such as cubic meters (m³) or cubic centimeters (cm³). The volume of a rectangular prism is given by the formula shown below.

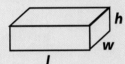

Volume = length × width × height
$V = lwh$

Example

A topaz crystal is a rectangular prism like the one shown. You can find the volume of the prism by using the steps below.

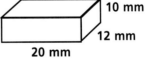

10 mm

12 mm

20 mm

Write the formula for the volume of a rectangular prism:	$V = lwh$
Substitute dimensions:	$= 20 \text{ mm} \times 12 \text{ mm} \times 10 \text{ mm}$
Simplify:	$= 2400 \text{ mm}^3$

ANSWER The volume of the rectangular prism is 2400 cubic millimeters.

Using Significant Figures

The **significant figures** in a decimal are the digits that are warranted by the accuracy of a measuring device.

When you perform a calculation with measurements, the number of significant figures to include in the result depends in part on the number of significant figures in the measurements. When you multiply or divide measurements, your answer should have only as many significant figures as the measurement with the fewest significant figures.

Example

Using a balance and a graduated cylinder filled with water, you determined that a marble has a mass of 8.0 grams and a volume of 3.5 cubic centimeters. To calculate the density of the marble, divide the mass by the volume.

Write the formula for density: $\text{Density} = \dfrac{\text{mass}}{\text{Volume}}$

Substitute measurements: $= \dfrac{8.0 \text{ g}}{3.5 \text{ cm}^3}$

Use a calculator to divide: $\approx 2.285714286 \text{ g/cm}^3$

ANSWER Because the mass and the volume have two significant figures each, give the density to two significant figures. The marble has a density of 2.3 grams per cubic centimeter.

Using Scientific Notation

Scientific notation is a shorthand way to write very large or very small numbers. For example, 73,500,000,000,000,000,000,000 kg is the mass of the Moon. In scientific notation, it is 7.35×10^{22} kg.

Example

You can convert from standard form to scientific notation.

Standard Form	Scientific Notation
720,000	7.2×10^5
5 decimal places left	Exponent is 5.
0.000291	2.91×10^{-4}
4 decimal places right	Exponent is −4.

You can convert from scientific notation to standard form.

Scientific Notation	Standard Form
4.63×10^7	46,300,000
Exponent is 7.	7 decimal places right
1.08×10^{-6}	0.00000108
Exponent is −6.	6 decimal places left

Note-Taking Handbook

Note-Taking Strategies

Taking notes as you read helps you understand the information. The notes you take can also be used as a study guide for later review. This handbook presents several ways to organize your notes.

Content Frame

1. Make a chart in which each column represents a category.
2. Give each column a heading.
3. Write details under the headings.

NAME	GROUP	CHARACTERISTICS	DRAWING
snail	mollusks	mantle, shell	
ant	arthropods	six legs, exoskeleton	
earthworm	segmented worms	segmented body, circulatory and digestive systems	
heartworm	roundworms	digestive system	
sea star	echinoderms	spiny skin, tube feet	
jellyfish	cnidarians	stinging cells	

categories

details

Combination Notes

1. For each new idea or concept, write an informal outline of the information.
2. Make a sketch to illustrate the concept, and label it.

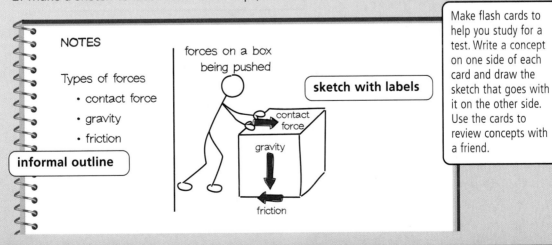

NOTES

Types of forces
- contact force
- gravity
- friction

informal outline

forces on a box being pushed

sketch with labels

contact force

gravity

friction

Make flash cards to help you study for a test. Write a concept on one side of each card and draw the sketch that goes with it on the other side. Use the cards to review concepts with a friend.

Main Idea and Detail Notes

1. In the left-hand column of a two-column chart, list main ideas. The blue headings express main ideas throughout this textbook.

2. In the right-hand column, write details that expand on each main idea.

You can shorten the headings in your chart. Be sure to use the most important words.

When studying for tests, cover up the detail notes column with a sheet of paper. Then use each main idea to form a question—such as "How does latitude affect climate?" Answer the question, and then uncover the detail notes column to check your answer.

MAIN IDEAS	DETAIL NOTES
1. Latitude affects climate. *(main idea 1)*	1. Places close to the equator are usually warmer than places close to the poles. *(details about main idea 1)* 1. Latitude has the same effect in both hemispheres.
2. Altitude affects climate. *(main idea 2)*	2. Temperature decreases with altitude. 2. Altitude can overcome the effect of latitude on temperature. *(details about main idea 2)*

Main Idea Web

1. Write a main idea in a box.
2. Add boxes around it with related vocabulary terms and important details.

You can find definitions near highlighted terms.

definition of *work*
Work is the use of force to move an object.

formula
Work = force · distance

main idea
Force is necessary to do work.

The joule is the unit used to measure work.
definition of *joule*

Work depends on the size of a force.
important detail

Mind Map

1. Write a main idea in the center.

2. Add details that relate to one another and to the main idea.

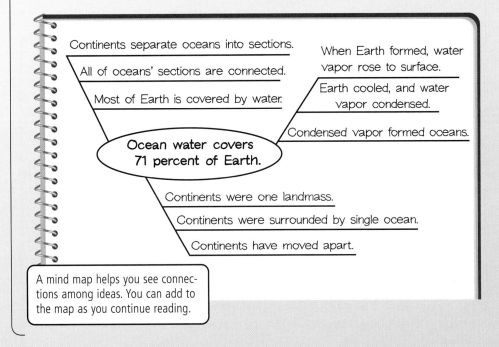

Continents separate oceans into sections.

All of oceans' sections are connected.

Most of Earth is covered by water.

When Earth formed, water vapor rose to surface.

Earth cooled, and water vapor condensed.

Condensed vapor formed oceans.

Ocean water covers 71 percent of Earth.

Continents were one landmass.

Continents were surrounded by single ocean.

Continents have moved apart.

A mind map helps you see connections among ideas. You can add to the map as you continue reading.

Supporting Main Ideas

1. Write a main idea in a box.

2. Add boxes underneath with information—such as reasons, explanations, and examples—that supports the main idea.

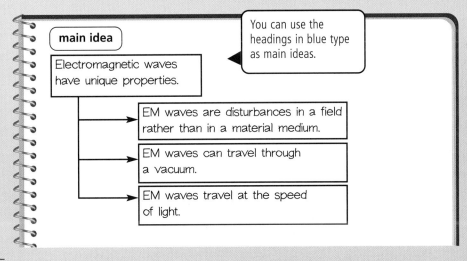

main idea

Electromagnetic waves have unique properties.

You can use the headings in blue type as main ideas.

EM waves are disturbances in a field rather than in a material medium.

EM waves can travel through a vacuum.

EM waves travel at the speed of light.

Outline

1. Copy the chapter title and headings from the book in the form of an outline.
2. Add notes that summarize in your own words what you read.

Cell Processes

> **1st key idea**

> **1st subpoint of I**

> **2nd subpoint of I**

I. Cells capture and release energy.

   A. All cells need energy.

   B. Some cells capture light energy.

> **1st detail about B**

> **2nd detail about B**

      1. Process of photosynthesis

      2. Chloroplasts (site of photosynthesis)

      3. Carbon dioxide and water as raw materials

      4. Glucose and oxygen as products

   C. All cells release energy.

      1. Process of cellular respiration

      2. Fermentation of sugar to carbon dioxide

      3. Bacteria that carry out fermentation

II. Cells transport materials through membranes.

   A. Some materials move by diffusion.

      1. Particle movement from higher to lower concentrations

      2. Movement of water through membrane (osmosis)

   B. Some transport requires energy.

      1. Active transport

      2. Examples of active transport

Correct Outline Form

Include a title.

Arrange key ideas, subpoints, and details as shown.

Indent the divisions of the outline as shown.

Use the same grammatical form for items of the same rank. For example, if A is a sentence, B must also be a sentence.

You must have at least two main ideas or subpoints. That is, every A must be followed by a B, and every 1 must be followed by a 2.

Concept Map

1. Write an important concept in a large oval.
2. Add details related to the concept in smaller ovals.
3. Write linking words on arrows that connect the ovals.

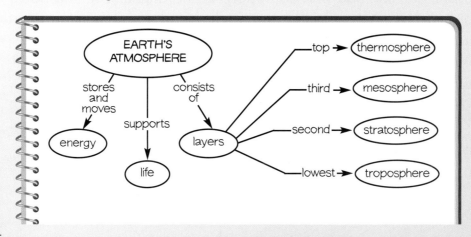

The main ideas or concepts can often be found in the blue headings. An example is "The atmosphere stores and moves energy." Use nouns from these concepts in the ovals, and use the verb or verbs on the lines.

Venn Diagram

1. Draw two overlapping circles, one for each item that you are comparing.
2. In the overlapping section, list the characteristics that are shared by both items.
3. In the outer sections, list the characteristics that are peculiar to each item.
4. Write a summary that describes the information in the Venn diagram.

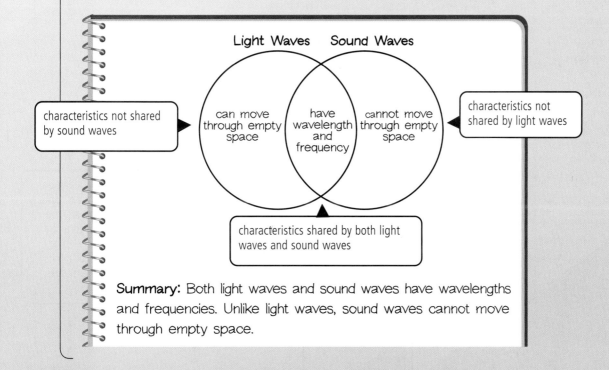

characteristics not shared by sound waves

characteristics not shared by light waves

characteristics shared by both light waves and sound waves

Summary: Both light waves and sound waves have wavelengths and frequencies. Unlike light waves, sound waves cannot move through empty space.

Vocabulary Strategies

Important terms are highlighted in this book. A definition of each term can be found in the sentence or paragraph where the term appears. You can also find definitions in the Glossary. Taking notes about vocabulary terms helps you understand and remember what you read.

Description Wheel

1. Write a term inside a circle.
2. Write words that describe the term on "spokes" attached to the circle.

When studying for a test with a friend, read the phrases on the spokes one at a time until your friend identifies the correct term.

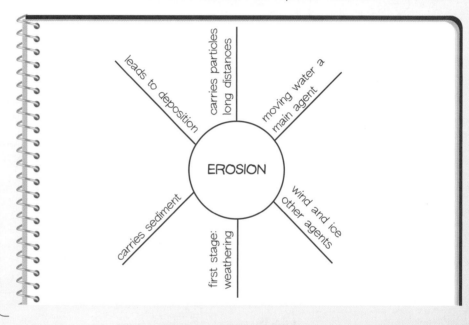

Four Square

1. Write a term in the center.
2. Write details in the four areas around the term.

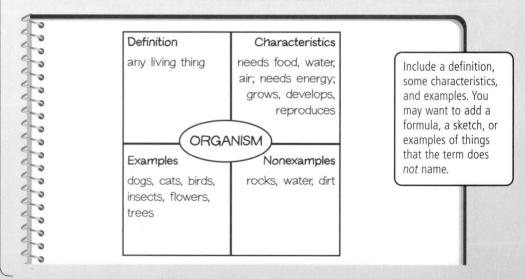

Include a definition, some characteristics, and examples. You may want to add a formula, a sketch, or examples of things that the term does *not* name.

Frame Game

1. Write a term in the center.
2. Frame the term with details.

Include examples, descriptions, sketches, or sentences that use the term in context. Change the frame to fit each new term.

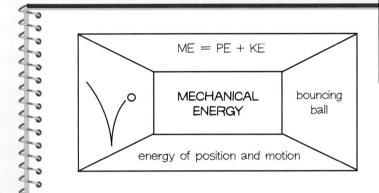

$$ME = PE + KE$$

MECHANICAL ENERGY — bouncing ball

energy of position and motion

Magnet Word

1. Write a term on the magnet.
2. On the lines, add details related to the term.

You can also use phrases or sentences on the lines.

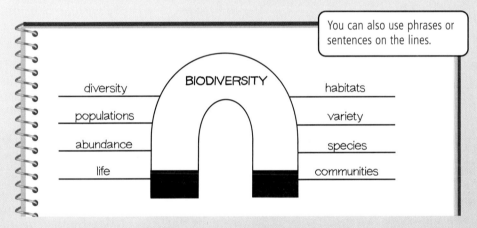

BIODIVERSITY

diversity	habitats
populations	variety
abundance	species
life	communities

Word Triangle

1. Write a term and its definition in the bottom section.
2. In the middle section, write a sentence in which the term is used correctly.
3. In the top section, draw a small picture to illustrate the term.

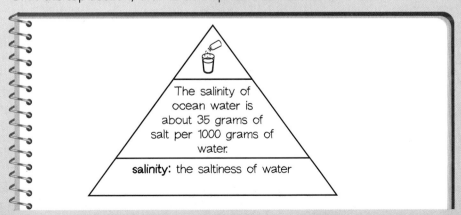

The salinity of ocean water is about 35 grams of salt per 1000 grams of water.

salinity: the saltiness of water

Appendix

Properties of Common Minerals

In this table, minerals are arranged alphabetically, and the most useful properties for identification are printed in *italic* type. Most minerals can be identified by means of two or three of the properties listed below. For some minerals, density is important; for others, cleavage is characteristic; and for others, the crystal shapes identify the minerals. The colors listed are the most common for each mineral.

Name	Hardness	Color	Streak	Cleavage	Remarks
Apatite	5	Green, brown	White	Poor in one direction	Nonmetallic (glassy) luster. Sp. gr. 3.1 to 3.2.
Augite	5–6	Dark green to black	Greenish	*Two directions, nearly at 90°*	Nonmetallic (glassy) luster. *Stubby four- or eight-sided crystals.* Common type of pyroxene. Sp. gr. 3.2 to 3.4.
Beryl	7.5–8	*Bluish-green, yellow, pink, colorless*	White	Imperfect in one direction	Nonmetallic (glassy) luster. *Hardness, greenish color, six-sided crystals.* Aquamarine and emerald are gem varieties. Sp. gr. 2.6 to 2.8.
Biotite mica	2.5–3	Black, brown, dark green	White	*Perfect in one direction*	Nonmetallic (glassy) luster. *Thin elastic films peel off easily.* Sp. gr. 2.8 to 3.2.
Calcite	*3*	White, colorless	White	*Perfect, three directions, not at 90° angles*	Nonmetallic (glassy to dull) luster. *Fizzes in dilute hydrochloric acid.* Sp. gr. 2.7.
Chalcopyrite	3.5–4	*Golden yellow*	Greenish black	Poor in one direction	Metallic luster. *Hardness distinguishes from pyrite.* Sp. gr. 4.1 to 4.3.
Chlorite	2–2.5	*Greenish*	Pale green to gray or brown	Perfect in one direction	Nonmetallic (glassy to pearly) luster. *Nonelastic flakes.* Sp. gr. 2.6 to 3.3.
Copper	2.5–3	*Copper red*	Copper	None	*Metallic luster on fresh surface. Dense.* Sp. gr. 8.9.
Corundum	9	Brown, pink, blue	White	None, parting resembles cleavage	Nonmetallic (glassy to brilliant) luster. *Barrel-shaped, six-sided crystals with flat ends.* Sp. gr. 4.0.
Diamond	10	Colorless to pale yellow	White	Perfect, four directions	Nonmetallic (brilliant to greasy) luster. *Hardest of all minerals.* Sp. gr. 3.5.

Sp. gr. = specific gravity

Name	Hardness	Color	Streak	Cleavage	Remarks
Dolomite	3.5–4	Pinkish, colorless, white	White	*Perfect, three directions, not at 90° angles*	Nonmetallic luster. *Scratched surface fizzes in dilute hydrochloric acid. Cleavage surfaces curved. Sp. gr. 2.8 to 2.9.*
Feldspar (Orthoclase)	*6*	*Salmon pink, red, white,* light gray	White	*Good, two directions, 90° intersection*	Nonmetallic (glassy) luster. *Hardness, color, and cleavage taken together are diagnostic.* Sp. gr. 2.6.
Feldspar (Plagioclase)	6	*White to light gray,* can be salmon pink	White	*Good, two directions, about 90°*	Nonmetallic (glassy to pearly) luster. *If striations are visible, they are diagnostic.* Sp. gr. 2.6 to 2.8.
Fluorite	4	Varies	White	*Perfect, four directions*	Nonmetallic (glassy) luster. In cubes or octahedrons as crystals. Sp. gr. 3.2.
Galena	2.5	*Lead gray*	Lead gray	*Perfect, three directions, at 90° angles*	*Metallic luster.* Occurs as crystals and masses. *Dense.* Sp. gr. 7.4 to 7.6.
Gold	2.5–3	*Gold*	Gold	None	Metallic luster. *Dense.* Sp. gr. 15.0 to 19.3.
Graphite	1–2	*Dark gray to black*	Grayish black	*Perfect in one direction*	Metallic or nonmetallic (earthy) luster. *Greasy feel, marks paper.* This is the "lead" in a pencil (mixed with clay). Sp. gr. 2.2.
Gypsum	*2*	Colorless, white, gray, yellowish, reddish	White	*Perfect in one direction*	Nonmetallic (glassy to silky) luster. *Can be scratched easily by a fingernail.* Sp. gr. 2.3.
Halite	2–2.5	Colorless, white	White	*Perfect, three directions, at 90° angles*	Nonmetallic (glassy) luster. *Salty taste.* Sp. gr. 2.2.
Hematite	5–6 (may appear softer)	*Reddish-brown, gray, black*	*Reddish*	None	Metallic or nonmetallic (earthy) luster. *Dense.* Sp. gr. 5.3.
Hornblende	5–6	*Dark green to black*	Brown to gray	*Perfect, two directions at angles of 56° and 124°*	Nonmetallic (glassy to silky) luster. Common type of amphibole. Long, slender, six-sided crystals. Sp. gr. 3.0 to 3.4.
Kaolinite	2	White, gray, yellowish	White	*Perfect in one direction*	Nonmetallic (dull, earthy) luster. Claylike masses. Sp. gr. 2.6.
Limonite group	4–5.5	*Yellow, brown*	Yellowish brown	None	Nonmetallic (earthy) luster. Rust stains. Sp. gr. 2.9 to 4.3.
Magnetite	5.5–6.5	*Black*	Black	None	Metallic luster. Occurs as eight-sided crystals and granular masses. *Magnetic. Dense.* Sp. gr. 5.2.

Sp. gr. = specific gravity

Properties of Common Minerals *continued*

Name	Hardness	Color	Streak	Cleavage	Remarks
Muscovite mica	2–2.5	Colorless in thin films; silvery, yellowish, and greenish in thicker pieces	White	Perfect in one direction	Nonmetallic (glassy to pearly) luster. *Thin elastic films peel off readily.* Sp. gr. 2.8 to 2.9.
Olivine	6.5–7	*Yellowish, greenish*	White	*None*	*Nonmetallic (glassy) luster. Granular.* Sp. gr. 3.3 to 4.4.
Opal	5–6.5	Varies	White	None	*Nonmetallic (glassy to pearly) luster. Conchoidal fracture.* Sp. gr. 2.0 to 2.2.
Pyrite	6–6.5	*Brass yellow*	Greenish black	None	Metallic luster. *Cubic crystals and granular masses. Dense.* Sp. gr. 5.0 to 5.1.
Quartz	7	*Colorless, white; varies*	White	None	Nonmetallic (glassy) luster. *Conchoidal fracture. Six-sided crystals common.* Many varieties. Sp. gr. 2.6.
Serpentine	3–5	*Greenish (variegated)*	White	None or good in one direction, depending on variety	*Nonmetallic (greasy, waxy, or silky) luster. Conchoidal fracture.* Sp. gr. 2.5 to 2.6.
Sphalerite	3.5–4	*Yellow, brown, black*	Yellow to light brown	*Perfect, six directions*	*Nonmetallic (brilliant to resinous) luster.* Sp. gr. 3.9 to 4.1.
Sulfur	1.5–2.5	*Yellow*	Yellow	Poor, two directions	Nonmetallic (glassy to earthy) luster. Granular. Sp. gr. 2.0 to 2.1.
Talc	1	Apple-green, gray, white	White	Perfect in one direction	Nonmetallic (pearly to greasy) luster. Nonelastic flakes, *greasy feel.* Sp. gr. 2.7 to 2.8.
Topaz	8	Varies	White	Perfect in one direction	Nonmetallic (brilliant to glassy) luster. *Crystals commonly striated length-wise.* Sp. gr. 3.4 to 3.6.
Tourmaline	7–7.5	*Black; varies*	White	None	Nonmetallic (glassy) luster. *Crystals often have triangular cross sections. Conchoidal fracture.* Sp. gr. 3.0 to 3.3.

Sp. gr. = specific gravity

APPENDIX

Topographic Map Symbols

The U.S. Geological Survey uses the following symbols to mark human-made and natural features on all of the topographic maps the USGS produces.

Primary highway, hard surface ....

Secondary highway, hard surface ....

Light-duty road, hard or improved surface...

Unimproved road ....

Trail ....

Railroad: single track ....

Railroad: multiple track ....

Bridge ....

Drawbridge ....

Tunnel ....

Footbridge ....

Overpass—Underpass ....

Power transmission line with located tower ..

Landmark line (labeled as to type)..............

Dam with lock ....

Canal with lock ....

Large dam...

Small dam: masonry—earth ....

Buildings (dwelling, place of employment, etc.)..

School—Church—Cemeteries.......................

Buildings (barn, warehouse, etc.)....................

Tanks; oil, water, etc. (labeled only if water)....

Wells other than water (labeled as to type)....

U.S. mineral or location monument—Prospect...

Quarry—Gravel pit ....

Mine shaft—Tunnel or cave entrance...........

Campsite—Picnic area...............................

Located or landmark object—Windmill..........

Exposed wreck..

Rock or coral reef..

Foreshore flat ....

Rock: bare or awash....................................

Benchmarks...

Road fork—Section corner with elevation ...

Checked spot elevation ....

Unchecked spot elevation............................

Boundary: national....................................

   State ....

   county, parish, municipio.........................

   civil township, precinct, town, barrio....

   incorporated city, village, town, hamlet.

   reservation, national or state ....

   small park, cemetery, airport, etc. ....

   land grant ....

Township or range line, U.S. land survey

Section line, U.S. land survey ....

Township line, not U.S. land survey ....

Section line, not U.S. land survey...............

Fence line or field line................................

Section corner: found—indicated................

Boundary monument: land grant—other...

Index contour   Intermediate contour

Supplementary cont   Depression contours

Cut—Fill.........   Levee ....

Mine dump .....   Large wash ......

Dune area ....   Distorted surface

Sand area ....   Gravel beach ...

Glacier ....   Intermittent streams

Seasonal streams   Aqueduct tunnel

Water well—Spring   Falls................

Rapids............   Intermittent lake

Channel ....   Small wash ...

Sounding—Depth curve ..   Marsh (swamp)

Dry lake bed ...   Land subject to controlled flooding

Woodland......   Mangrove........

Submerged marsh   Scrub ....

Orchard ....   Wooded marsh

Vineyard........   Many buildings ......

Areas revised since previous edition ....

Source: U.S. Geological Survey

Properties of Rocks and Earth's Interior

Scheme for Sedimentary Rock Identification

TEXTURE	GRAIN SIZE	COMPOSITION	COMMENTS	ROCK NAME	MAP SYMBOL
Clastic (fragmental)	Pebbles, cobbles, and/or boulders embedded in sand, silt, and/or clay	Mostly quartz, feldspar, and clay minerals; may contain fragments of other rocks and minerals	Rounded fragments	Conglomerate	
			Angular fragments	Breccia	
	Sand (0.2 to 0.006 cm)		Fine to coarse	Sandstone	
	Silt (0.006 to 0.0004 cm)		Very fine grain	Siltstone	
	Clay (less than 0.0004 cm)		Compact; may split easily	Shale	

CHEMICALLY AND/OR ORGANICALLY FORMED SEDIMENTARY ROCKS

TEXTURE	GRAIN SIZE	COMPOSITION	COMMENTS	ROCK NAME	MAP SYMBOL
Crystalline	Varied	Halite	Crystals from chemical precipitates and evaporites	Rock Salt	
	Varied	Gypsum		Rock Gypsum	
	Varied	Dolomite		Dolostone	
Bioclastic	Microscopic to coarse	Calcite	Cemented shell fragments or precipitates of biologic origin	Limestone	
	Varied	Carbon	From plant remains	Coal	

Scheme for Metamorphic Rock Identification

TEXTURE	GRAIN SIZE	COMPOSITION	TYPE OF METAMORPHISM	COMMENTS	ROCK NAME	MAP SYMBOL
FOLIATED — MINERAL ALIGNMENT	Fine	MICA QUARTZ FELDSPAR AMPHIBOLE GARNET PYROXENE	Regional (Heat and pressure increase with depth)	Low-grade metamorphism of shale	Slate	
	Fine to medium			Foliation surfaces shiny from microscopic mica crystals	Phyllite	
				Platy mica crystals visible from metamorphism of clay or feldspars	Schist	
FOLIATED — BANDING	Medium to coarse			High-grade metamorphism; some mica changed to feldspar; segregated by mineral type into bands	Gneiss	
NONFOLIATED	Fine	Variable	Contact (Heat)	Various rocks changed by heat from nearby magma/lava	Hornfels	
	Fine to coarse	Quartz	Regional or Contact	Metamorphism of quartz sandstone	Quartzite	
		Calcite and/or dolomite		Metamorphism of limestone or dolostone	Marble	
	Coarse	Various minerals in particles and matrix		Pebbles may be distorted or stretched	Metaconglomerate	

Scheme for Igneous Rock Identification

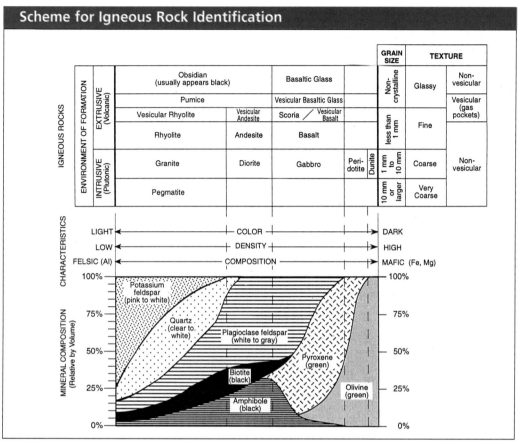

								GRAIN SIZE	TEXTURE	
IGNEOUS ROCKS	ENVIRONMENT OF FORMATION	EXTRUSIVE (Volcanic)	Obsidian (usually appears black)		Basaltic Glass			Non-crystalline	Glassy	Non-vesicular
			Pumice		Vesicular Basaltic Glass					Vesicular (gas pockets)
			Vesicular Rhyolite	Vesicular Andesite	Scoria / Vesicular Basalt			less than 1 mm	Fine	
			Rhyolite	Andesite	Basalt					Non-vesicular
		INTRUSIVE (Plutonic)	Granite	Diorite	Gabbro	Peri-dotite	Dunite	1 mm to 10 mm	Coarse	
			Pegmatite					10 mm or larger	Very Coarse	

CHARACTERISTICS

LIGHT ◄————— COLOR ————► DARK

LOW ◄————— DENSITY ————► HIGH

FELSIC (Al) ◄————— COMPOSITION ————► MAFIC (Fe, Mg)

MINERAL COMPOSITION (Relative by Volume)

- Potassium feldspar (pink to white)
- Quartz (clear to white)
- Plagioclase feldspar (white to gray)
- Biotite (black)
- Amphibole (black)
- Pyroxene (green)
- Olivine (green)

Inferred Properties of Earth's Interior

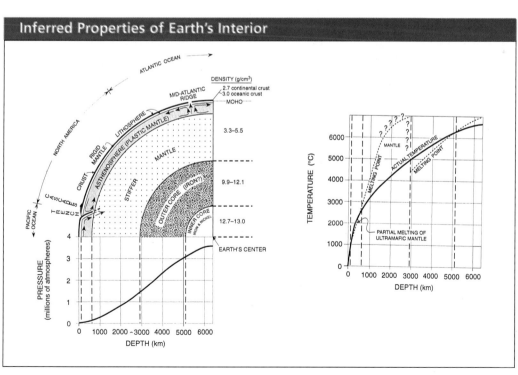

Time Zones

Because Earth rotates, noon can occur in one location at the same moment that the Sun is setting in another location. To avoid confusion in transportation and communication, officials have divided Earth into 24 time zones. Within a time zone, clocks are set to the same time of day.

Time zones are centered on lines of longitude, but instead of running straight, their boundaries often follow political boundaries. The starting point for the times zones is centered on the prime meridian (0°). The time in this zone is generally called Greenwich Mean Time (GMT), but it is also called Universal Time (UT) by astronomers and Zulu Time (Z) by meteorologists. The International Date Line is centered on 180° longitude. The calendar date to the east of this line is one day earlier than the date to the west.

In the map below, each column of color represents one time zone. The color beige shows areas that do not match standard zones. The labels at the top show the times at noon GMT. Positive and negative numbers at the bottom show the difference between the local time in the zone and Greenwich Mean Time.

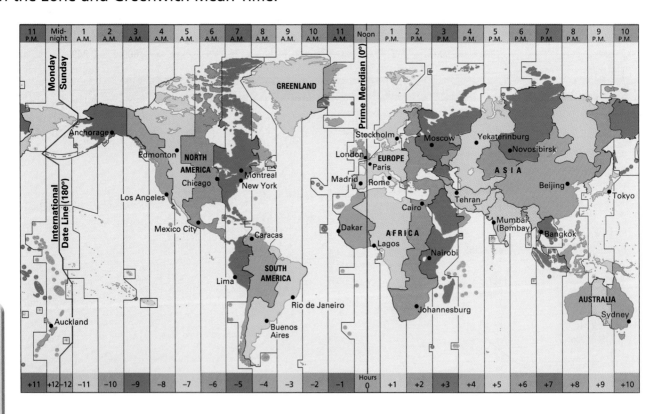

Characteristics of Planets

Some data about the planets and Earth's satellite, the Moon, are listed below. Some data, such as the tilt of Mercury and the mass of Pluto, are not known as well as other data. One astronomical unit (AU) is Earth's average distance from the Sun, or 149,597,870 kilometers. For comparison, Earth's mass is 5.97×10^{24} kilograms, and Earth's diameter is 12,756 kilometers.

Eccentricity is a measure of how flattened an ellipse is. An ellipse with an eccentricity of 0 is a circle. An ellipse with an eccentricity of 1 is completely flat.

Venus, Uranus, and Pluto rotate backward compared to Earth. If you use your left thumb as one of these planets' north pole, your fingers curve in the direction the planet turns.

Characteristics of Planets

Characteristic	Mercury	Venus	Earth	Mars	Jupiter	Saturn	Uranus	Neptune	Pluto	Moon
Mean distance from Sun (AU)	0.387	0.723	1.00	1.52	5.20	9.55	19.2	30.1	39.5	
Period of revolution (Earth years)	0.241 (88 Earth days)	0.615 (225 Earth days)	1.00	1.88	11.9	29.4	83.7	164	248	0.075 (27.3 Earth days)
Eccentricity of orbit	0.206	0.007	0.017	0.093	0.048	0.056	0.046	0.009	0.249	0.055
Diameter (Earth = 1)	0.382	0.949	1.00	0.532	11.21	9.45	4.01	3.88	0.180	0.272
Volume (Earth = 1)	0.06	0.86	1.00	0.15	1320	760	63	58	0.006	0.02
Period of rotation	58.6 Earth days	243 Earth days	23.9 hours	24.6 hours	9.93 hours	10.7 hours	17.2 hours	16.1 hours	6.39 Earth days	27.3 Earth days
Tilt of axis (°) (from perpendicular to orbit)	0.1 (approximate)	2.6	23.45	25.19	3.12	26.73	82.14	29.56	60.4	6.67
Mass (Earth = 1)	0.0553	0.815	1.00	0.107	318	95.2	14.5	17.1	0.002	0.0123
Mean density (g/cm³)	5.4	5.2	5.5	3.9	1.3	0.7	1.3	1.6	2	3.3

Seasonal Star Maps

Your view of the night sky changes as Earth orbits the Sun. Some constellations appear throughout the year, but others can be seen only during certain seasons. And over the course of one night, the constellations appear to move across the sky as Earth rotates.

When you go outside to view stars, give your eyes time to adjust to the darkness. Avoid looking at bright lights. If you need to look toward a bright light, preserve your night vision in one eye by keeping it closed.

The star maps on pages R61–R64 show parts of the night sky in different seasons. If you are using a flashlight to view the maps, you should attach a piece of red balloon over the lens. The balloon will dim the light and also give it a red color, which affects night vision less than other colors. The following steps will help you use the maps:

1. Stand facing north. To find this direction, use a compass or turn clockwise 90° from the location where the Sun set.

2. The top map for each season shows some constellations that appear over the northern horizon at 10 P.M. During the night, the constellations rotate in a circle around Polaris, the North Star.

3. Now turn so that you stand facing south. The bottom map for the season shows some constellations that appear over the southern horizon at 10 P.M.

WINTER SKY to the NORTH, *January 15*

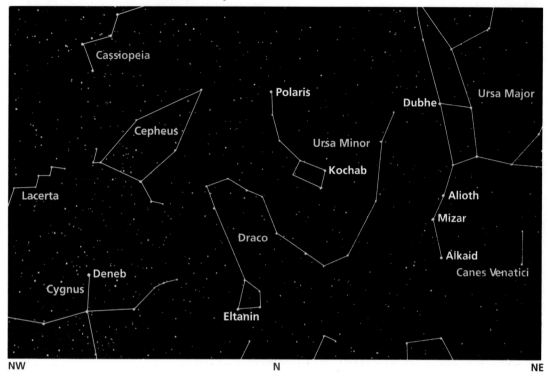

NW   N   NE

WINTER SKY to the SOUTH, *January 15*

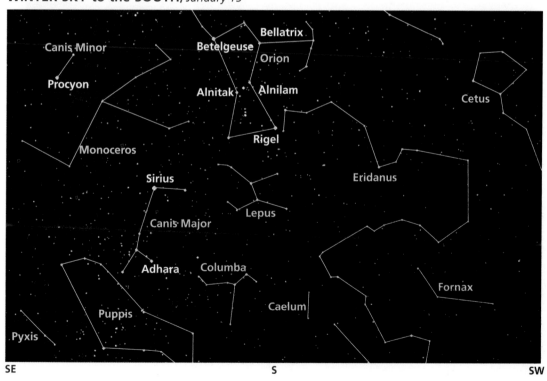

SE   S   SW

Seasonal Star Maps *continued*

SPRING SKY to the NORTH, *April 15*

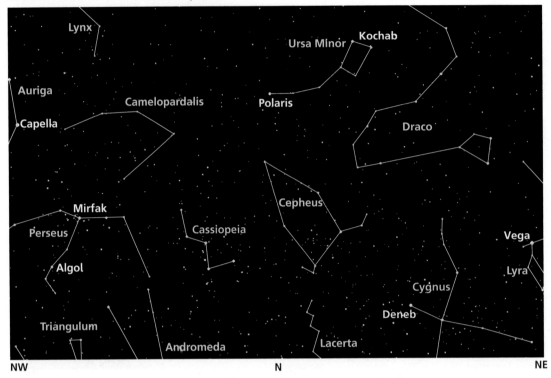

NW   N   NE

SPRING SKY to the SOUTH, *April 15*

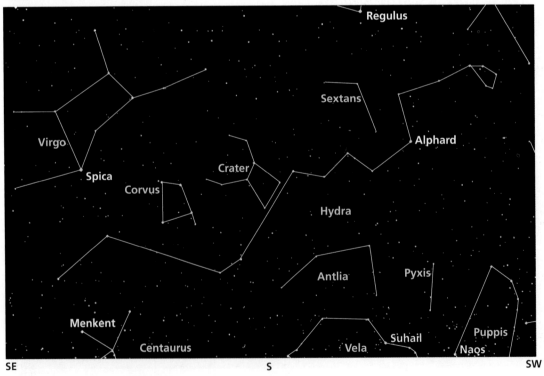

SE   S   SW

SUMMER SKY to the NORTH, *July 15*

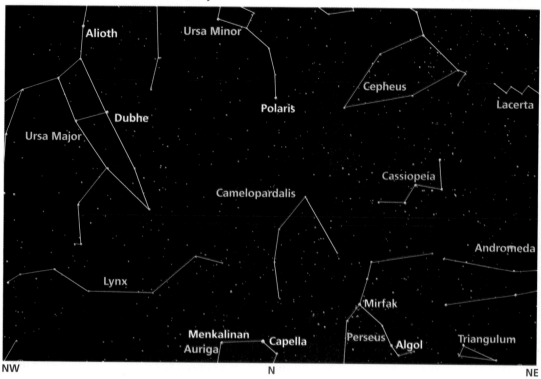

SUMMER SKY to the SOUTH, *July 15*

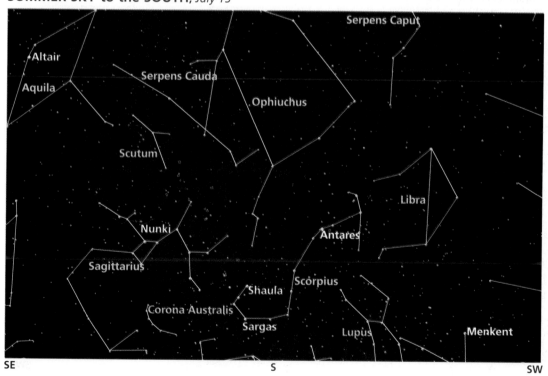

Seasonal Star Maps *continued*

AUTUMN SKY to the NORTH, *October 15*

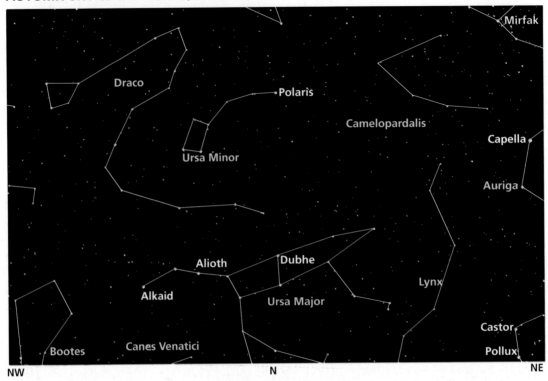

NW   N   NE

AUTUMN SKY to the SOUTH, *October 15*

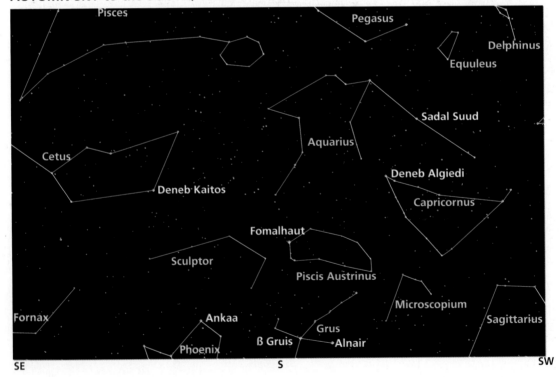

SE   S   SW

The Hertzsprung-Russell Diagram

The Hertzsprung-Russell (H-R) Diagram is a graph that shows stars plotted according to brightness and surface temperature. Most stars fall within a diagonal band called the main sequence. In the main-sequence stage of a star's life cycle, brightness is closely related to surface temperature. Red giant and red supergiant stars appear above the main sequence on the diagram. These stars are bright in relation to their surface temperatures because their huge surface areas give off a lot of light. Dim white dwarfs appear below the main sequence.

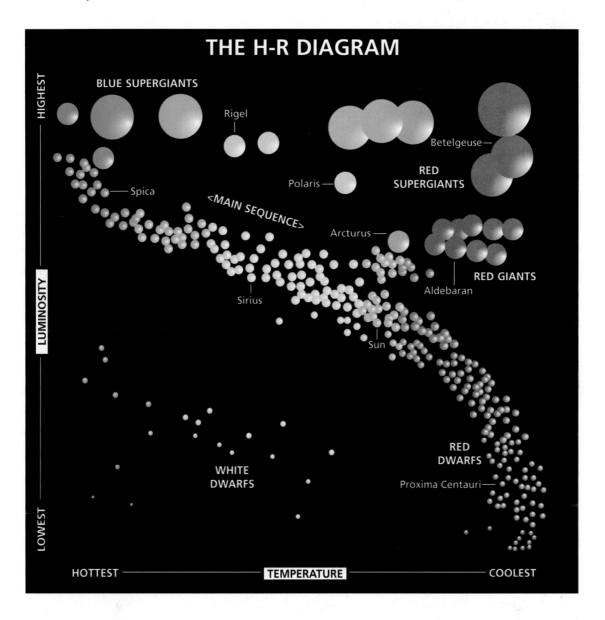

The Periodic Table of the Elements

1

1
H
Hydrogen
1.008

Period

Each row of the periodic table is called a **period**. As read from left to right, one proton and one electron are added from one element to the next.

2

3	4
Li	**Be**
Lithium	Beryllium
6.941	9.012

11	12
Na	**Mg**
Sodium	Magnesium
22.990	24.305

3	**4**	**5**	**6**	**7**	**8**	**9**
21	22	23	24	25	26	27
Sc	**Ti**	**V**	**Cr**	**Mn**	**Fe**	**Co**
Scandium	Titanium	Vanadium	Chromium	Manganese	Iron	Cobalt
44.956	47.87	50.942	51.996	54.938	55.845	58.933
39	40	41	42	43	44	45
Y	**Zr**	**Nb**	**Mo**	**Tc**	**Ru**	**Rh**
Yttrium	Zirconium	Niobium	Molybdenum	Technetium	Ruthenium	Rhodium
88.906	91.224	92.906	95.94	(98)	101.07	102.906
57	72	73	74	75	76	77
La	**Hf**	**Ta**	**W**	**Re**	**Os**	**Ir**
Lanthanum	Hafnium	Tantalum	Tungsten	Rhenium	Osmium	Iridium
138.906	178.49	180.95	183.84	186.207	190.23	192.217
89	104	105	106	107	108	109
Ac	**Rf**	**Db**	**Sg**	**Bh**	**Hs**	**Mt**
Actinium	Rutherfordium	Dubnium	Seaborgium	Bohrium	Hassium	Meitnerium
(227)	(261)	(262)	(266)	(264)	(269)	(268)

Row 4 leftmost (Group 1, 2):

19	20
K	**Ca**
Potassium	Calcium
39.098	40.078

37	38
Rb	**Sr**
Rubidium	Strontium
85.468	87.62

55	56
Cs	**Ba**
Cesium	Barium
132.905	137.327

87	88
Fr	**Ra**
Francium	Radium
(223)	(226)

Group

Each column of the table is called a **group**. Elements in a group share similar properties. Groups are read from top to bottom.

58	59	60	61	62
Ce	**Pr**	**Nd**	**Pm**	**Sm**
Cerium	Praseodymium	Neodymium	Promethium	Samarium
140.116	140.908	144.24	(145)	150.36
90	91	92	93	94
Th	**Pa**	**U**	**Np**	**Pu**
Thorium	Protactinium	Uranium	Neptunium	Plutonium
232.038	231.036	238.029	(237)	(244)

 Metal   Metalloid   Nonmetal   **Fe** Solid   **Hg** Liquid   Gas

APPENDIX

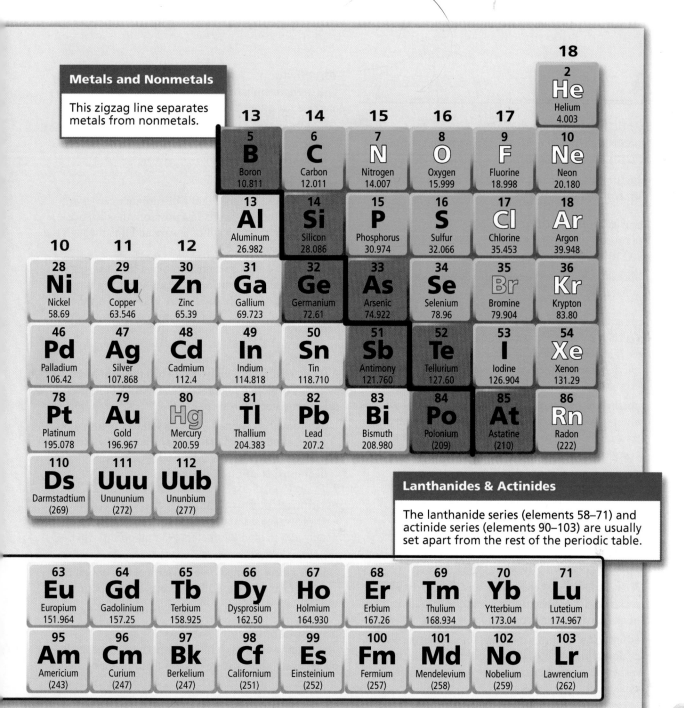

Metals and Nonmetals

This zigzag line separates metals from nonmetals.

18
2 **He** Helium 4.003

13	14	15	16	17
5 **B** Boron 10.811	6 **C** Carbon 12.011	7 **N** Nitrogen 14.007	8 **O** Oxygen 15.999	9 **F** Fluorine 18.998

| 13 **Al** Aluminum 26.982 | 14 **Si** Silicon 28.086 | 15 **P** Phosphorus 30.974 | 16 **S** Sulfur 32.066 | 17 **Cl** Chlorine 35.453 | 18 **Ar** Argon 39.948 |

10	11	12
28 **Ni** Nickel 58.69	29 **Cu** Copper 63.546	30 **Zn** Zinc 65.39
46 **Pd** Palladium 106.42	47 **Ag** Silver 107.868	48 **Cd** Cadmium 112.4
78 **Pt** Platinum 195.078	79 **Au** Gold 196.967	80 **Hg** Mercury 200.59
110 **Ds** Darmstadtium (269)	111 **Uuu** Unununium (272)	112 **Uub** Ununbium (277)

31 **Ga** Gallium 69.723	32 **Ge** Germanium 72.61	33 **As** Arsenic 74.922	34 **Se** Selenium 78.96	35 **Br** Bromine 79.904	36 **Kr** Krypton 83.80
49 **In** Indium 114.818	50 **Sn** Tin 118.710	51 **Sb** Antimony 121.760	52 **Te** Tellurium 127.60	53 **I** Iodine 126.904	54 **Xe** Xenon 131.29
81 **Tl** Thallium 204.383	82 **Pb** Lead 207.2	83 **Bi** Bismuth 208.980	84 **Po** Polonium (209)	85 **At** Astatine (210)	86 **Rn** Radon (222)

Lanthanides & Actinides

The lanthanide series (elements 58–71) and actinide series (elements 90–103) are usually set apart from the rest of the periodic table.

| 63 **Eu** Europium 151.964 | 64 **Gd** Gadolinium 157.25 | 65 **Tb** Terbium 158.925 | 66 **Dy** Dysprosium 162.50 | 67 **Ho** Holmium 164.930 | 68 **Er** Erbium 167.26 | 69 **Tm** Thulium 168.934 | 70 **Yb** Ytterbium 173.04 | 71 **Lu** Lutetium 174.967 |
| 95 **Am** Americium (243) | 96 **Cm** Curium (247) | 97 **Bk** Berkelium (247) | 98 **Cf** Californium (251) | 99 **Es** Einsteinium (252) | 100 **Fm** Fermium (257) | 101 **Md** Mendelevium (258) | 102 **No** Nobelium (259) | 103 **Lr** Lawrencium (262) |

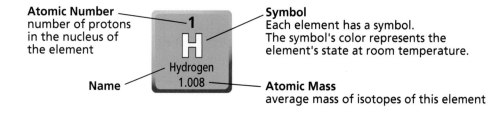

Atomic Number number of protons in the nucleus of the element

1 **H** Hydrogen 1.008

Symbol Each element has a symbol. The symbol's color represents the element's state at room temperature.

Name

Atomic Mass average mass of isotopes of this element

APPENDIX

Glossary

A

abiotic factor (ay-by-AHT-ihk)
A nonliving physical or chemical part of an ecosystem. (p. D10)

factor abiótico Una parte física o química sin vida de un ecosistema.

abrasion (uh-BRAY-zhuhn)
The process of wearing something down by friction. (p. A116)

abrasión El proceso de desgaste de algo por efecto de la fricción.

absorption (uhb-SAWRP-shuhn)
The disappearance of a wave into a medium. When a wave is absorbed, the energy transferred by the wave is converted into another form of energy, usually thermal energy. (p. C93)

absorción La desaparición de una onda dentro de un medio. Cuando se absorbe una onda, la energía transferida por la onda se convierte a otra forma de energía, normalmente a energía térmica.

acoustics (uh-KOO-stihks)
The scientific study of sound; the behavior of sound waves inside a space. (p. C55)

acústica El estudio científico del sonido; el comportamiento de las ondas sonoras dentro de un espacio.

adaptation
A characteristic, a behavior, or any inherited trait that makes a species able to survive and reproduce in a particular environment. (p. xxxi)

adaptación Una característica, un comportamiento o cualquier rasgo heredado que permite a una especie sobrevivir o reproducirse en un medio ambiente determinado.

alluvial fan (uh-LOO-vee-uhl)
A fan-shaped deposit of sediment at the base of a slope, formed as water flows down the slope and spreads at the bottom. (p. A153)

abanico aluvial Un depósito de sedimentos en forma de abanico situado en la base de una pendiente; se forma cuando el agua baja por la pendiente y se dispersa al llegar al pie de la misma.

amplification
The strengthening of an electrical signal, often used to increase the intensity of a sound wave. (p. C55)

amplificación El fortalecimiento de una señal eléctrica, a menudo se usa para aumentar la intensidad de una onda sonora.

amplitude
The maximum distance that a disturbance causes a medium to move from its rest position; the distance between a crest or trough of a wave and line through the center of a wave. (p. C17)

amplitud La distancia máxima que se mueve un medio desde su posición de reposo debido a una perturbación; la distancia entre una cresta o valle de una onda y una línea que pasa por el centro de la onda.

asteroid
A small, solid, rocky body that orbits the Sun. Most asteroids orbit in a region between Mars and Jupiter called the asteroid belt. (p. E103)

asteroide Un pequeño cuerpo sólido y rocoso que orbita alrededor del Sol. La mayoría de los asteroides orbitan en una región entre Marte y Júpiter denominada cinturón de asteroides.

astronomical unit AU
Earth's average distance from the Sun, which is approximately 150 million kilometers (93 million mi). (p. E81)

unidad astronómica ua
La distancia promedio de la Tierra al Sol, la cual es de aproximadamente 150 millones de kilómetros (93 millones de millas).

atmosphere (AT-muh-SFEER)
The outer layer of gases of a large body in space, such as a planet or star; the mixture of gases that surrounds the solid Earth; one of the four parts of the Earth system. (p. A10)

atmósfera La capa externa de gases de un gran cuerpo que se encuentra en el espacio, como un planeta o una estrella; la mezcla de gases que rodea la Tierra sólida; una de las cuatro partes del sistema terrestre.

atom
The smallest particle of an element that has the chemical properties of that element. (p. B16)

átomo La partícula más pequeña de un elemento que tiene las propiedades químicas de ese elemento.

axis of rotation
An imaginary line about which a turning body, such as Earth rotates. (p. E44)

eje de rotación Una línea imaginaria alrededor de la cual gira un cuerpo, como lo hace la Tierra.

B

barrier island
A long, narrow island that develops parallel to a coast as a sandbar builds up above the water's surface. (p. A160)

isla barrera Una isla larga y angosta que se desarrolla paralelamente a la costa al crecer una barra de arena hasta rebasar la superficie del agua.

big bang
The moment in time when the universe started to expand out of an extremely hot, dense state, according to scientific theory. (p. E138)

la gran explosión De acuerdo a la teoría científica, el momento en el tiempo en el cual el universo empezó a expandirse a partir de un estado extremadamente caliente y denso.

biodiversity
The number and variety of living things found on Earth or within an ecosystem. (p. D91)

biodiversidad La cantidad y variedad de organismos vivos que se encuentran en la Tierra o dentro de un ecosistema.

biology
The scientific study of life and all living things; ecology, zoology, and botany are examples of biological sciences.

biología El estudio científico de la vida y de todos los organismos vivos; la ecología, la zoología y la botántica son ejemplos de ciencias biológicas.

bioluminescence
The production of light by living organisms. (p. C89)

bioluminiscencia La producción de luz por parte de organismos vivos.

biome (BY-OHM)
A region of Earth that has a particular climate and certain types of plants. Examples are tundra, taiga, desert, grassland, temperate and tropical forests. (p. D30)

bioma Una región de la Tierra que tiene un clima particular y ciertos tipos de plantas. La tundra, la taiga, el desierto, la estepa, la selva tropical y el bosque templado son ejemplos de biomas.

biosphere (BY-uh-SFEER)
All living organisms on Earth in the air, on the land, and in the waters; one of the four parts of the Earth system. (p. A11)

biosfera Todos los organismos vivos de la Tierra, en el aire, en la tierra y en las aguas; una de las cuatro partes del sistema de la Tierra.

biotic factor (by-AHT-ihk)
A living thing in an ecosystem. (p. D10)

factor biótico Un organismo vivo en un ecosistema.

black hole
The final stage of an extremely massive star, which is invisible because its gravity prevents any form of radiation from escaping. (p. E126)

hoyo negro La etapa final de una estrella de enorme masa, la cual es invisible porque su gravedad evita que cualquier tipo de radiación escape.

boiling
A process by which a substance changes from its liquid state to its gas state. The liquid is heated to a specific temperature at which bubbles of vapor form within the liquid. (p. B54)

ebullición Un proceso mediante el cual una sustancia cambia de su estado líquido a su estado gaseoso se calienta el líquido a una determinada temperatura a la cual se forman burbujas de vapor dentro del líquido.

boiling point
The temperature at which a substance changes from its liquid state to its gas state through boiling. (p. B54)

punto de ebullición La temperatura a la cual una sustancia cambia de su estado líquido a su estado gaseoso mediante ebullición.

C

calorie
The amount of energy needed to increase the temperature of one gram of water by one degree Celsius. (p. B112)

caloría La cantidad de energía que se necesita para aumentar la temperatura de un gramo de agua un grado centígrado.

carbon cycle
The continuous movement of carbon through Earth, its atmosphere, and the living things on Earth. (p. D18)

ciclo del carbono El movimiento continuo del carbono en la Tierra, su atmósfera y todos los seres vivos en ella.

carrying capacity

The maximum size that a population can reach in an ecosystem. (p. D65)

capacidad de carga El tamaño máximo que una población puede alcanzar en un ecosistema.

cell

The smallest unit that is able to perform the basic functions of life. (p. xxxi)

célula La unidad más pequeña capaz de realizar las funciones básicas de la vida.

chemical change

A change of one substance into another substance. (p. B46)

cambio químico La transformación de una sustancia a otra sustancia.

chemical property

A characteristic of a substance that describes how it can form a new substance. (p. B46)

propiedad química Una característica de una sustancia que describe como puede formar una nueva sustancia.

chemical weathering

The breakdown or decomposition of rock that takes place when minerals change through chemical processes. (p. A118)

meteorización química La descomposición de las rocas que ocurre cuando los minerales cambian mediante procesos químicos.

classification

The systematic grouping of different types of organisms by their shared characteristics.

clasificación La agrupación sistemática de diferentes tipos de organismos en base a las características que comparten.

cleavage

The property of a mineral that describes its tendency to break along flat surfaces. (p. A53)

clivaje La propiedad de un mineral que describe su tendencia a romperse a lo largo de una superficie plana.

climate

The characteristic weather conditions in an area over a long period of time.

clima Las condiciones meteorológicas características de un lugar durante un largo período de tiempo.

comet

A body that produces a coma of gas and dust; a small, icy body that orbits the Sun. (p. E104)

cometa Un cuerpo que produce una coma de gas y polvo; un cuerpo pequeño y helado que se mueve en órbita alrededor del Sol.

commensalism (kuh-MEHN-suh-lihz-uhm)

An interaction between two species in which one species benefits without harming the other; a type of symbiosis. (p. D59)

comensalismo Una interacción entre dos especies en la cual una especie se beneficia sin causar daño a la otra; un tipo de simbiosis.

community

All the populations that live and interact with each other in a particular place. The community can live in a place as small as a pond or a park, or it can live in a place as large as a rain forest or the ocean. (p. D48)

comunidad Todas las poblaciones que viven e interactúan entre sí en un lugar. La comunidad puede vivir en un lugar tan pequeño como una laguna o un parque o en un lugar tan grande como un bosque tropical o el océano.

competition

The struggle between two or more living things that depend on the same limited resource. (p. D55)

competencia La lucha entre dos o más organismos vivos que dependen del mismo recurso limitado.

compound

A substance made up of two or more different types of atoms bonded together. (p. B23)

compuesto Una sustancia formada por dos o más diferentes tipos de átomos enlazados.

concave

Curved inward toward the center, like the inside of a spoon. (p. C116)

cóncavo Dicho de una superficie con curvatura hacia dentro, como la parte interna de una cuchara.

condensation

The process by which a gas becomes a liquid. (p. B55)

condensación El proceso mediante el cual un gas se convierte en un líquido.

conduction

The process by which energy is transferred from a warmer object to a cooler object by means of physical contact. (p. B117)

conducción El proceso mediante el cual se transfiere energía de un objeto más caliente a un objeto más frío por medio de contacto físico.

conductor
1. A material that transfers energy easily. (p. B117)
2. A material that transfers electric charge easily.

> **conductor** 1. Un material que transfiere energía fácilmente. 2. Un material que transfiere cargas eléctricas fácilmente.

coniferous (koh-NIHF-uhr-uhs)
A term used to describe cone-bearing trees and shrubs that usually keep their leaves or needles during all the seasons of the year; examples are pine, fir, and spruce trees. (p. D32)

> **conífero** Un término usado para describir a los árboles y los arbustos que producen conos o piñas y que generalmente conservan sus hojas o agujas durante todas las estaciones del año; el pino, el abeto y la picea son ejemplos de coníferas.

conservation
The process of saving or protecting a natural resource. (p. D99)

> **conservación** El proceso de salvar o proteger un recurso natural.

consumer
A living thing that gets its energy by eating other living things in a food chain; consumers are also called heterotrophs. (p. D24)

> **consumidor** Un organismo vivo que obtiene su energía alimentándose de oros organismos vivos en una cadena alimentaria; los consumidores también son llamados heterótrofos.

constellation
A group of stars that form a pattern in the sky. (p. E12)

> **constelación** Un grupo de estrellas que forman un patrón en el cielo.

contour interval
On a topographic map, the difference in elevation from one contour line to the next. (p. A26)

> **equidistancia entre curvas de nivel** En un mapa topográfico, la diferencia en elevación de una curva de nivel a la siguiente.

contour line
A line on a topographic map that joins points of equal elevation. (p. A25)

> **curva de nivel** Una línea en un mapa topográfico que une puntos de igual elevación.

convection
A process by which energy is transferred in gases and liquids, occurring when a warmer, less dense area of gas or liquid is pushed up by a cooler, more dense area of the gas or liquid. (pp. B118, E116)

> **convección** Un proceso mediante el cual se transfiere energía en los gases y los líquidos; ocurre cuando un área más fría y más densa del gas o del líquido empuja hacia arriba un área más caliente y menos densa de gas o de líquido.

convex
Curved outward, like the underside of a spoon. (p. C116)

> **convexo** Dicho de una superficie con curvatura hacia afuera, como la parte externa de una cuchara.

cooperation
A term used to describe an interaction between two or more living things in which they are said to work together. (p. D57)

> **cooperación** Un término que describe la interacción entre dos o más organismos vivos en la cual se dice que trabajan juntos.

cornea (KAWR-nee-uh)
A transparent membrane that covers the eye. (p. C127)

> **córnea** Una membrana transparente que cubre el ojo.

corona
The outer layer of the Sun's atmosphere. (p. E116)

> **corona** La capa exterior de la atmósfera del Sol.

crest
The highest point, or peak, of a wave. (p. C17)

> **cresta** El punto más alto, o el pico, de una onda.

crystal
A solid substance in which the atoms are arranged in an orderly, repeating, three-dimensional pattern. (p. A46)

> **cristal** Una sustancia sólida en la cual los átomos están organizados en un patrón tridimensional y ordenado que se repite.

cycle
n. A series of events or actions that repeat themselves regularly; a physical and/or chemical process in which one material continually changes locations and/or forms. Examples include the water cycle, the carbon cycle, and the rock cycle.

v. To move through a repeating series of events or actions.

> **ciclo** *s.* Una serie de eventos o acciones que se repiten regularmente; un proceso físico y/o químico en el cual un material cambia continuamente de lugar y/o forma. Ejemplos: el ciclo del agua, el ciclo del carbono y el ciclo de las rocas.

D

data

Information gathered by observation or experimentation that can be used in calculating or reasoning. *Data* is a plural word; the singular is *datum*.

datos Información reunida mediante observación o experimentación y que se puede usar para calcular o para razonar.

decibel dB

The unit used to measure the intensity of a sound wave. (p. C52)

decibel La unidad que se usa para medir la intensidad de una onda sonora.

deciduous (dih-SIHJ-oo-uhs)

A term used to describe trees and shrubs that drop their leaves when winter comes; examples are maple, oak, and birch trees. (p. D33)

caducifolio Un término usado para describir árboles y arbustos que dejan caer sus hojas cuando llega el invierno; el arce, el roble y el abedul son ejemplos de árboles caducifolios.

decomposer

An organism that feeds on and breaks down dead plant or animal matter. (p. D25)

organismo descomponedor Un organismo que se alimenta de y degrada materia vegetal o animal.

degree

Evenly divided units of a temperature scale. (p. B106)

grado Unidades de una escala de temperatura distribuidas uniformemente.

delta

An area of land at the end, or mouth, of a river that is formed by the buildup of sediment. (p. A153)

delta Un área de tierra al final, o en la desembocadura, de un río y que se forma por la acumulación de sedimentos.

density

A property of matter representing the mass per unit volume. (p. A54)

densidad Una propiedad de la materia que representa la masa por unidad de volumen.

deposition (DEHP-uh-ZISH-uhn)

The process in which transported sediment is laid down. (p. A145)

sedimentación El proceso mediante el cual se deposita sedimento que ha sido transportado.

desertification (dih-ZUR-tuh-fih-KAY-shuhn)

The expansion of desert conditions in areas where the natural plant cover has been destroyed. (p. A133)

desertificación La expansión de las condiciones desérticas en áreas donde la vegetación natural ha sido destruida.

diffraction

The spreading out of waves as they pass through an opening or around the edges of an obstacle. (p. C26)

difracción La dispersión de las ondas al pasar por una apertura o alrededor de los bordes de un obstáculo.

diffuse reflection

The reflection of parallel light rays in many different directions. (p. C114)

reflexión difusa La reflexión de rayos de luz paralelos en muchas direcciones diferentes.

diversity

A term used to describe the quality of having many differences. *Biodiversity* describes the great variety and many differences found among living things.

diversidad Un término usado para describir la cualidad de tener muchas diferencias. La biodiversidad describe la gran variedad y las muchas diferencias encontradas entre organismos vivos.

divide

A continuous high line of land—or ridge—from which water drains to one side or the other. (p. A151)

línea divisoria de aguas Una línea continua de tierra alta, o un cerro, desde donde el agua escurre hacia un lado o hacia el otro.

DNA

The genetic material found in all living cells that contains the information needed for an organism to grow, maintain itself, and reproduce. Deoxyribonucleic acid (dee-ahk-see-ry-boh-noo-KLEE-ihk).

ADN El material genético que se encuentra en todas las céulas vivas y que contiene la información necesaria para que un organismo crezca, se mantenga a sí mismo y se reproduzca. Ácido desoxiribunucleico.

Doppler effect

A change in the observed frequency of a wave, occurring when the source of the wave or the observer is moving. Changes in the frequency of light are often measured by observing changes in wavelength, whereas changes in the frequency of sound are often detected as changes in pitch. (pp. C50, E136)

efecto Doppler Un cambio en la frecuencia observada de una onda que ocurre cuando la fuente de la onda o el observador están en movimiento. Los cambios en la frecuencia de la luz a menudo se miden observando los cambios en la longitud de onda, mientras que los cambios en la frecuencia del sonido a menudo se detectan como cambios en el tono.

drainage basin

An area of land in which water drains into a stream system. The borders of a drainage basin are called divides. (p. A151)

cuenca tributaria Un área de tierra en la cual el agua escurre a un sistema de corrientes. Los límites de una cuenca tributaria se denominan líneas divisorias de aguas.

dune

A mound of sand built up by wind. (p. A161)

duna Un montículo de arena formado por el viento.

E

echolocation

The sending out of high-pitched sound waves and the interpretation of the returning echoes. (p. C59)

ecolocación El envío de ondas sonoras de tono alto y la interpretación de los ecos que regresan.

eclipse

An event during which one object in space casts a shadow onto another. On Earth, a lunar eclipse occurs when the Moon moves through Earth's shadow, and a solar eclipse occurs when the Moon's shadow crosses Earth. (p. E63)

eclipse Un evento durante el cual un objeto en el espacio proyecta una sombra sobre otro. En la Tierra, un eclipse lunar ocurre cuando la Luna se mueve a través de la sombra de la Tierra, y un eclipse solar ocurre cuando la sombra de la Luna cruza la Tierra.

ecology

The scientific study of how living things interact with each other and their environment. (p. D9)

ecología El estudio científico de cómo interactúan los organismos vivos entre sí y con su medio ambiente.

ecosystem

All the living and nonliving things that interact in a particular environment. An ecosystem can be as small as a meadow or a swamp or as large as a forest or a desert. (p. D9)

ecosistema Todos los organismos vivos y las cosas que interactúan en un medio ambiente específico. Un ecosistema puede ser tan pequeño como un prado o un pantano, o tan grande como un bosque o un desierto.

electromagnetic radiation

(ih-LEHK-troh-mag-NEHT-ihk)
Energy that travels across distances as certain types of waves. Types of electromagnetic radiation are radio waves, microwaves, infrared radiation, visible light, ultraviolet radiation, x-rays, and gamma rays. (p. E15)

radiación electromagnética Energía que viaja a través de las distancias en forma de ciertos tipos de ondas. Las ondas de radio, las microondas, la radiación infrarroja, la luz visible, la radiación ultravioleta, los rayos X y los rayos gama son tipos de radiación electromagnética.

electromagnetic spectrum EM spectrum

The range of all electromagnetic frequencies, including the following types (from lowest to highest frequency): radio waves, microwaves, infrared light, visible light, ultraviolet light, x-rays, and gamma rays. (p. C80)

espectro electromagnético La escala de todas las frecuencias electromagnéticas, incluyendo los siguientes tipos (de la frecuencia más baja a la más alta): ondas de radio, microondas, luz infrarroja, luz visible, luz ultravioleta, rayos X y rayos gamma.

electromagnetic wave EM wave

A type of wave, such as a light wave or radio wave, that does not require a medium to travel; a disturbance that transfers energy through a field. (p. C73)

onda electromagnética Un tipo de onda, como una onda luminosa o de radio, que no requiere un medio para propagarse; una perturbación que transfiere energía a través de un campo.

element

A substance that cannot be broken down into a simpler substance by ordinary chemical changes. An element consists of atoms of only one type. (p. A45)

elemento Una sustancia que no puede descomponerse en otra sustancia más simple por medio de cambios químicos normales. Un elemento consta de átomos de un solo tipo.

elevation

A measure of how high something is above a reference point, such as sea level. (p. A25)

elevación Una medida de lo elevado que está algo sobre un punto de referencia, como el nivel del mar.

ellipse

An oval or flattened circle. (p. E81)

elipse Un óvalo o círculo aplanado.

energy

The ability to do work or to cause a change. For example, the energy of a moving bowling ball knocks over pins; energy from food allows animals to move and to grow; and energy from the Sun heats Earth's surface and atmosphere, which causes air to move. (p. B72)

energía La capacidad para trabajar o causar un cambio. Por ejemplo, la energía de una bola de boliche en movimiento tumba los pinos; la energía proveniente de su alimento permite a los animales moverse y crecer; la energía del Sol calienta la superficie y la atmósfera de la Tierra, lo que ocasiona que el aire se mueva.

energy efficiency

A measurement of usable energy after an energy conversion; the ratio of usable energy to the total energy after an energy conversion. (p. B83)

eficiencia energética Una medida de la energía utilizable después de una conversión energética; la razón entre la energía utilizable y el total de energía después una conversión energética.

energy pyramid

A model used to show the amount of energy available to living things in an ecosystem. (p. D28)

pirámide de energía Un modelo usado para mostrar la cantidad de energía disponible para organismos vivos en un ecosistema.

environment

Everything that surrounds a living thing. An environment is made up of both living and nonliving factors. (p. xxxi)

medio ambiente Todo lo que rodea a un organismo vivo. Un medio ambiente está compuesto de factores vivos y factores sin vida.

equator

An imaginary east-west line around the center of Earth that divides the planet into the Northern Hemisphere and the Southern Hemisphere; a line set at 0° latitude. (p. A18)

ecuador Una línea imaginaria de este a oeste alrededor del centro de la Tierra y que divide al planeta en hemisferio norte y hemisferio sur; la línea está fijada a latitud 0°.

equinox (EE-kwhu-NAHKS)

In an orbit, a position and time in which sunlight shines equally on the Northern Hemisphere and the Southern Hemisphere; a time of year when daylight and darkness are nearly equal for most of Earth. (p. E46)

equinoccio En una órbita, la posición y el tiempo en los cuales la luz del Sol incide de la misma manera en el Hemisferio Norte y en el Hemisferio Sur; una época del año en la cual la luz del día y la oscuridad son casi iguales para la mayor parte de la Tierra.

erosion

The process in which sediment is picked up and moved from one place to another. (p. A145)

erosión El proceso en el cual el sedimento es recogido y transportado de un lugar a otro.

estuary

The lower end of a river where it meets the ocean and fresh and salt waters mix. (p. D36)

estuario La parte baja de un río donde desemboca en el océano y donde el agua dulce del río se mezcla con el agua salada del mar.

evaporation

A process by which a substance changes from its liquid state to its gas state by random particle movement. Evaporation usually occurs at the surface of a liquid over a wide range of temperatures. (p. B53)

evaporación Un proceso mediante el cual una sustancia cambia de su estado líquido a su estado gaseoso por medio del movimiento aleatorio de las partículas. La evaporación normalmente ocurre en la superficie de un líquido en una amplia gama de temperaturas.

exfoliation (ex-FOH-lee-AY-shuhn)

In geology, the process in which layers or sheets of rock gradually break off. (p. A116)

exfoliación En geología, el proceso en el cual capas u hojas de roca se desprenden gradualmente.

experiment

An organized procedure to study something under controlled conditions. (p. xxxviii)

experimento Un procedimiento organizado para estudiar algo bajo condiciones controladas.

extinction

The permanent disappearance of a species. (p. xxxi)

extinción La desaparición permanente de una especie.

extrusive igneous rock (ihk-STROO-sihv)
Igneous rock that forms as lava cools on Earth's surface. (p. A83)

> **roca ígnea extrusiva** Roca ígnea que se forma al enfriarse la lava sobre la superficie de la Tierra.

F

false-color image
A computer image in which the colors are not what the human eye would see. A false-color image can assign different colors to different types of radiation coming from an object to highlight its features. (p. A32)

> **imagen de color falso** Una imagen computacional en la cual los colores no son los que el ojo humano observaría. Una imagen de color falso puede asignar diferentes colores a los diferentes tipos de radiación que provienen de un objeto para hacer destacar sus características.

fiber optics
Technology based on the use of laser light to send signals through transparent wires called optical fibers. This technology is often used in communications. (p. C137)

> **fibra óptica** Tecnología basada en el uso de luz de láser para mandar señales por alambres transparentes llamados fibras ópticas. Esta tecnología se usa a menudo en comunicaciones.

field
An area around an object where the object can apply a force—such as gravitational force, magnetic force, or electrical force—on another object without touching it.

> **campo** Un área alrededor de un objeto donde el objeto puede aplicar una fuerza, como fuerza gravitacional, fuerza magnética o fuerza eléctrica, sobre otro objeto sin tocarlo.

floodplain
A flat area of land on either side of a stream that becomes flooded when a river overflows its banks. (p. A152)

> **planicie de inundación** Un área plana de tierra en cualquier costado de un arroyo que se inunda cuando un río se desborda.

fluorescence (flu-REHS-uhns)
A phenomenon in which a material absorbs electromagnetic radiation of one wavelength and gives off electromagnetic radiation of a different wavelength. (p. C91)

> **fluorescencia** Un fenómeno en el cual un material absorbe radiación electromagnética de una longitud de onda y emite radiación electromagnética de longitud de onda diferente.

focal length
The distance from the center of a convex lens to its focal point. (p. C123)

> **distancia focal** La distancia del centro de un lente convexo a su punto focal.

focal point
The point at which parallel light rays reflected from a concave mirror come together; the point at which parallel light rays refracted by a convex lens come together. (p. C117)

> **punto focal** El punto en el cual se unen los rayos paralelos de luz reflejados por un espejo cóncavo; el punto en el cual se unen los rayos paralelos de luz refractados por un lente convexo.

foliation
The arrangement of minerals within rocks into flat or wavy parallel bands; a characteristic of most metamorphic rocks. (p. A100)

> **foliación** La organización de minerales en bandas paralelas planas u onduladas en las rocas; una característica de la mayoría de las rocas metamórficas.

food chain
A model used to show the feeding relationship between a single producer and a chain of consumers in an ecosystem. In a typical food chain, a plant is the producer that is eaten by a consumer, such as an insect; then the insect is eaten by a second consumer, such as a bird. (p. D26)

> **cadena alimentaria** Un modelo usado para mostrar la relación de ingestión entre un solo productor y una cadena de consumidores en un ecosistema. En una cadena alimentaria típica, una planta es la productora que es ingerida por un consumidor como un insecto, y luego el insecto es ingerido por un segundo consumidor como un pájaro.

food web
A model used to show a feeding relationship in which many food chains overlap in an ecosystem. (p. D26)

> **red trófica** Un modelo usado para mostrar una relación de consumo en la cual muchas cadenas alimentarias se empalman en un ecosistema.

force
A push or a pull; something that changes the motion of an object. (p. xxxiii)

> **fuerza** Un empuje o un jalón; algo que cambia el movimiento de un objeto.

fossil
A trace or the remains of a once-living thing from long ago.

> **fósil** Un rastro o los restos de un organismo que vivió hace mucho tiempo.

fracture

The tendency of a mineral to break into irregular pieces. (p. A53)

fractura La tendencia de un mineral a romperse en pedazos irregulares.

freezing

The process by which a substance changes from its liquid state into its solid state. (p. B52)

congelación El proceso mediante el cual una sustancia cambia de su estado líquido a su estado sólido.

freezing point

The temperature at which a substance changes from its liquid state to its solid state through freezing. (p. B52)

punto de congelación La temperatura a la cual una sustancia cambia de su estado líquido a su estado sólido mediante congelación.

frequency

The number of waves that pass a fixed point in a given amount of time, usually one second; the number of cycles per unit time. (p. C17)

frecuencia El número de longitudes de onda (o crestas de onda) que pasan un punto fijo en un período de tiempo determinado, normalmente un segundo; el número de ciclos por unidad de tiempo.

friction

A force that resists the motion between two surfaces in contact. (p. xxxv)

fricción Una fuerza que resiste el movimiento entre dos superficies en contacto.

fusion

A process in which particles of an element collide and combine to form a heavier element, such as the fusion of hydrogen into helium that occurs in the Sun's core. (p. E116)

fusión Un proceso en el cual las partículas de un elemento chocan y se combinan para formar un elemento más pesado, como la fusión de hidrógeno en helio que ocurre en el núcleo del Sol.

G

galaxy

Millions or billions of stars held together in a group by their own gravity. (p. E10)

galaxia Millones o miles de millones de estrellas unidas en un grupo por su propia gravedad.

gamma rays

Part of the electromagnetic spectrum that consists of waves with the highest frequencies; electromagnetic waves with frequencies ranging from more than 10^{19} hertz to more than 10^{24} hertz. (p. C86)

rayos gamma Parte del espectro electromagnético que consiste de ondas con las frecuencias más altas; las ondas electromagnéticas con frecuencias de más de 10^{19} hertzios hasta más de 10^{24} hertzios.

gas

Matter with no definite volume and no definite shape. The molecules in a gas are very far apart, and the amount of space between them can change easily. (p. B28)

gas Materia sin volumen definido ni forma definida. Las moléculas en un gas están muy separadas unas de otras, y la cantidad de espacio entre ellas puede cambiar fácilmente.

gas giant

A large planet that consists mostly of gases in a dense form. The four large planets in the outer solar system—Jupiter, Saturn, Uranus, and Neptune—are gas giants. (p. E94)

gigante de gas Un planeta grande compuesto principalmente de gases en forma densa. Los cuatro planetas grandes en el sistema solar exterior—Júpiter, Saturno, Urano y Neptuno —son gigantes de gas.

genetic material

The nucleic acid DNA that is present in all living cells and contains the information needed for a cell's growth, maintenance, and reproduction.

material genético El ácido nucleico ADN, ue esta presente en todas las células vivas y que contiene la información necesaria para el crecimiento, el mantenimiento y la reproducción celular.

geographic information systems

Computer systems that can store, arrange, and display geographic data in different types of maps. (p. A33)

sistemas de información geográfica Sistemas computarizados que pueden almacenar, organizar y mostrar datos geográficos en diferentes tipos de mapas.

geosphere (JEE-uh-SFEER)

All the features on Earth's surface—continents, islands, and seafloor—and everything below the surface—the inner and outer core and the mantle; one of the four parts of the Earth system. (p. A12)

geosfera Todas las características de la superficie de la Tierra, es decir, continentes, islas y el fondo marino, y de todo bajo la superficie, es decir, el núcleo externo e interno y el manto; una de las cuatro partes del sistema de la Tierra.

glacier (GLAY-shuhr)
A large mass of ice that exists year-round and moves over land. (p. A165)

glaciar Una gran masa de hielo que existe durante todo el año y se mueve sobre la tierra.

gravity
The force that objects exert on each other because of their mass. (p. xxxv)

gravedad La fuerza que los objetos ejercen entre sí debido a su masa.

H

habitat
The natural environment in which a living thing gets all that it needs to live; examples include a desert, a coral reef, and a freshwater lake. (p. D46)

hábitat El medio ambiente natural en el cual un organismo vivo consigue todo lo que requiere para vivir; ejemplos incluyen un desierto, un arrecife coralino y un lago de agua dulce.

hardness
The resistance of a mineral or other material to being scratched. (p. A55)

dureza La resistencia de un mineral o de otro material a ser rayado.

heat
1. The flow of energy from an object at a higher temperature to an object at a lower temperature. (p. B110)
2. Energy that is transferred from a warmer object to a cooler object.

calor 1. El flujo de energía de un objeto a mayor temperatura a un objeto a menor temperatura. 2. Energía que se transfiere de un objeto más caliente a un objeto más frío.

hertz Hz
The unit used to measure frequency. One hertz is equal to one complete cycle per second. (p. C46)

hercio La unidad usada para medir frecuencia. Un hercio es igual a un ciclo completo por segundo.

humus (HYOO-muhs)
The decayed organic matter in soil. (p. A123)

humus La materia orgánica en descomposición del suelo.

hydrosphere (HY-druh-SFEER)
All water on Earth—in the atmosphere and in the oceans, lakes, glaciers, rivers, streams, and underground reservoirs; one of the four parts of the Earth system. (p. A10)

hidrosfera Toda el agua de la Tierra: en la atmósfera y en los océanos, lagos, glaciares, ríos, arroyos y depósitos subterráneos; una de las cuatro partes del sistema de la Tierra.

hypothesis
A tentative explanation for an observation or phenomenon. A hypothesis is used to make testable predictions. (p. xxxviii)

hipótesis Una explicación provisional de una observación o de un fenómeno. Una hipótesis se usa para hacer predicciones que se pueden probar.

I

igneous rock (IHG-nee-uhs)
Rock that forms as molten rock cools and becomes solid. (p. A78)

roca ígnea Roca que se forma al enfriarse la roca fundida y hacerse sólida.

image
A picture of an object formed by rays of light. (p. C115)

imagen Reproducción de la figura de un objeto formada por rayos de luz.

impact crater
A round pit left behind on the surface of a planet or other body in space after a smaller object strikes the surface. (p. E32)

cráter de impacto Un pozo circular en la superficie de un planeta u otro cuerpo en el espacio que se forma cuando un objeto más pequeño golpea la superficie.

incandescence (IHN-kuhn-DEHS-uhns)
1. The production of light by materials having high temperatures. (p. C89) 2. Light produced by an incandescent object.

incandescencia 1. La producción de luz por parte de materiales a altas temperaturas. 2. La luz producida por un objeto incandescente.

infrared light
Part of the electromagnetic spectrum that consists of waves with frequencies between those of microwaves and visible light. (p. C84)

luz infrarroja Parte del espectro electromagnético que consiste de ondas con frecuencias entre las de las microondas y las de la luz visible.

insulator
1. A material that does not transfer energy easily. (p. B117) 2. A material that does not transfer electric charge easily.

aislante 1. Un material que no transfiere energía fácilmente. 2. Un material que no transfiere cargas eléctricas fácilmente.

intensity
The amount of energy of a wave, per wavelength. Intensity is associated with the amplitude of a sound wave and with the quality of loudness produced by the sound wave. (p. C52)

intensidad La cantidad de energía de una onda sonora, por longitud de onda. La intensidad está asociada con la amplitud de una onda sonora y con la calidad del volumen producido por la onda sonora.

interaction
The condition of acting or having an influence upon something. Living things in an ecosystem interact with both the living and nonliving parts of their environment. (p. xxxi)

interacción La condición de actuar o influir sobre algo. Los organismos vivos en un ecosistema interactúan con las partes vivas y las partes sin vida de su medio ambiente.

interference
The meeting and combining of waves; the adding or subtracting of wave amplitudes that occurs as waves overlap. (p. C27)

interferencia El encuentro y la combinación de ondas; la suma o la resta de amplitudes de onda que ocurre cuando las ondas se traslapan.

intrusive igneous rock (ihn-TROO-sihv)
Igneous rock that forms as magma cools below Earth's surface. (p. A83)

roca ígnea intrusiva Roca ígnea que se forma al enfriarse el magma bajo la superficie de la Tierra.

J

joule (jool) J
A unit used to measure energy and work. One calorie is equal to 4.18 joules of energy; one joule of work is done when a force of one newton moves an object one meter. (p. B112)

julio Una unidad que se usa para medir la energía y el trabajo. Una caloría es igual a 4.18 julios de energía; se hace un joule de trabajo cuando una fuerza de un newton mueve un objeto un metro.

K

kettle lake
A bowl-shaped lake that was formed as sediment built up around a block of ice left behind by a glacier. (p. A169)

lago kettle Un lago en forma de tazón que se formó al acumularse sedimento alrededor de un bloque de hielo que quedó tras el paso de un glaciar.

kinetic energy
The energy of motion. A moving object has the most kinetic energy at the point where it moves the fastest. (p. B74)

energía cinética La energía del movimiento. Un objeto que se mueve tiene su mayor energía cinética en el punto en el cual se mueve con mayor rapidez.

kinetic theory of matter
A theory stating that all matter is made of particles in motion. (p. B104)

teoría cinética de la materia Una teoría que establece que toda materia está compuesta de partículas en movimiento.

L

lander
A craft designed to land on a planet's surface. (p. E28)

módulo de aterrizaje Una nave diseñada para aterrizar en la superficie de un planeta.

laser (LAY-zuhr)
A device that produces an intense, concentrated beam of light that can be brighter than sunlight. Lasers are often used in medicine and communications. (p. C135)

láser Un aparato que produce un intenso rayo de luz concentrado que es más brillante que la luz del Sol. Los láseres se usan a menudo en la medicina y las comunicaciones.

latitude
The distance in degrees north or south from the equator. (p. A18)

latitud La distancia en grados norte o sur a partir del ecuador.

lava
Molten rock that reaches a planet's surface through a volcano. (p. A62)

lava Roca fundida que llega a la superficie de un planeta a través de un volcán.

law

In science, a rule or principle describing a physical relationship that always works in the same way under the same conditions. The law of conservation of energy is an example.

ley En las ciencias, una regla o un principio que describe una relación física que siempre funciona de la misma manera bajo las mismas condiciones. La ley de la conservación de la energía es un ejemplo.

law of conservation of energy

A law stating that no matter how energy is transferred or transformed, it continues to exist in one form or another. (p. B82)

ley de la conservación de la energía Una ley que establece que no importa cómo se transfiere o transforma la energía, toda la energía sigue presente en alguna forma u otra.

law of reflection

A law of physics stating that the angle at which light strikes a surface (the angle of incidence) equals the angle at which it reflects off the surface (the angle of reflection). (p. C114)

ley de la reflexión Una ley de la física que establece que el ángulo al cual la luz incide sobre una superficie (el ángulo de incidencia) es igual al ángulo al cual se refleja (ángulo de reflexión) de la superficie.

lens

A transparent optical tool that refracts light. (p. C121)

lente Una herramienta óptica transparente que refracta la luz.

light-year

The distance light travels in one year, which is about 9.5 trillion kilometers (6 trillion mi). (p. E122)

año luz La distancia que viaja la luz en un año, la cual es de casi 9.5 billones de kilómetros (6 billones de millas).

limiting factor

A factor or condition that prevents the continuing growth of a population in an ecosystem. (p. D64)

factor limitante Un factor o una condición que impide el crecimiento continuo de una población en un ecosistema.

liquid

Matter that has a definite volume but does not have a definite shape. The molecules in a liquid are close together but not bound to one another. (p. B28)

líquido Materia que tiene un volumen definido pero no tiene una forma definida. Las moléculas en un líquido están cerca unas de otras pero no están ligadas.

loess (LOH-uhs)

Deposits of fine-grained, wind-blown sediment. (p. A162)

loes Depósitos de sedimento de grano fino transportado por el viento.

longitude

The distance in degrees east or west of the prime meridian. Longitude lines are numbered from 0° to 180°. (p. A19)

longitud La distancia en grados al este o al oeste del primer meridiano. Las líneas de longitud están numeradas de 0° a 180°.

longitudinal wave (LAHN-jih-TOOD-uhn-uhl)

A type of wave in which the disturbance moves in the same direction that the wave travels. (p. C14)

onda longitudinal Un tipo de onda en la cual la perturbación se mueve en la misma dirección en la que viaja la onda.

longshore current

The overall direction and movement of water as waves strike the shore at an angle. (p. A159)

corriente litoral La dirección y el movimiento general del agua conforme las olas golpean la costa en ángulo.

longshore drift

The zigzag movement of sand along a beach, caused by the action of waves. (p. A159)

deriva litoral El movimiento en zigzag de la arena a lo largo de una playa, ocasionado por la acción de las olas.

luminescence

The production of light without the high temperatures needed for incandescence. (p. C89)

luminiscencia La producción de luz sin las altas temperaturas necesarias para la incandescencia.

luster

The property of a mineral that describes the way in which light reflects from its surface. Major types of luster are metallic and nonmetallic. (p. A52)

brillo La propiedad de un mineral que describe la manera en la cual la luz se refleja en su superficie. Los principales tipos de brillo son metálico y no metálico.

M

magma

Molten rock beneath Earth's surface. (p. A62)

magma Roca fundida que se encuentra bajo la superficie de la Tierra.

main sequence

The stage in which stars produce energy through the fusion of hydrogen into helium. (p. E126)

secuencia principal La etapa en la cual las estrellas producen energía mediante la fusión de hidrógeno en helio.

map legend

A chart that explains the meaning of each symbol used on a map; also called a key. (p. A17)

clave del mapa Una tabla que explica el significado de cada símbolo usado en un mapa.

map scale

The comparison of distance on a map with actual distance on what the map represents, such as Earth's surface. Map scale may be expressed as a ratio, a bar scale, or equivalent units. (p. A17)

escala del mapa La comparación de la distancia en un mapa con la distancia real en lo que el mapa representa, como la superficie de la Tierra. La escala del mapa puede expresarse como una azón, una barra de escala o en unidades equivalentes.

mare (MAH-ray)

A large, dark plain of solidified lava on the Moon. The plural form of mare is maria (MAH-ree-uh). (p. E53)

mare Una planicie grande y oscura de lava solidificada en la Luna. El plural de mare es maría.

mass

A measure of how much matter an object is made of. (p. B10)

masa Una medida de la cantidad de materia de la que está compuesto un objeto.

mass wasting

The downhill movement of loose rock or soil. (p. A147)

movimiento de masa El desplazamiento cuesta abajo de suelo o de roca suelta.

matter

Anything that has mass and volume. Matter exists ordinarily as a solid, a liquid, or a gas. (p. B9)

materia Todo lo que tiene masa y volumen. Generalmente la materia existe como sólido, líquido o gas.

mechanical wave

A wave, such as a sound wave or a seismic wave, that transfers kinetic energy through matter. (p. C11)

onda mecánica Una onda, como una onda sonora o una onda sísmica, que transfiere energía cinética a través de la materia.

mechanical weathering

The breakdown of rock into smaller pieces of the same material without any change in its composition. (p. A116)

meteorización mecánica El desmoronamiento de las rocas en pedazos más pequeños del mismo material, sin ningún cambio en su composición.

medium

A substance through which a wave moves. (p. C11)

medio Una sustancia a través de la cual se mueve una onda.

melting

The process by which a substance changes from its solid state to its liquid state. (p. B51)

fusión El proceso mediante el cual una sustancia cambia de su estado sólido a su estado líquido.

melting point

The temperature at which a substance changes from its solid state to its liquid state through melting. (p. B51)

punto de fusión La temperatura a la cual una sustancia cambia de su estado sólido a su estado líquido mediante fusión.

metamorphic rock (MEHT-uh-MAWR-fihk)

Rock formed as heat or pressure causes existing rock to change in structure, texture, or mineral composition. (p. A78)

roca metamórfica Roca formada cuando el calor o la presión ocasionan que la roca existente cambie de estructura, textura o composición mineral.

metamorphism (MEHT-uh-MAWR-FIHZ-uhm)

The process by which a rock's structure or mineral composition is changed by pressure or heat. (p. A96)

metamorfismo El proceso mediante el cual la estructura o la composición mineral de una roca cambia debido a la presión o al calor.

meteor

A brief streak of light produced by a small particle entering Earth's atmosphere at a high speed. (p. E105)

meteoro Un breve rayo luminoso producido por una partícula pequeña que entra a la atmósfera de la Tierra a una alta velocidad.

meteorite

A small object from outer space that passes through Earth's atmosphere and reaches the surface. (p. E105)

meteorito Un pequeño objeto del espacio exterior que pasa a través de la atmósfera de la Tierra y llega a la superficie.

microwaves
Part of the electromagnetic spectrum that consists of waves with higher frequencies than radio waves, but lower frequencies than infrared waves. (p. C83)

microondas Parte del espectro electromagnético que consiste de ondas con frecuencias mayores a las ondas de radio, pero menores a las de las ondas infrarrojas.

mineral
A substance that forms in nature, is a solid, has a definite chemical makeup, and has a crystal structure. (p. A43)

mineral Una sustancia sólida formada en la naturaleza, de composición química definida y estructura cristalina.

mixture
A combination of two or more substances that do not combine chemically but remain the same individual substances. Mixtures can be separated by physical means. (p. B23)

mezcla Una combinación de dos o más sustancias que no se combinan químicamente sino que permanecen como sustancias individuales. Las mezclas se pueden separar por medios físicos.

molecule
A group of atoms that are held together by covalent bonds so that they move as a single unit. (p. B18)

molécula Un grupo de átomos que están unidos mediante enlaces covalentes de tal manera que se mueven como una sola unidad.

moraine (muh-RAYN)
A deposit of till left behind by a retreating glacier. Moraines can form along a glacier's sides and at its end. (p. A168)

morrena Un depósito de sedimentos glaciares dejado por un glaciar que retrocede. Las morrenas pueden formarse en los costados de un glaciar o en su extremo.

mutualism (MYOO-choo-uh-LIHZ-uhm)
An interaction between two species in which both benefit; a type of symbiosis. (p. D58)

mutualismo Una interacción entre dos especies en la cual ambas se benefician; un tipo de simbiosis.

N

natural resource
Any type of matter or energy from Earth's environment that humans use to meet their needs. (p. D84)

recurso natural Cualquier tipo de materia o energía del medio ambiente de la Tierra que usan los humanos para satisfacer sus necesidades.

nebula (NEHB-yuh-luh)
A cloud of gas and dust in space. Stars form in nebulae. (p. E125)

nebulosa Una nube de gas y polvo en el espacio. Las estrellas se forman en las nebulosas.

neutron star
A dense core that may be left behind after a higher-mass star explodes in a supernova. (p. E126)

estrella de neutrones Un núcleo denso que puede resultar después de que una estrella de mayor masa explota en una supernova.

niche (nihch)
The role a living thing plays in its habitat. A plant is a food producer, whereas an insect both consumes food as well as provides food for other consumers. (p. D47)

nicho El papel que juega un organismo vivo en su hábitat. Una planta es un productor de alimento mientras que un insecto consume alimento y a la vez sirve de alimento a otros consumidores.

nitrogen cycle
The continuous movement of nitrogen through Earth, its atmosphere, and the living things on Earth. (p. D19)

ciclo del nitrógeno El movimiento continuo de nitrógeno por la Tierra, su atmósfera y los organismos vivos de la Tierra.

nutrient (NOO-tree-uhnt)
A substance that an organism needs to live. Examples include water, minerals, and materials that come from the breakdown of food particles.

nutriente Una sustancia que un organismo necesita para vivir. Ejemplos incluyen agua, minerales y sustancias que provienen de la descomposición de partículas de alimento.

O

optics (AHP-tihks)
The study of light, vision, and related technology. (p. C113)

óptica El estudio de la luz, la visión y la tecnología relacionada a ellas.

orbit

n. The path of an object in space as it moves around another object due to gravity; for example, the Moon moves in an orbit around Earth. (p. E10)

v. To revolve around, or move in an orbit; for example, the Moon orbits Earth.

órbita *s.* La trayectoria de un objeto en el espacio a medida que se mueve alrededor de otro objeto debido a la gravedad; por ejemplo, la Luna se mueve en una órbita alrededor de la Tierra.

orbitar *v.* Girar alrededor de algo, o moverse en una órbita; por ejemplo, la Luna orbita la Tierra.

ore

A rock that contains enough of a valuable mineral to be mined for a profit. (p. A64)

mena Una roca que contiene suficiente mineral valioso para ser extraído con fines lucrativos.

organism

An individual living thing, made up of one or many cells, that is capable of growing and reproducing. (p. xxxi)

organismo Un individuo vivo, compuesto de una o muchas células, que es capaz de crecer y reproducirse.

P

parallax

The apparent shift in the position of an object when viewed from different locations. (p. E123)

paralaje El cambio aparente en la posición de un objeto cuando se observa desde diferentes puntos.

parasitism (PAR-uh-suh-tihz-uhm)

A relationship between two species in which one species is harmed while the other benefits; a type of symbiosis. (p. D59)

parasitismo Una relación entre dos especies en la cual una especie es perjudicada mientras que la otra se beneficia; un tipo de simbiosis.

particle

A very small piece of matter, such as an atom, molecule, or ion.

partícula Una cantidad muy pequeña de materia, como un átomo, una molécula o un ión.

penumbra

A region of lighter shadow that may surround an umbra; for example, the spreading cone of lighter shadow cast by a space object. (p. E63)

penumbra Una región de sombra más tenue que puede rodear a una umbra; por ejemplo, la sombra más tenue cónica proyectada por un objeto espacial.

photosynthesis (foh-toh-SIHN-thih-sihs)

The process by which green plants and other producers use simple compounds and energy from light to make sugar, an energy-rich compound. (p. D23)

fotosíntesis El proceso mediante el cual las plantas verdes y otros productores usan compuestos simples y energía de la luz para producir azúcares, compuestos ricos en energía.

physical change

A change in a substance that does not change the substance into a different one. (p. B44)

cambio físico Un cambio en una sustancia que no transforma la sustancia a otra sustancia.

physical property

A characteristic of a substance that can be observed without changing the identity of the substance. (p. B41)

propiedad física Una característica de una sustancia que se puede observar sin cambiar la identidad de la sustancia.

pioneer species

The first species to move into a lifeless environment. Plants like mosses are typical pioneer species on land. (p. D66)

especie pionera La primera especie que ocupa un medio ambiente sin vida. Las plantas como los musgos son típicas especies pioneras terrestres.

pitch

The quality of highness or lowness of a sound. Pitch is associated with the frequency of a sound wave—the higher the frequency, the higher the pitch. (p. C45)

tono La cualidad de un sonido de ser alto o bajo. El tono está asociado con la frecuencia de una onda sonora: entre más alta sea la frecuencia, más alto es el tono.

planet

A spherical body, larger than a comet or asteroid, that orbits the Sun, or a similar body that orbits a different star.

planeta Un cuerpo esférico, más grande que un cometa o un asteroide, que orbita alrededor del Sol, o un cuerpo similar que orbita alrededor de una estrella distinta.

polarization (POH-luhr-ih-ZAY-shuhn)

A way of filtering light so that all of the waves vibrate in the same direction. (p. C96)

polarización Una manera de filtrar la luz para que todas las ondas vibren en la misma dirección.

pollution

The release of harmful substances into the air, water, or land. (p. D91)

contaminación La descarga de sustancias nocivas al aire, al agua o a la tierra.

population

A group of organisms of the same species that live in the same area. For example, a desert will have populations of different species of lizards and cactus plants. (p. D46)

población Un grupo de organismos de la misma especie que viven en la misma área. Por ejemplo, un desierto tendrá poblaciones de distintas especies de lagartijas y de cactus.

population density

A measure of the number of organisms that live in a given area. The population density of a city may be given as the number of people living in a square kilometer. (p. D86)

densidad de población Una medida de la cantidad de organismos que viven un área dada. La densidad de población de una ciudad puede expresarse como el número de personas que viven en un kilómetro cuadrado.

potential energy

Stored energy; the energy an object has due to its position, molecular arrangement, or chemical composition. (p. B75)

energía potencial Energía almacenada; o la energía que tiene un objeto debido a su posición, arreglo molecular o composición química.

predator

An animal that hunts other animals and eats them. (p. D55)

predador Un animal que caza otros animales y se los come.

prey

An animal that other animals hunt and eat. (p. D55)

presa Un animal que otros animales cazan y se comen.

primary colors

Three colors of light—red, green, and blue—that can be mixed to produce all possible colors. (p. C98)

colores primarios Tres colores de luz, rojo, verde y azul, que se pueden mezclar para producir todos los colores posibles.

primary pigments

Three colors of substances—cyan, yellow, and magenta—that can be mixed to produce all possible colors. (p. C99)

pigmentos primarios Tres colores de sustancias, cian, amarillo y magenta, que se pueden mezclar para producir todos los colores posibles.

prime meridian

An imaginary north-south line that divides the planet into the Eastern Hemisphere and the Western Hemisphere. The prime meridian passes through Greenwich, England. (p. A19)

primer meridiano Una línea imaginaria de norte a sur que divide al planeta en hemisferio oriental y hemisferio occidental. El primer meridiano pasa a través de Greenwich, Inglaterra.

prism

An optical tool that uses refraction to separate the different wavelengths that make up white light. (p. C97)

prisma Una herramienta óptica que usa la refracción para separar las diferentes longitudes de onda que componen la luz blanca.

probe

A spacecraft that is sent into a planet's atmosphere or onto a solid surface. (p. E29)

sonda espacial Una nave espacial enviada a la atmósfera de un planeta o a una superficie sólida.

producer

An organism that captures energy from sunlight and transforms it into chemical energy that is stored in energy-rich carbon compounds. Producers are a source of food for other organisms. (p. D23)

productor Un organismo que capta energía de la luz solar y la transforma a energía química que se almacena en compuestos de carbono ricos en energía. Los productores son una fuente de alimento para otros organismos.

projection

A representation of Earth's curved surface on a flat map. (p. A20)

proyección Una representación de la superficie curva de la Tierra en un mapa plano.

pupil

The circular opening in the iris of the eye that controls how much light enters the eye. (p. C127)

pupila La apertura circular en el iris del ojo que controla cuánta luz entra al ojo.

GLOSSARY

Q

quasar
The very bright center of a distant galaxy. (p. E133)

quásar El centro muy brillante de una galaxia distante.

R

radiation (ray-dee-AY-shuhn)
Energy that travels across distances in the form of electromagnetic waves. (p. B119)

radiación Energía que viaja a través de la distancia en forma de ondas electromagnéticas.

radio waves
The part of the electromagnetic spectrum that consists of waves with the lowest frequencies. (p. C82)

ondas de radio La parte del espectro electromagnético que consiste de las ondas con las frecuencias más bajas.

recrystallization
The process by which bonds between atoms in minerals break and re-form in new ways during metamorphism. (p. A97)

recristalización El proceso mediante el cual los enlaces entre los átomos de los minerales se rompen y se vuelven a formar de diferentes maneras durante el metamorfismo.

reflection
The bouncing back of a wave after it strikes a barrier. (p. C25)

reflexión El rebote de una onda después de que incide sobre una barrera.

refraction
The bending of a wave as it crosses the boundary between two mediums at an angle other than 90 degrees. (p. C25)

refracción El doblamiento de una onda a medida que cruza el límite entre dos medios a un ángulo distinto a 90 grados.

regular reflection
The reflection of parallel light rays in the same direction. (p. C114)

reflexión especular La reflexión de rayos de luz paralelos en la misma dirección.

relief
In geology, the difference in elevation between an area's high and low points. (p. A25)

relieve En geología, la diferencia en elevación entre los puntos altos y bajos de un área.

relief map
A map that shows the differences in elevation in an area. Relief maps can show elevations through the use of contour lines, shading, colors, and, in some cases, three-dimensional materials. (p. A16)

mapa de relieve Un mapa que muestra las diferencias en elevación de un área. Los mapas de relieve pueden mostrar elevaciones mediante del uso de curvas de nivel, sombreado, colores y, en algunos casos, materiales tridimensionales.

remote sensing
A method of using scientific equipment to gather information about something from a distance. Most remote-sensing methods make use of different types of electromagnetic radiation. (p. A30)

sensoramiento remoto Un método de reunir información sobre algo a distancia usando equipo científico. La mayoría de los métodos de sensoramiento remoto hacen uso de diferentes tipos de radiación electromagnética.

resonance
The strengthening of a sound wave when it combines with an object's natural vibration. (p. C48)

resonancia El fortalecimiento de una onda sonora cuando se combina con la vibración natural de un objeto.

retina (REHT-uhn-uh)
A light-sensitive membrane at the back of the inside of the eye. (p. C127)

retina Una membrana sensible a la luz en la parte trasera del interior del ojo.

revolution
The motion of one body around another, such as Earth in its orbit around the Sun; the time it takes an object to go around once. (p. E45)

revolución El movimiento de un cuerpo alrededor de otro, como la Tierra en su órbita alrededor del Sol; el tiempo que le toma a un objeto dar la vuelta una vez.

ring
In astronomy, a wide, flat zone of small particles that orbit around a planet's equator. (p. E97)

anillo En astronomía, una zona ancha y plana de pequeñas partículas que orbitan alrededor del ecuador de un planeta.

rock
A naturally formed solid that is usually made up of one or more types of minerals. (p. A75)

roca Un sólido formado de manera natural y generalmente compuesto de uno o más tipos de minerales.

rock cycle

The set of natural, repeating processes that form, change, break down, and re-form rocks. (p. A78)

ciclo de las rocas La serie de procesos naturales y repetitivos que forman, cambian, descomponen y vuelven a formar rocas.

S

sandbar

A ridge of sand built up by the action of waves and currents. (p. A160)

barra de arena Una colina de arena que se forma por la acción de las olas y las corrientes.

satellite

An object that orbits a more massive object. (p. E23)

satélite Un objeto que orbita un objeto de mayor masa.

scattering

The spreading out of light rays in all directions as particles reflect and absorb the light. (p. C95)

dispersión La disipación de los rayos de luz en todas las direcciones a medida que las partículas reflejan y absorben la luz.

season

One part of a pattern of temperature changes and other weather trends over the course of a year. Astronomical seasons are defined and caused by the position of Earth's axis relative to the direction of sunlight. (p. E46)

estación Una parte de un patrón de cambios de temperatura y otras tendencias meteorológicas en el curso de un año. Las estaciones astronómicas se definen y son causadas por la posición del eje de la Tierra en relación a la dirección de la luz del Sol.

sediment

Solid materials such as rock fragments, plant and animal remains, or minerals that are carried by water or by air and that settle on the bottom of a body of water or on the ground. (p. A89)

sedimento Materiales sólidos como fragmentos de rocas, restos de plantas y animales o minerales que son transportados por el agua o el aire y que se depositan en el fondo de un cuerpo de agua o en el suelo.

sedimentary rock (SEHD-uh-MEHN-tuh-ree)

Rock formed as pieces of older rocks and other loose materials get pressed or cemented together or as dissolved minerals re-form and build up in layers. (p. A78)

roca sedimentaria Roca que se forma cuando los pedazos de rocas más viejas y otros materiales sueltos son presionados o cementados o cuando los minerales disueltos vuelven a formarse y se acumulan en capas.

sensor

A mechanical or electronic device that receives and responds to a signal, such as light. (p. A31)

sensor Un dispositivo mecánico o electrónico que recibe y responde a una señal, como la luz.

sinkhole

An open basin that forms when the roof of a cavern becomes so thin that it falls in. (p. A155)

sumidero Una cuenca abierta que se forma cuando el techo de una caverna se vuelve tan delgado que se desploma.

slope

A measure of how steep a landform is. Slope is calculated as the change in elevation divided by the distance covered. (p. A25)

pendiente Una medida de lo inclinada de una formación terrestre. La pendiente se calcula dividiendo el cambio en la elevación por la distancia recorrida.

soil horizon

A soil layer with physical and chemical properties that differ from those of soil layers above or below it. (p. A124)

horizonte del suelo Una capa del suelo con propiedades físicas y químicas que difieren de las de las capas del suelo superior e inferior a la misma.

soil profile

The soil horizons in a specific location; a cross section of soil layers that displays all soil horizons. (p. A124)

perfil del suelo Los horizontes del suelo en un lugar específico; una sección transversal de las capas del suelo que muestra todos los horizontes del suelo.

solar cell

A type of technology in which light-sensitive materials convert sunlight into electrical energy. (p. B88)

celda solar Un tipo de tecnología en el cual materiales sensibles a la luz convierten luz solar a energía eléctrica.

solar system
The Sun and its family of orbiting planets, moons, and other objects. (p. E10)

> **sistema solar** El Sol y su familia de planetas, lunas y otros objetos en órbita.

solar wind
A stream of electrically charged particles that flows out in all directions from the Sun's corona. (p. E119)

> **viento solar** Una corriente de partículas eléctricamente cargadas que fluye hacia fuera de la corona del Sol en todas las direcciones.

solid
Matter that has a definite shape and a definite volume. The molecules in a solid are in fixed positions and are close together. (p. B28)

> **sólido** La materia que tiene una forma definida y un volumen definido. Las moléculas en un sólido están en posiciones fijas y cercanas unas a otras.

solstice (SAHL-stihs)
In an orbit, a position and time during which one hemisphere gets its maximum area of sunlight, while the other hemisphere gets its minimum amount; the time of year when days are either longest or shortest, and the angle of sunlight reaches its maximum or minimum. (p. E46)

> **solsticio** En una órbita, la posición y el tiempo durante los cuales un hemisferio obtiene su área máxima de luz del Sol, mientras que el otro hemisferio obtiene su cantidad mínima; la época del año en la cual los días son los más largos o los más cortos y el ángulo de la luz del Sol alcanza su máximo o su mínimo.

sonar
Instruments that use echolocation to locate objects underwater; acronym for "sound navigation and ranging." (p. C59)

> **sonar** Instrumentos que usan la ecolocación para localizar objetos bajo agua; acrónimo en inglés para "navegación y determinación de distancias por sonido".

sound
A type of wave that is produced by a vibrating object and that travels through matter. (p. C37)

> **sonido** Un tipo de onda que es producida por un objeto que vibra y que viaja a través de la materia.

space station
A satellite in which people can live and work for long periods. (p. E24)

> **estación espacial** Un satélite en el cual la gente puede vivir y trabajar durante períodos largos.

species
A group of living things that are so closely related that they can breed with one another and produce offspring that can breed as well. (p. xxxi)

> **especie** Un grupo de organismos que están tan estrechamente relacionados que pueden aparearse entre sí y producir crías que también pueden aparearse.

specific heat
The amount of energy required to raise the temperature of one gram of a substance by one degree Celsius. (p. B113)

> **calor específico** La cantidad de energía que se necesita para aumentar la temperatura de un gramo de una sustancia un grado centígrado.

spectrum (SPEHK-truhm)
1. Radiation from a source separated into a range of wavelengths. 2. The range of colors that appears in a beam of visible light when it passes through a prism. See also electromagnetic radiation. (p. E16)

> **espectro** 1. Radiación de una fuente separada en una gama de longitudes de onda. 2. La gama de colores que aparece en un haz de luz visible cuando éste pasa a través de un prisma. Ver también radiación electromagnética.

states of matter
The different forms in which matter can exist. Three familiar states are solid, liquid, and gas. (p. B27)

> **estados de la materia** Las diferentes formas en las cuales puede existir la materia. Los tres estados conocidos son sólido, líquido y gas.

streak
The color of a mineral powder left behind when a mineral is scraped across a surface; a method for classifying minerals. (p. A51)

> **raya** El color del polvo que queda de un mineral cuando éste se raspa a lo largo de una superficie; un método para clasificar minerales.

sublimation
The process by which a substance changes directly from its solid state to its gas state without becoming a liquid first. (p. B53)

> **sublimación** El proceso mediante el cual una sustancia cambia directamente de su estado sólido a su estado gaseoso sin convertirse primero en líquido.

substance
Matter of a particular type. Elements, compounds, and mixtures are all substances.

> **sustancia** La materia de cierto tipo. Los elementos, los compuestos y las mezclas son sustancias.

succession (suhk-SEHSH-uhn)
A natural process that involves a gradual change in the plant and animal communities that live in an area. (p. D66)

> **sucesión** Un proceso natural que involucra un cambio gradual en las comunidades de plantas y animales que viven en un área.

sunspot
A darker spot on the photosphere of the Sun. A sunspot appears dark because it is cooler than the surrounding area. (p. E118)

> **mancha solar** Una mancha oscura en la fotosfera del Sol. Una mancha solar se ve oscura porque es más fría que el área que la rodea.

sustainable
A term that describes the managing of certain natural resources so that they are not harmed or used up. Examples include maintaining clean groundwater and protecting top soil from erosion. (p. D102)

> **sostenible** Un término que describe el manejo de ciertos recursos naturales para que no se deterioren o se terminen. Ejemplos incluyen mantener limpia el agua subterránea y proteger de la erosión a la capa superficial del suelo.

symbiosis (sihm-bee-OH-sihs)
The interaction between individuals from two different species that live closely together. (p. D58)

> **simbiosis** La interacción entre individuos de dos especies distintas que viven en proximidad.

system
A group of objects or phenomena that interact. A system can be as simple as a rope, a pulley, and a mass. It also can be as complex as the interaction of energy and matter in the four parts of the Earth system.

> **sistema** Un grupo de objetos o fenómenos que interactúan. Un sistema puede ser algo tan sencillo como una cuerda, una polea y una masa. También puede ser algo tan complejo como la interacción de la energía y la materia en las cuatro partes del sistema de la Tierra.

T

technology
The use of scientific knowledge to solve problems or engineer new products, tools, or processes.

> **tecnología** El uso de conocimientos científicos para resolver problemas o para diseñar nuevos productos, herramientas o procesos.

tectonics
The processes in which the motion of hot material under a crust changes the crust of a space body. Earth has a specific type of tectonics called plate tectonics. (p. E86)

> **tectónica** Los procesos en los cuales el movimiento del material caliente bajo una corteza cambia la corteza de un cuerpo espacial. La Tierra tiene un tipo específico de tectónica denominado tectónica de placas.

telescope
A device that gather visible light or another form of electromagnetic radiation. (p. E17)

> **telescopio** Un aparato que reúne luz visible u otra forma de radiación electromagnética.

temperature
A measure of the average amount of kinetic energy of the particles in an object. (p. B105)

> **temperatura** Una medida de la cantidad promedio de energía cinética de las partículas en un objeto.

terrestrial planet
Earth or a planet similar to Earth that has a rocky surface. The four planets in the inner solar system—Mercury, Venus, Earth, and Mars—are terrestrial planets. (p. E85)

> **planeta terrestre** La Tierra o un planeta parecido a la Tierra que tiene una superficie rocosa. Los cuatro planetas en el sistema solar interior — Mercurio, Venus, la Tierra y Marte — son planetas terrestres.

theory
In science, a set of widely accepted explanations of observations and phenomena. A theory is a well-tested explanation that is consistent with all available evidence.

> **teoría** En las ciencias, un conjunto de explicaciones de observaciones y fenómenos que es ampliamente aceptado. Una teoría es una explicación bien probada que es consecuente con la evidencia disponible.

thermal energy
The energy an object has due to the motion of its particles; the total amount of kinetic energy of particles in an object. (p. B111)

> **energía térmica** La energía que tiene un objeto debido al movimiento de sus partículas; la cantidad total de energía cinética de las partículas en un objeto.

thermometer
A device for measuring temperature. (p. B107)

> **termómetro** Un aparato para medir la temperatura.

till
Sediment of different sizes left directly on the ground by a melting, or retreating, glacier. (p. A168)

    sedimentos glaciares Sedimentos de diferentes tamaños depositados directamente en el suelo por un glaciar que se derrite o retrocede.

topography
All natural and human-made surface features of a particular area. (p. A24)

    topografía Todas las características de superficie de origen natural y humano en un área particular.

transmission (trans-MIHSH-uhn)
The passage of a wave through a medium. (p. C93)

    transmisión El paso de una onda a través de un medio.

transverse wave
A type of wave in which the disturbance moves at right angles, or perpendicular, to the direction in which the wave travels. (p. C13)

    onda transversal Un tipo de onda en el cual la perturbación se mueve en ángulo recto, o perpendicularmente, a la dirección en la cual viaja la onda.

trough (trawf)
The lowest point, or valley, of a wave (p. C17)

    valle El punto más bajo de una onda.

U

ultrasound
Sound waves with frequencies above 20,000 hertz, the upper limit of typical hearing levels in humans, used for medical purposes, among other things. (p. C46)

    ultrasonido Ondas sonoras con frecuencias superiores a 20,000 hertzios, el límite superior de los niveles auditivos típicos de los humanos. Estas ondas tienen usos médicos, entre otros.

ultraviolet light
The part of the electromagnetic spectrum that consists of waves with frequencies higher than those of visible light and lower than those of x-rays. (p. C85)

    luz ultravioleta La parte del espectro electromagnético que consiste de ondas con frecuencias superiores a las de luz visible y menores a las de los rayos X.

umbra
The dark, central region of a shadow, such as the cone of complete shadow cast by an object. (p. E63)

    umbra La región central y oscura de una sombra, como la sombra completa cónica proyectada por un objeto.

universe
Space and all the matter and energy in it. (p. E10)

    universo El espacio y toda la materia y energía que hay dentro de él.

urban
A term that describes a city environment.

    urbano Un término que describe el medio ambiente de una ciudad.

V

vacuum
A space containing few or no particles of matter. (p. C41)

    vacío Un espacio que no contiene partículas de materia o bien contiene muy pocas.

variable
Any factor that can change in a controlled experiment, observation, or model. (p. R30)

    variable Cualquier factor que puede cambiar en un experimento controlado, en una observación o en un modelo.

vibration
A rapid, back-and-forth motion. (p. C37)

    vibración Un movimiento rápido hacia delante y hacia atrás.

visible light
The part of the electromagnetic spectrum that consists of waves detectable by the human eye. (p. C84)

    luz visible La parte del espectro electromagnético que consiste de ondas detectables por el ojo humano.

volcanism
The process of molten material moving from a space body's hot interior onto its surface. (p. E86)

    vulcanismo El proceso del movimiento de material fundido del interior caliente de un cuerpo espacial a su superficie.

volume
An amount of three-dimensional space, often used to describe the space that an object takes up. (p. B11)

    volumen Una cantidad de espacio tridimensional; a menudo se usa este término para describir el espacio que ocupa un objeto.

W

water cycle
The continuous movement of water through Earth, its atmosphere, and the living things on Earth. (p. D17)

ciclo del agua El movimiento continuo de agua por la Tierra, su atmósfera y los organismos vivos de la Tierra.

wave
A disturbance that transfers energy from one place to another without requiring matter to move the entire distance. (p. C9)

onda Una perturbación que transfiere energía de un lugar a otro sin que sea necesario que la materia se mueva toda la distancia.

wavelength
The distance from one wave peak or crest to the next peak or crest. Wavelength can be measured as the distance from any part of one wave to the identical part of the next wave. (pp. C17, E16)

longitud de onda La distancia entre el pico o la cresta de una onda y el siguiente pico o cresta. La longitud de onda se puede medir como la distancia entre cualquier parte de una onda y la parte idéntica de la siguiente onda.

weathering
The process by which natural forces break down rocks. (p. A115)

meteorización El proceso por el cual las fuerzas naturales fragmentan las rocas.

weight
The force of gravity on an object. (p. B11)

peso La fuerza de la gravedad sobre un objeto.

X, Y, Z

x-rays
The part of the electromagnetic spectrum that consists of waves with high frequencies and high energies; electromagnetic waves with frequencies ranging from more than 10^{16} hertz to more than 10^{21} hertz. (p. C86)

rayos X La parte del espectro electromagnético que consiste de las ondas con altas frecuencias y altas energías; las ondas electromagnéticas con frecuencias de más de 10^{16} hertzios hasta más de 10^{21} hertzios.

Index

Page numbers for definitions are printed in **boldface** type.
Page numbers for illustrations, maps, and charts are printed in *italics*.

INDEX

M

INDEX

U

ultrasound, C2–5, **C46,** C47, C58–60
ultrasound scanner, C2–5, C60, *C60*
ultraviolet light, C81, *C81,* **C85,** *C85*
ultraviolet waves, E16, *E16*
umbra, **E63,** *E63–64*
United Nations Environment Programme, D102
United States Geological Survey (USGS), A27
Unit Projects
    astronomy and archaeology, E67
    collision of galaxies, E134
    gem cutting, A67
    gravity and plant growth, E35
    landscape architecture, A137
    life on the dunes, A164
    mapping for an Olympic Stadium, A35
    rocks from space, A81
    surface of Mars, E93
units of measurement
    British thermal unit (BTU), B91
    calorie, **B112**
    centimeter, B12
    decibel, **C52**
    degree, **B106**
    gram, B10
    hertz, **C46,** C47, C81
    joule, **B112**
    kilogram, B10
    meter, B12
    newton, B11
    pound, B11
    wavelength, **C17,** C30
universe, E9–10, **E10,** *E11*
    early astronomy, E9
    expansion, E135–137, *E137,* E140
    formation, E139
    looking back in time, E136, *E136*
    origins, E138–139
unmanned space exploration, E26
Uranus, E94, E98, *E98*
    color, E98
    density, E98
    diameter, E98
    distance from Sun, E98
    mass, E98
    moons, E98
    orbit of Sun, E98
    rings, E98
    rotation, E98
    size, E79, *E80*
    temperature, E98
urban areas, *D86,* D86–87
    population of, D86
urban planning, *D88*
U.S. Forest Service, D103
U.S. Geological Survey, D74

V

vacuum, **C41,** C75
    EM waves and, C75
vacuum flask, B98, *B120,* B121
valleys, A152
variables, **R30,** R31, R32
    controlled, R17
    dependent, **R30,** R31
    independent, **R30**
Venus, E85–88, *E90,* E90–91
    atmosphere, E32, E88, E90
    craters, E91
    day/night cycle, E90
    diameter, E90
    distance from Sun, E90
    erosion, E91
    exploration, E28
    mass, E90
    orbit of Sun, E14, E90
    rotation, E90
    size, E79, *E80*
    temperature, E90
    volcanoes, E86, *E87,* E90–91
Very Large Array radio telescopes, E18, *E18*
vibration, **C37,** C38–39, C40
views of earth, A6–39
    Internet Activity, A7
    mapping, A30–34
    maps and globes, A15–22, A36
    note-taking strategies, A8
    topography, A24–29
    using technology, A9–14, A30–34, A36
    vocabulary strategies, A8
visible light, C81, *C81,* **C84,** *C135,* E15–18, *E16,* E20–21.
    See also optics.
vision, C126–130
    correction of, C129–130
    farsightedness, C129, *C129,* C130
    formation of images, *C127,* C128
    nearsightedness, C129, *C129,* C130
vitamin E molecule, B18
vocabulary strategies, R50–51
    description wheels, A42, A114, B102, *B102,* C36,
        C36, C112, *C112,* E114, R50, *R50*
    four squares, A144, B8, *B8,* C8, *C8,* C112, *C112,* D44,
        D44, R50, *R50*
    frame games, B70, *B70,* C72, *C72,* C112, *C112,* D8,
        D8, E42, R51, *R51*
    magnet words, A74, A114, B40, *B40,* D80, *D80,* E8,
        R51, *R51*
    word triangles, A8, A114, E78, R51, *R51*
vocal cords, C38, *C38*
volcanism, E86, **E86,** *E87,* E108
    atmospheres, E88
    Mars, E91
    Mercury, E89
    Venus, E90
volcanoes, A12, A148. *See also* lava.
volume, **B11,** B34, B41, R43, **R43**
    calculating, B12–13
    Chapter Investigation, B14–15
    displacement, B13, *B13*
    of liquid, B13
    as physical property, B41, B42
Voyager 2 spacecraft, E26, E99

Acknowledgments

Photography

Cover © David Nunuk/Photo Researchers; **i** © David Nunuk/Photo Researchers; **iii** *left (top to bottom)* Photograph of James Trefil by Evan Cantwell; Photograph of Rita Ann Calvo by Joseph Calvo; Photograph of Linda Carnine by Amilcar Cifuentes; Photograph of Sam Miller by Samuel Miller; *right (top to bottom)* Photograph of Kenneth Cutler by Kenneth A. Cutler; Photograph of Donald Steely by Marni Stamm; Photograph of Vicky Vachon by Redfern Photographics; **vi** © Steve Starr, Boston Inc./PictureQuest; **vii** Stephen Alvarez/National Geographic Image Collection; **viii** © David Leahy/Getty Images; **ix** AP/Wide World Photos; **x** © Chip Simons/Getty Images; **xi** © Alan Kearney/Getty Images; **xii** © Jeff Schultz/Alaska Stock.com; **xiii** © Wolcott Henry/National Geographic Image Collection; **xiv** © Roger Ressmeyer/Corbis; **xv** Courtesy of NASA/JPL/Caltech; **xx–xxi** Photographs by Sharon Hoogstraten; **xii** © Jeff Schultz/Alaska Stock.com; **xiii** © Wolcott Henry/National Geographic Image Collection; **xxx–xxxi** © Georgette Duowma/Taxi/Getty Images; **xxxii–xxxiii** © Aflo Foto Agency; **xxxiv–xxxv** © Larry Hamill/age fotostock america, inc.; **xxxvi** © Vince Streano/Corbis; **xxxvii** © Roger Ressmeyer/Corbis; **xxxviii** *left* University of Florida Lightning Research Laboratory; *center* © Roger Ressmeyer/Corbis; **xxxix** *center* © Mauro Fermariello/ Science Researchers; *bottom* © Alfred Pasieka/Photo Researchers; **xl–xli** © Stocktrek/ Corbis; *center* NOAA; **xli** *top* © Alan Schein Photography/Corbis; *right* Vaisala Oyj, Finland; **xlvii** © The Chedd-Angier Production Company.

Earth's Surface

Divider © Per Breiehagen/Getty Images; **A2–A3** Courtesy of NASA/JPL/Caltech; **A3** *top* Carla Thomas/NASA; *bottom* Diamonds North Resources, Ltd.; **A4** *top* Carla Thomas/NASA; *bottom* © The Chedd-Angier Production Company; **A5** © William Whitehurst/Corbis; **A6–A7** NASA; **A7** *top left* © NASA; *center left* SeaWiFS Project/NASA Goddard Space Flight Center; *bottom left* National Air & Space Museum/Smithsonian Institution; *top right* Courtesy of L. Sue Baugh; *center right* Bike Map courtesy of Chicagoland Bicycle Federation. Photograph by Sharon Hoogstraten; *bottom right* NASA Goddard Space Flight Center; **A9** Photograph by Sharon Hoogstraten; **A10–A11** NASA; **A10** *bottom left* © David Parker/Photo Researchers; *bottom center* © R. Wickllund/ OAR/National Undersea Research Program; **A11** *bottom center* University of Victoria, Victoria, British Columbia, Canada; *bottom right* © Peter and Georgina Bowater/Stock Connection/PictureQuest; **A12** © Photodisc/Getty Images; **A13** Photograph by Sharon Hoogstraten; **A14** © A. Ramey/PhotoEdit/PictureQuest; **A15** Photograph by Sharon Hoogstraten; **A16** U.S. Geological Survey; **A19** © David Parker/Photo Researchers; **A20** Photograph by Sharon Hoogstraten; **A23** © Jerry Driendl/Getty Images; **A24** Photograph by Sharon Hoogstraten; **A25** *top* © Stan Osolinski/Getty Images; *bottom* U.S. Geological Survey; **A26, A28** *top left* U.S. Geological Survey; *bottom left, center right, bottom right* Photographs by Sharon Hoogstraten; **A30, A31** *top right* © Space Imaging; *bottom background* © Paul Morrell/Getty Images; *bottom left* National Oceanic and Atmospheric Administration/Department of Commerce; **A32** *top left, top center* Eros Data Center/U.S. Geological Survey; *bottom right* Photograph by Sharon Hoogstraten; **A34** Photo courtesy of John D. Rogie, 1997; **A35** © Lynn Radeka/SuperStock Images; **A36** *top* NASA; *lower center* U.S. Geological Survey; *bottom left, background,* © Paul Morrell/Getty Images; *bottom left* National Oceanic and Atmospheric Administration/ Department of Commerce; **A38** U.S. Geological Survey; **A40–A41** © Steve Starr, Boston Inc./ PictureQuest; **A41** *top right, center right* Photographs by Sharon Hoogstraten; *bottom right* © Dan Suzio/Photo Researchers; **A43** Photograph by Sharon Hoogstraten; **A44** © Andrew J. Martinez/Photo Researchers; **A45** *left* © Astrid & Hanns-Freider/Photo Researchers; *center* © Charles D. Winters/Photo Researchers; **A46** Photograph by Sharon Hoogstraten; **A47** *top left, center* © Charles D. Winters/Photo Researchers; *top right* Photograph by Malcolm Hjerstedt. Courtesy of F. John Barlow/SANCO Publishing; *bottom left* © Biophoto Associates/Photo Researchers; *bottom center* © Dorling Kindersley; *bottom right* © Phil Degginger/Color Pic, Inc.; *top* © David Young Wolff/PhotoEdit; *bottom* © Doug Martin/Photo Researchers; **A49** *background* © Joyce Photographics/Photo Researchers; *top* © Dorling Kindersley; **A50, A51** Photographs by Sharon Hoogstraten; **A52** *top left* © Charles D. Winters/Photo Researchers; *top right* © Mark A. Schneider/Photo Researchers; *bottom* Photograph by Sharon Hoogstraten; **A53, A54** Photographs by Sharon Hoogstraten; **A55** *top, center right* Photographs by Sharon Hoogstraten; *bottom right* © Thomas Hunn/Visuals Unlimited; **A56** Photograph by Sharon Hoogstraten; **A57** *top left, center* © Mark A. Schneider/Visuals Unlimited; *top right* Photograph by Sharon Hoogstraten; **A58** *top left* © Martin Miller/Visuals Unlimited; *bottom left, right* Photographs by Sharon Hoogstraten; **A59, A60** Photographs by Sharon Hoogstraten; **A61** *top left* © Geoff Tompkinson/Photo Researchers; *center left* © A.J. Copely/Visuals Unlimited; *bottom left* © Charles D. Winters/Photo Researchers; *top right* © Charles Falco/Photo Researchers; *center right, bottom right* © Dorling Kindersley; **A63** *top right, center left* © Mark A. Schneider/Photo Researchers; *center right* © Andrew J. Martinez/Photo Researchers; *bottom right* © M. Claye/Photo Researchers; **A65** *top* © Mervyn P. Lawes/Corbis; *bottom* Photograph by Sharon Hoogstraten; **A66** Newmont Mining Corp.; **A67** *top left* © Dorling Kindersley; *top right* © Louis Goldman/Photo Researchers; *center left, bottom left* © Dorling Kindersley; **A68** *center* © Charles D. Winters/Photo Researchers; *bottom left* © Astrid & Hanns-Freider/ Photo Researchers; *bottom right top* © Photodisc/Getty Images; *bottom right middle* © Dorling Kindersley; *bottom right* © Photodisc/Getty Images; **A70** *left* NASA/Science Photo Library; *right* NASA; **A72–A73** Stephen Alvarez/NGS Image Collection; **A73** *top, center* Photographs by Sharon Hoogstraten; *bottom* Courtesy of L. Sue Baugh; **A75** Photograph by Sharon Hoogstraten; **A76** *top left* © Dorling Kindersley; *top right* © Doug Martin/Photo Researchers; *bottom* © The Image Bank/Getty Images; **A77** *top* © James Lyon/Lonely Planet Images; *bottom* Photograph by Sharon Hoogstraten; **A79** *center left, bottom* © Andrew J. Martinez/Photo Researchers; *center right* © Arthur R. Hill/Visuals Unlimited; **A81** *background* Arne Danielsen, Norway; *left* © Charles O'Rear/ Corbis; *right* © Detlev Van Ravenswaay/ Photo Researchers; **A82** Photograph by Sharon Hoogstraten; **A83** *top left* © Arthur R. Hill/Visuals Unlimited; *top center, top right* © Joyce Photographics/Photo Researchers; *bottom center* © Mark Schneider/Visuals Unlimited; *bottom right* © Dorling Kindersley; **A84** *top* © Andrew J. Martinez/Photo Researchers; *bottom* © Breck P. Kent; **A85** Photograph by Sharon Hoogstraten; **A86, A87** © Francois Gohier/Photo Researchers; **A88** *background* © Dr. Juero Aleon/Photo Researchers; **A89** Photograph by Sharon Hoogstraten; **A91** *left* © Carolyn Iverson/Photo Researchers; *right* © Ted Clutter/Pennsylvania State Museum Collection/Photo Researchers; **A92** *top left* Photograph by Sharon Hoogstraten; *center* Courtesy of L. Sue Baugh; *bottom right* © Norbert Wu/Norbert Wu Productions/ PictureQuest; *bottom left;* National Oceanic and Atmospheric Administration **A93** *top* © Look GMBH/eStockPhotography/PictureQuest; *bottom* © Corbis; **A94** Photograph by Sharon Hoogstraten; **A95** *left* © 1991 Ned Haines/ Photo Researchers; *center* © Wayne Lawler/Photo Researchers; *right* © Jim Steinberg/Photo Researchers; **A96** Photograph by Sharon Hoogstraten; **A97** *right (top to bottom)* © Andrew J. Martinez 1995/Photo Researchers; © Andrew J. Martinez 1995/Photo Researchers; Boltin Picture Library; © Breck P. Kent; © 1996 Andrew J. Martinez/Photo Researchers; **A98** Photograph by Sharon Hoogstraten; **A100** *top left* The Boltin Picture Library; *top right* Photograph courtesy of John Longshore; *bottom left* © E.R. Degginger/Color-Pic, Inc.; *bottom right* © Patricia Tye/Photo Researchers; **A102** *top* Will Hart/PhotoEdit; *center, bottom* Photographs by Sharon Hoogstraten; **A103** © Corbis; **A104** *top left, top center* © Andrew J. Martinez/Photo Researchers; *upper center section left* Arthur R. Hill/Visuals Unlimited; *lower center section, left* © Andrew J. Martinez/Photo Researchers; *right* Photograph by Sharon Hoogstraten; *bottom left, center* © Andrew J. Martinez/Photo Researchers; *bottom right* © Breck P. Kent; **A106** © G.R. Roberts Photo Library; **A108** *top* © Chris Butler/Photo Researchers; *bottom* © Detlev van Ravenswaay/Photo Researchers; **A109** *top* © Jim Brandenburg/Minden Pictures; *center* J.W. Schopf/University of California, Los Angeles; *bottom* Japan Meteorological Agency; **A110** *top left* © Simon Fraser/Photo Researchers; *top right* © Chase Studios/Photo Researchers; *bottom* Courtesy of the Ocean Drilling Program; **A111** *top* NASA Goddard Space Flight Center; *bottom* STS-113 Shuttle Crew/NASA; **A112–A113** © Wendy Conway/Alamy Images; **A113** *top right, center* Photographs by Sharon Hoogstraten; **A115** Photograph by Sharon Hoogstraten; **A117** *background* © Photodisc/Getty Images; *inset top* © Susan Rayfield/Photo Researchers; *inset center, bottom left* Photographs courtesy of Sara Christopherson; *inset bottom right* © Kirkendall-Spring Photographer; **A118** Photograph by Sharon Hoogstraten; **A119** *top left* © Bettmann/Corbis; *top right* © Runk/Schoenberger/ Grant Heilman

Photography; *bottom* © Cheyenne Rouse/Visuals Unlimited; **A121** *background* © Ecoscene/Corbis; *inset* © Michael Nicholson/Corbis; **A122** Photograph by Sharon Hoogstraten; **A123** *left* © Joel W. Rogers/Corbis; *right* © Barry Runk/Grant Heilman Photography; **A124** © Barry Runk/Grant Heilman Photography; **A125** *top left* © Sally A. Morgan/Corbis; *top right* © Peter Falkner/Photo Researchers; *bottom left* © Tony Craddock/ Photo Researchers; *bottom left* © Tui de Roy/Bruce Coleman, Inc.; **A128** © Barry Runk/Grant Heilman Photography; **A129** © Jim Strawser/Grant Heilman Photography; **A130** *top left* © Larry Lefever/Grant Heilman Photography; *center right, bottom left* Photograph by Sharon Hoogstraten; **A132** © Cameron Davidson/Stock Connection, Inc./Alamy Images; **A133** AP/Wide World Photos; **A134** *top* © Steve Strickland/ Visuals Unlimited; *bottom* Betty Wald/Aurora; **A135** Photograph by Sharon Hoogstraten; **A136** *left* © Charles O'Rear/Corbis; *right* © Larry Lefever/Grant Heilman Photography; **A137** *center inset* Courtesy of Teska Associates, Evanston. Illinois; **A138** *top right* © Runk/Schoenberger/Grant Heilman Photography; *bottom* © Larry Lefever/Grant Heilman Photography; **A140** © Barry Runk/Grant Heilman Photography; **A142–A143** A.C. Waltham/Robert Harding Picture Library/Alamy Images; **A143** *center right* Photograph by Sharon Hoogstraten; **A145** © Bernhard Edmaier/Photo Researchers; **A146** Photograph by Sharon Hoogstraten; **A147** AP/Wide World Photos; **A148** *top* Photograph by L.M. Smith, Waterways Experiment Station, U.S. Army Corps of Engineers. Courtesy, USGS; *bottom* © Thomas Rampton/Grant Heilman Photography; **A149** © Troy and Mary Parlee/Alamy Images; **A150** Photograph by Sharon Hoogstraten; **A151** © Bill Ross/Corbis; **A152** *top* © Kevin Horan/Stock Boston /PictureQuest; *bottom* © Yann Arthus-Bertrand/Corbis; **A153** © 1992 Tom Bean; **A154** © Charles Kennard/Stock Boston/PictureQuest; **A155** © Reuters NewMedia, Inc./Corbis; **A156** © Peter Bowater/Alamy Images; **A158** © John and Lisa Merrill/Getty Images; **A159** © Robert Perron; **A160** Photograph by Sharon Hoogstraten; **A161** © Tim Barnwell/Picturesque/ PictureQuest; **A162** © John Shaw/Bruce Coleman, Inc.; **A163** *top* © 1994 Tom Bean; *right* © Goodshoot/Alamy Images; **A164** *background* © Gustav Verderber/Visuals Unlimited; *inset left* © Gary Meszaros/Bruce Coleman, Inc.; *inset right* © Lee Rentz/Bruce Coleman, Inc.; **A165** Photograph by Sharon Hoogstraten; **A167** *left* © Bernard Edmaier/Photo Researchers; *right* © ImageState-Pictor/PictureQuest ; **A168** *top* © Norman Barett/Bruce Coleman, Inc.; *bottom* © Jim Wark/Airphoto; **A169** *top* © 1990 Tom Bean; *bottom* Photograph by Sharon Hoogstraten; **A171** © Charles W. Campbell/ Corbis; **A172** *top* © Bernhard Edmaier/Photo Researchers; *center* © John and Lisa Merrill/Getty Images; **A174** © Tom Bean.

Matter and Energy

Divider © Scott T. Smith/Corbis; **B2–B3, B3** Courtesy of NASA/JPL/Caltech; **B4** *top* © Babakin Space Center, The Planetary Society; *bottom* © The Chedd-Angier Production Company; **B6–B7** © Steve Allen/Brand X Pictures; **B7, B9** Photographs by Sharon Hoogstraten; **B10** *left* © Antonio Mo/Getty Images; *right* © ImageState/Alamy; **B11** © Tom Stewart/Corbis; **B12, B13** Photographs by Sharon Hoogstraten; **B14** *top* © Stewart Cohen/ Getty Images; *bottom* Photograph by Sharon Hoogstraten; **B14–B15, B15** Photographs by Sharon Hoogstraten; **B16** © Royalty-Free/Corbis; **B17** Photograph by Sharon Hoogstraten; **B18** © NatPhotos/Tony Sweet/Digital Vision; **B19** © Jake Rajs/Getty Images; **B20** Courtesy IBM Archives; **B21** Photograph by Sharon Hoogstraten; **B22** *left* © James L. Amos/Corbis; *right* © Omni Photo Communications, Inc./Index Stock; **B23** © Richard Laird/Getty Images; **B24** Photograph by Sharon Hoogstraten; **B25** © Royalty-Free/Corbis; **B26** © Nik Wheeler/Corbis; **B27** Photograph by Sharon Hoogstraten; **B30** © Robert F. Sisson/Getty Images; **B31** Photograph by Sharon Hoogstraten; **B34** *top* Photograph by Sharon Hoogstraten; *bottom left* © James L. Amos/Corbis; *bottom right* © Royalty-Free/Corbis; **B36** Photographs by Sharon Hoogstraten; **B38–B39** © David Leahy/Getty Images; **B39, B41** Photographs by Sharon Hoogstraten; **B42** Photograph by Sharon Hoogstraten; *right* © Dan Lim/Masterfile; **B45** *top left* © Maryellen McGrath/Bruce Coleman Inc.; *top center* © Jean-Bernard Vernier/Corbis Sygma; *top right* © Angelo Cavalli/Getty Images; *bottom* © Garry Black/Masterfile; *inset* Photograph by Sharon Hoogstraten; **B46** © Mark C. Burnett/Stock, Boston Inc./PictureQuest; **B47** Photograph by Sharon Hoogstraten; **B48** © J. Westrich/Masterfile; **B49** *left* © Owen Franken/Corbis; *right* © Erich Lessing/Art Resource, New York; **B50** © ImageState/Alamy; **B51** *left* © Brand X Pictures; *right* © Peter Bowater/ Alamy; **B52** © Royalty-Free/Corbis; **B53** © Winifred Wisniewski/Frank Lane Picture Agency/Corbis; **B54** © A. Pasieka/Photo Researchers; **B55** © Sean Ellis/Getty Images; **B56** © Royalty-Free/Corbis; *bottom* Photograph by Sharon Hoogstraten; **B57, B58** Photographs by Sharon Hoogstraten; **B59** © Lawrence Livermore National Laboratory/Photo Researchers; **B60** *top left* © SPL/Photo Researchers; *top right* © Felix St. Clair Renard/Getty Images; *bottom* © David Young-Wolff/PhotoEdit; **B61** Photograph by Sharon Hoogstraten; **B62** © Alan Towse/Ecoscene/Corbis; **B63** © Robert Essel NYC/Corbis; *inset* © The Cover Story/Corbis; **B64** *top left* © Dan Lim/Masterfile; *top right* © Mark C. Burnett/Stock, Boston Inc./PictureQuest; *bottom* © David Young-Wolff/PhotoEdit; **B66** © Winifred Wisniewski/Frank Lane Picture Agency/Corbis; **B68–B69** AP/Wide World Photos; **B69, B71** Photographs by Sharon Hoogstraten; **B72** © Alan Schein Photography/Corbis; **B73** *top* © Patrick Ward/Corbis; *bottom* © NASA/Photo Researchers; **B74** AP/Wide World Photos; **B75** *top* © George H. H. Huey/Corbis; *bottom* Photograph by Sharon Hoogstraten; **B76** *top* © Vladimir Pcholkin/Getty Images; *bottom* © Thomas Beach; **B77** © Adam Gault/Digital Vision; **B78** © Bill Aron/PhotoEdit; **B79** © TempSport/Corbis; **B80** © Robert Cameron/Getty Images; **B81** *left* © Gunter Marx Photography/Corbis; *right* © Lester Lefkowitz/Corbis; **B82** © Left Lane Productions/Corbis; **B83** © Dorling Kindersley; **B84** *top* © Grant Klotz/Alaska Stock Images/PictureQuest; *bottom* Photograph by Sharon Hoogstraten; **B85, B86** Photographs by Sharon Hoogstraten; **B87** *top left* © Royalty-Free/Corbis; *top right* Thinkstock, LLC; *bottom* AP/Wide World Photos; **B88** © AFP/Corbis; *inset* © John Farmar; Cordaiy Photo Library Ltd./Corbis; **B89** *top* © Sally A. Morgan; Ecoscene/Corbis; *bottom* Photograph by Sharon Hoogstraten; **B90** © Joe Sohm/Visions of America, LLC/PictureQuest; **B91** © Michael S. Lewis/Corbis; **B92** *top* © Vladimir Pcholkin/Getty Images; *bottom* © AFP/Corbis; **B96** © Don Farrall/Getty Images; **B97** *top left* © Sheila Terry/Photo Researchers; *top center, top right* © Dorling Kindersley; *bottom* © SEF/Art Resource, New York; **B98** *top left* Mary Evans Picture Library; *top right, bottom* © Dorling Kindersley; **B99** © Mark Wiens/Masterfile; **B100–B101** © Steve Bloom/stevebloom.com; **B101, B103** Photographs by Sharon Hoogstraten; **B104** © Tracy Frankel/Getty Images; **B105** Photographs by Sharon Hoogstraten; **B106** © Daryl Benson/Masterfile; *inset* © Spencer Grant/PhotoEdit; **B107** Photograph by Sharon Hoogstraten; **B108** *top* © Steve Vidler/SuperStock; *bottom* © Chase Jarvis/Getty Images; **B109** © FogStock/Alamy; *inset* © Gordon Wiltsie/Getty Images; **B110** © David Bishop/Getty Images; **B111** Thinkstock, LLC; **B112** Photograph by Sharon Hoogstraten; **B113** © Richard Bickel/Corbis; **B115** *top left* © Jeremy Samuelson/FoodPix; *bottom left* © William Reavell-StockFood Munich/StockFood; *right* © Martin Jacobs/FoodPix; **B116** Photograph by Sharon Hoogstraten; **B117** © Brand X Pictures/Alamy; **B119** © ImageState Royalty Free/Alamy; **B120** *top left* E.C. Humphrey; *top right* Creatas®; *bottom* © Uwe Walz Gdt/age fotostock america, inc.; **B122** *top* © Nancy Ney/Corbis; *bottom* Photograph by Sharon Hoogstraten; **B123** Photograph by Sharon Hoogstraten; **B124** *top* Photographs by Sharon Hoogstraten; *bottom* Thinkstock, LLC.

Waves, Sound, and Light

Divider © David Pu'u/Corbis; **C2–C3** © Paul Kuroda/SuperStock; **C3** *left* © B. Benoit/Photo Researchers; *right* © Powerstock/SuperStock; **C4** *top* © Stephen Frink/Corbis; *bottom* © The Chedd-Angier Production Company; **C5** © George Stetten, M.D., Ph.D; **C6–C7** © Peter Sterling/Getty Images; **C7, C9** Photographs by Sharon Hoogstraten; **C11** Photograph courtesy of Earthquake Engineering Research Institute Reconnaissance Team; **C12** © Michael Krasowitz/Getty Images; **C13** Photograph by Sharon Hoogstraten; **C15** © John Lund/Getty Images; **C16** © Greg Huglin/Superstock; **C17** © Arnulf Husmo/Getty Images; **C19** Richard Olsenius/National Geographic Image Collection; **C20** Photograph by Sharon Hoogstraten; **C22** *top* © 1990 Robert Mathena/ Fundamental Photographs, NYC; *bottom* Photographs by Sharon Hoogstraten; **C23, C24** Photographs by Sharon Hoogstraten; **C25** © 2001 Richard Megna/Fundamental Photographs, NYC; **C26** © 1972 FP/Fundamental Photographs, NYC; *bottom* Photograph by Sharon Hoogstraten; **C27** © 1998 Richard Megna/Fundamental Photographs, NYC; **C28** © Hiroshi Hara/Photonica; **C29** Takaaki Uda, Public Works Research Institute, Japan/NOAA; **C30** *bottom center* © 2001 Richard Megna/Fundamental Photographs, NYC; *bottom right* © 1972 FP/Fundamental Photographs, NYC; **C34–C35** © Chip Simons/Getty Images; **C35, C37** Photographs by Sharon Hoogstraten; **C39** © Susumu Nishinaga/Photo Researchers; **C41** Photographs by Sharon Hoogstraten; **C42** © Jeff Rotman/Getty Images; **C43** © John Terence Turner/Getty Images; **C44** *left* © Reuters NewMedia Inc./Corbis; *background* © Jason Hindley/Getty Images; **C45** Photograph by Sharon Hoogstraten; **C47** *left (top to bottom)* © Will Crocker/Getty Images; © Dorling Kindersley; © Photodisc/Getty Images; © Dorling Kindersley; © Photodisc/Getty Images; © Stephen Dalton/Animals Animals; © Steve Bloom/Getty Images; *top right* © Don Smetzer/Getty Images; *bottom right* Brian Gordon Green/National Geographic Image Collection; **C48** Photograph by Sharon Hoogstraten; **C49** © Dorling Kindersley; **C50** © Michael Melford/Getty Images; **C52** © Tom Main/Getty Images; **C53** Photograph by Sharon Hoogstraten; **C55** *left* © Roger Ressmeyer/Corbis; *right* Symphony Center, Home of the Chicago Symphony Orchestra; **C56** © Yehoash Raphael, Kresge Hearing Research Institute, The University of Michigan; **C57** © Chris Shinn/Getty Images; **C58** Photograph by Sharon Hoogstraten; **C59** *top left* © Stephen Dalton/OSF/Animals Animals; *top right* © Paulo de Oliveira/Getty Images;

bottom left © AFP/Corbis; bottom right U.S. Navy photo by Photographer's Mate 3rd Class Lawrence Braxton/Department of Defense; **C60** © Fotos; **C63** © Andrew Syred/Photo Researchers; **C64** top left © Reuters NewMedia Inc./Corbis; bottom Photographs by Sharon Hoogstraten; **C65** Photograph by Sharon Hoogstraten; **C66** bottom left © Stephen Dalton/OSF/Animals Animals; bottom right © Paulo de Oliveira/Getty Images; **C68** © Photodisc/Getty Images; **C70–C71** © Alan Kearney/Getty Images; **C71** top, center Photographs by Sharon Hoogstraten; bottom The EIT Consortium/NASA; **C73** Photograph by Sharon Hoogstraten; **C75** NASA, The Hubble Heritage Team, STScI, AURA; **C76** Photograph by Sharon Hoogstraten; **C78** top Palomar Observatory/Caltech; center NASA/MSFC/SAO; bottom NASA/CXC/ASU/J. Hester et al; background NASA/JHU/AUI/R. Giacconi et al.; **C79** Photograph by Sharon Hoogstraten; **C80** left © China Tourism Press/Getty Images; center © David Nunuk/Photo Researchers; right © Dr. Arthur Tucker/Photo Researchers; **C81** left to right © Jeremy Woodhouse/Getty Images; © Sinclair Stammers/Photo Researchers; © Hugh Turvey/Photo Researchers; © Alfred Pasieka/Photo Researchers; **C84** Photograph by Sharon Hoogstraten; **C85** top © Dr. Arthur Tucker/Photo Researchers; bottom © Thomas Eisner, Cornell University; **C86** © Martin Spinks; **C87** © Photodisc/Getty Images; inset © David Young-Wolff/Getty Images; **C88** Robert F. Sisson/National Geographic Image Collection; **C89** © George D. Lepp/Corbis; **C90** top © Raymond Blythe/OSF/Animals Animals; bottom Photograph by Sharon Hoogstraten; **C92** © Traffic Technologies; **C93** Photograph by Sharon Hoogstraten; **C94** © Jeff Greenberg/Visuals Unlimited; **C95** © Raymond Gehman/Corbis; **C96** © Charles Swedlund; **C97** top © Ace Photo Agency/Phototake; bottom © Dorling Kindersley; **C98** Photograph by Sharon Hoogstraten; **C100** top © Michael Newman/PhotoEdit; bottom Photographs by Sharon Hoogstraten; **C101** Photographs by Sharon Hoogstraten; **C102** center right Robert F. Sisson/National Geographic Image Collection; bottom © Ace Photo Agency/Phototake; **C106** top The Granger Collection, New York; bottom © Jack and Beverly Wilgus; **C107** top The Granger Collection, New York; center left Diagram of the eye from the *Opticae thesaurus. Alhazeni Arabis libri septem, nunc primum editi* by Ibn al-Haytham (Alhazen). Edited by Federico Risnero (Basleae, 1572), p. 6. Private collection, London; center right Courtesy of NASA/JPL/Caltech; bottom © Royal Greenwich Observatory/Photo Researchers; **C108** top © Stock Connection/Alamy; center © Florian Marquardt; bottom © Museum of Holography, Chicago; **C109** top © Bettmann/Corbis; bottom © Bob Masini/Phototake; **C110–C111** © Tom Raymond/Getty Images; **C111** top, center Photographs by Sharon Hoogstraten; bottom © Philippe Plailly/Photo Researchers; **C112** Photograph by Sharon Hoogstraten; **C114** © Laura Dwight/Corbis; **C115** Photograph by Sharon Hoogstraten; **C116** © Michael Newman/PhotoEdit; **C117** Photographs by Sharon Hoogstraten; **C118** Peter McBride/Aurora; **C119** Photograph by Sharon Hoogstraten; **C120** © Richard H. Johnston/Getty Images; **C122** © Kim Heacox/Getty Images; background © Photodisc/Getty Images; **C123** © T. R. Tharp/Corbis; **C124** top © Ruddy Gold/age photostock america, inc.; bottom Photograph by Sharon Hoogstraten; **C125** Photographs by Sharon Hoogstraten; **C126** © CMCD, 1994; **C128** Photograph by Sharon Hoogstraten; **C130** © Argentum/Photo Researchers; **C131** Photograph by Sharon Hoogstraten; **C133** top © Andrew Syred/Photo Researchers; center Lunar and Planetary Institute, CIRS/Library; bottom NASA; **C134** Photograph by Sharon Hoogstraten; **C135** Use of Canon Powershot S45 courtesy of Canon USA; **C136** © Philippe Psaila/Photo Researchers; **C137** top © Photodisc/Getty Images; bottom © Tom Stewart/corbisstockmarket.com; **C138** Bradley C. Edwards, Ph.D.; **C139** top © Photodisc/Getty Images; center © PhotoFlex.com; bottom © Michael Goldman/Photis/PictureQuest; **C140** © Michael Newman/PhotoEdit.

Ecology

Divider © Richard du Toit/Nature Picture Library; **D2, D3** background © Mark Thiessen/National Geographic Image Collection; **D3** top © Frank Oberle/Getty Images; bottom © Hal Horwitz/Corbis; **D4** top (both) © Lawrence J. Godson; bottom Chedd-Angier Production Company; **D6, D7** © Jeff Schultz/Alaska Stock.com; **D7** top Photograph by Ken O'Donoghue; center Photograph by Frank Siteman; **D9** Photograph by Frank Siteman; **D10** © Mark Allen Stack/Tom Stack & Associates; **D11** left © Jim Brandenburg/Minden Pictures; right © Ted Kerasote/Photo Researchers, Inc.; **D12** bottom left © Grant Heilman Photography; **D13** © Frans Lemmens/Getty Images; **D14** top © Michael J. Doolittle/The Image Works, Inc.; bottom Photograph by Ken O'Donoghue; **D16** Photograph by Ken O'Donoghue; **D19** Photograph by Frank Siteman; **D21** © Randy Wells/Corbis; **D22** Photograph by Frank Siteman; **D23** left © Eric Crichton/Corbis; top right © E.R. Degginger/Color-Pic, Inc.; bottom right © T.E. Adams/Visuals Unlimited, Inc.; **D24** © Anthony Mercieca Photo/Photo Researchers, Inc.; **D25** top © Fred Bruemmer/DRK Photo; bottom Photograph by Ken O'Donoghue; **D27** background © Raymond Gehman/Corbis; **D29** left © Arthur Gurmankin & Mary Morina/Visuals Unlimited, Inc.; top right © Carmela Leszczynski/Animals Animals; **D30** © Charles Melton/Visuals Unlimited, Inc.; **D31** © Michio Hoshino/Minden Pictures; **D32** top left © Tom Bean; top right © E.R. Degginger/Color-Pic, Inc.; bottom © Joe McDonald/Visuals Unlimited, Inc.; **D33** left © David Wrobel/Visuals Unlimited, Inc.; right © Tom Bean; **D34** left © Owaki-Kulla/Corbis; right © Frans Lanting/Minden Pictures; **D35** top Photograph by Ken O'Donoghue; bottom © Stephen Dalton/Photo Researchers, Inc.; **D36** left © Aaron Horowitz/Corbis; center © Hans Pfletschinger/Peter Arnold, Inc.; right © Arthur Gurmankin & Mary Morina/Visuals Unlimited, Inc.; **D37** left © Paul Rezendes; center © Richard Herrmann/Visuals Unlimited, Inc.; right © Norbert Wu; **D42, D43** © Wolcott Henry/National Geographic Image Collection; **D43** top Photograph by Frank Siteman; center Photograph by Ken O'Donoghue; **D45** Photograph by Frank Siteman; **D46** left and center © Frans Lanting/Minden Pictures; right © Robin Karpan/Visuals Unlimited, Inc.; **D50** © Walt Anderson/Visuals Unlimited, Inc.; **D51** ©Alan & Linda Detrick/Photo Researchers, Inc.; **D52** top © Patrick J. Endres/Visuals Unlimited, Inc.; bottom left Photograph by Frank Siteman; bottom right Photograph by Ken O'Donoghue; **D53** Photograph by Ken O'Donoghue; **D54** © Spencer Grant/PhotoEdit, Inc.; **D55** © Gary Braasch; **D56** top © Joe McDonald/Visuals Unlimited, Inc.; bottom © Stephen J. Krasemann/Photo Researchers, Inc.; **D57** top Photograph by Ken O'Donoghue; bottom © Michael Fogden/Bruce Coleman Inc.; **D58** © Michael & Patricia Fogden/Minden Pictures; **D59** © Bradley Sheard; **D60** clockwise from top © S.J. Krasemann/Peter Arnold, Inc.; © Ray Coleman/Visuals Unlimited, Inc.; © Astrid & Hanns-Frieder Michler/Science Photo Library; © E.R. Degginger/Color-Pic, Inc.; © Dwight R. Kuhn; © Phil Degginger/Color-Pic, Inc.; **D61** © Arthur Morris/Visuals Unlimited, Inc.; **D62** left © Kevin Fleming/Corbis; inset © David M. Dennis/Animals Animals; **D63** Photograph by Ken O'Donoghue; **D64** top © Shin Yoshino/Minden Pictures; bottom © Tim Fitzharris/Minden Pictures; **D65** Photograph by Frank Siteman; **D66** bottom (background) © Leo Collier/Getty Images; **D67** bottom (background) © David R. Frazier/Getty Images; **D69** © A. & J. Visage/Peter Arnold, Inc.; **D70** top left © Frans Lanting/Minden Pictures; **D74** bottom left Denver Public Library, Western History Collection, call#F-4659; top center © James Randklev/Getty Images; bottom right Library of Congress, Prints and Photographs Division (LC-USZ62-16709 DLC) cph 3a18915; **D75** top left © H.H. French/Corbis; top right © Bill Ross/Corbis; center left The Bancroft Library, University of California, Berkeley; center right © Corbis; bottom © Michael Sewell/Peter Arnold, Inc.; **D76** top left © Alfred Eisenstaedt/Getty Images; top right © Tom Bean/DRK Photo; center right © David Muench/Corbis; bottom left © Kevin Schafer/Corbis; bottom right Habitat Quality for San Joaquin Kit Fox on Managed and Private Lands reprinted from ESRI Map Book, Vol. 16 and used herein with permission. Copyright © 2001 ESRI. All rights reserved.; **D77** top © Tom Soucek/Alaska Stock Images; bottom © Richard Galosy/Bruce Coleman, Inc.; **D78, D79** ©Alex Maclean/Photonica; **D79** top and center Photographs by Ken O'Donoghue; **D81** Photograph by Frank Siteman; **D83** © Ray Pfortner/Peter Arnold, Inc.; **D84** Photograph by Ken O'Donoghue; **D85** top © John Elk III; bottom © Ted Spiegel/Corbis; **D86** background © ChromoSohm/Sohm/Photo Researchers, Inc.; insets Courtesy, USGS: EROS Data Center; **D87** © Mark E. Gibson/Visuals Unlimited, Inc.; **D88** © David Zimmerman/Corbis; **D89** © David Young-Wolff/PhotoEdit, Inc.; **D90** left © Richard Stockton/Iguazu Falls/Index Stock Imagery, Inc.; right © Bill Ross/Corbis; **D91** Photograph by Ken O'Donoghue; **D92** bottom © Tom Bean/DRK Photo; inset © Jenny Hager/The Image Works, Inc.; **D93** bottom © Natalie Fobes/Corbis; inset © Natalie Fobes/Getty Images; **D95** © Kent Foster Photgraphs/Visuals Unlimited, Inc.; **D96** top © Andrew J. Martinez/Photo Researchers, Inc.; inset © D. Cavagnaro/Visuals Unlimited, Inc.; **D97** © Tom Edwards/Visuals Unlimited, Inc.; **D98** Photographs by Ken O'Donoghue and Frank Siteman; **D99** © Frank Pedrick/The Image Works, Inc.; **D100** © Joe McDonald/Visuals Unlimited, Inc.; **D101** top (background) © Jim Wark/Airphoto; top (inset) Photograph by Scott Williams/U.S. Fish and Wildlife Service; bottom (background) © Tom Bean/Corbis; bottom (insets) Courtesy, San Diego State University, Soil Ecology and Restoration Group; **D102** © Melissa Farlow/National Geographic Image Collection; **D103** © Klein/Hubert/Peter Arnold, Inc.; **D104** top © Janis Miglavs; bottom © David Young-Wolff/PhotoEdit, Inc.; **D105** © Kevin Schafer/Corbis; **D106** top Tom Myers/Photo Researchers, Inc.; bottom Photograph by Frank Siteman; **D108** center left © Natalie Fobes/Corbis; center right © Kent Foster Photographs/Visuals Unlimited, Inc.; bottom left © Joe McDonald/Visuals Unlimited, Inc.; bottom right © Klein/Hubert/Peter Arnold, Inc.

Space Science

Divider © David Nunuk/Photo Researchers; **E2–E3** © Charles O'Rear/Corbis; **E3** top right © D. Nunuk/Photo Researchers; **E4** © The Chedd-Angier Production Company; **E4–E5** © David Parker/Photo Researchers; **E5** top center NASA/JPL; **E6–E7** NASA; **E7, E9** Photographs by Sharon

...gstraten; **E11** Johnson Space Center/NASA; **E12** Photograph by Sharon Hoogstraten; **E13** *top* © Roger Ressmeyer/Corbis; *bottom* Photograph Sharon Hoogstraten; **E15** Photograph by Sharon Hoogstraten; **E16** *center left* Kapteyn Laboratorium/Photo Researchers; *center* National Optical Astronomy Observatories/Photo Researchers; *center right* A. Wilson (UMD) et al., CXC/NASA; **E18** © Roger Ressmeyer/Corbis; **E19** *top left* NASA Johnson Space Center; *top right* © STScI/NASA/ Photo Researchers; **E20** *top left* © ImageState-Pictor/PictureQuest; **E20–E21, E22** Photographs by Sharon Hoogstraten; **E23** *bottom, inset* NASA; **E24** Courtesy of NASA/JSC; **E25** *top* NASA; *bottom* Photograph by Sharon Hoogstraten; **E27** Photograph by Bill Ingalls/NASA; **E30** *left, inset* Chris Butler/Photo Researchers; **E31** NASA; **E32** Courtesy of V.R. Sharpton University of Alaska-Fairbanks and the Lunar and Planetary Institute; **E33** Photograph by Sharon Hoogstraten; **E34** NASA; **E35** *background* © Jan Tove Johansson/Image State-Pictor/ PictureQuest; *left inset* Andy Fyon, Ontariowildflower.com (Division of Professor Beaker's Learning Labs); *right inset* NASA; **E36** *top* Photograph by Sharon Hoogstraten; *center* © Roger Ressmeyer/Corbis; *bottom* NASA; **E40–E41** © Roger Ressmeyer/Corbis; **E41** *top right, center right* Photographs by Sharon Hoogstraten; *bottom right* NASA Goddard Space Flight Center; **E43** *left* NASA; *right* Photograph by Sharon Hoogstraten; **E44** *top* © 2003 The Living Earth Inc.; *bottom* Photograph by Sharon Hoogstraten; **E45** Photograph by Sharon Hoogstraten; **E47** NASA/JSC; **E49** © Arnulf Husmo/Getty Images; **E50** *top* © Christian Perret/jump; *bottom left, bottom right* Photograph by Sharon Hoogstraten; **E51, E52** Photographs by Sharon Hoogstraten; **E53** Courtesy of NASA and the Lunar and Planetary Institute; **E54** USGS Flagstaff, Arizona; **E55** *top right* Photograph by Sharon Hoogstraten; *bottom right* NASA; *right inset* NASA and the Lunar and Planetary Institute; **E58** Photograph by Steve Irvine; **E59** © DiMaggio/Kalish/Corbis; **E61** *background* Lunar Horizon View/NASA; **E62** Photograph by Sharon Hoogstraten; **E63** *top* © Roger Ressmeyer/Corbis; *bottom* Photograph by Jean-Francois Guay; **E64** *center* NASA/Getty Images; *bottom left* © Fred Espenak; **E65** *top* © Jeff Greenberg/MRP/Photo Researchers; *bottom* © 1999 Ray Coleman/Photo Researchers; **E67** *top left* © Peter Duke; *right inset* © David Parker/Photo Researchers; *bottom left* Public Domain; *bottom center* Barlow Aerial Photography, Ignacio, CO; **E68** *top left* © 2003 The Living Earth, Inc.; *center left* Photograph courtesy of NASA and the Lunar and Planetary Institute; **E70** *left* USGS Flagstaff, Arizona; *right* NASA Goddard Space Flight Center; **E72** Courtesy of Adler Planetarium & Astronomy Museum, Chicago, Illinois; **E73** *top left* © Stapleton/Corbis; *center* © Science Museum/Science & Society Picture Library; *right* provided by Roger Bell, University of Maryland, and Michael Briley, University of Wisconsin, Oshkosh; *bottom* Courtesy of Adler Planetarium & Astronomy Museum, Chicago, Illinois; **E74** *top left* © Harvard College Observatory/Photo Researchers; *top right* Robert Williams and the Hubble Deep Field Team (STScI) and NASA; *bottom* © Fermi National Accelerator Laboratory/Photo Researchers; **E75** *top* Ann Feild (STScI); *bottom* © NASA/Photo Researchers; **E76–E77** Courtesy of NASA/JPL/University of Arizona; **E77** *top right, center right* Photographs by Sharon Hoogstraten; **E79, E82** Photographs by Sharon Hoogstraten; **E83** *left* Photo © Calvin J. Hamilton; *right* Courtesy of NASA/JPL/Caltech; **E84** NASA; **E85** *top* Photograph by Sharon Hoogstraten; *bottom* Johnson Space Center NASA; **E87** *background* Mark Robinson/Mariner 10/NASA; *top right* NASA; *top left* © Walt Anderson/Visuals Unlimited; *bottom left* NASA/ JPL/Malin Space Science Systems; **E88** Photograph by Sharon Hoogstraten; **E89** *top* USGS; *bottom* Courtesy of NASA/JPL/ Northwestern University; **E90** *top, center, bottom* NASA; **E91** NASA/JSC; **E92** Courtesy of NASA/JPL/Caltech; **E93** *left* Courtesy of NASA/JPL/Malin Space Science Systems; *right* MAP-A-Planet/NASA; *right inset* NASA/Goddard Space Flight Center Scientific Visualization Studio; **E94, E95** Courtesy of NASA/JPL/Caltech; **E96** *top* Courtesy of NASA/JPL/Caltech; *bottom* Photograph by Sharon Hoogstraten; **E97** *top* NASA; *bottom* NASA and the Hubble Heritage Team (STScI/AURA); **E98** *top* E. Karkoschka(LPL) and NASA; *bottom* © Calvin J. Hamilton; **E99** *top* Courtesy of NASA/JPL/Caltech; *center* NASA; **E100** near.jhuapl.edu; **E101** Hubble Space Telescope, STScI-PR96-09a/NASA; **E102** *top, left, inset* NASA; *bottom left* Courtesy of NASA/JPL/Caltech; *bottom left inset* NASA; *top right* © NASA/ JPL/Photo Researchers; *top right inset, bottom right, bottom right inset* NASA; **E103** Courtesy of NASA/JPL/Caltech; **E104** *background* © 1997 Jerry Lodriguss; *right* Courtesy of NASA/JPL/ Caltech; **E105** Fred R. Conrad/The New York Times; **E106** *top left* © James L. Amos/Corbis; *bottom left* Photograph by Sharon Hoogstraten; **E107** Photograph by Sharon Hoogstraten; **E108** *top* NASA; *bottom* Courtesy of NASA/JPL/Caltech; **E112–E113** David Malin Images/Anglo- Australian Observatory; **E113** *top left* © Jerry Schad/Photo Researchers; *center left* Photograph by Sharon Hoogstraten; **E115** Photograph by Sharon Hoogstraten; **E117** Photograph by Jay M. Paschoff, Bryce A. Babcock, Stephan Martin, Wendy Carlos, and Daniel B. Seaton © Williams College; **E118** *left* © John Chumack/Photo Researchers; *right* © NASA/Photo Researchers; **E119** © Patrick J. Endres/Alaskaphotographics.com; **E120** *top* © Dave Robertson/Masterfile; *left bottom, right bottom* Photograph by Sharon Hoogstraten; **E121, E122, E123** Photographs by Sharon Hoogstraten; **E125** *top* © Dorling Kindersley; *bottom* ESA and J. Hester (ASU),NASA; **E126** J. Hester et al./NASA/CXC/ASU; **E127** Hubble Heritage Team/AURA/STScI/NASA; **E129** © MPIA-HD, Birkle, Slawik/Photo Researchers; **E130** Photograph by Sharon Hoogstraten; **E131** © Allan Morton/Dennis Milon/Photo Researchers; *bottom* Photograph by Sharon Hoogstraten; **E132** David Malin Images /Anglo-Australian Observatory; **E133** Walter Jaffe/Leiden Observatory, Holland Ford/JHU/STScI, and NASA; **E134** *left* NASA and Hubble Heritage Team (STScI); *center* NASA, H. Ford (JHU), G. Illingworth (UCSC/LO), M. Clampin (STScI), G. Hartig (STScI), the ACS Science Team, and ESA; **E135** Photograph by Sharon Hoogstraten; **E136** © Jason Ware; **E138** Photograph by Sharon Hoogstraten; **E139** N. Benitez (JHU), T. Broadhurst (The Hebrew University), H. Ford (JHU), M. Clampin (STScI), G. Hartig (STScI), G. Illingworth (UCO/Lick Observatory), the AGS Science Team and ESA/NASA; **E140** *top* David Malin Images/Anglo-Australian Observatory; *bottom* N. Benitez (JHU), T. Broadhurst (The Hebrew University), H. Ford (JHU), M. Clampin (STScI), G. Hartig (STScI), G. Illingworth (UCO/Lick Observatory), the AGS Science Team and ESA/NASA; **E142** *left* Hubble Heritage Team (AURA/STScI/NASA); *right* Anglo-Australian Observatory/David Malin Images.

Backmatter
R28 © Photodisc/Getty Images.

Illustrations and Maps
Accurate Art Inc. **A39, A107, A175, B127, C33, E106;** Ampersand Design Group **B29, B115, C139;** Argosy **C10, C13, C14, C18, C19, C25, C30, C55, C61;** Julian Baum **E57, E117, E127, E128, E131, E140;** Richard Bonson/Wildlife Art Ltd. **A83, D28, D47, D49, D60** *(background)*, **D70** *(top right);* Peter Bull/Wildlife Art Ltd. **A160, A162, A167, A169, E26, E27, E47, E48, E68;** Eric Chadwick **C98, C99;** Bill Cigliano **E67, E137;** Steve Cowden **C12, C51, C54, C82, E48;** Sandra Doyle/Wildlife Art Ltd. **D27** *(all),* **D38** *(bottom);* Stephen Durke **A45, A53, B10, B11, B18, B20, B22, B30, B32, B33, B34, B81, E12, E14, E18;** Chris Forsey **A99;** Luigi Galante **A127, A138, D66–D67** *(all insets),* **D70** *(bottom);* Dan Gonzalez **D88, D94;** David A. Hardy **A12, A84, A86, A104, E11, E32, E80, E83, E95, E108;** Gary Hincks **A63, A79, A80, A149, A153, D12** *(bottom right),* **D17, D18, D20, D36–D37** *(background),* **D38** *(center),* **D83;** Dan Maas/Maas Digital **E28, E36;** Mapquest.com, Inc. **A17, A18, A23, A32, A33, A34, A36, A64, A88, A110, A125, A166, A170, B114, D31, D47** *(top right),* **D49** *(top),* **D85, E64, R58;** Morgan, Cain & Assoc. **A128;** Laurie O'Keefe **D29;** Mike Saunders **A117, A120, A138;** Space.comCanada.Inc. **E61–E64;** Dan Stuckenschneider **C62, C77, C91, C102, C133, C135, C136, C140, E17, E36, R11–R19, R22, R32;** Raymond Turvey **A159;** Bart Vallecoccia **C38, C39, C126, C127, C129, C135, C140;** Rob Wood **A117, A154;** Ron Wood/Wood Ronsaville Harlin **E56, E68.**

ACKNOWLEDGMENTS